Microsoft® Exchange Server 2007 Administrator's Pocket Consultant, Second Edition

William Stanek

PUBLISHED BY
Microsoft Press
A Division of Microsoft Corporation
One Microsoft Way
Redmond, Washington 98052-6399

Library of Congress Control Number: 2008923654

Printed and bound in the United States of America.

1 2 3 4 5 6 7 8 9   QWE   3 2 1 0 9 8

Distributed in Canada by H.B. Fenn and Company Ltd.

A CIP catalogue record for this book is available from the British Library.

Microsoft Press books are available through booksellers and distributors worldwide. For further
information about international editions, contact your local Microsoft Corporation office or contact
Microsoft Press International directly at fax (425) 936-7329. Visit our Web site at
www.microsoft.com/mspress. Send comments to mspinput@microsoft.com.

Microsoft, Microsoft Press, Active Directory, ActiveSync, Authenticode, Entourage, Excel,
Forefront, Hotmail, InfoPath, Internet Explorer, MSN, Outlook, PowerPoint, SharePoint, Tahoma,
Windows, and Windows Vista are either registered trademarks or trademarks of Microsoft
Corporation in the United States and/or other countries. Other product and company names
mentioned herein may be the trademarks of their respective owners.

The example companies, organizations, products, domain names, e-mail addresses, logos, people,
places, and events depicted herein are fictitious. No association with any real company, organization,
product, domain name, e-mail address, logo, person, place, or event is intended or should be
inferred.

This book expresses the author's views and opinions. The information contained in this book is
provided without any express, statutory, or implied warranties. Neither the authors, Microsoft
Corporation, nor its resellers, or distributors will be held liable for any damages caused or alleged to
be caused either directly or indirectly by this book.

Acquisitions Editor: Martin DelRe
Developmental Editor: Karen Szall
Project Editor: Maria Gargiulo
Editorial Production: Interactive Composition Corporation
Cover: Tom Draper Design

Body Part No. X14-86389

Contents at a Glance

Table of Contents

What do you think of this book? We want to hear from you!

Microsoft is interested in hearing your feedback so we can continually improve our books and learning resources for you. To participate in a brief survey, please visit:

www.microsoft.com/learning/booksurvey

What do you think of this book? We want to hear from you!

Microsoft is interested in hearing your feedback so we can continually improve our books and learning resources for you. To participate in a brief survey, please visit:

www.microsoft.com/learning/booksurvey

Acknowledgments

You know you've been at this thing called writing a long time when people ask how many books you've written and you just have no idea. (This number is somewhere over 70 for those who may be wondering.) For me, it's always been about the craft of writing. I love writing, and I love challenging projects most of all. When I began my research for the original *Microsoft Exchange Server 2007 Administrator's Pocket Consultant* back in 2005, I had no idea how challenging this project would be. To say that Exchange Server 2007 is completely different from its predecessors is a considerable understatement. Exchange Server 2007 represents a massive top-to-bottom overhaul of Exchange Server, and every corner of Exchange Server has been tweaked, over-hauled, or replaced entirely. In fact, I'll go so far as to say that Exchange Server 2007 seems more like an entirely different product than a new release of Exchange Server—and Exchange Server 2007 SP1 and later have even more features, which I cover in this new edition.

Exchange Server has evolved into a comprehensive messaging and collaboration platform that is completely integrated with Active Directory and fully scalable to meet the needs of the most demanding environments. What's more, just about every facet of Exchange Server 2007 is completely customizable, and many of the customizations can be performed only from the command line. With literally thousands of customizations and an extensive role-based architecture that can easily span multiple servers even in small businesses, the challenge in writing a day-to-day administrator's guide to Exchange Server 2007 lay in figuring out the best way to approach and organize the material as well as in determining the essential information so that I could provide you, the reader, with all the essential details in one portable, precise, and concise guide. With that in mind, I had to carefully review the text, making sure I organized the material appropriately, focused on the core topics, and included all the tips, tricks, and techniques you've come to expect from the pocket consultants. The result is the book you hold in your hand, which I hope you'll agree is one of the best practical, portable guides to Exchange Server 2007.

As I've stated in *Windows Vista Administrator's Pocket Consultant* and in *Microsoft Windows Command-Line Administrator's Pocket Consultant*, the team at Microsoft Press is top-notch. On this project, I worked with Karen Szall, Devon Musgrave, Maria Gargiulo, Martin DelRe, and others. Everyone was great to work with and very supportive of my unique approach to this book. Martin DelRe in particular believed in the book from the beginning and was really great to work with. Completing and publishing the book wouldn't have been possible without their help!

Unfortunately for the writer (but fortunately for readers), writing is only one part of the publishing process. Next came editing and author review. I must say, Microsoft Press has the most thorough editorial and technical review process I've seen anywhere—and

I've written a lot of books for many different publishers. John Pierce was the project editor and Becka McKay was the copy editor. I believe this was the first time I worked with John, and it turned out to be a good experience. Thank you!

I would also like to thank Lucinda Rowley and everyone else at Microsoft who has helped at many points of my writing career and been there when I needed them the most. Thank you also for shepherding my many projects through the publishing process!

Thanks also to Studio B literary agency and my agents, David Rogelberg and Neil Salkind. David and Neil are great to work with.

I hope I haven't forgotten anyone, but if I have, it was an oversight. *Honest.*;-)

Introduction

Microsoft Exchange Server 2007 Administrator's Pocket Consultant, Second Edition, is designed to be a concise and compulsively usable resource for Exchange Server 2007 administrators. This is the readable resource guide that you'll want on your desk at all times. The book covers everything you need to perform the core administrative tasks for Exchange Server 2007 with SP1 or later, whether your servers are running on Windows Server 2003 or Windows Server 2008. Because the focus is on giving you maximum value in a pocket-sized guide, you don't have to wade through hundreds of pages of extraneous information to find what you're looking for. Instead, you'll find exactly what you need to get the job done.

In short, the book is designed to be the one resource you turn to whenever you have questions regarding Exchange Server 2007 administration. To this end, the book zeroes in on daily administrative procedures, frequently used tasks, documented examples, and options that are representative although not necessarily inclusive. One of the goals is to keep the content so concise that the book remains compact and easy to navigate while at the same time ensuring that the book is packed with as much information as possible—making it a valuable resource. Thus, instead of a hefty 1,000-page tome or a lightweight 100-page quick reference, you get a valuable resource guide that can help you quickly and easily perform common tasks, solve problems, and implement advanced Exchange Server 2007 technologies such as EdgeSync subscriptions, local continuous replication, Outlook Anywhere, SMTP connectors, and Active Directory site links.

Who Is This Book For?

Microsoft Exchange Server 2007 Administrator's Pocket Consultant, Second Edition, covers the Standard and Enterprise editions of Exchange Server 2007. The book is designed for the following readers:

- Current Exchange Server 2007 administrators
- Current Windows administrators who want to learn Exchange Server 2007
- Administrators upgrading to Exchange Server 2007 from Exchange 2000
- Administrators upgrading to Exchange Server 2007 from Exchange 2003
- Administrators transferring from other messaging servers
- Managers and supervisors who have been delegated authority to manage mailboxes or other aspects of Exchange Server 2007

To pack in as much information as possible, I had to assume that you have basic networking skills and a basic understanding of e-mail and messaging servers. With this in mind, I don't devote entire chapters to explaining why e-mail systems are needed or how they work. I don't devote entire chapters to installing Exchange Server 2007, either. I do, however, provide complete details on the components of Exchange organizations and how you can use these components to build a fully redundant and highly available messaging environment. You will also find complete details on all the essential Exchange administration tasks.

I also assume that you are fairly familiar with Windows Server. If you need help learning Windows Server, I highly recommend that you buy *Windows Server 2008 Administrator's Pocket Consultant* or *Windows Server 2008 Inside Out*.

How Is This Book Organized?

Microsoft Exchange Server 2007 Administrator's Pocket Consultant, Second Edition, is designed to be used in the daily administration of Exchange Server 2007. As such, the book is organized by job-related tasks rather than by Exchange Server 2007 features. If you are reading this book, you should be aware of the relationship between Pocket Consultants and Administrator's Companions. Both types of books are designed to be part of an administrator's library. While Pocket Consultants are the down-and-dirty, in-the-trenches books, Administrator's Companions are the comprehensive tutorials and references that cover every aspect of deploying a product or technology in the enterprise.

Speed and ease of reference is an essential part of this hands-on guide. The book has an expanded table of contents and an extensive index for finding answers to problems quickly. Many other quick reference features have been added as well. These features include quick step-by-step instructions, lists, tables with fast facts, and extensive cross-references. The book is broken down into both parts and chapters.

Part I, "Exchange Server 2007 Administration Fundamentals," provides an overview of Exchange servers and Exchange clients. Chapter 1 provides an overview of Exchange Server 2007 administration concepts, tools, and techniques. Chapter 2 discusses deploying Exchange Server. Chapter 3 covers Exchange client setup and management. Chapter 4 extends the Exchange client discussion and looks at mobile Microsoft Office Outlook users as well as Exchange Active Sync, Outlook Web Access, and Outlook Anywhere. With more and more users working on the road or from home, this chapter helps ensure that you can give these mobile users the best support possible.

In Part II, "Exchange Server 2007 Administration Essentials," I cover the fundamental tasks you need for Exchange Server administration. Chapter 5 details how Exchange environments are organized, how information is stored in Exchange Server, and how Exchange Server works. The chapter also explores Exchange message queues and Exchange Server service management. Chapter 6 discusses Windows PowerShell and Exchange Management Shell, providing the essential background for using these powerful command-line environments for Exchange Server administration. Chapter 7 takes a look at creating and managing users and contacts. You'll learn all about Exchange aliases, enabling and disabling exchange mail for individual users, forwarding mail offsite, and more. Chapter 8 discusses mailbox administration, including techniques for configuring special-purpose resource mailboxes, moving mailboxes, and configuring mailbox delivery restrictions. In Chapter 9, you'll find a detailed discussion of how to use distribution groups and address lists. You'll also learn how to manage these resources. The final chapter in this part covers implementing Exchange security.

In Part III, "Server and Group Administration," I discuss advanced tasks for managing and maintaining Exchange organizations. Chapter 11 provides the essentials for managing the Exchange information store, implementing local continuous replication, managing storage groups, and using full-text indexing. Chapter 12 examines administration of mailbox and public folder databases. The chapter also covers how to recover disconnected mailboxes and deleted messaging items. Chapter 13 discusses how you can use messaging resource management to help retain messaging content that your organization may need for business or legal reasons and how to delete messages that are no longer needed. Chapter 14 looks at how you can use public folders in the enterprise.

Chapter 15 provides a comprehensive discussion of deploying and managing Hub Transport servers and Edge Transport servers. The chapter examines SMTP connectors, Active Directory sites, Active Directory links, and connecting to Exchange 2000 and Exchanged 2003 routing groups. The chapter also examines configuring EdgeSync subscriptions, journal rules, transport rules, and antispam features. Chapter 16 provides a comprehensive discussion of deploying and managing Client Access servers. The chapter examines HTTP virtual servers, POP3, IMAP4, and Outlook Anywhere. The chapter also examines configuring Exchange Server features for mobile devices including Autodiscovery, Direct Push, Exchange ActiveSync Mailbox Policy, Remote Device Wipe, Password Recovery, Direct File Access, Remote File Access, and WebReady Document Viewing.

Part IV, "Exchange Server 2007 Optimization and Maintenance," discusses optimization and maintenance. Chapter 17 discusses troubleshooting essentials as well as Exchange maintenance, monitoring, and queuing. You'll learn key techniques for using message tracking, protocol logging, and connectivity logging for troubleshooting. You'll also learn techniques for automated monitoring and managing Exchange message queues—both of which can help ensure that your Exchange organization runs smoothly. Finally, Chapter 18 details how to back up and restore Exchange Server. You'll learn key techniques that can help you reliably back up and, more important, recover Exchange Server in case of failure.

Conventions Used in This Book

I've used a variety of elements to help keep the text clear and easy to follow. You'll find code terms and listings in monospace type, except when I tell you to actually type a command. In that case, the command appears in **bold** type. When I introduce and define a new term, I put it in *italics*.

Other conventions include:

- **Notes** To provide details on a point that needs emphasis.

- **Best Practices** To examine the best technique to use when working with advanced configuration and administration concepts.

- **Cautions** To warn you of potential problems you should look out for.

- **More Info** To provide more information on the subject.

- **Real World** To provide real-world advice when discussing advanced topics.

- **Security Alerts** To point out important security issues.

- **Tips** To offer helpful hints or additional information.

I truly hope you find that *Microsoft Exchange Server 2007 Administrator's Pocket Consultant*, Second Edition provides everything you need to perform essential administrative tasks as quickly and efficiently as possible. You're welcome to send your thoughts to me at williamstanek@aol.com, or visit *http://www.williamstanek.com/*. Thank you.

Support

Every effort has been made to ensure the accuracy of this book. Microsoft Press provides corrections for books through the World Wide Web at the following address: *http://www.microsoft.com/mspress/support/*.

If you have comments, questions, or ideas about this book, please send them to Microsoft Press using either of the following methods:

Postal Mail:

Microsoft Press
Attn: Editor, Microsoft Exchange Server 2007 Administrator's Pocket Consultant,
Second Edition
One Microsoft Way
Redmond, WA 98052-6399

E-mail:

mspinput@microsoft.com

Please note that product support isn't offered through the mail addresses. For support information, visit Microsoft's Web site at *http://support.microsoft.com/*.

Part I

Exchange Server 2007 Administration Overview

In this part:

Chapter 1
Microsoft Exchange Server 2007 Administration Overview

Exchange Server 2007 completely redefines the Exchange Server messaging platform and provides the essential foundation on which small, medium, and large organizations can build their next-generation IT infrastructure. Every Exchange Server 2007 implementation has three layers in its architecture:

- **Network layer**   The network layer provides the basic foundation for computer-to-computer communications and essential name resolution features. The network layer has both physical and logical components. The physical components include the IP addresses, the IP subnets, LAN or WAN links used by messaging systems as well as the routers that connect these links, and the firewalls that protect the infrastructure. The logical components are the DNS zones that define the naming boundaries and contain the essential resource records required for name resolution.

- **Active Directory layer**   The Active Directory layer provides the basic foundation necessary for authentication, authorization, and replication. The Active Directory layer has both physical and logical components. The physical components include the domain controllers, global catalog servers, and site links used for authentication, authorization, and replication. The logical components include the Active Directory forests, sites, domains, and organizational units that are used to group objects for the purposes of resource sharing, centralized management, and replication control. The logical components also include the users and groups that are part of the Active Directory infrastructure.

- **Messaging layer**   The messaging layer provides the basic foundation for messaging and collaboration. The messaging layer has both physical and logical components. The physical components include individual Exchange servers that determine how messages are delivered and mail connectors that determine how messages are routed outside an Exchange server's routing boundaries. The logical components specify the organizational boundaries for messaging, the mailboxes used for storing messages, the public folders used for storing data, and the distribution lists used for distributing messages to multiple recipients.

As you get started with Exchange Server 2007, you should concentrate on these areas:

- How Exchange Server 2007 works with your hardware
- What versions and editions of Exchange Server 2007 are available and how they meet your needs

- How Exchange Server 2007 works with Windows–based operating systems
- How Exchange Server 2007 works with Active Directory
- What administration tools are available

Exchange Server 2007 and Your Hardware

Before you deploy Exchange Server 2007, you should carefully plan the messaging architecture. As part of your implementation planning, you need to look closely at preinstallation requirements and the hardware you will use. Exchange Server is no longer the simple messaging server that it once was. It is now a complex messaging platform with many components that work together to provide a comprehensive solution for routing, delivering, and accessing e-mails, voice mails, faxes, contacts, and calendar information.

Successful Exchange Server administration depends on three things:

- Good Exchange administrators
- Strong architecture
- Appropriate hardware

The first two ingredients are covered: you're the administrator, you're smart enough to buy this book to help you through the rough spots, and you've enlisted Exchange Server 2007 to provide your high-performance messaging needs. This brings us to the issue of hardware. Exchange Server 2007 should run on a system with adequate memory, processing speed, and disk space. You also need an appropriate data-and-system protection plan at the hardware level.

Key guidelines for choosing hardware for Exchange Server are as follows:

- **Memory**   Exchange Server 2007 has been tested and developed for maximum memory configurations of 32 gigabytes (GB) for Mailbox servers and 8 GB for all other server roles. The minimum random access memory (RAM) is 2 GB. In most cases, you'll want to have at least twice the recommended minimum amount of memory. The primary reason for this is performance. Most of the single-server Exchange installations I run use 4 GB of RAM as a starting point, even in small installations. In multiple Exchange server installations, the Mailbox server should have at least 2 GB of RAM plus 5 megabytes (MB) of RAM per mailbox. For all Exchange server configurations, the paging file should be at least equal to the amount of RAM in the server plus 10 MB.

- **CPU**   64-bit versions run on the x64 family of processors from AMD and Intel, including AMD64 and Intel Extended Memory 64 Technology (Intel EM64T). Exchange Server 2007 provides solid benchmark performance with Intel Xeon 3.66 GHz, AMD Opteron 2.6 GHz, and AMD Athlon 2.6 GHz. Any of these CPUs provide good starting points for the average Exchange Server system. You can achieve significant performance improvements with a high level of processor cache. Look closely at the L1, L2, and L3 cache options available—a higher cache can yield much better performance overall.

The primary advantages of 64-bit processors over 32-bit processors have to do with memory limitations and data access. Because 64-bit processors can exceed the 4-GB memory limit of 32-bit processors, they can store greater amounts of data in main memory, providing direct access to and faster processing of data. In addition, 64-bit processors can process data and execute instruction sets that are twice as large as 32-bit processors. Accessing 64 bits of data (versus 32 bits) offers a significant advantage when processing complex calculations that require a high level of precision.

> **Note**   Exchange Server 2007 32-bit versions run on Intel x86 or compatible hardware, and are used for testing, training, and evaluation only. 64-bit versions do not support Intel Itanium.

- **SMP**   Exchange Server 2007 supports symmetric multiprocessors, and you'll see significant performance improvements if you use multiple CPUs. Microsoft tested and developed Exchange Server 2007 for use with dual-core and multicore CPUs as well. The minimum, recommended, and maximum number of CPUs—whether single core, dual core, or multicore—depends on a server's Exchange roles (see "Exchange Server Messaging Roles" in Chapter 2, "Deploying Microsoft Exchange Server 2007."). Still, if Exchange Server is supporting a small organization with a single domain, one CPU should be enough. If the server supports a medium or large organization or handles mail for multiple domains, you might want to consider adding processors. An alternative would be to distribute the workload to virtual servers on different systems.

- **Disk drives**   The data storage capacity you need depends entirely on the number and size of the data that will pass through, be journaled on, or stored on the Exchange server. You need enough disk space to store all data and logs, plus workspace, system files, and virtual memory. Input/output (I/O) throughput is just as important as drive capacity. In most cases, small computer system interface (SCSI) drives are faster than integrated device electronics/enhanced integrated drive electronics (IDE/EIDE) and are, therefore, recommended. Rather than use one large drive, you should use several smaller drives, which allow you to configure fault tolerance with redundant array of independent disks (RAID).

- **Data protection**   Add protection against unexpected drive failures by using RAID. For data, use RAID 0 or RAID 5. For logs, use RAID 1. RAID 0 (disk striping without parity) offers good read/write performance, but any failed drive means that Exchange Server can't continue operation on an affected database until the drive is replaced and data is restored from backup. RAID 1 (disk mirroring) creates duplicate copies of data on separate drives, and you can rebuild the RAID unit to restore full operations. RAID 5 (disk striping with parity) offers good protection against single drive failure, but has poor write performance. For best performance and fault tolerance, RAID 0 + 1 is recommended, which consists of disk mirroring and disk striping without parity.

- **Uninterruptible power supply**   Exchange Server 2007 is designed to maintain database integrity at all times and can recover information using transaction logs. This doesn't protect the server hardware, however, from sudden power loss or power spikes, both of which can seriously damage hardware. To prevent this, connect your server to an uninterruptible power supply (UPS). A UPS gives you time to shut down the server or servers properly in the event of a power outage. Proper shutdown is especially important on servers using write-back caching controllers. These controllers temporarily store data in cache. Without proper shutdown, this data can be lost before it is written to disk.

If you follow these hardware guidelines and modify them for specific messaging roles, as discussed in the next section, you'll be well on your way to success with Exchange Server 2007.

Microsoft Exchange Server 2007 Editions

Several editions of Exchange Server 2007 are available, including Exchange Server 2007 Standard Edition and Exchange Server 2007 Enterprise Edition. The various server editions support the same core features and administration tools, which means you can use the techniques discussed throughout this book regardless of which Exchange Server 2007 edition you are using. For reference, the specific feature differences between Standard Edition and Enterprise Edition are as follows:

- **Exchange Server 2007 Standard Edition**   Designed to provide essential messaging services for small to medium-sized organizations and branch office locations. This server edition supports up to five storage groups (with one of the storage groups, called the Recovery Storage group, reserved for database recovery operations) and a maximum of five databases per storage group. Each database is limited to a maximum size of 16 terabytes (TB)–limited only by hardware. In addition, Windows clustering is not supported, and neither advanced compliance capabilities or unified messaging features are included. Also, although local continuous replication is available, cluster continuous replication and standby continuous replication are not available.

- **Exchange Server 2007 Enterprise Edition**   Designed to provide essential messaging services for organizations with increased availability, reliability, and manageability needs. This server edition supports up to 50 storage groups (with one of the storage groups, called the Recovery Storage group, reserved for database recovery operations). Although a maximum of five databases per storage group is allowed, you can create only 50 databases in total on a particular server. Each database is limited to a maximum size of 16 terabytes (TB)–limited only by hardware. Windows clustering is fully supported, and both advanced compliance capabilities and unified messaging features are included.

Note   Throughout this book, I refer to Exchange Server in different ways, and each has a different meaning. Typically, I refer to the software product as *Exchange Server*. If you see this term, you can take it to mean *Microsoft Exchange Server 2007*. When necessary, I use *Exchange Server 2007* to draw attention to the fact that I am discussing a feature that's new or has changed in the most recent version of the product. Each of these terms means essentially the same thing. If I refer to a previous version of Exchange Server, I always do so specifically, such as Exchange Server 2003. Finally, I often use the term *Exchange server* (note the lowercase *s* in server) to refer to an actual server computer, as in "There are eight Exchange servers in this routing group."

Real World   Microsoft provides a single binary for each supported platform—one for x64 systems and one for x86 systems—and the same binary files are used for both the Standard and the Enterprise editions. The license key provided during installation is what determines which edition is established during installation.

You can use product keys in new ways with Exchange Server 2007. Unlike earlier releases of Exchange Server, you can use a valid product key to go from a trial edition to a Standard Edition or Enterprise Edition of Exchange Server 2007 without having to reinstall. Using a valid product key, you can also upgrade from Standard Edition to Enterprise Edition. You can also relicense an Exchange Server by entering a new product key for the installed edition, which is useful if you accidentally used the same product key on multiple servers and want to correct the mistake.

There are several caveats. When you change the product key on a Mailbox server, you must restart the Microsoft Exchange Information Store service to apply the change. When you change the product key on an Edge Transport server, you must resubscribe the server in the Exchange organization to apply the change. Additionally, you cannot use product keys to downgrade editions. To downgrade editions, you must uninstall Exchange Server and then reinstall Exchange Server.

A client accessing an Exchange server requires a Client Access License (CAL). With either Exchange Server edition, the client can use a Standard CAL, an Enterprise CAL, or both. The Standard CAL allows for the use of e-mail, shared calendaring, contacts, task management, Outlook Web Access, and Exchange Active Sync. The Enterprise CAL allows for the use of unified messaging, advanced compliance capabilities, and antivirus/antispam protection. A client must have both a Standard CAL and an Enterprise CAL to make full use of all Exchange Server features.

Beyond the editions and CALs, Exchange Server 2007 has several variants. Exchange Server 2007 RTM is the original release. This variant runs only on Windows Server 2003 with at least Release 2 or Service Pack 1 (SP1) installed. Exchange Server 2007 SP1 is a full product re-release of Exchange Server 2007 with Service Pack 1 already integrated. You can install Exchange Server 2007 SP1 on servers running Exchange Server 2007 RTM as an in-place upgrade. For new installations, however, you do not need to install Exchange Server 2007 RTM and then install SP1. Instead, you simply install Exchange Server 2007 SP1 and then apply any updates or additional service packs as necessary.

Exchange Server 2007 SP1 runs on Windows Server 2008 as well as Windows Server 2003 with at least Release 2 or Service Pack 1. With Windows Server 2008, you cannot upgrade a server running Windows Server 2003 and any Exchange Server 2007 release to Windows Server 2008. You must install Windows Server 2008 and then install Exchange Server 2007 SP1 or later.

To install Exchange Server 2007, the system partition and all disk partitions used by Exchange must be formatted using the NT file system (NTFS). Additional preinstallation requirements are as follows:

- The domain controller with the Schema Master role must be running at least Windows Server 2003 Service Pack 1 (SP1).

- All domains in the Active Directory forest where Exchange Server 2007 will be installed or in which recipients will be hosted must have the domain functional level set to Windows 2000 Server native or higher.

- For forest-to-forest delegation and free/busy availability selection across forests, you must establish a trust between the forests that have Exchange Server installed, and the minimum forest functional level for these forests must be Windows Server 2003.

- The domain must be configured to use multiple label DNS names, such as cpandl.com or adatum.local, rather than single-label DNS names, such as cpandl or adatum.

Note   Using Active Directory with Exchange Server 2007 is covered in more detail in the "Exchange Server and Active Directory" section of this chapter and the "Integrating Exchange Server Roles with Active Directory" section of Chapter 2.

Exchange Server 2007 requires Microsoft Management Console 3.0 or later, the Microsoft .NET Framework version 2.0 or later, and the Windows PowerShell for the Exchange Management Shell. The Exchange Management Shell is a new, task-based, command-line shell for system administration. If you want to manage Exchange Server 2007 from a workstation, you'll need to install Windows PowerShell for the Exchange Management Shell and the Exchange Server 2007 management tools.

Real World   Different versions of the Exchange Server 2007 management tools are available. The management tools for Exchange Server 2007 RTM and all previous versions of Exchange are not supported for installation on a computer running Windows Vista or Windows Server 2008. With Windows Vista or Windows Server 2008, you must use the Exchange Server 2007 SP1 or later tools. Microsoft provides both 32-bit and 64-bit management tools. On a 32-bit system, you must install and use the 32-bit tools. You can use 32-bit tools to manage remote Exchange installations on servers running 64-bit operating systems.

Exchange Server 2007 uses the Windows Installer and has a fully integrated installation process. This means you can configure Exchange Server 2007 much like you can any other application you install on the operating system. The installation can be performed remotely from a command shell as well as locally.

Chapter 2 provides detailed instructions for installing Exchange Server 2007. With an initial installation, Windows Installer will first check the system configuration to determine the status of required services and components, which includes checking the Active Directory configuration and the availability of components, such as IIS (Internet Information Server), as well as operating system service packs, installation permissions for the default install path, memory, and hardware.

After checking the system configuration, the installer allows you to select the roles to install. Whether you use the Standard or Enterprise Edition, you have similar options. You can:

- Install an internal messaging server by selecting the individual server roles to install and combining the Mailbox role, Client Access role, Hub Transport role, and Unified Messaging role as required for your environment. In many cases, you'll want an internal Exchange server to also be configured as a domain controller with a global catalog.

  > **Note**   For details on how the various server roles are used, see Chapter 2, which also provides guidelines for sizing and positioning the various server roles.

- Install a Messaging server in a perimeter zone outside the organization's main network by selecting only the Edge Transport role. Edge Transport servers are not members of the Active Directory forest and are not configured on domain controllers.

- Install a clustered Mailbox server by selecting the Active Clustered Mailbox role or Passive Clustered Mailbox role, as appropriate.

- Install the management tools.

- Specify the path for the Exchange Server installation files.

- Specify the path for the Exchange Server installation.

If you want to change the configuration after installation, you can use Exchange Server 2007 maintenance mode, as discussed in "Adding, Modifying, or Uninstalling Server Roles" in Chapter 2.

Exchange Server 2007 includes the following antispam and antivirus capabilities:

- **Connection filtering**   Allows administrators to configure IP Block lists and IP Allow lists, as well as providers who can supply these lists.

- **Content filtering**   Uses intelligent message filtering to scan message content and identify spam. Spam can be automatically deleted, quarantined, or filed as junk e-mail.

> **Tip**   Using the Exchange Server management tools, administrators can manage messages sent to the quarantine mailbox and take appropriate actions, such as deleting messages, flagging them as false positives, or allowing them to be delivered as junk e-mail. Messages delivered as junk e-mail are converted to plain text to strip out any potential viruses they might contain.

- **IP Reputation Service**   Provides Exchange Server 2007 customers with exclusive access to an IP Block list provided by Microsoft.

- **Outlook Junk E-mail Filter list aggregation**   Allows the junk e-mail filter lists of individual Outlook users to be propagated to Exchange servers.

- **Recipient filtering**   Allows administrators to replicate recipient data from the enterprise to the server running the Edge Transport role. This server can then perform recipient lookups on incoming messages and block messages that are for nonexistent users.

- **Sender ID verification**   Verifies that incoming e-mail messages are from the Internet domain from which they claim to come. Exchange verifies the sender ID by examining the sender's IP address and comparing it to the related security record on the sender's public domain name system (DNS) server.

- **Sender reputation scoring**   Helps to determine the relative trustworthiness of unknown senders through sender ID verification and by examining message content and sender behavior history. A sender can then be added temporarily to the Blocked Senders list.

Although these antivirus and antispam features are fairly extensive, they are not comprehensive in scope. For comprehensive antivirus protection, you'll need to install Forefront Security for Exchange Server. Forefront Security for Exchange Server helps protect Exchange servers from viruses, worms, and other malware using multiple antivirus scan engines and file filtering capabilities. Forefront Security provides distributed protection for Exchange servers with the Mailbox server, Hub Transport server, and Edge Transport server roles. Although you can install Forefront Security on Exchange servers with these roles to gain substantial antivirus protection, you do not need to install Forefront Security on Exchange servers with only the Client Access Server or Unified Messaging Server role.

You can use the Forefront Security Setup program to install the administrator console, the server components, or both on a local or remote computer. When prompted for an installation location during setup, choose Local Installation to install on a local computer or choose Remote Installation to install on a remote computer, and then click Next. Then choose Server–Admin Console And Scanner Components as the type of installation to install the Forefront Security server components on an Exchange server. Or choose Client–Admin Console Only to install only the administrator console on the computer. For clustered Exchange servers, you must perform a local installation of Forefront Security on each node in the cluster, starting with the primary active node.

Forefront Security has two operating modes:

- **Secure mode**   This is the default mode. In this mode, messages and attachments delivered from the quarantine mailbox are rescanned for viruses and filter matches.

- **Compatibility mode**   This mode allows messages matching filter criteria to be redelivered. In this mode, messages and attachments delivered from the quarantine mailbox are rescanned for viruses but are not rescanned for filter matches.

You can set the operating mode during installation and change it at any time using the administrator console.

Exchange Server and Windows

When you install Exchange Server and Forefront Security for Exchange Server on a server operating system, Exchange Server and Forefront Security make extensive modifications to the environment. These modifications include new system services, integrated authentication, and new security groups.

Services for Exchange Server

When you install Exchange Server and Forefront Security for Exchange Server on Windows, multiple services are installed and configured on the server. Table 1-1 provides a summary of key services, how they are used, and with which server components they are associated.

Table 1-1   Summary of Key Services Used by Exchange Server 2007

Service Name	Description	Server Role
AdoNavSvc	Navigates the objects in Active Directory for Forefront Security.	Forefront Security
FSEMailPickup	Provides mail pickup services for Forefront.	Forefront Security
FSEIMC	Connects to the Simple Mail Transfer Protocol (SMTP) stack to ensure that messages are scanned by Forefront. Works with the Microsoft Exchange Transport service.	Forefront Security
FSCMonitor	Monitors the information store, SMTP/IMS, and Forefront processes to ensure that Forefront provides continuous protection.	Forefront Security

Table 1-1   Summary of Key Services Used by Exchange Server 2007

Service Name	Description	Server Role
FSCStatisticsService	Coordinates all real-time, manual, IMC, and SMTP scanning activities, and is the agent to which the Forefront Security administrator connects.	Forefront Security
FSCController	Controls interaction between Forefront Security and the Microsoft Exchange Information Store. Ensures that Forefront initializes properly with the information store. FSCController starts and stops with the information store.	Forefront Security
Secure Socket Tunneling Protocol Service	Provides support for Secure Socket Tunneling Protocol (SSTP) for securely connecting to remove computers.	Client Access
IIS Admin	Enables the server to administer Web services. Required to support HTTP SSL and World Wide Web publishing services.	Client Access
Microsoft Exchange Active Directory Topology	Provides Active Directory topology information to Exchange services. If this service is stopped, most Exchange servers will not be able to start.	Hub Transport, Mailbox, Client Access, Unified Messaging
Microsft Exchange ADAM	Maintains the Active Directory ADAM data store.	Edge Transport
Microsoft Exchange Anti-Spam Update	Maintains the antispam data for Forefront Security on an Exchange server.	
Microsoft Exchange EdgeSync	Provides EdgeSync services between Hub and Edge servers.	Hub Transport, Edge Transport
Microsoft Exchange File Distribution	Distributes Exchange data to other Exchange servers.	
Microsoft Exchange IMAP4	Provides IMAP4 services to clients.	Client Access
Microsoft Exchange Information Store	Manages the Microsoft Exchange Information Store. This includes mailbox stores and public folder stores.	Mailbox
Microsoft Exchange Mail Submission Service	Submits messages from the Mailbox server to the Hub Transport servers.	Mailbox
Microsoft Exchange Mailbox Assistants	Manages assistants that are responsible for calendar updates and booking resources.	Mailbox
Microsoft Exchange Monitoring	Provides support for monitoring and diagnostics.	

Table 1-1   Summary of Key Services Used by Exchange Server 2007

Service Name	Description	Server Role
Microsoft Exchange POP3	Provides Post Office Protocol version 3 (POP3) services to clients.	Client Access
Microsoft Exchange Replication Service	Provides replication functionality used for continuous replication.	Mailbox
Microsoft Search (Exchange)	Provides searches services for mailboxes, address lists, and so on.	Mailbox
Microsoft Exchange Search Indexer	Controls indexing of mailboxes to improve search performance.	Mailbox
Microsoft Exchange Service Host	Provides a host for essential Exchange services.	
Microsoft Exchange Speech Engine	Provides speech processing services for Microsoft Exchange. If this service is stopped, speech recognition services will not be available to Unified Messaging clients.	Unified Messaging
Microsoft Exchange System Attendant	Provides monitoring, maintenance, and Active Directory lookup services.	Mailbox, Client Access
Microsoft Exchange Transport	Provides mail transport services.	Hub Transport, Edge Transport
Microsoft Exchange Transport	Provides search capability for Exchange transport log files.	Hub Transport, Edge Transport
Microsoft Exchange Unified Messaging	Enables voice and fax messages to be stored in Exchange and gives users telephone access to e-mail, voice mail, calendar, contacts, or an automated attendant.	Unified Messaging
World Wide Web Publishing Services	Provides Web connectivity and administration features for IIS.	Client Access

Exchange Server Authentication and Security

In Exchange Server 2007, e-mail addresses, distribution groups, and other directory resources are stored in the directory database provided by Active Directory. Active Directory is a directory service running on Windows domain controllers. When there are multiple domain controllers, the controllers automatically replicate directory data with each other using a multimaster replication model. This model allows any domain controller to process directory changes and then replicate those changes to other domain controllers.

The first time you install Exchange Server 2007 in a Windows domain, the installation process updates and extends Active Directory to include objects and attributes used by Exchange Server 2007. Unlike previous releases of Exchange, this process does not include updates for the Active Directory Users And Computers Snap-In for Microsoft Management Console (MMC), and you no longer use Active Directory Users And Computers to manage mailboxes, messaging features, messaging options, or e-mail addresses associated with user accounts. You now perform these tasks in the Exchange Management Console only.

Exchange Server 2007 fully supports the Windows Server security model and relies on this security mechanism to control access to directory resources. This means you can control access to mailboxes and membership in distribution groups and you can perform other Exchange security administration tasks through the standard Windows Server permission set. For example, to add a user to a distribution group, you simply make the user a member of the distribution group in Active Directory Users And Computers.

Because Exchange Server uses Windows Server security, you can't create a mailbox without first creating a user account that will use the mailbox. Every Exchange mailbox must be associated with a domain account—even those used by Exchange for general messaging tasks. For example, the SMTP and System Attendant mailboxes that Exchange Server uses are associated by default with the built-in System user. In the Exchange Management Console, you can create a new user account as part of the process of creating a new mailbox.

To support coexistence between Exchange 2000 Server or Exchange Server 2003 and Exchange Server 2007, all Exchange Server 2007 servers are automatically added to a single administrative group when you install Exchange Server 2007. This administrative group is recognized in the Exchange System Manager in Exchange Server 2003 as "Exchange Administrative Group." Although Exchange 2000 Server and Exchange Server 2003 use administrative groups to gather Exchange objects for the purposes of delegating permission to manage those objects, Exchange Server 2007 does not use administrative groups. Instead, you manage Exchange servers according to their roles and the type of information you want to manage using the Exchange Management Console. You'll learn more about this in Chapter 5, "Microsoft Exchange Server 2007 Administration Essentials."

Exchange Server Security Groups

In Exchange Server 2003, the Delegation Wizard allowed you to create security roles for Exchange Full Administrators, Exchange Administrators, and Exchange View-Only Administrators. Exchange Server 2007 uses predefined universal security groups to separate administration of Exchange permissions from administration of other permissions. When you add an administrator to one of these security groups, the administrator inherits the permissions permitted by that role.

The predefined security groups have permissions to manage the following types of Exchange data in Active Directory:

- **Organization Configuration node**   This type of data is not associated with a specific server and is used to mange policies, address lists, and other types of organizational configuration details.

- **Server Configuration node**   This type of data is associated with a specific server and is used to manage the server's messaging configuration.

- **Recipient Configuration node**   This type of data is associated with mailboxes, mail-enabled contacts, and distribution groups.

The predefined groups are as follows:

- **Exchange Organization Administrators**   Members of this group have full access to all Exchange properties and objects in the Exchange organization.

- **Exchange Recipient Administrators**   Members of this group have permissions to modify any Exchange property on an Active Directory user, contact, group, dynamic distribution list, or public folder object. Members of this group can also manage unified messaging mailbox settings and client access mailbox settings.

- **Exchange Server Administrators**   Members of this group have access to only local server Exchange configuration data, either in Active Directory or on the physical computer on which Exchange 2007 is installed. This allows members to administer a particular server but not to perform operations that have global impact in the Exchange organization.

- **Exchange View-Only Administrators**   Members of this group have read-only access to the entire Exchange organization tree in the Active Directory configuration container and read-only access to all the Windows domain containers that have Exchange recipients.

- **Exchange2003Interop**   Members of this group are granted send-to and receive-from permissions, which are necessary for routing group connections between Exchange Server 2007 and Exchange 2000 Server or Exchange Server 2003. Exchange 2000 Server and Exchange Server 2003 bridgehead servers must be made members of this group to allow proper mail flow in the organization. For more information on interoperability, see Chapter 2.

Exchange Server and Active Directory

Unlike Exchange 2000 Server and Exchange Server 2003, Exchange Server 2007 is tightly integrated with Active Directory. Not only does Exchange Server 2007 store information in Active Directory, but it also uses the Active Directory routing topology to determine how to route messages within the organization. Routing to and from the organization is handled using transport servers.

Understanding How Exchange Stores Information

Exchange stores four types of data in Active Directory: schema data (stored in the Schema partition), configuration data (stored in the Configuration partition), domain data (stored in the Domain partition), and application data (stored in application-specific partitions). In Active Directory, schema rules determine what types of objects are available and what attributes those objects have. When you install the first Exchange server in the forest, the Active Directory preparation process adds many Exchange-specific object classes and attributes to the schema partition in Active Directory. This allows Exchange-specific objects, such as agents and connectors, to be created. It also allows you to extend existing objects, such as users and groups, with new attributes, such as those attributes that allow user objects to be used for sending and receiving e-mail. Every domain controller and global catalog server in the organization has a complete copy of the Schema partition.

During the installation of the first Exchange server in the forest, Exchange configuration information is generated and stored in Active Directory. Exchange configuration information, like other configuration information, is also stored in the Configuration partition. For Active Directory, the configuration information describes the structure of the directory, and the Configuration container includes all of the domains, trees, and forests, as well as the locations of domain controllers and global catalogs. For Exchange, the configuration information is used to describe the structure of the Exchange organization. The Configuration container includes lists of templates, policies, and other global organization-level details. Every domain controller and global catalog server in the organization has a complete copy of the Configuration partition.

In Active Directory, the Domain partition stores domain-specific objects, such as users and groups, and the stored values of attributes associated with those objects. As you create, modify, or delete objects, Exchange stores the details about those objects in the Domain partition. During the installation of the first Exchange server in the forest, Exchange objects are created in the current domain. Whenever you create new recipients or modify Exchange details, the related changes are reflected in the Domain partition as well. Every domain controller has a complete copy of the Domain partition for the domain for which it is authoritative. Every global catalog server in the forest maintains information about a subset of every Domain partition in the forest.

Understanding How Exchange Routes Messages

Within the organization, Hub Transport servers use the information about sites stored in Active Directory to determine how to route messages, and can also route messages across site links. The Hub Transport server does this by querying Active Directory about its site membership and the site membership of other servers, and then uses the information it discovers to route messages appropriately. Because of this, when you are deploying an Exchange Server 2007 organization, no additional configuration is required to establish routing in the Active Directory forest.

For mail delivery within the organization, additional routing configuration is only necessary in these specific scenarios:

- If you deploy Exchange Server 2007 in an existing Exchange 2000 Server or Exchange Server 2003 organization, you must configure a two-way routing group connector from the Exchange routing group to each Exchange Server 2003 routing group that communicates with Exchange Server 2007. You must also suppress link state updates for the same.

- If you deploy an Exchange Server 2007 organization with multiple forests, you must install Exchange Server 2007 in each forest and then connect the forests using appropriate cross-forest trusts. The trust allows users to see address and availability data across the forests.

- In an Exchange Server 2007 organization, if you want direct mail flow between Exchange servers in different forests, you must configure SMTP send connectors and SMTP receive connectors on the Hub Transport servers that should communicate directly with each other.

The organization's Mail Transport servers handle mail delivery outside the organization and receipt of mail from outside servers. You can use two types of Mail Transport servers: Hub Transport servers and Edge Transport servers. You deploy Hub Transport servers within the organization. You can optionally deploy Edge Transport servers in the organization's perimeter network for added security.

With Hub Transport servers, no other special configuration is needed for message routing to external destinations. You must configure only the standard mail setup, which includes identifying DNS servers to use for lookups. With Edge Transport servers, you can optimize mail routing and delivery by configuring one-way synchronization from the internal Hub Transport servers to the perimeter network's Edge Transport servers. Beyond this, no other special configuration is required for mail routing and delivery.

Using the Graphical Administration Tools

Exchange Server 2007 provides several types of tools for administration. The graphical tools are the ones you'll use most frequently. Exchange Server and Forefront Security for Exchange have separate management consoles. If you follow the instructions for installing Exchange Server in Chapter 2, you'll be able to access these consoles by selecting Start, choosing Programs or All Programs, and then using the Microsoft Exchange Server 2007 menu.

Exchange Server 2007 has several graphical tools that replace or combine features of the graphical tools in previous Exchange Server editions. The Exchange Management

Console, shown in Figure 1-1, replaces Exchange System Manager. As discussed further in Chapter 17, "Microsoft Exchange Server 2007 Maintenance, Monitoring, and Queuing," and Chapter 18, "Backing Up and Restoring Microsoft Exchange Server 2007," the Toolbox node in the Exchange Management Console provides access to a suite of related tools, including:

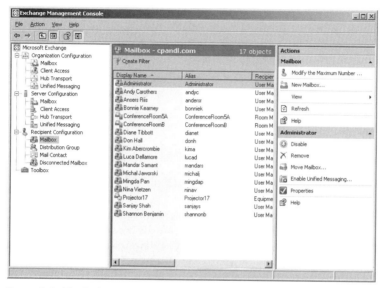

Figure 1-1   The Exchange Management Console.

- **Best Practices Analyzer**   Checks the configuration and health of your Exchange organization to ensure that it complies with current best practices recommended by Microsoft. Because best practices are periodically updated, the tool includes an update facility to ensure that the most current best practices are in place.

- **Database Recovery Management**   Assists administrators in restoring server availability. Also provides step-by-step recovery procedures,

- **Database Troubleshooter**   Helps troubleshoot problems related to mounting data stores as well as other problems related to Exchange databases and transaction logs that prevent recovery.

- **Details Templates Editor**   Helps administrators customize client-side GUI presentation of object properties accessed through address lists. You can use this tool to customize the presentation of contacts, users, groups, public folders, and more in the client interface.

- **Mail Flow Troubleshooter**   Helps troubleshoot problems related to mail flow and transport configuration by providing suggested resolutions for symptoms observed by administrators.

- **Message Tracking**   Allows administrators to track messages as they are routed through the Exchange organization.

- **Public Folder Management Console**   Allows administrators to manage public folders using a graphical interface rather than the command line.

- **Queue Viewer**   Allows administrators to track message queues and mail flow. Also allows administrators to manage message queuing and remove messages.

- **Performance Monitor**   Allows administrators to graph system performance. Also allows administrators to create performance logs and alerts. Wide arrays of Exchange performance objects are available for tracking performance.

- **Performance Troubleshooter**   Helps troubleshoot problems related to performance by identifying possible bottlenecks and providing suggested solutions.

- **Routing Log Viewer**   Helps administrators troubleshoot routing problems on transport servers by providing information about routing topology.

Other administration tools that you might want to use with Exchange Server are summarized in Table 1-2.

Table 1-2   Quick Reference Administration Tools to Use with Exchange Server 2007

Administrative Tool	Purpose
Active Directory Cleanup Wizard	Identify and merge multiple accounts that refer to the same person.
Computer Management	Start and stop services, manage disks, and access other system management tools.
Configure Your Server	Add, remove, and configure Windows services for the network. Windows Server 2003 only.
DNS	Manage the DNS service.
Event Viewer	Manage events and logs.
IIS Manager	Manage Web servers used by Exchange.
Microsoft Network Monitor	Monitor network traffic and troubleshoot networking problems.
Server Manager	Add, remove, and configure roles, role services, and features. Windows Server 2008 only.

You access most of the tools listed in Table 1-2 from the Administrative Tools program group. Click Start, point to Programs or All Programs, and then point to Administrative Tools.

Using the Command-Line Administration Tools

The graphical tools provide just about everything you need to work with Exchange Server. Still, there are many times when you might want to work from the command line, especially if you want to automate installation, administration, or maintenance with scripts. To help with all your command-line needs, Exchange Server includes the Exchange Management Shell.

The Exchange Management Shell is an extension shell for the Microsoft Command Shell that includes a wide array of built-in commands for working with Exchange Server. Microsoft Command Shell commands are referred to as cmdlets (pronounced *commandlets*) to differentiate these commands from less powerful commands built into the command prompt and from more full-featured utility programs that can be invoked at the command prompt.

> **Note**   For ease of reading and reference, I'll usually refer to command prompt commands, command shell cmdlets, and command-line invoked utilities simply as commands.

The Exchange Management Shell, shown in Figure 1-2, is accessible by selecting Start, choosing Programs or All Programs, choosing Microsoft Exchange Server 2007, and then choosing Exchange Management Shell.

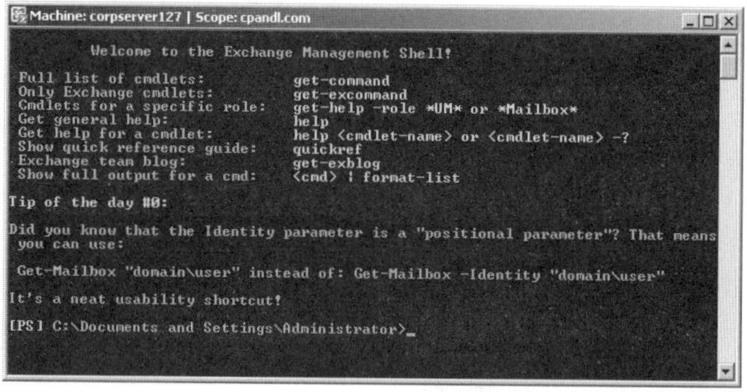

Figure 1-2   The Exchange Management Shell.

The basics of working with the Exchange Management Shell are fairly straightforward:

- Type **get-command** to get a full list of all available cmdlets on the server.
- Type **get-excommand** to get a full list of all Exchange-specific cmdlets available.
- Type **help** *cmdletName* to get help information, where *cmdletName* is the name of the command you are looking up.

You'll find a comprehensive discussion of the Exchange Management Shell and Microsoft Command Shell in Chapter 6, "Configuring Microsoft Exchange Server with Exchange Management Shell," as well as examples of using cmdlets for Exchange Server management throughout the book.

Chapter 2
Deploying Microsoft Exchange Server 2007

Before you deploy Exchange Server 2007, you should carefully plan the messaging architecture. As part of your implementation planning, you need to look closely at the roles your Exchange servers will perform and modify the hardware accordingly to meet the requirements of these roles on a per-server basis. Exchange Server is no longer the simple messaging server that it once was. It is now a complex messaging platform with many components that work together to provide a comprehensive solution for routing, delivering, and accessing e-mails, voice mails, faxes, contacts, and calendar information.

Exchange Server Messaging Roles

With Exchange Server Setup, you can deploy servers with specific roles throughout the enterprise. Prior to setup and configuration, you need to decide how you will use Exchange Server 2007, what roles you will deploy, and where you will locate those roles. Afterward, you can plan for your deployment and then roll out Exchange Server.

Understanding Exchange Server Messaging Roles

As discussed in Chapter 1, "Microsoft Exchange Server 2007 Administration Overview," Exchange Server 2007 implementations have three layers in their architecture: a network layer, an Active Directory layer, and a messaging layer. The messaging layer is where you define and deploy the Exchange Server roles. The Exchange servers at the core of the messaging layer can operate in the following roles:

- **Mailbox Server** A back-end server that hosts mailboxes, public folders, and related messaging data, such as address lists, resource scheduling, and meeting items. Using Microsoft Outlook, as discussed in Chapter 3, "Managing Microsoft Exchange Server 2007 Clients," local users can connect directly to the Mailbox server and check their messages. The Mailbox Server role is the only role that you can cluster.

- **Client Access Server** A middle-tier server that accepts connections to Exchange Server from a variety of different clients. This server hosts the protocols used by clients when checking messages remotely or over the Internet. Using Outlook Anywhere, Outlook Web Access, or Exchange ActiveSync, as discussed in Chapter 4, "Managing Mobile Messaging Users," remote users can connect to the Client Access server and check their messages.

- **Unified Messaging Server**   A middle-tier server that integrates a private branch eXchange (PBX) system with Exchange Server 2007, allowing voice messages and faxes to be stored with e-mail in a user's mailbox. Unified messaging supports call answering with automated greetings and message recording, fax receiving, and dial-in access. With dial-in access, users can use Outlook Voice Access to check voice mail, e-mail, and calendar information; to review or dial contacts; and to configure preferences and personal options.

- **Hub Transport Server**   Previously called a bridgehead server, this is a mail routing server that handles mail flow, routing, and delivery within the Exchange organization. This server processes all mail that is sent inside the organization before it is delivered to a mailbox in the organization or routed to users outside the organization. Processing ensures that senders and recipients are resolved and filtered as appropriate, content is filtered and has its format converted if necessary, and attachments are screened. To meet any regulatory or organizational compliance requirements, the Hub Transport server can also record, or journal, messages and add disclaimers to them.

- **Edge Transport Server**   An additional mail routing server that routes mail into and out of the Exchange organization. This server is designed to be deployed in an organization's perimeter network and is used to establish a secure boundary between the organization and the Internet. This server accepts mail coming into the organization from the Internet and from trusted servers in external organizations, processes the mail to protect against some types of spam messages and viruses, and routes all accepted messages to a Hub Transport server inside the organization.

These five roles are the building blocks of Exchange organizations. Table 2-1 provides an overview of the supported processor configurations for these roles. Processors can be single core, dual core, or multiple core. Following this, a dedicated Mailbox server can have up to eight single-core, dual-core, or multi-core processors, but a server with Mailbox and other roles combined can only have up to four single-core, dual-core, or multi-core processors.

Table 2-1   Processor Configurations for Exchange Server 2007 Roles

Server Role	Minimum	Recommended	Maximum
Edge Transport	1	2	4
Hub Transport	1	4	8
Client Access	1	4	4
Unified Messaging	1	4	4
Mailbox	1	4	8
Multiple server roles	1	4	4

In a nonclustered environment, you can combine all of the roles except the Edge Transport Server role on a single server. Given this, one of the most basic Exchange organizations you can create is one that includes a single Exchange server that provides the Mailbox Server, Client Access Server, and Hub Transport Server roles. These three roles are the minimum required for routing and delivering messages to both local and remote messaging clients. For added security and protection, you can deploy the Edge Transport Server role in a perimeter network on one or more separate servers.

Deploying Mailbox Servers: The Essentials

The underlying functionality of a Mailbox server is similar to that of a database server. Every mailbox-enabled recipient defined in the organization has a mailbox that is used to store messaging data. Groups of related mailboxes are organized using storage groups, and each storage group can have one or more storage databases associated with it.

To provide failure protection, you can configure the Mailbox Server role as a cluster resource, allowing the messaging workload of a failed server to automatically shift to another server in a cluster. Exchange Server 2007 has several enhancements that may change the way you use clustering for messaging servers, including:

- **Continuous replication**   With continuous replication, Exchange Server 2007 uses its built-in asynchronous replication technology to create copies of storage groups and then keep the copies up-to-date using transaction log shipping and replay. In a nonclustered environment, you can use local continuous replication to create local copies of storage groups. In a clustered environment, you can use cluster continuous replication to make sure that logs on an active node are copied to a passive node. With Exchange Server 2007 SP1 or later, you also have the option of using standby continuous replication to copy logs on an active node to a standby node.

- **Single-copy clusters**   With single-copy clusters, all Mailbox servers in a cluster use shared storage, allowing multiple servers to manage a single copy of your storage groups. Because Mailbox servers now have their own network identity, not the identity of the cluster node, failover is smoother than with previous versions of Exchange and allows a clustered mailbox to be logically disconnected from the failed node and placed under the control of a new host node.

Note   On Windows Server 2003, cluster continuous replication requires remote streaming backup for seed operations, such as when you use the Update-Storage-GroupCopy cmdlet. To enable remote streaming backup, you must set the Enable Remote Streaming Backup value in the Registry to 1. This DWORD value is stored under HKLM\System\CurrentControlSet\Services\MSExchangeIS\ParametersSystem. You cannot use this feature on Windows Server 2008. Windows Server 2008 doesn't support remote streaming backup and restore operations because they aren't fully secure.

For a successful deployment of a Mailbox server, the storage subsystem must meet the storage capacity requirements and must be able to perform the expected number of input/output (I/O) operations per second. Storage capacity requirements are determined by the number of mailboxes hosted on a server and the total storage size allowed per mailbox. For example, if a server hosts 1,000 mailboxes that you allow to store up to 2 gigabytes (GB) each, you'll need to ensure there are at least 2 terabytes (TB) of storage capacity above and beyond the storage needs of the operating system and Exchange itself.

I/O performance of the storage subsystem is measured in relation to the latency (delay) for each read/write operation to be performed. The more mailboxes you store on a specific drive or drive array, the more read/write operations performed and the greater the potential delay. To improve performance, you can organize mailboxes into multiple storage groups and store the related database and transaction log files on separate disk drives.

I/O performance in Exchange Server 2007 running on 64-bit architecture is improved substantially over Exchange Server 2003 running on 32-bit architecture. On Mailbox servers, 64-bit architecture enables a database cache size of up to approximately 90 percent of total random access memory (RAM). A larger cache increases the probability that data requested by a client will be serviced out of memory instead of by the storage subsystem.

> **Real World**   Because of 64-bit architecture and new cache optimizations for the Extensible Storage Engine, Exchange Server 2007 can perform read and write operations with up to 1,024 kilobytes (KB) of data versus 64 KB of data previously. This increases the ability to read and write larger I/O and means fewer I/O operations are necessary to service requests for data.
>
> To further improve database read and write performance during I/O operations, the streaming database file and installable file system have been removed and the database page size has been increased from 4 KB to 8 KB. Removing the streaming database file and installable file system reduces overhead associated with maintaining a database. Using 8-KB database pages increases the likelihood that messages can be stored in a single database page, which also reduces the overhead associated with maintaining a database. Further, each storage group has its own transaction log, making the database file and its associated transaction log the basic unit of backup and restore operations. See Chapter 5, "Microsoft Exchange Server 2007 Administration Essentials," for more information on data storage. See Chapter 18, "Backing Up and Restoring Microsoft Exchange Server 2007," for information on backup and recovery.

Deploying Client Access Servers: The Essentials

Client Access servers handle many of the stateless messaging tasks in an Exchange implementation, and the underlying functionality is similar to that of an application server that makes extensive use of Web services. Unlike Mailbox servers, Client Access servers don't perform a great deal of I/O operations, and the primary potential bottle-necks for these servers are the processors, memory, and network. I/O operations on Client Access servers are primarily limited to protocol logging, content conversion, and paging operations. As content conversion is performed in the TMP folder, you can improve performance by ensuring that this folder is not on the same physical disk as the paging file and operating system.

Note   When you work with Windows Server 2003, Client Access servers require three Internet Information Services (IIS) 6.0 components: Enable Network COM+ Access, IIS Admin Service, and the World Wide Web Service. You can install these IIS 6.0 components through the Add Or Remove Programs utility in Control Panel. When working with Windows Server 2008, you must install IIS 7.0 with the standard default components as well as these additional components: IIS 6 metabase com-patibility, IIS 6 management console, dynamic content compression, basic authenti-cation, digest authentication, and Windows authentication.

Client Access servers provide access through the Internet Message Access Protocol 4 (IMAP4), Post Office Protocol version 3 (POP3), and Hypertext Transfer Protocol (HTTP) Internet protocols. Exchange Server 2007 allows remote access using Outlook Anywhere, Outlook Web Access, and Exchange ActiveSync. To allow full configuration for remote access, you must install the World Wide Web Service, ASP.NET, and the RPC Over HTTP Proxy Windows networking component prior to installing Exchange Server 2007. For more information on remote access to Exchange Server 2007, see Chapter 4.

Deploying Unified Messaging Servers: The Essentials

Unified messaging allows you to integrate voice mail, fax, and e-mail functionality so that the related data can be stored in a user's Exchange mailbox. To implement Unified Messaging, your organization must have a PBX that is connected to the local area network (LAN), and you must deploy a Unified Messaging server running Exchange Server 2007. Once deployed, the job of the Unified Messaging server is to provide call answering, fax receiving, subscriber access, and auto-attendant features that allow access to content over the telephone and storage of content received from the PBX.

Although some current PBXs, referred to as IP-PBXs, are Internet Protocol–capable, all other PBXs require a separate Internet Protocol/Voice over Internet Protocol (IP/VoIP) gateway to connect to the LAN. After you connect a PBX to the LAN, you can link it to Exchange by deploying and appropriately configuring the Unified Messaging Server role. Prior to installing the Unified Messaging Server role, you must install Microsoft Speech service, Microsoft Windows Media Encoder, and Microsoft Windows Media Audio Voice Code.

Note   With Windows Server 2003, Unified Messaging servers require Microsoft Core XML Services (MSXML) 6.0 or later. MSXML 6.0 supports the XML 1.0 and XML Schema 1.0 W3C Recommendations and is compatible with System.Xml 2.0. The MSXML 6.0 SDK is available as a free download from the Microsoft Web site.

With Windows Server 2008, Unified Messaging servers require Windows Media Encoder. Windows Media Encoder is used to encode voice messages and other audio files. Windows Media Encoder is available when you install the Desktop Experience feature using the Add Features Wizard. In Server Manager, click the Features node and then click Add Features to start the Add Features Wizard.

Similar to Client Access servers, Unified Messaging servers don't perform a great deal of I/O operations, and the primary potential bottlenecks for these servers are the processors, memory, and network. I/O operations on Unified Messaging servers are primarily limited to access to routing details and dial plans, which include auto-attendant and mail policy settings.

Deploying Transport Servers: The Essentials

The Hub Transport and Edge Transport roles are similar. You use both for messaging routing, and both have a similar set of filters to protect the organization from spam and viruses. The key difference is in where you place servers with these roles. You place a server with the Hub Transport role in the internal network and configure it as a member of the organizational domain. If used, you place a server with the Edge Transport role in the organization's perimeter network and you do not configure it as a member of the organizational domain.

For computers with the Hub Transport or Edge Transport role, the server cannot have the Simple Mail Transfer Protocol (SMTP) or Network News Transfer Protocol (NNTP) service installed. Although you install Edge Transport servers outside the Active Directory forest, you must have a domain name system (DNS) suffix configured and you must be able to perform name resolution from the Edge Transport server to any Hub Transport servers.

Tip   Transports servers store all incoming mail in a database file called mail.que until it is routed. This database has an associated transaction log in which changes are first committed. For optimal performance, you should place the database and the transaction log on separate disks.

Transport servers perform protocol logging, message tracking, and content conversion. Protocol logging allows you to verify whether a protocol is performing as expected and whether any issues need attention. Message tracking creates logs that track messages sent and received. Incoming mail from the Internet is converted to Messaging Application Programming Interface (MAPI) prior to being delivered. As content conversion is performed in the TMP folder, you can improve performance by ensuring that the TMP folder is not on the same physical disk as the paging file and operating system.

Note   When working with Edge Transport servers and Windows Server 2008, you must install Active Directory Lightweight Directory Service as a server role prior to installing Exchange Server 2007. Use the Add Roles Wizard to configure this role. In Server Manager, click the Roles node and then click Add Roles to start the Add Roles Wizard.

Integrating Exchange Server Roles with Active Directory

Exchange Server 2007 makes extensive use of Active Directory. Each Exchange Server 2007 role must access Active Directory to retrieve information about recipients and other Exchange server roles. Each Exchange server role uses Active Directory in other ways as well, as discussed in the sections that follow.

Note   As discussed in Chapter 1 of *Windows Server 2008 Administrator's Pocket Consultant* (Microsoft Press, 2008), you can configure Windows Server 2008 domain controllers as read-only or read-writeable. As long as writeable domain controllers and writeable global catalog servers are available, Exchange Server 2007 can work in an environment where you've deployed read-only domain controllers and read-only global catalog servers. However, Exchange Server 2007 does not make use of read-only domain controllers or read-only global catalog servers.

Using Hub Transport Servers with Active Directory

Hub Transport servers contact Active Directory when they perform message categorization. The Categorizer queries Active Directory to perform recipient lookup, retrieves the information needed to locate a recipient's mailbox (according to the mailbox store in which it is created), and determines any restrictions or permissions that may apply to the recipient. The Categorizer also queries Active Directory to expand the membership of distribution lists and to perform the Lightweight Directory Access Protocol (LDAP) query processing when mail is sent to a dynamic distribution list.

After the Categorizer determines the location of a mailbox, the Hub Transport server uses Active Directory site configuration information to determine the routing topology and locate the site in which the mailbox is located. If the mailbox is in the same Active Directory site as the Hub Transport server, the Hub Transport server delivers the message directly to the user's mailbox. If the mailbox is in a different Active Directory site from the Hub Transport server, the Hub Transport server delivers the message to a Hub Transport server in the remote Active Directory site.

Hub Transport servers store all configuration information in Active Directory. This configuration information includes the details of any transport or journaling rules and connectors. When this information is needed, a Hub Transport server accesses it in Active Directory.

Using Client Access Servers with Active Directory

Client Access servers receive connections from the Internet for users who access their mailboxes using Outlook Web Access, POP3, IMAP4, or Exchange ActiveSync. When a user connection is received, the Client Access server contacts Active Directory to authenticate the user and to determine the location of the user's mailbox. If the user's mailbox is in the same Active Directory site as the Client Access server, the user is connected to his or her mailbox. If the user's mailbox is in an Active Directory site other than the one the Client Access server is located in, the connection is redirected to a Client Access server in the same Active Directory site as the user's mailbox.

Using Unified Messaging Servers with Active Directory

Unified Messaging servers access Active Directory to retrieve global configuration information, such as dial plans and IP gateway details. When a message is received by the Unified Messaging server, the server searches for Active Directory recipients to match the telephone number to a recipient address. When the server has resolved this information, it can determine the location of the recipient's mailbox and then submit the message to the appropriate Hub Transport server for submission to the mailbox.

Using Mailbox Servers with Active Directory

Mailbox servers are service locations for e-mails, voice mails, and faxes. For outgoing mail, Mailbox servers can access Active Directory to retrieve information about the location of Hub Transport servers in their site. Then they can use this information to forward messages for routing. Mailbox servers also store configuration information about mailbox users, mailbox stores, agents, address lists, and policies in Active Directory. Mailbox servers retrieve this information to enforce recipient policies, mailbox policies, system policies, and global settings.

Using Edge Transport Servers with Active Directory

You deploy Edge Transport servers in perimeter networks and they are not domain members. Because of this, Edge Transport servers do not have direct access to the organization's internal Active Directory servers for the purposes of recipient lookup or categorization. Thus, unlike Hub Transport servers, Edge Transport servers cannot contact an Active Directory server to help route messages.

To route messages into the organization, an administrator can configure a subscription from the Edge Transport server to the Active Directory site that allows it to store recipient and configuration information about the Exchange organization in its Active Directory Application Mode (ADAM) data store. After an Edge Transport server is subscribed to an Active Directory site, it is associated with the Hub Transport servers in that site for the purposes of message routing. Thereafter, Hub Transport servers in the organization route messages being delivered to the Internet to the site associated with the Edge Transport server, and Hub Transport servers in this site relay the messages to the Edge Transport server. The Edge Transport server, in turn, routes the messages to the Internet.

The EdgeSync service running on Hub Transport servers is a one-way synchronization process that pushes information from Active Directory to the Edge Transport server. Periodically, the EdgeSync service synchronizes the data to keep the Edge Transport server's data store up-to-date. The EdgeSync service also establishes the connectors needed to send and receive information that is being moved between the organization and the Edge Transport server and between the Edge Transport server and the Internet. The key data pushed to the Edge Transport server includes:

- Accepted domains
- Valid recipients
- Safe senders
- Send connectors
- Available Hub Transport servers

After the initial replication is performed, the EdgeSync service synchronizes the data periodically. Configuration information is synced once every hour. Recipient information is synced once every four hours. If necessary, administrators can initiate an immediate synchronization using the Start-EdgeSynchronization cmdlet in the Exchange Management Shell.

> **Note** During synchronization, objects may be added to, deleted from, or modified in the Edge Transport server's ADAM data store. To protect the integrity and security of the organization, no information is ever pushed from the Edge Transport server's ADAM data store to Active Directory.

Integrating Exchange Server 2007 into Existing Exchange Organizations

Existing Exchange 2000 Server and Exchange Server 2003 installations can coexist with Exchange Server 2007 installations. Generally, you do this by integrating Exchange Server 2007 into your existing Exchange 2000 Server or Exchange Server 2003 organization. Integration requires:

- Preparing Active Directory and the domain for the extensive Active Directory changes that will occur when you install Exchange Server 2007.
- Configuring Exchange Server 2007 so that it can communicate with Exchange Server 2000 and Exchange Server 2003 servers.

You cannot upgrade existing Exchange 2000 Server and Exchange Server 2003 servers and organizations to Exchange Server 2007. You must install Exchange Server 2007 on new hardware, and then move the mailboxes from your existing installations to the new installation. See "Transitioning to Exchange Server 2007" later in this chapter for more details.

Preparing Active Directory for Exchange Server 2007

Exchange Server 2007 can be integrated into Exchange 2000 Server and Exchange Server 2003 organizations. If you have any servers running Exchange 2000 Server or Exchange Server 2003, you need to prepare Active Directory and the domain for the extensive Active Directory changes that will occur when you install Exchange Server 2007. You do this by completing the following steps:

1. Run Setup with the /PrepareLegacyExchangePermissions option. To success-fully run this command, you must be a member of the Exchange Admins groups and the domain in which you run this command must be able to contact all domains in the forest.

2. After all permissions have replicated across your entire Exchange organization, run Setup with the /PrepareSchema option to connect to the schema master and update the schema with attributes for Exchange Server 2007. To run this com-mand, you must be a member of the Schema Admins group and the Exchange Admins group. You must run this command on a computer in the same Active Directory domain and same Active Directory site as the schema master. The schema master is located in the forest root domain.

3. After all schema changes have been made, run Setup with the /PrepareAD option to configure global Exchange objects in Active Directory, create Exchange Universal Security groups in the root domain, and prepare the current domain for Exchange Server 2007. To run this command, you must be a member of the Enterprise Admins group. When completed, the root domain should have a new organizational unit called Microsoft Exchange Security Groups, and this organizational unit should contain the following groups: Exchange Organization Administrators, Exchange Recipient Administrators, Exchange View-Only Administrators, Exchange Servers, and Exchange2003Interop.

4. Finalize security settings for Exchange Server 2007 by preparing the local domain by running Setup with the /PrepareDomain option, or preparing all domains by running setup with the /PrepareAllDomains option. To run this command, you must be a member of the Domain Admins groups for the local domain or the Enterprise Admins group.

Configuring Exchange Server 2007 for Use with Existing Exchange Organizations

All the Exchange 2007 server roles are supported for coexistence with a native-mode Exchange organization. In the Exchange System Manager for Exchange 2000 Server and Exchange Server 2003, all Exchange servers are displayed as members of the Exchange Administrative Group. Exchange Server 2007 servers are also displayed as members of the Exchange Routing Group. These groups are created only for purposes of coexistence with Exchange 2000 Server and Exchange Server 2003.

When managing Exchange servers, you should use the administrative tools for that Exchange Server version. Exchange Server 2007 doesn't use Active Directory Users And Computers for recipient management, and instead uses only the Exchange Management Console and the Exchange Management Shell for this purpose. The Exchange Management Console and the Exchange Management Shell are the primary management tools for Exchange Server 2007.

Mailboxes located on Exchange 2000 Server and Exchange Server 2003 servers are also displayed in the Exchange Management Console. You can manage the Exchange 2000 Server and Exchange Server 2003 mailbox properties using the Exchange Management Console or the Exchange Management Shell. However, you can use only the Exchange Management Shell to move mailbox recipients from Exchange 2000 Server and Exchange Server 2003 to Exchange 2007.

When deploying Exchange Server 2007 in an Exchange 2000 Server or Exchange Server 2003 organization, keep the following in mind:

- If you want to use the Exchange Server 2007 Client Access Server role, you must deploy a Client Access Server role in each Active Directory site that contains the Mailbox Server role. Clients will see the Microsoft Office Outlook Web Access or Exchange ActiveSync version that is on their mailbox store.

- If you want to use the Hub Transport Server role, you must configure a two-way routing group connector from the Exchange Routing Group to each Exchange Server 2003 routing group that communicates directly with Exchange Server 2007. You must also suppress link state updates for each Exchange Routing Group that communicates with Exchange Server 2007.

- If you want to use the Unified Messaging Server role, you must deploy the Exchange Server 2007 Hub Transport Server role in the same Active Directory site as the Unified Messaging Server role. Keep in mind that Exchange Server 2003 mailboxes cannot be unified messaging–enabled.

- If you want to use the Mailbox Server role, you must deploy the Exchange Server 2007 Hub Transport Server role in the same Active Directory site as the Mailbox Server role.

- If you want to use the Edge Transport Server role, you must configure SMTP connectors to accept mail from and send mail to the Internet. Four connector configurations are needed: Internet Send Connector, Internet Receive Connector, Legacy Send Connector, and Legacy Receive Connector. Other modifications are required to mail Exchange and smart host records. Further, you can synchronize the Edge Transport server's ADAM data with Active Directory only if the Exchange Server 2007 Active Directory preparation process has been performed.

Moving to Exchange Server 2007

Most organizations have existing Exchange installations. When moving those installations to Exchange Server 2007, you cannot perform an in-place upgrade. Instead, you must install new Exchange Server 2007 servers into the existing organization and then either migrate or transition to Exchange Server 2007.

- Migration from Exchange 2000 Server or Exchange Server 2003 to Exchange Server 2007 involves installing Exchange Server 2007 on new hardware and then moving the mailboxes from your existing installations to the new installation. In a migration, only mailbox data is moved and any Exchange configuration data is not maintained.

- Transitioning from Exchange 2000 Server or Exchange Server 2003 to Exchange Server 2007 is a multiple-phase process that allows for the retention of Exchange configuration and mailbox data. During these transitioning processes, the Exchange organization is considered to be operating in a coexistence mode.

Migrating to Exchange Server 2007

Migration from Exchange 2000 Server or Exchange Server 2003 to Exchange Server 2007 moves the mailboxes from your existing installations to your new Exchange Server 2007 installations. In a migration, only mailbox data is moved and any Exchange configuration data is not maintained.

The steps you perform to migrate from Exchange 2000 Server or Exchange Server 2003 to Exchange Server 2007 are as follows:

1. Install Exchange Server 2007 on new hardware, and make it a member of the appropriate domain in the forest. At a minimum, you should install the Client Access Server role, the Hub Transport Server role, and the Mailbox Server role. You can install these roles on a single server or on multiple servers. If you plan to have an Edge Transport server in your Exchange 2007 organization, you must install the Edge Transport Server role on a separate computer.

2. Move mailboxes from your existing Exchange Server 2003 or Exchange 2000 Server installations to the new Exchange Server 2007 Mailbox server or servers.

3. If you want to remove your Exchange 2000 Server or Exchange Server 2003 servers, you must first remove Exchange Server 2003 routing groups and all connectors to these routing groups. Also, keep the following in mind:

   ❑ Exchange Server 2007 does not support the following Exchange 2000 Server features: Microsoft Mobile Information Server, Instant Messaging service, Exchange Chat service, Exchange 2000 Conferencing Server, Key Management service, cc:Mail connector, or MS Mail connector. If you require any of these features, you must retain at least one computer running Exchange 2000 Server in your organization.

   ❑ Exchange Server 2007 does not support the Novell GroupWise connector for Exchange Server 2003 or the use of the Inter-Organization Replication tool to share free/busy and public folder data across forests. If you require these features, you must keep at least one Exchange Server 2003 server in your organization.

4. Remove your old Exchange Server 2003 or Exchange 2000 Server server from the organization.

Transitioning to Exchange Server 2007

The steps you perform to transition from Exchange 2000 Server or Exchange Server 2003 to Exchange Server 2007 depend on the forest configuration. To transition from a single forest organization to a single forest organization or to deploy Exchange Server 2007 in an Exchange resource forest and then transition to Exchange Server 2007, follow these steps:

1. Install Exchange Server 2007 on new hardware, and make it a member of the appropriate domain in the forest. At a minimum, you should install the Client Access Server role, the Hub Transport Server role, and the Mailbox Server role. You can install these roles on a single server or on multiple servers. If you plan to have an Edge Transport server in your Exchange 2007 organization, you must install the Edge Transport Server role on a separate computer.

2. Move mailboxes from your existing Exchange Server 2003 or Exchange 2000 Server installations to the new Exchange Server 2007 Mailbox server or servers.

3. For any public folders in your existing Exchange 2000 Server or Exchange Server 2003 organization that you want to maintain, create a replica on your Exchange Server 2007 Mailbox server or servers. You must create the replica using Exchange System Manager in the Exchange 2000 Server or Exchange Server 2003 organization. Exchange will then replicate the public folder data to the Exchange Server 2007 Mailbox server or servers.

   Note   You do not need to create replicas for the offline address book (OAB) or free/busy system folders. When you install the first Exchange Server 2007 server, Exchange creates these replicas.

4. If you want to remove your Exchange 2000 Server or Exchange 2003 Server servers, you must first remove Exchange Server 2003 routing groups and all connectors to these routing groups. Also, keep the following in mind:

   ❑ Exchange Server 2007 does not support the following Exchange 2000 Server features: Microsoft Mobile Information Server, Instant Messaging service, Exchange Chat service, Exchange 2000 Conferencing Server, Key Management service, cc:Mail connector, or MS Mail connector. If you require any of these features, you must retain at least one computer running Exchange 2000 Server in your organization.

   ❑ Exchange Server 2007 does not support the Novell GroupWise connector for Exchange Server 2003 or the use of the Inter-Organization Replication tool to share free/busy and public folder data across forests. If you require these features, you must keep at least one Exchange Server 2003 server in your organization.

5. Remove your old Exchange Server 2003 or Exchange 2000 Server server from the organization.

In some cases, you may want to have one or more forests that contain accounts and a separate resource forest for your Exchange organization. Although configuring a separate resource forest provides clear separation between accounts and your Exchange organization, it requires a great deal of predeployment planning and additional work to maintain. In the Exchange forest, you must disable any user accounts with mailboxes and then associate these disabled user accounts, and all other user accounts, with the user accounts in your other forests. To do this, you must install Microsoft Integration Identity Server 2003 or later, or the Identity Integration Feature Pack 1a or later for Microsoft Windows Server Active Directory and then use its GAL Synchronization feature to create mail-enabled contacts that represent recipients from other forests.

To transition from a single forest organization to a resource forest organization, follow these steps:

1. Create a new Active Directory forest, and then create a one-way, outgoing forest trust from this forest to your existing forest. This ensures that the Exchange Server 2007 resource forest trusts the existing forest. You will need the trust so that you can move mailboxes from servers in the existing forest to servers in the Exchange Server 2007 forest.

2. In the Exchange Server 2007 forest, install Exchange Server 2007 on new hardware, and make it a member of the appropriate domain in this forest. At a minimum, you should install the Client Access Server role, the Hub Transport Server role, and the Mailbox Server role. You can install these roles on a single server or on multiple servers. If you plan to have an Edge Transport server in your Exchange Server 2007 organization, you must install the Edge Transport Server role on a separate computer.

3. Move all mailboxes from the existing forest to the Exchange Server 2007 forest. You must move all mailboxes. If you do not move all mailboxes, you will be in an unsupported hybrid forest scenario.

4. To complete the transition, follow steps 3 through 5 from the procedure previously described under "Transitioning to Exchange Server 2007."

Running and Modifying Exchange Server 2007 Setup

Exchange Server 2007 Setup is the program you use to perform installation tasks for Exchange Server 2007. You use Exchange Server 2007 Setup to install Exchange Server roles and the Exchange management tools. When you want to manage the Exchange server configuration, you use Add Or Remove Programs in Control Panel. Tasks you can perform with these utilities include:

- Installing Exchange Server roles and management tools
- Adding server roles or management tools
- Maintaining existing components
- Uninstalling Exchange Server

Installing New Exchange Servers

You can install multiple Exchange Server roles on a single computer. For servers deployed within the organization, you can deploy any combination of the Mailbox, Client Access, Hub Transport, and Unified Messaging roles on a single computer. You cannot combine the Edge Transport role with other roles, however, because this is an optional role for the organization's perimeter network and you must install it separately from other roles.

In clustered environments, you use one of the modified cluster Mailbox Server roles rather than the standard Mailbox Server role. For clustered servers, you must use either the active clustered Mailbox role or the passive clustered Mailbox role, depending on whether you are configuring an active node or a passive node in the cluster as a Mailbox server. You cannot install a clustered Mailbox server on a server with any other roles.

Often, small and medium organizations can deploy a single Exchange server per Active Directory site that hosts the Mailbox, Client Access, Hub Transport, and Unified Messaging roles and may not need to have an Edge Transport server in a perimeter zone. As the size and needs of the organization increase, however, it becomes more and more beneficial to host some roles on separate servers. Keep the following in mind:

- You can achieve increased efficiency for message routing and delivery by combining the Mailbox and Hub Transport roles on a single server.

■ You can achieve increased security by isolating the Client Access role and deploying it on a server other than one that also hosts the Mailbox and Hub Transport roles.

■ You can improve responsiveness for dial-in and voice access by isolating the Unified Messaging role and deploying it on a server other than one that also hosts the Mailbox and Hub Transport roles.

When you use multiple Exchange servers, you should deploy the roles in the following order:

1. Client Access server

2. Hub Transport server

3. Mailbox server

4. Unified Messaging server

For client access to work correctly, install at least one Client Access server in each Active Directory site that has a Mailbox server. For Hub Transport, Mailbox, and Unified Messaging servers, install at least one of each server role for each group of Active Directory sites that are well connected on a common LAN. For example, if the organization consists of Sites A and B, which are well connected on a common LAN, and Sites C and D, which are well connected on a common LAN, with wide area network (WAN) links connecting Sites A and B to Sites C and D, a minimal recommended implementation would be to have Hub Transport, Mailbox, and Unified Messaging servers only in Site A and Site C.

Because you install Edge Transport servers outside the Active Directory forest, you can deploy them at any time. By configuring multiple Edge Transport servers, you can ensure that if one server fails, Edge Transport services continue. If you also configure your Edge Transport servers with round-robin DNS, you can load-balance between them.

Installing Exchange Server

The Exchange Server 2007 installation process has changed considerably since Exchange Server 2003. The installation process now requires the .NET Framework version 2.0 or later, Microsoft Management Console version 3.0 or later, and Windows PowerShell Version 1.0 or later. In Setup, links are provided so that you can download and install the most recent versions of these applications. The installation process also requires Windows Installer 3.0 or later, which is included in Windows Server 2003 Release 2, Windows Server 2003 Service Pack 1, and later releases of Windows Server. Some Exchange server roles also require IIS components, as discussed previously.

Using Windows Installer helps to streamline and stabilize the installation process and makes modification of installation components easier. You can:

- Install additional roles or components by re-running the Installation Wizard.

- Maintain installed components. With Windows Server 2003, use Add Or Remove Programs in Control Panel. With Windows Server 2008, use the Programs And Feature page under Control Panel\Programs.

- Resume a failed installation or modification. With Windows Server 2003, use Add Or Remove Programs in Control Panel. With Windows Server 2008, use the Programs And Feature page under Control Panel\Programs.

For administration purposes, you can install the Exchange management tools on a workstation computer running Windows XP Service Pack 2 or later. This workstation must also have the Microsoft Command Shell installed.

Real World   To upgrade Exchange Server 2007 RTM to Exchange Server 2007 SP1 or later, run Setup from the Exchange 2007 SP1 or later media/folder. On the Start page, click Install Microsoft Exchange Server 2007 to start the Exchange Server 2007 Installation Wizard. Because you cannot specify which server roles to upgrade, accept all the default options to perform a full upgrade to Exchange Server 2007 SP1 or later.

Like Exchange Server 2007, Forefront Security for Exchange Server has several variants. Forefront Security for Exchange Server RTM is the original release. This variant only works with Exchange Server 2007 RTM and is incompatible with Exchange Server 2007 SP1. Before you can install Exchange Server 2007 SP1 or later, you must either remove any existing Forefront Security for Exchange Server RTM installations or upgrade existing Forefront Security for Exchange Server RTM installations to a later edition, such as Forefront Security for Exchange Server with SP1.

Throughout the rest of the book, I will assume you are installing and working with Exchange Server 2007 SP1 or later. For this reason, I will no longer differentiate between Exchange Server 2007 RTM and Exchange Server 2007 SP1 or later. I will, however, point out differences between Exchange Server 2007 administration on Windows Server 2003 and Exchange Server 2007 administration on Windows Server 2008.

To install Exchange Server roles on a server, complete the following steps:

1. Log on to the server using an administrator account. When you install the Mailbox, Hub Transport, Client Access, and Unified Messaging roles, you must use a domain account that is a member of the Enterprise Administrators group. If you've already prepared Active Directory, this account must also be a member of the Exchange Organization Administrators group.

2. Insert the Exchange Server 2007 DVD into the DVD-ROM drive. If Autorun is enabled, Exchange Server 2007 Setup should start automatically. Otherwise, double-click Setup.exe on the root folder of the DVD.

3. On the Start page, click the links for steps 1, 2, and 3, each in turn. This will help you download and install the .NET Framework version 2.0 or later, Microsoft Management Console version 3.0 or later, and Microsoft PowerShell Version 1.0 or later.

4. On the Start page, click Step 4: Install Microsoft Exchange. In the Exchange Server 2007 Installation Wizard, read the introductory text, and then click Next.

5. On the License Agreement page, select I Accept The Terms In The License Agreement, and then click Next.

6. On the Error Reporting page, choose Yes if you'd like to send error reports automatically to Microsoft or No if you would like to turn off automatic error reporting. Click Next.

7. On the Installation Type page, click Custom Exchange Server Installation and then click Next.

8. On the Server Role Selection Page, select the server roles that you want to install on the computer. When you select one or more roles, the wizard selects the Management Tools option automatically to install the Exchange management tools. The default installation location for Exchange Server and all its components is %SystemDrive%\Program Files\Microsoft\Exchange Server. If you want to change the path for the Exchange Server 2007 installation, click Browse, locate the relevant folder in the folder tree, and then click OK. Click Next.

    Note   When you are installing production versions of Exchange Server 2007, the Management Tools option installs the 64-bit management tools. Although you can manage Exchange Server 2007 remotely from a 32-bit Windows Vista or 32-bit Windows Server 2008 installation, you must do so using 32-bit tools. You can download the 32-bit management tools from the Microsoft Downloads site.

9. If you selected Mailbox Role, Client Access Role, Hub Transport Role, or Unified Messaging Role, and if this is the first Exchange 2007 server in your organization, on the Exchange Organization page, type a name for your Exchange organization or accept the default value of First Organization. Click Next.

10. If you selected Mailbox Role, and if this is the first Exchange 2007 server in your organization, you'll next see the Client Settings page. If you have client computers that are running Outlook 2003 and earlier or Entourage, select the Yes option so that Exchange will create a public folder database on the mailbox server. If all of your client computers are running Outlook 2007, public folders are optional, because the OAB and free/busy information are maintained separately. If you

select the No option, Exchange will not create a public folder database on the mailbox server. You can add a public folder database later if desired. Click Next.

11. On the Readiness Checks page, Setup then checks to see whether Exchange is ready to be installed with the roles you selected. Review the status to determine whether the organization and server role prerequisite checks completed successfully. You must complete any required prerequisites before continuing. Once checks are completed successfully, click Install to install Exchange Server 2007.

12. On the Completion page, click Finish. When the installation completes, you may need to restart the server. Restart the server if prompted and then verify the installation by doing the following on the server:

   ❑ Start the Exchange Management Shell, and type **get-ExchangeServer** to display a list of all Exchange roles installed on that server.

   ❑ Review the application logs for events from Exchange Setup. These events have event IDs 1003 and 1004, with the source as MSExchangeSetup.

   ❑ Review the Exchange Setup logs in the %SystemRoot%\Exchange-SetupLogs folder. Because these logs contain standard text, you can perform a search using the keyword "error" to find any setup errors that occurred.

Real World   With a new Exchange Server 2007 implementation, each new recipient object (such as a mailbox, contact, distribution list, mailbox-agent, or mail-enabled public folder) will have a special attribute called legacyDN that corresponds to the new administrative group for the Exchange Server 2007 server. Because of this legacyDN, Microsoft Outlook will request a full OAB download from the Exchange Server 2007 server for each user in this organization that logs on. In a large organization, this could mean multiple simultaneous OAB downloads, which, in turn, could cause high network utilization.

To complete the installation for an initial deployment of Exchange into an organization, you'll need to perform the following tasks:

■ For Client Access servers:

   ❑ If you plan to use ActiveSync for mobile messaging clients, as discussed in Chapter 4, configure direct push, authentication, and mobile devices.

   ❑ Configure the Outlook Web Access URL, authentication, and display options.

   ❑ Enable the server for POP3 and IMAP4, as appropriate.

■ For Edge Transport servers:

   ❑ Export the Edge Transport server subscription file, and import it on Hub Transport servers, as discussed in Chapter 15, "Managing Hub Transport and Edge Transport Servers."

- ❑ If you are using Edge Transport servers with Exchange 2000 Server or Exchange Server 2003 organizations, you must manually configure the necessary connectors, as discussed previously.

- ❑ Configure a postmaster mailbox for each mail domain.

- ❑ Configure DNS MX resource records for each accepted domain.

- ❑ Configure antispam, junk e-mail, and safe sender features, as appropriate.

- ■ For Hub Transport servers:

  - ❑ Configure domains for which you will accept e-mail. You will need an accepted domain entry for each SMTP domain for which you will accept e-mail, as discussed in Chapter 15.

  - ❑ If you also deployed the Edge Transport Server role, you will need to subscribe to the Edge Transport server so that the EdgeSync service can establish one-way replication of recipient and configuration information from Active Directory to the Active Directory ADAM store on the Edge Transport server. See Chapter 15 for details.

  - ❑ Create a postmaster mailbox so that you can receive mail addresses to the postmaster address, as discussed in Chapter 15.

  - ❑ Configure DNS MX resource records for each accepted domain.

- ■ For Mailbox servers:

  - ❑ Configure OAB distribution for Outlook 2007 clients, as discussed in Chapter 9, "Working with Distribution Groups and Address Lists."

  - ❑ Configure OAB distribution for Outlook 2003 or earlier clients, as discussed in Chapter 9.

  - ❑ Configure storage groups and databases, as discussed in Chapter 11, "Managing Microsoft Exchange Server 2007 Data and Storage Groups."

- ■ For Unified Messaging servers:

  - ❑ Configure a unified messaging dial plan, and add the server to it.

  - ❑ Configure Unified Messaging hunt groups.

  - ❑ Enable users for unified messaging, as appropriate.

  - ❑ Configure your IP/VoIP gateways or IP-PBXs to work with Exchange server.

  - ❑ Configure a Unified Messaging IP gateway in Exchange server.

  - ❑ As desired, create auto-attendant and mailbox policies and configure additional dial plans, gateways, and hunt groups.

Adding, Modifying, or Uninstalling Server Roles

After you install an Exchange server with its initial role or roles, you can add new roles or remove existing roles. The technique you use with Windows Server 2003 is different from the one for Windows Server 2008.

With Windows Server 2003, use Add Or Remove Programs and then follow these steps:

1. In Control Panel, double-click Add Or Remove Programs. In Add Or Remove Programs, click the Microsoft Exchange Server 2007 entry to display the Change and Remove buttons.

2. To add roles or the management tools to an installation, click Change to start the Exchange Server 2007 Setup in update maintenance mode. You will then be able to use Setup to add roles to the server or to install the management tools, if they weren't previously installed. Simply select the check boxes for the roles you want to add, click Next, and then follow the prompts.

3. To remove roles from an installation, click Remove to start the Exchange Server 2007 Setup in modify maintenance mode. You will then be able to use Setup to remove roles from the server. Simply clear the check boxes for the roles you want to remove, click Next, and then follow the prompts.

With Windows Server 2008, use Programs And Features and follow these steps:

1. In Control Panel, click the Uninstall A Program link under Programs. In Programs And Features, select the Microsoft Exchange Server 2007 entry to display the Change and Uninstall buttons.

2. Click Change to start the Exchange Server 2007 Setup in update maintenance mode. You will then be able to use Setup to add or remove roles. Select the check boxes for the roles you want to add. Clear the check boxes for roles you want to remove. Click Next, and then follow the prompts.

Before you can remove the Mailbox role from a server, you must move or delete all mailboxes hosted in mailbox databases on the server and all offline address books hosted in public folder databases on the server. If the public folder database is the last one in the Exchange organization—which may be the case if you are uninstalling Exchange on a test or development server—you will need to use the Exchange Management Shell to delete the public folder database once you've emptied it.

To remove the last public folder database in the Exchange organization, type the following command at the Exchange Management Shell prompt:

```
get-publicfolderdatabase | remove-publicfolderdatabase
 -oktoremovelastpublicfolderdatabase
```

You'll see the following warning prompt:

```
Confirm
Are you sure you want to perform this action? Removing Public Folder
Database "CORPSVR127\Second Storage Group\Public Folder Database".
[Y] Yes  [A] Yes to All  [N] No  [L] No to All  [S] Suspend  [?] Help
(default is "Y"):
```

Carefully read the details regarding which public folder database you are removing. Press Y to proceed. You'll then see the following additional warning prompt:

```
Confirm
You are attempting to remove the last public folder database in the
organization. If you remove this database, all its contents will be lost
and only users running Outlook 2007 or later will be able to connect
to your Exchange organization. Are you sure that you want to delete
the last public folder database?
[Y] Yes  [A] Yes to All  [N] No  [L] No to All  [S] Suspend  [?] Help
(default is "Y"):
```

Carefully read the details regarding which public folder database you are removing. Press Y to proceed. You'll see a final warning similar to the following:

```
WARNING: The specified database has been removed. You must remove the
database file located in C:\Program Files\Microsoft\Exchange Server\
Mailbox\Second Storage Group\Public Folder Database.edb
from your computer manually if it exists.
```

Chapter 3
Managing Microsoft Exchange Server 2007 Clients

As a Microsoft Exchange administrator, you need to know how to configure and maintain Exchange clients. With Microsoft Exchange Server 2007, you can use any mail client that supports standard mail protocols. For ease of administration, however, you'll want to choose a specific client for on-site users as a standard and supplement it with a specific client for off-site or mobile users. The on-site and off-site clients can be the same. I recommend focusing on Microsoft Windows Mail, Microsoft Office Outlook 2007, and Outlook Web Access. Each client supports a slightly different set of features and messaging protocols, and each client has its advantages and disadvantages, including the following:

- With Outlook 2007, you get a full-featured client that on-site, off-site, and mobile users can use. Outlook 2007 is part of the 2007 Microsoft Office system of applications, and is the only mail client spotlighted here that features full support for the latest messaging features in Exchange Server. Corporate and workgroup users often need its rich support for calendars, scheduling, voice mail, and e-mail management.

- With Windows Mail, you get a lightweight client that's best suited for off-site or mobile users. Windows Mail is the replacement for Outlook Express and is installed by default with Windows Vista. Although Windows Mail supports standard messaging protocols for POP3 and IMAP4, the client doesn't support HTTP mail, calendars, scheduling, voice mail, or key messaging features of Exchange Server. Windows Mail is, however, fairly easy to configure.

- With Outlook Web Access, you get a mail client that you can access securely through a standard Web browser. With Microsoft Internet Explorer 5.0 or later, Outlook Web Access supports most of the features found in Outlook 2007, including calendars, scheduling, and voice mail. With other browsers, the client functionality remains the same, but some features, such as voice mail, might not be supported. You don't need to configure Outlook Web Access on the client, and it's ideal for users who want to access e-mail while away from the office.

Outlook 2007 is the most common Exchange client for corporate and workgroup environments. With the Outlook Anywhere feature of Exchange, which eliminates the need for a virtual private network (VPN) to securely access Exchange Server over the Internet by using a remote procedure call (RPC) over Hypertext Transfer Protocol (HTTP) connection, Outlook 2007 might also be your client of choice for off-site and mobile users. The catch with Outlook Anywhere is that the feature is not enabled by default, requires additional components, and is supported only when Exchange Server 2007 is running on Microsoft Windows Server 2003 or later releases of Windows Server.

Windows Mail and Outlook Web Access, on the other hand, aren't designed for corporate users and are really meant for off-site or mobile users. Both clients are easy to configure and require relatively little back-end configuration. In fact, you can quickly and easily configure Exchange Server to work with these clients.

This chapter shows you how to manage Outlook 2007 and Windows Mail. Chapter 4, "Managing Mobile Messaging Users," describes using Outlook 2007, Outlook Web Access, and Outlook Anywhere.

Configuring Mail Support for Outlook 2007 and Windows Mail

You can install both Outlook 2007 and Windows Mail as clients on a user's computer. The following sections look at these topics:

- Configuring Outlook 2007 and Windows Mail for the first time
- Adding Internet mail accounts to Outlook 2007 and Windows Mail
- Reconfiguring Outlook 2007 mail support
- Setting advanced mail options

Configuring Outlook 2007 for the First Time

You can install Outlook 2007 as a stand-alone product or as part of the 2007 Office system. Outlook 2007 can be used to connect to the following types of e-mail servers:

- **Microsoft Exchange Server**   Connects directly to Exchange Server; best for users who are connected to the organization's local area network (LAN). Users will have full access to Exchange Server. If users plan to connect to Exchange Server using Outlook Anywhere, this is the option to choose as well. With Exchange Server, users can check mail on an e-mail server and download the mail to their inbox. They can access any private or public folders to which they have been granted permissions.

- **POP3**   Connects to Exchange or another Post Office Protocol 3 (POP3) e-mail server through the Internet; best for users who are connecting from a remote location, such as a home or a remote office, using dial-up or broadband Internet access. With POP3, users can check mail on an e-mail server and download it to their inboxes. Users can't, however, synchronize mailbox folders or access private or public folders on the server. By using advanced configuration settings, the user can elect to download the mail and leave it on the server for future use.

By leaving the mail on the server, the user can check mail on a home computer and still download it to an office computer later.

- **IMAP4**   Connects to Exchange or another Internet Message Access Protocol Version 4 (IMAP4) e-mail server through the Internet; best for users who are connecting from a remote location, such as a home or a remote office, using dial-up or broadband Internet access. Also well suited for users who have a single computer, such as a laptop, that they use to check mail both at the office and away from it. With IMAP4, users can check mail on an e-mail server and synchronize mailbox folders. Users can also download only message headers and then access each e-mail individually to download it. Unlike POP3, IMAP4 has no option to leave mail on the server. IMAP4 also lets users access public and private folders on an Exchange server.

- **HTTP**   Connects to an HTTP e-mail server, such as MSN Hotmail, through the Internet; best as an additional e-mail configuration option. Here, users can have an external e-mail account with a Web-based e-mail service that they can check in addition to corporate e-mail.

- **Additional Server Types**   Connects to a third-party mail server or other types of mail servers. If your organization has multiple types of mail servers, including Exchange Server, you'll probably want to configure a connection to Exchange Server first and then add additional e-mail account configurations later.

Unlike earlier releases of Outlook, Outlook 2007 is fairly easy to configure. To begin, log on to the computer as the user whose e-mail you are configuring. If the computer is part of a domain, you should log on using the user's domain account. If you are configuring e-mail for use with a direct Exchange Server connection rather than a POP3, IMAP4, or HTTP connection, you should ensure that the user's mailbox has been created. If the user's mailbox has not been created, auto-setup will fail, as will the rest of the account configuration.

> **Note**   You can configure both Outlook 2007 and Windows Mail on the same computer. If you configure Windows Mail after configuring Outlook 2007, Windows Mail assumes you may be migrating from Outlook 2007 to Windows Mail and offers to import Outlook mail after you complete the initial e-mail setup. If you configure Outlook 2007 after configuring Windows Mail, Outlook 2007 does not offer to import mail from Windows Mail. If you want to import mail from Windows Mail or another program to Outlook 2007, you'll need to use the Import And Export Wizard, which you can start by selecting File and then clicking Import And Export.

The first time you start Outlook 2007, the application runs the Outlook 2007 Startup Wizard. You can use the Startup Wizard to configure e-mail for Exchange Server, POP3, IMAP4, and HTTP mail servers, as discussed in the sections that follow.

First-Time Configuration: Connecting to Exchange Server

You can use the Startup Wizard to configure e-mail for Exchange Server in Outlook 2007 by completing the following steps:

1. Start Outlook 2007 and click Next on the Welcome page.

   Note If you've previously configured Outlook Express or Windows Mail, you'll see the E-Mail Upgrade Options page. You can then elect to upgrade from or not upgrade from Outlook Express or Windows Mail. If you elect to upgrade, Outlook 2007 will attempt to import e-mail messages, address books, and settings from the e-mail programs detected during initial setup.

2. When prompted as to whether you would like to configure an e-mail account, verify that Yes is selected, and then click Next.

3. The next page of the wizard varies depending on the computer's current configuration:

   ❑ For computers that are part of a domain and for users that have an existing Exchange Server mailbox, the Startup Wizard uses the new Auto Account Setup feature to automatically discover the required account information, as shown in Figure 3-1.

   ❑ For computers that are part of a domain and for users for which you have not created an Exchange mailbox, you must exit the wizard by clicking Cancel, create the user's Exchange mailbox, and then restart Outlook 2007 to restart the Startup Wizard.

   ❑ For computers that are part of a workgroup or for which you are logged on locally, Outlook 2007 assumes that you want to configure the user to use an Internet e-mail account. You must next enter the user's account name, e-mail address, and password. Then type and confirm the user's password.

4. When you click Next, the Startup Wizard, taking advantage of the new Auto Account Setup feature, attempts to automatically discover the rest of the information needed to configure the account and then uses the settings to log on to the server. If the auto-configuration and server logon are successful, click Finish, and skip the remaining steps in this procedure. The wizard will then set up the user's Exchange mailbox on the computer as appropriate.

5. If auto-configuration is not successful, click Next so that the wizard can attempt to establish an unencrypted connection to the server. If the auto-configuration and server logon are successful this time, click Finish, and then skip the remaining steps in this procedure.

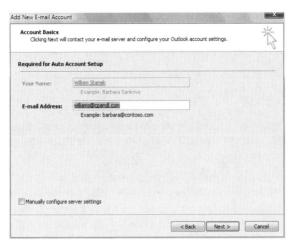

Figure 3-1   The Microsoft Outlook Startup Wizard automatically fills in your account information when you are logged on to a domain.

6. If auto-configuration fails twice, you'll see a prompt to confirm the user's e-mail address. If the e-mail address is incorrect, change it to the correct one, and then click Retry. If the auto-configuration and server logon are successful this time, click Finish, and then skip the remaining steps in this procedure.

7. If all attempts at auto-configuration fail, you can try to configure settings manually. The wizard automatically selects the Manually Configure Server Settings check box. Click Next. On the Choose E-Mail Service page, select Internet E-Mail, Microsoft Exchange, or Other. Use Other to configure Outlook 2007 to connect to the Outlook Mobile Service. Click Next. On the next wizard page, complete the necessary information for the type of e-mail service you selected. If necessary, click More Settings, and then use the Properties dialog box provided to configure the additional required settings. When you are finished, click OK to close the Properties dialog box, and then click Finish to complete the mail configuration.

First-Time Configuration: Connecting to Internet E-mail Servers

When a user is logged on to a domain, Outlook 2007 will automatically attempt to configure itself for use with the user's Exchange mailbox as part of its initial configuration. This configuration works for internal users but not for remote users who need to access Exchange using POP3 or IMAP4. For these users, you can complete the first-time configuration of Outlook 2007 by completing the following steps:

1. In the Startup Wizard, when you are prompted as to whether you would like to configure an e-mail account, verify that Yes is selected, and then click Next.

2. Select the Manually Configure Server Settings Or Additional Server Types check box, and then click Next.

3. On the Choose E-Mail Service page, select Internet E-Mail and then click Next.

4. In the Your Name text box, type the name that will appear in the From field of outgoing messages for this user, such as **William Stanek**.

5. In the E-Mail Address text box, type the e-mail address of the user. Be sure to type the e-mail user name as well as the domain name, such as **williams@cpandl.com**.

6. From the Account Type list, select the type of protocol to use for the incoming mail server as POP3, IMAP4, or HTTP. The advantages and disadvantages of these protocols are as follows:

   ❑ POP3 is used to check mail on an e-mail server and download it to the user's inbox. The user can't access private or public folders on the server. By using advanced configuration settings, the user can elect to download the mail and leave it on the server for future use. By leaving the mail on the server, the user can check mail on a home computer and still download it to an office computer later.

   ❑ IMAP4 is used to check mail on an e-mail server and download message headers. The user can then access each e-mail individually and download it. Unlike POP3, IMAP4 has no option to leave mail on the server. IMAP4 also lets users access public and private folders on an Exchange server. It is best suited for users who have a single computer, such as a laptop, that they use to check mail both at the office and away from it.

   ❑ HTTP is used to check mail on a Web-based e-mail server, such as Hotmail or MSN. The user can then access e-mail through Outlook 2007 instead of through a Web browser.

7. If you select POP3 or IMAP4, you must enter the fully qualified domain name for the incoming and outgoing mail servers. Although these entries are often the same, some organizations have different incoming and outgoing mail servers. If you are not certain of your mail servers' fully qualified domain names, contact your network administrator.

   Note If you're connecting to Exchange with POP3 or IMAP4, enter the fully qualified domain name for the Exchange server instead of the host name. For example, you would use MailServer.cpandl.com instead of MailServer.

8. If you select HTTP, a server URL is required. With Hotmail or MSN, the required URL is entered for you. With other services, you must enter the required URL.

9. Under Logon Information, type the user's log on name and password. If the mail server requires secure logon, select the Require Logon Using Security Password Authentication check box.

10. To verify the settings, click Test Account Settings. Outlook 2007 will then send a test message to the specified mail server. If the test fails, note the errors and make corrections as necessary.

11. If necessary, click More Settings, and then use the Properties dialog box provided to configure the additional required settings. When you are finished, click Next, and then click Finish to complete the configuration. If other e-mail applications are configured on the computer, the Windows Mail Import Wizard is started and you have the option of importing the user's messages and address book.

Configuring Windows Mail for the First Time

Windows Mail is installed with Windows Vista. It runs the Internet Connection Wizard the first time you start the application. You configure the user's Internet connection for startup by completing the following steps:

1. In the Display Name text box, type the name that will appear in the From field of outgoing messages for this user, such as **William Stanek**. Click Next.

2. Type the e-mail address of the user. Be sure to type the e-mail user name as well as the domain name, such as **williams@cpandl.com**. Click Next.

3. As shown in Figure 3-2, select the type of protocol to use for the incoming mail server as POP3 or IMAP4. The advantages and disadvantages of these protocols are as follows:

   ❑ POP3 is used to check mail on an e-mail server and download it to the user's inbox. The user can't access private or public folders on the server. By using advanced configuration settings, the user can elect to download the mail and leave it on the server for future use. By leaving the mail on the server, the user can check mail on a home computer and still download it to an office computer later.

   ❑ IMAP4 is used to check mail on an e-mail server and download message headers. The user can then access each e-mail individually and download it. Unlike POP3, IMAP4 has no option to leave mail on the server. IMAP4 also lets users access public and private folders on an Exchange server. It is best suited for users who have a single computer, such as a laptop, that they use to check mail both at the office and away from it.

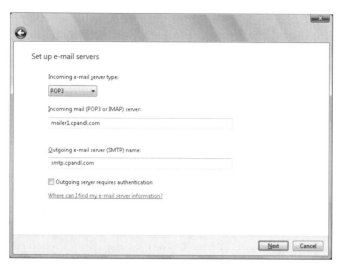

Figure 3-2   Specify incoming and outgoing mail server options with the Internet Connection Wizard.

4. If you select POP3 or IMAP4, you must enter the fully qualified domain name for the incoming and outgoing mail servers. Although these entries are often the same, some organizations have different incoming and outgoing mail servers. If you are not certain of your mail servers' fully qualified domain names, contact your network administrator.

> **Note**   If you're connecting to Exchange with POP3 or IMAP4, enter the fully qualified domain name for the Exchange server instead of the host name. For example, you would use MailServer.cpandl.com instead of MailServer.

5. If the mail server requires a user name and password when a user sends mail in addition to when a user retrieves mail, select the Outgoing Server Requires Authentication check box. Click Next.

> **Note**   To enhance security, most mail servers should require a user name and password for both sending and receiving mail. If a password isn't required for sending mail, the mail server may be vulnerable to exploitation.

6. On the Internet Mail Logon page, type the account name and password for the user for logging on to the POP3 or IMAP4 server, or have the user type this information. The account name is usually the same as the e-mail user name. For some mail servers, however, you might need to enter the name of the domain as well. You type this information in the form: *domain\e-mail_alias*, such as **technology\williams**. In some cases, you might need to type this information in the form: *domain/e-mail_alias*, such as **technology/williams**.

7. Click Next, and then click Finish to complete the configuration. If other e-mail applications are configured on the computer, the Windows Mail Import Wizard is started and you have the option of importing the user's messages and address book.

Configuring Outlook 2007 for Exchange

If you didn't configure Outlook 2007 to use Exchange Server the first time it was started, don't worry: You can change the Outlook 2007 configuration to use Exchange. It does take a bit of extra work, however.

To get started, you should close Outlook 2007, if it is started, and then follow these steps to configure Outlook 2007 to use Exchange:

1. Start the Mail utility. Click Start, and then click Control Panel. In Control Panel, click Classic View and then double-click Mail. If you are using a 64-bit operating system, the Mail utility is listed under the 32-bit Control Panel. In Control Panel, click Classic View, double-click 32-Bit Control Panel, and then double-click Mail.

2. In the Mail Setup–Outlook dialog box, click E-Mail Accounts. The Accounts Settings dialog box appears.

3. In the Account Settings dialog box, the E-Mail tab is selected by default. Click New.

4. On the Choose E-Mail Service page, select Microsoft Exchange, POP3, IMAP, Or HTTP and then click Next.

5. Follow steps 3–7 outlined previously in the section of this chapter entitled "First-Time Configuration: Connecting to Exchange Server."

6. When you finish the previous procedure, close the Mail Setup–Outlook dialog box, and then start Outlook 2007. If you elected to use a local copy of the user's mailbox (as per the default configuration), Outlook 2007 begins creating this local copy. The creation process can take several minutes.

Adding Internet Mail Accounts to Outlook 2007 and Windows Mail

Through e-mail account configuration, Outlook 2007 supports only one Exchange Server account at a time. If you need access to multiple Exchange mailboxes, you must configure access to these mailboxes as discussed in the section "Accessing Multiple Exchange Server Mailboxes" later in the chapter.

Although you can configure only one Exchange e-mail account at a time, both Outlook 2007 and Windows Mail allow you to retrieve mail from multiple Internet servers. For example, you could configure Outlook 2007 to check mail on the corporate Exchange server, a personal account on Earthlink, and a personal account on MSN Hotmail.

Adding Internet Mail Accounts in Outlook 2007

You add Internet mail accounts to Outlook 2007 by completing the following steps:

1. Display the Account Settings dialog box by selecting Tools and then selecting Account Settings.

2. In the Account Settings dialog box, the E-Mail tab is selected by default. Click New.

3. On the Choose E-Mail Service page, select Microsoft Exchange, POP3, IMAP, Or HTTP and then click Next.

4. Follow steps 2–11 outlined previously in the section of this chapter entitled "First-Time Configuration: Connecting to Internet E-mail Servers."

Adding Internet Mail Accounts in Windows Mail

With Windows Mail, you add Internet mail accounts by completing the following steps:

1. On the Tools menu, click Accounts. In the Internet Accounts dialog box, click Add.

2. Select E-Mail Account as the account type, and then click Next.

3. Follow the steps outlined previously in the section of this chapter entitled "Configuring Windows Mail for the First Time."

Repairing and Changing Outlook 2007 Mail Accounts

When you first configure Outlook 2007 on a computer, you can configure it to connect to an Exchange Server, Internet e-mail, or other e-mail server. With Exchange Server, the underlying Mailbox server is transparent to users—they are connected automatically to the appropriate Mailbox server. If a user's mailbox is moved to a different server within the Exchange organization, the user is connected to this server automatically the next time he or she starts Outlook 2007. If, for some reason, a user has a problem connecting to Exchange Server or needs to get updated configuration settings, you can accomplish this with a repair operation. Repairing the user's account restarts the Auto Account Setup feature.

With non-Exchange servers, access to e-mail very much depends on the account and server configuration remaining the same. If the account or server configuration changes, the account configuration in Outlook 2007 must be updated. The easiest way to do this is with a repair operation.

To start a repair, follow these steps:

1. Log on as the domain account of the user for which you are repairing e-mail.

2. In Outlook 2007, display the Account Settings dialog box by selecting Tools, and then selecting Account Settings.

3. In the Account Settings dialog box, the E-Mail tab lists all currently configured e-mail accounts by name. Select the account to repair, and then click Repair.

4. On the Auto Account Setup page, check the account settings. With Exchange accounts for domain users, you cannot change the displayed information. With other accounts, you can modify the user's e-mail address and password, which may be necessary.

5. When you click Next, the Repair E-Mail Account Wizard will contact the mail server and try to determine the correct account settings. If the auto-configuration and server logon are successful, click Finish. Skip the remaining steps in this procedure.

6. If auto-configuration is not successful, click Next so that the wizard can attempt to establish an unencrypted connection to the server. If the auto-configuration and server logon are successful this time, click Finish, and then skip the remaining steps in this procedure.

7. If auto-configuration fails twice, you can try to configure settings manually. Select the Manually Configure Settings check box, and then click Next.

8. Use the fields provided to update the mail account configuration. If you need to configure additional settings beyond the user, server, and logon information, click More Settings, and then use the Properties dialog box provided to configure the additional required settings. When you are finished, click OK to close the Properties dialog box.

9. Check the new settings by clicking Test Account Settings.

10. Click Next, and then click Finish.

In some cases, if you've incorrectly configured Exchange, you might not be able to start Outlook 2007 and access the Account Settings dialog box. In this case, you can repair the settings using the following procedure:

1. Start the Mail utility. Click Start, and then click Control Panel. In Control Panel, click Classic View and then double-click Mail. If you are using a 64-bit operating system, the Mail utility is listed under the 32-Bit Control Panel. In Control Panel, click Classic View, double-click 32-Bit Control Panel and then double-click Mail.

2. In the Mail Setup–Outlook dialog box, click E-Mail Accounts. The Accounts Settings dialog box appears.

3. In the Account Settings dialog box, the E-Mail tab is selected by default. Click the incorrectly configured Exchange account and then do the following:

   ❑ Click Change to modify the Exchange settings using the techniques discussed previously.

   ❑ Click Remove to remove the Exchange settings so that they are no longer used by Outlook 2007.

4. When you are finished, close the Mail Setup–Outlook dialog box, and then start Outlook 2007.

For POP3, IMAP4, and HTTP, you can change a user's e-mail configuration at any time by completing the following steps:

1. In Outlook 2007, display the Account Settings dialog box by selecting Tools, and then selecting Account Settings.

2. In the Account Settings dialog box, the E-Mail tab lists all currently configured e-mail accounts by name. Select the account you want to work with, and then click Change.

3. Use the fields provided to update the mail account configuration. If you need to configure additional settings beyond the user, server, and logon information, click More Settings, and then use the Properties dialog box provided to configure the additional required settings. When you are finished, click OK to close the Properties dialog box.

4. Check the new settings by clicking Test Account Settings.

5. Click Next, and then click Finish.

Leaving Mail on the Server with POP3

If the user connects to an Internet e-mail server, an advantage of POP3 is that it lets the user leave mail on the server. By doing this, the user can check mail on a home computer and still download it to an office computer later.

Leaving Mail on the Server: Outlook 2007

With Outlook 2007, you can configure POP3 accounts to leave mail on the server by completing the following steps:

1. Start Outlook 2007. Then, on the Tools menu, click Account Settings.

2. In the Account Settings dialog box, select the POP3 mail account you want to modify, and then click Change.

3. Click More Settings to display the Internet E-Mail Settings dialog box.

4. In the Internet E-Mail Settings dialog box, click the Advanced tab, as shown in Figure 3-3.

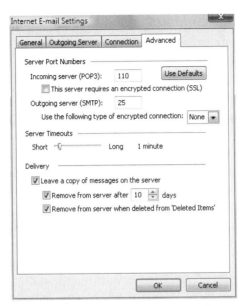

Figure 3-3   Use the Advanced tab to configure how and when mail should be left on the server.

5. Use the options below Delivery to configure how and when mail should be left on the server. To enable this option, select the Leave A Copy Of Messages On The Server check box. The additional options depend on the client configuration. Options you might see include the following:

    ❏ **Remove From Server After *N* Days**   Select this option if you're connecting to an Internet service provider (ISP) and want to delete messages from the server after a specified number of days. By deleting ISP mail periodically, you ensure that your mailbox size doesn't exceed your limit.

    ❏ **Remove From Server When Deleted From "Deleted Items"**   Select this option to delete messages from the server when you delete them from the Deleted Items folder. You'll see this option with Internet-only Outlook 2007 configurations.

6. Click OK when you've finished changing the account settings.

7. Click Next, and then click Finish. Click Close to close the Account Settings dialog box.

Leaving Mail on the Server: Windows Mail

With Windows Mail, you can configure POP3 accounts to leave mail on the server by completing the following steps:

1. Start Windows Mail. Then, on the Tools menu, click Accounts.

2. Select the POP3 mail account you want to modify, and then click Properties.

3. In the Properties dialog box, click the Advanced tab.

4. Use the options below Delivery to configure how and when mail should be left on the server. To enable this option, select Leave A Copy Of Messages On The Server. The additional options depend on the client configuration. Options you might see include the following:

   ❑ **Remove From Server After N Days** Select this option if you're connecting to an ISP and want to delete messages from the server after a specified number of days. By deleting ISP mail periodically, you ensure that your mailbox size doesn't exceed your limit.

   ❑ **Remove From Server When Deleted From "Deleted Items"** Select this option to delete messages from the server when you delete them from the Deleted Items folder. You'll see this option with Internet-only Outlook 2007 configurations.

5. Click OK, and then click Close.

Checking Private and Public Folders with IMAP4 and UNIX Mail Servers

With IMAP4, you can check public and private folders on a mail server. This option is enabled by default, but the default settings might not work properly with UNIX mail servers.

Checking Folders: Outlook 2007

With Outlook 2007, you can check or change the folder settings used by IMAP4 by completing the following steps:

1. Start Outlook 2007. Then, on the Tools menu, click Account Settings.

2. In the Account Settings dialog box, select the IMAP4 mail account you want to modify, and then click Change.

3. Click More Settings to display the Internet E-Mail Settings dialog box.

4. In the Internet E-mail Settings dialog box, click the Advanced tab, as shown in Figure 3-4.

5. If the account connects to a UNIX mail server, enter the path to the mailbox folder on the server, such as **~williams/mail**. Don't end the folder path with a forward slash (/), and then click OK.

6. Click Next, and then click Finish.

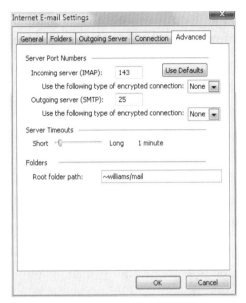

Figure 3-4   Use the Advanced tab to configure how folders are used with IMAP4 mail accounts.

Checking Folders: Windows Mail

With Windows Mail, you can check or change the folder settings used by IMAP4 by completing the following steps:

1. Start Windows Mail. Then, on the Tools menu, click Accounts.

2. Select the IMAP4 mail account you want to modify, and then click Properties.

3. In the Properties dialog box, select the IMAP4 tab.

4. If the account connects to a UNIX mail server, enter the path to the mailbox folder on the server, such as **~williams/mail**. Don't end the folder path with a forward slash (/).

5. To automatically check for new messages in all public, private, and hidden folders, make sure the Check For New Messages In All Folders check box is selected.

6. To store sent items, draft messages, deleted items, and junk e-mail on the IMAP4 server, select the Store Special Folders On IMAP4 Server check box, and then type the name for these folders. The default names are Sent Items, Drafts, Deleted Items, and Junk E-Mail, respectively.

7. Click OK, and then click Close.

Managing the Exchange Server Service in Outlook 2007

Whenever you use Outlook 2007 to connect to Exchange Server, you can use the Exchange Server Service to optimize the way mail is handled. This service has many advanced configuration and management options, including those for the following:

- E-mail delivery and processing
- Remote mail
- Scheduled connections
- Multiple mailboxes

Each of these options is examined in the sections that follow.

Managing Delivery and Processing E-Mail Messages

When Outlook 2007 uses Exchange Server, you have strict control over how e-mail is delivered and processed. Exchange mail can be delivered in one of three ways:

- Server mailboxes
- Server mailboxes with local copies
- Personal folders

Exchange mail can be processed by any of the information services configured for use in Outlook 2007. These information services include the following:

- Microsoft Exchange
- Internet e-mail

Let's look at how you use each of these delivery and processing options.

Using Server Mailboxes

Server mailboxes are the default configuration option. With server mailboxes, new e-mail is delivered to a mailbox on the Exchange server, and you can view or receive new mail only when you're connected to Exchange. Server mailboxes are best suited for corporate users with dedicated connections and users who can remotely access Exchange through a dial-up connection or through Outlook Anywhere (RPC over HTTP).

With server mailboxes, you have the option of storing a local copy of e-mail on the user's computer in addition to the e-mail stored on Exchange Server, or you can store e-mail only on the Exchange server. The default configuration is to use a local copy of the user's mailbox. In most cases, this is a good configuration. You might want to change this configuration if the user's computer has limited hard disk space or if the user doesn't have a dedicated computer. Another reason for changing this configuration is if the user makes use of multiple computers for e-mail and you don't want local copies of mail stored on several different computers.

Changing the configuration doesn't necessarily mean storing e-mail only on the server. Three caching configurations are available:

- **Download Full Items** Downloads the full text of a message, including the header, body, and attachments, at the same time. All messages are fully cached on the user's computer for possible offline use. This option is best when a user is connected directly to the LAN or has a continuous remote access connection over dial-up, wireless, or broadband.

- **Download Headers And Then Full Items** Downloads all message headers first and then full items. When a user opens a message, the message body and any attachments are downloaded. The message is then fully cached on the user's computer for possible offline use. This option lets users quickly see all message headers without having to download the full message text.

- **Download Headers** Downloads only message headers. When a user opens a message, the message body is retrieved. If a user tries to open a message attachment, the attachment is retrieved at that time. Only message headers are cached. The message body and attachments are not cached. Use this option when the user has an unreliable or slow connection.

With any of these caching options, you can also select On Slow Connections Download Only Headers. This additional option downloads only message headers when a slow link is detected. The full item is downloaded when opened. Whether the item is stored depends on the other caching options selected in combination with this option.

> **Tip**   You can think of local copies as mirror images of the user's mailbox on Exchange Server. Local copies of Exchange mailboxes are stored in .ost files. With Windows Vista, the default location of an .ost file is *%LocalAppData%*\Microsoft\Outlook, where *%LocalAppData%* is a user-specific environment variable that points to a user's local application data.

When caching is enabled, you can easily change the caching options by following these steps:

1. Start Outlook 2007. Click File, and then click Cached Exchange Mode.

2. Select the caching option you want to use. You can select only one caching option at a time.

3. To add slow-link detection and handling, select On Slow Connections Download Only Headers.

To configure how server mailboxes and local copies of server mailboxes are used, complete the following steps:

1. Log on as the user for whom you are configuring e-mail.

2. Start Outlook 2007. Then, on the Tools menu, click Account Settings. The Account Settings dialog box appears.

3. Select the Exchange mail account you want to modify, and then click Change. This starts the Change E-Mail Account Wizard.

4. If the user should store e-mail only on the server, clear the Use Cached Exchange Mode check box. Otherwise, if the user should store e-mail on the server and cache mail locally, select the Use Cached Exchange Mode check box.

5. Click Next, and then click Finish.

Using Personal Folders

An alternative to using server mailboxes is to use personal folders. Personal folders are stored in a file on the user's computer. With personal folders, mail delivered to the user's inbox is no longer stored on the server. Users have personal folders when Outlook 2007 is configured to use Internet e-mail or other e-mail servers. Users might also have personal folders if the auto-archive feature is used to archive messages.

> **Real World**   Personal folders are stored in .pst files. With Windows Vista, the default location of a .pst file is *%LocalAppData%*\Microsoft\Outlook, where *%LocalAppData%* is a user-specific environment variable that points to a user's local application data. Personal folders are best suited for mobile users who check mail through dial-up connections and who might not be able to use a dial-up connection to connect directly to Exchange.
>
> Users with personal folders lose the advantages that server-based folders offer—namely, single-instance storage and the ability to have a single point of recovery in case of failure. In addition, .pst files have many disadvantages. They get corrupted more frequently and, on these occasions, you must use the Inbox Repair Tool to restore the file. If the hard disk on a user's computer fails, you can recover the mail only if the .pst file has been backed up. Unfortunately, most workstations aren't backed up regularly (if at all), and the onus of backing up the .pst file falls on the user, who might or might not understand how to do this.

Determining the Presence of Personal Folders   You can determine the presence of personal folders by following these steps:

1. Start Outlook 2007. On the Tools menu, click Account Settings.

2. In the Account Settings dialog box, click the Data Files tab.

3. The location of the data file associated with each e-mail account is listed. If the file name ends in .pst, the account is using a personal folder.

Creating New or Opening Existing Personal Folders   If personal folders aren't available and you want to configure them, follow these steps:

1. Start Outlook 2007. On the Tools menu, click Account Settings.

2. In the Account Settings dialog box, click the Data Files tab.

3. Click Add. The New Outlook Data File dialog box appears.

4. Office Outlook Personal Folders File (.pst) should be selected by default. Click OK, and the Create Or Open Outlook Data File dialog box appears, as shown in Figure 3-5.

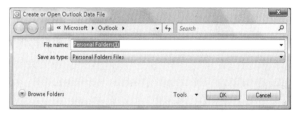

Figure 3-5   Use the Create Or Open Outlook Data File dialog box to search for an existing .pst file or to create a new one.

5. You can now create a new .pst file or open an existing .pst file:

   ❑ To create a new .pst file in the default folder, type the file name in the text box provided, and then click OK. In the Create Microsoft Personal Folders dialog box, specify a password, verify a password for the .pst file, and click OK.

   ❑ To create a new .pst file in a nondefault folder, click Browse Folders to expand the dialog box. Browse for the folder you want to use, type the file name in the text box provided, and then click OK. In the Create Microsoft Personal Folders dialog box, specify a password, verify a password for the .pst file, and click OK.

   ❑ To open an existing .pst file, click Browse Folders to expand the dialog box. Browse to the folder containing the .pst file. Select the .pst file, and then click OK. In the Personal Folders dialog box, you can use the options provided to change the current password or compact the personal folder, and then click OK.

   Note   It is important to be aware that Exchange Server does not ship with any password recovery utility for .pst files. If a user sets a password on a .pst file and forgets it, the Exchange administrator has no way to reset it. You might find third-party vendors who make password-cracking or recovery tools, but they are not guaranteed to work and they are not supported by Microsoft.

6. Click Close. The personal folder you've selected or created is displayed in the Outlook 2007 folder list. You should see related subfolders as well.

Delivering Mail to Personal Folders   When you deliver mail to a personal folder, Outlook 2007 saves e-mail messages only locally on your computer. As a result, Outlook 2007 removes the messages from Exchange Server and you can access the messages only on the currently logged-on computer. If you want mail to be delivered to a personal folder, complete the following steps:

1. Start Outlook 2007. On the Tools menu, click Account Settings.

2. In the Account Settings dialog box, click the Data Files tab.

3. Select the .pst file to use in the list of data files provided, and then click Set As Default.

4. When prompted to confirm, click Yes. Click Close.

5. Exit and restart Outlook 2007. Outlook 2007 will now use personal folders.

If you want mail to resume using server-stored mail, complete the following steps:

1. Start Outlook 2007. On the Tools menu, click Account Settings.

2. In the Account Settings dialog box, click the Data Files tab.

3. Select the .ost file to use in the list of data files provided, and then click Set As Default.

4. When prompted to confirm, click OK. Click Close.

5. Exit and restart Outlook 2007. Outlook 2007 will now use personal folders.

Backing Up Personal Folders   The Personal Folders Backup Tool is available as a free download on the Microsoft Office Online Web site. Be sure to exit Outlook 2007 before installing this tool. After you download and install this backup tool, you can back up a user's personal folders by completing the following steps:

1. Log on as the user, and then start Outlook 2007.

2. In Outlook 2007, on the File menu, click Backup.

3. Click Options. Select the check boxes for the personal folders you want to back up.

4. Click Browse. Navigate to the location where you want to save the backup, and then click Open.

5. To remind users to create personal folder backups, select the Remind Me To Backup Every ... Days check box, specify the reminder interval, and then click OK.

6. Click Save Backup.

7. Exit Outlook 2007 so that the backup process can begin.

Restoring Backed Up Personal Folder Data   After you've created a backup of a personal folder, you can recover any backed up messages or data by following these steps:

1. In Outlook 2007, open the .pst file as discussed in "Creating New or Opening Existing Personal Folders."

2. Drag messages or data entries from the backup personal folder to the current personal folder. You'll restore the selected items.

To recover the entire .pst file from backup, follow these steps:

1. In Outlook 2007, on the Tools menu, click Account Settings.

2. In the Account Settings dialog box, click the Data Files tab. Write down the name and folder location of the damaged .pst file.

3. Exit Outlook 2007.

4. In Windows Explorer, rename the damaged .pst file.

5. In Windows Explorer, copy the backup .pst file to the folder containing the original .pst file.

6. In Windows Explorer, give the backup .pst file the original name of the .pst file.

7. Restart Outlook 2007.

Accessing Multiple Exchange Server Mailboxes

Earlier in the chapter, I discussed how users could check multiple Internet mail accounts in Outlook 2007. You might have wondered whether users could check multiple Exchange mailboxes as well—and they can. Users often need to access multiple Exchange mailboxes for many reasons:

- Help desk administrators might need access to the help desk mailbox in addition to their own mailboxes.

- Managers might need temporary access to the mailboxes of subordinates who are on vacation.

- Mailboxes might need to be set up for long-term projects and project members need access to those mailboxes.

- Resource mailboxes might need to be set up for accounts payable, human resources, corporate information, and so on.

Normally, a one-to-one relationship exists between user accounts and Exchange mailboxes. You create a user account and assign a mailbox to it; only this user can access the mailbox directly through Exchange. To change this behavior, you must do the following:

1. Log on to Exchange as the owner of the mailbox.

2. Delegate access to the mailbox to one or more additional users.

3. Have users with delegated access log on to Exchange and open the mailbox.

The sections that follow examine each of these steps in detail.

Logging On to Exchange as the Mailbox Owner

Logging on to Exchange as the mailbox owner allows you to delegate access to the mailbox. Before you can do this, however, you must complete the following steps:

1. Create a domain user account for the mailbox, if one doesn't already exist.

2. Log on as the user. You'll need to know the account name and password for the domain.

3. Start Outlook 2007. Make sure that mail support is configured to use Exchange Server. If necessary, configure this support, which creates the mail profile for the user.

4. After you configure Outlook 2007 to use Exchange Server, you should be able to log on to Exchange Server as the mailbox owner.

Tip   With multiple mailbox users, you should configure the mailbox to deliver mail to the server rather than to a personal folder. In this way, the mail is available to be checked by one or more mailbox users.

Delegating Mailbox Access

After you've logged on as the mailbox owner, you can delegate access to the mailbox by completing these steps:

1. In Outlook 2007, on the Tools menu, click Options. On the Delegates tab, click Add.

2. The Add Users dialog box appears, as shown in Figure 3-6. To add users, double-click the name of a user who needs access to the mailbox. Repeat this step as necessary for other users, and then click OK when you're finished.

3. In the Delegate Permissions dialog box, assign permissions to the delegates for the Calendar, Tasks, Inbox, Contacts, Notes, and Journal items. The available permissions are as follows:

   ❏ **None**   No permissions

   ❏ **Reviewer**   Grants read permission only

   ❏ **Author**   Grants read and create permissions

   ❏ **Editor**   Grants read, create, and modify permissions

   Note   If the user needs total control over the mailbox, you should grant the user Editor permission for all items.

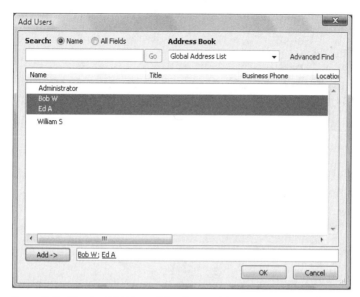

Figure 3-6   Use the Add Users dialog box to delegate access to mailboxes.

4. Click OK twice. These changes take place when the user restarts Outlook 2007.

5. Delegated users can access the mailbox and send mail on behalf of the mailbox owner. To change this behavior, set folder permissions as described in the section of this chapter entitled "Granting Permission to Access Folders Without Delegating Access."

Opening Additional Exchange Mailboxes

The final step is to let Exchange Server know about the additional mailboxes the user wants to open. To do this, follow these steps:

1. Have the user who wants access to additional mailboxes log on and start Outlook 2007.

2. In Outlook 2007, on the Tools menu, click Account Settings.

3. Select the Microsoft Exchange Server account, and then click Change.

4. Click More Settings to display the Microsoft Exchange Server dialog box.

5. In the Change E-Mail Account Wizard, click More Settings.

6. In the Microsoft Exchange dialog box, on the Advanced tab, click Add. Then type the name of a mailbox to open. Generally, this is the same as the mail alias for the user or account associated with the mailbox. Click OK, repeat this step to add other mailboxes, and click OK again.

7. Click Next, and then click Finish.

8. Click Close. The additional mailboxes are displayed in the Outlook 2007 folder list.

Granting Permission to Access Folders Without Delegating Access

When a mailbox is stored on the server, you can grant access to individual folders in the mailbox. Granting access in this way allows users to add the mailbox to their mail profiles and work with the folder. Users can perform tasks only for which you've granted permission.

To grant access to folders individually, follow these steps:

1. Right-click the folder for which you want to grant access, and then select Change Sharing Permissions. This displays the Permissions tab, as shown in Figure 3-7.

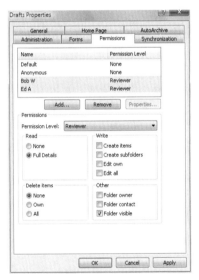

Figure 3-7   Grant access to a folder through the Permissions tab.

2. The Name and Permission Level lists display account names and their permissions on the folder. Two special names might be listed:

   ❏ **Default**   Provides default permissions for all users

   ❏ **Anonymous**   Provides permissions for anonymous users, such as those who anonymously access a published public folder through the Web

3. If you want to grant users permission that differs from the default permission, click Add.

4. In the Add Users dialog box, double-click the name of a user who needs access to the mailbox. Click Add to put the name in the Add Users list. Repeat this step as necessary for other users, and click OK when finished.

5. In the Name and Role lists, select one or more users whose permissions you want to modify. Afterward, use the Roles list to assign permissions or select individual permission items. The roles are defined as follows:

    ❑ **Owner**   Grants all permissions in the folder. Users with this role can create, read, modify, and delete all items in the folder. They can create subfolders and change permissions on folders as well.

    ❑ **Publishing Editor**   Grants permission to create, read, modify, and delete all items in the folder. Users with this role can create subfolders as well.

    ❑ **Editor**   Grants permission to create, read, modify, and delete all items in the folder.

    ❑ **Publishing Author**   Grants permission to create and read items in the folder, to modify and delete items the user created, and to create subfolders.

    ❑ **Author**   Grants permission to create and read items in the folder and to modify and delete items the user created.

    ❑ **Nonediting Author**   Grants permission to create and read items in the folder.

    ❑ **Reviewer**   Grants read-only permission.

    ❑ **Contributor**   Grants permission to create items but not to view the contents of the folder.

    ❑ **None**   Grants no permission in the folder.

6. When you're finished granting permissions, click OK.

Using Mail Profiles to Customize the Mail Environment

The mail profile used with Outlook 2007 determines which information services are available and how they are configured. A default mail profile is created when you install and configure Outlook 2007 for the first time. This mail profile is usually called Outlook.

The active mail profile defines the service setup for the user who is logged on to the computer. You can define additional profiles for the user as well. You can use these additional profiles to customize the user's mail environment for different situations. Here are two scenarios:

- A manager needs to check the Technical Support and Customer Support mailboxes only on Mondays when she writes summary reports. On other days, the manager doesn't want to see these mailboxes. To solve this problem, you create two mail profiles: Support and Standard. The Support profile displays the manager's mailbox as well as the Technical Support and Customer Support mailboxes. The Standard profile displays only the manager's mailbox. The manager can then switch between these mail profiles as necessary.

- A laptop user wants to check Exchange mail directly while connected to the LAN. When at home, the user wants to use remote mail with scheduled connections. On business trips, the user wants to use Simple Mail Transfer Protocol (SMTP) and POP3. To solve this problem, you create three mail profiles: On-Site, Off-Site, and Home. The On-Site profile uses the Exchange Server service with a standard configuration. The Off-Site profile configures Exchange Server for remote mail and scheduled connections. The Home profile doesn't use the Exchange information service and uses the Internet mail service instead.

Common tasks you'll use to manage mail profiles are examined in the sections that follow.

Creating, Copying, and Removing Mail Profiles

You manage mail profiles through the Mail utility. To access this utility and manage profiles, follow these steps:

1. Start the Mail utility. Click Start, and then click Control Panel. In Control Panel, click Classic View and then double-click Mail. If you are using a 64-bit operating system, the Mail utility is listed under the 32-bit Control Panel. In Control Panel, click Classic View, double-click 32-Bit Control Panel, and then double-click Mail.

2. In the Mail Setup–Outlook dialog box, click Show Profiles.

3. As Figure 3-8 shows, you should see a list of mail profiles for the current user. Mail profiles for other users aren't displayed. You can now perform the following actions:

   ❑ Click Add to create a new mail profile using the Account Settings Wizard.

   ❑ Delete a profile by selecting it and clicking Remove.

   ❑ Copy an existing profile by selecting it and clicking Copy.

   ❑ View a profile by selecting it and clicking Properties.

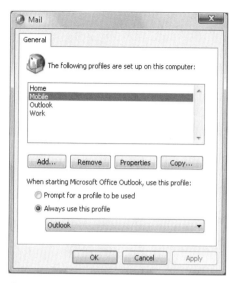

Figure 3-8   To add, remove, or edit mail profiles, click Show Profiles to display this dialog box.

Selecting a Specific Profile to Use on Startup

You can configure Outlook 2007 to use a specific profile on startup or to prompt for a profile to use. To start with a specific profile, follow these steps:

1. Start the Mail utility. Click Start, and then click Control Panel. In Control Panel, click Classic View and then double-click Mail. If you are using a 64-bit operating system, the Mail utility is listed under the 32-bit Control Panel. In Control Panel, click Classic View, double-click 32-Bit Control Panel, and then double-click Mail.

2. In the Mail Setup–Outlook dialog box, click Show Profiles.

3. Select Always Use This Profile, and then use the drop-down list to choose the startup profile. Click OK.

To prompt for a profile before starting Outlook 2007, follow these steps:

1. Start the Mail utility. Click Start, and then click Control Panel. In Control Panel, click Classic View and then double-click Mail. If you are using a 64-bit operating system, the Mail utility is listed under the 32-bit Control Panel. In Control Panel, click Classic View, double-click 32-Bit Control Panel, and then double-click Mail.

2. In the Mail Setup–Outlook dialog box, click Show Profiles.

3. Select Prompt For A Profile To Be Used, and then click OK.

The user will be prompted for a profile the next time Outlook 2007 is started.

Chapter 4

Managing Mobile Messaging Users

In our increasingly connected world, most users want to be able to access e-mail, calendars, contacts, and scheduled tasks no matter what time it is or where they are. With Microsoft Exchange Server 2007, you can make anywhere, anytime access to Exchange data a real possibility. How? Start by using Exchange's built-in Web and mobile access features to allow users to connect to Exchange over the Internet and from cellular networks. Afterward, configure your network to allow direct dial-up or secure anywhere connections from Outlook 2007, and then create Microsoft Outlook profiles that use these configurations.

Web access, mobile access, and secure anywhere access are implemented separate features that are available when you install the Client Access Server role for Exchange Server 2007. These features include Exchange ActiveSync, Outlook Web Access, and Outlook Anywhere. Although Exchange ActiveSync and Outlook Web Access were available in earlier releases of Exchange Server, Outlook Anywhere is a new feature that builds on the remote procedure call (RPC) over Hypertext Transfer Protocol (HTTP) feature introduced in the previous Exchange Server release.

Mastering Outlook Web Access Essentials

Outlook Web Access is a standard Exchange Server 2007 technology that allows users to access their mailboxes and shared non-mail data using a Web browser. The technology works with standard Internet protocols, including Web Distributed Authoring and Versioning (WebDAV).

WebDAV is an extension to HTTP that allows remote clients to create and manage server-based files, folders, and data. When users access mailboxes and shared non-mail data over the Web, an HTTP virtual server hosted by Exchange Server 2007 is working behind the scenes to grant access and transfer files to the browser. Because you don't need to configure Outlook Web Access on the client, it's ideally suited for users who want to access e-mail while away from the office.

When you install the Client Access Server role for Exchange Server 2007, Outlook Web Access is automatically configured for use. This makes Outlook Web Access fairly easy to manage, but there are some essential concepts that you should know to manage it more effectively. This section explains these concepts.

Note   For detailed information on managing the related server components, see Chapter 16, "Managing Client Access Servers." At a minimum, to ensure that proper security procedures are in place, you'll want to configure Exchange ActiveSync Mailbox Policy. You may also want to configure how Outlook Web Access is used with public and private computers.

Getting Started with Outlook Web Access

Outlook Web Access and a default HTTP virtual server are installed automatically when you install the Client Access Server role for Exchange Server 2007. In most cases, you only need to open the appropriate ports on your organization's firewall, as discussed in Chapter 16, to allow users to access mailboxes and shared non-mail data over the Web. After that, you simply tell users the Uniform Resource Locator (URL) path that they need to type into their browser's Address text box. The users can then access Outlook Web Access when they're off-site.

Outlook Web Access is optimized for screen resolutions of 800 × 600 or higher. Two different versions are available:

- **Light**   Provides a basic experience with a simplified user interface that supports accessibility for blind and low vision users. No Premium-only features are available. In addition, calendar options are limited and messages can only be composed as plain text.

- **Premium**   Provides a rich experience with performance that closely approximates Microsoft Office Outlook 2007, including a folder hierarchy that you can expand or collapse, drag-and-drop functionality, move and copy functionality, and shortcut menus that you can access by right-clicking. In addition, you can use all of the following Premium-only features: appearance color schemes, calendar views, file shares integration, notifications, personal distribution lists, public folder access, reading pane, recover deleted items, reminders, search, secure signed and encrypted e-mail with S/MIME, server side rules, spelling checker, voice mail options, and WebReady Document viewing. Premium does not, however, support accessibility for blind and low-vision users.

Outlook Web Access uses Hypertext Markup Language (HTML) 3.2, JavaScript [European Computer Manufacturers Association (ECMA)] script. Because Premium uses some Windows-specific application programming interfaces (APIs), Outlook Web Access Premium can only be used on computers running Windows. These Windows-specific extensions provide features that improve performance and the user experience.

The API for Microsoft Internet Explorer 6.0 has extensions for Outlook Web Access as well. These extensions allow Internet Explorer to compress message data using GZip compression technology, provided that Exchange is running on Microsoft Windows Server 2003 or later. GZip compression gives about a 30 percent performance improvement when transferring data.

Table 4-1 provides an overview of browser versions that have been tested for compatibility with Outlook Web Access Light and Outlook Web Access Premium. Because the supported versions may change over time, be sure to reference current documentation.

Table 4-1   Browsers and Operating Systems to Use with Outlook Web Access

Operating System	Outlook Web Access Light Supported Browsers	Outlook Web Access Premium Supported Browsers
Windows 98	Internet Explorer 5.01, 5.5, 6 and later	Internet Explorer 6 and later
Windows ME	Internet Explorer 5.5, 6 and later	Internet Explorer 6 and later
Windows 2000	Internet Explorer 5.01, 5.5, 6 and later	Internet Explorer 6 and later
Windows XP	Internet Explorer 6 and later, Mozilla Firefox 1.8, Opera 7.54	Internet Explorer 6 and later
Windows Server 2003	Internet Explorer 6 and later, Mozilla Firefox 1.8, Opera 7.54	Internet Explorer 6 and later
Mac OS 9	Internet Explorer 5.01, Netscape Navigator 7.1	-
Mac OS 10.3	Safari 1.2	-
Sun Solaris 9, x86	Mozilla Firefox 1.8, Netscape Navigator 7.1	-
Linux Red Hat Desktop	Mozilla Firefox 1.8, Netscape Navigator 7.1	-
HP/UX 11i	Mozilla Firefox 1.8, Netscape Navigator 7.1	-

With Exchange Server 2007, the preferred way to share documents is to use Windows File Shares and Windows SharePoint Services. Collectively these are referred to as shared non-mail data. Exchange Server 2007 de-emphasizes the role of public folders. Public folders are no longer required for access to the global address list or the offline address book. The reason for this is that Exchange Server 2003 provides these features through a Web-based distribution point. Microsoft Office Outlook 2007 and later clients use Web-based distribution points for the global address list and the offline address book automatically. The primary way users can work with public folders is through Microsoft Outlook 2007. As an administrator, you can work with public folders using Microsoft Outlook 2007 and the Exchange Management Shell.

Connecting to Mailboxes and Shared Non-Mail Data Over the Web

With Outlook Web Access, you can easily access mailboxes and shared non-mail data over the Web and the corporate intranet. To access a user's mailbox, type the Exchange Outlook Web Access URL into Internet Explorer's Address text box, and then enter the user name and password for the mailbox you want to access. The general steps are as follows:

1. In a Web browser, type **https://*servername.yourdomain.com*/owa**, where *servername* is a placeholder for the HTTP virtual server hosted by Exchange Server 2007 and *yourdomain.com* is a placeholder for your external domain name. For example, if your Client Access server is configured to use *mail* as the external DNS name and your external domain is *cpandl.com*, you would type **https://mail.cpandl.com/owa**.

2. At the security prompt, the user will need to specify whether he is using a public or shared computer, or a private computer. If the browser supports Outlook Web Access Premium, the user can elect to use Outlook Web Access Light by selecting the Use Outlook Web Access Light check box.

3. Type the user name in domain\username format, such as **cpandl\williams**, and password, and then click the Log On button.

Exchange Server uses the computer type to determine the period of inactivity to allow before logging the user off automatically. With a private computer, the user will be allowed a longer period of inactivity before being logged off. With a public or share computer, Exchange Server will log the user off more quickly to prevent the user's data from being compromised.

> **Note** By default, Client Access servers are configured to use Secure HTTP (HTTPS) for Outlook Web Access. This is a change from earlier releases of Exchange Server. When you install Exchange Server 2007, a security certificate is issued for the Client Access server automatically. Because this default certificate is not issued by a trusted certificate authority, users will see a warning that there is a problem with the Web site's security certificate. At the warning prompt, the user should click the Continue To This Website link. The user will only see this warning again if they clear their SSL certificate cache.

Once a user has accessed her mailbox in OWA, she can access public folders and any shared non-mail data that is available as well. With Exchange Server 2007, shared non-mail data includes documents shared using Windows File Shares and Windows SharePoint Services.

To access public folders, follow these steps:

1. In the left pane of the OWA window, click Public Folders.

2. Under Public Folders, you'll see a list of the available top levels to which you have access.

3. Select folders to navigate their contents and open items by double-clicking.

To access shared non-mail data, follow these steps:

1. In the left pane of the OWA window, click Documents.

2. Under Documents, click Open Location.

3. In the Open Location dialog box, type the address of the Windows file share or Windows SharePoint Services server to access and then click Open.

Working with Outlook Web Access

After you enter the Exchange Outlook Web Access URL into Internet Explorer's Address text box and enter the user name and password for the mailbox you want to access, you'll see the view of Outlook Web Access compatible with your browser. Figure 4-1 shows the Premium view of Outlook Web Access. Most users with Internet Explorer 6.0 or later see this view of Outlook Web Access automatically. If their browsers don't support a necessary technology for the Premium view, or if this technology has been disabled, they might see the Light view instead. If they can right-click and see a shortcut menu, they have the Premium view.

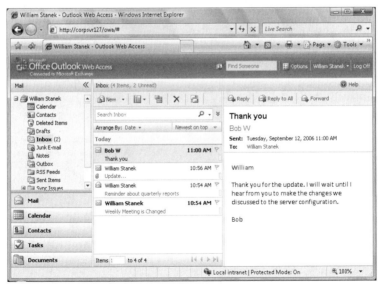

Figure 4-1   Outlook Web Access has nearly all of the features of Outlook 2007.

As shown in Figure 4-1, the latest version of Outlook Web Access has a toolbar that provides quick access to the following key features:

- **Address Book**   Displays the Address Book, which provides quick access to address lists and contacts. Any tracked resources, such as conference rooms or projectors, are available as well. If you click a contact or resource in an address list, the e-mail address and availability information are displayed.

- **Address Book Search**   Search the Address Book for a specific contact or resource. Simply enter as much of the name as is necessary to uniquely identify the contact or resource, and then press Enter. If multiple matches are found, you'll see a shortcut menu with a list of matches. Clicking a match displays the properties for that item.

- **Options**   Configure Outlook Web Access properties or view current configuration details.

- **User Mailbox**   Lists the name of the current mailbox. Clicking the current mailbox name displays the Open Other Mailbox dialog box. If you have been granted permission to access another mailbox or delegated permission to access a folder within a mailbox, as discussed in Chapter 3, "Managing Microsoft Exchange Server 2007 Clients," you can open the mailbox and access any authorized folders using this feature. Simply enter the mailbox name in the text box provided, and then click Open.

- **Log Off**   Logs off the current user and ends the Outlook Web Access session. As a recommended best practice, you should advise all users to log off from their Outlook Web Access sessions when they are finished.

In addition to being able to manage their inbox, calendar, contacts, tasks, shared non-mail data, public folders, and mailbox rules, users can set the following Outlook Web Access options by clicking Options in the task pane, making whatever changes are desired, and then clicking Save:

- **About**   Lists the current configuration being used by the Outlook Web Access server and the Outlook Web Access client. This information is useful for troubleshooting.

- **Calendar Options**   Allows you to specify when the first day of the week is and when the workday starts and ends for the purposes of calendar scheduling. Reminder options allow you to enable or disable reminders for calendars and tasks. Automatic calendaring options specify how meeting requests, notifications, and responses are handled.

- **Change Password**   Allows users to change their domain passwords. After changing their passwords, users may need to re-enter their credentials and log on again.

- **Deleted Items**   Controls whether the Deleted Items folder is emptied on logoff. If necessary, you can recover items that were recently emptied and move them back to the Deleted Items folder.

- **General Settings**   Allows you to configure e-mail name resolution, appearance, and accessibility options. E-mail name resolution options allow you to specify whether the global address list or your personal contacts are checked first when resolving e-mail addresses in messages you are composing. By default, the global address list is checked first. Appearance options allow you to select the color scheme used by Outlook Web Access. The default color scheme is blue.

    Note   Under General Settings, accessibility options allow you to optimize Outlook Web Access for blind and low-vision users. By selecting Use The Blind And Low Vision Experience, you ensure that Outlook Web Access Light is used rather than Outlook Web Access Premium.

- **Junk E-Mail**   Allows you to filter junk e-mail and to manage Safe Sender, Blocked Sender, and Safe Recipient lists.

- **Messaging Options**   Allows you to set key messaging options. By default, 50 items are displayed per page, but you can set this to anywhere from 5 to 100 items per page. You can also edit your e-mail signature, preferred message format, and preferred font to use for messages. The default font is 10-point Tahoma. Message tracking options allow you to specify how to respond to requests for read receipts. Reading pane options allow you to specify whether and how messages are marked as read.

- **Mobile Devices**   Allows you to manage mobile devices. You can remove mobile devices you are no longer using, display a device password, and retrieve related access logs. If you lose a mobile device, you can start a remote device wipe to protect your information. All data is removed the next time the device connects to Exchange Server, returning the device to its factory default condition. If a user initiates a remote wipe in Outlook Web Access, the user will receive a confirmation e-mail when the device acknowledges the remote wipe request. If an administrator initiates a remote wipe on a user's behalf, the administrator and the user will receive a confirmation e-mail when the device acknowledges the remote wipe request.

- **Out Of Office Assistant**   Allows you to specify whether you are in the office or out of the office. If out of the office, you can enter the text of the AutoReply message to be sent to anyone who sends you e-mail. Separate messages can be configured for internal recipients and external recipients. With external recipients, you have the option of sending auto-reply messages only to those in your contacts list.

- **Regional Settings** Allows you to set the language, dates, and time formats to use with Outlook Web Access.

- **Spelling Options** Allows you to set options for the spelling checker, including the dictionary language. The default language is set per the browser's language setting.

Listing 4-1 shows an example of the details on the About page, which can be helpful for troubleshooting. If a user is having problems with Outlook Web Access, you can instruct the user to click Options, scroll through the options, and then select About. If he has a non-e-mail related problem and is able to send e-mail, he can click Copy To Clipboard, and then paste the contents of the Clipboard into an e-mail message by pressing Ctrl+V.

Listing 4-1 Outlook Web Access Configuration Details

```
Mailbox owner: William Stanek [williams@cpandl.com]
User-Agent: Mozilla/4.0
(compatible; MSIE 7.0; Windows NT 6.0; WOW64; SLCC1;
.NET CLR 2.0.50727; .NET CLR 3.0.04506; Media Center PC 5.0)
Outlook Web Access experience: Premium
User language: English (United States)
User time zone: (GMT-08:00) Pacific Time (US & Canada)
Exchange mailbox address: /o=First Organization/ou=Exchange
Administrative Group (FYDIBOHF23SPDLT)/cn=Recipients/cn=williams
Outlook Web Access host address: https://mailserver25.cpandl.com/owa
Outlook Web Access version: 8.1.240.5
Outlook Web Access host name: mailserver25.cpandl.com
S/MIME control: not installed
Client Access server name: MAILSERVER25.cpandl.com
Exchange Client Access server .NET Framework version: 2.0.50727.1434
Client Access server operating system version: Microsoft Windows NT 6.0.60
01 Service Pack 1, v.745
Client Access server operating system language: en-US
Microsoft Exchange Client Access server version: 8.1.240.0
Client Access server language: en-US
Client Access server time zone: Pacific Standard Time
Microsoft Exchange Client Access server platform: 64bit
Mailbox server name: MAILSERVER25.cpandl.com
Mailbox server Microsoft Exchange version: 8.1.240.0
Other Microsoft Exchange server roles currently installed on the Client
Access server: Mailbox, Hub Transport, Unified Messaging
Authentication type associated with this Outlook Web Access session: Basic
Public logon: No
```

Enabling and Disabling Web Access for Users

Exchange Server 2007 enables Outlook Web Access for each user by default. If necessary, you can disable Outlook Web Access for specific users. To do this, complete the following steps:

1. Start Exchange Management Console by clicking Start, clicking All Programs, clicking Microsoft Exchange Server 2007, and then selecting Exchange Management Console.

2. Expand Recipient Configuration and then select Mailbox.

3. You should now see a list of users with Exchange mailboxes in the organization. Double-click the user's name to open the Properties dialog box for the user account.

4. On the Mailbox Features tab, the enabled mobile and Web access features for the user are displayed, as shown in Figure 4-2.

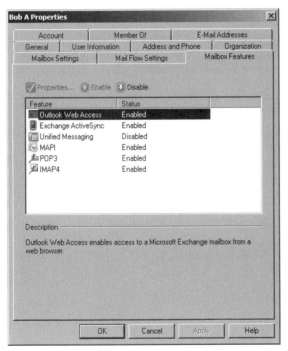

Figure 4-2   Use the Mailbox Features tab to manage a user's mobile and Web access settings.

    ❏ To disable Outlook Web Access for this user, under Feature, select Outlook Web Access, and then click Disable.

    ❏ To enable Outlook Web Access for this user, under Feature, select Outlook Web Access, and then click Enable.

  5. Click OK.

Mastering Mobile Device and Wireless Access Essentials

Exchange Server 2007 supports wireless access for users with many types of mobile devices, including browser-enabled cell phones and Windows Mobile–powered devices. Exchange Server 2007 uses Exchange ActiveSync to provide mobile access functionality. The version of Exchange ActiveSync included in Exchange Server 2007 integrates functionality previously provided separately with Outlook Mobile Access and Exchange ActiveSync.

When you install Exchange Server 2007, Exchange ActiveSync is automatically configured for use. As with Outlook Web Access, this makes Exchange ActiveSync fairly easy to manage, but there are still some essential concepts you should know to manage it more effectively. This section explains these concepts.

> **Tip**   As an Exchange administrator, you can do many things to fine-tune the mobile access configuration for your organization, as discussed in Chapter 16. At a minimum, you'll want to ensure that the appropriate level of authentication is applied. You'll also want to create and apply Exchange ActiveSync Mailbox Policy.

Using Exchange ActiveSync

Using Exchange ActiveSync, users with mobile devices can access their e-mail, calendar, contacts, and scheduled tasks. Mobile access services have several key components:

- **Wireless synchronization access**   With wireless synchronization access, users can synchronize their mobile devices with Exchange Server. Synchronizing a device to Exchange allows users to keep their Exchange data current without being constantly connected to a wireless network.

- **Wireless browser access**   With wireless browsing, users connect to Exchange and browse their Exchange data using their mobile device. On the wireless device, browsing is enabled using the built-in Web browser. Users connect to the Internet using the services of their mobile device, and then browse Exchange using the Exchange ActiveSync URL, such as *https://exchange.cpandl.com/ Microsoft-Server-ActiveSync*.

Both wireless access components are installed by default on Exchange Server 2007, and no installation is required. Exchange ActiveSync browsing is possible because of the HTTP virtual server that is installed with Exchange.

Managing Wireless Synchronization and Exchange Server ActiveSync

Using Exchange Server ActiveSync, users whose mobile devices have Windows Mobile 5.0 and the Messaging and Security Feature Pack (MSFP) and later versions of Windows Mobile software can initiate synchronization with Exchange to keep their data up-to-date and receive notices from Exchange that trigger synchronization through the Direct Push feature. Direct Push is a key feature that you probably want to know a bit more about. It works like this:

1. The user configures her mobile device to synchronize with Exchange, selecting specific Exchange folders that he or she wants to keep up-to-date.

2. When a new message arrives in a designated sync folder, a control message is sent to the mobile device.

3. The control message initiates a data synchronization session, and the device performs background synchronization with Exchange.

Users with third-party synchronization software for their mobile devices can also sync with Exchange, provided the software is compatible with Exchange Server ActiveSync. After they are synchronized, users can then access their data while they are offline. In Exchange Server 2007, User Initiated Synchronization, Direct Push, and Synchronization Notification Receipt are all either enabled or disabled along with Exchange ActiveSync itself.

Exchange Server 2007 enables ActiveSync for each user by default. If necessary, you can disable ActiveSync for specific users. To do this, complete the following steps:

1. Start Exchange Management Console by clicking Start, clicking All Programs, clicking Microsoft Exchange Server 2007, and then selecting Exchange Management Console.

2. Expand Recipient Configuration and then select Mailbox.

3. You should now see a list of users with Exchange mailboxes in the organization. Double-click the user's name to open the Properties dialog box for the user account.

4. On the Mailbox Features tab, the enabled mobile and Web access features for the user are displayed, as shown previously in Figure 4-2:

   ❑ To disable Exchange ActiveSync for this user, under Feature, select Exchange ActiveSync, and then click Disable.

   ❑ To enable Exchange ActiveSync for this user, under Feature, select Exchange ActiveSync, and then click Enable.

5. Click OK.

> **Real World**   ActiveSync notifications are sent over wireless networks using the
> Internet. To take advantage of these services, users must subscribe to the Internet
> services of a wireless carrier. The actual process of receiving synchronization
> requests and sending synchronization notifications is handled through the HTTP
> virtual server configured for use with Exchange. Exchange ActiveSync is, in fact,
> configured as an ASP.NET application on the HTTP virtual server. For Exchange
> Server ActiveSync to work properly, the HTTP virtual server must be configured
> properly, as discussed in Chapter 16. If you want to learn more about Internet
> Information Services (IIS) and ASP.NET, I recommend *Microsoft IIS 7.0 Administrator's
> Pocket Consultant* (Microsoft Press, 2007).

To define organization-wide security and authentication options, you can use
Exchange ActiveSync policies. When you install Exchange Server 2007, a default
Exchange ActiveSync policy is created. Through Exchange ActiveSync policy settings,
you can precisely control mobile browsing capabilities for all users in the enterprise,
including:

- Whether passwords are required and how passwords must be configured

- Synchronization settings to include past calendar and e-mail items

- Permitted devices and device options, such as whether a device can use Wi-Fi,
  infrared, Bluetooth, or Internet sharing

For more information, see the section "Understanding and Using Exchange
ActiveSync Mailbox Policy" in Chapter 16.

Managing Wireless Browsing on Mobile Devices

Wireless browsing allows users to access their Exchange e-mail, calendar, contacts,
and scheduled tasks using the built-in Web browser of their mobile devices. To
browse Exchange, users must subscribe to the Internet services of a wireless
carrier and then access Exchange using the ActiveSync Access URL, such as
https://exchange.cpandl.com/Microsoft-Server-ActiveSync.

Wireless browsing is designed to be used with devices running Windows Mobile
software. If unsupported devices are allowed in ActiveSync policy, any device with a
wireless browser can be used to browse Exchange. However, because of some technology
incompatibilities with carrier gateways that alter the markup contained in message
data sent between Exchange and wireless devices, wireless browsing is supported only
with the following:

- HTML devices, such as Pocket PC 2002 or later and smart phones

- Extensible Hypertext Markup Language (XHTML) devices, such as cell phones,
  that use Wireless Application Protocol (WAP) 2.0 or later

- Compact Hypertext Markup Language (CHTML) devices, such as cell phones, that use iMode

In addition, the wireless device must be with a wireless carrier whose network uses Global System for Mobile Communications (GSM), General Packet Radio Service (GPRS), or Code Division Multiple Access (CDMA). With these supported devices running on a supported network, you can be sure that a user's wireless browsing experience is consistent from device to device.

When users access Exchange in their mobile browser, they'll have these key options:

- **Inbox**   Read, reply to, forward, or flag e-mail messages.

- **Calendar**   View calendar and scheduling information, such as meetings and appointments.

- **Contacts**   Find important contacts with their address, e-mail, and telephone information, or create new contacts.

- **Tasks**   Browse current tasks or create new ones.

- **Find Someone**   Find information on someone in Exchange's global address list.

- **Compose New**   Create new e-mail messages.

- **Preferences**   Configure Outlook Web Access preferences.

Note   With Exchange, Outlook Mobile Access is configured as an ASP.NET application on an HTTP virtual server being used with Exchange. For Outlook Mobile Access to work properly, the HTTP virtual server must be configured properly, as discussed in Chapter 16.

A user's mobile browsing capability is controlled by enabling or disabling his or her mailbox for use with Exchange ActiveSync. To enable mobile browsing for the organization, you must set an external browsing URL. You should also be sure to configure security and authentication options appropriately.

Configuring Mobile Device Access and Wireless Browsing

Configuring mobile devices to access Exchange is a multipart process. First, users need to subscribe to the Internet service offered by their wireless carrier and configure their mobile devices to use the service. Then they need to configure their device for synchronization, browsing, or both.

With a Pocket PC, the process of configuration synchronization works like this:

1. After you configure the mobile device to use the Internet service provided by the user's wireless carrier, on the Today screen, tap Start, and then tap ActiveSync. This displays the ActiveSync screen.

2. Tap Menu, and then tap Configure Server.

3. Tap anywhere within the address bar, and then type the Exchange ActiveSync URL, such as **https://exchange.microsoft.com/mobile**. Select This Server Requires An Encrypted (SSL) Connection.

4. Click Next. When prompted, enter your user name, password, and domain information.

5. Select the Save Password check box, and then click Next.

6. Select the types of information you want to sync with the server, such as inbox, calendar, and contacts, and then click Finish.

With a Pocket PC, the process of mobile browsing works like this:

1. After you configure the mobile device to use the Internet service provided by the user's wireless carrier, on the Today screen, tap Start, and then tap Internet Explorer. This displays the Internet Explorer screen.

2. Tap View, and then tap Address Bar to display the address bar in the browser window.

3. Tap anywhere within the address bar, and then type the Exchange ActiveSync URL, such as **https://exchange.microsoft.com/mobile**. You should automatically connect. If you don't, you might have to connect manually.

4. When prompted, provide your user name, password, and domain information.

Mastering Remote Mail and Outlook Anywhere Essentials

Two additional technologies you can use for mobile access are remote mail and Outlook Anywhere. These technologies require extra configuration for both Outlook clients and Exchange servers. This section discusses Outlook client configuration. See Chapter 16 for a discussion of Exchange server configuration.

Using Remote Mail and Outlook Anywhere

Remote mail and Outlook Anywhere are two of the least understood configuration options for Exchange Server. Using remote mail, you can configure Outlook 2007 to connect to Exchange Server using a dial-up connection to your organization's modem bank. Remote mail is useful in these scenarios:

■ Users at a branch office must connect to Exchange Server by means of dial-up connections.

■ Laptop users want to connect to Exchange Server through dial-up connections when out of the office. (Here, you might want to configure on-site and off-site mail profiles for the user. See the section in Chapter 3 entitled "Using Mail Profiles to Customize the Mail Environment.")

- Users working at home need to connect to Exchange Server by means of dial-up connections.

Outlook Anywhere is a technology that allows users to access Exchange Server over the Internet using Outlook 2007. With Outlook Anywhere, you don't need to use a virtual private network (VPN) to securely connect Outlook to Exchange Server. Instead of relying on VPN for security, Outlook Anywhere takes advantage of security features of Microsoft Windows, Outlook 2007, and Exchange Server 2007 to ensure that communications are secure.

Outlook Anywhere builds on the RPC over HTTP feature introduced with Exchange Server 2003 and Outlook 2003. It provides additional, more dynamic communication protocols for remotely accessing Exchange Server, including RPC over HTTP, with or without SSL encryption, and RPC over Transmission Control Protocol/Internet Protocol (TCP/IP), with or without SSL encryption.

- With RPC over HTTP, remote procedure calls (RPC) are nested within HTTP packets, which can either be encrypted with Secure Sockets Layer (SSL) or not encrypted with SSL, and then transmitted.

- With RPC over TCP/IP, remote procedure calls are nested within standard TCP/IP packets, which can either be encrypted with SSL or not encrypted with SSL, and then transmitted.

In most cases, RPC over TCP/IP is more efficient and resilient than RPC over HTTP. By adding SSL encryption to either technique, you ensure that data transmitted between Outlook and Exchange Server is encrypted and, therefore, protected.

Outlook Anywhere is useful in these scenarios:

- Users at a branch office must connect to Exchange Server over a broadband connection, such as a digital subscriber line (DSL) or a cable modem, and you don't have a VPN, or you want to simplify the connection process by eliminating the need for a VPN.

- Laptop users want to connect to Exchange Server through broadband or T1 connections when out of the office without having to use VPNs. (Here, you might want to configure on-site and off-site mail profiles for the user. See the section in Chapter 3 entitled "Using Mail Profiles to Customize the Mail Environment.")

- Users working at home need to connect to Exchange Server by means of broadband connections without having to use a VPN.

Enabling remote mail and Outlook Anywhere requires separate client and server configurations. As discussed in "Creating Outlook Profiles for Dial-Up Connections to Corporate Networks" and "Configuring Outlook Profiles for Outlook Anywhere" later in this chapter, configuring Outlook 2007 for use with remote mail or Outlook Anywhere is fairly easy—all you need to do is properly configure a related mail profile. What isn't so easy is implementing the required back-end server configuration.

Remote mail requires a fairly complex server implementation on the back end to enable the technology for users, the discussion of which is beyond the scope of this book. You can deploy Outlook Anywhere by following the procedure discussed in Chapter 16.

Creating Outlook Profiles for Dial-Up Connections to Corporate Networks

You configure dial-up connections for Outlook 2007 (also called remote mail) by creating an Outlook profile that can be used for dial-up connections to the corporate network. Before you can create this profile, you must also configure the area code and dialing options to use with the computer's modem.

To configure the area code and dialing options, follow these steps:

1. Click Start, and then click Control Panel. In Control Panel, click Hardware And Sound, and then, under Phone And Modem Options, click Set Up Dialing Rules.

2. Using the selection list provided, specify the country or region you are located in, such as the United States.

3. Enter your area code, such as **212**.

4. Optionally, enter carrier codes, the number needed to dial in an outside line, or both.

5. Select either Tone Dialing or Pulse Dialing.

6. When you click OK, the Phone And Modem Options dialog box appears with the Dialing Rules tab selected. Review the configuration, and then click OK when you are finished.

To create the Outlook profile for remote mail, follow these steps:

1. Exit Outlook 2007. Start the Mail utility. (Click Start, and then click Control Panel. In Control Panel, click User Accounts, and then click Mail.)

2. In the Mail Setup–Outlook dialog box, click Show Profiles. Then, in the Mail window, click Add.

3. Type the name of the profile, such as **Remote Exchange**, and then click OK. This starts the Add New E-Mail Account Wizard.

4. You need to manually configure settings. Select the Manually Configure Server Settings check box, and then click Next.

5. Select Microsoft Exchange, and then click Next.

6. In the Microsoft Exchange Server text box, type the host name of the mail server, such as **mailer1**. You can also enter the fully qualified domain name (FQDN) of the mail server, such as **mailer1.cpandl.com**. Using the fully qualified domain name can help ensure a successful connection when the mail server is in a different domain or forest.

7. In the User Name text box, enter the user's domain logon name or domain user name, such as **Williams** or **William Stanek**. Click Check Name to confirm that you've entered the correct user name for the mailbox. You'll want to store a local copy of the user's e-mail on his computer, so ensure that the Use Cached Exchange Mode check box is selected.

8. Click More Settings. This displays the Microsoft Exchange Server dialog box.

9. With remote mail connections, you'll usually want to work offline and dial up only as necessary. Select Manually Control Connection State, and then select Work Offline And Use Dial-Up Networking, as shown in Figure 4-3.

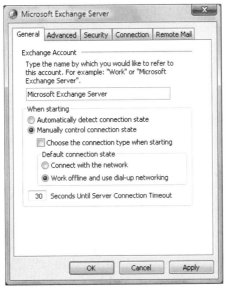

Figure 4-3   Use manual connection settings for working offline and dial-up networking.

10. If you want the user to be prompted for the connection type, select the Choose The Connection Type When Starting check box.

11. If you want to encrypt message traffic, click the Security tab, and under Encryption, select the Encrypt Data Between Microsoft Office Outlook And Microsoft Exchange check box.

12. On the Connection tab, choose Connect Using My Phone Line. Then, under Use The Following Dial-Up Networking Connection, choose an existing connection to use for remote mail, as shown in Figure 4-4. If no connection is available, click Add, and create a connection.

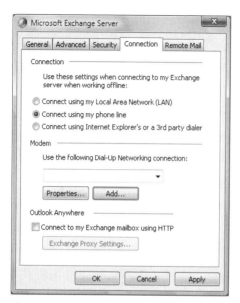

Figure 4-4 Connect using a phone line, and then specify the dial-up networking connection to use.

13. You now need to configure remote mail. Click the Remote Mail tab.

14. If you'd like to remotely send and receive all mail with Exchange, select Process Marked Items, and skip steps 15 and 16.

15. If you'd like to receive only mail that meets specific criteria, select Retrieve Items That Meet The Following Conditions, and then click Filter. This displays the Filter dialog box shown in Figure 4-5. When using filters, keep in mind that remote mail retrieves only messages that match all the conditions you specify.

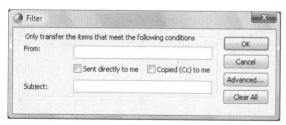

Figure 4-5 The Filter dialog box lets you filter mail so that it meets specified criteria.

16. Use the following options in the Filter dialog box to configure filters:

   ❑ **From** Enter names or e-mail addresses that must appear in the From text box of messages. You can use semicolons (;) to separate multiple names or e-mail addresses.

❑ **Sent Directly To Me**   Transfers messages with the user's name in the To text box.

> **Note**   When you select the Sent Directly To Me check box, messages sent to distribution lists that the user is a member of aren't transferred, so be sure that this is the behavior you want. If you want to transfer messages sent to distribution lists that the user is a member of, select the Copied (Cc) To Me check box as well.

❑ **Copied (Cc) To Me**   Transfers messages with the user's name in the Cc text box or messages sent to distribution lists of which the user is a member.

❑ **Subject**   Transfers messages with a specific subject. Multiple subjects can be entered as long as a semicolon separates each one.

❑ **Advanced**   Allows you to specify additional criteria for messages to be transferred, including size, date, and importance.

17. After you're finished configuring remote mail, click OK. In the Add New E-mail Account Wizard, click Next, and then click Finish.

18. In the Mail dialog box, select Prompt For A Profile To Be Used and then click OK.

Configuring Outlook Profiles for Outlook Anywhere

You configure Outlook 2007 to use Outlook Anywhere by completing the following steps:

1. Exit Outlook 2007. Start the Mail utility. Click Start, and then click Control Panel. In Control Panel, click User Accounts, and then click Mail.

2. In the Mail Setup–Outlook dialog box, click Show Profiles. Then, in the Mail window, click Add.

3. Type the name of the profile, such as **Outlook Anywhere**, and then click OK. This starts the Add New E-mail Account Wizard.

4. You need to manually configure settings. Select the Manually Configure Server Settings check box, and then click Next.

5. Select Microsoft Exchange, and then click Next.

6. In the Microsoft Exchange Server text box, type the host name of the mail server, such as **mailer1**. You can also enter the FQDN of the mail server, such as **mailer1.cpandl.com**. Using the fully qualified domain name can help ensure a successful connection when the mail server is in a different domain or forest.

7. In the User Name text box, enter the user's domain logon name or domain user name, such as **Williams** or **William Stanek**. Click Check Name to confirm that you've entered the correct user name for the mailbox. You'll want to store a local

copy of the user's e-mail on his computer, so ensure that the Use Cached Exchange Mode check box is selected.

8. Click More Settings. This displays the Microsoft Exchange dialog box.

9. With Outlook Anywhere connections, you'll usually want to manually control the connection state and connect to Exchange only when there is an active connection. On the General tab, select both Manually Control Connection State and Connect With The Network options.

10. If you want the user to be prompted for a connection type, select the Choose Connection Type When Starting check box.

11. If you want to encrypt message traffic, on the Security tab, under Encryption, select Encrypt Data Between Microsoft Office Outlook And Microsoft Exchange.

12. On the Connection tab, select Connect Using Internet Explorer's Or A Third Party Dialer.

13. Select the Connect To Microsoft Exchange Using HTTP check box. If this check box is unavailable, you might need to apply the most recent service packs for the operating system and Internet Explorer. Then repeat this procedure.

14. Click the Exchange Proxy Settings button to open the Exchange Proxy Settings dialog box, shown in Figure 4-6.

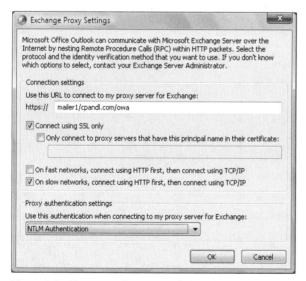

Figure 4-6   Connect to the Internet-facing Client Access server.

15. In the Use This URL To Connect To My Proxy Server For Exchange text box, enter the Exchange Outlook Web Access URL. Selecting the Connect Using SSL Only check box ensures that the connection to Exchange Server is secure and uses SSL.

16. The On Fast Networks and On Slow Networks check boxes allow you to configure the protocols used by Outlook Anywhere. When configuring these options, keep the following in mind:

    ❑ If you select neither check box, Outlook Anywhere always uses RPC over TCP/IP and doesn't try to use RPC over HTTP.

    ❑ If you select both check boxes, Outlook Anywhere first tries to use RPC over HTTP. If it experiences problems connecting or transmitting, it then tries to use RCP over TCP/IP.

    ❑ If you select only the Slow Network check box and Outlook Anywhere detects the user is on a slow network, it first tries to use RPC over HTTP and then tries to use RCP over TCP/IP. The definition of a slow network is configured in Group Policy. By default, a slow network is a network with a connection speed of 256 kilobits per second or less transmission speed.

    ❑ If you select only the Fast Network check box and Outlook Anywhere detects the user is on a fast network, it first tries to use RPC over HTTP and then tries to use RCP over TCP/IP.

17. NTLM Authentication is the default authentication technique. Using NT LAN Manager (NTLM) authentication ensures that the user's credentials are protected and encrypted when transmitted over the network.

18. After you finish configuring remote mail, click OK. In the Add New E-mail Account Wizard, click Next, and then click Finish.

19. In the Mail dialog box, select Prompt For A Profile To Be Used and then click OK.

Part II

Exchange Server 2007 Administration Essentials

In this part:

Chapter 5

Microsoft Exchange Server 2007 Administration Essentials

Whether you're using Microsoft Exchange Server 2007 for the first time or honing your skills, you'll need to master many key concepts to work effectively with Exchange Server. You'll need to know the following:

- How the Exchange environment is organized

- How information is stored in Exchange Server

- Which Windows processes are used with Exchange Server

- How Exchange Server works

You'll also need to know how to use the Exchange Management Console. These topics are all covered in this chapter.

Validating the Exchange Server Licensing

Unlike earlier releases of Exchange Server, with Exchange Server 2007 you do not enter a product key during initial setup: Instead, you provide the product key after installation using the Exchange Management Console. Until you enter a product key, Exchange Server 2007 runs in trial mode.

The product key you provide determines which edition is established on an Exchange server. You can use a valid product key to go from a trial edition to a Standard Edition or Enterprise Edition of Exchange Server 2007 without having to reinstall the program.

Using the Exchange Management Console, you can determine the established edition for an Exchange server and licensing by completing the following steps:

1. In Exchange Management Console, select the Server Configuration node.

2. In the main pane, right-click the server you want to work with and then select Properties.

3. In the Properties dialog box, the established edition and license details are listed on the General tab.

> **Real World**   You can determine the licensing configuration of multiple Exchange servers without accessing the properties of each server. In the Exchange Management Console, select the Server Configuration node. On the View menu, select Add/Remove Columns. This displays the Add/Remove Columns dialog box. In the Add/Remove Columns dialog box, under Available Columns, click Product ID, click

Add, and then click OK. This adds the Product ID to the displayed columns list. In the main pane of the Exchange Management Console, scroll left or right as necessary to display the Product ID column for your Exchange servers. If the Product ID is listed as Unlicensed, you have not yet provided a valid product key for the Exchange server. Otherwise, the Product ID is a generated ID for the Exchange server.

Using the Exchange Management Console, you can enter a product key by completing the following steps:

1. In Exchange Management Console, select the Server Configuration node and then select the server that requires the product key.

2. In the Action pane or on the Action menu, select Enter Product Key. This starts the Enter Product Key Wizard.

3. When prompted, type in the product key for the Exchange Server 2007 edition you want to establish, either Standard Edition or Enterprise Edition, and then click Enter.

   Note The product key is a 25-character alphanumeric string, grouped in sets of five characters separated by hyphens. You can find the product key on the Exchange Server 2007 DVD case.

4. The wizard validates the product key and displays any appropriate warnings. Read the information provided and then click Finish. Keep the following in mind:

   ❑ When you change the product key on a Mailbox server, you must restart the Microsoft Exchange Information Store service to apply the change.

   ❑ When you change the product key on an Edge Transport server, you must resubscribe the server in the Exchange organization to apply the change.

   ❑ You cannot use product keys to downgrade editions. To downgrade editions, you must uninstall Exchange Server and then reinstall Exchange Server.

Using the Exchange Management Shell, you can enter a server's product key using the Set-ExchangeServer cmdlet. Sample 5-1 shows the syntax and usage. For the identity parameter, you use the server's name, such as MailServer25.

Sample 5-1 Setting the Exchange product key syntax and usage

```
Syntax

Set-ExchangeServer -Identity 'ServerName'
-ProductKey 'ProductKey'
```

Usage

```
Set-ExchangeServer -Identity 'MailServer25'
-ProductKey 'AAAA-BBBB-CCCC-DDDD-EEEE'
```

Tip   Using a valid product key, you can go from Standard Edition to Enterprise Edition. You also can relicense an Exchange server by entering a new product key for the installed edition, which is useful if you accidentally used the same product key on multiple servers and want to correct the mistake. The best way to do this is to enter the desired product key using the Set-ExchangeServer cmdlet.

Understanding Exchange Server 2007 Organizations

The root of an Exchange environment is an *organization*. It's the starting point for the Exchange hierarchy, and its boundaries define the boundaries of any Exchange environment. Exchange Server 2007 organizations are quite different from Exchange Server 2003 organizations.

When you install Exchange Server 2007, you are not given the opportunity to join an existing organization or create a new organization. Instead, in a domain, you install the Exchange server within the organizational context of the domain in which the server is a member. The physical site boundaries and subnets defined for Active Directory are the same as those used by Exchange Server 2007, and the site details are determined according to the IP address assigned to the server.

Unlike Exchange Server 2003, Exchange Server 2007 uses Active Directory site-based routing instead of routing groups and configuration containers instead of administrative groups. The use of site-based routing and configuration containers substantially changes the way you configure and manage Exchange Server 2007.

Using Site-Based Routing Instead of Routing Groups

With Exchange Server 2007, site-based routing is possible because Exchange servers can determine their own Active Directory site membership and the Active Directory site membership of other servers by querying Active Directory. Using Active Directory for routing eliminates the need for Exchange to have its own routing infrastructure.

How Site-Based Routing Works

Mailbox and Unified Messaging servers use site membership information to determine which Hub Transport servers are located in the same site. This allows the Mailbox or Unified Messaging server to submit messages for routing and transport to a Hub Transport server that has the same site membership.

When a Client Access server receives a user connection request, it queries Active Directory to determine which Mailbox server is hosting the user's mailbox. The Client Access server then retrieves the site membership of that Mailbox server. If the Client Access server is not in the same site as the user's Mailbox server, the connection is redirected to a Client Access server in the same site as the Mailbox server.

Hub Transport servers retrieve information from Active Directory to determine how they should transport mail inside the organization. When a user sends a message, the Categorizer running on the Hub Transport server uses the header information about the message to query Active Directory for information about where the server must deliver the message. If the recipient's mailbox is located on a Mailbox server in the same site as the Hub Transport server, the server delivers the message directly to that mailbox. If the recipient's mailbox is located on a Mailbox server in a different site, the message is transferred to a Hub Transport server in that site and then that server delivers the message to the mailbox.

Exchange servers determine site membership by matching their assigned IP address to a subnet that is defined in Active Directory Sites And Services and associated with an Active Directory site. The Exchange server then uses this information to determine which domain controllers, Global Catalog servers, and other Exchange servers exist in that site and communicates with those directory servers for authentication, authorization, and messaging purposes. Exchange 2007 always tries to retrieve information about recipients from directory servers that are in the same site as the Exchange 2007 server.

> **Tip**   In Active Directory, you can associate a site with one or more IP subnets. Each subnet that is part of a site should be connected over reliable, high-speed links. You should configure any business locations connected over slow or unreliable links as part of separate sites. Because of this, individual sites typically represent well-connected local area networks (LANs) within an organization, and wide area network (WAN) links between business locations typically mark the boundaries of these sites. Sites cannot have overlapping subnet configurations. If subnets overlap, replication and message routing will not work correctly.

How IP Site Links Are Used

As Figure 5-1 shows, Active Directory sites are connected through IP site links. An IP site link can connect two or more sites. Each site link has a specific schedule, interval, and cost. The schedule and interval determine the frequency of Active Directory replication. The cost value determines the cost of using the link relative to other links that may be available. Active Directory replication uses the link with the lowest cost when multiple paths exist to a destination. The cost of a route is determined by adding together the cost of all site links in a transmission path. Administrators assign the cost value to a link based on relative network speed, available bandwidth, and reliability compared to other available connections. By default, IP site links always allow traffic to flow into or out of a site.

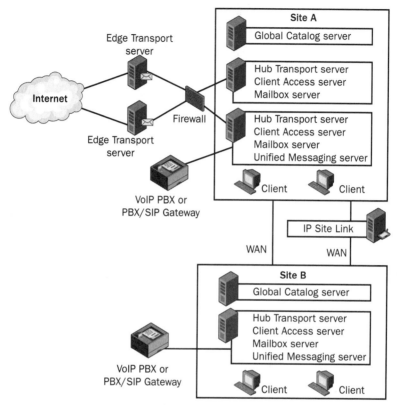

Figure 5-1   Message traffic between sites is routed over IP site links.

In large enterprises, message traffic may have to travel through multiple sites to get from the source site to a destination site. When transferring messages from one site to another site through other sites, a Hub Transport server always tries to connect directly to a Hub Transport server in the destination site. Because of this, messages are not relayed through each Hub Transport server in each site in the link path. Instead, they go directly from the Hub Transport server in the originating site across the link to the Hub Transport server in the destination site. If the originating server cannot connect directly to a Hub Transport server in the destination site, the originating Hub Transport server uses the link cost to determine the closest site at which to queue the message. This new feature is called *queue at point of failure*.

The Hub Transport server can also use the site link information to optimize routing of messages that users send to multiple recipients. Here, the Hub Transport server only expands a distribution list and creates multiple copies of a message when there are multiple paths in the routing topology. This new feature is called *delayed fan-out*.

Using Configuration Containers Instead of Administrative Groups

Exchange Server 2007 uses configuration containers instead of administrative groups to simplify the administrative model. As Figure 5-2 shows, you can view the logical structure of the Exchange organization in the Exchange Management Console. Start the Exchange Management Console by clicking Start, selecting All Programs, selecting Microsoft Exchange Server 2007, and selecting Exchange Management Console.

In the Exchange Management Console, under the Microsoft Exchange node, you'll find three top-level containers:

- **Organization Configuration** Used to view and manage the global settings for all servers and recipients in an organization. Settings are organized based on server role and applied globally throughout the organization.

- **Server Configuration** Used to view and manage the configuration of individual servers in an organization. Servers are organized by role.

- **Recipient Configuration** Used to view and manage recipients in an organization. Recipients are organized by type, independent of the mailbox server on which they are stored.

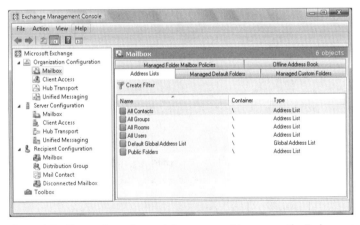

Figure 5-2 The configuration containers are used to manage the Exchange organization.

The sections that follow discuss these Exchange components and explain how they fit into the overall organizational structure.

Working with the Organization Configuration Node

With Exchange Server 2007, the scope of the organization is the same as the scope of your Active Directory organization. Because of this, Organization Configuration settings apply to all Exchange servers and Exchange recipients in all domains of your

Active Directory forest. When you select the Organization Configuration node, the results pane lists the identities that are currently configured as Exchange administrators, including the role and scope assigned, as shown in Figure 5-3.

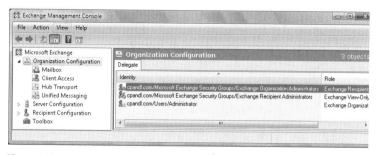

Figure 5-3   Organization Configuration extends to administrator roles as well as other organization-wide settings.

You can specify additional Exchange administrators by right-clicking the Organization Configuration node and selecting Add Delegate. You can remove Exchange administrators by right-clicking the administrator entry and selecting Remove. Other tips and techniques for managing administrative roles are discussed in Chapter 10, "Implementing Exchange Server 2007 Security."

The subnodes under the Organization Configuration node provide access to the most common organization-level settings you'll work with:

- **Mailbox**   Allows you to manage Mailbox Server role settings that apply to your entire Exchange 2007 organization. Mailbox Server role settings that you can manage include address lists, managed folders, mailbox policies, and offline address books. See Chapter 9, "Working with Distribution Groups and Address Lists," for more information.

- **Client Access**   Allows you to manage Client Access Server role settings that apply to your entire Exchange 2007 organization. Client Access Server role settings allow you to create and manage Exchange ActiveSync Mailbox policies. See Chapter 16, "Managing Client Access Servers," for more information.

- **Hub Transport**   Allows you to manage Hub Transport Server role settings that apply to your entire Exchange 2007 organization. Hub Transport Server role settings you can manage include remote and accepted domains, e-mail address policies, transport rules, journal rules, send connectors, and Edge subscriptions. See Chapter 15, "Managing Hub Transport and Edge Transport Servers," for more information.

- **Unified Messaging**   Allows you to manage Unified Messaging Server role settings that apply to your entire Exchange 2007 organization. Unified Messaging Server role settings you can manage include dial plans, gateways, mailbox policies, and auto-attendants.

With Exchange Server 2007 organizations, all organization information is stored in Active Directory. When you start the Exchange Management Console, the console obtains the Organization Configuration details from the authoritative domain controller to which your computer is currently connected. In some cases, such as when you need to work with recipients and objects in a specific site or domain, you may want to connect to a specific authoritative domain controller and obtain server and Organization Configuration details from this server.

You can specify the domain controller from which to obtain Organization Configuration details by completing the following steps:

1. Open Exchange Management Console.

2. Right-click the Organization Configuration node, and then select Modify Configuration Domain Controller. The Configuration Domain Controller dialog box appears, shown in Figure 5-4.

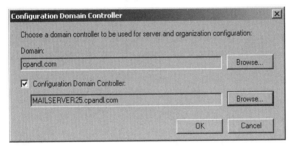

Figure 5-4   Specify the domain and domain controller to use.

3. In the Domain text box, click Browse, and then use the Select Domain dialog box to select the domain to use.

4. In the specified domain, by default you are connected to the first authoritative domain controller that responds to your request. To specify a configuration domain controller to use, select the Configuration Domain Controller checkbox and then click Browse. Use the Select Domain Controller dialog box to select the domain controller to use according to its site membership in the previously specified domain.

5. When you click OK, Exchange Management Console retrieves the topology information for the specified domain and site.

Working with the Server Configuration Node

Unlike Exchange Server 2003, all servers running Exchange Server 2007 have one or more server roles. You can deploy the Mailbox, Client Access, Hub Transport, and Unified Messaging Server roles together. You can also manage these roles together using the Server Configuration node in the Exchange Management Console. When you select the Server Configuration node in the Exchange Management Console, all

Exchange servers in your Exchange Server 2007 organization are listed in the results pane by name, Exchange Server 2007 roles installed, and Exchange Server version, as shown in Figure 5-5.

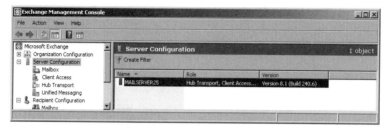

Figure 5-5   Server Configuration settings apply to individual servers according to their role.

You can work with the individual server entries in several ways:

- If you right-click a server entry, you'll see a shortcut menu with options for managing each configured role. Selecting one of those options opens the corresponding subnode under Server Configuration, and is the same as selecting the subnode and then selecting the server with which you want to work.

- If you right-click a server entry, and then select Properties, you'll see the Properties dialog box, shown in Figure 5-6. The General tab provides additional summary details on the server configuration, including the Exchange Server 2007 edition the server is running, the domain controllers being used by Exchange, and the Global Catalog servers being used by Exchange. Other server-specific configuration details are discussed elsewhere in this book.

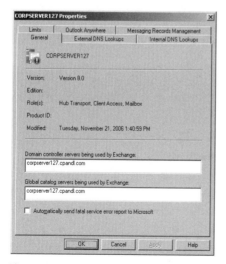

Figure 5-6   General properties provide additional configuration details for the selected server.

The subnodes under the Server Configuration node provide access to the most common settings you'll work with for individual servers according to their role:

- **Mailbox**   Allows you to manage the Mailbox configuration of a selected server. In the top pane, servers are listed by name, role, and Exchange version. If you select a server in the top pane, the related databases are listed according to the related storage groups and database file paths. See Chapter 11, "Managing Microsoft Exchange Server 2007 Data and Storage Groups," for more information.

- **Client Access**   Allows you to manage the Client Access configuration of a selected server. In the top pane, servers are listed by name, role, Exchange version, and Outlook Anywhere state. If you select a server in the top pane, you can view the Web sites and Uniform Resource Locators (URLs) used with Outlook Web Access, Exchange ActiveSync, and Offline Address Book Distribution. See Chapter 16 for more information.

- **Hub Transport**   Allows you to manage the Hub Transport configuration of a selected server. In the top pane, servers are listed by name, role, Exchange version, external postmaster address, and message tracking state. If you select a server in the top pane, you can view the Receive Connectors and their status. See Chapter 15 for more information.

- **Unified Messaging**   Allows you to manage the Unified Messaging configuration of a selected server. In the top pane, servers are listed by name, role, Exchange version, unified messaging status, and associated dial plans. If you select a server in the top pane, you can view the dial plans, IP gateways, mailbox policies, and auto-attendants for that server.

As with organization-level configuration details, the configuration details for individual servers are stored in Active Directory. You can specify the domain controller from which to obtain Server Configuration details by completing the following steps:

1. Open Exchange Management Console.

2. Right-click the Server Configuration node, and then select Modify Configuration Domain Controller. The Configuration Domain Controller dialog box appears, shown previously in Figure 5-4.

3. Follow steps 3–5 under "Working with the Organization Configuration Node."

Working with the Recipient Configuration Node

A recipient is an entity that can receive Exchange mail. Recipients include users, contacts, distribution groups, public folders, and resources. Types of resources used with Exchange include rooms and equipment used for scheduling.

You refer to recipients as either mailbox-enabled or mail-enabled. Mailbox-enabled recipients (users and resources) have mailboxes for sending and receiving e-mail messages. Mail-enabled recipients (contacts, distribution groups, and public folders) have e-mail addresses but no mailboxes. Thus, mail-enabled recipients can receive messages but can't send them.

In addition to users, contacts, groups, resources, and public folders, Exchange Server 2007 has two unique types of recipients: linked mailboxes and dynamic distribution groups. Basically, a linked mailbox represents a mailbox that is accessed by a user in a separate, trusted forest. A dynamic distribution group is a type of distribution group that you can use to build a list of recipients whenever mail addressed to the group is received, rather than having a fixed member list.

To manage recipients in your organization, you need to know these key concepts:

- **How e-mail policies are used**   E-mail address policies define the technique Exchange uses to create e-mail addresses for users, resources, contacts, and mail-enabled groups. For example, you can set a policy for users with Exchange mailboxes that creates e-mail addresses by combining an e-mail alias with @cpandl.com. Thus, during setup of an account for William Stanek, the e-mail alias williams is combined with @cpandl.com to create the e-mail address williams@cpandl.com.

- **How address lists are used**   You use address lists to organize recipients and resources, making it easier to find the ones that you want to use, along with their related information. During setup, Exchange creates a number of default address lists. The most commonly used default address list is the global address list, which lists all the recipients in the organization. You can create custom address lists as well.

- **How managed folders are used**   Every recipient has a default set of managed folders that are displayed in Outlook and related views of Outlook, such as Outlook Web Access. These folders include Inbox, Contacts, Drafts, Deleted Items, Junk E-mail, Outbox, and Sent Items. To the default folders, you can add custom managed folders. For example, if managers need to approve certain types of messages before the messages are sent, you could create a Pending Approval folder.

In the Exchange Management Console, Recipient Configuration settings apply to individual recipients in all domains of your Active Directory forest according to their type. The subnodes under the Recipient Configuration node provide access to recipients according to their type or state:

- **Mailbox**   Allows you to view and manage user mailboxes, room mailboxes, equipment mailboxes, and linked mailboxes. See Chapter 8, "Mailbox Administration," for more details.

- **Distribution Group**   Allows you to view and manage standard and dynamic distribution groups. See Chapter 9 for more details.

- **Mail Contact**   Allows you to view and manage mail contacts. See Chapter 7, "User and Contact Administration," for more details.

- **Disconnected Mailbox**   Allows you to view and manage disconnected mailboxes. A disconnected mailbox is a mailbox that is not associated with an Active Directory user account because it has been removed and marked for deletion. By default, when you remove a mailbox, it remains as a disconnected mailbox in Exchange for 30 days. At the end of the 30-day period, the mailbox is permanently removed. See Chapter 12, "Mailbox and Public Folder Database Administration," for more information.

When you select the Recipient Configuration node in the Exchange Management Console, or any related subnodes, Exchange recipients for your logon domain are listed in the results pane, as shown in Figure 5-7. Recipients are scoped to the logon domain by default rather than to all domains in the Active Directory forest, because an enterprise can have many thousands of recipients and you typically will not want to work with all recipients in all domains simultaneously.

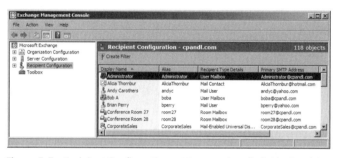

Figure 5-7   Recipient Configuration settings apply to individual recipients according to their type.

You can, however, configure the recipient scope so that you can:

- View all recipients in your Active Directory forest

- View all recipients in a domain other than your logon (default) domain

- View all recipients in a specific organizational unit (OU)

You can set the scope for recipient configuration by completing the following steps:

1. Open Exchange Management Console.

2. Right-click the Recipient Configuration node, and then select Modify Recipient Scope. The Recipient Scope dialog box appears, shown in Figure 5-8.

3. If you want to view all recipients in your Active Directory forest, select View All Recipients In Forest. Information about recipients for the forest is retrieved from the Global Catalog. If you'd like to specify a specific Global Catalog server to use, select the Global Catalog check box, click Browse, and then use the Select Global

Catalog dialog box to select the Global Catalog server to use according to its site membership in the forest.

Figure 5-8   Specify the scope for recipient configuration.

4. If you want to view all recipients in specific domain or organizational unit, select View All Recipients In Specified Organizational Unit. Information about recipients for the domain or organizational unit is retrieved from a domain controller in the domain or OU. If you'd like to specify a domain controller to use, select the Recipient Domain Controller check box, click Browse, and then use the Select Domain Controller dialog box to select the domain controller to use according to its site membership in the related domain.

5. When you click OK, the recipient information for the specified forest, domain, or OU is retrieved.

When you select the Recipient Configuration node in the Exchange Management Console, or any related subnodes, the maximum number of Exchange recipients you can view at any time is limited by default to 1,000. You can change the maximum number of recipients to display by completing the following steps:

1. Open Exchange Management Console.

2. Select the Recipient Configuration node or the subnode you want to work with, and then in the Actions pane, click Modify The Maximum Number Of Recipients To Display. This displays the Maximum Number Of Recipients To Display dialog box shown in Figure 5-9.

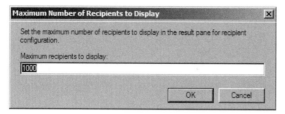

Figure 5-9 Specify the number of recipients to display.

3. In the text box provided, type the maximum number of recipients to display.

4. When you click OK, the recipient display is refreshed using the specified maximum number of recipients.

Understanding Data Storage in Exchange Server 2007

Depending on its role, Exchange Server stores information in several locations, including:

- Active Directory data store
- Exchange Server information store
- Exchange Server queues

Working with the Active Directory Data Store

The Active Directory data store contains all directory information for Exchange Server 2007 configuration and Exchange Server 2007 recipients as well as other important directory resources. Domain controllers maintain the data store in a file called Ntds.dit. The location of this file is set when Active Directory is installed and must be on an NTFS (NT file system) drive formatted for use with Microsoft Windows Server 2003. You can also save directory data separately from the main data store. This is true for some public data, such as logon scripts.

Two key concepts to focus on when looking at Active Directory are multimaster replication and Global Catalog servers.

Using Multimaster Replication

Domain controllers replicate most changes to the data store by using multimaster replication, which allows any domain controller to process directory changes and replicate those changes to other domain controllers. Replication is handled automatically for key data types, including the following:

- **Domain data** Contains information about objects within a domain, such as users, groups, and contacts.

- **Configuration data**   Describes the topology of the directory and includes a list of important domain information.

- **Schema data**   Describes all objects and data types that can be stored in the data store.

Using Global Catalogs

Active Directory information is also made available through Global Catalogs. You use Global Catalogs for information searches and, in some cases, domain logon. A domain controller designated as a Global Catalog server stores a full replica of all objects in the data store (for its host domain).

By default, the first domain controller installed in a domain is designated as the Global Catalog server. Consequently, if there is only one domain controller in the domain, the domain controller and the Global Catalog are on the same server. Otherwise, the Global Catalog is on the domain controller configured as such.

Information searches are one of the key uses of the Global Catalog. Searches in the Global Catalog are efficient and can resolve most queries locally, thus reducing the network load and allowing for quicker responses. With Exchange, the Global Catalog can be used to execute Lightweight Directory Access Protocol (LDAP) queries for dynamic distribution groups. Here, the members of the distribution group are based on the results of the query sent to the Global Catalog server rather than being fixed.

Why use LDAP queries instead of a fixed member list? The idea is to reduce administrative overheard by being able to dynamically determine what the members of a distribution group should be. Query-based distribution is most efficient when the member list is relatively small (fewer than 25 members). If the member list has potentially hundreds or thousands of members, however, dynamic distribution can be inefficient and might require a great deal of processing to complete.

Here's how dynamic distribution works:

1. When e-mail is received that is addressed to the group, the Exchange Categorizer (a transport component) sends the predefined LDAP query to the Global Catalog server for the domain.

2. The Global Catalog server executes the query and returns the resulting address set.

3. The Exchange Categorizer then uses the address list to generate the recipient list and deliver the message. If the Categorizer is unable to generate the list for any reason, for instance if the list is incomplete or an error was returned, the Categorizer might start the process over from the beginning.

> **Note**   To make the process more efficient, large organizations can use a dedicated expansion server. Here, LDAP queries are routed to the expansion server. The expansion server processes the query and returns the results.

Working with the Exchange Server Information Store

The Exchange information store contains mailbox and public folder data. To make the information store more manageable, Exchange Server 2007 allows you to organize it into multiple databases. You can then manage these databases individually or in logical groupings called storage groups.

Exchange Server uses transactions to control changes in storage groups. As with traditional databases, these transactions are recorded in a transaction log. Exchange Server then commits or rolls back changes based on the success of the transaction. In the case of failure, you can use the transaction log to restore the database. The facility that manages transactions is the Microsoft Exchange Information Store service (Store.exe).

When working with storage groups and Exchange Server 2007 Standard Edition, you should keep the following in mind:

- Each Mailbox server can have up to five storage groups (with one of the storage groups, called the recovery storage group, or RSG, reserved for database recovery operations).

- Each Mailbox server can have a maximum of five databases, with a maximum size per database of 16 terabytes (TB)—limited only by hardware. While a single storage group can have up to five databases, allocating five databases to one storage group would mean that you couldn't allocate additional databases to other storage groups.

When working with storage groups and Exchange Server 2007 Enterprise Edition, you should keep the following in mind:

- Each Mailbox server can have up to 50 storage groups (with one of the storage groups, the RSG, reserved for database recovery operations).

- A single storage group can have up to five databases, with a maximum size per database of 16 TB—limited only by hardware. However, the maximum number of databases that a single Mailbox server can have is 50 (with up to five reserved for the recovery storage group).

To create a new storage group with a mailbox or public folder database, you'll need about 50 megabytes (MB) of free disk space. The files required by the storage group use a minimum of 23 MB of disk space. Although the total disk space used is about 23 MB, you'll need the extra space during creation and for read/write operations.

The Exchange information store uses Extensible Storage Engine (ESE) databases for message storage. ESE is a revised and updated architecture for the JET database previously used with the Windows operating systems. Key concepts to focus on when working with the Exchange information store and storage groups are the following:

- What Exchange server data files are used
- How data is stored in Exchange database files

- What files are associated with storage groups
- How single-instance storage is used

What Exchange Server Data Files Are Used?

With Exchange Server 2007, Mailbox servers have a single database file for each mailbox or public folder database. Unlike Exchange Server 2003, Exchange Server 2007 does not use a streaming Internet content file with the .stm file extension. Although the .stm file was previously used to store message attachments, Exchange Server 2007 now stores attachments along with messages in the primary data file.

Because attachments are encapsulated and written in binary format, you don't need to convert them to Exchange format. Exchange Server uses a link table within the database to reference the storage location of attachments within it.

Two types of databases are available:

- **Mailbox databases**   Contain mailboxes
- **Public Folder databases**   Contain public folders

What Files Are Associated with Storage Groups?

As Figure 5-10 shows, each storage group has primary data files for each associated database and several other types of shared working files and transaction logs.

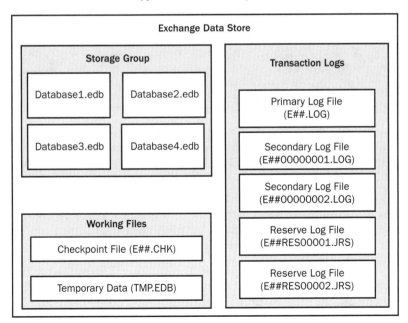

Figure 5-10   The Exchange data store has primary data files for each database as well as working files for the storage group.

These files are used as follows:

- **Primary data file (Database.edb)**   Physical database file that holds the contents of the data store. The name of the data file is the same as the name of the associated data store with the .edb file extension added.

- **Checkpoint file (E##.chk)**   Checkpoint file that tracks the point up to which the transactions in the log file have been committed to databases in the storage group. Generally, the name of the checkpoint file for the first storage group is E00.chk, the name of the checkpoint file for the second storage group is E01.chk, and so on.

- **Temporary data (Tmp.edb)**   Temporary workspace for processing transactions.

- **Primary log file (E##.log)**   Primary log file that contains a record of all changes that have yet to be committed to the database in the storage group. Generally, the name of the log file for the first storage group is E00.log, the name of the log file for the second storage group is E01.log, and so on.

- **Secondary log files (E##00000001.log, E##00000002.log, ...)**   Additional log files that are used as needed. Up to a billion unique log files can be created per storage group.

- **Reserve log files (E##Res00001.jrs, E##Res00002.jrs, ...)**   Files that are used to reserve space for additional log files if the primary log file becomes full.

By default, the primary data file, working files, and transaction logs are all stored in the same location. On a Mailbox server, you'll find these files in a per-storage group subfolder of the %SystemRoot%\Program Files\Microsoft\Exchange Server\Mailbox folder. Although these are the only files used for the data store, Exchange Server uses other files, depending on the roles for which you have configured the server.

How Is Data Stored in Exchange Database Files?

Exchange uses object-based storage. The primary data file contains several indexed tables, including a data table that contains a record for each object in the data store. Each referenced object can include object containers, such as mailboxes, and any other type of data that is stored in the data store.

Think of the data table as having rows and columns; the intersection of a row and a column is a field. The table's rows correspond to individual instances of an object. The table's columns correspond to folders. The table's fields are populated only if a folder has stored data. The data stored in fields can be a fixed or a variable length.

Records in the data table are stored in data pages that have a fixed size of 8 kilobytes (KB, or 8,192 bytes). The 8-KB page file size represents a change from the 4-KB data pages used with Exchange Server 2003. This change was made to improve performance.

In an Exchange database, each data page has a page header, data rows, and free space that can contain row offsets. The page header uses the first 96 bytes of each page, leaving 8,096 bytes for data and row offsets. Row offsets indicate the logical order of rows on a page, which means that offset 0 refers to the first row in the index, offset 1 refers to the second row, and so on. If a row contains long, variable-length data, the data may not be stored with the rest of the data for that row. Instead, Exchange can store an 8-byte pointer to the actual data, which is stored in a collection of 8-KB pages that aren't necessarily written contiguously. In this way, an object and all its stored values can be much larger than 8 KB.

The primary log file has a fixed size of 1 MB. The 1-MB log file size represents a change from the 5-MB log files used with Exchange Server 2003. This change was made so that Exchange Server 2007 could support continuous replication. When this log file fills up, Exchange creates additional (secondary) log files as necessary. The secondary log files are also limited to a fixed size of 1 MB. Exchange uses the reserve log files to reserve disk space for log files that it may need to create. As several reserve files are already created, this speeds up the transactional logging process when additional logs are needed.

How Is Single-Instance Storage Used?

Like previous versions, Exchange Server 2007 continues to use single-instance message storage on a per-database basis. With this technique, a message that's sent to multiple mailboxes is:

■ Stored once if all the mailboxes are in the same database.

■ Copied once to each database that contains a target mailbox.

In addition, if the databases are in different storage groups, Exchange Server writes the message to each database as well as to the transaction log set for each storage group. Thus, a message written to three databases that are in two different storage groups would use five times the disk space used by a message written to a single database in a single storage group. To better understand this, consider the following example:

A 2-MB message is sent to all company employees. The mailboxes for these employees are in mailbox databases A and B in storage group 1 and in mailbox database C in storage group 2. Exchange Server writes the message to the transaction log in storage groups 1 and 2 and then writes to the mailbox databases A, B, and C. Storing the original 2-MB messages thus requires 10 MB of disk space.

> **Note**   Needing 10 MB of disk space to store a 2-MB message might sound like an awful lot of space, but remember the hidden savings. That 2-MB message might have been sent to 1,000 employees, and without single-instance message storage, Exchange Server would use a whopping 2 GB of disk space.

Working with the Exchange Server Message Queues

Exchange Server message queues are temporary holding locations for messages that are waiting to be processed. Two general types of queues are used:

- **Persistent**   Persistent queues are always available even if no messages are waiting to be processed.

- **Nonpersistent**   Nonpersistent queues are only available when messages are waiting to be processed.

With Exchange Server 2007, both Hub Transport and Edge Transport servers store messages waiting to be processed in persistent and nonpersistent queues. Table 5-1 provides an overview of the queues used.

Table 5-1   Queues Used with Transport Servers

Queue Name	Server Role	Number of Queues	Queue Type
Mailbox delivery	Hub Transport	One for each unique destination Mailbox server	Nonpersistent
Poison message	Hub Transport, Edge Transport	One	Persistent
Remote delivery	Hub Transport	One for each unique remote Active Directory site	Nonpersistent
Remote delivery	Edge Transport	One for each unique destination Simple Mail Transfer Protocol (SMTP) domain and smart host	Nonpersistent
Submission	Hub Transport, Edge Transport	One	Persistent
Unreachable	Hub Transport, Edge Transport	One	Persistent

As Figure 5-11 shows, the various message queues are all stored in a single database. Like the Exchange information store, the message queues database uses the ESE for message storage as well as for data pages that have a fixed size of 8 KB.

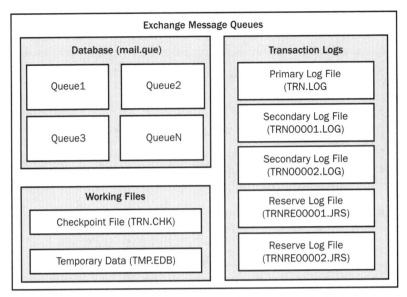

Figure 5-11   The Exchange message queues are all stored in a single database.

The database has a single data file associated with it and several other types of working files and transaction logs. These files are used as follows:

- **Primary data file (Mail.que)**   Physical database file that holds the contents of all message queues.

- **Checkpoint file (Trn.chk)**   Checkpoint file that tracks the point up to which the transactions in the log file have been committed to the database.

- **Temporary data (Tmp.edb)**   Temporary workspace for processing transactions.

- **Primary log file (Trn.log)**   Primary log file that contains a record of all changes that have yet to be committed to the database.

- **Secondary log files (TRN00001.log, TRN00002.log, ...)**   Additional log files that are used as needed.

- **Reserve log files (TRNRes00001.jrs, TRNRes00002.jrs, ...)**   Files that are used to reserve space for additional log files if the primary log file becomes full.

The facility that manages queuing transactions is the Microsoft Exchange Transport service (MSExchangeTransport.exe). Because logs used with message queues are not continuously replicated, these log files have a fixed size of 5 MB. When the primary log file for message queues fills up, Exchange creates additional (secondary) log files as necessary. Exchange uses the reserve log files to reserve disk space for log files that may need to be created. As several reserve files are already created, this speeds up the transactional logging process when additional logs are needed.

By default, the data file, working files, and transaction logs are all stored in the same location. On a Hub Transport or Edge Transport server, you'll find these files in the %SystemRoot%\Program Files\Microsoft\Exchange Server\TransportRoles\ data\Queue folder.

Using and Managing Exchange Server Services

Each Exchange server in the organization relies on a set of services for routing messages, processing transactions, replicating data, and much more. Table 1-1 in Chapter 1, "Microsoft Exchange Server 2007 Administration Overview," lists these services.

> **Tip**   Of all the Exchange services, the one service that relies on having a network connection at startup is the Microsoft Exchange Information Store service. If you start an Exchange server and the server doesn't have a network connection, the Microsoft Exchange Information Store service may fail to start. As a result, you may have to manually start the service. Sometimes, you'll find the service has a "Stopping" state. In this case, you'll have to wait until the server completely stops the service before you restart it.

To manage Exchange services, you'll use the Services node in the Computer Management console, which you start by completing the following steps:

1. Choose Start, point to Programs or All Programs, point to Administrative Tools, and then select Computer Management. Or, in the Administrative Tools folder, select Computer Management.

2. To connect to a remote Exchange server, right-click the Computer Management entry in the console tree, and then select Connect To Another Computer from the shortcut menu. You can now choose the Exchange server for which you want to manage services.

3. Expand the Services And Applications node and then select Services.

Figure 5-12 shows the Services view in the Computer Management console. The key fields of this window are used as follows:

- **Name**   The name of the service.
- **Description**   A short description of the service and its purpose.
- **Status**   The status of the service as started, paused, or stopped. (Stopped is indicated by a blank entry.)
- **Startup Type**   The startup setting for the service.

Note   Automatic services are started when the computer is started. Manual services are started by users or other services. Disabled services are turned off and can't be started.

- **Log On As**   The account the service logs on as. The default, in most cases, is the local system account.

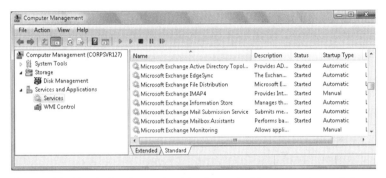

Figure 5-12   Use the Services node of the Computer Management console to manage Exchange Server services.

Note   It is important to note that on a new Exchange Server 2007 installation, some services are configured for a manual start for security reasons. Specifically, you'll find that the Microsoft Exchange Post Office Protocol version 3 (POP3), Microsoft Exchange Internet Messaging Access Protocol 4 (IMAP4), and Microsoft Search (Exchange) services are configured to start manually. If you use these services with Exchange, you'll need to configure them for automatic startup and then start them using the techniques discussed in this section.

Starting, Stopping, and Pausing Exchange Server Services

As an administrator, you'll often have to start, stop, or pause Exchange services. You manage Exchange services through the Computer Management console or through the Services console.

To start, stop, or pause services in the Computer Management console, follow these steps:

1. If necessary, connect to the remote Exchange server for which you want to manage services.

2. Expand the Services And Applications and then select Services.

3. Right-click the service you want to manipulate, and then select Start, Stop, or Pause, as appropriate. You can also choose Restart to have Windows stop and then start the service after a brief pause. Also, if you pause a service, you can use the Resume option to resume normal operation.

Tip   When services that are set to start automatically fail, the status is listed as blank and you'll usually receive notification in a pop-up window. Service failures can also be logged to the system's event logs. In Windows Server 2003, you can configure actions to handle service failure automatically. For example, you could have Windows Server 2003 attempt to restart the service for you. See the section of this chapter entitled "Configuring Service Recovery" for details.

Configuring Service Startup

Essential Exchange services are configured to start automatically and normally shouldn't be configured with another startup option. That said, if you're trouble-shooting a problem, you might want a service to start manually or you might want to temporarily disable a service.

You configure service startup by completing the following steps:

1. In the Computer Management console, connect to the Exchange server for which you want to manage services.

2. Expand the Services And Applications node and then select Services.

3. Right-click the service you want to configure, and then select Properties.

4. On the General tab, use the Startup Type drop-down list to choose a startup option, as shown in Figure 5-13. Select Automatic to start a service when the computer starts. Select Manual to allow services to be started manually. Select Disabled to disable the service. Click OK.

Note   The Disabled option doesn't stop the service if it's currently running. It just prevents the service from starting the next time you start the server. To stop the service, you must click Stop.

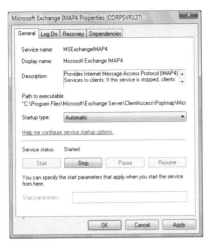

Figure 5-13   For troubleshooting, you might want to change the service startup option in the Properties dialog box.

Configuring Service Recovery

You can configure Windows services to take specific actions when a service fails. For example, you could attempt to restart the service or reboot the server. To configure recovery options for a service, follow these steps:

1. In the Computer Management console, connect to the computer for which you want to manage services.

2. Expand the Services And Applications node and then select Services.

3. Right-click the service you want to configure, and then select Properties.

4. On the Recovery tab, shown in Figure 5-14, you can configure recovery options for the first, second, and subsequent recovery attempts. The available options are as follows:

   ❑ Take No Action

   ❑ Restart The Service

   ❑ Run A File

   ❑ Restart The Computer

5. Configure other options based on your previously selected recovery options. If you elected to restart the service, you'll need to specify the restart delay. After stopping the service, Windows Server 2003 waits for the specified delay period before trying to start the service. In most cases, a delay of one to two minutes should be sufficient. Click OK.

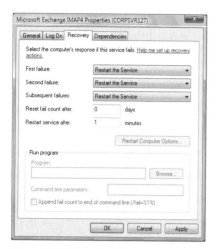

Figure 5-14   By using the Recovery tab in the Properties dialog box, you can configure services to automatically recover in case of failure.

When you configure recovery options for critical services, you might want to try to restart the service on the first and second attempts and then reboot the server on the third attempt.

Chapter 6
Configuring Microsoft Exchange Server with Exchange Management Shell

Microsoft Exchange Server 2007 introduces the Exchange Management Shell to compliment the expanding role of Exchange Server administrators and developers. The Exchange Management Shell is an extensible command-line environment for Exchange Server 2007 that builds on the existing framework provided by Windows PowerShell. When you install Exchange Server 2007 on a server, or when you install the Exchange Server management tools on a workstation, you install Windows PowerShell and the Exchange Management Shell as part of the process. This chapter introduces Windows PowerShell and its features, and then details the available commands and options of the Exchange Management Shell.

Using the Windows PowerShell

Anyone with a UNIX background is probably familiar with the concept of a command shell. Most UNIX-based operating systems have several full-featured command shells available, including Korn Shell (KSH), C Shell (CSH), and Bourne Shell (SH). Although Microsoft Windows operating systems have always had a command-line environment, they've lacked a full-featured command shell, and this is where Windows PowerShell comes into the picture.

Introducing the Windows PowerShell

Not unlike the less sophisticated Windows command prompt, the UNIX command shells operate by executing built-in commands, external commands, and command-line utilities and then returning the results in an output stream as text. The output stream can be manipulated in various ways, including redirecting the output stream so that it can be used as input for another command. This process of redirecting one command's output to another command's input is called piping, and it is a widely used shell-scripting technique.

The C Shell is one of the more sophisticated UNIX shells. In many respects, C Shell is a marriage of some of the best features of the C programming language and a full-featured UNIX shell environment. The Windows PowerShell takes the idea of a full-featured command shell built on a programming language a step further. It does this by implementing a scripting language based on C# and an object model based on the .NET Framework.

Basing the scripting language for Windows PowerShell on C# ensures that the scripting language can be easily understood by current C# developers and also allows new developers to advance to C#. Using an object model based on the .NET Framework allows the Windows PowerShell to pass complete objects and all their properties as output from one command to another. The ability to redirect objects is extremely powerful and allows for a much more dynamic manipulation of a result set. For example, not only can you get the name of a particular user, but you can also get the entire related user object. You can then manipulate the properties of this user object as necessary by referring to the properties you want to work with by name.

Running and Using Windows PowerShell

To invoke the Windows PowerShell, you must first open a command prompt window and then start the Windows PowerShell by typing **powershell** at the command line. To exit the Windows PowerShell and return to the command prompt, type **exit**.

Usually, when the shell starts, you will see a message similar to the following:

```
Windows PowerShell
Copyright (C) 2006 Microsoft Corporation. All rights reserved.
```

You can disable this message by starting the shell with the –nologo parameter, such as

```
powershell -nologo
```

Regardless of how you start the shell, you know you are using the Windows PowerShell because the command prompt title bar changes to Command Prompt–powershell and the current path is preceded by PS, as shown in Figure 6-1.

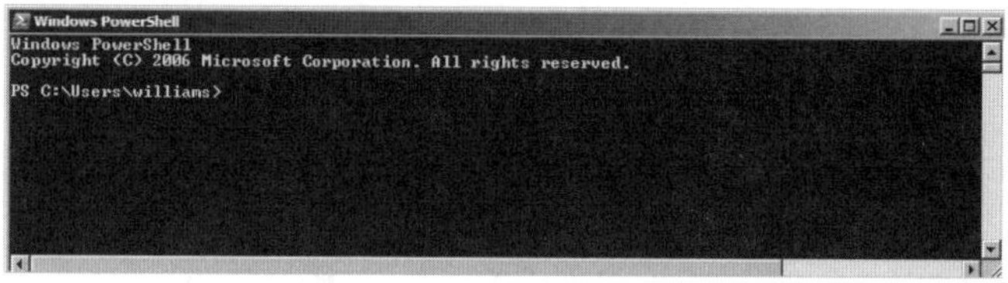

Figure 6-1 Start the Windows PowerShell.

When the shell starts, user and system profiles are run to set up the environment. The following is a listing and description of the profile files run, in the order of their execution:

1. %windir%\system32\WindowsPowerShell\v1.0\profile.ps1

   A system-wide profile executed for all users. This profile is used by the system administrator to configure common settings for the Windows PowerShell.

2. %windir%\system32\WindowsPowerShell\v1.0\Microsoft.PowerShell_profile.ps1

   A system-wide profile executed for all users. This profile is used by the system administrator to configure common settings for the Windows PowerShell.

3. %UserProfile%\Documents\WindowsPowerShell\profile.ps1

   A user-specific profile executed only for the current user. This profile is used by individual users to configure common settings for the Windows PowerShell.

4. %UserProfile%\Documents\WindowsPowerShell\
   Microsoft.PowerShell_profile.ps1

   A user-specific profile executed only for the current user. This profile is used by individual users to configure common settings for the Windows PowerShell.

You can start Windows PowerShell without loading profiles using the –noprofile parameter, such as:

```
powershell -noprofile
```

The first time you start Windows PowerShell, you typically will see a message indicating that scripts are disabled and that none of the listed profiles are executed. This is the default secure configuration for the Windows PowerShell. To enable scripts for execution, enter the following command at the shell prompt:

```
set-executionpolicy allsigned
```

This command sets the execution policy to require that all scripts have a trusted signature to execute. For a less restrictive environment, you can enter the following command:

```
set-executionpolicy remotesigned
```

This command sets the execution policy so that scripts downloaded from the Web execute only if they are signed by a trusted source. To work in an unrestricted environment, you can enter the following command:

```
set-executionpolicy unrestricted
```

This command sets the execution policy to run scripts regardless of whether they have a digital signature.

Running and Using Cmdlets

Windows PowerShell introduces the concept of a cmdlet (pronounced *commandlet*). A cmdlet is the smallest unit of functionality in the Windows PowerShell. You can think of a cmdlet as a built-in command. Rather than being highly complex, most cmdlets are quite simple and have a small set of associated properties.

You use cmdlets the same way you use any other commands and utilities. Cmdlet names are not case-sensitive. This means you can use a combination of both uppercase and lowercase characters. After starting the Windows PowerShell, you can enter the name of the cmdlet at the prompt and it will run in much the same way as a command-line command.

For ease of reference, cmdlets are named using verb-noun pairs. As Table 6-1 shows, the verb tells you what the cmdlet does in general. The noun tells you what specifically the cmdlet works with. For example, the get-variable cmdlet gets a named Windows PowerShell environment variable and returns its value. If you don't specify which variable to get as a parameter, get-variable returns a list of all Windows PowerShell environment variables and their values.

Table 6-1   Common Verbs Associated with Cmdlets and Their Meanings

Cmdlet Verb	Usage
New-	Creates a new instance of an item, such as a new mailbox.
Remove-	Removes an instance of an item, such as a mailbox.
Enable-	Enables a setting or mail-enables a recipient.
Disable-	Disables an enabled setting or mail-disables a recipient.
Set-	Modifies specific settings of an object.
Get-	Queries a specific object or a subset of a type of object, such as a specified mailbox or all mailbox users.

You can work with cmdlets in two ways:

- Executing commands directly at the shell prompt
- Running commands from within scripts

You can enter any command or cmdlet you can run at the Windows PowerShell command prompt into a script by copying the related command text to a file and saving the file with the .ps1 extension. You can then run the script in the same way you would any other command or cmdlet.

> **Note**   Windows PowerShell also includes a rich scripting language and allows the use of standard language constructs for looping, conditional execution, flow control, and variable assignment. Discussion of these features is beyond the scope of this book. A good resource is *Windows PowerShell Administrator's Pocket Consultant* (Microsoft Press, 2008).

From the Windows command-line environment or a batch script, you can execute Windows PowerShell cmdlets with the -command parameter. Typically when you do this, you will also want to suppress the Windows PowerShell logo and stop execution of profiles. After doing this, you can type the following command at a command prompt or insert it into a .BAT script:

```
powershell -nologo -noprofile -command get-service
```

Finally, when you are working with Windows PowerShell, it is important to remember that the current directory may not be part of the environment path. Because of this, you may need to use "./" when you run a script in the current directory, such as:

```
./runtasks
```

Running and Using Other Commands and Utilities

Because Windows PowerShell runs within the context of the Windows command prompt, you can run all Windows command-line commands, utilities, and graphical applications from within the Windows PowerShell. However, it is important to remember that the Windows PowerShell interpreter parses all commands before passing off the command to the command prompt environment. If the Windows PowerShell has a like-named command or a like-named alias for a command, this command, and not the expected Windows command, is executed. (See the "Using Cmdlet Aliases" section later in this chapter for more information on aliases.)

Non-Windows PowerShell commands and programs must reside in a directory that is part of the PATH environment variable. If the item is found in the path, it is run. The PATH variable also controls where the Windows PowerShell looks for applications, utilities, and scripts. In Windows PowerShell, you can work with Windows environment variables using $env. If you want to view the current settings for the PATH environment variable, you type $env:**path**. If you want to add a directory to this variable, you can use the following syntax:

```
$env:path += ";DirectoryPathToAdd"
```

where *DirectoryPathToAdd* is the directory path you want to add to the path, such as:

```
$env:path += ";C:\Scripts"
```

To have this directory added to the path every time you start the Windows PowerShell, you can add the command line as an entry in your profile. Keep in mind that cmdlets are like built-in commands rather than stand-alone executables. Because of this, they are not affected by the PATH environment variable.

Working with Cmdlets

Cmdlets provide the basic foundation for working with a computer from within the Windows PowerShell. Although there are many different cmdlets with many different available uses, cmdlets all have common features, which I'll examine in this section.

Using Windows PowerShell Cmdlets

At the Windows PowerShell prompt, you can get a complete list of cmdlets available by typing **help** *-*. To get help documentation on a specific cmdlet, type **help** followed by the cmdlet name, such as:

```
help get-variable
```

Table 6-2 provides a list of cmdlets you'll commonly use for administration. Although many other cmdlets are available, these are the ones you're likely to use the most.

Table 6-2   Cmdlets Commonly Used for Administration

Cmdlet Name	Description
ConvertFrom-SecureString	Exports a secure string to a safe format.
ConvertTo-SecureString	Creates a secure string from a normal string.
Get-Alias	Returns alias names for cmdlets.
Get-AuthenticodeSignature	Gets the signature object associated with a file.
Get-Credential	Gets a credential object based on a password.
Get-Date	Gets the current date and time.
Get-EventLog	Gets the log data from the Windows log files.
Get-ExecutionPolicy	Gets the effective execution policy for the current shell.
Get-Host	Gets host information.
Get-Location	Displays the current location.
Get-PSDrive	Gets the drive information for the specified PS drive.
Get-Service	Gets a list of services.
Import-Alias	Imports an alias list from a file.
New-Alias	Creates a new cmdlet-alias pairing.
New-Service	Creates a new service.
Push-Location	Pushes a location to the stack.
Read-Host	Reads a line of input from the host console.
Restart-Service	Restarts a stopped service.

Table 6-2   Cmdlets Commonly Used for Administration

Cmdlet Name	Description
Resume-Service	Resumes a suspended service.
Set-Alias	Maps an alias to a cmdlet.
Set-AuthenticodeSignature	Places an Authenticode signature in a script or other file.
Set-Date	Sets the system date and time on the host system.
Set-ExecutionPolicy	Sets the execution policy for the current shell.
Set-Location	Sets the current working location to a specified location.
Set-Service	Makes and sets changes to the properties of a service.
Start-Service	Starts a stopped service.
Start-Sleep	Suspends shell or script activity for the specified period.
Stop-Service	Stops a running service.
Suspend-Service	Suspends a running service.
Write-Output	Writes an object to the pipeline.

Using Cmdlet Parameters

All cmdlet parameters are designated with an initial dash (-). To reduce the amount of typing required, some parameters are position-sensitive, so that you can sometimes pass parameters in a specific order without having to specify the parameter name. For example, with get-service, you don't have to specify the -Name parameter, you can simply type the following:

```
Get-service ServiceName
```

where *ServiceName* is the name of the service you want to examine, such as:

```
Get-service MSExchangeIS
```

This command line returns the status of the Microsoft Exchange Information Store service. Because you can use wildcards, such as *, with name values, you can also type **get-service mse*** to return the status of all Microsoft Exchange–related services.

All cmdlets support the common set of parameters listed in Table 6-3. However, to use these parameters, you must run the cmdlet in such a way that these parameters are returned as part of the result set.

Table 6-3   Common Cmdlet Parameters

Parameter Name	Description
-Confirm	Pauses processes and requires the user to acknowledge the action before continuing. Remove- and Disable- cmdlets have this parameter.
-Debug	Provides programming-level debugging information about the operation.
-ErrorAction	Controls the command behavior when an error occurs.
-ErrorVariable	Sets the name of the variable (in addition to the standard error) in which to place objects for which an error has occurred.
-OutBuffer	Sets the output buffer for the cmdlet.
-OutVariable	Sets the name of the variable in which to place output objects.
-Verbose	Provides detailed information about the operation.
-WhatIf	Allows the user to view what would happen if a cmdlet were run with a specific set of parameters. Remove- and Disable- cmdlets have this parameter.

Understanding Cmdlet Errors

When you work with cmdlets, you'll encounter two standard types of errors:

- **Terminating errors**   Errors that halt execution
- **Nonterminating errors**   Errors that cause error output to be returned but do not halt execution

With both types of errors, you'll typically see error text that can help you resolve the problem that caused it. For example, an expected file might be missing or you may not have sufficient permissions to perform a specified task.

Using Cmdlet Aliases

For ease of use, Windows PowerShell lets you create aliases for cmdlets. An alias is an abbreviation for a cmdlet that acts as a shortcut for executing the cmdlet. For example, you can use the alias gsv instead of the cmdlet name get-service.

Table 6-4 provides a list of commonly used default aliases. Although there are many other aliases, these are the ones you'll use most frequently.

Table 6-4   Commonly Used Cmdlet Aliases

Alias	Cmdlet
clear, cls	Clear-Host
Diff	Compare-Object
cp, copy	Copy-Item
Epal	Export-Alias
Epcsv	Export-Csv
Foreach	ForEach-Object
Fl	Format-List
Ft	Format-Table
Fw	Format-Wide
Gal	Get-Alias
ls, dir	Get-ChildItem
Gcm	Get-Command
cat, type	Get-Content
h, history	Get-History
gl, pwd	Get-Location
gps, ps	Get-Process
Gsv	Get-Service
Gv	Get-Variable
Group	Group-Object
Ipal	Import-Alias
Ipcsv	Import-Csv
R	Invoke-History
Ni	New-Item
Mount	New-PSDrive
Nv	New-Variable
rd, rm, rmdir, del, erase	Remove-Item
Rv	Remove-Variable
Sal	Set-Alias
sl, cd, chdir	Set-Location

Table 6-4 Commonly Used Cmdlet Aliases

Alias	Cmdlet
sv, set	Set-Variable
Sort	Sort-Object
Sasv	Start-Service
Sleep	Start-Sleep
spps, kill	Stop-Process
Spsv	Stop-Service
write, echo	Write-Output

You can define additional aliases using the Set-Alias cmdlet. The syntax is:

```
Set-alias aliasName cmdletName
```

where *aliasName* is the alias you want to use and *cmdletName* is the cmdlet for which you are creating an alias. The following example creates a "go" alias for the get-process cmdlet:

```
Set-alias go get-process
```

To use your custom aliases whenever you work with Windows PowerShell, enter the related command line in your profile.

Using the Exchange Management Shell

The Exchange Management Shell is a command-line management interface built on the Windows PowerShell. You use the Exchange Management Shell to manage any aspect of Exchange Server 2007 configuration that you can manage in the Exchange Management Console. This means that you can typically use either tool to configure Exchange Server 2007. However, there are also some configuration settings that you can manage only by using the Exchange Management Shell.

Running and Using the Exchange Management Shell

After you've installed the Exchange management tools on a computer, you can start the Exchange Management Shell by clicking Start, pointing to All Programs, selecting Microsoft Exchange Server 2007, and then selecting the Exchange Management Shell. You know you are using the Exchange Management Shell because the command prompt title bar shows "Machine:" followed by the server name and the current scope. The current path is preceded by [PS], as shown in Figure 6-2.

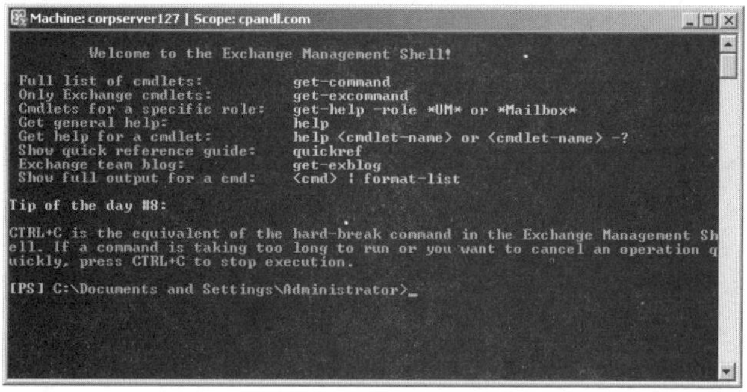

Figure 6-2   Use the Exchange Management Shell to manage Exchange Server from the command line.

When you start the Exchange Management Shell, it is initialized by a Microsoft Configuration (MCF1) file that instructs the shell to use administrator mode and obtain specific session settings about the Active Directory environment in which Exchange Server is being used. Because the Exchange Management Shell is an extension of the Windows PowerShell, user and system profiles are also run to set up the environment. If you want to use specific environment settings every time you use the Exchange Management Shell, you should put the settings in your user profile—either %UserProfile%\Documents\PSConfiguration\profile.ps1 or %UserProfile%\Documents\PSH\Microsoft.PowerShell_profile.ps1.

When you work with the Exchange Management Shell, all the Windows PowerShell cmdlets and aliases are available for your use. Although additional cmdlets are added, no additional aliases are added to the working environment. To end your session, you can exit the Exchange Management Shell by typing **exit**. Or you can close the shell window by clicking Close.

Working with Exchange Cmdlets

When you are working with the Exchange Management Shell, additional Exchange-specific cmdlets are available. As with Windows PowerShell cmdlets, you can get help information on Exchange cmdlets:

- To view a list of all Exchange cmdlets, type **get-excommand** at the shell prompt.

- To view Exchange cmdlets related to a specific server role, type **get-help –role** *RoleName* where *RoleName* is the name of the server role you want to examine. You can use the following role names:

    ❑ *UM* for cmdlets related to the Unified Messaging Server role

    ❑ *Mailbox* for cmdlets related to the Mailbox Server role

    ❑ *ClientAccess* for cmdlets related to the Client Access Server role

When you work with the Exchange Management Shell, you'll often work with Get-, Set-, Enable-, Disable-, New-, and Remove- cmdlets. These cmdlets all accept the -Identity parameter, which identifies the unique object with which you are working.

Typically, a cmdlet that accepts the -Identity parameter has it as its first parameter, allowing you to specify the identity, with or without the parameter name. When identities have names as well as aliases, you can specify either value as the identity. For example, you can use any of the following techniques to retrieve the mailbox object for the user William Stanek with the mail alias WilliamS:

```
get-mailbox -identity williams
get-mailbox -identity 'William Stanek'
get-mailbox Williams
get-mailbox "William Stanek"
```

With Get- cmdlets, you typically can return an object set containing all related items simply by omitting the identity. For example, if you type **get-mailbox** at the shell prompt without specifying an identity, you get a list of all mailboxes in the enterprise (up to the maximum permitted to return in a single object set).

By default, all cmdlets return data in table format. Because there are often many more columns of data than you can fit across the screen, you may need to switch to format-list output to see all of the data. To change to the format-list output, redirect the output using the pipe symbol (|) to the format-list cmdlet, as shown in this example:

```
get-mailbox -identity williams | format-list
```

You can abbreviate format-list as fl, as in this example:

get-mailbox –identity williams | fl

Either technique typically will ensure that you see much more information about the object or the result set than if you were retrieving table-formatted data.

Working with Object Sets and Redirecting Output

When you are working with the Exchange Management Shell, you'll often need to redirect the output of one cmdlet and pass it as input to another cmdlet. You can do this using the pipe symbol. For example, if you want to view mailboxes for a specific mailbox database rather than all mailboxes in the enterprise, you can pipe the output of get-mailboxdatabase to get-mailbox, as shown in this example:

```
get-mailboxdatabase -Identity "Engineering" | get-mailbox
```

Here, you use get-mailboxdatabase to get the mailbox database object for the Engineering database. You then send this object to the get-mailbox cmdlet as input, and get-mailbox iterates through all the mailboxes in this database. If you don't perform any other manipulation, the mailboxes for this database are listed as output, as shown here:

```
Name                 Alias              Server         ProhibitSendQuota
Administrator        Administrator      corpsvr127     unlimited
William S            williams           corpsvr127     unlimited
Tom G                tomg               corpsvr127     unlimited
David W              davidw             corpsvr127     unlimited
Kari F               karif              corpsvr127     unlimited
Connie V             conniev            corpsvr127     unlimited
Mike D               miked              corpsvr127     unlimited
```

You could also pipe this output to another cmdlet to perform an action on each individual mailbox in this database.

Working with Exchange Cmdlets

You use Exchange cmdlets to manage the configuration of your Exchange organization. These cmdlets work with objects matching a specific set of criteria. The sections that follow provide an overview of the most commonly used cmdlets with their most commonly used syntaxes.

Using General-Purpose Cmdlets

Several general-purpose cmdlets are provided. These cmdlets, along with their syntaxes, follow:

- **Get-ExchangeCertificate**   Retrieves a list of all public key certificates in the certificate store or details of a specified certificate. Each certificate has a thumbprint, which is a digest of the certificate data.

```
Get-ExchangeCertificate [-Domain 'DomainName']
[-Thumbprint 'Identifier']
```

- **Get-ExchangeServer**   Retrieves a list of all or specified Exchange servers.

```
Get-ExchangeServer -Domain 'DomainName'
[-DomainController 'DCName']
```

- **Get-Recipient**   Retrieves a list of all or specific recipients.

```
Get-Recipient [-RecipientType 'RecipientIdentifier']
  [-Identity 'Identifier'] [-DomainController 'DCName']
  [-OrganizationalUnit 'OUName'] [-Anr 'String']
```

Note   The -Anr parameter is used to specify a string on which to perform ambiguous name resolution. Any value entered is searched for within the specified objects.

Using Contact Management Cmdlets

You can work with contacts using the following cmdlets and command-line syntaxes:

- **Enable-MailContact**   Mail-enables a contact.

```
Enable-Mailcontact -Identity 'Identifier'
-externalEmailAddress 'EmailAddress'  [-Alias 'NewAlias']
[-DisplayName 'Name']  [-DomainController 'DCName']
[-MacAttachmentFormat 'Format'] [-MessageBodyFormat 'Format']
[-MessageFormat 'Format'] [-OrganizationalUnit 'OU']
[-PrimarySmtpAddress 'SmtpAddress']
[-UsePreferMessageFormat <$false|$true>]
```

- **Disable-MailContact**   Mail-disables a contact.

```
Disable-MailContact -Identity 'Alias'
[-DomainController 'DCName']
```

- **Get-MailContact**   Retrieves a list of all or specific mail-enabled contacts.

```
Get-MailContact [-Identity 'Identifier']
[-DomainController 'DCName'] [-OrganizationalUnit 'OUName']
[-Anr 'String'] [-ResultSize 'Size'] [-SortBy 'Value']
```

- **New-MailContact**   Creates a new mail-enabled contact.

```
New-MailContact -Name 'Name'
-ExternalEmailAddress 'ProxyAddress'
[-Alias 'NewAlias'] [-DisplayName 'Name']
[-DomainController 'DCName']
[-FirstName 'FirstName'] [-Initials 'Value']
[-LastName 'LastName'] [-MacAttachmentFormat 'Format']
[-MessageBodyFormat 'Format'] [-MessageFormat 'Format']
[-OrganizationalUnit 'OU'] [-PrimarySmtpAddress 'SmtpAddress']
[-TemplateInstance 'Instance']
[-UsePreferMessageFormat <$false|$true>]
```

■ **Set-MailContact**   Changes the specified properties of the specified mail-enabled contact.

```
Set-MailContact -Identity 'Identifier' [-Alias 'NewAlias']
[-AcceptMessagesOnlyFrom 'Recipient']
[-AcceptMessagesOnlyFromDLMembers 'Recipient']
[-DisplayName 'Name'] [-DomainController 'DCName']
[-EmailAddresses 'ProxyAddress']
[-EmailAddressPolicyEnabled <$false|$true>]
[-ExternalEmailAddress 'ProxyAddress']
[-GrantSendOnBehalfTo 'Mailbox']
[-HiddenFromAddressListsEnabled <$false|$true>]
[-MacAttachmentFormat 'Format'] [-MaxReceiveSize 'Size']
[-MaxRecipientPerMessage 'Size']
[-MaxSendSize 'Size'] [-MessageBodyFormat 'Format']
[-MessageFormat 'Format'] [-Name 'Name']
[-PrimarySmtpAddress 'SmtpAddress']
[-RejectMessagesFrom 'Recipient']
[-RejectMessagesFromDLMembers 'Recipient']
[-RequireSenderAuthenticationEnabled <$false|$true>]
[-SimpleDisplayName 'Name'] [-WindowsEmailAddress 'SmtpAddress']
```

■ **Get-Contact**   Retrieves a list of all or specific contacts, whether mail-enabled or not.

```
Get-Contact -Identity 'Identifier' [-DomainController 'DCName']
[-OrganizationalUnit 'OUName'] [-ResultSize 'Size']
[-SortBy 'Value']
```

■ **Set-Contact**   Changes or sets the specified properties of the specified contact.

```
Set-Contact -Identity 'Identifier' [-AssistantName 'Name']
[-City 'Name']
[-Company 'Name'] [-CountryOrRegion 'Name'] [-Department 'Name']
[-DisplayName 'Name'] [-DomainController 'DCName']
[-Fax 'FAXNUMBER']
[-FirstName 'Name'] [-HomePhone 'PhoneNumber']
[-Initials 'Value']
[-LastName 'Name'] [-Manager 'RecipientId']
[-MobilePhone 'PhoneNumber']
[-Name 'Name'] [-Notes 'Value'] [-Office 'Value']
[-Phone 'PhoneNumber']
[-PostalCode 'Code'] [-SimpleDisplayName 'Name']
[-StateOrProvince 'Value']
[-StreetAddress 'Value'] [-TelephoneAssistant 'Value']
[-Title 'Value']
[-WebPage 'Value'] [-WindowsEmailAddress 'SmtpAddress']
```

Using User Management Cmdlets

You can manage users using the following cmdlets and command-line syntaxes:

■ **Get-User**   Retrieves a list of all or specific Active Directory users.

```
Get-User [-Identity 'Identifier'] [-DomainController 'DCName']
[-OrganizationalUnit 'OUName'] [-ResultSize 'Size']
[-SortBy 'Value']
```

■ **Disable-MailUser**   Mail-disables the specified Active Directory user.

```
Disable-MailUser -Identity 'Identifier'
[-DomainController 'DCName']
```

■ **Enable-MailUser**   Mail-enables the specified Active Directory user.

```
Enable-MailUser -Identity 'Identifier'
-ExternalEmailAddress 'ProxyAddress'
[-Alias 'NewAlias'] [-DisplayName 'Name']
[-DomainController 'DCName']
[-MacAttachmentFormat 'Format'] [-MessageBodyFormat 'Format']
[-MessageFormat 'Format'] [-PrimarySmtpAddress 'SmtpAddress']
```

■ **Get-MailUser**   Retrieves a list of all or specified mail-enabled users.

```
Get-MailUser [-Identity 'Identifier']
[-DomainController 'DCName']
[-OrganizationalUnit 'OUName'] [-ResultSize 'Size']
[-SortBy 'Value']
```

■ **Remove-MailUser**   Removes the specified mail-enabled user.

```
Remove-MailUser -Identity 'Identifier'
[-DomainController 'DCName']
```

■ **Set-MailUser**   Sets the specified properties for the specified mail-enabled user.

```
Set-MailUser -Identity 'Identifier'
[-AcceptMessagesOnlyFrom 'Recipient']
[-AcceptMessagesOnlyFromDLMembers 'Recipient']
[-Alias 'NewAlias']
```

```
[-DisplayName 'Name'] [-DomainController 'DCName']
[-EmailAddresses 'ProxyAddress']
[-EmailAddressPolicyEnabled <$false|$true>]
[-ExternalEmailAddress 'ProxyAddress']
[-GrantSendOnBehalfTo 'Mailbox']
[-HiddenFromAddressListsEnabled <$false|$true>]
[-MacAttachmentFormat 'Format'] [-MaxReceiveSize 'Size']
[-MaxRecipientPerMessage 'Size']
[-MaxSendSize 'Size'] [-MessageBodyFormat 'Format']
[-MessageFormat 'Format'] [-Name 'Name']
[-PrimarySmtpAddress 'SmtpAddress']
[-RejectMessagesFrom 'Recipient']
[-RejectMessagesFromDLMembers 'Recipient']
[-RequireSenderAuthenticationEnabled <$false|$true>]
[-SimpleDisplayName 'Name'] [-WindowsEmailAddress 'SmtpAddress']
```

■ **Set-User**   Sets the specified properties for the specified user.

```
Set-User -Identity 'Identifier' [-AssistantName 'Name']
[-City 'Name']
[-Company 'Name'] [-CountryOrRegion 'Name'] [-Department 'Name']
[-DisplayName 'Name'] [-DomainController 'DCName']
[-Fax 'FAXNUMBER']
[-FirstName 'Name'] [-HomePhone 'PhoneNumber']
[-Initials 'Value']
[-LastName 'Name'] [-Manager 'RecipientId']
[-MobilePhone 'PhoneNumber']
[-Name 'Name'] [-Notes 'Value'] [-Office 'Value']
[-Phone 'PhoneNumber']
[-PostalCode 'Code'] [-SamAccountName 'Name']
[-SimpleDisplayName 'Name'] [-StateOrProvince 'Value']
[-StreetAddress 'Value'] [-TelephoneAssistant 'Value']
[-Title 'Value']
[-UserPrincipalName 'Name'] [-WebPage 'Value']
[-WindowsEmailAddress 'SmtpAddress']
```

Using Distribution Group Management Cmdlets

You can work with distribution groups using the following cmdlets and command-line syntaxes:

■ **Enable-DistributionGroup**   Mail-enables an existing universal distribution group.

```
Enable-DistributionGroup -Identity 'Identifier' [-Alias 'Alias']
[-DisplayName 'Name'] [-DomainController 'DCName']
```

■ **Disable-DistributionGroup**   Mail-disables a specified universal distribution group.

```
Disable-DistributionGroup -Identity 'Identifier'
[-DomainController 'DCName']
```

■ **Get-DistributionGroup**   Retrieves a list of all or specific mail-enabled universal distribution groups.

```
Get-DistributionGroup [-Identity 'Identifier']
[-DomainController 'DCName']
[-ManagedBy 'RecipientId'] [-OrganizationalUnit 'OUName']
[-ResultSize 'Size'] [-SortBy 'Value']
```

■ **New-DistributionGroup**   Creates the specified universal distribution group.

```
New-DistributionGroup -Name 'Name' -
SamAccountName 'SamAccountName'
[-Type 'GroupType'] [-Alias 'NewAlias'] [-DisplayName 'Name']
[-DomainController 'DCName'] [-ManagedBy 'RecipientId']
[-OrganizationalUnit 'OUName'] [-TemplateInstance 'Instance']
```

■ **Remove-DistributionGroup**   Removes the specified universal distribution group.

```
Remove-DistributionGroup [-Identity 'Identifier']
[-DomainController 'DCName']
```

■ **Set-DistributionGroup**   Changes the specified properties of the specified universal distribution group.

```
Set-DistributionGroup -Identity 'Identifier' [-Alias 'NewAlias']
[-AcceptMessagesOnlyFrom 'Recipient']
[-AcceptMessagesOnlyFromDLMembers 'Recipient']
[-DisplayName 'Name'] [-DomainController 'DCName']
[-EmailAddresses 'ProxyAddress']
[-EmailAddressPolicyEnabled <$false|$true>]
[-ExpansionServer 'Server'] [-GrantSendOnBehalfTo 'Mailbox']
[-HiddenFromAddressListsEnabled <$false|$true>]
```

```
[-ManagedBy 'RecipientId']
[-MaxReceiveSize 'Size'] [-MaxSendSize 'Size']
[-Name 'Name'] [-PrimarySmtpAddress 'SmtpAddress']
[-RejectMessagesFrom 'Recipient']
[-RejectMessagesFromDLMembers 'Recipient']
[-ReportToManagerEnabled <$false|$true>]
[-ReportToOriginatorEnabled <$false|$true>]
[-RequireSenderAuthenticationEnabled <$false|$true>]
[-SimpleDisplayName 'Name'] [-SamAccountName 'SamAccountName']
[-WindowsEmailAddress 'SmtpAddress']
```

- **Add-DistributionGroupMember**   Adds the specified recipient to the universal distribution group.

```
Add-DistributionGroupMember -Identity 'Identifier'
-Member 'RecipientID'
[-DomainController 'DCName']
```

- **Remove-DistributionGroupMember**   Removes the specified recipient from the universal distribution group.

```
Remove-DistributionGroupMember -Identity 'Identifier'
-Member 'RecipientID'
[-DomainController 'DCName']
```

- **Get-DistributionGroupMember**   Retrieves a list of all of the members of the specified distribution group.

```
Get-DistributionGroupMember -Identity 'Identifier'
[-DomainController 'DCName'] [-ResultSize 'Size']
```

- **Get-Group**   Retrieves a list of all security and distribution groups.

```
Get-Group [-Identity 'Identifier'] [-DomainController 'DCName']
[-OrganizationalUnit 'OUName'] [-ResultSize 'Size']
[-SortBy 'Value']
```

■ **Set-Group**   Sets the specified properties of the specified Windows group.

```
Set-Group -Identity 'Identifier' [-DisplayName 'NewDisplayName']
[-DomainController 'DCName'] [-ManagedBy 'RecipientId']
[-Name 'Name']
[-Notes 'Value'] [-SimpleDisplayName 'Name']
[-WindowsEmailAddress 'SmtpAddress']
```

■ **Get-DynamicDistributionGroup**   Retrieves a list of all or specific dynamic
distribution groups.

```
Get-DynamicDistributionGroup [-Identity 'Identifier']
[-DomainController 'DCName']
[-ManagedBy 'RecipientId'] [-OrganizationalUnit 'OUName']
[-ResultSize 'Size'] [-SortBy 'Value']
```

■ **New-DynamicDistributionGroup**   Creates the specified dynamic distribution
group.

```
New-DynamicDistributionGroup -Identity 'Identifier'
-IncludedRecipients 'Values' [-Alias 'Alias']
[-ConditionalCompany 'Values'] [-ConditionalDepartment 'Values']
[-ConditionalStateOrProvince 'Values'] [-DisplayName 'Name']
[-DomainController 'DCName'] [-OrganizationalUnit 'OUName']
[-RecipientContainer 'OUName'] [-TemplateInstance 'Instance']
```

■ **Remove-DynamicDistributionGroup**   Removes the specified dynamic
distribution group.

```
Remove-DynamicDistributionGroup [-Identity 'Identifier']
[-DomainController 'DCName']
```

■ **Set-DynamicDistributionGroup**   Changes the specified properties of the
specified dynamic distribution group.

```
Set-DynamicDistributionGroup -Identity 'Identifier'
[-Alias 'NewAlias']
[-AcceptMessagesOnlyFrom 'Recipient']
[-AcceptMessagesOnlyFromDLMembers 'Recipient']
[-ConditionalCompany 'Values'] [-ConditionalDepartment 'Values']
[-ConditionalStateOrProvince 'Values'] [-DisplayName 'Name']
[-DisplayName 'Name'] [-DomainController 'DCName']
```

```
[-EmailAddresses 'ProxyAddress']
[-EmailAddressPolicyEnabled <$false|$true>]
[-ExpansionServer 'Server'] [-ForceUpgrade <$false|$true>]
[-GrantSendOnBehalfTo 'Mailbox']
[-HiddenFromAddressListsEnabled <$false|$true>]
[-IncludedRecipients 'Recipients'] [-ManagedBy 'RecipientId']
[-MaxReceiveSize 'Size'] [-MaxSendSize 'Size']
[-Name 'Name'] [-Notes 'Value']
[-PrimarySmtpAddress 'SmtpAddress']
[-RecipientContainer 'OUName'] [-RecipientFilter 'String']
[-RejectMessagesFrom 'Recipient']
[-RejectMessagesFromDLMembers 'Recipient']
[-ReportToManagerEnabled <$false|$true>]
[-ReportToOriginatorEnabled <$false|$true>]
[-RequireSenderAuthenticationEnabled <$false|$true>]
[-SendOofMessageToOriginatorEnabled <$false|$true>]
[-SimpleDisplayName 'Name'] [-WindowsEmailAddress 'SmtpAddress']
```

Using Mailbox Management Cmdlets

You can work with mailboxes using the following cmdlets and command-line syntaxes:

- **Enable-Mailbox**   Mailbox-enables an existing Active Directory user account.

```
Enable-Mailbox -Identity 'Domain\UserName'
-Database 'MailboxDatabase'
[-ActiveSyncMailboxPolicy 'PolicyId'] [-Alias 'Alias']
[-DisplayName 'Name'] [-DomainController 'DCName']
[-ManagedFolderMailboxPolicy 'PolicyId']
[-ManagedFolderMailboxPolicyAllowed <$false|$true>]
[-PrimarySmtpAddress 'SmtpAddress']
```

- **Disable-Mailbox**   Mailbox-disables the specified user account.

```
Disable-Mailbox -Identity 'Identifier'
[-DomainController 'DCName']
```

- **Get-Mailbox**   Retrieves a list of all or specific mailboxes.

```
Get-Mailbox [-Identity 'Identifier'] |
[-Database 'DatabaseName']
[-DomainController 'DCName'] [-OrganizationalUnit 'OUName']
[-ResultSize 'Size'] [-SortBy 'Value']
```

- **Get-MailboxStatistics** Retrieves summary statistics for all or specific mailboxes, as long as the mailboxes have been logged on to at least once.

```
Get-MailboxStatistics [-Identity 'Identifier' |
-Database 'MailboxDatabase' | -Server 'Server']
[-DomainController 'DCName']
```

- **Move-Mailbox** Moves the mailbox of the specified user to the specified server.

```
Move-Mailbox -Identity 'Identifier'
-TargetDatabase 'Server\MailboxDatabase'
[-AllowMerge <$false|$true>] [-AttachmentFilenames 'Values']
[-BadItemLimit 'Limit'] [-ContentKeywords 'Values']
[-DomainController 'DCName'] [-EndDate 'DateTime']
[-ExcludeFolders 'MapiFoldePath'] [-GlobalCatalog 'GCName']
[-IgnorePolicyMatch <$false|$true>]
[-IgnoreRuleLimitErrors <$false|$true>]
[-IncludeFolders 'MapiFolderPath'] [-Locale 'Value']
[-MaxThreads 'Num']
[-NTAccountOU 'OUId'] [-PreserveMailboxSizeLimit <$false|$true>]
[-RecipientKeywords 'Values'] [-ReportFile 'LocalPath']
[-RetryInterval 'TimeSpan'] [-RetryTimeout 'TimeSpan']
[-SenderKeywords 'Values'] [-StartDate 'DateTime']
[-SubjectKeywords 'Values'] [-ValidateOnly <$false|$true>]
```

- **New-Mailbox** Creates the specified mailbox.

```
New-Mailbox -Name 'Name' -Database 'Server\MailboxDatabase'
[-ActiveSyncMailboxPolicy 'PolicyId'] [-Alias 'Alias']
[-DisplayName 'Name'] [-DomainController 'DCName']
[-FirstName 'Name'] [-Initials 'Value'] [-LastName 'Name']
[-ManagedFolderMailboxPolicy 'PolicyId']
[-ManagedFolderMailboxPolicyAllowed <$false|$true>]
[-OrganizationalUnit 'OUName']
[-ResetPasswordOnNextLogon <$false|$true>]
[-Password 'Password']
[-SamAccountName 'SamAccountName']
[-TemplateInstance 'Instance']
```

■ **Set-Mailbox**   Changes the specified properties of the specified mailbox.

```
Set-Mailbox -Identity 'Identifier'
[-AcceptMessagesOnlyFrom 'RecipientId']
[-AcceptMessagesOnlyFromDLMembers 'RecipientId']
[-Alias 'Alias']
[-AntispamBypassEnabled <$false|$true>]
[-ApplyMandatoryProperties <$false|$true>]
[-DeliverToMailboxAndForward <$false|$true>]
[-DisplayName 'Name']
[-DomainController 'DCName']
[-DowngradeHighPriorityMessagesEnabled <$false|$true>]
[-EmailAddresses 'ProxyAddresses']
[-EmailAddressPolicyEnabled <$false|$true>]
[-EndDateForRententionHold 'DateTime']
[-ExternalOofOptions 'Value']
[-ForwardingAddress 'RecipientId']
[-GrantSendOnBehalfTo 'MailboxId>']
[-HiddenFromAddressListsEnabled <$false|$true>]
[-IssueWarningQuota 'Size']
[-ManagedFolderMailboxPolicy 'MailboxPolicyId']
[-ManagedFolderMailboxPolicyAllowed <$false|$true>]
[-MaxBlockedSenders 'Value'] [-MaxSafeSenders 'Value']
[-MaxReceiveSize 'Size'] [-MaxSendSize 'Size'] [-Name 'Name']
[-Office 'Value'] [-OfflineAddressBook 'OfflineAddressBookId']
[-PrimarySmtpAddress 'SmtpAddress'] [-ProhibitSendQuota 'Size']
[-ProhibitSendReceiveQuota 'Size'] [-RecipientLimits 'Size']
[-RejectMessagesFrom 'RecipientId']
[-RejectMessagesFromDLMembers 'RecipientId']
[-RequireSenderAuthenticationEnabled <$false|$true>]
[-RemoveManagedFolderAndPolicy <$false|$true>]
[-RetainDeletedItemsFor 'Time']
[-RetainDeletedItemsUntilBackup <$false|$true>]
[-RetentionHoldEnabled <$false|$true>] [-SamAccountName 'Name']
[-SimpleDisplayName 'Name'] [-
StartDateForRetentionHold 'DateTime']
[-Type 'MailboxType'] [-UseDatabaseQuotaDefaults <$false|$true>]
[-UseDatabaseRetentionDefaults <$false|$true>]
[-WindowsEmailAddress 'SmtpAddress']
```

Using Database Management Cmdlets

You can manage Exchange databases using the following cmdlets and command-line syntaxes:

- **New-MailboxDatabase**   Creates a new mailbox database in the specified storage group.

```
New-MailboxDatabase -Name 'MailboxDatabase'
-StorageGroup 'StorageGroup'
[-CopyEdbFilePath 'EdbFilePath'] [-DomainController 'DCName']
[-EdbFilePath 'EdbFilePath'] [-HasLocalCopy <$false|$true>]
[-OfflineAddressBook 'OABId']
[-PublicFolderDatabase 'DatabaseId']
[-TemplateInstance 'Instance']
```

- **Remove-MailboxDatabase**   Removes the specified mailbox database.

```
Remove-MailboxDatabase -Identity 'MailboxDatabase'
[-DomainController 'DCName']
```

- **Set-MailboxDatabase**   Sets the specified properties of the specified mailbox database.

```
Set-MailboxDatabase [-Identity 'MailboxDatabase']
[-AllowFileRestore <$false|$true>]
[-DeletedItemRetention 'TimeSpan']
[-DomainController 'DCName']
[-EventHistoryRetentionPeriod 'TimeSpan']
[-IndexEnabled <$false|$true>] [-IssueWarningQuota 'Size']
[-JournalRecipient 'RecipientId'] [-MailboxRetention 'TimeSpan']
[-MaintenanceSchedule 'Schedule']
[-MountAtStartup <$false|$true>]
[-Name 'Name'] [-OfflineAddressBook 'OABId']
[-ProhibitSendQuota 'Size']
[-ProhibitSendReceiveQuota 'Size']
[-PublicFolderDatabase 'DatabaseId']
[-QuotaNotificationSchedule 'Schedule']
[-RetainDeletedItemsUntilBackup <$false|$true>]
```

- **Get-MailboxDatabase**   Retrieves a list of all or specified mailbox databases.

```
Get-MailboxDatabase [-Identity 'MailboxDatabase' |
-StorageGroup 'StorageGroup | -Server 'Server']
```

```
[-DomainController 'DCName' ]
[-IncludePreExchange2007 <$false|$true>]
[-Status <$false|$true>]
```

- **Clean-MailboxDatabase**   Scans Active Directory for disconnected mailboxes that are in the specified database and are not yet marked as disconnected.

```
Clean-MailboxDatabase -Identity 'MailboxDatabase'
[-DomainController 'DCName']
```

- **New-PublicFolderDatabase**   Creates a new Public Folder database in the specified storage group.

```
New-PublicFolderDatabase -Name 'PublicFolderDatabase'
-StorageGroup 'StorageGroup' [-CopyEdbFilePath 'EdbFilePath']
[-DomainController 'DCName'] [-EdbFilePath 'EdbFilePath']
[-HasLocalCopy <$false|$true>]
[-TemplateInstance 'Instance']
```

- **Remove-PublicFolderDatabase**   Removes the specified Public Folder database.

```
Remove-PublicFolderDatabase -Identity 'PublicFolderDatabase'
[-DomainController 'DCName'] [-RemoveLastAllowed <$false|$true>]
```

- **Set-PublicFolderDatabase**   Sets the specified properties of the specified Public Folder database.

```
Set-PublicFolderDatabase [-Identity 'PublicFolderDatabase']
[-AllowFileRestore <$false|$true>]
[-DeletedItemRetention 'TimeSpan']
[-DomainController 'DCName']
[-EventHistoryRetentionPeriod 'TimeSpan']
[-IssueWarningQuota 'Size'] [-ItemRetentionPeriod 'TimeSpan']
[-MaintenanceSchedule 'Schedule'] [-MaxItemSize 'Size']
[-MountAtStartup <$false|$true>] [-Name 'Name']
[-ProhibitPostQuota 'Size']
[-QuotaNotificationSchedule 'Schedule']
[-ReplicationMessageSize 'Size']
[-ReplicationSchedule 'Schedule']
[-RetainDeletedItemsUntilBackup <$false|$true>]
```

- **Get-PublicFolderDatabase**   Retrieves a list of all or specified Public Folder databases.

```
Get-PublicFolderDatabase [-Identity 'PublicFolderDatabase' |
-StorageGroup 'StorageGroup' | -Server 'Server']
[-DomainController 'DCName' ]
[-IncludePreExchange2007 <$false|$true>]
[-Status <$false|$true>]
```

- **Mount-Database**   Mounts the specified database.

```
Mount-Database -Identity 'MailboxDatabase'
[-DomainController 'DCName']
[-AcceptDataLoss <$false|$true>] [-Force <$false|$true>]
```

- **Dismount-Database**   Dismounts the specified database.

```
Dismount-Database -Identity 'MailboxDatabase'
[-DomainController 'DCName']
```

- **Enable-DatabaseCopy**   Enables local continuous backup for the specified database.

```
Enable-DatabaseCopy -Identity 'MailboxDatabase'
[-CopyEdbFilePath 'EdbFilePath'] [-DomainController 'DCName']
```

- **Move-DatabasePath**   Sets a new path for the specified database and moves the related files to that location.

```
Move-DatabasePath -Identity 'Database'
[-ConfigurationOnly <$false|$true>]
[-CopyEdbFilePath 'EdbFilePath']
[-EdbFilePath 'EdbFilePath'] [-DomainController 'DCName']
[-Force <$false|$true>]
```

Using Storage Group Management Cmdlets

You can manage Exchange storage groups using the following cmdlets and command-line syntaxes:

- **New-StorageGroup**   Creates the named storage group on the specified server.

```
New-StorageGroup -Name 'StorageGroupName' [-Server 'Server']
[-CircularLoggingEnabled <$false|$true>]
[-CopyLogFolderPath 'LocalPath']
[-CopySystemFolderPath 'LocalPath'] [-DomainController 'DCName']
[-HasLocalCopy <$false|$true>] [-LogFolderPath 'LocalPath']
[-ReplayLagTime 'Time'] [-StandbyMachine 'Server']
[-SystemFolderPath 'LocalPath'] [-TruncationLagTime 'Time']
[-ZeroDatabasePages <$false|$true>]
```

- **Get-StorageGroup**   Retrieves a list of all or specified storage groups.

```
Get-StorageGroup [-Identity 'StorageGroup']
[-DomainController 'DCName']
[-IncludePreExchange2007 <$false|$true>]
[-Status <$false|$true>]
```

- **Set-StorageGroup**   Changes the name of the specified storage group to the name value provided.

```
Set-StorageGroup -Identity 'StorageGroup'
[-CircularLoggingEnabled <$false|$true>]
[-DomainController 'DCName']
[-Name 'Name'] [-ZeroDatabasePages <$false|$true>]
```

- **Remove-StorageGroup**   Deletes the specified storage group.

```
Remove-StorageGroup -Identity 'StorageGroup'
[-DomainController 'DCName']
```

- **Move-StorageGroupPath**   Sets a new path for the specified storage group and moves the related files to that location. This requires dismounting and then remounting all databases in the storage group.

```
Move-StorageGroupPath -Identity 'StorageGroup'
[-ConfigurationOnly <$false|$true>]
[-CopyLogFolderPath 'OrigLogFolderPath']
[-CopySystemFolderPath 'OrigSystemFolderPath']
[-DomainController 'DCName']
[-Force <$false|$true>] [-LogFolderPath 'NewLogFolderPath']
[-SystemFolderPath 'NewSystemFolderPath']
```

- **Enable-StorageGroupCopy**   Enables local continuous backup for the specified storage group, provided that all databases within the storage group already have this feature enabled.

```
Enable-StorageGroupCopy -Identity 'StorageGroup'
[-CopyLogFolderPath 'LocalPath']
[-CopySystemFolderPath 'LocalPath']
[-DomainController 'DCName'] [-ReplayLagTime 'Time']
[-SeedingPostponed <$false|$true>] [-StandbyMachine 'Server']
[-TruncationLagTime 'Time']
```

- **Disable-StorageGroupCopy**   Disables the continuous backup of the specified storage group.

```
Disable-StorageGroupCopy -Identity 'StorageGroup'
[-DomainController 'DCName'] [-StandbyMachine 'Server']
```

- **Get-StorageGroupCopyStatus**   Gets the current status of the continuous backup feature for the specified storage group.

```
Get-StorageGroupCopyStatus -Identity 'StorageGroup'
[-DomainController 'DCName']
[-DumpsterStatistics <$false|$true>]
[-StandbyMachine 'Server']
```

- **Restore-StorageGroupCopy**   Restores a continuous backup of the specified storage group during recovery operations.

```
Restore-StorageGroupCopy -Identity 'StorageGroup'
[-DomainController 'DCName'] [-Force <$false|$true>]
[-ReplaceLocations <$false|$true>] [-StandbyMachine 'Server']
```

■ **Update-StorageGroupCopy**   Initiates or resynchronizes continuous backup of the specified storage group.

```
Update-StorageGroupCopy -Identity 'StorageGroup'
[-DataHostNames 'ServerNames']
[-DeleteExistingFiles <$false|$true>]
[-DomainController 'DCName'] [-Force <$false|$true>]
[-ManualResume <$false|$true>] [-StandbyMachine 'Server']
[-TargetPath 'DatabaseFilePath']
```

■ **Suspend-StorageGroupCopy**   Halts continuous backup of the specified storage group.

```
Suspend-StorageGroupCopy -Identity 'StorageGroup'
[-DomainController 'DCName']
[-ExecutionTime 'MaxTimeToWaitForResponse']
[-StandbyMachine 'Server'] [-SuspendComment 'Comment']
```

■ **Resume-StorageGroupCopy**   Resumes continuous backup of the specified storage group after backup has been suspended.

```
Resume-StorageGroupCopy -Identity 'StorageGroup'
[-DomainController 'DCName'] [-StandbyMachine 'Server']
```

Chapter 7
User and Contact Administration

One of your primary tasks as a Microsoft Exchange administrator is to manage user accounts and contacts. User accounts enable individual users to log on to the network and access network resources. In Active Directory, users are represented by User and InetOrgPerson objects. User objects represent standard user accounts; InetOrgPerson objects represent user accounts imported from non-Microsoft Lightweight Directory Access Protocol (LDAP) or X.500 directory services. User and InetOrgPerson are the only Active Directory objects that can have Exchange mailboxes associated with them. Contacts, on the other hand, are people that you or others in your organization want to get in touch with. Contacts can have street addresses, phone numbers, fax numbers, and e-mail addresses associated with them. Unlike user accounts, contacts don't have network logon privileges.

Understanding Users and Contacts

In Active Directory, users are represented as objects that can be mailbox-enabled or mail-enabled. A *mailbox-enabled* user account has an Exchange mailbox associated with it. Mailboxes are private storage areas for sending and receiving mail. A user's display name is the name Exchange presents in the global address list and in the From text box of e-mail messages.

Another important identifier for mailbox-enabled user accounts is the Exchange alias. The alias is the name that Exchange associates with the account for mail addressing. When your mail client is configured to use Exchange Server, you can type the alias or display name in the To, Cc, or Bcc text boxes of an e-mail message and have Exchange Server resolve the alias or name to the actual e-mail address.

Although most Microsoft Windows user accounts are mailbox-enabled, user accounts don't have to have mailboxes associated with them. You can create user accounts without assigning a mailbox. You can also create user accounts that are *mail-enabled* rather than mailbox-enabled, which means that the account has an off-site e-mail address associated with it but doesn't have an actual mailbox. Mail-enabled users have Exchange aliases and display names that Exchange Server can resolve to actual e-mail addresses. Internal users can send mail to the mail-enabled user account using the Exchange display name or alias, and the mail will be directed to the external address. Users outside the organization, however, can't use the Exchange alias to send mail to the user.

It's not always easy to decide when to create a mailbox for a user. To help you out, consider the following scenario:

1. You've been notified that two new users, Elizabeth and Joe, will need access to the domain.

2. Elizabeth is a full-time employee who starts on Tuesday. She'll work on-site and needs to be able to send and receive mail. People in the company need to be able to send mail directly to her.

3. Joe, on the other hand, is a consultant who is coming in to help out temporarily. His agency maintains his mailbox, and he doesn't want to have to check mail in two places. However, people in the company need to be able to contact him, and he wants to ensure that his external address is available.

4. You create a mailbox-enabled user account for Elizabeth. Afterward, you create a mail-enabled user account for Joe, ensuring that his Exchange information refers to his external e-mail address.

Mail-enabled users are one of several types of custom recipients that you can create in Exchange Server. Another type of custom recipient is a *mail-enabled contact*. You mail-enable a contact by specifying the external e-mail address that users can use to send e-mail to that contact.

Understanding the Basics of E-mail Routing

Exchange uses e-mail addresses to route messages to mail servers inside and outside the organization. When routing messages internally, Hub Transport servers use mail connectors to route messages to other Exchange servers, as well as to other types of mail servers that your company might use. Two standard types of connectors are used:

- Send connectors
- Receive connectors

Send and Receive connectors use Simple Mail Transfer Protocol (SMTP) as the default transport and provide a direct connection among Hub Transport servers in an organization. Hub Transport and Edge Transport servers can also receive mail from and send mail to other types of mail servers.

You can use these connectors to connect Hub Transport servers in an organization. When routing messages outside the company, Hub Transport and Edge Transport servers use mail gateways to transfer messages. The default gateway is SMTP.

Exchange Server 2007 uses directory-based recipient resolution for all messages that are sent from and received by users throughout the organization. The Exchange component responsible for recipient resolution is the Categorizer. The Categorizer must be able to associate every recipient in every message with a corresponding recipient object in Active Directory.

All senders and recipients must have a primary SMTP address. If the Categorizer discovers a recipient that does not have a primary SMTP address, it will either determine what the primary SMTP address should be or replace the non-SMTP address. Replacing a non-SMTP address involves encapsulating the address in a primary SMTP address that will be used while transporting the message.

Note Non-SMTP e-mail address formats include fax, X.400, and messages originating from Lotus Notes. The Categorizer encapsulates e-mail addresses using non-SMTP formats in the Internet Mail Connector Encapsulated Addressing (IMCEA) format. For example, the Categorizer encapsulates the fax address, FAX:888-555-1212 as IMCEA-FAX-888-555-1212@*yourdomain*.com. Any e-mail address that is longer than what SMTP allows is transmitted as extended properties in the XExch50 field.

In addition to primary SMTP e-mail addresses, you can configure alternative recipients and forwarding addresses for users and public folders. If there is an alternative recipient or forwarding address, redirection is required during categorization. You specify the addresses to which messages will be redirected in Active Directory, and redirection history is maintained with each message.

Managing User Accounts and Mail Features

With Exchange Server 2007, the Exchange Management Console and the Exchange Management Shell are the only administration tools you need to manage mailboxes, distribution groups, and mail contacts. You can use these tools to create and manage mail-enabled user accounts, mailbox-enabled user accounts, and mail-enabled contacts. The sections that follow examine techniques that you can employ to manage user accounts and the Exchange features of those accounts.

Note Domain administrators can create user accounts and contacts using Active Directory Users And Computers. If any existing user accounts need to be mail-enabled or mailbox-enabled, you perform these tasks using the Exchange management tools. If existing contacts need to be mail-enabled, you also perform this task using the Exchange management tools.

Finding Existing Mailboxes, Contacts, and Groups

In the Exchange Management Console, you can view current mailboxes, mail-enabled users, contacts, and groups by following these steps:

1. Start Exchange Management Console by clicking Start, pointing to All Programs, selecting Microsoft Exchange Server 2007, and clicking Exchange Management Console.

2. As shown in Figure 7-1, expand the Recipient Configuration node by double-clicking it.

3. Select the related Mailbox, Distribution Group, or Mail Contact node, as appropriate for the type of recipient with which you want to work.

4. By default, the Exchange Management Console displays only the recipients in the current domain or organizational unit. To view recipients in other domains or organizational units, right-click the Recipient Configuration node, and then select Modify Recipient Scope. Use the options provided to configure the scope to use, and then click OK.

5. By default, the maximum number of Exchange recipients you can view at any time is limited to 1,000. You can change the maximum number of recipients to display by right-clicking the Recipient Configuration node or the subnode you want to work with and then selecting Modify The Maximum Number Of Recipients To Display. Type the number of recipients to display, and then click OK.

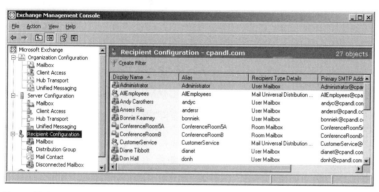

Figure 7-1   Access the Recipient Configuration node to work with mailboxes, distribution groups, and mail contacts.

Creating Mailbox-Enabled and Mail-Enabled User Accounts

You need to create a user account for each user who wants to use network resources. The following sections explain how to create domain user accounts that are either mailbox-enabled or mail-enabled, and how to add a mailbox to an existing user account. If a user needs to send and receive e-mail, you'll need to create a new mailbox-enabled account for the user or add a mailbox to the user's existing account. Otherwise, you can create a mail-enabled account.

Understanding Logon Names and Passwords

Before you create a domain user account, you should think for a moment about the new account's logon name and password. You identify all domain user accounts with a logon name. This logon name can be (but doesn't have to be) the same as the user's e-mail address. In Windows domains, logon names have two parts:

- **User name**   The account's text label
- **User domain**   The domain where the user account exists

For the user williams whose account is created in adatum.com, the full logon name for Windows is williams@adatum.com.

User accounts can also have passwords and public certificates associated with them. *Passwords* are authentication strings for an account. *Public certificates* combine a public and private key to identify a user. You log on with a password interactively. You log on with a public certificate using a smart card and a smart card reader.

Although Windows displays user names to describe privileges and permissions, the key identifiers for accounts are security identifiers (SIDs). SIDs are unique identifiers that Windows generates when you create accounts. SIDs consist of the domain's security ID prefix and a unique relative ID. Windows uses these identifiers to track accounts independently from user names. SIDs serve many purposes; the two most important are to allow you to easily change user names and to allow you to delete accounts without worrying that someone could gain access to resources simply by re-creating an account with the same user name.

When you change a user name, you tell Windows to map a particular SID to a new name. When you delete an account, you tell Windows that a particular SID is no longer valid. Afterward, even if you create an account with the same user name, the new account won't have the same privileges and permissions as the previous one because the new account will have a new SID.

Creating New Mail-Enabled User Accounts

Mail-enabled users are defined as custom recipients in Exchange Server. They have an Exchange alias and an external e-mail address, but do not have an Exchange mailbox. All e-mail messages sent to a mail-enabled user are forwarded to the remote e-mail address associated with the account.

In the Exchange Management Console, mail-enabled users are listed as such in the Recipient Configuration node and in the Mail Contact node. You can manage mail-enabled users through the Exchange Management Console and the Exchange Management Shell.

In the Exchange Management Console, you can create a new mail-enabled user by completing the following steps:

1. In Exchange Management Console, expand and then select the Recipient Configuration node.

Note If you want to create the user account in a domain other than the current one, you'll first need to set the scope for the Recipient Configuration node, as discussed previously in "Finding Existing Mailboxes, Contacts, and Groups."

2. Right-click the Recipient Configuration node, and then select New Mail User. This starts the New Mail User Wizard.

3. Click Next to accept the default selections on the Introduction page (to create a mail user).

4. On the User Information page, shown in Figure 7-2, the Organizational Unit text box shows where in Active Directory the user account will be created. By default, this is the Users container in the current domain. Because you'll usually need to create new user accounts in a specific organizational unit rather than in the Users container, click Browse. In the Select Organizational Unit dialog box, choose the location in which to store the account, and then click OK.

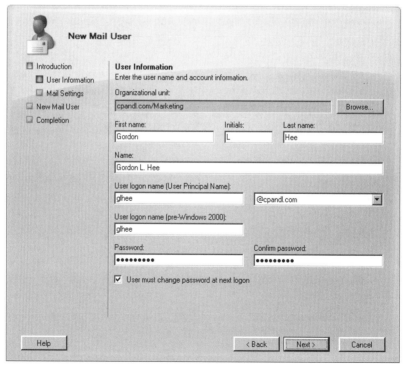

Figure 7-2 Configure the mail-enabled user's settings.

5. Type the user's first name, middle initial, and last name in the text boxes provided. These values are used to create the Name entry, which is the user's display name.

6. As necessary, make changes to the Name text box. For example, you might want to type the name in LastName FirstName MiddleInitial format or in FirstName MiddleInitial LastName format. The full name must be no more than 64 characters.

7. In the User Logon Name text box, type the user's logon name. Use the drop-down list to select the domain with which you want to associate the account. This sets the fully qualified logon name.

8. The first 20 characters of the logon name are used to set the pre-Windows 2000 logon name, which must be unique in the domain. If necessary, change the pre-Windows 2000 logon name.

9. Type and then confirm the password for the account. This password must follow the conventions of your organization's password policy. Typically, this means that the password must be at least six characters in length and must use three of the four available character types: lowercase letters, uppercase letters, numbers, and symbols.

10. If you want to ensure that the user changes the password at next logon, select the User Must Change Password At Next Logon check box. Click Next.

    As shown in Figure 7-3, the Exchange alias is set to the user's logon name by default. You can change this value by entering a new alias. The Exchange Management Console uses the alias to set the user's e-mail address.

    > **Note** Technically, the default value for the Exchange alias is set to the pre-Windows 2000 logon name, which is normally the same as the user logon name. However, if you change the pre-Windows 2000 logon name, the default Exchange alias will be set to the value you enter.

11. To the right of the External E-mail Address text box is an Edit button. Click the down arrow next to the Edit button to display two options:

    ❑ **SMTP Address** Select SMTP Address to associate a standard SMTP e-mail address with the user. Enter the e-mail address, and then click OK.

    ❑ **Custom Address** Click Custom Address to associate a custom e-mail address with the user. Enter the e-mail address, and then enter the e-mail address type. Click OK.

12. Click Next, and then click New. Exchange Management Console creates the new user and mail-enables it. If an error occurs, the user will not be created. You will need to correct the problem and repeat this procedure. Click Finish.

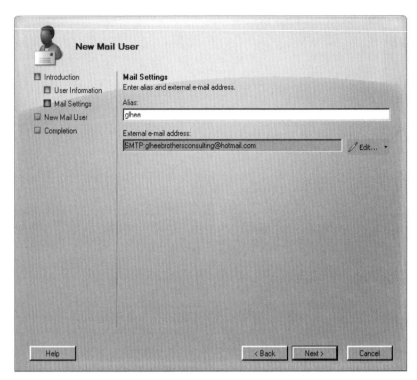

Figure 7-3   Configure the user's mail settings.

You can list all mail-enabled users by typing **get-mailuser** at the Exchange Management Shell prompt. Sample 7-1 provides the full syntax and usage for get-mailuser.

Sample 7-1   Get-MailUser cmdlet syntax and usage

```
Syntax
Get-MailUser [-Identity 'Identifier'] [-DomainController 'DCName']
[-OrganizationalUnit 'OUName'] [-ResultSize 'Size'] [-SortBy 'Value']
```

```
Usage

Get-MailUser -Identity 'bperry' | fl

Get-MailUser -OrganizationalUnit 'marketing'  | fl
```

You can create a new mail-enabled user account using the New-MailUser cmdlet. Sample 7-2 shows the syntax and usage. When prompted, provide a secure password for the user account.

Note   The syntax and usage are entered on multiple lines for ease of reference. You must enter the command-line values for a cmdlet on a single line.

Sample 7-2   New-MailUser cmdlet syntax and usage

Syntax
```
New-MailUser -Name 'DisplayName' -ExternalEmailAddress 'EmailAddress'
-Password 'Password' -UserPrincipalName 'logonName@domain'
[-Alias 'ExchangeAlias'] [-DisplayName 'Name']
[-DomainController 'DCName']
[-FirstName 'Name'] [-Initials 'Value'] [-LastName 'Name']
[-MacAttachmentFormat 'Format'] [-MessageBodyFormat 'Format']
[-OrganizationalUnit 'OrganizationalUnit']
[-PrimarySmtpAddress 'SmtpAddress']
[-ResetPasswordOnNextLogon <$false|$true>]
[-TemplateInstance 'Instance'] [-SamAccountName 'Name']
[-UsePreferMessageFormat <$false|$true>]
```

Usage
```
New-MailUser -Name 'Frank Miller' -Alias 'frankm'
-OrganizationalUnit 'cpandl.com/Technology'
-UserPrincipalName 'frankm@cpandl.com'
-SamAccountName 'frankm'
-FirstName 'Frank' -Initials '' -LastName 'Miller'
-ResetPasswordOnNextLogon $false
-ExternalEmailAddress 'SMTP:frankm@hotmail.com'
```

Mail-Enabling Existing User Accounts

When a user already has an account in Active Directory, you can mail-enable the account using the Exchange Management Console and the Exchange Management Shell. In the Exchange Management Console, you can mail-enable an existing user account by completing the following steps:

1. In Exchange Management Console, expand and then select the Recipient Configuration node.

    Note   If you want to create the user account in a domain other than the current one, you'll first need to set the scope for the Recipient Configuration node, as discussed previously in "Finding Existing Mailboxes, Contacts, and Groups."

2. Right-click the Recipient Configuration node, and then select New Mail User. This starts the New Mail User Wizard.

3. On the Introduction page, select Existing User, and then click Browse. This displays the Select User dialog box.

4. In the Select User dialog box, select the user account you want to mail-enable, and then click OK. User accounts for the current domain are listed by name and organizational unit.

    Note   Accounts listed don't yet have an Exchange mailbox or e-mail association. You'll need to change the scope, as discussed previously, if you don't see the user you want to use.

5. Click Next. On the Mail Settings page, the Exchange alias is set to the user's logon name by default. You can change this value by entering a new alias. The Exchange Management Console uses the alias to set the user's e-mail address.

6. To the right of the External E-mail Address text box is an Edit button. Click the down arrow next to the Edit button to display two options:

    ❑ **SMTP Address**   Select SMTP Address to associate a standard SMTP e-mail address with the user. Enter the e-mail address, and then click OK.

    ❑ **Custom Address**   Click Custom Address to associate a custom e-mail address with the user. Enter the e-mail address, and then enter the e-mail address type. Click OK.

7. Click Next, and then click New. Exchange Management Console mail-enables the user account you previously selected. If an error occurs, the user account will not be mail-enabled. You will need to correct the problem and repeat this procedure. Click Finish.

You can mail-enable an existing user account using the Enable-MailUser cmdlet. Sample 7-3 shows the syntax and usage. For the identity parameter, you can use the user's display name, logon name, or user principal name.

Sample 7-3   Enable-MailUser cmdlet syntax and usage

```
Syntax
Enable-MailUser -Identity 'Identity'
-ExternalEmailAddress 'EmailAddress'
[-Alias 'ExchangeAlias'] [-DisplayName 'Name']
[-DomainController 'DCName']
[-MacAttachmentFormat 'Format'] [-MessageBodyFormat 'Format']
[-MessageFormat 'Format'] [-PrimarySmtpAddress 'SmtpAddress']
```

Usage

```
Enable-MailUser -Identity 'cpandl.com/Marketing/Frank Miller'
-Alias 'frankm' -ExternalEmailAddress 'SMTP:frankm@hotmail.com'
```

Managing Mail-Enabled User Accounts

You can manage mail-enabled users in several ways. If a user account should no longer be mail-enabled, you can disable mail forwarding. To disable mail forwarding in the Exchange Management Console, right-click the Mail User and then select Disable. When prompted to confirm, click Yes. At the Exchange Management Shell prompt, you can disable mail forwarding using the Disable-MailUser cmdlet, as shown in Sample 7-4.

Sample 7-4   Disable-MailUser cmdlet syntax and usage

Syntax
```
Disable-MailUser -Identity 'Identity' [-DomainController 'DCName']
```

Usage

```
Disable-MailUser -Identity 'Frank Miller'
```

If you no longer need a mail-enabled user account, you can permanently remove it from Active Directory. To remove a mail-enabled user account in the Exchange Management Console, right-click the Mail User and then select Remove. When prompted to confirm, click Yes. At the Exchange Mananagement Shell prompt, you can remove a mail-enabled user account by using the Remove-MailUser cmdlet, as shown in Sample 7-5.

Sample 7-5   Remove-MailUser cmdlet syntax and usage

Syntax
```
Remove-MailUser -Identity 'Identity'
```

Usage

```
Remove-MailUser -Identity 'Frank Miller'
```

Creating New Domain User Accounts with Mailboxes

In the Exchange Management Console, you can create a new user account with a mailbox by completing the following steps:

1. In Exchange Management Console, expand and then select the Recipient Configuration node.

   Note If you want to create the user account in a domain other than the current one, you'll first need to set the scope for the Recipient Configuration node, as discussed previously in "Finding Existing Mailboxes, Contacts, and Groups."

2. Right-click the Recipient Configuration node, and then select New Mailbox. This starts the New Mailbox Wizard.

3. Click Next twice to accept the default selections on the Introduction page (to create a user mailbox) and the User Type page (to create a new user account with a mailbox).

4. On the Mailbox Information page, shown in Figure 7-4, the Organizational Unit text box shows where in Active Directory the user account will be created. By default, this is the Users container in the current domain. Because you'll usually need to create new user accounts in a specific organizational unit rather than the Users container, click Browse. Use the Select Organizational Unit dialog box to choose the location in which to store the account, and then click OK.

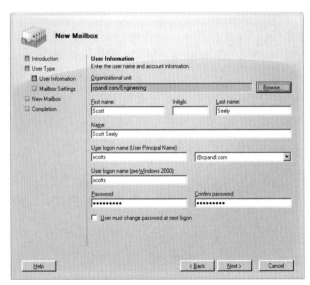

Figure 7-4   Configure the user's domain settings.

5. Type the user's first name, middle initial, and last name in the text boxes provided. These values are used to create the Name entry, which is the user's display name.

6. As necessary, make changes to the Name text box. For example, you might want to type the name in LastName FirstName MiddleInitial format or in FirstName MiddleInitial LastName format. The full name must be no more than 64 characters.

7. In the User Logon Name text box, type the user's logon name. Use the drop-down list to select the domain with which you want to associate the account. This sets the fully qualified logon name.

8. The first 20 characters of the logon name are used to set the pre-Windows 2000 logon name, which must be unique in the domain. If necessary, change the pre-Windows 2000 logon name.

9. Type and then confirm the password for the account. This password must follow the conventions of your organization's password policy. Typically, this means that the password must be at least six characters in length and must use three of the four available character types: lowercase letters, uppercase letters, numbers, and symbols.

10. If you want to ensure that the user changes the password at next logon, select the User Must Change Password At Next Logon check box. Click Next.

11. As shown in Figure 7-5, the Exchange alias is set to the user's logon name by default. You can change this value by entering a new alias. The Exchange Management Console uses the alias to set the user's e-mail address.

> **Note**   Technically, the default value for the Exchange alias is set to the pre-Windows 2000 logon name, which is normally the same as the user logon name. However, if you change the pre-Windows 2000 logon name, the default Exchange alias will be set to the value you enter.

12. Click the Browse button to the right of the Mailbox Database text box. In the Select Mailbox Database dialog box, choose the mailbox database in which the mailbox should be stored. Mailbox databases are listed by name as well as by associated storage group and server.

13. Click Next, and then click New to create the account and the related mailbox. If an error occurs during account or mailbox creation, the Exchange Management Console will create neither the account nor the related mailbox. You will need to correct the problem and repeat this procedure.

14. Click Finish. For all mailbox-enabled accounts, an SMTP e-mail address is configured automatically. You can also add additional addresses of the same type. For example, if Brian Johnson is the company's human resources administrator, he might have the primary SMTP addresses of brianj@adatum.com and an alternate SMTP address of resumes@adatum.com.

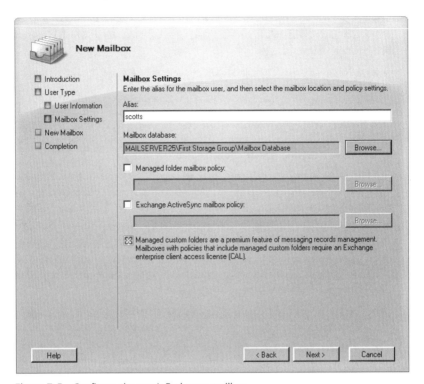

Figure 7-5 Configure the user's Exchange mailbox.

15. Creating the user account and mailbox isn't the final step. Next, you might want to do the following:

- ❑ Add detailed contact information for the user, such as business phone number and title.

- ❑ Add the user to security and distribution groups.

- ❑ Associate additional e-mail addresses with the account.

- ❑ Enable or disable Exchange features for the account.

- ❑ Modify the user's default delivery options, storage limits, and restrictions on the account.

In the Exchange Management Shell, you can create a user account with a mailbox using the New-Mailbox cmdlet. Sample 7-6 provides the syntax and usage. When prompted, enter a secure password for the new user account.

Sample 7-6   New-Mailbox cmdlet syntax and usage

```
Syntax
New-Mailbox -Name 'Name' -Database 'Server\MailboxDatabase'
[-ActiveSyncMailboxPolicy 'PolicyId'] [-Alias 'Alias']
[-DisplayName 'Name'] [-DomainController 'DCName']
[-FirstName 'Name'] [-Initials 'Value'] [-LastName 'Name']
[-ManagedFolderMailboxPolicy 'PolicyId']
[-ManagedFolderMailboxPolicyAllowed <$false|$true>]
[-OrganizationalUnit 'OUName']
[-ResetPasswordOnNextLogon <$false|$true>]
[-Password 'Password']
[-SamAccountName 'SamAccountName']
[-TemplateInstance 'Instance']
```

```
Usage

New-Mailbox -Name 'Shane S. Kim' -Alias 'shanek'
 -OrganizationalUnit 'cpandl.com/Engineering'
 -Database 'Corpsvr127\First Storage Group\Engineering'
 -UserPrincipalName 'shanek@cpandl.com' -SamAccountName 'shanek'
 -FirstName 'Shane' -Initials 'S' -LastName 'Kim'
 -ResetPasswordOnNextLogon $true
```

Adding Mailboxes to Existing Domain User Accounts

You don't have to create an Exchange mailbox when you create a user account. You can create a mailbox for a user account any time you determine the mailbox is needed. Using the Exchange Management Console, you can create mailboxes for multiple user accounts at the same time by using bulk creation mode, or you can create a single mailbox for a specific user by completing the following steps:

1. In Exchange Management Console, expand and then select the Recipient Configuration node.

   Note   If you want to create the user account in a domain other than the current one, you'll first need to set the scope for the Recipient Configuration node, as discussed previously in "Finding Existing Mailboxes, Contacts, and Groups."

2. Right-click the Recipient Configuration node, and then select New Mailbox. This starts the New Mailbox Wizard. Click Next on the New Mailbox page to accept the default action to create a user mailbox.

3. On the User Type page, select Existing Users, and then click Add. This displays the Select User dialog box. In the Select User dialog box, shown in Figure 7-6, select the user account or accounts you want to mailbox-enable, and then click OK. User accounts that are not yet mail-enabled or mailbox-enabled for the current domain are listed by name and organizational unit.

> **Note**   You can select multiple accounts individually by holding down the Ctrl key and then clicking the left mouse button on each object you want to select. You can select a series of accounts at once by holding down the Shift key, selecting the first object, and then clicking the last object.

4. Click Next. On the Mailbox Settings page, the Exchange alias is set to the logon name by default. When you are creating mailboxes for multiple accounts, you cannot change the default value. When you are creating a single mailbox for a specific user, you can change this value by entering a new alias. The Exchange alias is used to set the user's e-mail address.

5. Click the Browse button to the right of the Mailbox Database text box. In the Select Mailbox Database dialog box, choose the mailbox database in which the mailbox should be stored. Mailbox databases are listed by name as well as by associated storage group and server.

Figure 7-6   Find the user account you want to mailbox-enable.

6. Click Next, and then click New to create the mailbox or mailboxes for the selected user accounts. If an error occurs during mailbox creation, the mailbox or mailboxes are not created. You will need to correct the problem and repeat this procedure.

7. Click Finish.

In the Exchange Management Shell, you can add a mailbox to individual user accounts using the Enable-Mailbox cmdlet. Sample 7-7 provides the syntax and usage.

If you want to create mailboxes for multiple accounts, you'll need to enter a separate command for each account.

Sample 7-7   Enable-Mailbox cmdlet syntax and usage

```
Syntax
Enable-Mailbox -Identity 'Domain\UserName' -Database 'MailboxDatabase'
[-ActiveSyncMailboxPolicy 'PolicyId'] [-Alias 'Alias']
[-DisplayName 'Name'] [-DomainController 'DCName']
[-ManagedFolderMailboxPolicy 'PolicyId']
[-ManagedFolderMailboxPolicyAllowed <$false|$true>]
[-PrimarySmtpAddress 'SmtpAddress']
```

```
Usage

Enable-Mailbox -Identity 'cpandl.com/Engineering.com/Frank Lee'
-Database 'Corpsvr127\First Storage Group\Engineering'
-Alias 'frankl'
```

Setting or Changing the Display Name and Logon Name for User Accounts

All user accounts have a display name, a logon name, and a pre-Windows 2000 logon name. These names can be different from the mailbox name and mailbox alias used by Exchange Server.

You can set contact information for a user account by completing the following steps:

1. In Exchange Management Console, expand the Recipient Configuration node and then select the related Mailbox node.

2. Double-click the mailbox entry for the user with which you want to work.

3. On the User Information tab, use the following text boxes to set the user's display name and logon name:

   ❑ **First Name, Initials, Last Name**   Sets the user's full name

   ❑ **Name**   Sets the user's display name as seen in logon sessions and in Active Directory

   > **Note**   The Simple Display Name field sets the display name used by systems that cannot interpret all the characters in the regular display name. Because the Simple Display Name field only accepts ASCII characters, this ensures that the name is displayed correctly in all versions of the Exchange management interfaces.

4. Click OK to save your changes.

Setting or Changing Contact Information for User Accounts

You can set contact information for a user account by completing the following steps:

1. In Exchange Management Console, expand the Recipient Configuration node and then select the related Mailbox node.

2. Double-click the mailbox entry for the user with which you want to work.

3. On the User Information tab, use the Web Page text box to set the URL of the user's home page, which can be on the Internet or the company intranet.

4. Click the Address And Phone tab. Use the text boxes provided to set the user's business address or home address. Normally, you'll want to enter the user's business address. This way, you can track the business locations and mailing addresses of users at various offices.

5. Use the Phone Numbers text boxes to set the user's primary business telephone, pager, fax, home telephone, and mobile telephone numbers.

   Note   You need to consider privacy issues before entering private information, such as home addresses and home phone numbers, for users. Discuss the matter with your human resources and legal departments. You might also want to get user consent before releasing home addresses.

6. Click the Organization tab. As appropriate, type the user's title, company, department, and office.

7. To specify the user's manager, select the Manager check box, and then click Browse. In the Select Recipient User Or Contact dialog box, select the user's manager and then click OK. When you specify a manager, the user shows up as a direct report in the manager's account. Click Apply or OK to apply the changes.

Changing a User's Exchange Server Alias and Display Name

Each mailbox has an Exchange alias and display name associated with it. The Exchange alias is used with address lists as an alternative way of specifying the user in the To, Cc, or Bcc text boxes of an e-mail message. The alias also sets the primary SMTP address associated with the account.

   Tip   Whenever you change the Exchange alias, a new e-mail address can be generated and set as the default address for SMTP. The previous e-mail addresses for the account aren't deleted. Instead, these remain as alternatives to the defaults. To learn how to change or delete these additional e-mail addresses, see the section of this chapter entitled "Adding, Changing, and Removing E-mail Addresses."

To change the Exchange alias and mailbox name on a user account, complete the following steps:

1. In Exchange Management Console, expand the Recipient Configuration node and then select the related Mailbox node.

2. Double-click the mailbox entry for the user with which you want to work.

3. On the General tab, the first text box sets the mailbox name. Change this text box if you'd like the mailbox to have a different display name.

4. The Alias text box sets the Exchange alias. If you'd like to assign a new alias, enter the new Exchange alias in this text box. Click OK.

Adding, Changing, and Removing E-Mail Addresses

When you create a mailbox-enabled user account, default e-mail addresses are created. Any time you update the user's Exchange alias, a new default e-mail address can be created. However, the old addresses aren't deleted. They remain as alternative e-mail addresses for the account.

To add, change, or remove an e-mail address, follow these steps:

1. In Exchange Management Console, expand the Recipient Configuration node and then select the related Mailbox node.

2. Double-click the mailbox entry for the user with which you want to work.

3. On the E-mail Addresses tab, shown in Figure 7-7, you can use the following techniques to manage the user's e-mail addresses:

   ❑ **Create a new SMTP address**   Click Add. Enter the SMTP e-mail address, and then click OK.

   ❑ **Create a custom address**   Click the small arrow to the right of the Add button, and then select Custom Address. Enter the e-mail address, and then enter the e-mail address type. Click OK.

   > **Tip**   Use SMTP as the address type for standard Internet e-mail addresses. For custom address types, such as X.400, you must manually enter the address in the proper format.

   ❑ **Edit an existing address**   Double-click the address entry. Modify the settings in the Address dialog box, and then click OK.

   ❑ **Delete an existing address**   Select the address, and then click the Remove button.

   > **Note**   You can't delete the primary SMTP address without first promoting another e-mail address to the primary position. Exchange Server uses the primary SMTP address to send and receive messages.

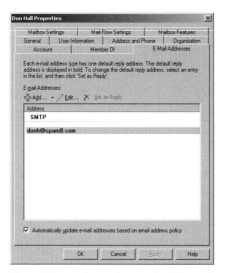

Figure 7-7 Configure the e-mail addresses for the user account.

Setting a Default Reply-To Address for a User Account

Each e-mail address type has one default reply address. This e-mail address sets the value of the Reply To text box. To change the default reply address, follow these steps:

1. In Exchange Management Console, expand the Recipient Configuration node and then select the related Mailbox node.

2. Double-click the mailbox entry for the user with which you want to work.

3. Click the E-mail Addresses tab. Current default e-mail addresses are highlighted with bold text. E-mail addresses that aren't highlighted are used only as alternative addresses for delivering messages to the current mailbox.

4. To change the current default settings, select an e-mail address that isn't highlighted, and then click Set As Reply.

Changing a User's Web, Wireless Service, and Protocol Options

When you create user accounts with mailboxes, global settings determine the Web, wireless services, and protocols that are available. You can change these settings for individual users at any time by completing the following steps:

1. In Exchange Management Console, expand the Recipient Configuration node and then select the related Mailbox node.

2. Double-click the mailbox entry for the user with which you want to work.

3. Click the Mailbox Features tab. As shown in Figure 7-8, configure the following
   Web, wireless services, and protocols for the user:

   ❑ **Outlook Web Access**   Permits the user to access the mailbox with a Web
   browser

   ❑ **Exchange ActiveSync**   Allows the user to synchronize the mailbox and to
   browse wireless devices

   ❑ **Unified Messaging**   Allows the user to access unified messaging features,
   such as the voice browser

   ❑ **MAPI**   Permits the user to access the mailbox with a Messaging Application Programming Interface (MAPI) e-mail client

   ❑ **POP3**   Permits the user to access the mailbox with a Post Office Protocol
   Version 3 (POP3) e-mail client

   ❑ **Internet Message Access Protocol Version 4 (IMAP4)**   Permits the user to
   access the mailbox with a (IMAP4) e-mail client

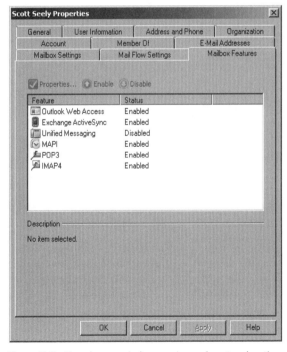

Figure 7-8   You change wireless service and protocol options for users in the
Properties dialog box for each user.

4. Select an option, and then click Enable or Disable, as appropriate, to change the status. If an option has configurable properties and you want to change the properties, select the option, and then click Properties. Click OK.

Requiring User Accounts to Change Passwords

Group Policy settings typically require users to periodically change their passwords. Sometimes, you may have to ensure that a user changes her password the next time she logs on. For example, if you have to reset a user's password and you give him the password over the phone, you may want the user to change the password the next time he logs on.

You can set a user account to require the password to be changed on next logon by completing the following steps:

1. In Exchange Management Console, expand the Recipient Configuration node and then select the related Mailbox node.

2. Double-click the mailbox entry for the user with which you want to work.

3. On the Account tab, select the User Must Change Password At Next Logon check box. Click OK.

You can use the Set-User cmdlet to perform the same task, following the syntax shown in Sample 7-8.

Sample 7-8   Requiring user password change

```
Syntax
Set-User -Identity 'UserIdentity'
-ResetPasswordOnNextLogon <$false|$true>
```

```
Usage

SetUser -Identity 'Frank Lee' -ResetPasswordOnNextLogon $true
```

Deleting Mailboxes from User Accounts

When you disable a mailbox for a user account using the Exchange management tools, you permanently remove all Exchange attributes from the user object in Active Directory and mark the primary mailbox for deletion. Exchange Server then deletes the mailbox according to the retention period you set on the account or on the mailbox database. Because you only removed the user account's Exchange attributes, the user account still exists in Active Directory.

In the Exchange Management Console, you can delete a mailbox from a user account and all related Exchange attributes by right-clicking the mailbox and selecting Disable. When prompted to confirm this action, click Yes.

You can use the Disable-Mailbox cmdlet to delete mailboxes while retaining the user accounts as well. Sample 7-9 shows the syntax and usage.

Sample 7-9   Disable-Mailbox cmdlet syntax and usage

```
Syntax
Disable-Mailbox -Identity 'Identifier' [-DomainController 'DCName']
```

```
Usage

Disable-Mailbox -Identity 'Frank Lee'
```

Deleting User Accounts and Their Mailboxes

When you delete a user account and its mailbox using the Exchange management tools, you permanently remove the account from Active Directory and mark the primary mailbox for deletion. Exchange Server then deletes the mailbox according to the retention period you set on the account or on the mailbox database.

After you delete an account, you can't create an account with the same name and have the account automatically retain the same permissions as the original account. This is because the SID for the new account won't match the SID for the old account. However, that doesn't mean that after you delete an account, you can never again create an account with that same name. For example, a person might leave the company only to return a short while later. You can create an account using the same naming convention as before, but you'll have to redefine the permissions for that account.

Because deleting built-in accounts could have far-reaching effects on the domain, Windows doesn't let you delete built-in user accounts. In the Exchange Management Console, you can remove other types of accounts and the mailboxes associated with those accounts by right-clicking the mailboxes and selecting Remove. When prompted to confirm this action, click Yes.

> **Note**   Because Exchange security is based on domain authentication, you can't have a mailbox without an account. If you still need the mailbox for an account you want to delete, you can disable the account using Active Directory Users And Computers. Disabling the account in Active Directory prevents the user from logging on, but you can still access the mailbox if you need to. To disable an account, right-click the account in Active Directory Users And Computers, and then select Disable Account. If you don't have permissions to use Active Directory Users And Computers, ask a domain administrator to disable the account for you.

You can use the Remove-Mailbox cmdlet to delete user accounts as well. Sample 7-10 shows the syntax. By default, the –Permanent flag is set to $false and mailboxes are retained in a disconnected state according to the mailbox retention policy. If you set the –Permanent flag to $true, the mailbox is removed from Exchange.

Sample 7-10   Remove-Mailbox cmdlet syntax and usage

```
Syntax
Remove-Mailbox -Identity 'UserIdentity' [ -Permanent <$false|$true>]
[-DomainController 'DCName']
```

```
Usage

Remove-Mailbox -Identity 'Frank Lee'

Remove-Mailbox -Identity 'Frank Lee' -Permanent $true
```

Managing Contacts

Contacts represent people with whom you or others in your organization want to get in touch. Contacts can have directory information associated with them, but they don't have network logon privileges.

The only difference between a standard contact and a mail-enabled contact is the presence of e-mail addresses. A mail-enabled contact has one or more e-mail addresses associated with it; a standard contact doesn't. When a contact has an e-mail address, you can list the contact in the global address list or other address lists. This allows users to send messages to the contact.

In the Exchange Management Console, mail-enabled contacts and mail-enabled users are both listed in the Mail Contact node. Mail-enabled contacts are listed with the recipient type Mail Contact, and mail-enabled users are listed with the recipient type Mail User.

Creating Mail-Enabled Contacts

You can create and mail-enable a new contact by completing the following steps:

1. In Exchange Management Console, expand the Recipient Configuration node and then select the related Mail Contact node.

2. Right-click the Mail Contact node, and then select New Contact. This starts the New Mail Contact Wizard.

3. Click Next to accept the default selection on the Introduction page to create a new contact.

4. On the Contact Information page, shown in Figure 7-9, the Organizational Unit text box shows where in Active Directory the contact will be created. By default, this is the Users container in the current domain. Because you'll usually need to create new contacts in a specific organizational unit rather than the Users container, click Browse. Use the Select Organizational Unit dialog box to choose the location in which to store the contact, and then click OK.

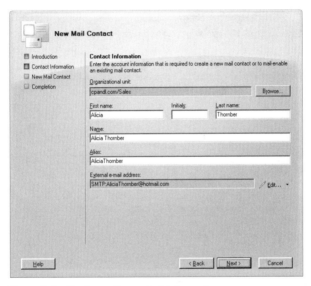

Figure 7-9 Configure the contact information.

5. Type the contact's first name, middle initial, and last name in the text boxes provided. These values are used to automatically create the following entries:

   ❏ **Contact Name** The Contact Name is the name used in Exchange Management Console.

   ❏ **Display Name** The Display Name is displayed in the global address list and other address lists created for the organization. It is also used when addressing e-mail messages to the contact.

   ❏ **Alias** The Alias is the Exchange alias for the contact. Aliases provide an alternate way of addressing users and contacts in To, Cc, and Bcc text boxes of e-mail messages.

6. To the right of the External E-mail Address text box is an Edit button. Click the down arrow next to the Edit button to display two options:

   ❑ **SMTP Address**   Select SMTP Address to associate a standard SMTP e-mail address with the contact. Enter the e-mail address, and then click OK.

   ❑ **Custom Address**   Click Custom Address to associate a custom e-mail address with the contact. Enter the e-mail address, and then enter the e-mail address type. Click OK.

7. Click Next, and then click New. Exchange Management Console creates the new contact and mail-enables it. If an error occurs, the contact will not be created. You will need to correct the problem and repeat this procedure.

8. Click Finish.

In the Exchange Management Shell, you can create a new mail-enabled contact using the New-MailContact cmdlet. Sample 7-11 provides the syntax and usage.

Sample 7-11   New-MailContact cmdlet syntax and usage

```
Syntax
New-MailContact -ExternalEmailAddress 'TYPE:EmailAddress'
[-Alias 'ExchangeAlias'] [-DisplayName 'Name']
[-DomainController 'DCName']
[-FirstName 'FirstName'] [-Initials 'Value']
[-LastName 'LastName'] [-MacAttachmentFormat 'Format']
[-MessageBodyFormat 'Format'] [-MessageFormat 'Format']
[-OrganizationalUnit 'OU'] [-PrimarySmtpAddress 'SmtpAddress']
[-TemplateInstance 'Instance']
[-UsePreferMessageFormat <$false|$true>]
```

```
Usage
New-MailContact -ExternalEmailAddress 'SMTP:jonash@hotmail.com'
 -Name 'Jonas Hasselberg' -Alias 'Jonas_Hasselberg'
 -OrganizationalUnit 'cpandl.com/Sales'
 -FirstName 'Jonas' -Initials '' -LastName 'Hasselberg'
```

Mail-Enabling Existing Contacts

You can mail-enable an existing contact by completing the following steps:

1. In Exchange Management Console, expand the Recipient Configuration and then select the related Mail Contact node.

2. Right-click the Mail Contact node, and then choose New Contact. This starts the New Mail Contact Wizard.

3. On the Introduction page, select Existing Contact, and then click Browse. This displays the Select Contact dialog box.

4. In the Select Contact dialog box, select the contact you want to mail-enable, and then click OK. Contacts for the current domain are listed by name and organizational unit. You'll need to change the scope, as discussed previously, if you don't see the contact you want to use.

5. Click Next. To the right of the External E-mail Address text box is an Edit button. Click the down arrow next to the Edit button to display two options:

   ❑ **SMTP Address** Click SMTP Address to associate a standard SMTP e-mail address with the contact. Enter the e-mail address, and then click OK.

   ❑ **Custom Address** Click Custom Address to associate a custom e-mail address with the contact. Enter the e-mail address, and then enter the e-mail address type. Click OK.

6. Click Next, and then click New. Exchange Management Console mail-enables the selected contact. If an error occurs, the contact will not be created. You will need to correct the problem and repeat this procedure.

7. Click Finish.

In the Exchange Management Shell, you can mail-enable an existing contact using the Enable-MailContact cmdlet. Sample 7-12 provides the syntax and usage.

Sample 7-12   Enable-MailContact cmdlet syntax and usage

```
Syntax
Enable-MailContact -Identity 'ContactIdentity'
 -ExternalEmailAddress 'TYPE:EmailAddress'
[-Alias 'ExchangeAlias']
[-DisplayName 'Name'] [-DomainController 'DCName']
[-MacAttachmentFormat 'Format'] [-MessageBodyFormat 'Format']
[-MessageFormat 'Format'] [-OrganizationalUnit 'OU']
[-PrimarySmtpAddress 'SmtpAddress']
[-UsePreferMessageFormat <$false|$true>]
```

```
Usage

Enable-MailContact -Identity 'cpand.com/Sales/Olinda Richard'
 -ExternalEmailAddress 'SMTP:olinda@msn.com'
 -Alias 'Olinda_Richard' -DisplayName 'Olinda Richard'
```

Setting or Changing a Contact's Name and Alias

All mail-enabled contacts and users have the following name components:

- **First Name, Initials, Last Name** The first name, initials, and last name of the contact

- **Exchange Name**   The name used in the Exchange Management Console
- **Display Name**   The name displayed in the global address list
- **Alias**   The Exchange alias for the contact

You can set or change name and alias information for a mail-enabled contact or user by completing the following steps:

1. In Exchange Management Console, expand the Recipient Configuration node and then select the related Mail Contact node.

2. Double-click the name of the mail-enabled contact or user you want to work with. The Properties dialog box appears.

3. On the General tab, the first text box sets the name used in Exchange Management Console. Change this text box if you'd like the mail-enabled contact or user to have a different name.

4. The Alias text box sets the Exchange alias. If you'd like to assign a new alias, enter the new Exchange alias in this text box.

5. On the Contact Information or User Information tab, use the following text boxes to set the full name and display name to use:

   ❑ **First Name, Initials, Last Name**   Sets the contact's full name

   ❑ **Name**   Sets the contact's display name as seen in the global address list

6. Click OK to save your changes.

Setting Additional Directory Information for Contacts

You can set additional directory information for a mail-enabled contact or user by completing the following steps:

1. In Exchange Management Console, expand the Recipient Configuration node and then select the related Mail Contact node.

2. Double-click the name of the mail-enabled contact or user you want to work with. The Properties dialog box appears.

3. On the Contact Information or User Information tab, use the Web Page text box to set the URL of the home page for the mail-enabled contact or user, which can be on the Internet or the company intranet.

4. On the Address And Phone tab, use the text boxes provided to set the business address or home address to use. Normally, you'll want to enter the business address rather than a personal address. This way, you can track the business locations and mailing addresses of contacts at various offices.

5. Use the Phone Numbers text boxes to set the primary business telephone, pager, fax, home telephone, and mobile telephone numbers.

6. On the Organization tab, type the title, company, department, and office, as appropriate.

7. To specify the manager of a mail-enabled contact or user, select the Manager check box, and then click Browse. In the Select Recipient User Or Contact dialog box, select the contact's manager. When you specify a manager, the contact shows up as a direct report in the manager's account. Click Apply or OK to apply the changes.

Changing E-mail Addresses Associated with Contacts

Mail-enabled contacts and users have several types of e-mail addresses associated with them:

- An internal, automatically generated e-mail address used for routing within the organization

- An external e-mail address to which mail routed internally is forwarded for delivery

You can change the e-mail addresses associated with a mail-enabled contact or user by completing the following steps:

1. In Exchange Management Console, expand the Recipient Configuration node and then select the related Mail Contact node.

2. Double-click the name of the mail-enabled contact or user you want to work with. The Properties dialog box appears.

3. On the E-mail Addresses tab, e-mail addresses are listed by protocol and type. If an e-mail address is also specified as an external address, it is listed according to its protocol type, such as SMTP or X.400, and under the External heading. You can use the following techniques to manage a contact's e-mail addresses:

   - ❏ **Create a new SMTP address**   Click the down arrow next to the Add button, and then select SMTP Address. Enter the e-mail address, and then click OK.

   - ❏ **Create a custom address**   Click the down arrow next to the Add button, and then select Custom Address. Enter the e-mail address, enter the e-mail address type, and click OK.

   - ❏ **Edit an existing address**   Double-click the address entry. Modify the settings in the Address dialog box, and then click OK.

   - ❏ **Delete an existing address**   Select the address, and then click the Remove button.

4. To set an e-mail address as the default Reply To address, select it, and then click Set As Reply.

5. To specify that an e-mail address is an external address, select it, and then click Set As External. Click OK.

Disabling Contacts and Removing Exchange Attributes

When you disable a contact using the Exchange management tools, you permanently remove the contact from the Exchange database, but you do not remove it from Active Directory. In the Exchange Management Console, you can remove contacts by right-clicking them and selecting Disable. When prompted to confirm this action, click Yes.

You can use the Disable-MailContact cmdlet to remove Exchange attributes from contacts while retaining the contact in Active Directory. Sample 7-13 shows the syntax and usage.

Sample 7-13   Disable-MailContact cmdlet syntax and usage

```
Syntax
Disable-MailContact -Identity 'ContactIdentity'
```

```
Usage

Disable-MailContact -Identity 'Lori Oviatt'
```

Deleting Contacts

When you delete a contact using the Exchange management tools, you permanently remove it from Active Directory and from the Exchange database. In the Exchange Management Console, you can delete contacts by right-clicking them and selecting Remove. When prompted to confirm this action, click Yes.

You can use the Remove-MailContact cmdlet to delete contacts as well. Sample 7-14 shows the syntax and usage.

Sample 7-14   Remove-MailContact cmdlet syntax and usage

```
Syntax
Remove-MailContact -Identity 'ContactIdentity'
```

```
Usage

Remove-Mailbox -Identity 'Lori Oviatt'
```

Chapter 8
Mailbox Administration

The difference between a good Microsoft Exchange administrator and a great one is the attention he or she pays to mailbox administration. Mailboxes are private storage places for sending and receiving mail, and they are created as part of private mailbox databases in Exchange. Mailboxes have many properties that control mail delivery, permissions, and storage limits. You can configure most mailbox settings on a per-mailbox basis. However, you cannot change some settings without moving mailboxes to a different mailbox database or changing the settings of the mailbox database itself. For example, you set the storage location on the Exchange file system, the default public folder database for the mailbox, and the default offline address book on a per-mailbox-database basis. Keep this in mind when performing capacity planning and when deciding which storage group and mailbox database to use for a particular mailbox.

Creating Special-Purpose Mailboxes

Exchange Server 2007 makes it easy to create several special-purpose mailbox types, including:

- **Room mailbox** A room mailbox is a mailbox for room scheduling.

- **Equipment mailbox** An equipment mailbox is a mailbox for equipment scheduling.

- **Linked mailbox** A linked mailbox is a mailbox for a user from a separate, trusted forest.

- **Forwarding mailbox** A forwarding mailbox is a mailbox that can receive mail and forward it off-site.

The sections that follow discuss techniques for working with these special-purpose mailboxes.

Using Room and Equipment Mailboxes

You use room and equipment mailboxes for scheduling purposes only. You'll find that:

- Room mailboxes are useful when you have conference rooms, training rooms, and other rooms for which you need to coordinate the use.

- Equipment mailboxes are useful when you have projectors, media carts, or other items of equipment for which you need to coordinate the use.

Every room and equipment mailbox must have a separate user account associated with it. Although these accounts are required so that the mailboxes can be used for scheduling, the accounts are disabled by default so that they cannot be used for logon. To ensure that the resource accounts do not get enabled accidentally, you'll need to coordinate closely with other administrators in your organization.

> **Note**   The Exchange Management Console doesn't show the enabled or disabled status of user accounts. The only way to check the status is to use domain administration tools.

Because the number of scheduled rooms and equipment grows as your organization grows, you'll want to carefully consider the naming conventions you use with rooms and equipment:

- With rooms, you'll typically want to use display names that clearly identify the rooms' physical locations. For example, you might have rooms named "Conference Room 28 on Fifth Floor" or "Building 83 Room 15."

- With equipment, you'll typically want to identify the type of equipment, the equipment's characteristics, and the equipment's relative location. For example, you might have equipment named "NEC HD Projector at Seattle Office" or "5th Floor Media Cart."

As with standard user mailboxes, room and equipment mailboxes have contact information associated with them. To make it easier to find rooms and equipment, you should provide as much information as possible. Specifically, you can make rooms easier for users to work with by using these techniques:

- If a room has a conference or call-in phone, enter this phone number as the business phone number on the Address And Phone tab of the Mailbox Properties dialog box.

- Specify the location details in the Office text box on the Organization tab of the Mailbox Properties dialog box.

- Specify the room capacity in the Resource Capacity text box on the Resource Information tab of the Mailbox Properties dialog box.

The business phone, location, and capacity are displayed in Microsoft Office Outlook.

After you've set up mailboxes for your rooms and equipment, scheduling the rooms and equipment is fairly straightforward. In Exchange, room and equipment availability is tracked using free/busy data. In Outlook, a user who wants to reserve rooms, equipment, or both simply makes a meeting request that includes the rooms and equipment that are required for the meeting.

The steps to schedule a meeting and reserve equipment are as follows:

1. In Outlook 2007, click New, and then select Meeting Request. Or press Ctrl+Shift+Q.

2. In the To text box, invite the individuals who should attend the meeting by typing their display names, Exchange aliases, or e-mail addresses, as appropriate (see Figure 8-1).

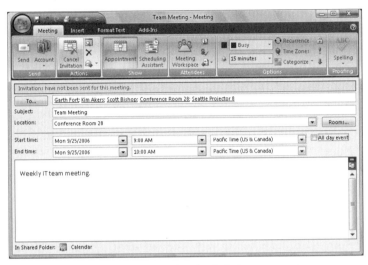

Figure 8-1   You can schedule a meeting that includes a reserved room and equipment.

3. Type the display name, Exchange alias, or e-mail address for any equipment you need to reserve.

4. Click the Rooms button to the right of the Location text box. The Select Rooms dialog box appears, as shown in Figure 8-2. By default, the Select Rooms dialog box uses the All Rooms address book. Rooms are added to this address book automatically when you create them.

5. Double-click the room you want to use. This adds the room to the Rooms list. Click OK to close the Select Rooms dialog box.

6. In the Subject text box, type the meeting subject.

7. Use the Start Time and End Time options to schedule the start and end times for the meeting.

8. Click Scheduling Assistant to view the free/busy data for the invited users and the selected resources.

9. After you type a message to accompany the meeting request, click Send.

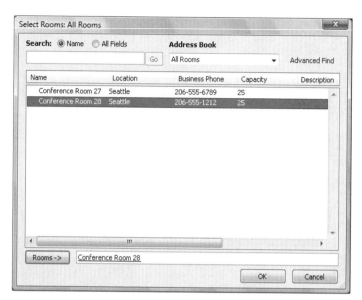

Figure 8-2 Select a room to use for the meeting.

Creating Room and Equipment Mailboxes

In the Exchange Management Console, you can create room and equipment mailboxes by completing the following steps:

1. In Exchange Management Console, expand the Recipient Configuration node and then select the related Mailbox node.

   Note If you want to create the user account for the room or equipment mailbox in a domain other than the current one, you'll first need to set the scope for the Mailbox node, as discussed in the "Finding Existing Mailboxes, Contacts, and Groups" section of Chapter 7, "User and Contact Administration."

2. Right-click the Mailbox node, and then select New Mailbox. This starts the New Mailbox Wizard.

3. On the Introduction page, select either Room Mailbox or Equipment Mailbox, as appropriate, and then click Next.

4. On the User Type page, verify that New User is selected, and then click Next. Each room or equipment must have a separate user account. This is necessary to track the unique free/busy data for the room or equipment.

5. On the Mailbox Information page, the Organizational Unit text box shows where in Active Directory the user account will be created. By default, this is the Users container in the current domain. As you'll usually need to create room and equipment accounts in a specific organizational unit rather than the Users container, click Browse. Use the Select Organizational Unit dialog box to choose the location in which to store the account, and then click OK.

6. Type a descriptive display name in the Name text box.

7. In the User Logon Name text box, type the logon name. Use the drop-down list to select the domain with which the account is to be associated. This sets the fully qualified logon name.

8. The first 20 characters of the logon name are used to set the pre-Microsoft Windows 2000 logon name, which must be unique in the domain. If necessary, change the pre-Windows 2000 logon name.

9. Type and then confirm the password for the account. Even though the account is disabled by default, this password must follow the conventions of your organization's password policy.

10. Click Next. On the Mailbox Settings page, the Exchange alias is set to the logon name by default. You can change this value by entering a new alias. The Exchange alias is used to set the user's e-mail address.

11. Click the Browse button to the right of the Mailbox Database text box. In the Select Mailbox Database dialog box, choose the mailbox database in which the mailbox should be stored. Mailbox databases are listed by name as well as by associated storage group and server.

12. Click Next, and then click New to create the account and the related mailbox. If an error occurs during account or mailbox creation, neither the account nor the related mailbox will be created. You will need to correct the problem and repeat this procedure.

13. Click Finish. For all mailbox-enabled accounts, a Simple Mail Transfer Protocol (SMTP) e-mail address is configured automatically.

In the Exchange Management Shell, you can create a user account with a mailbox for rooms and equipment using the New-Mailbox cmdlet. Sample 8-1 provides the syntax and usage. Although the account is disabled by default, you must enter a secure password for the account when prompted.

Note Note that for rooms, you must use the –Room parameter. For equipment, you must use the –Equipment parameter. By default, when you use either parameter, the related value is set as $true.

Sample 8-1   Creating Room and Equipment Mailboxes

```
Syntax
New-Mailbox -Name 'DisplayName' -Alias 'ExchangeAlias'
 -OrganizationalUnit 'OrganizationalUnit'
 -UserPrincipalName 'LogonName' -SamAccountName 'prewin2000logon'
 -FirstName '' -Initials '' -LastName ''
 -Database 'Server\MailboxDatabase'
 [-Room <$false|$true> | -Equipment <$false|$true> ]
```

```
Usage
New-Mailbox -Name 'Conference Room 27' -Alias 'room27'
 -OrganizationalUnit 'cpandl.com/Sales'
 -UserPrincipalName 'room27@cpandl.com' -SamAccountName 'room27'
 -FirstName '' -Initials '' -LastName ''
 -Database 'Corpsvr127\First Storage Group\Sales'
 -Room
```

Creating Linked Mailboxes

A linked mailbox is a mailbox that is accessed by a user in a separate, trusted forest. Typically, you'll use linked mailboxes when your organization's mailbox servers are in a separate resource forest and you want to ensure that users can access free/busy data across these forests.

All linked mailboxes have two user account associations:

- A unique user account in the same forest as the Mailbox server. The same forest user account is disabled automatically so that it cannot be used for logon.

- A unique user account in a separate forest for which you are creating a link. The separate forest user account is enabled so that it can be used for logon.

In the Exchange Management Console, you can create a linked mailbox by completing the following steps:

1. In Exchange Management Console, expand the Recipient Configuration node and then select the related Mailbox node.

2. Right-click the Mailbox node, and then select New Mailbox. This starts the New Mailbox Wizard.

3. On the Introduction page, select Linked Mailbox, and then click Next.

4. On the User Type page, verify that New User is selected, and then click Next.

5. On the Mailbox Information page, click Browse to create the new user account in a different container. Use the Select Organizational Unit dialog box to choose the location in which to store the account, and then click OK.

6. Type the user's first name, middle initial, and last name in the text boxes provided. These values are used to create the Name entry, which is the user's display name.

7. In the User Logon Name text box, type the user's logon name. Use the drop-down list to select the domain with which the account is to be associated. This sets the fully qualified logon name.

8. The first 20 characters of the logon name are used to set the pre-Windows 2000 logon name, which must be unique in the domain. If necessary, change the pre-Windows 2000 logon name.

9. Type and then confirm the password for the account. Although the account will not be used for logon, this password must follow the conventions of your organization's password policy.

10. Click Next. The Exchange alias is set to the logon name by default. Make sure the alias matches the one used in the resource forest.

11. Click the Browse button to the right of the Mailbox Database text box. In the Select Mailbox Database dialog box, choose the mailbox database in which the mailbox should be stored. Mailbox databases are listed by name as well as by associated storage group and server.

12. Click Next. On the Master Account page, click Browse to the right of the Linked Forest text box. In the Select Trusted Forest Or Domain dialog box, select the linked forest or domain in which the user's original account is located, and then click OK.

13. If you need additional administrative permissions to access the linked forest, select the Use The Following Windows Account check box. Then type the user name and password for an administrator account in this forest.

14. Click the Browse button to the right of the Linked Domain Controller text box. In the Select Domain Controller dialog box, select a domain controller in the linked forest, and then click OK.

15. Click the Browse button to the right of the Linked Master Account text box. Use the options in the Select User dialog box to select the original user account in the linked forest, and then click OK.

16. Click Next, and then click New to create the account and the related mailbox. If an error occurs during account or mailbox creation, neither the account nor the related mailbox will be created. You will need to correct the problem and repeat this procedure.

17. Click Finish. For all mailbox-enabled accounts, an SMTP e-mail address is configured automatically.

In the Exchange Management Shell, you can create a user account with a linked mailbox using the New-Mailbox cmdlet. Sample 8-2 provides the syntax and usage. You'll be prompted for two sets of credentials: one for the new user account and one for an administrator account in the linked forest.

Sample 8-2   Creating linked mailboxes

```
Syntax
New-Mailbox -Name 'DisplayName' -Alias 'ExchangeAlias'
 -OrganizationalUnit 'OrganizationalUnit'
 -Database 'Database'
 -UserPrincipalName 'LogonName' -SamAccountName 'prewin2000logon'
 -FirstName 'FirstName' -Initials 'Initial' -LastName 'LastName'
 -ResetPasswordOnNextLogon State
 -LinkedDomainController 'LinkedDC'
 -LinkedMasterAccount 'domain\user'
 -LinkedCredentials 'domain\administrator'
```

```
Usage
New-Mailbox -Name 'Wendy Richardson' -Alias 'wendyr'
 -OrganizationalUnit 'cpandl.com/Sales'
 -Database 'Corpsvr127\First Storage Group\Sales'
 -UserPrincipalName 'wendyr@cpandl.com' -SamAccountName 'wendyr'
 -FirstName 'Wendy' -Initials '' -LastName 'Richardson'
 -ResetPasswordOnNextLogon $true
 -LinkedDomainController 'CohoDC58'
 -LinkedMasterAccount 'coho\wrichardson'
 -LinkedCredentials 'coho\williams'
```

Creating Forwarding Mailboxes

Custom recipients, such as mail-enabled users and contacts, don't normally receive mail from users outside the organization because a custom recipient doesn't have an e-mail address that resolves to a specific mailbox in your organization. At times, though, you might want external users, applications, or mail systems to be able to send mail to an address within your organization and then have Exchange forward this mail to an external mailbox.

> **Tip**   In my organization, I've created forwarding mailboxes for pager alerts. This simple solution lets managers (and monitoring systems) within the organization quickly and easily send text pages to IT personnel. Here, I've set up mail-enabled contacts for each pager e-mail address, such as 8085551212@adatum.com, and then created a mailbox that forwards e-mail to the custom recipient. Generally, the display name of the mail-enabled contact is in the form Alert *User Name*, such as

Alert William Stanek. The display name and e-mail address for the mailbox are in the form Z *LastName* and AE-*MailAddress@myorg.com*, such as Z Stanek and AWilliamS@adatum.com, respectively. Afterward, I hide the mailbox so that it isn't displayed in the global address list or in other address lists, so users can see only the Alert William Stanek mailbox.

To create a user account to receive mail and forward it offsite, follow these steps:

1. Using Exchange Management Console, create a mail-enabled contact for the user. Name the contact X – *User Name*, such as X – William Stanek. Be sure to establish an external e-mail address for the contact that refers to the user's Internet address.

2. Using Exchange Management Console, create a mailbox-enabled user account in the domain. Name the account with the appropriate display name, such as William Stanek. Be sure to create an Exchange mailbox for the account, but don't grant any special permission to the account. You might want to restrict the account so that the user can't log on to any servers in the domain.

3. Using Exchange Management Console, access the Properties dialog box for the user's mailbox.

4. On the Mail Flow Settings tab, select Delivery Options, and then click Properties.

5. In the Delivery Options dialog box, select the Forward To check box, and then click Browse.

6. In the Select Recipient dialog box, select the mail-enabled contact you created earlier, and then click OK three times. You can now use the user account to forward mail to the external mailbox.

Managing Mailboxes: The Essentials

You often need to manage mailboxes the way you do user accounts. Some of the management tasks are fairly intuitive and others aren't. If you have questions, be sure to read the sections that follow.

Viewing Current Mailbox Size, Message Count, and Last Logon

You can use the Exchange Management Console to view who last logged on to a mailbox, last logon date and time, mailbox size, and message count by completing these steps:

1. In Exchange Management Console, expand the Recipient Configuration node and then select the related Mailbox node.

2. Double-click the mailbox with which you want to work.

3. On the General tab, the Last Logged On By text box shows who last logged on to the mailbox and the last logon date and time (see Figure 8-3).

4. On the General tab, the Total Items and Size (KB) areas show the number of messages in the mailbox and the current mailbox size in kilobytes, respectively.

Figure 8-3   View mailbox statistics.

If you want to view this same information for all mailboxes on a server, the easiest way is to use the Get-MailboxStatistics cmdlet. Sample 8-3 shows examples using this cmdlet.

Sample 8-3   Getting statistics for multiple mailboxes

```
Syntax
Get-MailboxStatistics [-Server  'Server' | -Identity 'Identity'
 | -Database  'Database']
```

```
Usage
Get-MailboxStatistics -Server  'corpsvr127'

Get-MailboxStatistics -Database
'Corpsvr127\First Storage Group\Engineering'

Get-MailboxStatistics -Identity 'cpandl\williams'
```

Setting Alternate Mailbox Display Names for Multilanguage Environments

In some cases, the full display name for a mailbox won't be available for display. This can happen when multiple language versions of the Exchange snap-in are installed on the network or when multiple language packs are installed on a system. Here, the system cannot interpret some or all of the characters in the display name and, as a result, doesn't show the display name. To correct this problem, you can set an alternate display name using a different character set. For example, you could use Cyrillic or Kanji characters instead of standard ANSI characters.

You can set an alternate display name for a mailbox by following these steps:

1. Open the Properties dialog box for the mailbox-enabled user account by double-clicking the user name in Exchange Management Console.

2. On the User Information tab, type the alternate display name in the Simple Display Name text box, and then click OK.

Hiding Mailboxes from Address Lists

Occasionally, you might want to hide a mailbox so that it doesn't appear in the global address list or other address lists. One reason for doing this is if you have administrative mailboxes that you use only for special purposes. To hide a mailbox from the address lists, follow these steps:

1. Open the Properties dialog box for the mailbox-enabled user account by double-clicking the user name in Exchange Management Console.

2. On the General tab, select the Hide From Exchange Address Lists check box, and then click OK.

Defining Custom Mailbox Attributes for Address Lists

Address lists, such as the global address list, make it easier for users and administrators to find available Exchange resources, including users, contacts, distribution groups, and public folders. The fields available for Exchange resources are based on the type of resource. If you want to add additional values that should be displayed or searchable in address lists, such as an employee identification number, you can assign these values as custom attributes.

Exchange provides 15 custom attributes, labeled Customer Attribute 1, Custom Attribute 2, and so on, through Custom Attribute 15. You can assign a value to a custom attribute by completing the following steps:

1. Open the Properties dialog box for the mailbox-enabled user account by double-clicking the user name in Exchange Management Console.

2. On the General tab, click Custom Attributes. The Custom Attributes dialog box appears.

3. Enter attribute values in the text boxes provided, and click OK twice.

Moving Mailboxes

To complete an upgrade, balance the server load, or manage drive space, you can move mailboxes from one server, storage group, or database to another server, storage group, or database:

- When your source and destination Mailbox servers are running Exchange Server 2007 and are in the same forest, you use the Exchange Management Console or the Move-Mailbox cmdlet to move the mailboxes. This might be necessary when you are seeking to balance the load on a particular server.

- When your source servers are running Exchange 2000 Server or Exchange Server 2003 and your destination servers are running Exchange Server 2007, you can use the Move-Mailbox cmdlet to move the mailboxes. This might be necessary when you are upgrading to Exchange Server 2007.

- When your source and destination servers are running Exchange Server 2007 but are in different forests, you can use the Move-Mailbox cmdlet to move the mailboxes. This might be necessary if you are implementing an Exchange resource forest or establishing a new forest.

The sections that follow discuss how to perform these various types of move tasks.

Moving Mailboxes: The Essentials

Moving mailboxes while they are actively being used isn't a good idea, as it may cause some disruption to the affected users. Typically, you'll want to move mailboxes at a time when they are less likely to be in use. You can use the move scheduling features in Exchange Server 2007 to do this when you use the Exchange Management Console.

When you move mailboxes from one server to another, or even to a different storage group on the same sever, keep in mind that the Exchange policies of the new mailbox database may be different from the old one. Because of this, consider the following issues before you move mailboxes to a new server or storage group:

- **General policy** Changes to watch out for include those in the default public folder database, the offline address book, and message settings. The risk is that the users whose mailboxes you move could lose or gain access to public folders. They might have a different offline address book, which might have different entries. This address book will also have to be downloaded in its entirety the first time the user's mail client connects to Exchange after the move.

- **Database policy** Changes to watch out for pertain to the maintenance interval and automatic mounting. If Exchange performs maintenance when these users are accessing their mail, they might have slower response times. If the mailbox database is configured so that it isn't mounted at startup, restarting the Exchange services could result in the users not being able to access their mailboxes.

■ **Limits** Changes to watch out for pertain to storage limits and deletion settings. Users might be prohibited from sending and receiving mail if their mailbox exceeds the storage limits of the new mailbox database. Users might notice that deleted items stay in their Deleted Items folder longer or are deleted sooner than expected if the Keep Deleted Items setting is different.

Moving Mailboxes Using the Exchange Management Console

When your source and destination Mailbox servers are running Exchange Server 2007 and are in the same forest, you can move mailboxes by completing these steps:

1. In Exchange Management Console, expand the Recipient Configuration node and then select the related Mailbox node.

2. Right-click the mailbox, and then select Move Mailbox. This starts the Move Mailbox Wizard, as shown in Figure 8-4.

> **Tip** You can select and move multiple mailboxes at the same time. To select multiple users individually, hold down the Ctrl key, and then click each user account that you want to select. To select a sequence of accounts, hold down the Shift key, select the first user account, and then click the last user account.

Figure 8-4 Use the Move Mailbox Wizard to move mailboxes.

3. Click the Browse button to the right of the Mailbox Database text box. In the Select Mailbox Database dialog box, choose the mailbox database to which the mailbox should be moved. Mailbox databases are listed by name as well as by associated storage group and server.

4. Click Next. If corrupted messages are found in a mailbox, specify how you'd like those messages to be handled. To skip the mailbox if corrupted messages are found, select Skip The Mailbox. To skip the corrupted messages if they are found but still move the mailbox, select Skip The Corrupted Messages.

5. If you elected to skip corrupted messages, you must also specify the maximum number of corrupted messages to skip. If this value is exceeded, the mailbox will not be moved.

6. Optionally, select the Global Catalog and Domain Controller check boxes and then use the Browse buttons to set the related servers to use for this mailbox move.

7. Click Next. If you want to move the mailboxes right away, select Immediately. To schedule the mailbox move, select At The Following Time, and then set the move date and time.

8. To specify the maximum length of time that the mailbox move can run, select the Cancel Tasks That Are Still Running After (Hours) check box, and then set the maximum number of hours the move task can run.

   Note   Cancelling a move after a maximum number of hours is designed to ensure that move tasks that are blocked or not proceeding as expected are cancelled. Most move operations should be completed in eight hours or less, but the exact duration depends on the number of mailboxes being moved, the size of the mailboxes, and the connection speed of the link connecting the source and destination mail servers.

9. When you click Next and then click Move, Exchange Server attempts to move the mailbox. If a problem occurs, you'll see an Error dialog box that lets you retry or cancel the operation.

Note   In the Exchange Management Console, you can't move mailboxes between forests. To move mailboxes among servers, the servers must be in the same forest.

Moving Mailboxes Using the Exchange Management Shell

In the Exchange Management Shell, you can move individual mailboxes using the Move-Mailbox cmdlet. Sample 8-4 provides the syntax and usage for using Move-Mailbox to move a specific mailbox from one server to another.

Sample 8-4   Moving individual mailboxes

```
Syntax
Move-Mailbox -Identity 'Identity' -TargetDatabase 'Database'
[-BadItemLimit 'Limit'] [-ContentKeywords 'Values']
[-DomainController 'DCName'] [-EndDate 'DateTime']
[-ExcludeFolders 'MapiFoldePath'] [-GlobalCatalog 'GCName']
[-IgnorePolicyMatch <$false|$true>]
[-IgnoreRuleLimitErrors <$false|$true>]
[-IncludeFolders 'MapiFolderPath'] [-Locale 'Value']
[-MaxThreads 'Num']
[-NTAccountOU 'OUId'] [-PreserveMailboxSizeLimit <$false|$true>]
[-RecipientKeywords 'Values'] [-ReportFile 'LocalPath']
[-RetryInterval 'TimeSpan'] [-RetryTimeout 'TimeSpan']
[-SenderKeywords 'Values'] [-StartDate 'DateTime']
[-SubjectKeywords 'Values'] [-ValidateOnly <$false|$true>]
```

```
Usage
Move-Mailbox -Identity 'cpandl\williams'
 -TargetDatabase 'Corpsvr127\First Storage Group\Engineering'
-BadItemLimit 50 -IgnorePolicyMatch $true
 -RetryTimeout '8:00:00' -RetryInterval '5:00'
```

If you want to move all mailboxes from one database to another, you can use the Get-Mailbox and Move-Mailbox cmdlets together, as shown in Sample 8-5.

Sample 8-5   Moving all mailboxes in a database

```
Syntax
Get-Mailbox -Database 'Database' | Move-Mailbox -Identity 'Identity'
 -TargetDatabase 'Database' [-BadItemLimit Number]
 [-DomainController 'DCName'] [-IgnorePolicyMatch Switch]
 [-RetryTimeout TimeSpan] [-RetryInterval TimeSpan]
```

```
Usage
Get-Mailbox -Database 'Corpsvr98\First Storage Group\Technology' |
 Move-Mailbox
-TargetDatabase 'Corpsvr127\First Storage Group\Engineering'
 -BadItemLimit 50 -IgnorePolicyMatch $true
-RetryTimeout '8:00:00' -RetryInterval '5:00'
```

If you are moving mailboxes between domains, you'll want to specify domain controllers and Global Catalogs to use in both the source and target domains, as shown in Sample 8-6. This ensures that performance and replication issues don't cause problems when moving mailboxes across domains.

Sample 8-6   Moving mailboxes across domains

```
Syntax
Move-Mailbox -Identity 'Identity' -TargetDatabase 'Database'
  [-SourceDomainController 'SourceDCName']
  [-DomainController 'TargetDCName']
  [-SourceGlobalCatalog 'SourceGCName']
  [-GlobalCatalog 'TargetGCName']
  [-BadItemLimit Number] [-DomainController 'DCName']
  [-IgnorePolicyMatch Switch] [-RetryTimeout TimeSpan]
  [-RetryInterval TimeSpan]
```

```
Usage
Move-Mailbox -Identity 'cpand1\williams'
  -TargetDatabase 'Corpsvr127\First Storage Group\Engineering'
  -SourceDomainController 'CohoDC27'] [-DomainController 'CityDC85']
  -SourceGlobalCatalog 'CohoGC18'] [-GlobalCatalog 'CityDC12']
  -BadItemLimit 50 -IgnorePolicyMatch $true
```

If you are moving mailboxes across forests, you must specify domain controllers and Global Catalogs to use in both the source and target forests, as shown in Sample 8-7. You must also specify the NT account organizational unit. When you perform the move mailbox task, you'll be prompted for administrator credentials to connect to the target database in the target forest. You must provide the account name and password for an administrator account in the target forest.

Sample 8-7   Moving mailboxes across forests

```
Syntax
Move-Mailbox -Identity 'Identity' -TargetDatabase 'Database'
  [-SourceDomainController 'SourceDCName']
  [-DomainController 'TargetDCName']
  [-SourceGlobalCatalog 'SourceGCName']
  [-GlobalCatalog 'TargetGCName']
  [-BadItemLimit Number] [-DomainController 'DCName']
  [-IgnorePolicyMatch Switch] [-RetryTimeout TimeSpan]
  [-RetryInterval TimeSpan]
```

```
Usage
Move-Mailbox -Identity 'cpand1\williams'
  -TargetDatabase 'Corpsvr127\First Storage Group\Engineering'
  -SourceDomainController 'CohoDC27'] [-DomainController 'CityDC85']
  -SourceGlobalCatalog 'CohoGC18'] [-GlobalCatalog 'CityDC12']
  -BadItemLimit 50 -IgnorePolicyMatch $true
```

Importing and Exporting Mailbox Data

As discussed in Chapter 3, "Managing Microsoft Exchange Server 2007 Clients," Exchange mail can be configured to use the following: server mailboxes, server mailboxes with local copies, or personal folders. Users who travel often may prefer to have personal folders where their mail is stored locally in .pst files. However, from an administration perspective, you'll find that mailboxes are easier to manage and protect when users have either server mailboxes or server mailboxes with local copies.

When you are working with the Exchange Management Shell, you can use the Import-Mailbox cmdlet to import mailbox data from a .pst file and the Export-Mailbox cmdlet to export mailbox data to a .pst file. Import and export operations are similar to mailbox move operations.

Sample 8-8 shows the syntax and usage for Import-Mailbox. The only required parameters are Identity and PstFolderPath. Most other parameters serve to limit what you are importing. For import operations, you'll typically want to create a copy of the user's .pst file and make this copy accessible on a desktop running a 32-bit operating system where the 32-bit Exchange management tools are installed. Once you've installed the 32-bit Exchange management tools on a desktop computer running a 32-bit operating system, you can access the Exchange Management Shell on the user's desktop and run this cmdlet. With Windows Vista, the default location of a .pst file is *%LocalAppData%* Microsoft\Outlook, where *%LocalAppData%* is a user-specific environment variable that points to a user's local application data.

Sample 8-8   Import-Mailbox cmdlet syntax and usage

```
Syntax
Import-Mailbox -Identity 'DestMailboxIdentifier'
 -PSTFolderPath 'PSTLocalPath'
[-AllowContentKeywords 'AllowedValues']
 [-AttachmentFilenames 'AllowedValues']
[-BadItemLimit 'Limit'] [-ContentKeywords 'BodyOrAttachmentValues']
[-EndDate 'DateTime'] [-ExcludeFolders 'MapiFoldePath']
[-GlobalCatalog 'GCName'] [-IncludeFolders 'MapiFolderPath']
[-Locale 'Value'] [-MaxThreads 'Num']
[-RecipientKeywords 'Values'] [-ReportFile 'LocalPath']
[-SenderKeywords 'Values'] [-StartDate 'DateTime']
[-SubjectKeywords 'Values'] [-ValidateOnly <$false|$true>]
```

```
Usage
Import-Mailbox -Identity 'cpandl.com/Engineering/williams'
 -PSTFolderPath 'c:\temp\william.pst'
```

Sample 8-9 shows the syntax and usage for Export-Mailbox. The only required parameters are Identity and PstFolderPath. Most other parameters serve to limit what you are exporting. When you are exporting to a .pst file, you'll want to run the command on a desktop running a 32-bit operating system where the 32-bit Exchange management tools are installed. Once you've installed the 32-bit Exchange management tools on a desktop computer running a 32-bit operating system, you can access the Exchange Management Shell on the user's desktop and run this cmdlet to store the exported data in a .pst file.

Sample 8-9 Export-Mailbox cmdlet syntax and usage

```
Syntax
Export-Mailbox -Identity 'SourceMailboxIdentifier'
-PSTFolderPath 'PSTLocalPath'
[-AllowContentKeywords 'AllowedValues']
 [-AttachmentFilenames 'AllowedValues']
[-BadItemLimit 'Limit'] [-ContentKeywords 'BodyOrAttachmentValues']
[-DeleteAssociatedMessages <$false|$true>]
 [-DeleteContent <$false|$true>]
[-EndDate 'DateTime'] [-ExcludeFolders 'MapiFoldePath']
[-GlobalCatalog 'GCName'] [-IncludeFolders 'MapiFolderPath']
[-Locale 'Value'] [-MaxThreads 'Num']
[-RecipientKeywords 'Values'] [-ReportFile 'LocalPath']
[-SenderKeywords 'Values'] [-StartDate 'DateTime']
[-SubjectKeywords 'Values'] [-ValidateOnly <$false|$true>]
```

```
Usage
Export-Mailbox -Identity 'cpandl.com/Engineering/williams'
 -PSTFolderPath 'c:\temp\william.pst'
```

Export-Mailbox has alternative syntax that allows you to export a mailbox or a subset of mail or folders and import it directly into a Recovered – Data subfolder of a specified folder in a specified mailbox. For example, you could use this technique to export the mail in Andy Carothers's mailbox into a SavedMail folder in Scotty Seely's mailbox. For this type of export operation, you do not have to run the cmdlet on a desktop running a 32-bit operating system where the 32-bit Exchange management tools are installed. Sample 8-10 provides the syntax and usage for an export/import.

Sample 8-10 Exporting and then importing Mailbox data

```
Syntax
Export-Mailbox -Identity 'SourceMailboxIdentifier'
-TargetFolder 'TargetMailboxFolder'
-TargetMailbox 'TargetMailboxIdentifier'
[-AllowContentKeywords 'AllowedValues']
 [-AttachmentFilenames 'AllowedValues']
[-BadItemLimit 'Limit'] [-ContentKeywords 'BodyOrAttachmentValues']
[-DeleteAssociatedMessages <$false|$true>]
 [-DeleteContent <$false|$true>]
[-EndDate 'DateTime'] [-ExcludeFolders 'MapiFoldePath']
[-GlobalCatalog 'GCName'] [-IncludeFolders 'MapiFolderPath']
[-Locale 'Value'] [-MaxThreads 'Num']
```

```
[-RecipientKeywords 'Values'] [-ReportFile 'LocalPath']
[-SenderKeywords 'Values'] [-StartDate 'DateTime']
[-SubjectKeywords 'Values'] [-ValidateOnly <$false|$true>]
```

Usage
```
Export-Mailbox -Identity 'cpandl.com/Engineering/andyc'
-TargetFolder 'SavedMail' -TargetMailbox
' cpandl.com/Engineering/andyc'
```

Configuring Mailbox Delivery Restrictions, Permissions, and Storage Limits

You use mailbox properties to set delivery restrictions, permissions, and storage limits. To change these configuration settings for mailboxes, follow the techniques discussed in this section.

Setting Message Size Restrictions for Contacts

You set message size restrictions for contacts in much the same way that you set size restrictions for users. Follow the steps listed in the section of this chapter entitled "Setting Message Size Restrictions on Delivery to and from Individual Mailboxes."

Setting Message Size Restrictions on Delivery to and from Individual Mailboxes

Using the When The Size Of Any Attachment Is Greater Than Or Equal To Limit transport rule condition, you can set restrictions regarding the size of message attachments and specify what action to take should a message have an attachment that exceeds this limit. You set individual delivery restrictions by completing the following steps:

1. Open the Properties dialog box for the mailbox-enabled user account by double-clicking the user name in Exchange Management Console.

2. On the Mail Flow Settings tab, double-click Message Size Restrictions. As shown in Figure 8-5, you can now set the following send and receive restrictions:

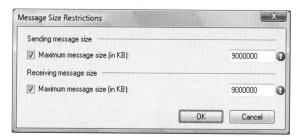

Figure 8-5   You can apply individual delivery restrictions on a per-user basis.

❑ **Sending Message Size** Sets a limit on the size of messages the user can send. If an outgoing message exceeds the limit, the message isn't sent and the user receives a nondelivery report (NDR).

❑ **Receiving Message Size** Sets a limit on the size of messages the user can receive. If an incoming message exceeds the limit, the message isn't delivered and the sender receives an NDR.

3. Click OK. The restrictions that you set override the global default settings.

Setting Send and Receive Restrictions for Contacts

You set message send and receive restrictions for contacts in the same way that you set these restrictions for users. Follow the steps listed in the section of this chapter entitled "Setting Message Send and Receive Restrictions on Individual Mailboxes."

Setting Message Send and Receive Restrictions on Individual Mailboxes

By default, user mailboxes are configured to accept messages from anyone. To override this behavior, you can:

- Specify that only messages from the listed users, contacts, or groups be accepted.

- Specify that messages from specific users, contacts, or groups listed be rejected.

- Specify that only authenticated users—meaning users who have logged on to the Exchange system or the domain—be accepted.

You set message send and receive restrictions by completing the following steps:

1. Open the Properties dialog box for the mailbox-enabled user account by double-clicking the user name in Exchange Management Console.

2. On the Mail Flow Settings tab, double-click Message Delivery Restrictions. As shown in Figure 8-6, you can now set message acceptance restrictions.

3. If you want to ensure that messages are accepted only from authenticated users, select the Require That All Senders Are Authenticated check box.

4. To accept messages from all e-mail addresses except those on the reject list, under Accept Messages From, select All Senders.

Figure 8-6   You can apply send and receive restrictions on messages on a per-user basis.

5. To specify that only messages from the listed users, contacts, or groups be accepted, select the Only Senders In The Following List option, and then add acceptable recipients:

   ❑ Click Add to display the Select Recipient dialog box.

   ❑ Select a recipient, and then click OK. Repeat as necessary.

   > **Tip**   You can select multiple recipients at the same time. To select multiple recipients individually, hold down the Ctrl key and then click each recipient that you want to select. To select a sequence of recipients, hold down the Shift key, select the first recipient, and then click the last recipient.

6. To specify that no recipients should be rejected, under Reject Messages From, select No Senders.

7. To reject messages from specific recipients, under Reject Messages From, select Senders In The Following List, and then add unacceptable recipients.

   ❑ Click Add to display the Select Recipients dialog box.

   ❑ Select a recipient, and then click OK. Repeat as necessary

8. Click OK.

Permitting Others to Access a Mailbox

Occasionally, users will need to access someone else's mailbox, and in certain situations, you should allow this. For example, if John is Susan's manager and Susan is going on vacation, John might need access to her mailbox while she's away. Another situation in which someone might need access to another mailbox is when you've set up special-purpose mailboxes, such as a mailbox for Webmaster@domain.com or a mailbox for Info@domain.com.

You can grant permissions for a mailbox in two way:

- You can grant access to a mailbox and its content.

- You can grant the right to send messages on behalf of the mailbox owner.

Using standard mail flow settings, you can grant or revoke access to these general permissions collectively. Granting someone the right to access a mailbox in this way also gives that person the right to view the mailbox and send messages on behalf of the mailbox owner. You can grant or revoke access through standard mail flow settings by completing the following steps:

1. Open the Properties dialog box for the mailbox-enabled user account by double-clicking the user name in Exchange Management Console.

2. On the Mail Flow Settings tab, double-click Delivery Options. The Grant This Permission To list box shows any users that currently have access permissions. You can now do the following:

   ❏ **Grant access** To grant the authority to access the mailbox, click Add, and then use the Select Recipient dialog box to choose the user or users who should have access to the mailbox.

   ❏ **Revoke access** To revoke the authority to access the mailbox, select an existing user name in the Grant This Permission To list box, and then click Remove.

3. Click OK.

If you want to grant access to a mailbox and its contents but not grant Send As permissions, use the Manage Full Access Permission Wizard. In the Exchange Management Console, right-click the mailbox you want to work with and then select Manage Full Access Permission. In the Manage Full Access Permission Wizard, click Add, and then use the Select Recipient dialog box to choose the user or users who should have access to the mailbox. To revoke the authority to access the mailbox, select an existing user name in the Security Principal list box and then click Remove. Click Manage to set the desired access permissions.

In the Exchange Management Shell, you can use the Add-MailboxPermission and Remove-MailboxPermission cmdlets to manage full access permissions. Samples 8-11 and 8-12 show examples of using these cmdlets. In these examples, the AccessRights parameter is set to FullAccess to indicate you are setting full access permissions on the mailbox.

Sample 8-11   Adding full access permissions

```
Syntax
Add-MailboxPermission -Identity 'UserBeingGrantedPermission'
 -User 'UserWhoseMailboxIsBeingConfigure' -AccessRights 'FullAccess'
```

```
Usage
Add-MailboxPermission -Identity 'CN=Scott Seely,
OU=Engineering,DC=cpandl,DC=com'
 -User 'CPANDL\boba' -AccessRights 'FullAccess'
```

Sample 8-12   Removing full access permissions

```
Syntax
Remove-MailboxPermission -Identity 'UserBeingGrantedPermission'
 -User 'UserWhoseMailboxIsBeingConfigure' -AccessRights 'FullAccess'
-InheritanceType 'All'
```

```
Usage
Remove-MailboxPermission -Identity 'CN=Scott Seely,
OU=Engineering,DC=cpandl,DC=com'
 -User 'CPANDL\boba' -AccessRights 'FullAccess' -InheritanceType 'All'
```

If you want to allow another user to send messages on behalf of the mailbox owner, you can do this using the Manage Send As Permission Wizard. In the Exchange Management Console, right-click the mailbox you want to work with and then select Manage Send As Permission. In the Manage Send As Permission Wizard, click Add, and then use the Select Recipient dialog box to choose the user or users who should have Send As permission on the mailbox. To revoke Send As permission, select an existing user name in the Security Principal list box, and then click Remove. Click Manage to set the desired access permissions.

In the Exchange Management Shell, you can use the Add-ADPermission and Remove-ADPermission cmdlets to manage Send As permissions. Sample 8-13 and 8-14 show examples using these cmdlets. In these examples, the ExtendedRights parameter is set to Send-As to indicate you are setting Send As permissions on the mailbox.

Sample 8-13   Adding Send As permissions

```
Syntax
Add-ADPermission -Identity 'UserBeingGrantedPermission'
 -User 'UserWhoseMailboxIsBeingConfigure' -ExtendedRights 'Send-As'
```

```
Usage
Add-ADPermission
 -Identity 'CN=Scott Seely,OU=Engineering,DC=cpandl,DC=com'
 -User 'CPANDL\boba' -ExtendedRights 'Send-As'
```

Sample 8-14 Removing Send As permissions

```
Syntax
Remove-ADPermission -Identity 'UserBeingRevokedPermission'
 -User 'UserWhoseMailboxIsBeingConfigure' -ExtendedRights 'Send-As'
-InheritanceType 'All' -ChildObjectTypes $null
 -InheritedObjectTypes $null
-Properties $null
```

```
Usage
Remove-ADPermission -
Identity 'CN=Scott Seely,OU=Engineering,DC=cpandl,DC=com'
 -User 'CPANDL\boba' -ExtendedRights 'Send-As' -InheritanceType 'All'
-ChildObjectTypes $null -InheritedObjectTypes $null
-Properties $null
```

Note Another way to grant access permissions to mailboxes is to do so through Outlook. Using Outlook, you have more granular control over permissions. You can allow a user to log on as the mailbox owner, delegate mailbox access, and grant various levels of access. For more information on this issue, see the sections of Chapter 3, "Managing Microsoft Exchange Server 2007 Clients," entitled "Accessing Multiple Exchange Server Mailboxes" and "Granting Permission to Access Folders Without Delegating Access."

Forwarding E-mail to a New Address

Any messages sent to a user's mailbox can be forwarded to another recipient. This recipient could be another user or a mail-enabled contact. You can also specify that messages should be delivered to both the forwarding address and the current mailbox.

To configure mail forwarding, follow these steps:

1. Open the Properties dialog box for the mailbox-enabled user account by double-clicking the user name in Exchange Management Console.

2. On the Mail Flow Settings tab, double-click Delivery Options.

3. To remove forwarding, in the Forwarding Address panel, clear the Forward To check box.

4. To add forwarding, select the Forward To check box, and then click Browse. Use the Select Recipient dialog box to choose the alternate recipient.

5. If messages should go to both the alternate recipient and the current mailbox owner, select the Deliver Messages To Both Forwarding Address And Mailbox check box (see Figure 8-7). Click OK.

Figure 8-7   Using the Delivery Options dialog box, you can specify alternate recipients for mailboxes and deliver mail to the current mailbox as well.

Setting Storage Restrictions on an Individual Mailbox

You can set storage restrictions on multiple mailboxes using global settings for each mailbox database or on individual mailboxes using per-user restrictions. Global restrictions are applied when you create a mailbox and are reapplied when you define new global storage restrictions. Per-user storage restrictions are set individually for each mailbox and override the global default settings.

Note   Storage restrictions apply only to mailboxes stored on the server. They don't apply to personal folders. Personal folders are stored on the user's computer.

You'll learn how to set global storage restrictions in Chapter 12, "Mailbox and Public Folder Database Administration." See the section of that chapter entitled "Setting Mailbox Database Limits and Deletion Retention."

You set individual storage restrictions by completing the following steps:

1. Open the Properties dialog box for the mailbox-enabled user account by double-clicking the user name in Exchange Management Console.

2. On the Mailbox Settings tab, double-click Storage Quotas. This displays the Storage Quotas dialog box, shown in Figure 8-8.

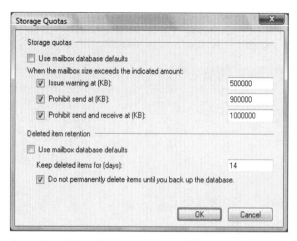

Figure 8-8   Using the Storage Quotas dialog box, you can specify storage limits and deleted item retention on a per-user basis when necessary.

3. To set mailbox storage limits, in the Storage Quotas panel, clear the Use Mailbox Database Defaults check box. Then set one or more of the following storage limits:

   ❑ **Issue Warning At (KB)**   This limit specifies the size, in kilobytes, that a mailbox can reach before a warning is issued to the user. The warning tells the user to clean out the mailbox.

   ❑ **Prohibit Send At (KB)**   This limit specifies the size, in kilobytes, that a mailbox can reach before the user is prohibited from sending any new mail. The restriction ends when the user clears out the mailbox and the mailbox size is under the limit.

   ❑ **Prohibit Send And Receive At (KB)**   This limit specifies the size, in kilobytes, that a mailbox can reach before the user is prohibited from sending and receiving mail. The restriction ends when the user clears out the mailbox and the mailbox size is under the limit.

   Caution   Prohibiting send and receive might cause the user to lose e-mail. When someone sends a message to a user who is prohibited from receiving messages, an NDR is generated and delivered to the sender. The original recipient never sees the e-mail. Because of this, you should rarely prohibit send and receive.

4. Click OK twice.

Setting Deleted Item Retention Time on Individual Mailboxes

When a user deletes a message in Microsoft Office Outlook 2007, the message is placed in the Deleted Items folder. The message remains in the Deleted Items folder until the user deletes it manually or allows Outlook to clear out the Deleted Items folder. With personal folders, the message is then permanently deleted and you can't restore it. With server-based mailboxes, the message isn't actually deleted from the Exchange information store. Instead, the message is marked as hidden and kept for a specified period of time called the *deleted item retention period*.

Default retention settings are configured for each mailbox database in the organization. You can change these settings, as described in the section of Chapter 12 entitled "Setting Mailbox Database Limits and Deletion Retention," or override the settings on a per-user basis by completing these steps:

1. Open the Properties dialog box for the mailbox-enabled user account by double-clicking the user name in Exchange Management Console.

2. On the Mailbox Settings tab, double-click Storage Quotas. This displays the Storage Quotas dialog box, shown previously in Figure 8-8.

3. In the Deleted Item Retention panel, clear the Use Mailbox Database Defaults check box.

4. In the Keep Deleted Items For (Days) text box, enter the number of days to retain deleted items. An average retention period is 14 days. If you set the retention period to 0, messages aren't retained and can't be recovered.

5. You can also specify that deleted messages should not be permanently removed until the mailbox database has been backed up. This option ensures that the deleted items are archived into at least one backup set. Click OK twice.

Real World   Deleted item retention is convenient because it allows the administrator the chance to salvage accidentally deleted e-mail without restoring a user's mailbox from backup. I strongly recommend that you enable this setting, either in the mailbox database or for individual mailboxes, and configure the retention period accordingly.

Chapter 9
Working with Distribution Groups and Address Lists

Distribution groups and address lists are extremely important in Microsoft Exchange Server 2007 administration. Careful planning of your organization's groups and address lists can save you countless hours in the long run. Unfortunately, most administrators don't have a solid understanding of these subjects, and the few who do spend most of their time on other duties. To save yourself time and frustration, study the concepts discussed in this chapter and then use the step-by-step procedures to implement the groups and lists for your organization.

Using Security and Distribution Groups

You use groups to grant permissions to similar types of users, to simplify account administration, and to make it easier to contact multiple users. For example, you can send a message addressed to a group, and the message will go to all the users in that group. Thus, instead of having to enter 20 different e-mail addresses in the message header, you enter one e-mail address for all of the group members.

Group Types, Scope, and Identifiers

Windows defines several different types of groups, and each of these groups can have a unique scope. In Active Directory domains, you use three group types:

- **Security** You use security groups to control access to network resources. You can also use user-defined security groups to distribute e-mail.

- **Standard distribution** Standard distribution groups have fixed membership, and you use them only as e-mail distribution lists. You can't use these groups to control access to network resources.

- **Dynamic distribution** Membership for dynamic distribution groups is determined based on a Lightweight Directory Access Protocol (LDAP) query; you use these groups only as e-mail distribution lists. The LDAP query is used to build the list of members whenever messages are sent to the group.

Note Dynamic distribution groups created for Exchange Server 2003 or Exchange 2000 Server are not compatible with Exchange Server 2007 and aren't displayed in the Exchange Management Console. You can resolve this by forcing an upgrade. See "Modifying Dynamic Distribution Groups Using Cmdlets" later in this chapter for details.

Security groups can have different scopes—*domain local, built-in local, global,* and *universal*—so that they are valid in different areas of your Active Directory forest. Previously, you could also create distribution groups with different scopes as well. To simplify group management, Exchange Server 2007 supports groups only with universal scope. You can mail-enable security groups with universal scope, and you can create new distribution groups with universal scope.

> **Real World**   If your organization has existing mail-enabled security groups or distribution groups with global scope, you will not be able to use those groups with Exchange Server 2007. You will either need to create a new architecture for your groups or convert those groups to universal groups. Using Active Directory Users And Computers, domain administrators can easily convert global groups to universal groups. They simply need to double-click the group entry, select Universal under Group Scope, and then click OK. However, some conversion restrictions apply. For example, you can convert a global group only if it isn't a member of another global group. In addition, pre-planning is recommended to determine the impact on Active Directory.

Groups with universal scope:

- Can contain user accounts from any domain in the forest as well as other groups from any domain in the forest.

- Can be put into other groups and assigned permissions in any domain in the forest.

When you work with dynamic distribution groups, keep in mind that the membership can include only members of the local domain, or it can include users and groups from other domains, domain trees, or forests. Scope is determined by the default apply-filter container you associate with the group when you create it. More specifically, the default apply-filter container defines the root of the search hierarchy and the LDAP query filters to recipients in and below the specified container. For example, if the apply-filter container you associate with the group is cpandl.com, the query filter is applied to all recipients in this domain. If the apply-filter container you associate with the organizational unit is Engineering, the query filter is applied to all recipients in or below this container.

As with user accounts, Windows uses unique security identifiers (SIDs) to track groups. This means that you can't delete a group, re-create it, and then expect all the permissions and privileges to remain the same. The new group will have a new SID, and all the permissions and privileges of the old group will be lost.

When to Use Security and Standard Distribution Groups

Exchange Server 2007 changes the rules about how you can use groups. Previously, you could use groups with different scopes, but now you can only use groups with universal scope. As a result, you might need to rethink how and when you use groups.

You must change the scope of any global group to universal before you can mail-enable it. Rather than duplicating your existing security group structure with distribution groups that have the same purpose, you might want to selectively mail-enable your universal security groups. For example, if you have a universal security group called Marketing, you don't need to create a MarketingDistList distribution group. Instead, you could enable Exchange mail on the original universal security group.

You can mail-enable built-in and predefined universal groups as well. Some of the groups you might want to consider mail-enabling include the following:

- Enterprise Admins

- Exchange Organization Administrators

- Exchange Public Folder Administrators

- Exchange Recipient Administrators

- Exchange View-Only Administrators

- Schema Admins

You might also want to mail-enable universal security groups that you previously defined. Then, if existing distribution groups serve the same purpose, you can delete the distribution groups.

When to Use Dynamic Distribution Groups

It's a fact of life that over time users will move to different departments, leave the company, or accept different responsibilities. With standard distribution groups, you'll spend a lot of time managing group membership when these types of changes occur—and that's where dynamic distribution groups come into the picture. With dynamic distribution groups, there isn't a fixed group membership and you don't have to add or remove users from groups. Instead, group membership is determined by the results of an LDAP query sent to your organization's Global Catalog (or dedicated expansion) server whenever mail is sent to the distribution group.

Dynamic distribution groups can be used with or without a dedicated expansion server. You'll get the most benefit from dynamic distribution without a dedicated expansion server when the member list returned in the results is relatively small (fewer than 25 members). In the case of potentially hundreds or thousands of members, however, dynamic distribution is inefficient and could require a great deal of processing to complete. To resolve this problem, you can shift the processing requirements from the Global Catalog server to a dedicated expansion server (a server whose only task is to expand the LDAP queries). However, it could still take several minutes to resolve and expand large distribution lists. For more information on expansion servers, see "Designating an Expansion Server" and "Modifying Dynamic Distribution Groups Using Cmdlets" later in this chapter.

One other thing to note about dynamic distribution is that you can associate only one specific query with each distribution group. For example, you could create separate groups for each department in the organization. You could have groups called QD-Accounting, QD-BizDev, QD-Engineering, QD-Marketing, QD-Operations, QD-Sales, and QD-Support. You could, in turn, create a standard distribution group or a dynamic distribution group called AllEmployees that contains these groups as members—thereby establishing a distribution group hierarchy.

When using multiple parameters with dynamic distribution, keep in mind that multiple parameters typically work as logical AND operations. For example, if you create a query with a parameter that matches all employees in the state of Washington with all employees in the Marketing department, the query results will not contain a list of all employees in Washington and all Marketing employees. Rather, the results will contain a list only of recipients who both are in Washington and are members of the Marketing group. In this case, you get the expected results by creating a dynamic distribution group for all Washington state employees, another dynamic distribution group for all Marketing employees, and a final group that has as members the other two distribution groups.

Working with Security and Standard Distribution Groups

As you set out to work with groups, you'll find that some tasks are specific to each type of group and some tasks can be performed with any type of group. Because of this, I've divided the group management discussion into three sections. In this section, you'll learn about the typical tasks you perform with security and standard distribution groups. The next section discusses tasks you'll perform only with dynamic distribution groups. The third section discusses general management tasks.

You can use the Exchange Management Console or the Exchange Management Shell to work with groups.

Creating Security and Standard Distribution Groups

You use groups to manage permissions and to distribute e-mail. As you set out to create groups, remember that you create groups for similar types of users. Consequently, the types of groups you might want to create include the following:

- **Groups for departments within the organization**   Generally, users who work in the same department need access to similar resources and should be a part of the same e-mail distribution lists.

- **Groups for roles within the organization**   You can also organize groups according to the users' roles within the organization. For example, you could use a group called Executives to send e-mail to all the members of the executive team and a group called Managers to send e-mail to all managers and executives in the organization.

- **Groups for users of specific projects** Often, users working on a major project need a way to send e-mail to all the members of the team. To solve this problem, you can create a group specifically for the project.

You can create groups two ways. You can mail-enable an existing universal security group or you can create an entirely new distribution group.

Mail-Enabling an Existing Universal Security Group

To mail-enable an existing universal security group, complete the following steps:

1. In Exchange Management Console, expand the Recipient Configuration node and then select the related Distribution Group node.

   Note Only recipients in the current domain or organization unit are displayed. To view recipients in other domains or organizational units, right-click the Recipient Configuration node and then select Modify Recipient Scope. Use the options provided to configure the scope to use and then click OK.

2. Right-click the Distribution Group node, and then select New Distribution Group. This starts the New Distribution Group Wizard.

3. On the Introduction page, select Existing Group, and then click Browse.

4. In the Select Group dialog box, shown in Figure 9-1, select the universal security group you want to mail-enable, and then click OK. Universal security groups for the current domain are listed by name and group type.

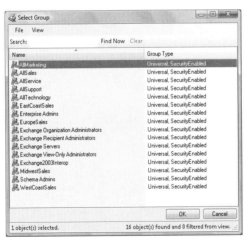

Figure 9-1 Use the Select Group dialog box to select the existing universal security group to mail-enable.

5. Click Next. On the Group Information page, the name details for the group are filled in automatically based on the details for the group you selected. You cannot change the group name or the pre-Windows 2007 group name.

6. Like users, groups have an Exchange alias. The Exchange alias is set to the group name by default. You can change this value by entering a new alias. The Exchange alias is used to set the group's e-mail address. If necessary, change the default alias.

7. Click Next, and then click New to create the group. An e-mail address is configured automatically for Simple Mail Transfer Protocol (SMTP). Exchange Server uses the SMTP address for receiving messages. After Exchange creates the group, click Finish.

8. Mail-enabling the group isn't the final step. Afterward, you might want to do the following:

   ❑ Add members to the group.

   ❑ Make the group a member of other groups.

   ❑ Assign a manager as a point of contact for the group.

   ❑ Set message size restrictions for messages mailed to the group.

   ❑ Limit users who can send to the group.

   ❑ Change or remove default e-mail addresses.

   ❑ Add additional e-mail addresses.

In the Exchange Management Shell, you can mail-enable a universal security group using the Enable-DistributionGroup cmdlet. Sample 9-1 provides the syntax and usage.

Sample 9-1   Enable-DistributionGroup cmdlet syntax and usage

```
Syntax
Enable-DistributionGroup -Identity 'GroupIdentity'
 -DisplayName 'DisplayName'
 -Alias 'ExchangeAlias'
```

```
Usage
Enable- DistributionGroup -Identity 'cpandl.com/Users/AllSales'
 -DisplayName 'All Sales'
 -Alias 'AllSales'
```

You can manage mail-enabled security groups in several ways. You can add or remove group members as discussed in the "Assigning and Removing Membership for

Individual Users, Groups, and Contacts" section of this chapter. If a group should no longer be mail-enabled, you can right-click it and select Disable to remove the Exchange settings from the group. If you no longer need a mail-enabled security group and it is not a built-in group, you can permanently remove it from Active Directory by right-clicking it and selecting Remove.

Using the Exchange Management Shell, you can disable a group's Exchange features using the Disable-DistributionGroup cmdlet, as shown in Sample 9-2.

Sample 9-2   Disable-DistributionGroup cmdlet syntax and usage

```
Syntax
Disable-DistributionGroup -Identity 'Identity'

Usage
Disable-DistributionGroup -Identity 'cpandl.com/Users/AllSales'
```

Creating a New Distribution Group

You can create a new distribution group by completing the following steps:

1. In Exchange Management Console, expand the Recipient Configuration node and then select the related Distribution Group node.

   Note   Only recipients in the current domain or organization unit are displayed. To view recipients in other domains or organizational units, right-click the Recipient Configuration node and then select Modify Recipient Scope. Use the options provided to configure the scope to use and then click OK.

2. Right-click the Distribution Group node, and then select New Distribution Group. This starts the New Distribution Group Wizard.

3. On the Introduction page, accept the default selection to create a new group, and click Next.

4. On the Group Information page, shown in Figure 9-2, the Organizational Unit field shows where in Active Directory the group will be created. By default, this is the Users container in the current domain. Because you'll usually need to create new groups in a specific organizational unit rather than the Users container, click Browse. Use the Select Organizational Unit dialog box to choose the location in which to store the account, and then click OK.

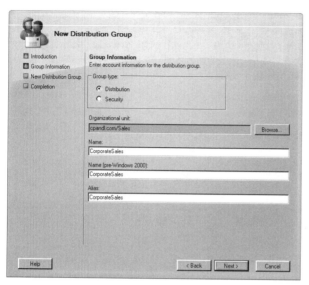

Figure 9-2 Configure the group's domain settings.

5. Select a group type—either Security or Distribution. Generally, you'll want to create a mail-enabled security group if you also want to use the group to manage access permissions. Otherwise, you'll want to create a distribution group to use the group only for mail distribution.

6. Type a name for the group. Group names aren't case-sensitive and can be up to 64 characters long.

7. The first 20 characters of the group name are used to set the pre–Windows 2000 group name. This group name must be unique in the domain. If necessary, change the pre–Windows 2000 group name.

8. Like users, groups have an Exchange alias. The Exchange alias is set to the group name by default. You can change this value by entering a new alias. The Exchange alias is used to set the group's e-mail address.

9. Click Next, and then click New to create the group. An e-mail address is configured automatically for SMTP. Exchange Server uses the SMTP address for receiving messages. Click Finish after creation of the group is complete.

10. Creating the group isn't the final step. Afterward, you might want to do the following:

   ❑ Add members to the group.

   ❑ Make the group a member of other groups.

   ❑ Assign a manager as a point of contact for the group.

- ❏   Set message size restrictions for messages mailed to the group.

- ❏   Limit users who can send to the group.

- ❏   Change or remove default e-mail addresses.

- ❏   Add additional e-mail addresses.

In the Exchange Management Shell, you can create a new distribution group using the New-DistributionGroup cmdlet. Sample 9-3 provides the syntax and usage. You can set the Type parameter to Distribution for a distribution group or to Security for a security group.

Sample 9-3   New-DistributionGroup cmdlet syntax and usage

```
Syntax
New-DistributionGroup –Name 'ExchangeName' –Type 'GroupType'
 -OrganizationalUnit 'OrganizationalUnit'
 -SamAccountName 'prewin2000logon'
 -DisplayName 'DisplayName'
 -Alias 'ExchangeAlias'
```

```
Usage
New-DistributionGroup –Name 'CorporateSales' –Type 'Distribution'
 -OrganizationalUnit 'cpandl.com/Sales'
 -SamAccountName 'CorporateSales'
 -DisplayName 'Corporate Sales'
 -Alias 'CorporateSales'
```

Assigning and Removing Membership for Individual Users, Groups, and Contacts

All users, groups, and contacts can be members of other groups. To configure a group's membership, follow these steps:

1. In Exchange Management Console, double-click the group entry. This opens the group's Properties dialog box.

2. On the Members tab, click Add to add objects to the group. The Select Recipient dialog box appears. You can now choose objects that should be members of this currently selected group. Select the recipients you want to add to the group and then click OK.

3. To remove a member from a group, select an object, and then click Remove. When you're finished, click OK.

In the Exchange Management Shell, you can add members to a group using the Add-DistributionGroupMember cmdlet. Sample 9-4 provides the syntax and usage.

Sample 9-4   Add-DistributionGroupMember cmdlet syntax and usage

```
Syntax
Add-DistributionGroupMember -Identity 'GroupIdentity'
 -Member 'RecipientIdentity'
```

```
Usage
Add-DistributionGroupMember -Identity 'cpandl.com/Users/CorpSales'
 -Member 'cpandl.com/Sales/Kim Akers'
```

In the Exchange Management Shell, you can remove members from a group using the Remove-DistributionGroupMember cmdlet. Sample 9-5 provides the syntax and usage.

Sample 9-5   Remove-DistributionGroupMember cmdlet syntax and usage

```
Syntax
Remove-DistributionGroupMember -Identity 'GroupIdentity'
 -Member 'RecipientIdentity'
```

```
Usage
Remove-DistributionGroupMember -Identity 'cpandl.com/Users/CorpSales'
 -Member 'cpandl.com/Sales/Kim Akers'
```

Working with Dynamic Distribution Groups

Just as there are tasks only for security and standard distribution groups, there are also tasks only for dynamic distribution groups. These tasks are discussed in this section.

Creating Dynamic Distribution Groups

With dynamic distribution groups, group membership is determined by the results of an LDAP query. You can create a dynamic distribution group and define the query parameters by completing the following steps:

1. In Exchange Management Console, expand the Recipient Configuration node and then select the related Distribution Group node.

2. Right-click the Distribution Group node, and then select New Dynamic Distribution Group. This starts the New Dynamic Distribution Group Wizard.

3. Click Next. On the Group Information page, the Organizational Unit field shows where in Active Directory the group will be created. By default, this is the Users container in the current domain. Because you'll usually need to create new groups in a specific organizational unit rather than the Users container, click Browse. Use the Select Organizational Unit dialog box to choose the location in which to store the account, and then click OK.

4. Type a name for the group. Group names aren't case-sensitive and can be up to 64 characters long.

5. The group name is used to set the display name. The display name is the name displayed in Microsoft Office Outlook address lists. If necessary, change the default display name.

6. Like users, groups have an Exchange alias. The Exchange alias is set to the group name by default. You can change this value by entering a new alias. The Exchange alias is used to set the group's e-mail address.

7. Click Next to display the Filter Settings page, shown in Figure 9-3. The container in which you apply the query filter defines the scope of the query, which is the LDAP query you define for the group filters to recipients in and below the specified container. The default apply-filter container is the one in which you are creating the group. To specify a different container for limiting the query scope, click Browse and then use the Select Organizational Unit dialog box to select a container. In most cases, you'll want to select the domain container.

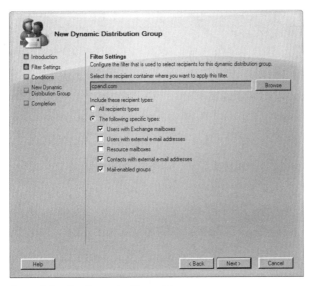

Figure 9-3   Configure the filter settings.

8. Use the Include These Recipient Types options to specify the types of recipients to include in the query. Select All Recipient Types or select The Following Specific Types, and then select the types of recipients you want to include in the dynamic distribution group.

9. Click Next. On the Conditions page, shown in Figure 9-4, you can now set the filter conditions. The following types of conditions are available as well as conditions for custom attributes:

□ **Recipient Is In A State Or Province**   Filters recipients based on the value of the State/Province text box on the Address And Phone tab in the related Properties dialog box. Click the related In The Specified State Or Province(s) link. In the Specify State Or Province dialog box, type a state or province to use as a filter condition, and then press Enter or click Add. Repeat as necessary, and then click OK.

□ **Recipient Is In A Department**   Filters recipients based on the value of the Department text box on the Organization tab in the related Properties dialog box. Click the related In The Specified Department(s) link. In the Specify Department dialog box, type a department to use as a filter condition, and then press Enter or click Add. Repeat as necessary, and then click OK.

□ **Recipient Is In A Company**   Filters recipients based on the value of the Company text box on the Organization tab in the related Properties dialog box. Click the related In The Specified Company(s) link. In the Specify Company dialog box, type a company name to use as a filter condition, and then press Enter or click Add. Repeat as necessary, and then click OK.

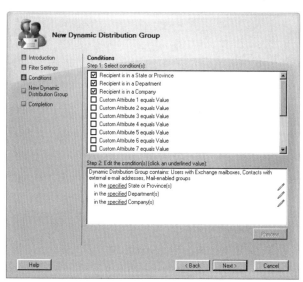

Figure 9-4   Set the filter conditions.

10. Click Preview to run the query and display a list of matching recipients by display name, alias, and organizational unit. Click OK.

11. Click Next and then click New to create the group. An e-mail address is configured automatically for SMTP. Exchange Server uses the SMTP address for receiving messages. Click Finish.

12. Creating the group isn't the final step. Afterward, you might want to do the following:

    ❑ Assign a manager as a point of contact for the group.

    ❑ Set message size restrictions for messages mailed to the group.

    ❑ Limit users who can send to the group.

    ❑ Change or remove default e-mail addresses.

    ❑ Add additional e-mail addresses.

In the Exchange Management Shell, you can create a dynamic distribution group using the New-DynamicDistributionGroup cmdlet. Sample 9-6 provides the syntax and usage.

Sample 9-6   New-DynamicDistributionGroup cmdlet syntax and usage

```
Syntax
New-DynamicDistributionGroup -Name 'ExchangeName'
 -OrganizationalUnit 'OrganizationalUnit' -DisplayName 'DisplayName'
 -Alias 'Alias' -IncludedRecipients 'RecipientTypes'
 -ConditionalCompany 'CompanyNameFilter1', 'CompanyNameFilter2',...
 -ConditionalDepartment 'DeptNameFilter1',' DeptNameFilter2', ...
 -ConditionalStateOrProvince 'StateNameFilter1', 'StateNameFilter2', ...
 -RecipientContainer 'ApplyFilterContainer'
```

```
Usage
New-DynamicDistributionGroup -Name 'CrossSales'
 -OrganizationalUnit 'cpandl.com/Users' -DisplayName 'CrossSales'
 -Alias 'CrossSales'
 -IncludedRecipients 'MailboxUsers, MailContacts, MailGroups'
 -ConditionalCompany 'City Power & Light'
 -ConditionalDepartment 'Sales','Marketing'
 -ConditionalStateOrProvince 'Washington'
 -RecipientContainer 'cpandl.com'
```

Changing Apply-To Filters

With dynamic distribution groups, the container in which you apply a query filter determines the scope of the query, which is the LDAP query you define for a group filters to recipients in and below the specified container. You can change the apply-filter container or modify the types of recipients to search for by completing the following steps:

1. In Exchange Management Console, double-click the dynamic distribution group entry. This opens the group's Properties dialog box.

2. On the Filter tab, the current apply-filter container is listed. To specify a different container for limiting the query scope, click Browse, and then use the Select Organizational Unit dialog box to select a container.

3. Use the Include These Recipient Types options to specify the type of recipients to include in the query. Select either All Recipient Types or select The Following Specific Types, and then select the types of recipients. Click OK.

Changing Filter Conditions

With dynamic distribution groups, the filter conditions determine the exact criteria that must be met for a recipient to be included in the dynamic distribution group. You can modify the filter conditions by completing the following steps:

1. In Exchange Management Console, double-click the dynamic distribution group entry. This opens the group's Properties dialog box.

2. On the Conditions tab, the current conditions are listed. The following types of conditions are available as well as conditions for custom attributes:

    ❑ **Recipient Is In A State Or Province**   Filters recipients based on the value of the State/Province field on the Address And Phone tab in the related Properties dialog box. Click the related In The Specified State Or Province(s) link. In the Specify State Or Province dialog box, add or remove states or provinces as necessary, and then click OK.

    ❑ **Recipient Is In A Department**   Filters recipients based on the value of the Department field on the Organization tab in the related Properties dialog box. Click the related In The Specified Department(s) link. In the Specify Department dialog box, add or remove departments as necessary, and then click OK.

    ❑ **Recipient Is In A Company**   Filters recipients based on the value of the Company field on the Organization tab in the related Properties dialog box. Click the related In The Specified Company(s) link. In the Specify Company dialog box, add or remove company names, and then click OK.

3. Click OK.

Designating an Expansion Server

When there are potentially hundreds or thousands of members, dynamic distribution groups are inefficient and could require a great deal of processing to complete. This is why the expansion process normally is handled by your organization's Global Catalog servers. However, in some cases, you might want a dedicated expansion server to handle expansion processing. The dedicated expansion server can be any Exchange server in your organization acting as a Global Catalog server, and you'll usually want to configure at least one dedicated expansion server per Active Directory site.

You can specify a dedicated expansion server for a dynamic distribution group by completing these steps:

1. In Exchange Management Console, double-click the dynamic distribution group entry. This opens the group's Properties dialog box.

2. On the Advanced tab, use the Expansion Server drop-down list to select the expansion server you want to use. If you can, select a specific Global Catalog server or allow any Global Catalog server to be used. Click OK.

Modifying Dynamic Distribution Groups Using Cmdlets

In the Exchange Management Shell, you can modify the filters and conditions associated with a dynamic distribution group using the Set-DynamicDistribution-Group cmdlet. This cmdlet has several other uses as well. You can use it to:

- Specify a dedicated expansion server to enhance query processing. Set the –ExpansionServer parameter to the identity of the Global Catalog server to use.

- Upgrade dynamic distribution groups created for Exchange 2003 and Exchange 2000 to allow incompatible dynamic distribution groups to be rewritten to work with Exchange Server 2007. Set –ForceUpgrade $true, and then modify any incompatible included recipients or recipient filters as necessary.

Sample 9-7 provides the syntax and usage for the Set-DynamicDistributionGroup cmdlet.

Sample 9-7   Set-DynamicDistributionGroup cmdlet syntax and usage

```
Syntax
Set-DynamicDistributionGroup -Identity 'GroupIdentity'
[-Alias 'NewAlias']
[-AcceptMessagesOnlyFrom 'Recipient']
[-AcceptMessagesOnlyFromDLMembers 'Recipient']
[-ConditionalCompany 'Values'] [-ConditionalDepartment 'Values']
[-ConditionalStateOrProvince 'Values'] [-DisplayName 'Name']
[-DisplayName 'Name'] [-DomainController 'DCName']
[-EmailAddresses 'ProxyAddress']
[-EmailAddressPolicyEnabled <$false|$true>]
[-ExpansionServer 'Server'] [-ForceUpgrade <$false|$true>]
[-GrantSendOnBehalfTo 'Mailbox']
[-HiddenFromAddressListsEnabled <$false|$true>]
[-IncludedRecipients 'Recipients'] [-ManagedBy 'RecipientId']
```

```
[-MaxReceiveSize 'Size'] [-MaxSendSize 'Size']
[-Name 'Name'] [-Notes 'Value'] [-PrimarySmtpAddress 'SmtpAddress']
[-RecipientContainer 'OUName'] [-RecipientFilter 'String']
[-RejectMessagesFrom 'Recipient']
[-RejectMessagesFromDLMembers 'Recipient']
[-ReportToManagerEnabled <$false|$true>]
[-ReportToOriginatorEnabled <$false|$true>]
[-RequireSenderAuthenticationEnabled <$false|$true>]
[-SendOofMessageToOriginatorEnabled <$false|$true>]
[-SimpleDisplayName 'Name'] [-WindowsEmailAddress 'SmtpAddress']
```

Usage
```
Set-DynamicDistributionGroup -Identity 'cpandl.com/Users/CrossSales'
 -IncludedRecipients 'Recipients'
 -ConditionalCompany 'City Power & Light'
 -ConditionalDepartment 'Sales','Accounting'
 -ConditionalStateOrProvince 'Washington','Idaho','Oregon'
 -RecipientContainer 'cpandl.com'
```

Usage
```
Set-DynamicDistributionGroup -Identity 'cpandl.com/Users/CrossSales'
 -ForceUpgrade $true
```

Usage
```
Set-DynamicDistributionGroup -Identity 'cpandl.com/Users/CrossSales'
 -ExpansionServer 'CorpSvr127'
```

Previewing Dynamic Distribution Group Membership

You can preview a dynamic distribution group to confirm its membership and determine how long it takes to return the query results.

■ In some cases, you might find that the membership isn't what you expected. If this happens, you'll need to change the query filters, as discussed earlier.

■ In other cases, you might find that it takes too long to execute the query and return the results. If this happens, you might want to rethink the query parameters. You might want to create several query groups.

To preview dynamic distribution group membership, follow these steps:

1. In Exchange Management Console, double-click the dynamic distribution group entry. This opens the group's Properties dialog box.

2. On the Conditions tab, click Preview.

3. When you are finished reviewing the results of the query, click OK twice.

Other Essential Tasks for Managing Groups

Previous sections covered tasks that were specific to a type of group. As an Exchange administrator, you'll find that you need to perform many additional group management tasks. These essential tasks are discussed in this section.

Changing a Group's Name Information

Each mail-enabled group has a display name, an Exchange alias, and one or more e-mail addresses associated with it. The display name is the name that appears in address lists. The Exchange alias is used to set the e-mail addresses associated with the group.

Whenever you change a group's naming information, new e-mail addresses can be generated and set as the default addresses for SMTP. These e-mail addresses are used as alternatives to e-mail addresses previously assigned to the group. To learn how to change or delete these additional e-mail addresses, see the section of this chapter entitled "Changing, Adding, or Deleting a Group's E-mail Addresses."

To change the group's Exchange name details, complete the following steps:

1. In Exchange Management Console, double-click the group entry. This opens the group's Properties dialog box.

2. On the General tab, the first text box shows the display name of the group. If necessary, type a new display name.

3. The Alias text box shows the Exchange alias. If necessary, type a new alias. Click OK.

   Note   When you change a group's display name, you give the group a new label. Changing the display name doesn't affect the SID, which is used to identify, track, and handle permissions independently from group names.

Changing, Adding, or Deleting a Group's E-mail Addresses

When you create a mail-enabled group, default e-mail addresses are created for SMTP and X.400. Any time you update the group's Exchange alias, new default e-mail addresses can be created. The old addresses aren't deleted, however; they remain as alternative e-mail addresses for the group.

To change, add, or delete a group's e-mail addresses, follow these steps:

1. In Exchange Management Console, double-click the group entry. This opens the group's Properties dialog box.

2. On the E-mail Addresses tab, you can use the following techniques to manage the group's e-mail addresses:

- ❏ **Create a new SMTP address**   Click the arrow to the right of Add, and then select SMTP Address. Enter the e-mail address, and then click OK.

- ❏ **Create a custom address**   Click the arrow to the right of Add, and then select Custom Address. Enter the e-mail address, and then enter the e-mail address type. Click OK.

> **Tip**   Use SMTP as the address type for standard Internet e-mail addresses. For custom address types, such as X.400, you must manually enter the address in the proper format.

- ❏ **Set a new Reply To address**   Select the address you want to be the new default, and then click Set As Reply.

- ❏ **Edit an existing address**   Double-click the address entry. Modify the settings in the Address dialog box, and then click OK.

- ❏ **Delete an existing address**   Select the address, and then click the Remove button.

Hiding Groups from Exchange Address Lists

By default, any mail-enabled security group or other distribution group that you create is shown in Exchange address lists, such as the global address list. If you want to hide a group from the address lists, follow these steps:

1. In Exchange Management Console, double-click the group entry. This opens the group's Properties dialog box.

2. On the Advanced tab, select the Hide Group From Exchange Address Lists check box. Click OK.

> **Note**   When you hide a group, it isn't listed in Exchange address lists. However, if a user knows the name of a group, he or she can still use it in the mail client. To prevent users from sending to a group, you must set message restrictions, as discussed in the section of this chapter entitled "Setting Usage Restrictions on Groups."

> **Tip**   Hiding group membership is different from hiding the group itself. In Outlook, users can view the membership of groups. In Exchange Server 2007, you cannot prevent viewing the group membership. In addition, membership of dynamic distribution groups is not displayed in global address lists because it is generated only when mail is sent to the group.

Setting Usage Restrictions on Groups

Groups are great resources for users in an organization. They let users send mail quickly and easily to other users in their department, business unit, or office. However, if you aren't careful, people outside the organization can use groups as well. Would your boss like it if spammers sent unsolicited e-mail messages to company employees through your distribution lists? Probably not—and you'd probably be sitting in the hot seat, which would be uncomfortable, to say the least.

To prevent unauthorized use of mail-enabled groups, you can specify that only certain users or members of a particular group can send messages to the group. For example, if you created a group called AllEmployees, of which all company employees were members, you could specify that only the members of AllEmployees could send messages to the group. You do this by specifying that only messages from AllEmployees are acceptable.

To prevent mass spamming of other groups, you could set the same restriction. For example, if you have a group called Technology, you could specify that only members of AllEmployees can send messages to that group.

> **Real World**   If you have users who telecommute or send e-mail from home using a personal account, you might be wondering how these users can send mail after you put a restriction in place. What I've done in the past is create a group called OffsiteEmailUsers and then added this as a group that can send mail to my mail-enabled groups. The OffsiteEmailUsers group contains separate mail-enabled contacts for each authorized off-site e-mail address.

Another way to prevent unauthorized use of mail-enabled groups is to specify that only mail from authenticated users is accepted. An authenticated user is any user accessing the system through a logon process. It does not include anonymous users or guests, and is not used to assign permissions. If you use this option, keep in mind that off-site users will need to log on to Exchange before they can send mail to restricted groups, which might present a problem for users who are at home or on the road.

You can set or remove usage restrictions by completing the following steps:

1. In Exchange Management Console, double-click the group entry. This opens the group's Properties dialog box.

2. On the Mail Flow Settings tab, double-click Message Delivery Restrictions.

3. If you want to ensure that messages are accepted only from authenticated users, select the Require That All Senders Are Authenticated check box.

4. To accept messages from all e-mail addresses except those on the reject list, under Accept Messages From, select All Senders.

5. To specify that only messages from the listed users, contacts, or groups be accepted, under Accept Messages From, select the Senders In The Following List option, and then add acceptable recipients:

   ❑ Click Add to display the Select Recipients dialog box.

   ❑ Select a recipient, and then click OK. Repeat as necessary.

   > **Tip** You can select multiple recipients at the same time. To select multiple recipients individually, hold down the Ctrl key, and then click each recipient that you want to select. To select a sequence of recipients, hold down the Shift key, select the first recipient, and then click the last recipient.

6. To specify that no recipients should be rejected, under Reject Messages From, select No Senders.

7. To reject messages from specific recipients, under Reject Messages From, select Senders In The Following List, and then add unacceptable recipients:

   ❑ Click Add to display the Select Recipients dialog box.

   ❑ Select a recipient, and then click OK. Repeat as necessary.

8. Click OK.

Setting Message Size Restrictions for Delivery to Groups

By default, messages of any size can be sent to distribution groups. You can change this behavior by limiting the size of messages that users can send to distribution groups. To do this, complete the following steps:

1. Open the Properties dialog box for the group by double-clicking the group name in Exchange Management Console.

2. On the Mail Flow Settings tab, double-click Message Size Restrictions.

3. Select the Maximum Message Size (In KB) check box.

4. In the text box provided, enter the maximum message size in kilobytes (KB). Be sure to set a size that allows the sending of suitably sized attachments. Click OK twice.

If a message addressed to the group exceeds the limit, the message isn't sent and the user receives a nondelivery report (NDR).

Setting Out-of-Office and Delivery Report Options for Groups

By default, distribution groups are configured so that delivery reports are sent to the person who sent the mail message. You can change this so that delivery reports are sent to the group owner or not sent at all. You can also specify out-of-office messages that are returned in response to messages from the sender. To set these options, complete the following steps:

1. Open the Properties dialog box for the group by double-clicking the group name in Exchange Management Console.

2. On the Advanced tab, if you want out-of-office messages to be delivered to the sender, select the Send Out-Of-Office Message To Originator check box.

3. If you want to stop sending delivery reports, select Do Not Send Delivery Reports. Alternately, you can send delivery reports to the group manager or the message originator. Click OK.

Deleting Groups

Deleting a group removes it permanently. After you delete a group, you can't create a group with the same name and automatically restore the permissions that the original group was assigned because the SID for the new group won't match the SID for the old group. You can reuse group names, but remember that you'll have to re-create all permissions settings.

Windows doesn't let you delete built-in groups. In the Exchange Management Console, you can remove other types of groups by right-clicking them and selecting Remove. When prompted, click Yes to delete the group. If you click No, the Exchange Management Console will not delete the group.

In the Exchange Management Shell, you can use the Remove-DistributionGroup cmdlet to remove distribution groups, as shown in Sample 9-8.

Sample 9-8   Remove-DistributionGroup cmdlet syntax and usage

```
Syntax
Remove-DistributionGroup -Identity 'Identity'
```

```
Usage
Remove-DistributionGroup -Identity 'cpandl.com/Users/AllSales'
```

To remove dynamic distribution groups, you can use the Remove-DynamicDistribution-Group cmdlet. Sample 9-9 shows the syntax and usage.

Sample 9-9   Remove-DynamicDistributionGroup cmdlet syntax and usage

```
Syntax
Remove-DynamicDistributionGroup -Identity 'Identity'
```

```
Usage
Remove-DynamicDistributionGroup -Identity 'cpandl.com/Users/
CrossSales'
```

Managing Online Address Lists

Address lists help administrators organize and manage Exchange recipients. You can use address lists to organize recipients by department, business unit, location, type, and other criteria. The default address lists that Exchange Server creates, as well as any new address lists that you create, are available to the user community. Users can navigate these address lists to find recipients to whom they want to send messages.

Using Default Address Lists

During setup, Exchange Server creates a number of default address lists, including the following:

- **Default Global Address List**   Lists all mail-enabled users, contacts, and groups in the organization.

- **Default Offline Address Book**   Provides an address list for viewing offline that contains information on all mail-enabled users, contacts, and groups in the organization.

- **All Contacts**   Lists all mail-enabled contacts in the organization.

- **All Groups**   Lists all mail-enabled groups in the organization.

- **All Rooms**   Lists all resource mailboxes for rooms.

- **Public Folders**   Lists all public folders in the organization.

- **All Users**   Lists all mail-enabled users in the organization.

The most commonly used address lists are the global address list and the offline address book.

In the Exchange Management Console, you access online address lists and offline address books by expanding the Organization Configuration node and then selecting the Mailbox node. As Figure 9-5 shows, the details pane then provides a group of tabs for managing organizational-level settings for mailbox servers. You use the Address Lists tab to manage online address lists and the Offline Address Book tab to manage offline address books.

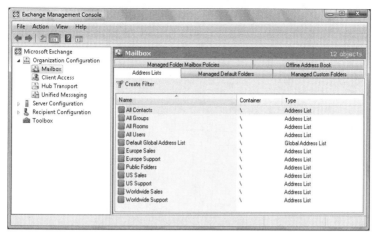

Figure 9-5   Access online address lists and offline address books under the Organization Configuration node.

Creating and Applying New Address Lists

You can create new address lists to accommodate your organization's special needs. For example, if your organization has offices in Seattle, Portland, and San Francisco, you might want to create separate address lists for each office.

To create an address list that users can select in their Outlook mail clients, follow these steps:

1. In Exchange Management Console, expand the Organization Configuration node and then select the related Mailbox node.

2. Right-click the Mailbox node in the console tree, and then select New Address List. This starts the New Address List Wizard.

3. Type a name for the address list, as shown in Figure 9-6. The name should describe the types of recipients that are viewed through the list. For example, if you're creating a list for recipients in the Boston office, you could call the list Boston E-mail Addresses.

4. The container on which you base the address list sets the scope of the list. The list will include recipients in address lists in and below the specified container. The default (root) container, \, specifies that all address lists are included by default. To specify a different container for limiting the list scope, click Browse, and then use the Select Address List dialog box to select a container. In most cases, you'll want to select the default (root) container.

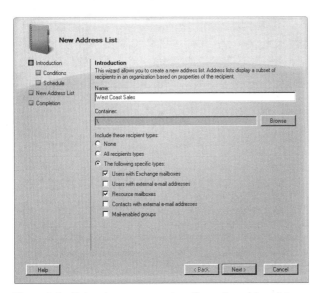

Figure 9-6 Determine a name and configure the address list.

5. Use the Include These Recipient Types options to specify the types of recipients to include in the query. Select either All Recipient Types or select The Following Specific Types, and then select the types of recipients. You can include mailbox users, mail-enabled contacts, mail-enabled groups, mail-enabled users, and resource mailboxes.

6. Click Next. On the Conditions page, you can now set the filter conditions. The following types of conditions are available as well as conditions for custom attributes:

   ❑ **Recipient Is In A State Or Province** Filters recipients to be included in the address list based on the value of the State/Province field on the Address And Phone tab in the related Properties dialog box. Click the related In The Specified State Or Province link. In the Specify State Or Province dialog box, type a state or province to use as a filter condition, and then press Enter or click Add. Repeat as necessary, and then click OK.

   ❑ **Recipient Is In A Department** Filters recipients to be included in the address list based on the value of the Department field on the Organization tab in the related Properties dialog box. Click the related In The Specified Department link. In the Specify Department dialog box, type a department to use as a filter condition, and then press Enter or click Add. Repeat as necessary, and then click OK.

❏ **Recipient Is In A Company**   Filters recipients to be included in the address list based on the value of the Company field on the Organization tab in the related Properties dialog box. Click the related In The Specified Company link. In the Specify Company dialog box, type a company name to use as a filter condition, and then press Enter or click Add. Repeat as necessary, and then click OK.

7. Click Next. If you want to create and apply the address list immediately, select Immediately. To schedule the address list creation and application, select At The Following Time, and then set the date and time to create and apply the list.

8. To specify the maximum length of time that the server can spend creating and applying the address list, select the Cancel Tasks That Are Still Running After (Hours) check box, and then set the maximum number of hours the address list task can run.

> **Note**   Cancelling after a maximum number of hours is designed to ensure that address list tasks that are blocked or not proceeding as expected are cancelled. Most address list tasks should be completed in two hours or less, but the exact duration depends on the number of recipients involved and the complexity of the filters.

9. Click Next, and then click New to create and schedule the address list to be created. After the address list is created, users will be able to use the new address list the next time they start Outlook. Click Finish.

In the Exchange Management Shell, creating and applying address lists are two separate tasks. You can create address lists using the New-AddressList cmdlet. You apply address lists using the Update-AddressList cmdlet. Sample 9-10 provides the syntax and usage for the New-AddressList cmdlet. Sample 9-11 provides the syntax and usage for the Update-AddressList cmdlet. For IncludedRecipients, you can include mailbox users, mail-enabled contacts, mail-enabled groups, mail-enabled users, and resource mailboxes.

> **Tip**   Exchange Server 2007 does not support Recipient Update Service (RUS). To replace the functionality of RUS, you can schedule the Update-AddressList and Update-EmailAddressPolicy cmdlets to run periodically using Task Scheduler.

Sample 9-10   New-AddressList cmdlet syntax and usage

```
Syntax
New-AddressList -Name 'ListName'
  -Container 'Container' -IncludedRecipients 'RecipientTypes'
  -ConditionalCompany 'CompanyNameFilter1', 'CompanyNameFilter2',...
  -ConditionalDepartment 'DeptNameFilter1',' DeptNameFilter2', ...
  -ConditionalStateOrProvince 'StateNameFilter1', 'StateNameFilter2', ...
```

```
Usage
New-AddressList -Name 'West Coast Sales'
  -Container '\'
  -IncludedRecipients 'MailboxUsers, MailContacts, MailGroups, MailUsers,
Resources'
  -ConditionalCompany 'City Power & Light'
  -ConditionalDepartment 'Sales','Marketing'
  -ConditionalStateOrProvince 'Washington','Idaho','Oregon'
```

Sample 9-11   Update-AddressList cmdlet syntax and usage

```
Syntax
Update-AddressList -identity 'ListIdentity'
```

```
Usage
Update-AddressList -Identity '\West Coast Sales'
```

Configuring Clients to Use Address Lists

Address books are available to clients that are configured for corporate or workgroup use. To set the address lists used by the client, complete these steps:

1. In Office Outlook 2007, from the Tools menu, select Address Book.

2. In the Address Book dialog box, from the Tools menu, select Options, and then set the following options to configure how address lists are used:

   ❑ **Show This Address List First**   Sets the address book that the user sees first whenever he or she works with the address book.

   ❑ **Keep Personal Addresses In**   Specifies the default address book for storing new addresses.

   ❑ **When Sending Mail, Check Names Using These Address Lists In The Following Order**   Sets the order in which Outlook searches address books when you send a message or click Check Names. Use the up and down arrows to change the list order.

3. Click OK.

Tip   When checking names, you'll usually want the global address list (GAL) to be listed before the user's own contacts or other types of address lists. This is important, because users will often put internal mailboxes in their personal address lists. The danger of doing this without first resolving names against the GAL is that although the display name might be identical, the *properties* of a mailbox might change. When changes occur, the entry in the user's address book is no longer valid and any mail sent will bounce back to the sender with a nondelivery receipt (NDR).

To correct this, the user should either remove that mailbox from his or her personal address list and add it based on the current entry in the GAL, or change the check names resolution order to use the GAL before any personal lists.

Updating Address List Configuration and Membership Throughout the Domain

Exchange Server doesn't immediately replicate changes to address lists throughout the domain. Instead, changes are replicated during the normal replication cycle, which means that some servers might temporarily have outdated address list information. Rather than waiting for replication, you can manually update address list configuration, availability, and membership throughout the domain. To do this, follow these steps:

1. In Exchange Management Console, expand the Organization Configuration node by double-clicking it, and then select the related Mailbox node.

2. In the details pane, right-click the address list you want to update, and then select Apply.

3. If you want to update the address list immediately, select Immediately. To schedule the address list creation and application, select At The Following Time, and then set the date and time to create and apply the list.

4. To specify the maximum length of time that the server can spend creating and applying the address list, select the Cancel Tasks That Are Still Running After (Hours) check box, and then set the maximum number of hours the address list task can run.

5. Click Next and then click Apply. Click Finish.

Sample 9-11 shows how to update and apply address lists.

Editing Address Lists

Although you can't change the properties of default address lists, you can change the properties of address lists that you create. To do this, complete the following steps:

1. In Exchange Management Console, expand the Organization Configuration node and then select the related Mailbox node.

2. In the details pane, right-click the address list you want to edit, and then select Edit. This starts the Edit Address List Wizard.

3. Modify the name as necessary, and then use the Include These Recipient Types options to specify the types of recipients to include in the query. Select All Recipient Types, or select The Following Specific Types and then select the types of recipients.

4. Click Next. On the Conditions page, you can manage the filter conditions.

5. Click Next. If you want to modify the address list but apply the changes as part of Exchange's regular housekeeping, select Do Not Apply. To apply the address list changes now, select Immediately. To schedule the address list creation and application, select At The Following Time, and then set the date and time to create and apply the list.

6. To specify the maximum length of time that the server can spend creating and applying the address list, select the Cancel Tasks That Are Still Running After (Hours) check box, and then set the maximum number of hours the address list task can run.

7. Click Next, and then click Edit to apply the changes.

8. Click Finish.

In the Exchange Management Shell, you can modify an address list using the Set-AddressList cmdlet. Sample 9-12 provides the syntax and usage. You can upgrade address lists created for Exchange Server 2003 and Exchange 2000 Server to allow incompatible address lists to be rewritten to work with Exchange Server 2007. Set –ForceUpgrade $true, and then modify any incompatible included recipients or recipient filters as necessary. After you update an address list, you can make the changes visible by using the update-AddressList cmdlet, as shown previously in Sample 9-11.

Sample 9-12 Set-AddressList cmdlet syntax and usage

```
Syntax
Set-AddressList [-Identity 'ListIdentity' | -Instance 'ListIdentity']
[-Name 'NewListName'] [-IncludedRecipients 'RecipientTypes']
[-ConditionalCompany 'CompanyNameFilter1', 'CompanyNameFilter2',... ]
[-ConditionalDepartment 'DeptNameFilter1', 'DeptNameFilter2', ... ]
[-ConditionalStateOrProvince 'StateNameFilter1', 'StateNameFilter2', ... ]
[-DisplayName 'Name'] [-DomainController 'DCName']
[-ForceUpgrade <$false|$true>]
```

```
Usage
Set-AddressList –Identity '\West Coast Sales' -Name 'Sales Team-West'
-IncludedRecipients 'MailboxUsers, MailContacts, MailGroups'
 -Company 'City Power & Light'
 -Department 'Sales','Marketing'
 -StateOrProvince 'Washington','Idaho','Oregon'
```

```
Usage
Set-AddressList –Identity '\West Coast Sales' -Name 'Sales Team-West'
 -IncludedRecipients 'MailboxUsers, MailContacts, MailGroups'
 -ForceUpgrade $true
```

Renaming and Deleting Address Lists

Although the Exchange Management Console will let you rename and delete default address lists, you really shouldn't do this. Instead, you should rename or delete only user-defined address lists.

■ **Renaming address lists**   To rename an address list, in Exchange Management Console, right-click its entry, and then select Edit. Type a new name in the Name text box. Click Next three times. Click Edit, and then click Finish.

■ **Deleting address lists**   To delete an address list, in Exchange Management Console, right-click its entry, and then select Remove. When prompted to confirm the action, click Yes.

In the Exchange Management Shell, you can remove address lists using the Remove-AddressList cmdlet. Sample 9-13 provides the syntax and usage. If you also want to remove address lists that reference the address list you are removing and match a portion of it (child address lists), you can set the Recursive parameter to $true. By default, the cmdlet does not remove child address lists of the specified list.

Sample 9-13   Remove-AddressList cmdlet syntax and usage

```
Syntax
Remove-AddressList -Identity 'ListIdentity'
[-DomainController 'DCName'] [-Recursive <$false|$true>]
```

```
Usage
Remove-AddressList -Identity '\West Coast Sales'
```

Managing Offline Address Books

You configure offline address books differently than online address lists. To use an offline address book, the client must be configured to have a local copy of the server mailbox, or you can use personal folders. Clients using Outlook 2003 or earlier versions of Outlook retrieve the offline address books from Exchange using the Mail Application Programming Interface (MAPI) protocol. Clients using Office Outlook 2007 or later versions of Outlook retrieve the offline address book from the designated offline address book (OAB) distribution point.

Note   An OAB distribution point is a virtual directory to which Office Outlook 2007 clients can connect to download the OAB. OAB distribution points are hosted by servers running Internet Information Services (IIS) as virtual directories. Each distribution point can have two URLs associated with it: one URL for internal (on-site) access and another for external (off-site) access. See Chapter 16, "Managing Client Access Servers," for details on configuring OAB distribution points.

Creating Offline Address Books

By default, the default offline address book includes all the addresses in the global address list. It does this by including the default Global Address List. All other offline address books are created by including the default Global Address List or a specific online address list as well.

You can create other custom offline address books by completing the following steps:

1. In Exchange Management Console, expand the Organization Configuration node by double-clicking it, and then select the related Mailbox node.

2. Right-click the Mailbox node in the console tree, and then select New Offline Address Book. This starts the New Offline Address Book Wizard.

3. Type a name for the address book, as shown in Figure 9-7. The name should describe the types of recipients that are viewed through the offline address book.

Figure 9-7   Set the name and configure the offline address book.

4. Offline address books are generated on designated mailbox servers. To specify the server to use to generate the address book, click Browse. In the Select Mailbox Server dialog box, select the mailbox server to use, and then click OK.

5. The default Global Address List is included by default. Clear the Include The Default Global Address List check box if you do not want to include it.

6. To include other address lists, select the Include The Following Address Lists check box. Click Add. In the Select Address List dialog box, click the address list to use, and then click OK. Repeat this step as necessary to include other address lists.

7. On the Distribution Points page, shown in Figure 9-8, select the distribution points to use. The default settings depend on the way Exchange Server was installed.

Figure 9-8   Configure distribution points for the offline address book.

8. To support Outlook 2007 and later clients, you must enable Web-based distribution. Select the Enable Web-Based Distribution check box, and then click Add. In the Select OAB Virtual Directory dialog box, select the OAB virtual directory to use, and then click OK. Repeat as necessary.

9. To support Outlook 2003 and other MAPI clients, you must enable public folder distribution. Select the Enable Public Folder Distribution check box.

10. Click Next, and then click New to create the offline address book.

11. Click Finish.

In the Exchange Management Shell, you can create offline address books using the New-OfflineAddressBook cmdlet. Sample 9-14 provides the syntax and usage.

Sample 9-14   New-OfflineAddressBook cmdlet syntax and usage

```
Syntax
New-OfflineAddressBook –Name 'ListName'
  -Server 'GenerationServer'
  -AddressLists 'AddressList1', 'AddressList2', ...
  -PublicFolderDistributionEnabled <$false|$true>
  -VirtualDirectories  'VirtualDir1', 'VirtualDir2', ...
```

```
Usage
New-OfflineAddressBook -Name 'Offline - West Coast Sales'
 -Server 'CorpSvr127'
 -AddressLists '\West Coast Sales'
 -PublicFolderDistributionEnabled $true
 -VirtualDirectories 'CORPSVR127\OAB (Default Web Site)'
```

Configuring Clients to Use an Offline Address Book

Offline address lists are available only when users are working offline. You can configure how clients use offline address books by completing the following steps:

1. Start Office Outlook 2007. Click Tools, select Send/Receive, and then select Download Address Book. The Offline Address Book dialog box appears.

2. Select the Download Changes Since Last Send/Receive check box to download only items that have changed since the last time you synchronized the address list. Clear this check box to download the entire contents of your address book.

3. Specify the information to download as:

   ❏ **Full Details**   Select this option to download the address book with all address information details. Full details are necessary if the user needs to encrypt messages when using remote mail.

   ❏ **No Details**   Select this option to download the address book without address information details. This reduces the download time for the address book.

4. If multiple address books are available, use the Choose Address Book drop-down list to specify which address book to download. Click OK.

Assigning a Time to Rebuild an Offline Address Book

The default offline address book is rebuilt daily at 1:00 A.M. Other offline address books are rebuilt daily at 5:00 A.M. You can change the time when the rebuild occurs by completing these steps:

1. In Exchange Management Console, expand the Organization Configuration node by double-clicking it, and then select the related Mailbox node.

2. In the details pane, right-click the offline address book you want to configure, and then select Properties.

3. Use the Update Schedule drop-down list to set the rebuild time. The available options are as follows:

   ❏ Run Daily At 1:00 A.M.

   ❏ Run Daily At 2:00 A.M.

- ❑ Run Daily At 3:00 A.M.
- ❑ Run Daily At 4:00 A.M.
- ❑ Run Daily At 5:00 A.M.
- ❑ Never Run
- ❑ Use Custom Schedule

> **Tip**   If you select Use Custom Schedule, click Customize to define your own rebuild schedule.

4. Click OK.

Rebuilding Offline Address Books Manually

Normally, offline address books are rebuilt at a specified time each day, such as 3:00 A.M. You can also rebuild offline address books manually. To do this, complete the following steps:

1. In Exchange Management Console, expand the Organization Configuration node by double-clicking it, and then select the related Mailbox node.

2. In the details pane, right-click the offline address book you want to rebuild, and then select Update.

3. When prompted to confirm the action, click Yes. Rebuilding address lists can take a long time. Be patient. Users will see the updates the next time they start Outlook.

Setting the Default Offline Address Book

Although you can create many offline address books, clients download only one. This address list is called the *default offline address book*, and you can set it by completing these steps:

1. In Exchange Management Console, expand the Organization Configuration node by double-clicking it, and then select the related Mailbox node.

2. In the details pane, right-click the offline address book you want to configure, and then select Set As Default. Users will use the new default offline address book the next time they start Outlook.

Changing Offline Address Book Properties

The offline address book is based on other address lists that you've created in the organization. You can modify the lists that are used to create the offline address book by completing the following steps:

1. In Exchange Management Console, expand the Organization Configuration node by double-clicking it, and then select the related Mailbox node.

2. In the details pane, right-click the offline address book you want to configure, and then select Properties.

3. On the Address Lists tab, you can make additional address lists a part of the master offline address book by clicking Add, selecting the list you want to use, and then clicking OK. If you no longer want an address list to be a part of the offline address book, select the address list, and then click the Remove button.

4. On the Distribution tab, to change the clients supported, select or clear the client-related check boxes as appropriate.

5. To enable or disable distribution points for Outlook 2007 clients, select or clear the Enable Web-Based Distribution check box, as appropriate. You can configure additional distribution points by clicking Add, selecting the distribution point you want to use, and then clicking OK. If you no longer want to use a distribution point, select the distribution point, and then click the Remove button.

6. To enable or disable distribution points for Outlook 2003 and other MAPI clients, select or clear the Enable Public Folder Distribution check box, as appropriate. Click OK.

In the Exchange Management Shell, you can modify offline address books using the Set-OfflineAddressBook cmdlet. Sample 9-15 provides the syntax and usage.

Sample 9-15 Set-OfflineAddressBook cmdlet syntax and usage

```
Syntax
Set-OfflineAddressBook -Identity 'ListIdentity'
[-IsDefault <$false|$true>]
[-AddressLists 'AddressList1', 'AddressList2', ...]
[-ApplyMandatoryProperties <$false|$true>]
[-DiffRetentionPeriod $null]
[-DomainController 'DCName']
[-Name 'NewAddressBookName']
[-PublicFolderDistributionEnabled <$false|$true>]
[-Schedule 'Schedule']
[-Versions 'Versions']
[-VirtualDirectories 'VirtualDir1', 'VirtualDir2', ...]


Usage
New-OfflineAddressBook -Identity '\Offline - West Coast Sales'
  -Name 'West Coast Sales - Offline'
  -AddressLists '\West Coast Sales'
  -PublicFolderDistributionEnabled $true
  -VirtualDirectories 'CORPSVR127\OAB (Default Web Site)'
```

Changing the Offline Address Book Server

In a large organization in which lots of users are configured to use offline folders, managing and maintaining offline address books can put a heavy burden on Exchange Server. To balance the load, you might want to designate a server other than your primary Exchange servers to manage and propagate offline address books.

You can change the offline address book server by completing these steps:

1. In Exchange Management Console, expand the Organization Configuration node by double-clicking it, and then select the related Mailbox node.

2. In the details pane, right-click the offline address book you want to configure, and then select Move. This starts the Move Offline Address Book Wizard.

3. The current offline address book server is listed in the Offline Address Book Server field. To use a different server, click Browse, and then, in the Select Mailbox Server dialog box, choose a different server. Click OK.

4. Click Move, and then click Finish.

In the Exchange Management Shell, you can change the offline address book server using the Move-OfflineAddressBook cmdlet. Sample 9-16 provides the syntax and usage.

Sample 9-16   Move-OfflineAddressBook cmdlet syntax and usage

```
Syntax
Move-OfflineAddressBook -Identity 'OfflineAddressBookIdentity'
 -Server 'Server'
```

```
Usage
Move-OfflineAddressBook -Identity '\Offline - West Coast Sales'
 -Server 'CorpSvr127'
```

Deleting Offline Address Books

If an offline address book is no longer needed, you can delete it as long as it isn't the default offline address book. Before you can delete the default offline address book, however, you must set another address book as the default.

You can delete an offline address book by completing the following steps:

1. In Exchange Management Console, expand the Organization Configuration node by double-clicking it, and then select the related Mailbox node.

2. In the details pane, right-click the offline address book you want to configure, and then select Remove.

3. When prompted to confirm, click Yes.

In the Exchange Management Shell, you can delete an offline address book using the Remove-OfflineAddressBook cmdlet. Sample 9-17 provides the syntax and usage. Set the Force parameter to $true to force the immediate removal of an offline address book.

Sample 9-17 Remove-OfflineAddressBook cmdlet syntax and usage

```
Syntax
Remove-OfflineAddressBook -Identity 'OfflineAddressBookIdentity'
[-Force <$false|$true>]
```

```
Usage
Remove-OfflineAddressBook -Identity '\Offline - West Coast Sales'
```

Chapter 10

Implementing Exchange Server 2007 Security

In this chapter, you'll learn how to implement Microsoft Exchange Server 2007 security and auditing. In Active Directory, you manage security using permissions. Users, contacts, and groups all have permissions assigned to them. These permissions control the resources that users, contacts, and groups can access. They also control the actions that users, contacts, and groups can perform. You use auditing to track the use of these permissions, as well as logons and logoffs. You manage Exchange administration permissions using either the Active Directory tools or the Exchange management tools.

Controlling Exchange Server Administration and Permissions

In Exchange Server 2007, management of permissions is greatly simplified over Exchange Server 2003. The reason for this change is that all Exchange information is now stored in Active Directory, and you can use the features of Active Directory to manage permissions across the Exchange organization.

Assigning Exchange Server Permissions to Users, Contacts, and Groups

Users, contacts, and groups are represented in Active Directory as objects. These objects have many attributes that determine how they are used. The most important attributes are the permissions assigned to the object. Permissions grant or deny access to objects and resources. For example, you can grant a user the right to create public folders but deny that same user the right to view the status of the information store.

Permissions assigned to an object can be applied directly to the object or they can be inherited from another object. Generally, objects inherit permissions from *parent objects*. A parent object is an object that is above another object in the object hierarchy. However, you can override inheritance. One way to do this is to assign permissions directly to an object. Another way is to specify that an object shouldn't inherit permissions.

In Exchange Server 2007, permissions are inherited through the organizational hierarchy. The root of the hierarchy is the *Organization node*. All other nodes in the tree inherit the Exchange permissions of this node. For example, the permissions on the Recipient Configuration node are inherited from the Organization node.

For the management of Exchange information and servers, Exchange Server 2007 uses several predefined groups. These predefined security groups have permissions to manage Exchange organization, Exchange server, and Exchange recipient data in Active Directory. In Active Directory Users And Computers, you can view and work with the administrator-related groups using the Microsoft Exchange Security Groups node (see Figure 10-1).

Tip   In Active Directory Users And Computers, there's a hidden container of Exchange objects called Microsoft Exchange System Objects. You can display this container by selecting Advanced Features on the View menu.

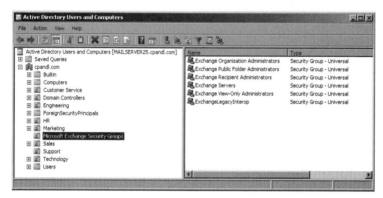

Figure 10-1   You can use Active Directory Users And Computers to manage Exchange administrator groups.

Understanding the Exchange Administration Groups

Table 10-1 lists predefined groups created in Active Directory for Exchange Server 2007. As the table shows, each group has a slightly different usage and purpose. Three of the seven groups are used by Exchange servers. These groups are: Exchange Install Domain Servers, Exchange Servers, and ExchangeLegacyInterop. You use the other groups for assigning administrator permissions. These groups are: Exchange Organization Administrators, Exchange Public Folder Administrators, Exchange Recipient Administrators, and Exchange View-Only Administrators.

Table 10-1   Security Groups Created for Exchange

Group	Group Type	Description
Exchange Install Domain Servers	Global Security Group	Members of this group include domain controllers on which Exchange is installed. You can see this group only when you select View and then click Advanced Features in Active Directory Users And Computers.
Exchange Organization Administrators	Universal Security Group	Members of this group have full access to all Exchange properties and objects in the Exchange organization.
Exchange Public Folder Administrators	Universal Security Group	Members of this group have permissions to modify public folder attributes and perform most public folder administration tasks.
Exchange Recipient Administrators	Universal Security Group	Members of this group have permissions to modify any Exchange property on an Active Directory user, contact, group, dynamic distribution list, or public folder object. Members of this group can also manage Unified Messaging mailbox settings and Client Access mailbox settings.
Exchange Servers	Universal Security Group	Members of this group can manage the Exchange information store, mail interchange, and mail queues. By default, all computers running Exchange Server 2007 are members of this group, and you shouldn't change this setup.
Exchange View-Only Administrators	Universal Security Group	Members of this group have read-only access to the entire Exchange organization tree in the Active Directory configuration container, and read-only access to all the Windows domain containers that have Exchange recipients.
ExchangeLegacy-Interop	Universal Security Group	Members of this group are granted Sent To and Receive From permissions, which are necessary for routing group connections between Exchange Server 2007 and Exchange 2000 Server or Exchange Server 2003. Exchange 2000 Server and Exchange Server 2003 bridgehead servers must be made members of this group to allow proper mail flow in the organization.

When working with Exchange-related groups, it is important to keep in mind that Exchange Organization Administrators grants the widest set of Exchange administration permissions possible. Members of this group can perform any Exchange administration task, including organization, server, and recipient management. Members of the Exchange Recipient Administrators group, on the other hand, can manage only recipient information, and Exchange Public Folder Administrators can manage only public folder information. Exchange View-Only Administrators can view Exchange organization, server, and recipient information, but cannot manage any aspects of Exchange.

Table 10-2 provides an overview of the group membership for the Exchange groups. Membership in a particular group grants the member the permissions of the group.

Table 10-2   Default Membership for Exchange Security Groups

Group	Member Of	Members
Exchange Install Domain Servers	Exchange Servers	Domain controllers on which Exchange is installed
Exchange Public Folder Administrators	Exchange View-Only Administrators	Exchange Organization Administrators
Exchange Organization Administrators	Administrators, Exchange Recipients Administrators, Exchange Public Folder Administrators	Administrator
Exchange Recipient Administrators	Exchange View-Only Administrators	Exchange Organization Administrators
Exchange Servers	Windows Authorization Access Group	Exchange Install Domain Servers, individual Exchange servers
Exchange View-Only Administrators		Exchange Recipient Administrators, Exchange Organization Administrators
ExchangeLegacyInterop		

Understanding how group membership affects permissions is extremely important. As an example, if you follow the membership of the Exchange Organization Administrators group, you can see why its members have the widest set of Exchange permissions. Its members are granted permissions of the Exchange Recipient Administrators group and Exchange Public Folder Administrators. Members of the Exchange Recipient Administrators and Exchange Public Folder Administrators groups are, in turn, members of the Exchange View-Only Administrators group. Because the Exchange Organization Administrators group is also a member of Administrators, its members gain all the permissions of this group and any groups of which Administrators is a member. In the local domain, members of the Administrators group have full administration privileges, allowing them to manage Active Directory information throughout the domain. Finally, Exchange Organization Administrators has as its only default member the built-in Administrator user. This means the only user account that, by default, has administrative permissions in Exchange is the built-in Administrator account. Other users that perform Exchange administrator tasks must be specifically granted permission to do so or be a member of a group that is granted permissions to do so.

Assigning Exchange Administrator Permissions in Active Directory Users and Computers

To grant Exchange administrator permissions to a user or group of users, all you need to do is make the user or group a member of the appropriate Exchange administrator group. The tool of choice for managing users in a domain is Active Directory Users And Computers. You can make users, contacts, computers, or other groups members of an Exchange administrator group by completing the following steps:

1. Click Start, point to All Programs, select Administrative Tools, and select Active Directory Users And Computers.

2. In Active Directory Users And Computers, double-click the Exchange administrator group you want to work with. This opens the group's Properties dialog box.

3. Click the Members tab, as shown in Figure 10-2.

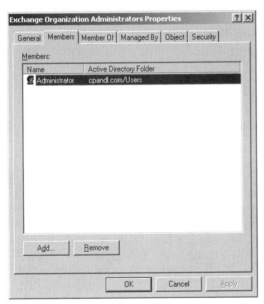

Figure 10-2   Use the Members tab to view and manage membership in the group.

4. To make a user or group a member of the selected group, click Add. The Select Users, Contacts, Computers, Or Groups dialog box appears, as shown in Figure 10-3.

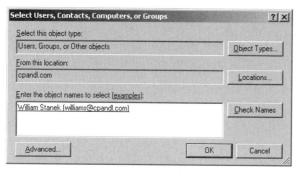

Figure 10-3   Specify the name of the user, contact, computer, or group to add.

5. Type the name of the account to which you want to grant permissions, and then click Check Names. If matches are found, select the account you want to use, and then click OK. If no matches are found, update the name you entered, and try searching again. Repeat this step as necessary. Click OK.

You can remove a user, contact, computer, or other group from an Exchange administrator group by completing the following steps:

1. Open Active Directory Users And Computers.

2. In Active Directory Users And Computers, double-click the Exchange administrator group with which you want to work. This opens the group's Properties dialog box.

3. On the Members tab, click the user or group you want to remove, and then click Remove. Click OK.

Understanding Advanced Exchange Server Permissions

Active Directory objects are assigned a set of permissions. These permissions are standard Microsoft Windows permissions, object-specific permissions, and extended permissions.

Table 10-3 summarizes the most common object permissions. Keep in mind that some permissions are generalized. For example, with Read Value(s) and Write Value(s), Value(s) is a placeholder for the actual type of value or values.

Table 10-3   Common Permissions for Active Directory Objects

Permission	Description
Full Control	Permits reading, writing, modifying, and deleting
List Contents	Permits viewing object contents
Read All Properties	Permits reading all properties of an object
Write All Properties	Permits writing to all properties of an object

Table 10-3   Common Permissions for Active Directory Objects

Permission	Description
Read Value(s)	Permits reading the specified value(s) of an object, such as general information or group membership
Write Value(s)	Permits writing the specified value(s) of an object, such as general information or group membership
Read Permissions	Permits reading object permissions
Modify Permissions	Permits modifying object permissions
Delete	Permits deleting an object
Delete Subtree	Permits deleting the object and its child objects
Modify Owner	Permits changing the ownership of the object
All Validated Writes	Permits all types of validated writes
All Extended Writes	Permits all extended writes
Create All Child Objects	Permits creating all child objects
Delete All Child Objects	Permits deleting all child objects
Add/Remove Self As Member	Permits adding and removing the object as a member
Send To	Permits sending to the object
Send As	Permits sending as the object
Change Password	Permits changing the password for the object
Receive As	Permits receiving as the object

Table 10-4 summarizes Exchange-specific permissions for objects. You use these extended permissions to control Exchange administration and use. If you want to learn more about other types of permissions, I recommend that you read *Windows Server 2008 Administrator's Pocket Consultant* (Microsoft Press, 2008) or *Windows Vista Administrator's Pocket Consultant* (Microsoft Press, 2007).

Table 10-4   Extended Permissions for Exchange Server

Permission	Description
Read Exchange Information	Permits reading general Exchange properties of the object
Write Exchange Information	Permits writing general Exchange properties of the object
Read Exchange Personal Information	Permits reading personal identification and contact information for an object

Table 10-4   Extended Permissions for Exchange Server

Permission	Description
Write Exchange Personal Information	Permits writing personal identification and contact information for an object
Read Phone and Mail Options	Permits reading phone and mail options of an object
Write Phone and Mail Options	Permits writing phone and mail options of an object
Allow Impersonation To Personal Exchange Info	Permits impersonating another user to access personal Exchange information
Allowed To Authenticate	Permits the object to authenticate in the domain

Assigning Advanced Exchange Server Permissions

In Active Directory, different types of objects can have different sets of permissions. Different objects can also have general permissions that are specific to the container in which they're defined. For troubleshooting or fine-tuning your environment, you may occasionally need to modify advanced permissions. You can set advanced permissions for Active Directory objects by following these steps:

1. Open Active Directory Users And Computers. If advanced features aren't currently being displayed, select Advanced Features on the View menu.

2. Right-click the user, group, or computer account with which you want to work.

    Caution   Only those administrators with a solid understanding of Active Directory and Active Directory permissions should manipulate advanced object permissions. Incorrectly setting advanced object permissions can cause problems that are difficult to track down.

3. Select Properties from the shortcut menu, and then click the Security tab in the Properties dialog box, as shown in Figure 10-4.

4. Users or groups with access permissions are listed in the Name list box. You can change permissions for these users and groups by doing the following:

    ❑   Select the user or group you want to change.

    ❑   Use the Permissions list box to grant or deny access permissions.

    ❑   When inherited permissions are dimmed, override inherited permissions by selecting the opposite permissions.

5. To set access permissions for additional users, computers, or groups, click Add. Then use the Select Users, Computers, Or Groups dialog box to add users, computers, or groups.

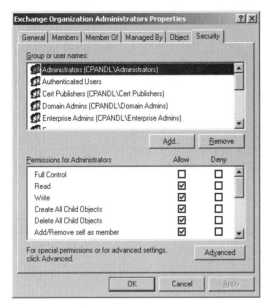

Figure 10-4   Use the Security tab to manage advanced permissions.

6. Select the user, computer, or group you want to configure in the Name list box, click Add, and then click OK. Then use the fields in the Permissions area to allow or deny permissions. Repeat for other users, computers, or groups. Click OK when you're finished.

Adding Exchange Administrator Permissions in the Exchange Management Console

In the Exchange Management Console, you add a new Exchange administrator role to assign administrative permissions for the Exchange organization. The level of permissions you set is determined by the role you assign a particular user or group.

Understanding Administration Roles

Adding Exchange permissions lets you assign any of the following administrative roles to users and groups:

- **Exchange Organization Administrator role**   Makes the user or group a member of the Exchange Organization Administrators group, which allows users or groups to fully administer the Exchange organization. Grant this role to users who need to manage the configuration of the organization, its servers, and its recipients.

- **Exchange Public Folder Administrator role**   Makes the user or group a member of the Exchange Public Folder Administrators group, which allows users or groups to fully administer public folders but not to manage the configuration of the organization or its servers. Grant this role to users or groups who are responsible for the day-to-day administration of public folders.

■ **Exchange Recipient Administrator role**   Makes the user or group a member of the Exchange Recipient Administrators group, which allows users or groups to fully administer Exchange recipients but not to manage the configuration of the organization or its servers. Grant this role to users or groups who are responsible for the day-to-day administration of Exchange recipients.

■ **Exchange View-Only Administrator role**   Makes this user or group a member of the Exchange View-Only Administrators group, which grants users or groups read-only access to the Exchange organization and read-only access to Windows domain containers that have Exchange recipients.

■ **Exchange Server Administrator role**   Makes the user or group a member of the Exchange Server Administrator role. This allows a user to manage the Exchange information store, mail interchange, and mail queues. To allow a user to fully administer the Exchange server, you must manually add the user or group to the built-in local Administrators group of the Exchange server.

To view the currently assigned Exchange permissions for users and groups, you select the Organization Configuration node in the Exchange Management Console, as shown in Figure 10-5, or type **get-exchangeadministrator** at the Exchange Management Shell prompt.

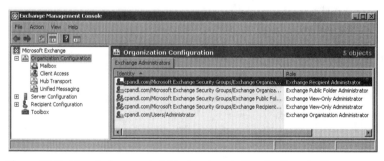

Figure 10-5   View Exchange administrators by selecting the Organization Configuration node.

Adding Exchange Permissions to a User or Group

In the Exchange Management Console, you can assign permissions to a user or group for administering the Exchange environment by completing the following steps:

1. Right-click the Organization Configuration node, and then select Add Exchange Administrator. This starts the Add Exchange Administrator Wizard, as shown in Figure 10-6.

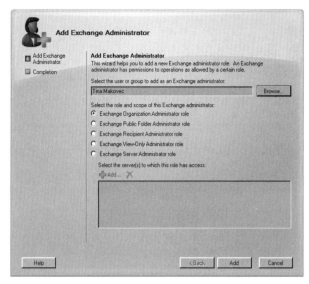

Figure 10-6   Use the Add Exchange Administrator Wizard to assign Exchange administrator permissions.

2. On the Add Exchange Administrator page, click Browse to display the Select User Or Group dialog box.

3. Select the user or group to which you want to assign permissions, and then click OK.

4. Select the role to add using the options provided. If you are assigning the Exchange Server Administrator role, click Add. Use the Select Exchange Server dialog box to select the Exchange server on which to add permissions, and then click OK.

5. Click Add, and then click Finish. When you are configuring the Exchange Server Administrator role, you must next manually add the user or group to the built-in local Administrators group of the Exchange server to allow the user or group to fully administer the Exchange server.

In the Exchange Management Shell, you can assign Exchange permissions using the Add-ExchangeAdministrator cmdlet. Sample 10-1 provides the syntax and usage. You can set the –Role parameter to PublicFolderAdmin, RecipientAdmin, ServerAdmin, ViewOnlyAdmin, or OrgAdmin.

Sample 10-1   Add-ExchangeAdministrator cmdlet syntax and usage

```
Syntax for Organization, Public Folder, and Recipient Admins
Add-ExchangeAdministrator -Identity 'UserOrGroupID'
  -Role 'Role'
```

```
Usage
Add-ExchangeAdministrator -Identity 'cpandl.com/Users/Arlene Huff'
 - Role 'RecipientAdmin'
```

```
Syntax for Server Admins
Add-ExchangeAdministrator -Identity 'UserOrGroupID'
 -Role 'ServerAdmin' -Scope 'Server'
```

```
Usage
Add-ExchangeAdministrator -Identity 'cpandl.com/Users/William Stanek'
 -Role 'ServerAdmin' -Scope 'CORPSVR127'
```

Removing Exchange Permissions

In the Exchange Management Console, you can remove the administrator permissions you have assigned to a user or group by completing the following steps:

1. Select the Organization Configuration node.

2. Right-click the user or group for which you want to remove permissions, and then select Remove.

3. When prompted to confirm, click Yes. When you are configuring the Exchange Server Administrator role, you must next manually remove the user or group from the built-in local Administrators group of the Exchange server to fully remove administrative access to the Exchange server.

In the Exchange Management Shell, you can remove Exchange permissions using the Remove-ExchangeAdministrator cmdlet. Sample 10-2 provides the syntax and usage. You can set the –Role parameter to PublicFolderAdmin, RecipientAdmin, ServerAdmin, ViewOnlyAdmin, or OrgAdmin.

Sample 10-2   Remove-ExchangeAdministrator cmdlet syntax and usage

```
Syntax for Organization, Public Folder, and Recipient Admins
Remove-ExchangeAdministrator -Identity 'UserOrGroupID'
 -Role 'Role'
```

```
Usage
Remove-ExchangeAdministrator -Identity 'cpandl.com/Users/Arlene Huff'
 - Role 'RecipientAdmin'
```

```
Syntax for Server Admins
Remove-ExchangeAdministrator -Identity 'UserOrGroupID'
 -Role 'ServerAdmin' -Scope 'Server'
```

```
Usage
Remove-ExchangeAdministrator -Identity 'cpandl.com/Users/Arlene Huff'
 -Role 'ServerAdmin' -Scope 'CORPSVR127'
```

Auditing Exchange Server Usage

Auditing lets you track what's happening with Exchange Server. You can use auditing to collect information related to information logons and logoffs, permission use, and much more. Any time an action that you've configured for auditing occurs, this action is written to the system's security log, where it's stored for your review. You can access the security log from Event Viewer.

Using Auditing

You enable auditing in the domain through Group Policy. You can think of group policies as sets of rules that help you manage resources. You can apply group policies to domains, organizational units within domains, and individual systems. Policies that apply to individual systems are referred to as *local group policies* and are stored only on the local system. Other group policies are linked as objects in Active Directory.

You can audit Exchange activity by enabling auditing in a Group Policy Object applied to your Exchange servers. This policy object can be a local Group Policy Object or an Active Directory Group Policy Object. You manage a server's local Group Policy Object using the Local Security Policy tool. You manage Active Directory Group Policy using the Group Policy Management Console (GPMC). GPMC is included as a Windows Feature with Windows Vista and later versions of the Windows operating system. After you add GPMC as a feature, you can access it on the Administrative Tools menu.

Configuring Auditing

You can enable Exchange auditing by completing the following steps:

1. Start the Group Policy Management Console by clicking Start, All Programs, Administrative Tools, Group Policy Management. You can now navigate through the forest and domains in the organization to view individual Group Policy Objects.

2. To specifically audit users' actions on Exchange Server, you should consider creating an organizational unit (OU) for Exchange servers and then define auditing policy for a Group Policy Object applied to the OU. After you've created the OU or if you have an existing OU for Exchange servers, right-click the related policy object, and then select Edit to open the policy object for editing in Group Policy Management Editor.

3. As shown in Figure 10-7, access the Audit Policy node by working your way down through the console tree. Expand Computer Configuration, Policies, Windows Settings, Security Settings, and Local Policies. Then select Audit Policy.

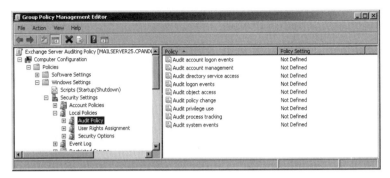

Figure 10-7   Use the Audit Policy node in Group Policy Management Editor to enable auditing.

4. You should now see the following auditing options:

- ❏ **Audit Account Logon Events**   Tracks user account authentication during logon. Account logon events are generated on the authenticating computer when a user is authenticated.

- ❏ **Audit Account Management**   Tracks account management by means of Active Directory Users And Computers. Events are generated any time user, computer, or group accounts are created, modified, or deleted.

- ❏ **Audit Directory Service Access**   Tracks access to Active Directory. Events are generated any time users or computers access the directory.

- ❏ **Audit Logon Events**   Tracks local logon events for a server or workstation.

- ❏ **Audit Object Access**   Tracks system resource usage for mailboxes, information stores, and other types of objects.

- ❏ **Audit Policy Change**   Tracks changes to user rights, auditing, and trust relationships.

- ❏ **Audit Privilege Use**   Tracks the use of user rights and privileges, such as the right to create mailboxes.

- ❏ **Audit Process Tracking**   Tracks system processes and the resources they use.

- ❏ **Audit System Events**   Tracks system startup, shutdown, and restart, as well as actions that affect system security or the security log.

5. To configure an auditing policy, double-click or right-click its entry, and then select Security. This opens a Properties dialog box for the policy.

6. Select the Define These Policy Settings check box, and then select the Success check box, the Failure check box, or both. Success logs successful events, such as successful logon attempts. Failure logs failed events, such as failed logon attempts.

7. Repeat steps 5 and 6 to enable other auditing policies. The policy changes won't be applied until the next time you start the Exchange server.

Part III

Server and Group Administration

In this part:

Chapter 11

Managing Microsoft Exchange Server 2007 Data and Storage Groups

As a Microsoft Exchange Server 2007 administrator, one of your most important tasks is managing the information store. Each mailbox server deployed in an organization has an information store, which contains storage groups and databases. This chapter focuses on the management of storage groups. You'll learn the following:

- How to enable, create, and use storage groups

- How to manage databases and their related transaction logs

- How to improve mailbox server availability

- How to manage full-text indexing of Exchange databases

To learn how to manage databases, see Chapter 12, "Mailbox and Public Folder Database Administration."

Navigating the Information Store

Storage groups allow you to group databases logically, giving you the option of managing an entire storage group (with all its databases) or managing databases individually. Each mailbox server has at least one storage group by default, and you can create additional storage groups as needed. One additional storage group, called the recovery storage group, is always reserved for database recovery operations.

Using Storage Groups and Databases

On the surface, storage groups and databases seem to be the most fundamental Exchange Server components. Yet, as you dig deeper, the reasons for creating additional storage groups and databases become clear. You use storage groups as containers for mailbox databases, which hold user mailboxes, and for public folder databases, which hold public folders.

Mailbox databases continue to be the primary type of database used with Exchange Server. Exchange Server 2007 also supports public folder databases. However, Exchange Server 2007 de-emphasizes public folders because Microsoft Office Outlook 2007 does not use public folders for accessing free/busy data or the Offline Address Book (OAB). Instead, Outlook 2007 accesses this information from the organization's Client Access servers. How does this work? Client Access servers provide Outlook Web

Access services, which in turn allow clients to access mail, free/busy data, OAB data, and other Exchange data using Hypertext Transfer Protocol (HTTP).

> **Tip** For sharing information and collaborating in an Exchange 2007 organization, you should configure Windows SharePoint Services Version 3 or later. With SharePoint Services, you can create shared team calendars, document libraries, discussion boards, and more.

Outlook 2003 clients and earlier clients require a public folder database to connect to Exchange Server. These clients use public folders to access free/busy information and the OAB. If you have Outlook 2003 or earlier clients and other Messaging Application Programming Interface (MAPI) clients, these clients can continue to access public folders on mailbox servers running Exchange Server 2007. You manage public folder configuration using the Public Folder Management Console and the Exchange Management Shell.

> **Note** Exchange Server 2007 does not support public folder access using Network News Transport Protocol (NNTP) or public folder access using Internet Mail Access Protocol 4 (IMAP4). Exchange Server 2007 also does not support non-MAPI top-level folders in your public folder databases. The only way to maintain this functionality in an Exchange 2007 organization is to maintain a server running Exchange 2000 Server or Exchange Server 2003.

When you install the first mailbox server in the organization, this server's information store typically has two default storage groups:

- First Storage Group, which contains the default mailbox database
- Second Storage Group, which contains the default public folder database

However, the specific configuration depends on your responses during setup. When you are installing the first mailbox server, Setup prompts you to specify whether any client computers run Outlook 2003 and earlier or Entourage. If you answer yes, the Second Storage Group with a public folder database is created. If you answer no, the Second Storage Group with a public folder database is not created.

> **Note** In an Exchange organization with existing Exchange 2000 or 2003 servers, you are not prompted about clients running Outlook 2003 and earlier or Entourage. In a mixed organization like this, Setup creates the Second Storage Group with a public folder database automatically to ensure backward compatibility.

When you install additional mailbox servers in the organization, these servers have only one default storage group, First Storage Group, which contains the default mailbox database. The reason for this default configuration is that the decision whether a public folder database is needed in the organization is determined only when you install the first mailbox server. When you install additional mailbox servers, you are not prompted about clients running Outlook 2003 and earlier or Entourage. A key reason for this is that only one public folder database is required in an Exchange organization and any other public folder databases are optional.

Configuring Storage Groups and Databases for Availability

Storage groups have several types of files associated with them. As Table 11-1 shows, these files include one or more checkpoint files, a temporary working file, and one or more transaction log files. Depending on the state of Exchange Server, you might see other working files as well. When you create a storage group, you can specify separate folder locations to use for transaction logs and system files.

Table 11-1   System and Data Files Used by Storage Groups

Type of File	File Name	Description
System Files		
Temporary data	Tmp.edb	Temporary workspace for processing transactions
Checkpoint file	E##.chk	Checkpoint file that tracks the point up to which the transactions in the log file have been committed
Transaction Log Files		
Primary log file	E##.log	Primary log file that contains a record of all changes that have yet to be committed
Secondary log files	E##00000001.log, E##00000002.log, ...	Additional log files used as needed
Reserve log files	E##Res00001.jrs, E##Res00002.jrs, ...	Files used to reserve space for additional log files if the primary log file becomes full

You create mailbox and public folder databases within storage groups. Each storage group can have multiple databases associated with it. You use Exchange databases to ease the administrative burden that comes with managing large installations. For example, instead of having a single 800-gigabyte (GB) database for the entire organization, you can create eight 100-GB databases that you can manage more easily.

> **Tip**   As a best practice, 100 GB is, in fact, the largest recommended size for Exchange Server 2007 databases. If you enable local continuous replication (LCR), as discussed later in this section, the largest recommended database size is 200 GB. When it comes to backup and recovery, you will find that these database sizes typically work well in helping you meet any Service Level Agreements (SLAs) you might have.

When you create a mailbox or public folder database, you specify the name for the database, and this name sets the name of the primary database file as well. For example, if you create a mailbox database called MarketingDept, the primary database file is set as MarketingDept.edb. With Exchange Server 2007, the default location for database files is the same as the log folder used by the storage group itself. If you want a database to be in a different location, you can specify the location you want to use.

The many files associated with storage groups and databases provide granular control over Exchange Server, and if you configure the data files properly, they can help you scale your Exchange organization efficiently while ensuring optimal performance. To see how, consider the scenarios listed in Table 11-2, which outline some ways that small, medium, and large organizations can configure mailbox servers based on performance needs.

Table 11-2   Configuring Exchange Data Files for Small, Medium, and Large Organizations

Organization Size	Performance Needs	Recommendation
Small	Low	Place all data files on the same drive. Consider using redundant array of independent disks such as RAID 1 or RAID 5 to protect the data.
	High	Place all databases on a single drive. Place all transaction logs and system files on a different drive. Consider using RAID 5 for databases and RAID 1 for transaction logs.
Medium	Low	Place all databases on a single drive, using RAID 5 to protect the drive in case of failure. Place all transaction logs and system files on a different drive, using RAID 1 to protect the drive in case of failure.
	High	Place all databases on a single drive, using RAID 5 to protect the drive in case of failure. Place all transaction logs on a different drive, using RAID 1 to protect the drive in case of failure. Place all system files on a third drive.
Large	Low	Organize data according to storage groups, placing all the data for each storage group on separate drives. Use RAID 1 or RAID 5 to protect the drives.
	Moderate	Each storage group should have its own database drive. Use RAID 5 to protect the database drives in case of failure. Place transaction logs and system files for each storage group on different drives, using RAID 1 to protect the drives in case of failure.
	High	Each database should have its own drive. Use RAID 5 to protect the drive in case of failure. Place the transaction logs for each storage group on separate drives, using RAID 1 to protect each drive in case of failure. Place system files for each storage group on separate drives.

Improving Availability

You can also use storage groups to manage Exchange Server 2007 backup and recovery more effectively. When you perform backup operations on Exchange Server, you can back up each storage group separately. If you have a problem with Exchange Server, you can restore a specific storage group to resolve the problem instead of having to restore all the Exchange data. Log files are also useful in recovery. Each transaction in a log file is marked with a database instance ID, which enables you to recover individual databases within a single storage group.

Before you create storage groups, mailbox databases, or public folder databases on mailbox servers, you should consider how you will back up and recover your server. Your backup and recovery plan should take into account the requirements of any SLAs for Exchange Server.

To improve availability for the information store, Exchange Server 2007 introduces:

■ Local continuous replication (LCR)

■ Cluster continuous replication (CCR)

■ Standby continuous replication (SCR)

LCR, CCR, and SCR are designed for storage group replication. LCR is a single-server solution for asynchronous log shipping, replay, and recovery. CCR combines the asynchronous log shipping, replay, and recovery features with the failover and management features of the Cluster service and is designed for configurations in which you have clustered mailbox servers with dedicated active and passive nodes.

SCR is an extension of LCR and CCR. SCR uses the same log shipping, replay, and recovery features of LCR and CCR but is designed for configurations in which you use or enable the use of standby recovery servers, which can be stand-alone mailbox servers that don't use LCR or passive nodes in a failover cluster where no clustered mailbox server has been installed. With SCR, you can copy data from a single source server to multiple targets.

You use LCR, CCR, and SCR to create and maintain a copy of a storage group and its related database for disaster recovery. With LCR's single-server solution, the copy, or replica, of the storage group is created and maintained on a separate set of disks than those used by the storage group being replicated. These disks—like the original disks used by the storage group—must be connected to the server and cannot be located on another server. With CCR and SCR's multiple server solution, the copy of the storage group is created and maintained on the cluster or standby server.

> **Tip**   From an overall performance perspective, it is important to keep in mind that LCR, CCR, and SCR require approximately 30 to 40 percent additional processor and memory resources to maintain. Because of this significant additional load, you may want to add processors and memory to your mailbox servers prior to enabling LCR, CCR, or SCR.

Because you cannot combine storage group replication with public folder replication, and you cannot create multiple databases in an LCR-enabled, CCR-enabled, and SCR-enabled storage group, there are some strict rules for mailbox and public folder databases. These rules are as follows:

- With mailbox databases, LCR, CCR, and SCR are available only when each storage group has a single database. If a storage group has multiple databases, you cannot enable any of these continuous replication features and you will need to first delete or move the additional databases.

- With public folder databases, LCR, CCR, and SCR are available only when the Exchange 2007 organization has one public folder database. If your organization has more than one public folder database, public folder replication is used instead of these continuous replication features. Public folder replication occurs automatically whenever there are two or more public folder databases, even if there are no public folders to replicate.

You enable and disable continuous replication on a per-storage group basis. When you enable continuous replication for a storage group with an existing database, the database it contains is enabled automatically to use continuous replication. For storage groups, continuous replication allows you to configure separate backup locations for transaction logs and system files. For databases, continuous replication allows you to configure a unique backup location for the passive copy of the database file. The best guideline to follow when determining whether to use separate storage locations is this: if you store transaction logs, system files, and databases separately for each storage group, you should strongly consider using separate backup locations as well. This will help ensure the server's drives can keep up with the expected read/write performance levels.

When you enable continuous replication, it becomes your first line of defense for disaster recovery. To recover a database, you can revert the passive copy of the data and do not have to restore from backup. After you revert the passive copy, it becomes the active copy and you can replay transaction logs, if they are available, to fully restore the database. You can also make backups of the passive copy rather than the active copy, giving you an additional backup option that should reduce any downtime related to backups.

After you've enabled continuous replication, you'll need to manage your continuous replication-enabled storage groups and databases in a slightly different way than storage groups and databases without continuous replication. For example, moving a storage group or database with LCR requires that you:

1. Suspend LCR.
2. Move the storage group or database.
3. Resume LCR.

You'll also want to regularly verify the continuous replication copies to ensure that they are valid and usable. Typically, you'll schedule verification to run during off-peak usage hours. See the section "Verifying Your Local Continuous Replication Copies" later in this chapter for more information.

Controlling the Information Store

The Exchange information store contains storage groups and databases. You can create and manage storage groups in a variety of ways.

Creating Storage Groups

You can create a storage group by completing the following steps:

1. In Exchange Management Console, expand the Server Configuration node, and then select the related Mailbox node.

2. In the details pane, right-click the mailbox server you want to manage, and then select New Storage Group from the shortcut menu. You should now see the New Storage Group Wizard, as shown in Figure 11-1.

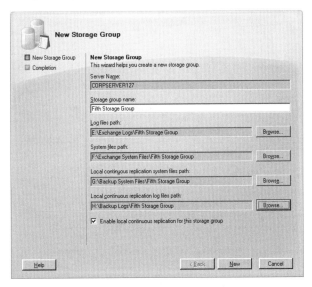

Figure 11-1   Set the storage group name and file locations.

3. The Server Name text box is set based on the server you selected. In the Storage Group Name text box, type a descriptive name for the storage group. If you want to follow the default naming convention, name each storage group in sequence, as in Second Storage Group, Third Storage Group, and so on.

4. Click Browse to the right of the Log Files Path text box. Use the Browse For Folder dialog box to select a location for the transaction logs, and then click OK. If you need to create a new folder, navigate to the location where you'd like to place the folder, click Make New Folder, type the name of the new folder, press Enter, and then click OK. You can't store files for additional storage groups in the same directory in which you have an existing storage group.

> **Tip** Each storage group has its own set of transaction logs. These logs are used to perform transactional processing within Exchange Server. To improve performance, you could place each set of transaction logs on a physically separate drive. The number of transaction log drives should equal the number of storage groups you're using. For example, if a server uses two storage groups, the server should have two transaction log drives. To protect transaction log drives against failure, you should mirror them as well. RAID 1 (disk mirroring) is recommended over RAID 5 (disk striping with parity) because you'll have better write performance with RAID 1 in most instances— and the transaction log drives are frequently written to on busy servers.

5. Click Browse to the right of the System Files Path text box, select a location for the system files that the storage group will use, and then click OK.

6. If you want to enable LCR for the storage group, select the Enable Local Continuous Replication For This Storage Group check box, and then set the backup locations for transaction logs and system files using the Browse buttons provided. Click each Browse button in turn, select a backup location, and then click OK.

> **Note** When you add a database to a storage group for which LCR has been enabled, you can enable LCR for the database. The default database backup location is the backup system files folder. You can set a different backup location if desired.

7. Click New to create the storage group, and then click Finish. You can now add databases to the storage group as appropriate.

In the Exchange Management Shell, you can create storage groups using the new-StorageGroup cmdlet. Sample 11-1 provides the syntax and usage.

Sample 11-1 new-StorageGroup cmdlet syntax and usage

```
Syntax
new-StorageGroup -Server 'CORPSVR127' -Name 'Third Storage Group'
  -LogFolderPath 'FolderPath'
  -SystemFolderPath 'FolderPath'
  -HasLocalCopy <$false|$true>]
[ -CopyLogFolderPath 'FolderPath']
[ -CopySystemFolderPath 'FolderPath']
```

```
Usage
new-StorageGroup -Server 'CORPSVR127' -Name 'Third Storage Group'
 -LogFolderPath 'E:\Exchange Logs\Third Storage Group'
 -SystemFolderPath 'F:\Exchange System Files\Third Storage Group'
 -HasLocalCopy $true
 -CopyLogFolderPath 'H:\Backup System Files\Third Storage Group'
 -CopySystemFolderPath 'G:\Backup Logs\Third Storage Group'
```

Enabling Local Continuous Replication for an Existing Storage Group

When a storage group contains a single database, you can enable LCR to improve availability. LCR is used to replicate transaction logs and system files, thereby enabling log replay and faster recovery in case of failure. For optimal performance, you'll want to configure LCR to use separate backup locations for transaction logs and system files.

> **Note**   If your Exchange 2007 organization has more than one public folder database, you cannot enable LCR for your public folder databases. When there are multiple public folder databases, public folder replication occurs automatically, even if there are no public folders to replicate. Additionally, although LCR can be enabled on a mailbox server that is configured as an SCR source, LCR and SCR targets cannot be combined on the same mailbox server.

You can enable LCR for a storage group by completing the following steps:

1. In Exchange Management Console, expand the Server Configuration node, and then select the related Mailbox node.

2. In the details pane, select the mailbox server you want to manage. You should see a list of storage groups that are available on the server.

3. Right-click the storage group you want to change, and then select Enable Local Continuous Replication from the shortcut menu. You should now see the Enable Storage Group Local Continuous Replication Wizard.

4. Click Next. On the Set Paths page, shown in Figure 11-2, click Browse to the right of the Local Continuous Backup System Files Path text box, select a location for the backup system files, and then click OK.

5. Click Browse to the right of the Local Continuous Backup Log Files Path text box, select a location for the backup log files, and then click OK. Click Next.

6. If the storage group has a database associated with it, you'll see the Mailbox Database or Public Folder Database page next. Click Browse, select the backup location for the related database file, and then click OK. The default location is the backup system files folder. Click Next.

7. Click Enable, and then click Finish.

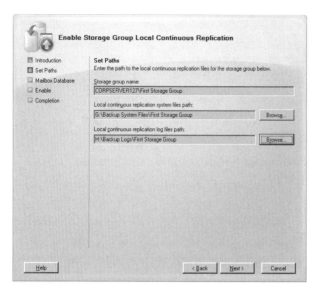

Figure 11-2   Set the backup location for the storage group.

In the Exchange Management Shell, you can enable LCR for a storage group using the enable-StorageGroupCopy cmdlet. If the storage group has a database for which LCR should be enabled as well, you can use the enable-DatabaseCopy cmdlet to do this. Always run enable-DatabaseCopy prior to running enable-StorageGroupCopy. Samples 11-2 and 11-3 provide the syntax and usage for these cmdlets.

Sample 11-2   enable-DatabaseCopy cmdlet syntax and usage

```
Syntax
enable-DatabaseCopy -Identity 'DatabaseIdentity'
  -CopyEdbFilePath 'FilePath'
```

```
Usage
enable-DatabaseCopy -Identity 'CORPSVR127\Third Storage
Group\MarketingMail'
  -CopyEdbFilePath 'J:\DBCopies\Third Storage
Group\MarketingMail.edb'
```

Sample 11-3   enable-StorageGroupCopy cmdlet syntax and usage

```
Syntax
enable-StorageGroupCopy -Identity 'StorageGroupIdentity'
  -CopyLogFolderPath 'FolderPath'
  -CopySystemFolderPath 'FolderPath'
```

Usage
```
enable-StorageGroupCopy -Identity 'CORPSVR127\Third Storage Group'
 -CopyLogFolderPath 'H:\Backup System Files\Third Storage Group'
 -CopySystemFolderPath 'G:\Backup Logs\Third Storage Group'
```

Disabling, Suspending, or Resuming Local Continuous Replication

After you've configured LCR, you can manage it in two key ways. If you no longer want to create backups, you can disable this feature. If you want to temporarily disable backups, as may be necessary when you are performing maintenance, you can suspend backups temporarily and then resume them.

To disable LCR for a storage group, follow these steps:

1. In Exchange Management Console, expand the Server Configuration node, and then select the related Mailbox node.

2. In the details pane, select the mailbox server you want to manage. You should see a list of storage groups that are available on the server.

3. Right-click the storage group, and then select Disable Local Continuous Replication.

4. When prompted to confirm the action, click Yes.

5. As necessary, manually delete the backup copies from the backup locations.

To temporarily suspend and then resume LCR for a storage group, follow these steps:

1. In Exchange Management Console, expand the Server Configuration node, and then select the related Mailbox node.

2. In the details pane, select the mailbox server you want to manage. You should see a list of storage groups that are available on the server.

3. Right-click the storage group, and then select Suspend Local Continuous Replication.

4. When prompted to confirm the action, type a comment to record in the application event log, and then click Yes.

5. As necessary, perform maintenance or recovery operations. When you are finished, right-click the storage group, and then select Resume Local Continuous Replication.

6. When prompted to confirm the action, click Yes.

In the Exchange Management Shell, you can disable, suspend, and resume local continuous replication for a storage group using the disable-StorageGroupCopy, suspend-StorageGroupCopy, and resume-StorageGroupCopy cmdlets, respectively. Samples 11-4 through 11-6 provide the syntax and usage for these cmdlets.

Sample 11-4   disable-StorageGroupCopy cmdlet syntax and usage

```
Syntax
disable-StorageGroupCopy -Identity StorageGroupIdentity'
```

```
Usage
disable-StorageGroupCopy -Identity 'CORPSVR127\Third Storage Group'
```

Sample 11-5   suspend-StorageGroupCopy cmdlet syntax and usage

```
Syntax
suspend-StorageGroupCopy -Identity 'StorageGroupIdentity'
 -SuspendComment 'Comment'
```

```
Usage
suspend-StorageGroupCopy -Identity 'CORPSVR127\Third Storage Group'
 -SuspendComment 'Suspending LCR for maintenance'
```

Sample 11-6   resume-StorageGroupCopy cmdlet syntax and usage

```
Syntax
resume-StorageGroupCopy -Identity 'StorageGroupIdentity'
```

```
Usage
resume-StorageGroupCopy -Identity 'CORPSVR127\Third Storage Group'
```

Initiating or Resynchronizing Local Continuous Replication

The update-StorageGroupCopy cmdlet allows an administrator to manually initiate or resynchronize LCR. Manually initiating or resynchronizing LCR creates or re-establishes a baseline copy of logs, system files, and the related database, allowing you to overwrite a corrupted LCR copy or invalid baseline. An example of when you might want to resynchronize the LCR copy is when you've recovered a database or server.

Manually initiating or resynchronizing LCR can be a lengthy process because Exchange must reseed the entire target database with data. Depending on the size of the data being continuously replicated, this process could take anywhere from a few minutes to a few hours to complete. The update-StorageGroupCopy cmdlet requires that no Exchange files exist in the target location when you run it and that you have suspended the LCR. With the update-StorageGroup cmdlet, you set the Delete-ExistingFiles parameter to true to delete the existing files. After you've resynchronized the LCR copy, you can resume LCR copying. Sample 11-7 provides the syntax and usage for a resynchronization script.

Sample 11-7   Resynchronizing local continuous replication syntax and usage

```
Syntax
suspend-StorageGroupCopy -Identity 'StorageGroupIdentity'
 -SuspendComment 'Comment'
update-StorageGroupCopy -Identity 'StorageGroupIdentity'
 [-DeleteExistingFiles <$false|$true>]
resume-StorageGroupCopy -Identity 'StorageGroupIdentity'
```

```
Usage
suspend-StorageGroupCopy -Identity 'CORPSVR127\Third Storage Group'
 -SuspendComment 'Suspending LCR for resync'
update-StorageGroupCopy -Identity 'CORPSVR127\Third Storage Group'
 -DeleteExistingFiles $true
resume-StorageGroupCopy -Identity 'CORPSVR127\Third Storage Group'
```

To manually initiate or resynchronize LCR using the Exchange Management Console, follow these steps:

1. In Exchange Management Console, expand the Server Configuration node, and then select the related Mailbox node.

2. In the details pane, select the mailbox server you want to manage. You should see a list of storage groups that are available on the server.

3. Right-click the storage group, and then select Update Local Continuous Replication.

4. You must delete existing log files in the target path before starting the update. For this reason, select the Delete Any Existing Log Files In The Target Path check box before clicking Next to continue.

5. Click Update to begin the update process. The update process can take a long time. Do not close the console while the update is in progress.

6. Typically, you'll see several prompts regarding existing files. If obsolete files are found, you are prompted to delete them. Click Yes when prompted. If an existing target database is found, you'll be prompted to delete it so that the update can begin. Click Yes when prompted only if you are certain you want to completely update the copy database.

7. Click Finish.

Moving Storage Groups

As discussed earlier, the transaction log location and system path have an important role in managing Exchange Server performance. The transaction log location determines where primary, secondary, and reserved log files are stored. The system path determines where check files are stored and where temporary transactions are processed. If you enable LCR, you can have separate backup locations for transaction logs and system files as well.

You can change the locations for transaction logs, system files, and backups for an existing storage group by completing the following steps:

1. In Exchange Management Console, expand the Server Configuration node, and then select the related Mailbox node.

2. In the details pane, select the Mailbox server you want to manage. You should see a list of storage groups that are available on the server.

3. If you have enabled LCR for the storage group, right-click the storage group, and then select Suspend Local Continuous Replication. When prompted to confirm the action, type a comment to record in the application event log, and then click Yes.

4. Right-click the storage group you want to change, and then select Move Storage Group Path from the shortcut menu. You should now see the Move Storage Group Path Wizard, as shown in Figure 11-3.

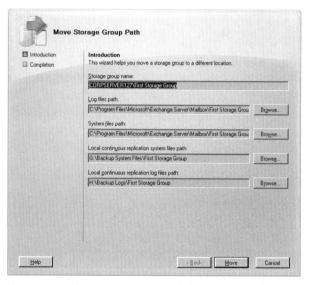

Figure 11-3   Move the storage group's files to new locations.

5. Click Browse to the right of the Log Files Path text box, select a new location for the storage group's transaction logs, and then click OK. The folder location must already exist. If the folder location doesn't exist, you'll need to create it in Windows Explorer or click New Folder in the Browse window.

6. Click Browse to the right of the System Files Path text box, select a new location for the storage group's system files, and then click OK. The folder location must already exist. If the folder location doesn't exist, you'll need to create it in Windows Explorer or click New Folder in the Browse window. If you don't place

the system files on a separate drive, you should place them on the same drive as the transaction logs.

7. If you have enabled LCR for the storage group, set the backup locations for transaction logs and system files using the Browse buttons provided. Click each Browse button in turn, select a backup location, and then click OK.

8. Click Move. Exchange will validate the paths you've provided and then move the files. Click Finish when this process completes.

> **Note**   If you've enabled LCR but replication has not yet begun, you may see an error stating that the backup paths are invalid. This occurs because there are no backup files to copy at this time, and you can ignore the error.

9. If LCR is enabled for the storage group, right-click the storage group, and then select Resume Local Continuous Replication. When prompted to confirm the action, click Yes.

In the Exchange Management Shell, you can move storage groups using the move-StorageGroupPath cmdlet. Sample 11-8 provides the syntax and usage. With LCR, you must suspend copying before moving the storage group and then resume copying after moving the storage group.

Sample 11-8   move-StorageGroupPath cmdlet syntax and usage

```
Syntax
move-StorageGroupPath -Identity 'StorageGroupIdentity'
 -LogFolderPath 'NewFolderPath'
 -SystemFolderPath 'NewFolderPath'
 [ -CopyLogFolderPath 'NewFolderPath']
 [ -CopySystemFolderPath 'NewFolderPath']
```

```
Usage
move-StorageGroupPath -Identity 'CORPSVR127\Third Storage Group'
 -LogFolderPath 'E:\Exchange Logs\Third Storage Group'
 -SystemFolderPath 'F:\Exchange System Files\Third Storage Group'
 -CopyLogFolderPath 'H:\Backup System Files\Third Storage Group'
 -CopySystemFolderPath 'G:\Backup Logs\Third Storage Group'
```

Tracking Local Continuous Replication Status

You can track the status of LCR on a per-storage group basis. The status details provided allow you to quickly determine the overall health of an LCR copy:

- **Disabled**   LCR is disabled for the storage group and its related database.

- **Broken**   Verification failed, as the database or logs were incompatible with each other or the storage group is improperly configured for LCR.

- **Seeding** Database seeding is in progress.

- **Stopped** Transaction log copying is stopped.

- **Copying** Transaction log replay is suspended but copying is enabled.

- **Healthy** LCR is currently healthy and operating normally.

Queuing details can help you determine whether Exchange is able to keep the LCR copy current. If the copy queue length is more than 5, or if the replay queue length is more than 20, Exchange is not able to keep up with the demands required by LCR copying. To resolve this, you'll need to determine the cause of the performance bottleneck. Typically, the bottleneck will be the drive to which you are writing the LCR copy. You may be able to resolve this problem by moving the LCR copies to new disks.

Although the usual suspect is the drive to which you are writing the LCR copy, the problem could also be with the server's CPUs and RAM. If the computer's CPUs are consistently at 80 percent utilization or higher, you'll need to correct this problem by adding CPUs or installing faster CPUs. If the computer's available physical memory is consistently low, you'll need to correct this problem by adding virtual memory, RAM, or both.

To use the Exchange Management Console to view LCR statistics, follow these steps:

1. In Exchange Management Console, expand the Server Configuration node, and then select the related Mailbox node.

2. In the details pane, select the mailbox server you want to manage. You should see a list of storage groups that are available on the server.

3. Right-click the storage group you want to work with, and then select Properties.

4. In the Properties dialog box, select the Local Continuous Replication tab and review the displayed statistics.

In the Exchange Management Shell, you view LCR statistics using the get-Storage-GroupCopyStatus cmdlet. Sample 11-9 provides the syntax and usage for this cmdlet.

Sample 11-9 get-StorageGroupCopyStatus cmdlet syntax and usage

```
Syntax
get-StorageGroupCopyStatus -Identity 'StorageGroupIdentity'
```

```
Usage
get-StorageGroupCopyStatus -Identity 'CORPSVR127\Third Storage Group'
```

```
Example Output
Identity: CORPSVR127\Third Storage Group
StorageGroupName: Third Storage Group
SummaryCopyStatus: Broken
Broken: True
BrokenMessage: InvalidFilePath: StorageGroup CORPSVR127\Third Storage
  Group, path Third Storage Group.
```

```
Seeding: False
ReplaySuspend: False
ReplaySuspendComment:
CopySuspend: False
CopySuspendComment:
CopyQueueLength: 0
ReplayQueueLength: 0
LatestAvailableLogTime: 2/17/2007 3:17:55 AM
LastCopyNotificationedLogTime: 2/17/2007 3:17:55 AM
LastCopiedLogTime: 2/17/2007 3:17:55 AM
LastInspectedLogTime: 2/17/2007 3:17:55 AM
LastReplayedLogTime: 2/17/2007 3:17:55 AM
LastLogGenerated: 3
LastLogCopied: 3
LastLogInspected: 3
LastLogReplayed: 3
LatestFullBackupTime:
LatestIncrementalBackupTime:
SnapshotBackup:
IsValid: True
ObjectState: Unchanged
```

As you can see from the example output, the get-StorageGroupCopyStatus cmdlet provides detailed tracking information. Table 11-3 provides a summary of these statistics.

Table 11-3   Summary of LCR Statistics

LCR Statistic	Statistic Description
Broken	When set to True, indicates that verification of the database or logs identified an inconsistency that prevents replication, or that there is a configuration or access problem with the active or passive copy.
BrokenMessage	When Broken is True, this statistic identifies the condition that caused replication to become broken, such as an invalid file path.
CopyQueueLength	Shows the number of transaction log files waiting to be copied to the backup log folder. A copy is not considered completed until it has been checked for corruption.
CopySuspend	When True, indicates that log copying has been halted for the passive copy. This prevents the backup log folder from changing.
CopySuspendComment	Shows the optional administrator comment, providing a reason why log copy activity was suspended.

Table 11-3   Summary of LCR Statistics

LCR Statistic	Statistic Description
Identity	Shows the server and name of the queried storage group.
LastCopiedLogTime	Shows the time of the last successful copy of a transaction log file.
LastCopyNotificationedLogTime	Shows the time the last copy notification occurred.
LastInspectedLogTime	Shows the time of the last successful inspection of a transaction log file.
LastLogCopied	Shows the last log generation number that was successfully copied to the backup log folder.
LastLogGenerated	Shows the last log generation number that was known to be generated on the active copy of the database.
LastLogInspected	Shows the last log generation number that was inspected.
LastLogReplayed	Shows the last log generation number that was successfully replayed into the passive copy of the database.
LastReplayedLogTime	Shows the time of the last successful replay of a transaction log file.
LatestAvailableLogTime	Shows the time of the most recently detected new transaction log file.
LatestFullBackupTime	Shows the time of the last full backup.
LatestIncrementalBackupTime	Shows the time of the last incremental backup.
ReplayQueueLength	Shows the number of transaction log files waiting to be replayed into the passive copy.
ReplaySuspend	When True, indicates that replay has been suspended for the passive copy. This prevents log replay.
ReplaySuspendComment	Shows the optional administrator comment, providing a reason why replay activity was halted.
Seeding	When True, indicates that seeding is in progress.
SnapshotBackup	Shows the time of the last snapshot backup.
StorageGroupName	Shows the name of the queried storage group.
SummaryCopyStatus	Shows the current overall status of LCR.

Verifying Your Local Continuous Replication Copies

When you use LCR, you should regularly verify the LCR copies to ensure that they are valid and usable. You can do this using the /K parameter of the Extensible Storage Engine Utility (Eseutil.exe). Before you run Eseutil, however, you should suspend LCR. After verification, you should resume LCR.

If you configure these tasks as a script that runs as a scheduled task, you'll be able to easily schedule verification to run during off-peak usage hours. Be sure to redirect the output of Eseutil to a log file so that you can determine whether errors were generated. Sample 11-10 provides the syntax and usage for a verification script.

> **Note**   By default, Eseutil.exe is located in %SystemDrive%\Program Files\Microsoft\Exchange Server\bin. This folder path must be part of the file path for the user under which the scheduled task runs. Eseutil.exe has other parameters that you can use for maintenance and repair. Related topics are covered in Chapter 12 and in Chapter 18, "Backing Up and Restoring Microsoft Exchange Server 2007."

Sample 11-10   Verifying LCR syntax and usage

```
Syntax
suspend-StorageGroupCopy -Identity 'StorageGroupIdentity'
 -SuspendComment 'Comment'
eseutil /k 'LogFilePrefix' >> TransLogFilePath
eseutil /k 'DatabaseFilePath' >> DBLogFilePath
resume-StorageGroupCopy -Identity 'StorageGroupIdentity'
```

```
Usage
suspend-StorageGroupCopy -Identity 'CORPSVR127\Third Storage Group'
 -SuspendComment 'Suspending LCR for maintenance'
eseutil /k 'E00'  >> C:\tlogs.log
eseutil /k 'J:\DBCopies\Third Storage Group\MarketingMail.edb'  >>
C:\db.log resume-StorageGroupCopy -Identity 'CORPSVR127\
Third Storage Group'
```

Enabling and Disabling Circular Logging

Circular logging allows Exchange Server to overwrite transaction log files after it has committed the data they contain to the database. Overwriting old transactions reduces the disk space requirements for Exchange Server, yet makes it impossible to recover Exchange Server up to the last transaction. If you enable circular logging, you can recover Exchange Server only up to the last full backup.

You control circular logging at the storage group level, which allows each storage group to have a different policy for logging. You cannot enable circular logging if LCR is enabled.

To enable or disable circular logging, complete the following steps:

1. In Exchange Management Console, expand the Server Configuration node, and then select the related Mailbox node.

2. In the details pane, select the mailbox server you want to manage. You should see a list of storage groups that are available on the server.

3. Right-click the storage group you want to change, and then select Properties from the shortcut menu.

4. Select or clear the Enable Circular Logging check box, as appropriate, and then click OK.

Caution   If you enable circular logging, you are limiting your recovery options for Exchange Server. As mentioned previously, you will be able to recover Exchange Server only up to the last full backup. Thus, you won't be able to successfully apply changes contained in differential or incremental backups that were created after the last full backup.

In the Exchange Management Shell, you can enable or disable circular logging using the –CircularLoggingEnabled parameter of the set-StorageGroupCopy cmdlet. Sample 11-11 provides the syntax and usage for this parameter and cmdlet.

Sample 11-11   Enabling or Disabling circular logging syntax and usage

```
Syntax
set-StorageGroupCopy -Identity 'StorageGroupIdentity'
 -CircularLoggingEnabled <$false|$true>]

Usage
set-StorageGroupCopy -Identity 'CORPSVR127\Third Storage Group'
 -CircularLoggingEnabled true$
```

Renaming Storage Groups

Renaming storage groups is simple. Right-click the storage group, and select Properties from the shortcut menu. In the Properties dialog box, delete the current name, type a new one, and then click OK. What you don't see are the repercussions of renaming, and this is what you need to be aware of.

All objects in Active Directory are located by a unique identifier that uses the directory namespace and works through each element in the directory hierarchy to a particular object. When you change the name of a storage group, you change the namespace for all the objects in that storage group, which includes databases, mailboxes, and more. Thus, the simple act of renaming a storage group has a definite impact on Exchange Server.

In the Exchange Management Shell, you can rename a storage group using the –Name parameter of the set-StorageGroupCopy cmdlet. Sample 11-12 provides the syntax and usage for this parameter and cmdlet.

Sample 11-12   Renaming a storage group

```
Syntax
set-StorageGroupCopy -Identity 'StorageGroupIdentity'
 -Name 'Name'
```

```
Usage
set-StorageGroupCopy -Identity 'CORPSVR127\Third Storage Group'
-Name 'Storage Group 3'
```

Deleting Storage Groups

Before attempting to delete a storage group, you must delete or move the databases it contains. Exchange Server allows you to delete storage groups only when they are empty (that is, only when they contain no databases).

When the storage group is empty, right-click the storage group, and then select Remove from the shortcut menu to remove it. When prompted, confirm the action by clicking Yes.

In the Exchange Management Shell, you can remove a storage group using the remove-StorageGroupCopy cmdlet. Sample 11-13 provides the syntax and usage for this cmdlet.

Sample 11-13   remove-StorageGroup cmdlet syntax and usage

```
Syntax
remove-StorageGroupCopy -Identity 'StorageGroupIdentity'
```

```
Usage
remove-StorageGroupCopy -Identity 'CORPSVR127\Third Storage Group'
```

Content Indexing

Content indexing is a built-in Exchange feature. Every Exchange server in your organization supports and uses some type of indexing. To manage indexing more effectively, use the techniques discussed in this section.

Understanding Indexing

Content indexing enables fast searches and lookups through server-stored mailboxes and public folders. Exchange Server supports two types of indexing:

- Standard indexing
- Full-text indexing

The Exchange Server storage engine automatically implements and manages standard indexing. Standard indexing is used with searches for common key fields, such as message subjects. Users take advantage of standard indexing every time they use the Find feature in Microsoft Office Outlook. With server-based mail folders, standard indexing is used to quickly search To, From, Cc, and Subject fields. With public folders, standard indexing is used to quickly search From and Subject fields.

As you probably know, users can perform advanced searches in Office Outlook as well. In Office Outlook, all they need to do is select the Advanced Find option from the Tools menu, enter their advanced search parameters, and then click Find Now. When Exchange Server receives an advanced query without full-text indexing, it searches through every message in every folder. This means that as Exchange mailboxes and public folders grow, so does the time it takes to complete an advanced search. With standard searching, Exchange Server is unable to search through message attachments.

With full-text indexing, Exchange Server builds an index of all searchable text in a particular mailbox or public folder database before users try to search. The index can then be updated or rebuilt at a predefined interval. Then, when users perform advanced searches, they can quickly find any text within a document or attachment.

> **Note**   Full-text indexes work only with server-based data. If users have personal folders, Exchange Server doesn't index the data in these folders.

The drawback of full-text indexing is that it's resource-intensive. As with any database, creating and maintaining indexes requires CPU time and system memory, which can affect Exchange performance. Full-text indexes also use disk space. A newly created index uses approximately 20 percent of the total size of the Exchange database. This means that a 1-GB database would have an index of about 200 megabytes (MB).

Each time you update an index, the file space that the index uses increases. Don't worry—only changes in the database are stored in the index updates. This means that the additional disk space usage is incremental. For example, if the original 1-GB database grew by 50 MB, the index would use about 210 MB of disk space (200 MB for the original index and 10 MB for the update).

Managing Full-Text Indexing

Unlike earlier releases of Exchange, Exchange Server 2007 doesn't allow administrators to control how indexing works. With Exchange Server 2007, the Microsoft Search (Exchange) service provides the full-text indexing of databases, and Microsoft Exchange Search provides search services. These services provide automated full-text indexing.

Full-text indexes are stored as part of the Exchange system files. Because of this, whatever folder location you use for Exchange system files will have a CatalogData-<GUID> subfolder for each storage group, which contains all the full-text indexing data for the related storage group and all its related databases. By default, you'll find full-text index files for the First Storage Group in the %SystemDrive%\Program Files\Microsoft\Exchange Server\Mailbox\First Storage Group\CatalogData-<GUID> folder, the index files for the Second Storage Group in the %SystemDrive%\Program Files\Microsoft\Exchange Server\Mailbox\Second Storage Group\CatalogData-<GUID> folder, and so on.

> **Note**   Exchange maintains full-text indexes as part of the database maintenance schedule. See the "Setting the Maintenance Interval" section of Chapter 12 for more information.

As part of the recovery process for a mailbox or public folder database, you may want to rebuild the related full-text index catalog to ensure it is current. You may also want to rebuild the full-text index after you've made substantial changes to a database or if you suspect the full-text index is corrupted.

You can rebuild an index manually at any time. Exchange Server rebuilds an index by re-creating it. This means that Exchange Server takes a new snapshot of the database and uses this snapshot to build the index from scratch. To manually rebuild an index, follow these steps:

1. Log on to the Exchange server using an account with administrator privileges.

2. Open an administrator command prompt.

3. At the command prompt, stop the Microsoft Exchange Search service by typing **net stop MsExchangeSearch**.

4. Use Windows Explorer to delete the CatalogData-<GUID> subfolder, which contains the full-text index for the database.

5. At the command prompt, start the Microsoft Exchange Search service by typing **net start MsExchangeSearch**.

Chapter 12
Mailbox and Public Folder Database Administration

Databases are containers for information. Microsoft Exchange Server 2007 uses two types of databases: *mailbox databases*, which store a server's mailboxes, and *public folder databases*, which store a server's public folders. The information in a particular database isn't exclusive to either mailboxes or public folders—Exchange Server maintains related information within databases as well. Within mailbox databases, you'll find information about Exchange logons and mailbox usage. Within public folder databases, you'll find information about Exchange logons, public folder instances, and replication. Mailbox and public folder databases also maintain information about full-text indexing. Understanding how to manage databases and the information they contain is the subject of this chapter.

Using Mailbox Databases

Each Mailbox server installed in the organization has an information store. The information store can hold multiple storage groups. Although you can create multiple mailbox databases within each storage group, you should do so only if you do not plan to use the local continuous replication (LCR) or other continuous replication copy features discussed in Chapter 11, "Managing Microsoft Exchange Server 2007 Data and Storage Groups." Each mailbox database has a database file associated with it. This file is stored in a location that you specify when you create or modify the mailbox database.

Understanding Mailbox Databases

Mailboxes are the delivery location for messages coming into an organization. They contain messages, message attachments, and other types of information that the user might have placed in the mailbox. Mailboxes, in turn, are stored in mailbox databases.

A default mailbox database is created on each Mailbox server in the organization. The default mailbox database is meant to be a starting point, and most Exchange organizations can benefit from having additional mailbox databases, especially as the number of users in the organization grows. There are many reasons for creating additional mailbox databases, but the key reasons are the following:

- To provide a smaller unit of recovery in case of failure. Each mailbox database has its own database, which is backed up as part of a storage group. During recovery, you can restore the entire storage group or individual databases within the storage group. By restoring only a specific mailbox database, you reduce the impact on the user community.

■ To impose a different set of mailbox rules on different sets of users. Each additional mailbox database can have its own property settings for maintenance, storage limits, deleted item retention, indexing, security, and policies. By placing a user's mailbox in one mailbox database instead of another, you can apply a different set of rules.

■ To optimize Exchange performance. Each mailbox database can have its own storage location. By placing the mailbox databases on different drives, you can improve the performance of Exchange Server 2007.

■ To create separate mailbox databases for different purposes. For example, you might want to create a mailbox database called General In-Out to handle all general-purpose mailboxes being used throughout the organization. These general-purpose mailboxes could be set up for Postmaster, Webmaster, Technical Support, Customer Support, and other key functions.

When you create a mailbox database, you specify the following information:

■ What the name of the database should be

■ Where the database file is to be located

■ When maintenance on the database should occur

■ Any limitations on mailbox size

■ Whether deleted items and mailboxes should be retained

Each mailbox database has a default Offline Address Book (OAB) and a default public folder database associated with it. Microsoft Office Outlook 2007 clients access the default OAB and default public folder hierarchy on your organization's Client Access servers using Hypertext Transfer Protocol (HTTP). Outlook 2003 clients access the OAB as part of the public folder data using Messaging Application Programming Interface (MAPI).

Creating Mailbox Databases

You can create mailbox databases using the New Mailbox Database Wizard. If the storage group in which you create the database has LCR enabled, the database will have this feature enabled as well, provided that it is the only database in the storage group. The default database file path and default copy file path are set automatically to be the same as those used for system files and backup system files, respectively.

To create a mailbox database, complete the following steps:

1. In Exchange Management Console, expand the Server Configuration node, and then select the related Mailbox node.

2. In the details pane, select the Mailbox server you want to manage. You should see a list of storage groups that are available on the server.

3. Right-click the storage group you want to change, and then select New Mailbox Database from the shortcut menu. You should now see the New Mailbox Database Wizard as shown in Figure 12-1.

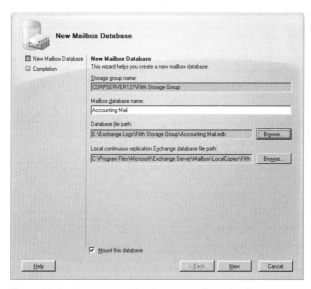

Figure 12-1   Enter a name for the new mailbox database.

4. In the Mailbox Database Name text box, type a name for the mailbox database.

5. Click Browse to the right of the Database File Path text box. Use the Exchange Database dialog box to select a new location for the database file, and then click Save.

> **Note**   The folder location must already exist. If the folder location doesn't exist, you'll need to create it in Windows Explorer first, and then set the location.

6. If you have enabled LCR for the storage group, set the backup locations for the database file using the Browse button provided. Click Browse, select a backup location, and then click OK.

7. If you want to mount the database so that it can be used, select the Mount This Database check box.

8. Click New to create the mailbox database, and then click Finish. You can now modify the properties of the mailbox database as necessary.

In the Exchange Management Shell, you can create mailbox databases using the new-MailboxDatabase cmdlet. Sample 12-1 provides the syntax and usage.

Note   Note that you use a separate cmdlet to mount the database. See the section "Mounting and Dismounting Databases" later in this chapter for details.

Sample 12-1   new-MailboxDatabase cmdlet syntax and usage

```
Syntax
new-MailboxDatabase -Name 'Name'
 -StorageGroup 'StorageGroupID'
 -CopyEdbFilePath 'FilePath'
 -EdbFilePath 'FilePath'
 -HasLocalCopy <$false|$true>
 [ -OfflineAddressBook 'OABIdentity']
 [ -PublicFolderDatabase 'PublicFolderIdentity']
 [-TemplateInstance 'Instance']
```

```
Usage
new-MailboxDatabase -Name 'Accounting Database'
 -StorageGroup 'CORPSVR127\First Storage Group'
 -EdbFilePath 'K:\Databases\First Storage Group\AccountingMail.edb'
```

Setting the Default Public Folder Database and Default Offline Address Book

Mailbox databases have different types of information associated with them, including a default public folder database and a default OAB. You set these options for mailbox databases using the Client Settings tab of the related Properties dialog box. To view this dialog box and update the messaging options, follow these steps:

1. In Exchange Management Console, right-click the mailbox database, and then select Properties.

2. In the Properties dialog box, click the Client Settings tab.

   Note   If you can't update the text boxes on the Client Settings tab, it means that a policy has been applied to the mailbox database. You must directly edit or remove the policy and then make the necessary changes.

3. The Default Public Folder Database text box shows the full path to the public folder database that the mailbox database is using. If you've created public folder databases, you might want to change the default public folder database as well. In this case, click Browse, select the public folder database that points to the public folder tree that you want to use, and then click OK.

4. The Offline Address Book text box shows the OAB for the mailbox database. OABs contain information regarding mail-enabled users, contacts, and groups in the organization, and are used when users aren't connected to the network. If

you've created additional OABs beyond the global default, you can specify one of these additional OABs as the default for the mailbox database. Click Browse, select the OAB you want to use, and then click OK. Click OK again to apply the changes.

In the Exchange Management Shell, you can set the default public folder database and default OAB for mailbox databases using the set-MailboxDatabase cmdlet. Sample 12-2 provides the syntax and usage.

Sample 12-2   Using the set-MailboxDatabase cmdlet to set defaults

```
Syntax
set-MailboxDatabase -Identity 'MailboxDatabaseIdentity'
 [ -OfflineAddressBook 'OABIdentity']
 [ -PublicFolderDatabase 'PublicFolderIdentity']
```

```
Usage
set-MailboxDatabase -Identity 'CORPSVR127\First Storage Group\
Accounting DB'
 -OfflineAddressBook '\US Corporate'
 -PublicFolderDatabase 'CORPSVR127\First Storage Group\PublicFolderDB'
```

Setting Mailbox Database Limits and Deletion Retention

Mailbox database limits are designed to control the amount of information that users can store in their mailboxes. Users who exceed the designated limits might receive warning messages and might be subject to certain restrictions, such as the inability to send messages.

Deleted item retention is designed to ensure that messages and mailboxes that might be needed in the future aren't permanently deleted. If retention is turned on, you can retain deleted messages and mailboxes for a specified period before they are permanently deleted and are nonrecoverable.

An average retention period for messages is about 14 days. The minimum retention period for mailboxes should be seven days. In most cases, you'll want deleted messages to be maintained for five to seven days and deleted mailboxes to be maintained for three to four weeks. A five- to seven-day interval is used for messages because users usually realize within a few days that they shouldn't have deleted a message. A three- to four-week interval is used for mailboxes because several weeks can (and often do) pass before users realize that they need a deleted mailbox. To understand why, consider the following scenario.

Sally leaves the company. A coworker gives permission to delete Sally's user account and mailbox. Three weeks later, Sally's boss realizes that she was the only person who received and archived the monthly reports e-mailed from corporate headquarters. The only way to get reports for previous years is to recover Sally's mailbox.

To view or set limits and deletion retention for a mailbox database, follow these steps:

1. In Exchange Management Console, right-click the mailbox database, and then select Properties.

2. In the Properties dialog box, on the Limits tab (shown in Figure 12-2), use the following options to set storage limits and deleted item retention:

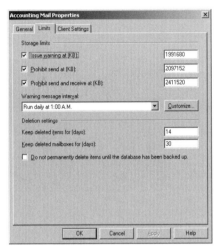

Figure 12-2   Use the Limits tab to set storage limits and deleted item retention for individual mailboxes and entire mailbox databases.

❑ **Issue Warning At (KB)**   Sets the size limit, in kilobytes, that a mailbox can reach before Exchange Server issues a warning to the user. The warning tells the user to clear out the mailbox.

❑ **Prohibit Send At (KB)**   Sets the size limit, in kilobytes, that a mailbox can reach before the user is prohibited from sending any new mail. The restriction ends when the user clears out the mailbox and the total mailbox size is under the limit.

❑ **Prohibit Send And Receive At (KB)**   Sets the size limit, in kilobytes, that a mailbox can reach before the user is prohibited from sending and receiving mail. The restriction ends when the user clears out the mailbox and the total mailbox size is under the limit.

> **Caution**   Prohibiting send and receive might cause users to lose e-mail. When a user sends a message to a user who is prohibited from receiving messages, a nondelivery report (NDR) is generated and delivered to the sender. The recipient never sees the e-mail. Because of this, you should prohibit send and receive only in very rare circumstances.

❑ **Warning Message Interval** Sets the interval for sending warning messages to users whose mailboxes exceed the designated limits. The default interval is daily at 1 A.M.

❑ **Keep Deleted Items For (Days)** Sets the number of days to retain deleted items. An average retention period is 14 days. If you set the retention period to 0, deleted messages aren't retained and you can't recover them.

❑ **Keep Deleted Mailboxes For (Days)** Sets the number of days to retain deleted mailboxes. The default setting is 30 days. You'll want to keep most deleted mailboxes for at least seven days to allow the administrators to extract any data that might be needed. If you set the retention period to 0, deleted mailboxes aren't retained and you can't recover them.

❑ **Do Not Permanently Delete Mailboxes And Items Until The Database Has Been Backed Up** Ensures that deleted mailboxes and items are archived into at least one backup set before they are removed.

3. Click OK to save the settings.

In the Exchange Management Shell, you can set limits for mailbox databases using the set-MailboxDatabase cmdlet. Sample 12-3 provides the syntax and usage.

Note Use the following format for single-event schedules: Startday.Hour:Minute [AM/PM]-End.Hour:Minute [AM/PM]. You can enter names of weekdays in full or abbreviate them. You can also use a 24-hour clock, and if you do do this, you must omit the AM/PM designator. Example with the AM/PM designator: **Mon.5:00 AM-Fri.7:00 PM**. Example with out the AM/PM designator: **Mon.05:00-Fri.19:00**.

Sample 12-3 Using the set-MailboxDatabase cmdlet to set limits

```
Syntax
Set-MailboxDatabase [-Identity 'MailboxDatabaseIdentity']
[-AllowFileRestore <$false|$true>] [-DeletedItemRetention NumberDays]
[-DomainController 'DCName']
[-EventHistoryRetentionPeriod NumberDays]
[-IndexEnabled <$false|$true>] [-IssueWarningQuota LimitKB]
[-JournalRecipient 'RecipientId'] [-MailboxRetention NumberDays]
[-MaintenanceSchedule 'Schedule'] [-MountAtStartup <$false|$true>]
[-Name 'Name'] [-OfflineAddressBook 'OABId']
[-ProhibitSendQuota LimitKB]
[-ProhibitSendReceiveQuota LimitKB]
[-PublicFolderDatabase 'DatabaseId']
[-QuotaNotificationSchedule 'Schedule']
[-RetainDeletedItemsUntilBackup <$false|$true>]
```

```
Usage
set-MailboxDatabase
-Identity 'CORPSVR127\First Storage Group\Accounting DB'
 -IssueWarningQuota 1991680
 -DeletedItemRetention 14
 -MailboxRetention 30
 -ProhibitSendQuota 2097152
 -ProhibitSendReceiveQuota 2411520
 -QuotaNotificationSchedule 'Sun.01:00-Sat.23:00'
 -RetainDeletedItemsUntilBackup $true
```

Recovering Deleted Mailboxes

Tasks related to deleting mailboxes are covered in Chapter 7, "User and Contact Administration," in the "Deleting Mailboxes from User Accounts" and "Deleting User Accounts and Their Mailboxes" sections. When you delete a mailbox from a user account, the mailbox is retained as a disconnected mailbox according to the mailbox retention setting. You can reconnect the mailbox to the original user account or another user account, if necessary. When you delete a user account and the related mailbox, the mailbox is retained as a disconnected mailbox according to the mailbox retention setting. You can connect the mailbox to an existing user account, if necessary.

To recover a deleted mailbox, complete the following steps:

1. In Exchange Management Console, expand the Recipient Configuration node, and then select the related Disconnected Mailbox node.

2. Deleted mailboxes are listed by the mailbox user's display name, storage group, and mailbox database. Right-click the deleted mailbox you want to recover, and then select Connect. This starts the Connect Mailbox Wizard.

    Note Deleted mailboxes aren't necessarily marked as such immediately. It may take 15 minutes to an hour before the mailbox is marked as deleted and listed accordingly.

3. On the Introduction page, select the type of mailbox you are recovering, and then click Next. The available options are: User Mailbox, Room Mailbox, Equipment Mailbox, and Linked Mailbox.

4. On the Mailbox Settings page, select Existing User, and then click Browse. Use the Select User dialog box to select the user account with which you want to associate the mailbox, and then click OK. You can connect a disconnected mailbox to a user account only if the account doesn't already have a mailbox associated with it.

Note   If you previously removed the mailbox, rather than disabling it, the user account associated with the mailbox was deleted as well. Because each user account has a unique security identifier associated with it, you can't simply re-create the user account to get back the same set of permissions and privileges. That said, however, if you want to connect the mailbox to a user account with the same name, you can do this by re-creating the account in Active Directory Users And Computers. The account will then be available when you select Existing User and click Browse.

5. The Exchange alias is set to the logon name by default. You can change this value by entering a new alias. The Exchange alias is used to set the user's e-mail address.

6. Click Next, and then click Connect.

You can use the connect-Mailbox cmdlet to perform the same task following the syntax shown in Sample 12-4.

Sample 12-4   connect-Mailbox cmdlet syntax and usage

```
Syntax
connect-Mailbox -Identity 'OrigMailboxIdentity'
-Database 'DatabaseIdentity'
-User 'NewUserIdentity'
[-ActiveSyncMailboxPolicy 'PolicyId'] [-Alias 'Alias']
[-DisplayName 'Name'] [-DomainController 'DCName']
[-ManagedFolderMailboxPolicy 'PolicyId']
[-ManagedFolderMailboxPolicyAllowed <$false|$true>]
[-Equipment <$false|$true>] [-Room <$false|$true>]
```

```
Usage
connect-Mailbox -Identity 'Molly Dempsey'
 -Database 'CORPSVR127\First Storage Group\Accounting DB'
-User 'CPANDL\mollyd'
 -Alias 'mollyd'
```

Recovering Deleted Items from Mailbox Databases

You can recover deleted items from mailbox databases as long as you've set a deleted item retention period for the database from which the items were deleted and the retention period hasn't expired. If both of these conditions are met, you can recover deleted items from mailbox databases.

To use Outlook for recovery, complete the following steps:

1. Log on as the user who deleted the message, and then start Outlook.

2. Click Deleted Items, and then, from the Tools menu, select Recover Deleted Items. The Recover Deleted Items From dialog box appears.

3. Select the items you want to recover, and then click Recover Selected Items.

To use Outlook Web Access (OWA) for recovery, complete these steps:

1. In a Web browser, type ***https://servername.yourdomain.com/owa***, where *servername* is a placeholder for the HTTP virtual server hosted by Exchange Server 2007 and *yourdomain.com* is a placeholder for your external domain name, such as https://mail.cpandl.com/owa.

2. Next, log on as the user (or have the user log on). At the security prompt, specify whether the user is using a public or shared computer or a private computer. Type the user name in *domain\username* format, such as **cpandl\bertk**, type the password, and then click Log On.

3. On the toolbar, click Options and in the Options panel, click Deleted Items.

4. In the Recover Deleted Items list, you'll see a list of recoverable items. Select the items you want to recover, and then click Recover To Deleted Items Folder.

5. Items you've recovered are copied to the Deleted Items folder. Click Mail in the left pane and then click Deleted Items.

6. In the Deleted Items folder, right-click items you want to keep and select Move To Folder.

7. In the Move Or Copy To Folder dialog box, select the folder to which the item should be moved and then click Move.

Using Public Folder Databases

This section explains how to create public folder databases and set basic public folder database properties. It doesn't go into detail on managing the many facets of public folders. That topic is covered in Chapter 14, "Accessing and Managing Public Folders."

Understanding Public Folder Databases

Public folders are used to share messages and files in an organization. You manage public folder databases much differently than mailbox databases. For starters, public folder databases must have a public folder tree associated with them. This public folder tree must be unique and can be assigned to a single public folder database only. Users access items that are stored in public folders through the public folder tree.

Each Mailbox server in your Exchange 2007 organization can have a maximum of one public folder database, and this is the default public folder database associated with the mailbox databases configured on that server. Exchange Server 2007 doesn't support creating multiple public folder databases on a Mailbox server. One of the primary reasons for this is that MAPI mail clients, such as Microsoft Office Outlook 2003, can access only their default public folder tree.

Unlike mailbox databases, which are completely separate from one another, you can replicate public folder databases from one Mailbox server to another. Replication allows mailbox users to access public data, regardless of which Mailbox server they are using. Having multiple Mailbox servers, each with a public folder database that is replicated, helps to distribute the workload.

When an Exchange 2007 organization has a single public folder database, you can configure LCR to create backups of public folder data. When an Exchange 2007 organization has two or more public folder databases, you cannot use LCR. Instead, replication occurs automatically between the public folder databases using public folder replication.

Creating Public Folder Databases

You can create public folder databases using the New Public Folder Database Wizard. If the storage group in which you create the database has LCR enabled, the database will have this feature enabled as well, provided that it is the only public folder database in the Exchange 2007 organization. The default database file path and default copy file path are set automatically to be the same as those used for system files and backup system files, respectively.

To create a public folder database, complete the following steps:

1. In Exchange Management Console, expand the Server Configuration node, and then select the related Mailbox node.

2. In the details pane, select the Mailbox server you want to manage. You should see a list of storage groups that are available on the server.

3. Right-click the storage group you want to change, and then select New Public Folder Database from the shortcut menu. You should now see the New Public Folder Database Wizard, as shown in Figure 12-3.

4. In the Public Folder Database Name text box, type a name for the public folder database.

5. Click Browse to the right of the Database File Path text box. Use the Exchange Database dialog box to select a new location for the database file, and then click Save.

   > **Note**   The folder location must already exist. If the folder location doesn't exist, you'll need to create it in Windows Explorer first, and then set the location.

6. If you want to mount the database so that it can be used, select the Mount This Database check box.

7. Click New to create the public folder database, and then click Finish. You can now modify the properties of the public folder database as necessary.

Figure 12-3   Enter a name for the new public folder database.

In the Exchange Management Shell, you can create public folder databases using the new-PublicFolderDatabase cmdlet. Sample 12-5 provides the syntax and usage.

Note   Note that a separate cmdlet is used to mount the database. See the section "Mounting and Dismounting Databases" later in this chapter for details.

Sample 12-5   new-PublicFolderDatabase cmdlet syntax and usage

```
Syntax
new-PublicFlderDatabase –Name 'Name'
 -StorageGroup 'StorageGroupID'
[-CopyEdbFilePath 'EdbFilePath']
[-DomainController 'DCName']
[-EdbFilePath 'EdbFilePath']
[-HasLocalCopy <$false|$true>]
[-TemplateInstance 'Instance']
```

```
Usage
new-PublicFolderDatabase –Name 'Public Folder Database'
 -StorageGroup 'CORPSVR192\Fourth Storage Group'
 -EdbFilePath 'K:\Databases\Fourth Storage Group\PublicFolderDatabase.edb'
```

Setting Public Folder Database Limits

Storage limits are designed to control the amount of information that users can post to public folders. As with mailbox databases, users who exceed the designated limits might receive warning messages and might be subject to certain restrictions, such as the inability to post messages.

Because public folders help users share messages, documents, and ideas, they're an important part of any Exchange organization. Over time, however, public folders can become cluttered, which reduces their usefulness. To minimize clutter, you can set an age limit on items that are posted to public folders. Items that reach the age limit expire and Exchange Server removes them permanently from the public folder.

When you set the age limit, keep in mind the type of information stored in the related public folders. For example, if you have a public folder database for general discussion and file sharing, you might want the age limit to be a few weeks. However, if you have a public folder database for projects, you might want the age limit to extend throughout the life of the project, which could be months or years.

The age limit and the deleted item retention are two separate values. Deleted item retention is designed to ensure that postings and documents that could be needed in the future aren't permanently deleted. When retention is turned on, deleted items are retained for a specified period before they are permanently deleted and made unrecoverable.

The age limit applies to deleted items as well. If a deleted item reaches the age limit, it's permanently deleted along with other items that have reached their age limit.

To set the storage limits, age limits, and deleted item retention for a public folder database, follow these steps:

1. In Exchange Management Console, right-click the public folder database, and then select Properties.

2. In the Properties dialog box, click the Limits tab, as shown in Figure 12-4. Use the following options to set the limits:

    ❑ **Issue Warning At (KB)**   Sets the size, in kilobytes, of the data that a user can post to the public folder database before a warning is issued. The warning tells the user to clean out the public folder database.

    ❑ **Prohibit Post At (KB)**   Sets the maximum size, in kilobytes, of the data that a user can post to the public folder database. The restriction ends when the total size of the user's data is under the limit.

    ❑ **Maximum Item Size (KB)**   Sets the maximum size, in kilobytes, for postings to the database.

    ❑ **Warning Message Interval**   Sets the interval for sending warning messages to users whose total data size exceeds the designated limits. The default interval is daily at midnight.

❑ **Keep Deleted Items For (Days)**   Sets the number of days to retain deleted items. An average retention period is 14 days. If you set the retention period to 0, deleted postings aren't retained and you can't recover them.

❑ **Do Not Permanently Delete Items Until The Database Has Been Backed Up**   Ensures that deleted items are archived into at least one backup set before they are removed.

❑ **Age Limit For All Folders In This Public Folder Database (Days)**   Sets the number of days to retain postings in the database. Postings older than the limit are automatically deleted.

Caution   If you set an age limit, be sure that all users who post to the public folder know about it. Otherwise, they'll be surprised when data is removed, and they could lose important work.

3. Click OK to save the settings.

Figure 12-4   Use the Limits tab to set the storage limits, age limits, and deleted item retention for a public folder database.

In the Exchange Management Shell, you can set limits for public folder databases using the set-PublicFolderDatabase cmdlet. Sample 12-6 provides the syntax and usage.

Sample 12-6   Using set-PublicFolderDatabase to set limits

```
Syntax
set-PublicFolderDatabase -Identity 'PublicFolderDatabaseIdentity'
[-AllowFileRestore <$false|$true>] [-DeletedItemRetention NumberDays]
[-DomainController 'DCName']
[-EventHistoryRetentionPeriod 'TimeSpan']
```

```
[-IssueWarningQuota LimitKB] [-ItemRetentionPeriod 'TimeSpan']
[-MaintenanceSchedule 'Schedule'] [-MaxItemSize LimitKB]
[-MountAtStartup <$false|$true>] [-Name 'Name']
[-ProhibitPostQuota LimitKB]
[-QuotaNotificationSchedule 'Schedule']
[-ReplicationMessageSize 'Size']
[-ReplicationPeriod 'Interval'] [-ReplicationSchedule 'Schedule']
[-RetainDeletedItemsUntilBackup <$false|$true>]
```

Usage
```
set-PublicFolderDatabase
-Identity 'CORPSVR127\Fourth Storage Group\Public DB'
 -IssueWarningQuota 1991680
 -DeletedItemRetention 14
 -MaxItemSize 10240
 -ItemRetentionPeriod 'Unlimited'
 -ProhibitPostQuota 2097152
 -QuotaNotificationSchedule 'Mon.5:00 AM-Fri.7:00 PM'
 -RetainDeletedItemsUntilBackup $true
```

Configuring Public Folder Replication

With Exchange Server 2007, public folder data is replicated automatically when there are two or more public folder databases. Because each mailbox server can have only one public folder database, you must install and configure at least two mailbox servers in your Exchange 2007 organization for automatic public folder replication to occur.

To control how replication works, follow these steps:

1. In Exchange Management Console, right-click the public folder database, and then select Properties.

2. In the Properties dialog box, on the Replication tab (shown in Figure 12-5), use the following options to configure replication:

   ❑ **Replication Interval**   Determines when changes to public folders are replicated. Select a specific time (Always Run, Run Every Hour, Run Every 2 Hours, Run Every 4 Hours, or Never Run) or select Use Custom Schedule and then click Customize to define the schedule.

   ❑ **Replication Interval For "Always Run" (Minutes)**   Sets the interval (in minutes) that's used when you select Always Run as the replication option. The default is 15 minutes.

   ❑ **Replication Message Size Limit (KB)**   Sets the size limit (in kilobytes) for messages that are replicated. Messages over the size limit aren't replicated. The default size limit is 300 kilobytes (KB).

3. Click OK to save the settings.

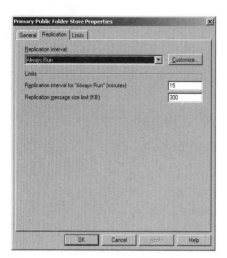

Figure 12-5 Use the Replication tab to configure replication of public folder data.

In the Exchange Management Shell, you can control replication of public folder data using the set-PublicFolderDatabase cmdlet. Sample 12-7 provides the syntax and usage.

Sample 12-7 Using set-PublicFolderDatabase to control replication

```
Syntax
set-PublicFolderDatabase -Identity 'PublicFolderDatabaseIdentity'
  [-ReplicationMessageSize LimitKB]
  [-ReplicationPeriod Interval]
  [-ReplicationSchedule 'Schedule']
```

```
Usage
set-PublicFolderDatabase -
Identity 'CORPSVR127\Fourth Storage Group\Public DB'
  -ReplicationMessageSize 300
  -ReplicationPeriod 15
  -ReplicationSchedule 'Always'
```

Configuring Public Folder Referrals

In a large organization with multiple public folder replicas in multiple locations, it is important to consider how clients access public folder data. By default, when a user accesses a public folder using Outlook or another client, his or her default public folder database determines which public folder replica the client should access. If the content exists on the Exchange server that handles the client request, the client accesses the local replica. Otherwise, Exchange redirects the client through a referral process to another public folder database that has a copy of the requested content.

The request and referral process works like this:

1. Outlook requests content in a public folder. If the content exists in the default public folder database, Exchange connects Outlook to the replica and Outlook retrieves the content. Otherwise, Exchange returns a replica list to Outlook sorted by relative priority.

2. Outlook attempts to access each replica in the list, starting with the replica with the highest relative priority. If that replica contains the desired content, Outlook retrieves the content. Otherwise, Outlook continues through the replica list until it has tried to access all replicas in the list. If Outlook fails to find a replica with the requested content, it displays an error to the user.

By default, Exchange and Outlook use the infrastructure provided by Active Directory to determine relative priority of replicas. In Active Directory, you use subnets to represent the physical structures of a network. Links between sites, referred to as *site links,* have an associated cost, which sets the relative priority of the link. Active Directory uses this relative priority to route requests and data across sites links. Typically, the site link or set of site links with the lowest cost is used.

Note   A good resource for learning more about site-based routing is *Windows Server 2008 Inside Out* (Microsoft Press, 2008). See Chapter 32, "Configuring Active Directory Sites and Replication" and Chapter 37 "Active Directory Site Administration."

Ideally, if you are having problems with replica referrals, you should work with your organization's chief IT architect or a senior Windows administrator to resolve the problem. Explain the problems you are seeing—or users are experiencing—to help the architect or administrator resolve the problem by better optimizing the way site links are used. Keep in mind that site link costs primarily are used for routing Active Directory replication traffic and communications, and it may not be possible to make changes to improve performance for public folder referrals.

Note   In mixed environments where you have Exchange Server 2007 and supported earlier releases of Exchange, Microsoft recommends assigning users a default public folder database on a server running Exchange Server 2007. When a client is referred to a server running Exchange Server 2000 and Exchange 2003 Server, Exchange and Outlook manage public folder referrals using routing group connectors and the related configuration settings.

An alternative to using Active Directory site link costs is to create a custom list that assigns a server referral cost. However, Microsoft recommends using a custom list of referrals only in a limited number of situations, such as when you have specific requirements that cannot be resolved using Active Directory site link costs.

When you create a custom list of referrals, you set the referral cost of each server with a public folder database. The referral cost is a value between 1 and 100. The server with the lowest referral cost is first on the referral list, the server with the second lowest referral cost is listed second on the referral list, and so on. Because each public folder database has its own custom list, the user's default public folder database settings will determine which custom list of referrals is used.

To view and manage the public folder referral configuration of a particular public folder database, follow these steps:

1. In Exchange Management Console, right-click the public folder database, and then select Properties.

2. In the Properties dialog box, on the Public Folder Referral tab, you'll see the current referral configuration and any custom list that has been created (if applicable).

3. If you want the database to use Active Directory site link costs for referrals, select Use Active Directory Site Costs, and then click OK.

4. If you want the database to use a custom list for referrals, select Use Custom List and then add referral servers to the list by clicking Add, specifying a referral server, assigning a referral cost, and then clicking OK.

You can configure custom referrals using the Set-PublicFolderDatabase cmdlet in the Exchange Management Shell. Sample 12-8 provides the syntax and usage.

Sample 12-8   Using set-PublicFolderDatabase to configure custom referrals

```
Syntax
set-PublicFolderDatabase -Identity 'PublicFolderDatabaseIdentity'
  [-UseCustomReferralServerList <$false|$true>]
  [-CustomReferralServerList 'ServerA:Cost', 'ServerB :Cost', ...]
```

```
Usage for Enabling Custom Referrals
set-PublicFolderDatabase
  -Identity 'CORPSVR127\Fourth Storage Group\Public DB'
  -UseCustomReferralServerList $true
  -CustomReferralServerList 'MailServer27:10', 'MailServer72:20'
```

```
Usage for Disabling Custom Referrals
set-PublicFolderDatabase
-Identity 'CORPSVR127\Fourth Storage Group\Public DB'
  -UseCustomReferralServerList $false
```

Recovering Deleted Items from Public Folder Databases

You can recover deleted items from public folder databases as long as you've set a deleted item retention period for the public folder database from which the items were deleted and the retention period for this database hasn't expired. If both of these conditions are met, you can recover deleted items by completing the following steps:

1. Log on to the domain using either an account with administrative privileges in the domain or an account with full control over the public folder from which you need to recover items.

> **Tip** Outlook only displays public folders when you fully expand the folder list in the left pane. In Outlook 2007, you'll find a Folder List button in the lower right corner of the left pane. Click this button to expand the folder list.

2. After starting Outlook, access the Public Folders node, and then select the public folder from which you need to recover an item.

3. On the Tools menu, select Recover Deleted Items. The Recover Deleted Items From dialog box appears.

4. Select the items you want to recover, and then click Recover Selected Items.

Managing Databases

Now that you know how to create and use databases, let's look at some general techniques you'll use to manage them.

Mounting and Dismounting Databases

You can access only databases that are mounted. If a database isn't mounted, the database isn't available for use. This means that an administrator has probably dismounted the database or that the drive on which the database is located isn't online.

> **Real World** A dismounted database could also point to problems with the database, transaction log, and system files used by the database. During startup, Exchange Server 2007 obtains a list of database files registered in Active Directory and then checks for the related files before mounting each database. If files are missing or corrupted, Exchange Server 2007 will be unable to mount the database. Exchange Server 2007 then generates an error and logs it in the application event log on the Exchange server. The most common error is Event ID 9547. An example of this error follows:
>
> ```
> The Active Directory indicates that the database file
> D:\Exchsrvr\mdbdata\Marketing.edb exists for the Microsoft Exchange
> Database /o=My Organization/ou=First Administrative Group/
> cn=Configuration/cn=Servers/ cn=MAILER2/
> cn=Marketing, however no such files exist on the disk.
> ```
>
> This error tells you that the Exchange database (Marketing.edb) is registered in Active Directory, but Exchange Server 2007 is unable to find the file on the disk. When Exchange Server 2007 attempts to start the corrupted mailbox database, you'll see an additional error as well. The most common error is Event ID 9519. An example of this error follows:
>
> ```
> Error 0xfffffb4d starting database First Storage Group\Marketing on
> the Microsoft Exchange Information Store.
> ```

This error tells you that Exchange Server 2007 couldn't start the Marketing database. To recover the mailbox database, you must restore the database file, as discussed in Chapter 18, "Backing Up and Restoring Microsoft Exchange Server 2007," in the section "Recovering Exchange Server." If you are unable to restore the database file, you can re-create the database structures in the Exchange Management Console by mounting the database. When you mount the database, Exchange Server 2007 creates a new database file, and, as a result, all the data in the database is lost and cannot be recovered. Exchange Server 2007 displays a warning before mounting the database and re-creating the database file. Click Yes only when you are absolutely certain that you cannot recover the database.

Determining the Status of Databases

Mailbox and public folder databases have several associated states, including:

- Mounted
- Dismounted
- Backup In Progress
- Online Maintenance In Progress
- Replication In Progress

You can determine the status of a database by following these steps:

1. In Exchange Management Console, expand the Server Configuration node, and then select the related Mailbox node.

2. In the details pane, select the Mailbox server you want to examine. You should see a list of storage groups that are available on the server.

3. For each storage group, you should see a list of available databases. The icon to the left of the database name indicates the mount status. If the icon shows a gray down arrow, the database isn't mounted. Otherwise, the database is mounted.

4. To determine the status of the database, right-click the database, and then select Properties. In the Properties dialog box, the status is listed on the General tab.

In the Exchange Management Shell, you can determine the status of all or specific databases using the get-MailboxDatabase and get-PublicFolderDatabase cmdlets. Sample 12-9 provides the syntax and usage for these cmdlets. To see status details, you must specify the status flags associated with each state you want to see as part of the formatted output. The Mounted, Dismounted, Backup In Progress, Online Maintenance In Progress, and Replication In Progress status values are then listed as True or False.

Sample 12-9   Getting database status details

```
Syntax
get-MailboxDatabase [-Identity 'MailboxDatabase' |
-StorageGroup 'StorageGroup | -Server 'Server']
[-DomainController 'DCName']
[-IncludePreExchange2007 <$false|$true>]
[-Status <$false|$true>] | format-table Name,StorageGroup,
Mounted,BackupInProgress,OnlineMaintenanceInProgress

get-PublicFolderDatabase [-Identity 'PublicFolderDatabase' |
-StorageGroup 'StorageGroup | -Server 'Server']
[-DomainController 'DCName' ]
[-IncludePreExchange2007 <$false|$true>]
[-Status <$false|$true>] |
format-table Name, StorageGroup, Mounted, BackupInProgress,
 OnlineMaintenanceInProgress,ReplicationInProgress
```

```
Usage for specific database and server
get-MailboxDatabase -Identity 'CORPSVR127\Storage Group 2\Eng DB'
 -Status | format-table Name,StorageGroup,
 Mounted,BackupInProgress,OnlineMaintenanceInProgress
```

```
Usage for all databases on a server
get-MailboxDatabase -Server 'CORPSVR127' -Status | format-table
 Name,StorageGroup, Mounted, BackupInProgress,
 OnlineMaintenanceInProgress
```

```
Usage for all databases
get-MailboxDatabase -Status | format-table Name,StorageGroup,
 Mounted,BackupInProgress,OnlineMaintenanceInProgress
```

Dismounting and Mounting Databases

You should rarely dismount an active database, but if you need to do so, follow these steps:

1. In Exchange Management Console, expand the Server Configuration node, and then select the related Mailbox node.

2. In the details pane, select the Mailbox server you want to manage. You should see a list of storage groups that are available on the server.

3. For each storage group, you should see a list of available databases. The icon to the left of the database name indicates the mount status. If the icon shows a gray down arrow, the database is already dismounted.

4. If LCR is enabled for the storage group in which the database is stored, right-click the storage group, and then select Suspend Local Continuous Replication. When prompted to confirm the action, type a comment to record in the application event log, and then click Yes.

5. Right-click the database you want to dismount, select Dismount Database, and then confirm the action by clicking Yes. Exchange Server dismounts the database. Users accessing the database will no longer be able to work with their server-based folders.

After you've dismounted a database and performed maintenance, recovery, or other procedures as necessary, you can remount the database by completing the following steps:

1. In Exchange Management Console, expand the Server Configuration node, and then select the related Mailbox node.

2. In the details pane, select the Mailbox server you want to manage. You should see a list of storage groups that are available on the server. For each storage group, you should see a list of available databases.

3. The icon to the left of the database name indicates the mount status. You should see a gray down arrow indicating that the database isn't mounted. If so, right-click the database, and then select Mount Database.

4. The new database isn't accessible to users that are currently logged on to Exchange server. Users need to exit and then restart Outlook before they can access the newly mounted database.

5. If LCR is enabled for the related storage group, right-click the storage group, and then select Resume Local Continuous Replication. When prompted to confirm the action, click Yes.

In the Exchange Management Shell, you can dismount and mount databases using the dismount-Database and mount-Database cmdlets, respectively. Sample 12-10 provides the syntax and usage for these cmdlets.

Sample 12-10 Dismounting and mounting databases

```
Syntax
dismount-Database -Identity 'DatabaseIdentity'

mount-Database -Identity 'DatabaseIdentity'
```

Usage for dismounting a database
```
dismount-Database -Identity 'CORPSVR127\Storage Group 2\Eng DB'
```

Usage for mounting a database
```
mount-Database -Identity 'CORPSVR127\Storage Group 2\Eng DB'
```

Specifying Whether a Database Should Be Automatically Mounted

Normally, Exchange Server automatically mounts databases on startup. You can, however, change this behavior. For example, if you're recovering an Exchange server from a complete failure, you might not want to mount databases until you've completed recovery. In this case, you can disable automatic mounting of databases.

To enable or disable automatic mounting of a database, complete the following steps:

1. In Exchange Management Console, expand the Server Configuration node, and then select the related Mailbox node.

2. In the details pane, select the Mailbox server you want to manage. You should see a list of storage groups that are available on the server. For each storage group, you should see a list of available databases.

3. Right-click the database you want to work with, and then select Properties.

4. To ensure that a database isn't mounted on startup, select the Do Not Mount This Database At Start-Up check box.

5. To mount the database on startup, clear the Do Not Mount This Database At Start-Up check box. Click OK.

In the Exchange Management Shell, you can enable or disable automatic mounting at startup using the set-MailboxDatabase and set-PublicFolderDatabase cmdlets. Sample 12-11 provides the syntax and usage for controlling automatic mounting.

Sample 12-11   Controlling automatic mounting

Syntax
```
set-MailboxDatabase -Identity 'DatabaseIdentity'
 -MountAtStartup <$false|$true>

set-PublicFolderDatabase -Identity 'DatabaseIdentity'
 -MountAtStartup <$false|$true>
```

Usage
```
set-MailboxDatabase -Identity 'CORPSVR127\Storage Group 2\Eng DB'
 -MountAtStartup $false
```

Setting the Maintenance Interval

You should run maintenance routines against databases on a daily basis. The maintenance routines organize the databases, clear out extra space, and perform other essential housekeeping tasks. By default, Exchange Server runs maintenance tasks daily from 1:00 A.M. to 5:00 A.M. If this conflicts with other activities on the Exchange server, you can change the maintenance schedule by following these steps:

1. In Exchange Management Console, right-click the database you want to work with, and then select Properties.

2. On the General tab in the Properties dialog box, use the Maintenance Schedule list to set a new maintenance time. Select a time (such as Run Daily From 11:00 P.M. To 3:00 A.M.) or select Use Custom Schedule. Click OK.

Tip   If you want to set a custom schedule, select Use Custom Schedule, and then click Customize. You can now set the times when maintenance should occur.

In the Exchange Management Shell, you can configure the maintenance schedule for a database by using the set-MailboxDatabase and set-PublicFolderDatabase cmdlets. Sample 12-12 provides the syntax and usage. In the example, replication is configured to occur between Friday at 9:00 PM and Monday at 1:00 AM.

Sample 12-12   Setting the maintenance schedule

```
Syntax
set-MailboxDatabase -Identity 'DatabaseIdentity'
 -MaintenanceSchedule Schedule

set-PublicFolderDatabase -Identity 'DatabaseIdentity'
 -MaintenanceSchedule Schedule
```

```
Usage
set-MailboxDatabase -Identity 'CORPSVR127\Storage Group 2\Eng DB'
 -MaintenanceSchedule 'Fri.9:00 PM-Mon.1:00 AM'
```

Moving Databases

As discussed earlier, each database has a database file associated with it, and the location of this file has an important role in managing Exchange Server performance. If you enable LCR, you can have separate backup locations for the database file as well.

You can change the database file and local continuous backup locations for a database by completing the following steps:

1. In Exchange Management Console, expand the Server Configuration node, and then select the related Mailbox node.

2. In the details pane, select the Mailbox server you want to manage. You should see a list of storage groups that are available on the server.

3. If LCR is enabled for the storage group, right-click the storage group, and then select Suspend Local Continuous Replication. When prompted to confirm the action, type a comment to record in the application event log, and then click Yes.

4. Right-click the database you want to move, and then select Move Database Path from the shortcut menu. You should now see the Move Database Path Wizard, as shown in Figure 12-6.

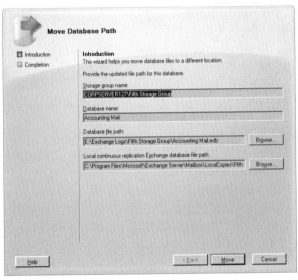

Figure 12-6   Move the database and its backup to new locations.

5. Click Browse to the right of the Database File Path text box, select a new location for the database file, and then click Save. The folder location must already exist. If the folder location doesn't exist, you'll need to create it in Windows Explorer before trying to move the file.

6. If LCR is enabled for the related storage group, set the backup location for the database file using the Browse button provided. Select a backup location, and then click Save.

7. Click Move. Exchange will validate the paths you've provided and then move the files. Click Finish when this process completes.

> **Note** If you've enabled LCR but replication has not yet begun, you may see an error stating that the backup paths are invalid. This occurs because there are no backup files to copy at this time, and you can ignore the error.

8. If LCR is enabled for the related storage group, right-click the storage group, and then select Resume Local Continuous Replication. When prompted to confirm the action, click Yes.

In the Exchange Management Shell, you can move databases using the move-Database-Path cmdlet. Sample 12-13 provides the syntax and usage. With LCR, you must suspend copying of the related storage group before moving the database and then resume copying after moving the database.

Sample 12-13 move-DatabasePath cmdlet syntax and usage

```
Syntax
move-DatabasePath -Identity 'DatabaseIdentity'
[-ConfigurationOnly <$false|$true>] [-CopyEdbFilePath 'EdbFilePath']
[-EdbFilePath 'EdbFilePath'] [-DomainController 'DCName']
[-Force <$false|$true>]
```

```
Usage
move-DatabasePath -Identity 'CORPSVR127\Third Storage Group\Sales DB'
 -CopyEdbFilePath 'I:\ReplCopies\First Storage Group\AccountingMail.edb'
 -EdbFilePath 'K:\Databases\First Storage Group\SalesMail.edb'
```

Renaming Databases

To rename a database, follow these steps:

1. In Exchange Management Console, right-click the database, and then select Properties.

2. In the Properties dialog box, type the new name for the database. Click OK.

> **Note** All objects in Active Directory are located by a unique identifier. This identifier uses the directory namespace and works through each element in the directory hierarchy to a particular object. When you change the name of a database, you change the namespace for all the objects in the database.

In the Exchange Management Shell, you can rename databases using the −Name parameter of the set-MailboxDatabase and set-PublicFolderDatabase cmdlets. Sample 12-14 provides the syntax and usage.

Sample 12-14   Renaming a database

```
Syntax
set-MailboxDatabase -Identity 'DatabaseIdentity'
 -Name 'NewName'

set-PublicFolderDatabase -Identity 'DatabaseIdentity'
 -Name 'NewName'
```

```
Usage
set-MailboxDatabase -Identity 'CORPSVR127\Storage Group 2\Eng DB'
 -Name 'Engineering Mail Database'
```

Deleting Databases

Deleting a database removes the database and all the public folders or mailboxes it contains. Before you delete a database, make sure that you no longer need the items it contains. If they are necessary, you should move them to a new database. You move mailboxes as described in Chapter 8, "Mailbox Administration," in the section "Moving Mailboxes." With public folders, public folder data is replicated between or among the public folder databases automatically. As long as all data has been replicated, you could remove a public folder database from a Mailbox server without losing data. However, because each Mailbox server can only have one public folder database, you'd need to create a new public folder database to ensure that users with mailboxes on the server can access public folder data.

After you've moved items that you might need, you can delete the database by completing the following steps:

1. In Exchange Management Console, right-click the database you want to delete, and then select Remove from the shortcut menu.

2. When prompted, confirm the action by clicking Yes.

In the Exchange Management Shell, you can delete databases using the remove-MailboxDatabase and remove-PublicFolderDatabase cmdlets. Sample 12-15 provides the syntax and usage.

Sample 12-15   Removing databases

```
Syntax
remove-MailboxDatabase -Identity 'DatabaseIdentity'

remove-PublicFolderDatabase -Identity 'DatabaseIdentity'
```

```
Usage
remove-MailboxDatabase -Identity 'CORPSVR127\Storage Group 2\Eng DB'
```

Chapter 13
Implementing Managed Folders and Managed Records

Microsoft Exchange Server 2007 implements messaging resource management to help retain messaging content that your organization may need for business or legal reasons, as well as to delete messages that are no longer needed. You specify the retention period and the types of messaging content to which management settings should apply using managed folders. A managed folder is simply a Microsoft Office Outlook folder to which you can apply retention policies. Messaging records management is configured globally for your Exchange 2007 organization and implemented on a per-server basis by enabling records management enforcement.

Introducing Messaging Records Management

Exchange Server 2007 uses two types of managed folders: managed default folders and managed custom folders. Managed default folders include the standard folders available in Outlook 2007. Managed custom folders are additional folders that you can create and deploy.

You can work with managed folders in several ways. If you want to control the contents of managed folders, you apply managed content settings. For example, you can apply managed content settings to the Inbox folder, specifying that Exchange Server should automatically delete or move its contents to another folder after 90 days. Although managed default folders appear in Outlook 2007 automatically, managed custom folders do not. To add a managed custom folder to a mailbox, you must create a Managed Folder Mailbox policy that deploys the folder. You can use a single Managed Folder Mailbox policy to deploy multiple managed custom folders.

Users add messaging content to managed folders according to the written policies of your organization. For example, you might have a Pending Approval folder used to track team or project messages that require approval prior to being sent. After a user receives permission to send a pending message, she should send out the message to her team and then place a copy of the message in the Approved Messages folder. You might also have a Legal Hold folder for messages and documents that users are legally required to hold for a certain period. You might want to automatically manage these items by creating copies and then deleting them when they are no longer needed.

By automating records management, Exchange Server 2007 helps your organization comply with legal requirements while minimizing the impact on administrators. The process relies on users to classify their own messaging content. Users can file items by placing them in the managed folder that is appropriate for that type of content, or messaging content can be sorted into the appropriate folder by using rules in Outlook 2007 or Outlook 2003. This ensures that messaging content is classified according to users' wants, and helps eliminate the mishandling of messaging content that can occur with completely automated messaging management solutions.

Managed folders are similar to the other folders in users' mailboxes, except that users cannot remove, rename, or delete the folders after Exchange Server has deployed them. The only exception is when you've set up a hosted Web services site that allows users to select the managed folders they want to use. You can create hosted Web services for managed folders using the Microsoft Exchange Server 2007 Software Developers Kit (SDK).

Exchange Server periodically processes messaging content that users put in managed folders according to the retention policies you define. You can configure retention policies by content age and by message type, and you can apply them to any of the folders in user mailboxes. When messages reach a retention limit, Exchange Server can retain required messaging content and delete unneeded messaging content without requiring administrator intervention.

You can retain any messaging content that you want to keep by applying managed content settings that create journal copies of the content in another location. This can be any location with a Simple Mail Transfer Protocol (SMTP) e-mail address, including another Exchange mailbox.

You can configure Exchange Server to delete any messaging content that is no longer needed by specifying a deletion action. You can delete content permanently or delete it so that users can still recover it. You can also move content to a managed folder that is set up for user review prior to deletion, or you can mark content as Expired in the user's mailbox in Outlook 2007. This, in turn, ensures that the user is prompted to take any required action.

When you apply managed content settings, you can also specify that messaging content should be journaled. A journal is an automatically forwarded copy of an item saved in an alternate location. Typically, you'll journal copies of items to a mailbox specifically set up for this purpose. You can use journaling to help your organization meet additional compliance or regulatory requirements.

Implementing Records Management

You can implement messaging records management by completing the following procedures:

1. Select a managed default folder to which you want to add messaging records management, or create a managed custom folder, as discussed in the section "Managing Mailbox Folders."

2. Define and apply managed content settings to the managed folder, as discussed in the section "Managing Content Settings."

3. Create and apply managed folder mailbox policies to managed custom folders, as discussed in the section "Deploying Managed Custom Mailbox Folders."

4. Apply managed folder mailbox policy to user mailboxes, as discussed in the section "Applying Managed Mailbox Policy to User Mailboxes."

5. Schedule the Managed Folder Assistant to apply the settings to user mailboxes, as discussed in the section "Applying Records Management to a Mailbox Server."

Each of these procedures is discussed in the sections that follow.

Managing Mailbox Folders

You configure managed mailbox folders at the organization level. This means your Exchange 2007 organization has a single managed folder configuration and you can apply this configuration to all Mailbox servers throughout the organization by enabling records management as desired on a per-server basis. As discussed in the sections that follow, you work with managed default folders and managed custom folders in different ways.

Viewing and Configuring Managed Default Folders

Exchange Server 2007 has a predefined set of managed default folders. Managed default folders are folders that are available automatically in user mailboxes in Outlook 2007. As an administrator, you do not have to create managed default folders and you cannot rename or delete these predefined folders.

In the Exchange Management Console, you can view and configure the available managed default folders by completing the following steps:

1. In Exchange Management Console, expand the Organization Configuration node, and then select the related Mailbox node.

2. In the details pane, click the Managed Default Folders tab. As shown in Figure 13-1, the available default managed folders are as follows:

   ❑ **Calendar**   Stores calendar items, including appointments and meetings

   ❑ **Contacts**   Stores business and personal contacts

   ❑ **Deleted Items**   Stores items that have been deleted from other folders

   ❑ **Drafts**   Stores messages that a user has saved as a draft

   ❑ **Entire Mailbox**   Provides a reference to all folders in user mailboxes

> **Note**   Managed content settings that you apply to Entire Mailbox apply to all the managed custom folders that users manually create at the root level of the mailbox folder hierarchy, as well as to all managed default folders not managed by means of a policy.

- ❏ **Inbox**   Stores incoming messages
- ❏ **Journal**   Stores journal entries for making notes or tracking what the user is doing throughout the day
- ❏ **Junk E-mail**   Stores e-mail that Outlook has filtered because it is suspected junk e-mail or that the user has specifically identified as junk e-mail
- ❏ **Notes**   Stores general notes
- ❏ **Outbox**   Stores outgoing messages before they are sent
- ❏ **RSS Feeds**   Stores Really Simple Syndication (RSS) feeds to which the user has subscribed
- ❏ **Sent Items**   Stores messages that Outlook has sent
- ❏ **Sync Issues**   Stores messages related to Outlook and Exchange synchronization
- ❏ **Tasks**   Stores to-do tasks

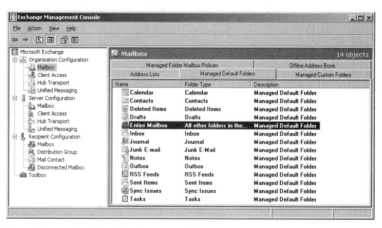

Figure 13-1   View the default managed folders.

3. You can view the general properties of a particular folder by right-clicking it and selecting Properties. This displays a Properties dialog box similar to the one shown in Figure 13-2.

4. To add a comment to display when the folder is viewed in Outlook, type the comment in the text box provided.

5. If you want to prevent users from minimizing the comment, select the Do Not Allow Users To Minimize Comment In Outlook check box. Click OK.

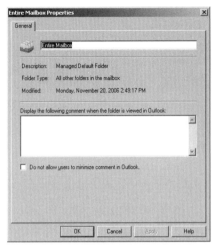

Figure 13-2   View and set properties of a default managed folder.

Viewing and Configuring Managed Custom Folders

In addition to the predefined managed default folders, Exchange 2007 allows you to create managed custom folders that can be used according to your organization's policies. Unlike managed default folders, managed custom folders are not automatically available in user mailboxes in Microsoft Office Outlook 2007. After you create a custom managed mailbox and apply managed content settings as appropriate, you make the folder available by adding it to a managed folder mailbox policy.

In the Exchange Management Console, you can view and configure managed custom folders by completing the following steps:

1. In Exchange Management Console, expand the Organization Configuration node, and then select the related Mailbox node.

2. In the details pane, on the Managed Custom Folders tab, you see the available custom managed folders.

3. To delete a custom folder that you no longer want to use, right-click the folder, and then select Remove. When prompted, confirm the action by clicking Yes.

4. To set a comment to display when the folder is viewed in Outlook, right-click the folder, and then select Properties. Type the comment in the text box provided. If you want to prevent users from minimizing the comment, select the Do Not Allow Users To Minimize Comment In Outlook check box. Click OK.

In the Exchange Management Console, you can create a managed custom folder by completing the following steps:

1. In Exchange Management Console, expand the Organization Configuration node, and then select the related Mailbox node.

2. In the details pane, on the Managed Custom Folders tab, right-click an open area of the window, and select New Managed Custom Folder. This starts the New Managed Custom Folder Wizard, as shown in Figure 13-3.

Figure 13-3   Create a managed custom folder.

3. Managed custom folders can have an Exchange name, which is displayed in Exchange, and a display name, which is displayed in Outlook. By default, both names are set to the value you type in the Name field. If you want the folder to have a different display name, change the display name.

4. Managed custom folders can have a storage limit that users are prevented from exceeding. To set a storage limit, select the Storage Limit (KB) For This Folder And Its Subfolders check box, and then type the desired limit as a value in kilobytes (KB), such as 500000.

5. To set a comment to display when the folder is viewed in Outlook, type the comment in the text box provided. If you want to prevent users from minimizing the comment, select the Do Not Allow Users To Minimize This Comment In Outlook check box.

6. Click New to create the folder, and then click Finish.

Using the Exchange Management Shell to Work with Managed Folders

In the Exchange Management Shell, you can work with managed folders using the following cmdlets:

- **New-ManagedFolder**   Creates a new managed custom folder

- **Get-ManagedFolder**   Displays a list of all managed folders or a specified managed folder

- **Set-ManagedFolder**   Sets properties of managed folders

- **Remove-ManagedFolder**   Removes managed custom folders

Samples 13-1 through 13-4 provide the syntax and usage for these cmdlets.

Sample 13-1   New-ManagedFolder cmdlet syntax and usage

```
Syntax
New-ManagedFolder -Name 'ExchangeName'
 -FolderName 'Pending OutlookName'
 -StorageQuota 'Limit'
 -Comment 'Comment'
 -MustDisplayComment <$false|$true>
```

```
Usage
New-ManagedFolder -Name 'Pending Approval'
 -FolderName 'Pending Approval'
 -StorageQuota '500000KB'
 -Comment 'All messages pending approval should be placed in this
folder.'
 -MustDisplayComment $true
```

Sample 13-2   Get-ManagedFolder cmdlet syntax and usage

```
Syntax
get-ManagedFolder [-Identity 'FolderIdentity' | -Mailbox
'MailboxIdentity']
```

```
Usage
get-ManagedFolder

get-ManagedFolder -Identity 'Pending Approval'

get-ManagedFolder -Mailbox 'cpand\tedb'
```

Sample 13-3   Set-ManagedFolder cmdlet syntax and usage

```
Syntax
Set-ManagedFolder -Identity 'FolderIdentity'
 -Name 'ExchangeName'
 -FolderName 'OutlookName'
 -StorageQuota 'Limit'
 -Comment 'Comment'
 -MustDisplayComment <$false|$true>
```

```
Usage
Set-ManagedFolder -Identity 'Pending Approval'
 -FolderName 'Pending For Approval'
 -StorageQuota 'Unlimited'
 -Comment 'Folder for messages pending approval.'
 -MustDisplayComment $false
```

Sample 13-4   Remove-ManagedFolder cmdlet syntax and usage

```
Syntax
Remove-ManagedFolder -Identity 'FolderIdentity'
```

```
Usage
Remove-ManagedFolder -Identity 'Pending For Approval'
```

When you are working with mailboxes, you'll often want to determine whether and how managed folders are being used. You can determine the managed folder configuration for a specific mailbox by using the following command line:

```
get-ManagedFolder -Mailbox 'MailboxIdentity'
```

where *MailboxIdentity* is the name of the mailbox you want to examine, such as:

```
get-ManagedFolder -Mailbox 'cpand\tedb'
```

The output returned from this command is a list of managed folders (if any). To examine detailed information about custom folders applied to a mailbox, simply format the output into a table list as shown in the following example:

```
get-ManagedFolder -Mailbox 'cpand\tedb' | fl
```

Managing Content Settings

In Exchange Server 2007, you control the contents of managed folders using Managed Content Settings policy. You can create policies that control how long Exchange Server retains the items in managed folders and their subfolders and specify the action the server takes at the end of the retention period. You can use policies to automatically:

- Move all messaging content from one folder to another or move messaging content of a specific type from one folder to another.

- Mark messaging content as being past retention limits and require the user to take action.

- Permanently delete all messaging content from a folder or delete messaging content of a specific type from a folder.

- Move all messaging content of a specific type to the Deleted Items folder.

The sections that follow discuss techniques for applying, removing, and reviewing managed content settings.

Applying Managed Content Settings

In the Exchange Management Console, you can apply managed content settings by completing the following steps:

1. In Exchange Management Console, expand the Organization Configuration node, and then select the related Mailbox node.

2. In the details pane, click the Managed Default Folders or the Managed Custom Folders tab as appropriate.

3. Right-click the managed folder you want to work with, and then select New Managed Content Settings. This starts the New Managed Content Settings Wizard.

4. On the Introduction page, shown in Figure 13-4, type a name for the Managed Content Settings policy in the box provided.

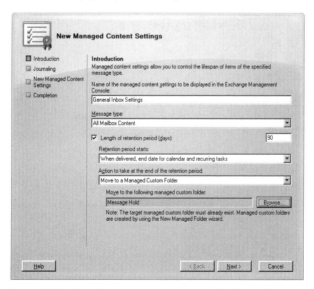

Figure 13-4   Specify how to control managed folder content.

5. Use the Message Type list to specify the type of content to which the policy should apply. The available options are:

- ❏ All Mailbox Content
- ❏ Calendar Items
- ❏ Contacts
- ❏ Documents
- ❏ Faxes
- ❏ Journal Items
- ❏ Meeting Requests, Responses, And Cancellations
- ❏ Missed Calls
- ❏ Notes
- ❏ Posts
- ❏ RSS Items
- ❏ Tasks
- ❏ Voicemail

6. You can now specify when the policy is applied:

- ❏ To apply the policy to all matching messaging content as soon as it is put in the selected folder, clear the Retention Period (Days) check box.
- ❏ To apply the policy to all matching messaging content after a specified period, select the Retention Period (Days) check box, and then enter the retention period.

7. Use the Retention Period Starts list to specify whether the retention period starts when an item is delivered to the folder or when items are moved from the folder to another folder.

8. Use the Action To Take When Retention Period Ends list to specify the action Exchange Server should take when the retention period ends. The available options are:

- ❏ **Move To Deleted Items Folder** Moves items of the specified types to the Deleted Items folder.
- ❏ **Move To A Managed Custom Folder** Allows you to move items of the specified types to a managed custom folder. After selecting this option, click Browse to select the existing managed custom folder to use.
- ❏ **Delete And Allow Recovery** Deletes items of the specified types. Although these items are not moved to the Deleted Items folder, they are available for recovery using the Recover Deleted Items feature in Outlook 2007.

❑ **Permanently Delete**   Permanently deletes items of the specified types. Items are not moved to the Deleted Items folder, nor are they available for recovery.

❑ **Mark As Past Retention Limit**   Marks items of the specified types as being past the retention limit. Messages are displayed shaded and with a strikethrough font. Users are prompted to resolve by moving or deleting the items.

9. Click Next. On the Journaling page, shown in Figure 13-5, you can configure optional journaling options for the previously specified messaging content types. Journaling is used to forward copies of messaging items automatically to an alternate location. To enable and configure journaling, do the following:

❑ Select the Forward Copies To check box, and then click Browse.

❑ In the Select Recipient dialog box, select the recipient to which Exchange Server should forward journal copies.

❑ Type an identifying label that should be assigned to the copies.

❑ Select a journal message format.

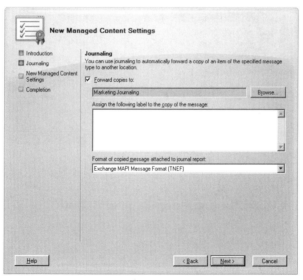

Figure 13-5   Set journaling options as necessary.

10. Click Next, and then click New to create the policy. Click Finish to complete the process.

In the Exchange Management Shell, you can use the new-ManagedContentSettings cmdlet to perform the same task. Sample 13-5 provides the syntax and usage.

Sample 13-5   New-ManagedContentSettings cmdlet syntax and usage

```
Syntax
new-ManagedContentSettings -Name 'SettingName'
 -FolderName 'FolderName'
 -RetentionAction ['MoveToFolder'|'MoveToDeletedItems'|
     'DeleteAndAllowRecovery'|'PermanentlyDelete'|
     'MarkAsPastRetentionLimit']
 -AddressForJournaling 'MailboxIdentity'
 -AgeLimitForRetention 'Limit'
 -JournalingEnabled [$true|$false|$null]
 -MessageFormatForJournaling ['UseTnef'|'UseMsg']
 -RetentionEnabled [$true|$false|$null]
 -LabelForJournaling 'Label'
 -MessageClass 'ExactNameListedInStep6'
 -MoveToDestinationFolder ['FolderName'|$null]
 -TriggerForRetention ['WhenDelivered'|'WhenMoved']
```

```
Usage
new-ManagedContentSettings -Name 'General Inbox Settings'
 -FolderName 'Inbox'
 -RetentionAction 'MoveToFolder'
 -AddressForJournaling 'cpandl.com/Users/Marketing Journaling'
 -AgeLimitForRetention '90'
 -JournalingEnabled $true
 -MessageFormatForJournaling 'UseTnef'
 -RetentionEnabled $true
 -LabelForJournaling 'Journaled Messaging Content'
 -MessageClass 'All Mailbox Content'
 -MoveToDestinationFolder 'Message Hold'
 -TriggerForRetention 'WhenDelivered'
```

Reviewing, Modifying, and Deleting Managed Content Settings

In the Exchange Management Console, you can review, modify, and delete managed content settings by completing the following steps:

1. In Exchange Management Console, expand the Organization Configuration node, and then select the related Mailbox node.

2. In the details pane, click the Managed Default Folders or the Managed Custom Folders tab as appropriate.

3. As Figure 13-6 shows, you can expand any folder to which you have applied managed content settings to view a list of related policy names.

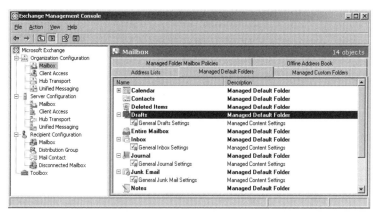

Figure 13-6   View policies applied to folders.

4. You can now:

   ❏ **Delete the managed content settings**   To delete the managed content settings, right-click the settings, and select Remove. When prompted to confirm, click Yes.

   ❏ **View the managed content settings configuration**   To view managed content settings configuration, right-click the settings, and then select Properties.

   ❏ **Modify the managed content settings configuration**   To modify the managed content settings configuration, right-click the settings, and then select Properties. Use the options on the General tab to configure the managed content settings. Use the options on the Journaling tab to configure journaling for the related folder.

In the Exchange Management Shell, you can use the get-ManagedContentSettings, set-ManagedContentSettings, and remove-ManagedContentSettings cmdlets to perform the same tasks. Samples 13-6 through 13-8 provide the syntax and usage.

Sample 13-6   Get-ManagedContentSettings cmdlet syntax and usage

```
Syntax
get-ManagedContentSettings [-Identity 'SettingsIdentity']

get-ManagedContentSettings [-FolderName 'FolderName']
```

Usage
```
get-ManagedContentSettings

get-ManagedContentSettings -Identity 'General Inbox Settings'

get-ManagedContentSettings -FolderName 'Inbox'
```

Sample 13-7   Set-ManagedContentSettings cmdlet syntax and usage

Syntax
```
set-ManagedContentSettings -Identity 'SettingsIdentity'
 -Name 'NewNameForContentSettings'
 -AddressForJournaling 'MailboxIdentity'
 -AgeLimitForRetention 'Limit'
 -JournalingEnabled [$true|$false|$null]
 -MessageFormatForJournaling ['UseTnef'|'UseMsg']
 -RetentionAction   ['MoveToFolder'|'MoveToDeletedItems'|
     'DeleteAndAllowRecovery'|'PermanentlyDelete'|
     'MarkAsPastRetentionLimit']
 -RetentionEnabled [$true|$false|$null]
 -LabelForJournaling 'Label'
 -MoveToDestinationFolder ['FolderName'|$null]
 -TriggerForRetention ['WhenDelivered'|'WhenMoved']
```

Usage
```
set-ManagedContentSettings -Identity 'General Inbox Settings'
 -Name 'Managed Content Settings for Inbox'
 -AddressForJournaling 'cpandl.com/Users/Marketing Journaling'
 -AgeLimitForRetention '90'
 -JournalingEnabled $true
 -LabelForJournaling 'Journaled Messaging Content'
 -MessageClass 'All Mailbox Content'
 -MessageFormatForJournaling 'UseMsg'
 -MoveToDestinationFolder $null
 -RetentionAction 'MoveToDeletedItems'
 -RetentionEnabled $true
 -TriggerForRetention 'WhenDelivered'
```

Sample 13-8   Remove-ManagedContentSettings cmdlet syntax and usage

Syntax
```
remove-ManagedContentSettings  -Identity 'SettingsIdentity'
```

Usage
```
remove-ManagedContentSettings  -Identity 'General Inbox Settings'
```

Deploying Managed Custom Mailbox Folders

Exchange Server automatically deploys managed default mailbox folders to user mailboxes. To deploy managed custom mailbox folders to user mailboxes, you must create a Managed Folder Mailbox policy and apply it to the folders. You can deploy all your custom folders with a single policy.

Creating Managed Folder Mailbox Policies

In the Exchange Management Console, you can create a Managed Folder Mailbox policy by completing the following steps:

1. In Exchange Management Console, expand the Organization Configuration node, and then select the related Mailbox node.

2. In the details pane, on the Managed Folder Mailbox Policies tab, right-click an open area of the window, and select New Managed Folder Mailbox Policy. This starts the New Managed Folder Mailbox Policy Wizard, as shown in Figure 13-7.

Figure 13-7   Create a new policy.

3. In the Policy Name text box, type a descriptive name for the policy.

4. Click Add.

5. Use the Select Managed Folder dialog box to select the managed folders to add to the policy. The policy can include any default folders and custom folders you've created. Click OK when you are finished.

Tip   You can select multiple folders in the Select Managed Folder dialog box. To select multiple folders individually, hold down the Ctrl key, and then click each folder that you want to select. To select a sequence of folders, hold down the Shift key, select the first folder, and then click the last folder.

6. Click New to create the policy, and then click Finish.

In the Exchange Management Shell, you can use the new-ManagedFolderMailbox-Policy cmdlet to perform the same task. Sample 13-9 provides the syntax and usage.

Sample 13-9   New-ManagedFolderMailboxPolicy cmdlet syntax and usage

```
Syntax
new-ManagedFolderMailboxPolicy -Name 'PolicyName'
 -ManagedFolderLinks 'FolderName1', 'FolderName2', ...
```

```
Usage
new-ManagedFolderMailboxPolicy
 -Name 'Deploy Pending Approval and Message Hold folders'
 -ManagedFolderLinks 'Pending Approval','Message Hold'
```

Reviewing, Modifying, and Deleting Managed Folder Mailbox Policies

In the Exchange Management Console, you can review, modify, and delete Managed Folder Mailbox policies by completing the following steps:

1. In Exchange Management Console, expand the Organization Configuration node, and then select the related Mailbox node.

2. In the details pane, click the Managed Folder Mailbox Policies tab. Exchange Management Console lists current policies by name. To delete a policy, right-click the settings, and select Remove. When prompted to confirm, click Yes.

3. To view or modify the policy, right-click the settings, and then select Properties. The Properties dialog box shows the currently associated folders. To delete a folder, select it, and then click the Delete button. To add a folder, click the Add button. Click OK when finished.

In the Exchange Management Shell, you can use the get-ManagedFolderMailboxPolicy, set-ManagedFolderMailboxPolicy, and remove-ManagedFolderMailboxPolicy cmdlets to perform the same tasks. Samples 13-10 through 13-12 provide the syntax and usage.

Sample 13-10   get-ManagedFolderMailboxPolicy cmdlet syntax and usage

```
Syntax
get-ManagedFolderMailboxPolicy [-Identity 'PolicyName']
```

Usage
```
get-ManagedFolderMailboxPolicy

get-ManagedFolderMailboxPolicy
-Identity 'Deploy Pending Approval and Message Hold folders'
```

Sample 13-11   set-ManagedFolderMailboxPolicy cmdlet syntax and usage

Syntax
```
set-ManagedFolderMailboxPolicy -Identity 'PolicyName'
 -ManagedFolderLinks 'FolderName1', 'FolderName2', ...
```

Usage
```
set-ManagedFolderMailboxPolicy
 -Identity 'Deploy Pending Approval and Message Hold folders'
 -ManagedFolderLinks 'Legal Hold','Finance Hold'
```

Sample 13-12   remove-ManagedFolderMailboxPolicy cmdlet syntax and usage

Syntax
```
remove-ManagedFolderMailboxPolicy -Identity 'PolicyName'
```

Usage
```
remove-ManagedFolderMailboxPolicy
-Identity 'Deploy Pending Approval and Message Hold folders'
```

Applying Managed Mailbox Policy to User Mailboxes

Now that you've configured records management, you need to apply your managed mailbox policy to user mailboxes. Although a Mailbox server can have multiple managed mailbox policies, each individual mailbox can have only one managed mailbox policy applied to it at a time.

You can enable, temporarily disable, or permanently remove a managed mailbox policy. When you enable policy, the Managed Folder Assistant performs the following tasks the next time it applies messaging records management settings:

- Creates the necessary managed custom folder or folders in the specified mailbox

- Moves or removes items in managed folders according to their retention settings

- Journals items in managed folders to other locations as appropriate

You can specify the one managed mailbox policy that Exchange should apply to a mailbox by following these steps:

1. In Exchange Management Console, expand the Recipient Configuration node and then select the related Mailbox node.

2. Right-click the mailbox you want to manage and then select Properties.

3. On the Mailbox Settings tab, double-click Messaging Records Management.

4. In the Messaging Records Management dialog box, select the Managed Folder Mailbox Policy check box and then click Browse.

5. In the Select Managed Folder Mailbox Policy dialog box, select the managed mailbox policy that Exchange should apply and then click OK.

6. Click OK again to apply the settings.

In the Exchange Management Shell, you can apply managed mailbox policy using the Set-Mailbox cmdlet, as shown in Sample 13-13. Use the Identity parameter to identify the mailbox to which Exchange should apply managed mailbox policy and the ManagedFolderMailboxPolicy parameter to specify the identity of the policy to apply.

Sample 13-13   Applying managed mailbox policy

```
Syntax
Set-mailbox -Identity 'MailboxIdentity'
  -ManagedFolderMailboxPolicy 'PolicyName'
```

```
Usage
Set-mailbox -Identity 'cpandl\mollyh'
  -ManagedFolderMailboxPolicy 'General Inbox Settings'
```

When a user goes on vacation or at other times when you don't want Exchange to apply managed mailbox policy, you can temporarily turn off messaging records management by following these steps:

1. In Exchange Management Console, expand the Recipient Configuration node and then select the related Mailbox node.

2. Right-click the mailbox you want to manage and then select Properties.

3. On the Mailbox Settings tab, double-click Messaging Records Management.

4. In the Messaging Records Management dialog box, select the Enabled Retention Hold check box.

5. Select the Start Date check box and then select a start date and time for the retention hold.

6. Select the End Date check box and then select an end date and time for the retention hold.

7. Click OK twice to apply the settings.

Note You should set both a start and an end date for retention hold whenever possible. With a start and end date, Exchange turns on the retention hold on the start date and turns off retention hold on the end date. However, if you don't set an end date, Exchange applies the retention hold to the mailbox until you turn the feature off or remove managed mailbox policy.

In the Exchange Management Shell, you can temporarily turn off managed mailbox policy using the Set-Mailbox cmdlet as shown in Sample 13-14. Set the RetentionHold-Enabled parameter to $true to enable retention hold and then use the StartDateForRetentionHold and EndDateForRetentionHold parameters to set the respective start and end dates for the retention hold.

Sample 13-14   Using retention hold

```
Syntax
Set-mailbox -Identity 'MailboxIdentity'
 –RetentionHoldEnabled <$false|$true>
 -StartDateForRetentionHold 'Date' –EndDateForRetentionHold 'Date'
```

```
Usage
Set-mailbox -Identity 'cpandl\tedb' –RetentionHoldEnabled $true
 -StartDateForRetentionHold '05-16-2010'
 –EndDateForRetentionHold '05-30-2010'

Set-mailbox -Identity 'cpandl\tedb' –RetentionHoldEnabled $false
```

When you no longer want Exchange to apply managed mailbox policy to a mailbox, you can remove messaging records management. When you remove the policy, the Managed Folder Assistant performs the following tasks the next time it applies messaging records management settings:

■ Removes mailbox policy settings from managed folders

■ Removes empty managed custom folders

■ Converts managed custom folders with items to standard folders

You can remove the policy by following these steps:

1. In Exchange Management Console, expand the Recipient Configuration node and then select the related Mailbox node.

2. Right-click the mailbox you want to manage, and then select Properties.

3. On the Mailbox Settings tab, double-click Messaging Records Management.

4. In the Messaging Records Management dialog box, clear the Managed Folder Mailbox Policy check box, and then click OK.

In the Exchange Management Shell, you can remove managed mailbox policy from a mailbox by using the Set-Mailbox cmdlet as shown in Sample 13-15.

Sample 13-15 Removing managed mailbox policy

```
Syntax
Set-mailbox -Identity 'MailboxIdentity'
  -RemovedManagedFolderAndPolicy <$false|$true>
```

```
Usage
Set-mailbox -Identity 'cpandl\tedb' -RetentionHoldEnabled $true
  -RemovedManagedFolderAndPolicy $true
```

Applying Records Management to a Mailbox Server

After you've configured records management for your organization and applied policy as appropriate to user mailboxes, you can begin managing records on the individual Mailbox servers in your organization. In Exchange Server 2007, the Managed Folder Assistant is responsible for applying records management settings. The Assistant does this by:

- Creating the necessary managed custom folders in user mailboxes

- Moving or removing items according to their retention settings

- Journaling items in mailboxes to other locations

Each Mailbox server in your organization has a Managed Folder Assistant, which runs according to a schedule you specify. It attempts to process all of the mailboxes on a server in the specified amount of time. If it does not finish during the allotted time, it automatically resumes processing where it left off the next time it runs.

In the Exchange Management Console, you can enable records management and schedule the Managed Mailbox Assistant to run by completing the following steps:

1. In Exchange Management Console, expand the Server Configuration node, and then select the related Mailbox node.

2. Right-click the Mailbox server you want to configure, and then select Properties. In the Properties dialog box, click the Messaging Records Management tab as shown in Figure 13-8.

3. Select Use Custom Schedule from the list, and then click Customize.

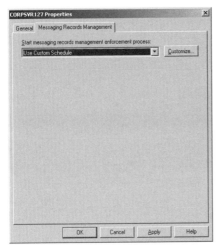

Figure 13-8   Enable records management.

4. In the Schedule dialog box, select the times and days during which you want the Managed Folder Assistant to run. Click OK to close the Schedule dialog box, and then click OK to close the server's Properties dialog box.

In the Exchange Management Console, you can disable records management by completing the following steps:

1. In Exchange Management Console, expand the Server Configuration node, and then select the related Mailbox node.

2. Right-click the Mailbox server you want to configure, and then select Properties.

3. In the Properties dialog box, click the Messaging Records Management tab.

4. In the Start Messaging Records Management Enforcement Process list, select Never. Click OK.

In the Exchange Management Shell, you can enable and disable records management using the -ManagedFolderAssistantSchedule parameter of the set-MailboxServer cmdlet. Sample 13-16 provides the syntax and usage. Note that it is easiest to schedule run times using a 24-hour clock.

Sample 13-16   Enabling and disabling records management

```
Syntax
set-MailboxServer -Identity 'ServerIdentity'
  -ManagedFolderAssistantSchedule 'Schedule'
```

Usage for enabling records management
```
set-MailboxServer -Identity 'CorpSvr127'
 -ManagedFolderAssistantSchedule 'Sun.01:00-Sun.05:00',
'Wed.01:00-Wed.05:00'
```

Usage for disabling records management
```
set-MailboxServer -Identity 'CorpSvr127'
 -ManagedFolderAssistantSchedule $null
```

In the Exchange Management Shell, you can manually start and stop records management using the start-ManagedFolderAssistant and stop-ManagedFolderAssistant cmdlets, respectively. When you start the Assistant manually, any current processing of mailboxes stops and the Assistant reprocesses all mailboxes on the server. Sample 13-17 provides the syntax and usage.

Sample 13-17 Starting and stopping records management manually

Syntax
```
start-ManagedFolderAssistant -Identity 'ServerIdentity'

stop-ManagedFolderAssistant -Identity 'ServerIdentity'
```

Usage
```
start-ManagedFolderAssistant -Identity 'CorpSvr127'
```

Real World If you no longer want to use messaging records management, you can remove all records management settings from a Mailbox server by deleting all managed custom folders and all managed mailbox polices. When you remove all managed custom folders and all managed mailbox policies, the Managed Folder Assistant performs the following tasks the next time it runs for all mailboxes with records management enabled: removes mailbox policy settings from managed folders, removes empty managed custom folders, and converts managed custom folders with items to standard folders. When you are sure the Managed Folder Assistant has run, you can turn off this feature as well.

Chapter 14

Accessing and Managing Public Folders

You use public folders to share messaging content and documents within an organization. Public folders are stored in a hierarchical structure referred to as a *public folder tree*. There is a direct correspondence between public folder databases and public folder trees. Each Mailbox server in a Microsoft Exchange 2007 organization can have one public folder database, and all Mailbox servers share the same public folder tree. Exchange 2007 does not support any alternate public folder trees. If you want users to have access to alternate public folder trees, you must retain a computer running Exchange 2000 Server or Exchange Server 2003 in your Exchange 2007 organization.

Accessing Public Folders

A public folder server is a Mailbox server with a public folder database. When your Exchange 2007 organization has more than one public folder database, public folder servers replicate public folder data automatically between and among these databases to create public folder replicas. Replicas provide redundancy in case of server failure and help to distribute the user load. All replicas of a public folder are equal. There is no master replica. This means that you can directly modify replicas of public folders. The public folder server with which you are working replicates the folder changes automatically to other servers.

Public folder trees define the structure of an organization's public folders. The public folder tree has two subtrees:

- Default public folders, also referred to as the default public folder tree.
- System public folders, also referred to as the system public folder tree.

The default public folder tree has its own hierarchy, which is separate from the system public folder tree. You can make the default public folder tree accessible to users based on criteria you set, and then users can create folders and manage their content. E-mail clients, such as Microsoft Outlook 2003, can access public folders using Messaging Application Programming Interface (MAPI). Newer clients, such as Office Outlook 2007, can access public folders using Hypertext Transfer Protocol (HTTP). The actual technology that makes it possible to create, edit, and manage messaging content and documents on remote servers is Web Distributed Authoring and Versioning (WebDAV).

To maintain security, each public folder in the default public folder tree can have specific usage rules. For example, you could create public folders called CompanyWide,

Marketing, and Engineering. Whereas you would typically make the CompanyWide folder accessible to all users, you would make the Marketing folder accessible only to users in the marketing department, and the Engineering folder accessible only to users in the engineering department.

In contrast, users cannot directly access or create folders in the system public folder tree. Exchange uses the folders in the system public folder tree to store and share specific types of system data stored in the public folder tree, including offline address books, Schedule+ free/busy information, and organizational forms. Thus, while client applications can use system folders to store and retrieve certain types of data, such as an offline address book, client applications do not have a direct management interface, such as is available with the default public folder tree.

Accessing Public Folders in Mail Clients

You can access public folders from just about any e-mail client, provided that the client is MAPI-compliant or supports Web distribution points, such as Outlook 2007. When you configure Outlook 2007 for Exchange Server, users have direct access to the default public folders tree. When you configure Outlook 2007 for Internet-only use, users can access public folders using only Internet Messaging Access Protocol 4 (IMAP4) and you must have retained a computer running Exchange 2000 Server or Exchange Server 2003 in your Exchange 2007 organization.

If Outlook is configured properly, users can access public folders by completing the following steps:

1. Start Outlook 2007. If the Folder list isn't displayed, click Go, and then select Folder List.

2. In the Folder list, expand Public Folders, and then expand All Public Folders to get a complete view of the available top-level folders. A top-level folder is simply a folder at the next level below the tree root.

Note Chapter 3, "Managing Microsoft Exchange Server 2007 Clients," discusses techniques you can use to configure Outlook. Refer to the section of that chapter entitled "Configuring Mail Support for Outlook 2007 and Windows Mail."

Accessing Public Folders Through the Information Store

Exchange 2007 automatically configures Web sharing and access controls. As an administrator, you can access public folders through the Exchange information store using either the Public Folder Management Console or the Exchange Management Shell.

The Public Folder Management Console provides easy access to both the default public folders and the system public folders. In the Exchange Management Console, you can start the Public Folder Management Console by selecting the Toolbox node in the left pane and then double-clicking the Public Folder Management Console entry in the main pane.

The Public Folder Management Console allows you to manage public folders on one server at a time. To connect to a specific server or set a default server, complete the following steps:

1. In Public Folder Management Console, select the Public Folders node in the console tree and then click Connect To Server on the Action menu or in the Action pane.

2. In the Connect To Server dialog box, click Browse. In the Select Public Folder Servers dialog box, only Mailbox servers with public folder databases are available for selection. Select the server to use and then click OK.

3. If you want the currently selected server to be the default server whenever you use Public Folder Management Console, select the Set As Default Server check box.

4. Click Connect to connect to the server. If you set the server as the default, this setting is saved for the user account on the computer that is running the console. If you start the console on another computer or use a different account, the default server may be different.

Once you've accessed the Public Folder Management Console and connected to a server, you'll be able to work with the default public folder tree and the system public folder tree. As shown in Figure 14-1, both trees are accessible in the left pane. By double-clicking expandable nodes, you can navigate through successive levels of the public folder hierarchy. The interface doesn't display individual items stored in folders; the interface only displays public folders and subfolders.

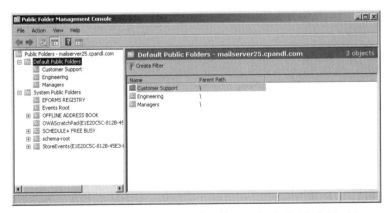

Figure 14-1   View and work with the public folder tree in the Public Folder Management Console.

When you select a folder containing subfolders in the left pane, the console displays details regarding the subfolders in the main pane. By default, the console only displays the subfolder name and parent path. You can display additional details by clicking Add/Remove Columns on the View menu, selecting columns to display in the Available Columns list, and then clicking Add. Additional details you can display include: the age limit in days, the hidden from address list flag, the local replica age limit in days, the mail-enabled flag, and a list of replicas.

At the Exchange Management Shell prompt, you can get information about the public folder database by using the Get-PublicFolder cmdlet. When you are working with this cmdlet, you use the –Identity parameter to identify the folder with which you want to work:

- \ represents the root of the default public folder tree (also known as the IPM_SUBTREE).

- *FolderName* represents a specific named folder.

- \\NON_IPM_SUBTREE represents the root of the hidden system public folder tree.

Sample 14-1 provides the syntax and usage for getting information about a folder. As the sample output shows, the Exchange Management Shell returns configuration details for the folder identity.

Sample 14-1   Getting information about a public folder

```
Syntax
Get-PublicFolder -Identity 'FolderIdentity' | fl
```

```
Usage
Get-PublicFolder -Identity '\' | fl
```

```
Output
Schema                           :
Microsoft.Exchange.Data.Mapi.PublicFolderSchema
AgeLimit                         :
EntryId                          :
HasSubFolders                    : True
HiddenFromAddressListsEnabled    : False
LocalReplicaAgeLimit             :
MailEnabled                      : False
MaxItemSize                      : 102040 KB
Name                             : IPM_SUBTREE
ParentPath                       :
PerUserReadStateEnabled          : True
PostStorageQuota                 :
Replicas                         : {}
ReplicationSchedule              : {}
```

```
RetainDeletedItemsFor            : 90 days
StorageQuota                     :
UseDatabaseAgeDefaults           : True
UseDatabaseQuotaDefaults         : True
UseDatabaseReplicationSchedule   : False
UseDatabaseRetentionDefaults     : True
Identity                         : \
IsValid                          : True
OriginatingServer                : mailserver25.cpandl.com
```

You can use the –Recurse parameter to examine recursively the folder and its subfolders. When you use this parameter, you should redirect the output through the Format-List command and name the folder details that you want to examine. You can examine any of the properties previously listed in Sample 14-1 by specifying the property names to return in a comma-separated list. For example, if you want to return a list of all sub-folders of the public folder root formatted by the Name and MailEnabled properties, you could use the following command:

```
Get-PublicFolder –Identity '\' -Recurse | Format-List
Name,MailEnabled
```

The output would look similar to the following:

```
Name        : IPM_SUBTREE
MailEnabled : False

Name        : Projects
MailEnabled : False

Name        : SavedData
MailEnabled : False

Name        : Teams
MailEnabled : False
```

If you suspect a replication problem with public folders, you could compare the configuration details for public folders on your Mailbox servers using the Get-PublicFolder cmdlet. Just specify the –Server parameter and the identity of the server you want to work with, such as:

```
Get-PublicFolder –Server 'CorpSvr272' -Recurse | fl

Get-PublicFolder –Server 'CorpSvr185' -Recurse | fl
```

To get information about a specific public folder on a server, you can use the –Server parameter to identify the server with which you want to work and the –Identity parameter to identify the public folder to examine.

```
Get-PublicFolder –Identity '\Managers' –Server 'CorpSvr272' | fl
```

Real World   You can trace most problems with Web sharing of public folders to individuals who inadvertently change the access settings. If you restore the original settings, users should regain access to the public folder. Note that only Exchange Server can initialize Web sharing for public folders. If Exchange Server isn't sharing public folders correctly, you might have incorrectly configured Microsoft Internet Information Services (IIS) or Outlook Web Access. For details on working with IIS, HTTP virtual servers, and Outlook Web Access, see Chapter 16, "Managing Client Access Servers."

Creating and Working with Public Folders

The following sections examine techniques you can use to create and work with public folders. Both users and administrators can create and work with public folders using Outlook. Administrators can also create and work with public folders using the Public Folder Management Console or the Exchange Management Shell.

Creating Public Folders in Microsoft Outlook

Both administrators and authorized users can create public folders in the default public folder tree using Outlook. To do this, complete the following steps:

1. Start Outlook 2007. If the Folder list isn't displayed, click Go, and then select Folder List.

2. Expand Public Folders in the Folder list, and then right-click All Public Folders.

3. Select New Folder. You'll see the Create New Folder dialog box, as shown in Figure 14-2.

4. Enter a name for the public folder, and then use the Folder Contains list box to choose the type of item you want to place in the folder. Public folders can contain:

   ❑ Calendar Items

   ❑ Contact Items

   ❑ InfoPath Form Items

   ❑ Journal Items

   ❑ Mail And Post Items

   ❑ Note Items

   ❑ Task Items

Figure 14-2   Create a new public folder in the default public folder tree.

5. Select where to place the folder. To create the folder as a top-level folder, select All Public Folders. Otherwise, expand All Public Folders, and then select the folder in which you want to place the public folder.

6. Click OK. Complete, as necessary, the following tasks, as explained in the section of this chapter entitled "Managing Public Folder Settings."

   ❑ Control replication and set messaging limits.

   ❑ Set client permissions.

   ❑ Propagate public folder settings.

Creating Public Folders Using the Public Folder Management Console

As an administrator, you can use Public Folder Management Console to create public folders by completing the following steps:

1. In Exchange Management Console, start Public Folder Management Console by selecting the Toolbox node in the left pane and then double-clicking the Public Folder Management Console entry in the main pane.

2. In the left pane, you have access to default public folders and system public folders. Navigate through successive levels of the public folder hierarchy by double-clicking expandable nodes until you get to the folder in which you want to create your folder.

3. Right-click the folder in which you want to create a folder, and then select New Public Folder. This starts the New Public Folder Wizard.

4. On the New Public Folder page, shown in Figure 14-3, type the display name for the public folder. The Path box shows the path to the folder you are creating in the public folder hierarchy. If the path is a backslash ("\"), you are creating a new top-level folder. Otherwise, you are creating a subfolder of an existing folder.

5. Click New to create the public folder and then click Finish.

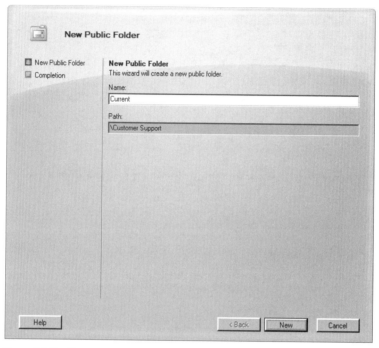

Figure 14-3   Create a new public folder for the organization.

Creating Public Folders Using the Exchange Management Shell

As an administrator, you can create public folders within the default public folder tree using the New-PublicFolder cmdlet. Use the –Name parameter to set the name of the public folder and the –Path parameter to create the folder under a particular folder. If you omit the –Path parameter, Exchange creates the folder as a top-level folder under the default public folders root. Sample 14-2 provides the syntax and usage for the New-PublicFolder cmdlet.

Sample 14-2   New-PublicFolder cmdlet syntax and usage

Syntax
```
New-PublicFolder -Name 'FolderName'
  [-Path 'ParentFolderName']
  [-Server 'Server']
```

Usage
```
New-PublicFolder -Name 'Projects'
```

Determining Public Folder Size, Item Count, and Last Access Time

In Outlook, you can determine the size in kilobytes of a public folder by completing the following steps:

1. Start Outlook 2007. If the Folder list isn't displayed, click Go, and then select Folder List.

2. Expand Public Folders in the Folder list, and then expand All Public Folders.

3. Right-click the public folder with which you want to work, and then select Properties.

4. On the General tab of the Public Folder Properties dialog box, click Folder Size. The Folder Size dialog box lists the total size of the selected public folder, including all subfolders and the individual size of each subfolder.

Using the Public Folder Management Console, you can determine the size, item count, and last access time of a top-level public folder by completing the following steps:

1. In Public Folder Management Console, select the Default Public Folders node or the System Public Folders node as appropriate for the type of public folder you want to work with.

2. In the main pane, right-click a top-level public folder to examine, and then select Properties.

3. On the General tab of the Properties dialog box, you'll see the key details for the selected public folder as shown in Figure 14-4.

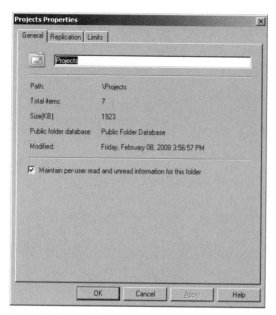

Figure 14-4 Get information about the public folder using the Properties dialog box.

In the Exchange Management Shell, you can view the total number of items contained in and the last access time of public folders using the Get-PublicFolderStatistics cmdlet as shown in the following example:

```
Get-PublicFolderStatistics
```

The output will be similar to the following:

```
Name              ItemCount         LastAccessTime
----              ---------         --------------
Projects          19292             03/15/2007 3:38:21 PM
SavedData         791               03/17/2007 7:21:35 AM
Teams             895               02/01/2007 2:45:18 PM
```

If you use the –Identity parameter to examine a specific public folder and format the output as a list, you can see additional details, including total item size and deleted item size. Sample 14-3 shows the syntax and usage. Keep in mind that if you omit the –Identity parameter, you'll view details for all public folders.

Sample 14-3 Getting usage statistics for public folders

```
Syntax
Get-PublicFolderStatistics [-Identity 'FolderIdentity']
  [-Server 'Server']
```

```
Usage
Get-PublicFolderStatistics -Identity '\Projects' | fl
```

```
Output
AdminDisplayName         : Customer Support
AssociatedItemCount      : 4
ContactCount             : 52
CreationTime             : 4/22/2009 7:14:08 PM
DeletedItemCount         : 24
EntryId                  : 000000001A447390AA6611CD9BC800AA002FC45A030
                           032952AC3E
                           164D2419EE9E7A08CCB68910001907875400000
ExpiryTime               :
FolderPath               : Customer Support
IsDeletePending          : False
ItemCount                : 789
LastAccessTime           : 12/8/2008 11:24:00 AM
LastModificationTime     : 12/22/2008 9:14:09 AM
Name                     : Customer Support
OwnerCount               : 12
TotalAssociatedItemSize  : 9823B
TotalDeletedItemSize     : 1281904B
TotalItemSize            : 397719508223B
ServerName               : MAILSERVER25
StorageGroupName         : Second Storage Group
DatabaseName             : Public Folder Database
Identity                 : 000000001A447390AA6611CD9BC800AA002FC45A030
                           032952AC3E
                           164D2419EE9E7A08CCB68910001907875400000
IsValid                  : True
OriginatingServer        : mailserver25.cpandl.com
```

Adding Items to Public Folders Using Outlook

Exchange 2007 supports standard public folders and mail-enabled public folders. Authorized users can post items to public folders through any compliant application. Let's briefly look at how you could use Outlook to post items to public folders.

In Outlook, authorized users can post items to public folders by completing these steps:

1. Start Outlook 2007. If the Folder list isn't displayed, click Go, and then select Folder List.

2. Expand Public Folders and then All Public Folders in the Folder list. Then select the folder you want to use.

3. Click New, or press Ctrl+Shift+S. Notice that when a public folder is selected, the New button automatically changes to public folder post mode.

4. Type a subject for the message, and then type your message text. Add any necessary attachments.

5. Click Post.

Mail-Enabling Public Folders

Public folders are not mail-enabled by default. If you want authorized users to be able to submit items using standard e-mail, you can mail-enable a public folder using the Enable-MailPublicFolder cmdlet. If you later want to disable sending mail to a public folder, you can use the Disable-MailPublicFolder cmdlet. Samples 14-4 and 14-5 provide the syntax and usage for these cmdlets. Use the −Server parameter to specify the Mailbox server with a public folder database on which to perform the procedure.

Sample 14-4   Enable-MailPublicFolder cmdlet syntax and usage

```
Syntax
Enable-MailPublicFolder -Identity 'FolderIdentity'
  [-HiddenFromAddressListsEnabled <$false|$true>]
  [-Server 'Server']
```

```
Usage
Enable-MailPublicFolder -Identity '\Projects'
```

Sample 14-5   Disable-MailPublicFolder cmdlet syntax and usage

```
Syntax
Disable-MailPublicFolder -Identity 'FolderIdentity'
  [-Server 'Server']
```

```
Usage
Disable-MailPublicFolder -Identity '\Projects'
```

In the Public Folder Management Console, you can mail-enable a public folder by selecting the folder's parent in the left pane, clicking the folder in the main pane, and then clicking Mail Enable. Conversely, to disable sending mail to a public folder, select the folder's parent in the left pane, click the folder in the main pane, and then click Mail Disable. When prompted to confirm that you want to disable sending mail to the public folder, click Yes.

After you've mail-enabled a public folder, users simply address an e-mail to the public folder and the public folder receives the message as a posting. The default e-mail address is the same as the folder name, with any spaces converted to underscore characters ("_"). For example, if the public folder name was Current Projects and

Cpandl.com was the e-mail domain, the e-mail address of the public folder would be current_projects@cpandl.com.

In the Public Folder Management Console, you can view or set a public folder's e-mail–related properties by double-clicking the public folder in the main pane and using the additional tabs provided. As Figure 14-5 shows, Properties dialog boxes for mail-enabled public folders have the following additional tabs:

- **Exchange General**   Allows you to view or set general Exchange settings that include the Exchange alias, standard display name, and simple display name. You can also hide the public folder from the address list and add custom attributes using the options on this tab.

- **E-Mail Addresses**   Allows you to view or set the e-mail address or addresses associated with the public folder. The related procedures for public folders are similar to those for mailbox users. See "Adding, Changing, and Removing E-mail Addresses" in Chapter 7, "User and Contact Administration," for more information.

- **Mail Flow Settings**   Allows you to view and set delivery options, message size restrictions, and message delivery restrictions for the public folder. The related procedures for public folders are similar to those for mailbox users. See "Configuring Mailbox Delivery Restrictions, Permissions, and Storage Limits" in Chapter 8, "Mailbox Administration," for more information.

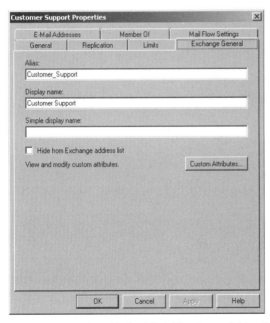

Figure 14-5   Mail-enabled public folders have additional properties and option tabs.

You can view information about mail-enabled public folders using the Get-MailPublicFolder cmdlet, and you can set any of the related properties using the Set-MailPublicFolder cmdlet. You can set all the highlighted parameters displayed as output for the Get-MailPublicFolder cmdlet by using their parameter names with the Set-MailPublicFolder cmdlet. Samples 14-6 and 14-7 provide the syntax and usage for these cmdlets.

Sample 14-6   Set-MailPublicFolder cmdlet syntax and usage

```
Syntax
Set-MailPublicFolder -Identity 'FolderIdentity'
 [-ParameterName 'ParameterValue']
```

```
Usage
Set-MailPublicFolder -Identity '\Projects' –Alias 'Projects'
```

Sample 14-7   Get-MailPublicFolder cmdlet syntax and usage

```
Syntax
Get-MailPublicFolder -Identity 'FolderIdentity'
```

```
Usage
Get-MailPublicFolder -Identity '\Projects'
```

```
Output
Schema      : Microsoft.Exchange.Data.Directory.Management.MailPublicFol
derSchema
Contacts                    : {}
DeliverToMailboxAndForward      : False
ExternalEmailAddress        : expf:PROJECTS6CB2F8154AD7266514255EB216467
DABEF5F9F
ForwardingAddress           :
PublicFolderType            : Mapi
RootUrl                     :
AcceptMessagesOnlyFrom      : {}
AcceptMessagesOnlyFromDLMembers   : {}
AddressListMembership           : {Default Global Address List,
Worldwide Sales, Europe Sales, US Sales, Europe Support, Public
Folders, West Coast Sales Teams}
Alias                   : Projects
OrganizationalUnit      : cpandl.com/
Microsoft Exchange System Objects
CustomAttribute1            :
CustomAttribute10           :
CustomAttribute11           :
CustomAttribute12           :
CustomAttribute13           :
```

```
CustomAttribute14          :
CustomAttribute15          :
CustomAttribute2           :
CustomAttribute3           :
CustomAttribute4           :
CustomAttribute5           :
CustomAttribute6           :
CustomAttribute7           :
CustomAttribute8           :
CustomAttribute9           :
DisplayName                : Projects
EmailAddresses             : {SMTP:Projects@cpandl.com, X400:c=US;a=;
                             p=First Organizati;o=Exchange;s=Projects;}
GrantSendOnBehalfTo            : {}
HiddenFromAddressListsEnabled    : False
MaxSendSize                : unlimited
MaxReceiveSize             : unlimited
EmailAddressPolicyEnabled       : True
PrimarySmtpAddress            : Projects@cpandl.com
RecipientType              : PublicFolder
RecipientTypeDetails          : PublicFolder
RejectMessagesFrom            : {}
RejectMessagesFromDLMembers      : {}
RequireSenderAuthenticationEnabled : False
SimpleDisplayName             :
WindowsEmailAddress           : projects@cpandl.com
Name                       : Projects
```

Managing Public Folder Settings

You should actively manage public folders. If you don't, you won't get optimal performance and users might encounter problems when reading from or posting to the folders. Each folder in a public folder tree has its own settings, and each time a folder is created, you should review and modify the following settings:

- Replication, messaging limits, deleted item retention, and quotas
- Client and Send As permissions

You might also want to designate folder administrators and propagate the changes you've made. This section of the chapter explains these and other public folder administration tasks. Don't forget that in the Public Folder Management Console, you can view or set a public folder's e-mail–related properties by using the related Properties dialog box. As discussed previously under "Mail-Enabling Public Folders," the related procedures are similar to those for mailbox users.

Controlling Folder Replication, Messaging Limits, Quotas, and Deleted Item Retention

Public folders inherit the replication, messaging limit, quota, and deleted item retention settings of the public folder database. The best way to control these settings for public folders is to set the appropriate options for the entire public folder database rather than for individual public folders, as discussed in the "Using Public Folder Databases" section of Chapter 12, "Mailbox and Public Folder Database Administration." That said, the Exchange Management Shell includes the Set-PublicFolder cmdlet for configuring these options for individual public folders.

Sample 14-8 provides the syntax and usage for this cmdlet. To override database settings for replication, messaging limit, quota, deleted item retention settings, or any combination thereof, you must first set the related "Use" parameter to $false, as shown in the example, and then set any desired default values as shown in the second example.

Sample 14-8   Using set-PublicFolder to set limits

```
Syntax
set-PublicFolder -Identity 'PublicFolderIdentity'
  [-AgeLimit LimitKB]
  [-HiddenFromAddressListsEnabled <$false|$true>]
  [-MaxItemSize LimitKB]
  [-Name 'Name']
  [-PerUserReadStateEnabled <$false|$true>]
  [-PostStorageQuota LimitKB]
  [-Replicas 'DatabaseID1', 'DatabaseID2', ...]
  [-ReplicationSchedule 'Schedule']
  [-RetainDeletedItemsFor NumberDays]
  [-Server 'Server']
  [-StorageQuota NumberDays]
  [-UseDatabaseAgeDefaults <$false|$true>]
  [-UseDatabaseQuotaDefaults <$false|$true>]
  [-UseDatabaseReplicationSchedule <$false|$true>]
  [-UseDatabaseRetentionDefaults <$false|$true>]
```

```
Usage
set-PublicFolder -Identity '\Projects'
  -UseDatabaseRetentionDefaults $false

set-PublicFolder -Identity '\Projects'
  -RetainDeletedItemsFor 120
```

You can also configure these values using the Public Folder Management Console. When you display a public folder's Properties dialog box by double-clicking the public folder in the main pane, you can use the options on the Replication and Limits tabs to set related values. To override default settings for the related public folder database, use the following techniques as appropriate for your desired configuration:

- On the Replication tab, clear the Use Public Folder Database Replication Schedule check box and then set the desired replication schedule.

- On the Limits tab, clear the Use Database Quota Defaults check box and then set the desired quota values.

- On the Limits tab, clear the Use Database Retention Defaults check box and then set the desired retention value.

- On the Limits tab, clear the Use Database Age Defaults check box and then set the desired age limit for replicas.

You can restore the default settings for the related public folder database simply by selecting the related check box or check boxes on the Replication tab, the Limits tab, or both.

Setting Client Permissions

You use client permissions to specify which users can access a particular public folder. By default, all users (except those accessing the folder anonymously over the Web) have permission to access the folder, read items in the folder, create items in the folder, and edit and delete items they've created. Anyone accessing the folder anonymously can create items but has no other permissions for viewing or editing items.

To change permissions for anonymous and authenticated users, you need to set a new permission level for the special users Anonymous and Default, respectively. Initially, anonymous users have the role of Contributor and authenticated users have the role of Author. These and other client-permission levels are defined as follows:

- **Owner**   Grants all permissions in the folder. Users with this role can create, read, modify, and delete all items in the folder. They can create subfolders and change permissions on folders as well.

- **Publishing Editor**   Grants permission to create, read, modify, and delete all items in the folder. Users with this role can create subfolders as well.

- **Editor**   Grants permission to create, read, modify, and delete all items in the folder.

- **Publishing Author**   Grants permission to create and read items in the folder, to modify and delete items the user created, and to create subfolders.

- **Author**   Grants permission to create and read items in the folder, as well as to modify and delete items that the user created.

- **Nonediting Author**   Grants permission to create and read items in the folder.

- **Reviewer** Grants read-only permission.

- **Contributor** Grants permission to create items but not to view the contents of the folder.

- **None** Grants no permission in the folder.

To set new roles for users or to modify existing client permissions, complete the following steps:

1. Start Outlook 2007. If the Folder list isn't displayed, click Go, and then select Folder List.

2. Expand Public Folders in the Folder list, and then expand All Public Folders.

3. Right-click the folder with which you want to work, and then select Properties.

4. On the Permissions tab (shown in Figure 14-6), the Name and Permission Level lists display account names and their permissions on the folder. If you want to grant users permissions that are different from the default permission, click Add.

Figure 14-6 Use the Permissions tab to set permissions and assign roles for users. The role controls the actions the user can perform.

5. In the Add Users dialog box, select the name of a user who needs access to the mailbox. Then click Add to put the name in the Add Users list. Repeat this step as necessary for other users. Click OK when you're finished.

6. In the Name and Permission Level lists, select one or more users whose permissions you want to modify. Then use the Permission Level list to assign a role or select individual permission items. When you're finished granting permissions, click OK.

In the Exchange Management Shell, you can work with permissions using the Get-PublicFolderClientPermission, Add-PublicFolderClientPermission, and Remove-PublicFolderClientPermission cmdlets. Samples 14-9 through 14-11 provide the syntax and usage for these cmdlets. Values for the –AccessRights parameter can be set to the name of the permission level desired. Specify the exact name, as listed previously, without spaces. If you want to create modified permission levels, you can add or remove individual access rights. Use the names exactly as shown on the Permissions tab, without spaces.

Sample 14-9   Get-PublicFolderClientPermission syntax and usage

```
Syntax
Get-PublicFolderClientPermission –Identity 'PublicFolderIdentity'
 [-Server 'Server']
 [-User 'UserIdentity']
```

```
Usage
Get-PublicFolderClientPermission –Identity '\Projects'
 -User 'William Stanek'
```

Sample 14-10   Add-PublicFolderClientPermission syntax and usage

```
Syntax
Add-PublicFolderClientPermission –Identity 'PublicFolderIdentity'
 -AccessRights 'PermLevelOrAccessRight'
 -User 'UserIdentity'
 [-Server 'Server']
```

```
Usage
Add-PublicFolderClientPermission –Identity '\Projects'
 -AccessRights 'PublishingEditor'
 -User 'William Stanek'

Add-PublicFolderClientPermission –Identity '\Projects'
 -AccessRights 'CreateItems'
 -User 'JimWilson'
```

Sample 14-11   Remove-PublicFolderClientPermission syntax and usage

```
Syntax
Remove-PublicFolderClientPermission –Identity 'PublicFolderIdentity'
 -AccessRights 'PermLevelOrAccessRight'
 -User 'UserIdentity'
 [-Server 'Server']
```

```
Usage
Remove-PublicFolderClientPermission -Identity '\Projects'
 -AccessRights 'PublishingEditor'
 -User 'William Stanek'

Remove-PublicFolderClientPermission -Identity '\Projects'
 -AccessRights 'CreateItems'
 -User 'Jim Wilson'
```

Granting and Revoking Send As Permissions for Public Folders

If you want to allow a user to send messages on behalf of the public folder, you can do
this using the Manage Send As Permission Wizard. In the Public Folder Management
Console, select the folder's parent in the left pane, click the folder in the main pane,
and then click Manage Send As Permission on the Action menu or in the Action pane.
In the Manage Send As Permission Wizard, click Add, and then use the Select
Recipient dialog box to choose the user or users who should have Send As permission
on the public folder. To revoke Send As permission, select an existing user name in the
Security Principal list box, and then click Remove. Click Manage to set the desired
access permissions.

In the Exchange Management Shell, you can use the Add-ADPermission and Remove-
ADPermission cmdlets to manage Send As permissions. Sample 14-12 and 14-13 show
examples using these cmdlets. Here, the ExtendedRights parameter is set to Send-As to
indicate that you are setting Send As permissions on the mailbox.

Sample 14-12   Adding Send As permissions for public folders

```
Syntax
Add-ADPermission -Identity 'PublicFolderIdentity'
 -User 'UserBeingGrantedPermission' -ExtendedRights 'Send-As'
```

```
Usage
Add-ADPermission
 -Identity 'CN=Managers,CN=Microsoft Exchange System Objects,
 DC=cpandl,DC=com' -User 'CPANDL\andyc' -ExtendedRights 'Send-As'
```

Sample 14-13   Removing send as permissions for public folders

```
Syntax
Remove-ADPermission -Identity 'PublicFolderIdentity'
 -User 'UserBeingRevokedPermission' -ExtendedRights 'Send-As'
 -InheritanceType 'All' -ChildObjectTypes $null
 -InheritedObjectTypes $null
 -Properties $null
```

```
Usage
Remove-ADPermission
-Identity 'CN=Managers,CN=Microsoft Exchange System Objects,
DC=cpandl,DC=com' -User 'CPANDL\andyc' -ExtendedRights 'Send-As'
-InheritanceType 'All' -ChildObjectTypes $null
-InheritedObjectTypes $null
-Properties $null
```

Propagating Public Folder Settings and Data

Any property changes you make to public folders aren't automatically applied to subfolders or replicated to other Mailbox servers hosting public folder replicas. You must either wait for the maintenance/replication interval to begin or manually propagate setting changes using the Update Hierarchy feature in Public Folder Management Console or the Update-PublicFolderHiearchy cmdlet.

In Public Folder Management Console, you can update the entire public folder hierarchy by selecting the Public Folders node in the left pane and then clicking Update Hierarchy on the Action menu or in the Action pane. Sample 14-14 provides the syntax and usage for the Update-PublicFolderHierarchy cmdlet.

Sample 14-14   Update-PublicFolderHierarchy syntax and usage

```
Syntax
Update-PublicFolderHierarchy -Server 'Server'
```

```
Usage
Update-PublicFolderHierarchy -Server 'CorpSvr257'
```

Similarly, changes users make to individual public folders aren't automatically replicated to other Mailbox servers hosting replicas. You must either wait for replication to begin or manually replicate data changes using the Update Content feature in Public Folder Management Console or the Update-PublicFolder cmdlet.

In Public Folder Management Console, you can update an individual public folder and its subfolders by selecting the parent folder in the left pane, clicking the folder in the main pane, and then clicking Update Content on the Action menu or in the Action pane. Sample 14-15 provides the syntax and usage for the Update-PublicFolder cmdlet.

Sample 14-15   Update-PublicFolder syntax and usage

```
Syntax
Update-PublicFolder -Identity 'PublicFolderIdentity'
 -Server 'Server'
```

```
Usage
Update-PublicFolder -Identity '\Projects'
 -Server 'CorpSvr257'
```

Manipulating, Renaming, and Recovering Public Folders

Public folders are stored as objects in Active Directory. You can manipulate public folders using standard techniques, such as cut, copy, and paste. Follow the procedures outlined in this section to manipulate, rename, and recover public folders.

Renaming Public Folders

To rename a public folder using Outlook, follow these steps:

1. In Outlook, right-click the public folder you want to rename.

2. Select Rename, type a new name, and then press Enter.

To rename a public folder using the Public Folder Management Console, follow these steps:

1. In Public Folder Management Console, select the parent folder in the left pane and then double-click the folder in the main pane.

2. On the General tab of the Properties dialog box, type a new name in the text box provided and then click OK.

   Note For mail-enabled public folders, you set the Exchange alias, the standard display name, and the simple display name on the Exchange General tab.

Copying and Moving Public Folders

You can copy and move public folders only within the same public folder tree. You can't copy or move a public folder to a different tree.

To create a copy of a public folder, follow these steps:

1. In Outlook, right-click the public folder with which you want to work, and then select Copy.

2. Right-click the folder into which you want to copy the folder, and then select Paste.

To move a public folder to a new location in the same tree, follow these steps:

1. In Outlook, right-click the public folder with which you want to work, and then select Cut.

2. Right-click the folder into which you want to move the folder, and then select Paste.

Deleting Public Folders

When you delete a public folder, you remove its contents, any subfolders it contains, and the contents of its subfolders. Before you delete a folder, however, you should ensure that any existing data that the folder contains is no longer needed and that you make a backup of the folder contents just in case.

Using Outlook, you delete public folders and their subfolders by completing the following steps:

1. In Outlook, right-click the public folder you want to remove, and then select Delete.

2. You'll be asked to confirm that you want to delete the folder and all subfolders. Click Yes.

Using the Public Folder Management Console, you delete public folders and their subfolders by completing the following steps:

1. In Public Folder Management Console, select the parent folder in the left pane and then select the folder that you want to delete in the main pane.

2. On the Action menu or in the Action pane, click Remove.

3. You'll be asked to confirm that you want to delete the folder and all subfolders. Click Yes.

Recovering Public Folders

You can recover deleted folders from public folder databases, provided that you've set a deleted item retention period for the public folder database from which the folders were deleted and the retention period hasn't expired. If both of these conditions are met, you can recover deleted folders by completing the following steps:

1. Log on to the domain using an account with administrative privileges in the domain or using an account with full control over the public folders you need to recover.

2. After starting Outlook, access the Public Folders node, and then select the parent node that contained the public folders. For example, with a top-level folder, you'd select the All Public Folders node, but with a subfolder of a top-level folder, you'd select the node for the top-level folder.

3. On the Tools menu, select Recover Deleted Items. The Recover Deleted Items From dialog box appears.

4. Select the folders you want to recover, and then click the Recover Selected Items button.

5. Each folder restored by the recovery operation has "(Recovered)" appended to the folder name. After you verify the contents of the folder, you can complete the recovery operation by doing the following:

❑ **Restoring the original folder name**   Right-click the folder, select Rename, type a new name, and then press Enter.

❑ **Restoring the folder's e-mail addresses**   Right-click the folder, and then select Properties. In the Properties dialog box, click the E-mail Addresses tab. Edit each e-mail address so that it's restored to its original value.

Chapter 15

Managing Hub Transport and Edge Transport Servers

You can configure your Microsoft Exchange Server 2007 organization with only Hub Transport servers for message routing and delivery or you can configure it with Hub Transport servers and Edge Transport servers. When you use only Hub Transport servers, these servers are responsible for:

- Messaging routing and delivery within the organization.

- Receiving messages from outside the organization and delivering them to Mailbox servers within the organization.

- Receiving messages from Mailbox servers within the organization and routing them to destinations outside the organization.

When you use Hub Transport and Edge Transport servers, message routing and delivery works like this:

- Hub Transport servers handle messaging routing and delivery within the organization.

- Edge Transport servers receive messages from outside the organization and route them to Hub Transport servers within the organization that, in turn, deliver them to your Mailbox servers.

- Hub Transport servers receive messages from Mailbox servers within the organization and route them to Edge Transport servers, which, in turn, route them to destinations outside the organization.

The primary mail protocol used by Exchange Server 2007 is Simple Mail Transfer Protocol (SMTP). This chapter discusses how transport servers use SMTP for routing and delivery, as well as how you can view and manage transport server configurations.

Working with SMTP Connectors, Sites, and Links

SMTP connectors, Active Directory sites, and Active Directory links all have important roles to play in determining how Exchange routes and delivers messages in your organization. You can work with connectors, sites, and links in a variety of ways, but first you need a strong understanding of how connectors are used.

Connecting Source and Destination Servers

Exchange Server 2007 uses SMTP connectors to represent logically the connection between a source server and a destination server. How you configure an SMTP connector determines how Exchange Server transports messages using that connection. Because each SMTP connector represents a one-way connection, Exchange Server uses both Send and Receive connectors.

A Send connector is a logical gateway through which transport servers send all outgoing messages. When you create a Send connector, it is stored in Active Directory or in Active Directory Application Mode (ADAM) as a connector object. Send connectors are not scoped to a single server. Multiple servers can use a single Send connector for sending messages. Send connectors deliver mail by either looking up a mail exchanger (MX) record on a Domain Name System (DNS) server or by using a smart host as a destination. By default with DNS MX records, the DNS server settings you configure on the Transport server are used for name resolution. You can configure different settings for internal and external DNS lookups if necessary. See the "Configuring Send Connector DNS Lookups" section of this chapter.

A Receive connector is a logical gateway through which all incoming messages are received. When you create a Receive connector, it is stored in Active Directory or in ADAM as a connector object. Unlike Send connectors, Receive connectors are scoped to a single server and determine how that server listens for connections. The permissions on a Receive connector determine from whom the connector will accept connections. The authentication mechanisms you configure for a Receive connector determine whether anonymous connections are allowed and the types of authentication that are permitted.

Exchange Server creates the Send and Receive connectors required for mail flow when you install your Hub Transport servers. If your organization also uses Edge Transport servers, Exchange creates the additional Send and Receive connectors required during the Edge Subscription process. You can also explicitly create Send and Receive connectors or automatically compute them from the organization topology using Active Directory sites and site-link information.

Viewing and Managing Active Directory Site Details

Hub Transport servers use Active Directory sites and the costs that are assigned to the Active Directory Internet Protocol (IP) site links to determine the least-cost routing path to other Hub Transport servers in the organization. After a Hub Transport server determines the least-cost routing path, the server routes messages over the link or links in this path, and in this way, a source Hub Transport server relays messages to target Hub Transport servers. By default, when there are multiple Active Directory sites between the source and destination server, the Hub Transport servers that are located in Active Directory sites along the path between the source server and the target server don't process or relay the messages in any way—with several exceptions:

- If you want messages to be processed en route, you can configure an Active Directory site as a hub site so that Exchange routes messages to the hub site to be processed by the site's Hub Transport servers before being relayed to a target server. The hub site must exist along the least-cost routing path between source and destination Hub Transport servers.

- If a message cannot be delivered to the target site, the Hub Transport server in the closest reachable site along the least-cost routing path of the target site queues the message for relay. The message is then relayed when the destination Hub Transport server becomes available.

> **Tip**   To determine which Active Directory and global catalog servers a Transport server is using, click the System Settings tab in the server's Properties dialog box. On an Edge Transport server, select Edge Transport. On a Hub Transport server, expand the Server Configuration node, and then select the Hub Transport node. Right-click the entry for the transport server, and then select Properties. In the Properties dialog box, click the System Settings tab.

You can use the Get-AdSite cmdlet to display the configuration details of an Active Directory site. If you do not provide an identity with this cmdlet, configuration information for all Active Directory sites is displayed.

Sample 15-1 provides the syntax and usage, as well as sample output, for the Get-AdSite cmdlet. Note that the output specifies whether the site is enabled as a hub site.

Sample 15-1   Get-AdSite cmdlet syntax and usage

```
Syntax
Get-AdSite [-Identity 'SiteIdentity']
  [-DomainController 'DCName']
```

```
Usage
Get-AdSite -Identity 'First-Seattle-Site' | fl
```

```
Output
HubSiteEnabled    : False
AdminDisplayName  :
ExchangeVersion   : 0.0 (6.5.6500.0)
Name              : First-Seattle-Site
DistinguishedName : CN=First-Seattle-Site,
                    CN=Sites,CN=Configuration,DC=cpandl,DC=com
Identity          : cpandl.com/Configuration/Sites/First-Seattle-Site
Guid              : dda814f3-2173-4943-bdd9-5ba8d6b6e5d7
ObjectCategory    : cpandl.com/Configuration/Schema/Site
ObjectClass       : {top, site}
```

```
WhenChanged        : 1/21/2008 6:36:00 PM
WhenCreated        : 1/21/2008 6:36:00 PM
OriginatingServer  : MAILSERVER25.cpand1.com
IsValid            : True
```

You can use the Set-AdSite cmdlet to configure an Active Directory site as a hub site to override the default message routing behavior. When a hub site exists along the least-cost routing path between source and destination Hub Transport servers, messages are routed to the hub site for processing before they are relayed to the destination server.

Sample 15-2 provides the syntax and usage, as well as sample output, for the Set-AdSite cmdlet. To enable a site as a hub site, set the –HubSiteEnabled parameter to $true. To disable a site as a hub site, set the –HubSiteEnabled parameter to $false. You must have Enterprise Administrator rights to use the –Name parameter to change a site's name.

Sample 15-2   Set-AdSite cmdlet syntax and usage

```
Syntax
Set-AdSite -Identity 'SiteIdentity'
  [-HubSiteEnabled <$true | $false>]
  [-DomainController 'DCName']
  [-Instance 'SiteIdentity']
  [-Name 'NewSiteName']
```

```
Usage
Set-AdSite -Identity 'First-Seattle-Site' –HubSiteEnabled $true
```

Viewing and Managing Active Directory Site Link Details

You can use the Get-AdSiteLink cmdlet to view the configuration information about an Active Directory IP site link. This configuration information includes the value of the Exchange-specific cost, the cost assigned to the Active Directory IP site link, and a list of the sites in the IP site link.

Note   A good resource to learn more about Active Directory sites and site links is *Windows Server 2008 Inside Out* (Microsoft, 2008). See Chapter 32, "Configuring Active Directory Sites and Replication," and Chapter 37, "Active Directory Site Administration."

Sample 15-3 provides the syntax and usage, as well as sample output, for the Get-AdSiteLink cmdlet. Use the Identity parameter to retrieve the configuration information about a specific IP site link. If you do not provide an identity, the configuration information about all IP site links is returned.

Sample 15-3   Get-AdSiteLink cmdlet syntax and usage

```
Syntax
Get-AdSiteLink [-Identity 'SiteIdentity']
 [-DomainController 'DCName']
```

```
Usage
Get-AdSiteLink -Identity 'PORTLANDSEATTLELINK' | fl
```

```
Output
Cost              : 100
ADCost            : 100
ExchangeCost      :
MaxMessageSize    : unlimited
Sites             : {First-Seattle-Site}
AdminDisplayName  :
ExchangeVersion   : 0.0 (6.5.6500.0)
Name              : PORTLANDSEATTLELINK
DistinguishedName : CN=PORTLANDSEATTLELINK,CN=IP,
                    CN=Inter-Site Transports,CN=Sites,
                    CN=Configuration,DC=cpandl,DC=com
Identity          : cpandl.com/Configuration/Sites/
                    Inter-Site Transports/IP/PORTLANDSEATTLELINK
Guid              : b304910a-4a2e-47af-8755-ac0e72653f9f
ObjectCategory    : cpandl.com/Configuration/Schema/Site-Link
ObjectClass       : {top, siteLink}
WhenChanged       : 1/21/2008 6:36:00 PM
WhenCreated       : 1/21/2008 6:36:00 PM
OriginatingServer : MAILSERVER25.cpandl.com
IsValid           : True
```

By default, Exchange Server 2007 determines the least-cost routing path by using the cost that is assigned to the Active Directory IP site links. You can change this behavior by using the Set-AdSiteLink cmdlet to configure an Exchange-specific cost for Active Directory IP site links. After you configure it, the Exchange-specific cost is used instead of the Active Directory-assigned cost to determine the Exchange routing path.

Sample 15-4 provides the syntax and usage, as well as sample output, for the Set-AdSiteLink cmdlet. When there are multiple wide area network (WAN) paths between sites, you can set a higher site-link cost if you want to reduce the likelihood that a link will be used. You can set a lower site-link cost if you want to increase the likelihood that a link will be used. You must have Enterprise Administrator rights to use the –Name parameter to change the name of a site link.

You can use the –MaxMessageSize parameter to set the maximum size for messages that are relayed across a specified link. The default value is "unlimited," which allows messages of any size to be relayed. You can specify the units for values using B for bytes,

KB for kilobytes, MB for megabytes, or GB for gigabytes. The valid range for maximum size is from 64 KB to the largest value in bytes that can be set using a 64-bit integer.

Sample 15-4 Set-AdSiteLink cmdlet syntax and usage

```
Syntax
Set-AdSiteLink -Identity 'SiteIdentity'
  [-DomainController 'DCName']
  [-ExchangeCost Cost]
  [-Instance 'SiteIdentity']
  [-MaxMessageSize <'Size' | 'Unlimited'>]
  [-Name 'NewSiteLinkName']
```

```
Usage
Set-AdSiteLink -Identity 'PORTLANDSEATTLELINK'
  -ExchangeCost 20

Set-AdSiteLink -Identity 'LASACRAMENTOLINK'
  -MaxMessaeSize 'Unlimited'

Set-AdSiteLink -Identity 'LASACRAMENTOLINK'
  -MaxMessaeSize '24MB'
```

Creating Send Connectors

Send connectors are the gateways through which Transport servers send messages. Exchange automatically creates the Send connectors required for mail flow. As an administrator, you can explicitly create Send connectors and then manage the configuration of these explicitly created Send connectors as necessary. You cannot, however, manage the configuration of Send connectors created implicitly by Exchange to enable mail flow. The key reasons for creating Send connectors are when you want to:

- Control explicitly how message routing works within domains or between domains.

- Control explicitly the hosts used as destinations or the way messages are routed over the Internet.

- Connect to an Exchange Server 2003 or Exchange 2000 Server routing group.

When you create Send connectors, you can encrypt message traffic sent over the link and require strict authentication. You can transmit messages to a designated server—called a smart host—or you can use DNS MX records to route messages. If you use a smart host, Exchange Server 2007 transfers messages directly to the smart host, which then sends out messages over an established link. The smart host allows you to route messages on a per-domain basis. If you use DNS MX records, Exchange Server 2007 performs a DNS lookup for each address to which the connector sends mail.

When you create a Send connector, you must either define the address space for the connector or link it to a specific Receive connector. The address space determines when the Send connector is used and the domain names to which the connector sends messages. For example, if you want to connect two domains in the same Exchange organization—dev.microsoft.com and corp.microsoft.com—you can create a Send connector in dev.microsoft.com, and then add an SMTP address type for the e-mail domain corp.microsoft.com.

Send connectors can be used by multiple Transport servers. When you create a Send connector within an Exchange 2007 organization, you can select the Hub Transport servers that are permitted to use the Send connector. When you create a Send connector on an Edge Transport server, the Send connector is configured for only that server.

To create a Send connector, complete the following steps:

1. Start Exchange Management Console. On an Edge Transport server, select Edge Transport. On a Hub Transport server, expand the Organization Configuration node, and then select Hub Transport.

2. On the Send Connectors tab in the details pane, right-click an open area, and then select New Send Connector. This starts the New SMTP Send Connector Wizard, shown in Figure 15-1.

Figure 15-1   Create a new SMTP Send connector.

3. In the Name text box, type a descriptive name for the connector, and then set the connector type. The available options are:

❑ **Custom**   Creates a Send connector that sends mail to the address spaces you specify. No default group permissions are set.

❑ **Internal**   Creates a Send connector for sending mail to another transport server in the organization and sets the default permissions so that the connector can be used by the Exchange Servers group.

❑ **Internet**   Creates a Send connector that sends mail to external users over the Internet. Used with Edge Transport servers only with default permissions for the Anonymous and Partners groups.

❑ **Legacy**   Creates a Send connector that sends mail to an Exchange 2003 or Exchange 2000 routing group and sets the default permissions so that the connector can be used by the Legacy Servers groups. Legacy connectors can only use smart hosts.

❑ **Partner**   Creates a Send connector that sends mail to partner domains. Partner domains cannot be configured as smart hosts. Only connections that authenticate with Transport Layer Security (TLS) are allowed by default. Partner domains must also be listed on the TLS Send Domain Secure list.

4. Click Next and on the Address Space page, click Add. In the Add Address Space dialog box, enter the domain name to which this connector will send mail. To use this connector to send e-mail to all subdomains of the address space, select the Include All Subdomains check box. Click OK to close the Add Address Space dialog box. Repeat as necessary to add more address spaces to this connector. If you make a mistake, select the address space, and then click Remove.

5. If you'd like to scope the Send connector to the current site, select the Scoped Send Connector check box. When a Send connector is scoped, only Hub Transport servers in the same Active Directory site as the Send connector's source servers consider that Send connector in routing decisions. Click Next to continue.

6. On the Network Settings page, select how you want to send e-mail with the Send connector. If you select Use Domain Name System (DNS) "MX" Records To Route Mail Automatically, the Send connector uses the DNS client service on the Transport server to query a DNS server and resolve the destination address. Skip steps 7–10

7. If you select Route Mail Through The Following Smart Hosts, you have to specify the smart hosts to which mail should be forwarded for processing. Click Add.

8. In the Add Smart Host dialog box, select either IP Address or Fully Qualified Domain Name (FQDN) to specify how to locate the smart host. If you select IP Address, enter the IP address of the smart host. If you select Fully Qualified Domain Name (FQDN), enter the full domain name of the smart host. The Transport server must be able to resolve the FQDN.

9. Click OK to close the Add Smart Host dialog box. Repeat steps 7–9 as necessary to add more smart hosts to this connector. If you make a mistake, select the smart host, and then click Edit or Remove as appropriate. When you are finished, click Next to continue.

10. After you've configured smart hosts, you'll see the Configure Smart Host Authentication Settings page next. On this page, select the method that you want to use to authenticate your servers to the smart host. Choose one of the following options, and then click Next:

  ❑ **Basic Authentication**   Standard authentication with wide compatibility. With basic authentication, the user name and password specified are passed as cleartext to the remote domain.

  ❑ **Basic Authentication Over TLS**   Transport Layer Security (TLS) authentication is combined with basic authentication to allow encrypted authentication for servers with smart cards or X.509 certificates.

  ❑ **Exchange Server Authentication**   Secure authentication for Exchange servers. With Exchange Server authentication, credentials are passed securely.

  ❑ **Externally Secured**   Secure authentication for Exchange servers. With externally secured authentication, credentials are passed securely using an external security protocol for which the server has been separately configured, such as Internet Protocol Security (IPsec).

  Note   With Basic Authentication or Basic Authentication Over TLS, you must provide the name and password for the account authorized to establish connectors to the designated smart hosts. All smart hosts must use the same user name and password.

11. When you are working with a Hub Transport server, you'll see the Source Server page next. If you are logged on to a Hub Transport, this server is added as the source server automatically. Click Add to associate the connector with Hub Transport servers and Edge Subscriptions. In the Select Hub Transport And Subscribed Edge Transport Servers dialog box, select the Hub Transport server or the Edge subscription that will be used as the source server for sending messages to the address space that you previously specified, and then click OK. Repeat as necessary to add additional Transport servers. If you make a mistake, select the server, and then click Remove. When you are finished, click Next to continue.

12. On the New Connector page, review the configuration summary for the connector. To modify the settings, click Back. To create the Send connector, click New.

13. On the Completion page, click Finish.

In the Exchange Management Shell, you can create Send connectors using the New-SendConnector cmdlet. The Usage parameter sets the Send connector type as Custom,

Internal, Internet, or Legacy. The AddressSpaces parameter sets the address spaces for the Send connector by FQDN or IP address. The DNSRoutingEnabled parameter determines whether DNS MX records are used for lookups or smart hosts are used. To use DNS MX records, set DNSRoutingEnabled to $true. To use smart hosts, set DNSRoutingEnabled to $false, and then use the SmartHosts parameter to designate the smart hosts.

Sample 15-5 provides the syntax and usage for the New-SendConnector cmdlet. With Basic Authentication or Basic Authentication Over TLS, you will be prompted to provide credentials. To scope the Send connector to the current Active Directory site, set the IsScopedConnector parameter to $true.

Sample 15-5   New-SendConnector cmdlet syntax and usage

```
Syntax
New-SendConnector -Name 'Name'
 [-AddressSpaces 'Addresses']
 [-AuthenticationCredential 'Credentials']
 [-ConnectionInactivityTimeout 'TimeSpan']
 [-Custom <$true | $false>]
 [-DNSRoutingEnabled <$true | $false>]
 [-DomainSecureEnabled <$true | $false>]
 [-Enabled <$true | $false>]
 [-Force <$true | $false>]
 [-ForceHELO <$true | $false>]
 [-Fqdn 'FQDN']
 [-IgnoreStartTLS <$true | $false>]
 [-Internal <$true | $false>]
 [-Internet <$true | $false>]
 [-IsScopedConnector <$true | $false>]
 [-LinkedReceiveConnector 'ReceiveConnectorIdentity']
 [-MaxMessageSize <'Size' | 'Unlimited'>]
 [-Partner <$true | $false>]
 [-Port PortNumber]
 [-ProtocolLoggingLevel <'None' | 'Verbose'>]
 [-RequireTLS <$true | $false>]
 [-SmartHostAuthMechanism <'None'|'BasicAuth'|'BasicAuthRequireTls'
                           |'ExchangeServer'|'ExternalAuthoritative'>]
 [-SmartHosts 'SmartHosts']
 [-SourceIPAddress 'IPAddress']
 [-SourceTransportServers 'TranportServers']
 [-TemplateInstance 'Instance']
 [-Usage <'Custom'|'Internal'|'Internet'|'Partner'>]
 [-UseExternalDNSServersEnabled <$true | $false>]


Usage for DNS MX records
New-SendConnector -Name 'Adatum.com Send Connector'
 -Usage 'Custom'
```

```
-AddressSpaces 'smtp:*.adatum.com;1'
-IsScopedConnector $true
-DNSRoutingEnabled $true
-UseExternalDNSServersEnabled $false
-SourceTransportServers 'CORPSVR127'
```

Usage for Smart hosts
```
New-SendConnector -Name 'Cohovineyards.com'
-Usage 'Custom'
-AddressSpaces 'smtp:*.cohovineyards.com;1'
-IsScopedConnector $false
-DNSRoutingEnabled $false
-SmartHosts '[192.168.10.52]'
-SmartHostAuthMechanism 'ExternalAuthoritative'
-UseExternalDNSServersEnabled $false
-SourceTransportServers 'CORPSVR127'
```

Viewing and Managing Send Connectors

The Exchange Management tools only provide access to the Send connectors you've explicitly created. On Hub Transport servers, Send connectors created by Exchange Server are not displayed or configurable. On Edge Transport servers, you can view and manage the internal Send connector used to connect to the Hub Transport servers in your Exchange organization.

To view the Send connectors and manage their configuration, start the Exchange Management Console. On an Edge Transport server, select Edge Transport, and then click the Send Connectors tab in the details pane. On a Hub Transport server, expand the Organization Configuration node, select Hub Transport, and then click the Send Connectors tab in the details pane. Send connectors you've created are listed by name and status. You can now:

- **Change a connector's properties**   To change a connector's properties, right-click the connector, and then select Properties. Use the Properties dialog box to manage the connector's properties.

- **Enable a connector**   To enable a connector, right-click it, and then select Enable.

- **Disable a connector**   To disable a connector, right-click it, and then select Disable.

- **Remove a connector**   To remove a connector, right-click it, and then select Remove.

In the Exchange Management Shell, you can view, update, or remove Send connectors using the Get-SendConnector, Set-SendConnector, or Remove-SendConnector cmdlets, respectively. Samples 15-6 through 15-8 provide the syntax and usage. With

Get-SendConnector, if you don't specify an identity, the cmdlet returns a list of all administrator-configured Send connectors.

Sample 15-6   Get-SendConnector cmdlet syntax and usage

```
Syntax
Get-SendConnector
Get-SendConnector -Identity 'ConnectorIdentity'
```

```
Usage
Get-SendConnector -Identity 'Adatum.com Send Connector'
```

Sample 15-7   Set-SendConnector cmdlet syntax and usage

```
Syntax
Set-SendConnector -Identity 'ConnectorIdentity'
  [-Name 'NewName']
  [-AddressSpaces 'Addresses']
  [-AuthenticationCredential 'Credentials']
  [-ConnectionInactivityTimeout 'TimeSpan']
  [-DNSRoutingEnabled <$true | $false>]
  [-DomainSecureEnabled <$true | $false>]
  [-Enabled <$true | $false>]
  [-Force <$true | $false>]
  [-ForceHELO <$true | $false>]
  [-Fqdn 'FQDN']
  [-IgnoreStartTLS <$true | $false>]
  [-IsScopedConnector <$true | $false>]
  [-LinkedReceiveConnector 'ReceiveConnectorIdentity']
  [-MaxMessageSize <'Size' | 'Unlimited'>]
  [-Port PortNumber]
  [-ProtocolLoggingLevel <'None' | 'Verbose'>]
  [-RequireTLS <$true | $false>]
  [-SmartHostAuthMechanism <'None'|'BasicAuth'|'BasicAuthRequireTls'
                            |'ExchangeServer'|'ExternalAuthoritative'>]
  [-SmartHosts 'SmartHosts']
  [-SourceIPAddress 'IPAddress']
  [-SourceTransportServers 'TranportServers']
  [-UseExternalDNSServersEnabled <$true | $false>]
```

```
Usage
Set-SendConnector -Name 'Adatum.com Send Connector'
 -AddressSpaces 'smtp:*.adatum.com;1'
 -DNSRoutingEnabled $true -SmartHosts
 -SmartHostAuthMechanism 'None'
 -SourceTransportServers 'CORPSVR127'
```

Sample 15-8   Remove-SendConnector cmdlet syntax and usage

```
Syntax
Remove-SendConnector –Identity 'ConnectorIdentity'
  [-Confirm <$true | $false>]
```

```
Usage
Remove-SendConnector -Identity 'Adatum.com Send Connector'
```

Configuring Send Connector DNS Lookups

You can configure different settings for internal and external DNS lookups by configuring a Transport server's External DNS Lookups and Internal DNS Lookups properties. External DNS Lookup servers are used to resolve the IP addresses of servers
outside your organization. Internal DNS Lookup servers are used to resolve IP
addresses of servers inside the organization.

To configure DNS Lookup servers, complete these steps:

1. Start Exchange Management Console. On an Edge Transport server, select Edge
   Transport. On a Hub Transport server, expand the Server Configuration node,
   and then select the Hub Transport node.

2. In the details pane, right-click the server and then select Properties.

3. On the External DNS Lookups tab, specify how external lookups should be
   performed:

   ❑ To use DNS settings from the server's network card or cards for external
      lookups, select Use Network Card DNS settings and then either choose All
      Available to use all configured settings or a specific network card to use the
      configured settings of that card.

   ❑ To use a specific DNS server for external lookups, click Use These DNS
      Servers. Then type the IP address of a DNS server to use for external look-
      ups, and then click Add. Repeat this process to specify multiple servers.

4. On the Internal DNS Lookups tab, specify how internal lookups should be
   performed:

   ❑ To use DNS settings from the server's network card or cards for internal
      lookups, select Use Network Card DNS settings and then either choose All
      Available to use all configured settings or a specific network card to use the
      configured settings of that card.

   ❑ To use a specific DNS server for internal lookups, click Use These DNS
      Servers. Then type the IP address of a DNS server to use for internal look-
      ups, and then click Add. Repeat this process to specify multiple servers.

5. Click OK to save your settings.

Setting Send Connector Limits

Send connector limits determine how mail is delivered once a connection has been established and the receiving computer has acknowledged that it's ready to receive the data transfer. After a connection has been established and the receiving computer has acknowledged that it's ready to receive the data transfer, Exchange Server attempts to deliver messages queued for delivery to the computer. If a message can't be delivered on the first attempt, Exchange Server tries to send the message again after a specified time. Exchange Server keeps trying to send the message at the intervals you've specified until the expiration time-out is reached. When the time limit is reached, the message is returned to the sender with a nondelivery report (NDR). The default expiration time-out is two days.

After multiple failed attempts to deliver a message, Exchange Server generates a delay notification and queues it for delivery to the user who sent the message. Notification doesn't occur immediately after failure. Instead, Exchange Server sends the delay notification message only after the notification delay interval and then only if the message hasn't already been delivered. The default delay notification is four hours.

With SMTP, you have much more control over outgoing connections than you do over incoming connections. You can limit the number of simultaneous connections and the number of connections per domain. These limits set the maximum number of simultaneous outbound connections. By default, the maximum number of connections is 1000 and the maximum number of connections by domain is 20.

You can view or change the Send connector limits by completing the following steps:

1. Start Exchange Management Console. On an Edge Transport server, select Edge Transport. On a Hub Transport server, expand the Server Configuration node, and then select the Hub Transport node.

2. In the details pane, right-click the server and then select Properties.

3. On the Limits tab, use the following options for retrying unsuccessful outbound connections:

   ❑ **Outbound Connection Failure Retry Interval (Minutes)**   Sets the retry interval for subsequent connection attempts to a remote server where previous connections have failed. The default is 10 minutes.

   ❑ **Transient Failure Retry Interval (Seconds)**   Sets the interval at which the server immediately retries when it encounters a connection failure with a remote server. The default is 300 seconds.

   ❑ **Transient Failure Retry Attempts**   Sets the maximum number of times that the server immediately retries when it encounters a connection failure with a remote server. The default is six. If you enter 0 as the number of retry attempts or the maximum number of attempts has been reached, the server no longer immediately retries a connection and instead waits according to the outbound connection failure retry interval.

4. When messages that cannot be delivered reach the Maximum Time Since Submission value, they expire, and Exchange Server generates a non-delivery report (NDR). To set the expiration time-out for messages, enter the desired message expiration value in the Maximum Time Since Submission (Days) text box. The default expiration time-out for messages is two days.

5. When messages are delayed longer than the allowed delay interval, Exchange Server sends a delay notification to the sender. To set the amount of time to wait before notifying senders of a delay, enter the desired wait time in the Notify Sender When Message Is Delayed More Than text box. The default wait time is four hours.

6. To remove outgoing connection limits, clear the Maximum Concurrent Outbound Connections check box. To set an outgoing connection limit, select the Maximum Concurrent Outbound Connections check box, and then type the limit value. The default limit is 1,000 outbound connections.

7. To remove outgoing connection limits per domain, clear the Maximum Concurrent Outbound Connections Per Domain check box. To set an outgoing connection limit per domain, select the Maximum Concurrent Outbound Connections Per Domain check box, and then type the limit value. The default limit is 20 outbound connections per domain.

8. Click OK to save your settings.

Creating Receive Connectors

Receive connectors are the gateways through which Transport servers receive messages. Exchange creates the Receive connectors required for mail flow automatically. The receive permissions on a Receive connector determine who is allowed to send mail through the connector.

As an administrator, you can explicitly create Receive connectors and then manage the configuration of those explicitly created Receive connectors as necessary. You cannot, however, manage the configuration of connectors created implicitly by Exchange to enable mail flow. The key reasons for creating SMTP connectors are when you want to:

- Control explicitly how messages are received within domains or between domains.

- Control explicitly the permitted incoming connections.

- Receive mail from an Exchange 2003 or Exchange 2000 routing group.

Unlike Send connectors, Receive connectors are used by only a single, designated Transport server. When you create a Receive connector within an Exchange 2007 organization, you can select the Hub Transport or Edge Transport server with which the connector should be associated and configure the specific binding for that connector. A binding is a combination of IP addresses and ports on which the Receive connector listens. You cannot create a Receive connector that duplicates the bindings of existing Receive connectors. Each Receive connector must have a unique binding.

> **Note** Exchange Server 2007 uses standard SMTP or Extended SMTP (ESMTP) to deliver mail. As the ESMTP standard is more efficient and secure than SMTP, SMTP connectors always try to initiate ESMTP sessions before trying to initiate standard SMTP sessions. SMTP connectors initiate ESMTP sessions with other mail servers by issuing an EHLO start command. SMTP connectors initiate SMTP sessions with other mail servers by issuing the HELO start command.

To create a Receive connector, complete the following steps:

1. Start Exchange Management Console. On an Edge Transport server, select Edge Transport. On a Hub Transport server, expand the Server Configuration node, and then select the Hub Transport node. On the Receive Connectors tab in the details pane, select the server on which you want to create the receive connection, and then click the server's Receive Connectors tab.

2. In the details pane, below Receive Connectors, right-click an open area, and then select New Receive Connector. This starts the New SMTP Receive Connector Wizard, shown in Figure 15-2.

Figure 15-2 Create a new SMTP Receive connector.

3. In the Name text box, type a descriptive name for the connector, and then set the connector type. The available options are:

    ❑ **Custom** Creates a Receive connector bound to a specific port or IP address on a server with multiple receive ports or IP addresses. Can also be used to specify a remote IP address from which the connector receives messages. No default group permissions are set.

    ❑ **Internal** Creates a Receive connector to receive messages from another Transport server in the organization. For Edge Transport servers, it sets the default permissions so that the connector can be used by the Exchange Servers group. For Hub Transport servers, it sets the default permissions so that the connector can be used by the Exchange Servers and Exchange Users groups.

    ❑ **Internet** Creates a Receive connector that accepts incoming connections from the Internet. Sets default permissions for the Anonymous group.

    ❑ **Client** Creates a Receive connector used to receive mail from users of Microsoft Exchange. Only connections from authenticated Microsoft Exchange users are accepted by default.

    ❑ **Partner** Creates a Receive connector used to receive mail from partner domains. Partner domains cannot be configured as smart hosts. Only connections that authenticate with Transport Layer Security (TLS) are allowed by default. Partner domains must also be listed on the TLS Receive Domain Secure list.

    ❑ **Legacy** Creates a Receive connector that accepts incoming connections from an Exchange 2003 or Exchange 2000 routing group and sets the default permissions so that the connector can be used by the Legacy Servers groups.

4. Click Next. For Custom, Partner, and Internet Receive connectors, you can specify the local IP addresses and the port on which mail can be received. By default, Custom and Internet Receive connectors are configured to receive mail over port 25 on all available IP addresses for which the server is configured. Port 25 is the default TCP port for SMTP. To use a different configuration, select the default entry on the Local Network Settings page, and then click Remove. You can now create new entries by clicking Add. In the Add Receive Connector Binding dialog box, select Use All Available IP Addresses to have the connector listen for connections on all the IP addresses that are assigned to the network adapters on the local server. Select Specify An IP Address if you want to type an IP address that is assigned to a network adapter on the local server and have the connector listen for connections only on this IP address. As necessary, modify the listen port value. Click OK.

5. For Custom, Partner, and Internet Receive connectors, you can specify the FDQN the Transport server provides in response to HELO or EHLO messages on the Local Network Settings page. In the Specify The FQDN This Connector Will Provide In Response To HELO Or EHLO text box, type the name that the server advertises, such as **mailserver83.cpandl.com**. Click Next.

6. On the Remote Network Settings page, you can specify the remote IP addresses from which the server can receive mail. By default, Receive connectors are configured to accept mail from all remote IP addresses, which is why the IP address range 0.0.0.0 – 255.255.255.255 is set as the default entry. You'll only want to change this behavior if you want to limit the servers that are permitted to send mail to the Transport server. To use a different configuration, select the default entry on the Remote Network Settings page, and then click Remove. To specify the remote servers by a range of IP addresses, click the small arrow next to Add and then select IP Range. In the Add Remote Servers – IP Address Range dialog box, enter a start IP address and an end IP address for the first acceptable range of IP addresses, and then click OK. Repeat this process as necessary to configure other acceptable IP address ranges. Click Next.

7. On the New Connector page, review the configuration summary for the connector. If you want to modify the settings, click Back. To create the Receive connector by using the settings in the configuration summary, click New.

8. On the Completion page, click Finish.

In the Exchange Management Shell, you can create Receive connectors using the New-ReceiveConnector cmdlet. The Usage parameter sets the Receive connector type as Custom, Internal, Internet, or Legacy. The Bindings parameter sets the internal IP addresses and ports on which to listen. The FQDN parameter sets the FQDN to advertise in response to HELO or EHLO messages. The RemoteIPRanges parameter provides a comma-separated list of acceptable IP address ranges. The Server parameter specifies the server on which to create the Receive connector.

As Sample 15-9 shows, the required parameters for the New-ReceiveConnector cmdlet depend on the type of Receive connector you are creating. Once you provide the required parameters, the remaining parameters can be used in the same way regardless of which type of Receive connector you are creating. With Basic Authentication or Basic Authentication Over TLS, you will be prompted to provide credentials.

Sample 15-9   New-ReceiveConnector cmdlet syntax and usage

```
Syntax
New-ReceiveConnector
 –Name 'Name'
 –Usage <Custom | Internet | Internal | Client | Partner>
```

```
New-ReceiveConnector
-Name 'Name'
-Bindings 'Bindings'
-RemoteIPRanges 'IPRange1', 'IPRange2', . . .

New-ReceiveConnector
-Name 'Name'
-Bindings 'Bindings'
-Internet <$true | $false >

New-ReceiveConnector
-Name 'Name'
-Client <$true | $false >
-RemoteIPRanges 'IPRange1', 'IPRange2', . . .

New-ReceiveConnector
-Name 'Name'
-Internal <$true | $false >
-RemoteIPRanges 'IPRange1', 'IPRange2', . . .

New-ReceiveConnector
-Name <String>
-Bindings 'Bindings'
-Partner <$true | $false >
-RemoteIPRanges 'IPRange1', 'IPRange2', . . .

  [-AuthMechanism <None | Tls | Integrated | BasicAuth |
   BasicAuthRequireTLS | ExchangeServer | ExternalAuthoritative>]
  [-Banner 'Banner']
  [-BinaryMimeEnabled <$true | $false>]
  [-Bindings 'Bindings']
  [-ChunkingEnabled <$true | $false >]
  [-Comment 'Comment']
  [-Confirm <$true | $false >]
  [-ConnectionInactivityTimeout 'TimeSpan']
  [-ConnectionTimeout 'TimeSpan']
  [-Custom <$true | $false >]
  [-DefaultDomain 'DefaultDomain']
  [-DeliveryStatusNotificationEnabled <$true | $false>]
  [-DomainController 'DCName']
  [-DomainSecureEnabled <$true | $false>]
  [-EightBitMimeEnabled  <$true | $false>]
  [-EnableAuthGSSAPI <$true | $false>]
  [-Enabled <$true | $false>]
  [-EnhancedStatusCodesEnabled <$true | $false>]
  [-Fqdn 'FQDN']
  [-LongAddressesEnabled <$true | $false>]
  [-MaxHeaderSize 'MaxHeaderBytes']
  [-MaxHopCount MaxHops]
```

```
[-MaxInboundConnection <'MaxConn' | 'Unlimited'>]
[-MaxInboundConnectionPercentagePerSource MaxPercentage]
[-MaxInboundConnectionPerSource <'MaxConnPerSource' | 'Unlimited'>]
[-MaxLocalHopCount MaxHops]
[-MaxLogonFailures MaxLogonFailures]
[-MaxMessageSize 'MaxMessageSize']
[-MaxProtocolErrors <'MaxErrors' | 'Unlimited'>]
[-MaxRecipientsPerMessage 'MaxRecipients']
[-MessageRateLimit <'RateLimit' | 'Unlimited'>]
[-OrarEnabled <$true | $false>]
[-PermissionGroups <None | AnonymousUsers | ExchangeUsers |
 ExchangeServers | ExchangeLegacyServers | Partners | Custom>]
[-PipeliningEnabled < $true | $false>]
[-ProtocolLoggingLevel <None | Verbose>]
[-RemoteIPRanges 'IPRange1', 'IPRange2', . . .]
[-RequireEHLODomain <$true | $false>]
[-RequireTLS < $true | $false>]
[-Server 'Server']
[-SizeEnabled <Disabled | Enabled | EnabledWithoutValue>]
[-TarpitInterval 'TimeSpan']
[-TemplateInstance 'Instance']
```

Usage
```
New-ReceiveConnector -Name 'Custom Receive Connector'
 -Usage 'Custom'
 -Bindings '0.0.0.0:425'
 -Fqdn 'mailserver85.cpandl.com'
 -RemoteIPRanges '0.0.0.0-255.255.255.255'
 -Server 'CORPSVR127'
```

Viewing and Managing Receive Connectors

To view all available Receive connectors, start the Exchange Management Console and expand the Server Configuration node. On an Edge Transport server, select Edge Transport. On a Hub Transport server, select Hub Transport. On the Receive Connectors tab in the details pane, select the server on which you want to create the Receive connector, and then click the server's Receive Connectors tab. Receive connectors are listed by name and status. You can now:

- **Change a connector's properties**   To change a connector's properties, right-click the connector, and then select Properties. Use the Properties dialog box to manage the connector's properties.

- **Enable a connector**   To enable a connector, right-click it, and then select Enable.

- **Disable a connector**   To disable a connector, right-click it, and then select Disable.

- **Remove a connector**   To remove a connector, right-click it, and then select Remove.

When configuring Receive connector properties, you can specify the security mechanisms that can be used for incoming connections on the Authentication tab. Use any combination of the following:

- **Transport Layer Security**   Allows encrypted authentications with TLS for servers with smart cards or X.509 certificates.

- **Enable Domain Security (Mutual Auth TLS)**   When TLS is enabled, you can also enable domain security to require mutual authentication.

- **Basic Authentication**   Allows basic authentication. With basic authentication, the user name and password specified are passed as cleartext to the remote domain.

- **Offer Basic Authentication Only After Starting TLS**   Allows basic authentication only within an encrypted TLS session.

- **Exchange Server Authentication**   Allows secure authentication for Exchange servers. With Exchange Server authentication, credentials are passed securely.

- **Integrated Windows Authentication**   Allows secure authentication using NT LAN Manager (NTLM) or Kerberos.

- **Externally Secured**   Allows secure external authentication. With externally secured authentication, credentials are passed securely using an external security protocol for which the server has been separately configured, such as IPsec.

Also when configuring Receive connector properties, you can specify the security group that is allowed to connect on the Permission Groups tab. Use any combination of the following:

- **Anonymous Users**   Allows unauthenticated, anonymous users to connect to the Receive connector.

- **Exchange Users**   Allows connections by authenticated users who are valid recipients in the organization.

- **Exchange Servers**   Allows connections by authenticated servers that are members of the Exchange Server Administrator group.

- **Legacy Exchange Servers**   Allows connections by authenticated servers that are members of the ExchangeLegacyInterop group.

- **Partners**   Allows connections by authenticated servers that are members of partner domains, as listed on the TLS Receive Domain Secure list.

In the Exchange Management Shell, you can view, update, or remove Receive connectors using the Get-ReceiveConnector, Set-ReceiveConnector, or Remove-ReceiveConnector cmdlets, respectively. Samples 15-10–15-12 provide the syntax and usage. With Get-ReceiveConnector, you can return a list of all available Receive connectors if you don't specify an identity or server. If you want to see only the Receive connectors configured on a particular server, use the Server parameter.

Sample 15-10 Get-ReceiveConnector cmdlet syntax and usage

```
Syntax
Get-ReceiveConnector [-Identity 'Server\ConnectorIdentity']
  [-Server 'Server']
```

```
Usage
Get-ReceiveConnector

Get-ReceiveConnector -Identity 'Corpsvr127\Adatum.com Receive
Connector'

Get-ReceiveConnector -Server 'Corpsvr127'
```

Sample 15-11 Set-ReceiveConnector cmdlet syntax and usage

```
Syntax
Set-ReceiveConnector -Identity 'Identity'
  [-AuthMechanism <None | Tls | Integrated | BasicAuth |
   BasicAuthRequireTLS | ExchangeServer | ExternalAuthoritative>]
  [-Banner 'Banner']
  [-BinaryMimeEnabled <$true | $false>]
  [-Bindings 'Bindings']
  [-ChunkingEnabled <$true | $false >]
  [-Comment 'Comment']
  [-Confirm <$true | $false >]
  [-ConnectionInactivityTimeout 'TimeSpan']
  [-ConnectionTimeout 'TimeSpan']
  [-Custom <$true | $false >]
  [-DefaultDomain 'DefaultDomain']
  [-DeliveryStatusNotificationEnabled <$true | $false>]
  [-DomainController 'DCName']
  [-DomainSecureEnabled <$true | $false>]
  [-EightBitMimeEnabled <$true | $false>]
  [-EnableAuthGSSAPI <$true | $false>]
  [-Enabled <$true | $false>]
  [-EnhancedStatusCodesEnabled <$true | $false>]
  [-Fqdn 'FQDN']
  [-LongAddressesEnabled <$true | $false>]
  [-MaxHeaderSize 'MaxHeaderBytes']
  [-MaxHopCount MaxHops]
  [-MaxInboundConnection <'MaxConn' | 'Unlimited'>]
  [-MaxInboundConnectionPercentagePerSource MaxPercentage]
  [-MaxInboundConnectionPerSource <'MaxConnPerSource' | 'Unlimited'>]
  [-MaxLocalHopCount MaxHops]
  [-MaxLogonFailures MaxLogonFailures]
```

```
[-MaxMessageSize 'MaxMessageSize']
[-MaxProtocolErrors <'MaxErrors' | 'Unlimited'>]
[-MaxRecipientsPerMessage 'MaxRecipients']
[-MessageRateLimit <'RateLimit' | 'Unlimited'>]
[-OrarEnabled <$true | $false>]
[-PermissionGroups <None | AnonymousUsers | ExchangeUsers |
 ExchangeServers | ExchangeLegacyServers | Partners | Custom>]
[-PipeliningEnabled < $true | $false>]
[-ProtocolLoggingLevel <None | Verbose>]
[-RemoteIPRanges 'IPRange1', 'IPRange2', . . .]
[-RequireEHLODomain <$true | $false>]
[-RequireTLS < $true | $false>]
[-Server 'Server']
[-SizeEnabled <Disabled | Enabled | EnabledWithoutValue>]
[-TarpitInterval 'TimeSpan']
```

```
Usage
set-ReceiveConnector -Identity 'Corpsvr127\Custom Receive Connector'
 -Bindings '0.0.0.0:425'
 -Fqdn 'mailserver85.cpandl.com'
 -RemoteIPRanges '0.0.0.0-255.255.255.255'
```

Sample 15-12   Remove-ReceiveConnector cmdlet syntax and usage

```
Syntax
Remove-ReceiveConnector -Identity 'ConnectorIdentity'
 [-Confirm <$true | $false >]
 [-DomainController 'DCName']
```

```
Usage
Remove-ReceiveConnector -Identity 'CorpSvr127\Adatum.com Receive
Connector'
```

Connecting to Exchange 2003 or Exchange 2000 Routing Groups

Although Exchange 2007 doesn't use routing groups, you must create routing group connectors to route messages between Exchange Server 2007 Hub Transport servers and Exchange Server 2003 or Exchange 2000 Server routing groups. You can manage routing group connectors only by using the Exchange Management Shell.

You can view, create, update, or remove routing group connectors using the Get-Routing-GroupConnector, New-RoutingGroupConnector, Set-RoutingGroupConnector, or Remove-RoutingGroupConnector cmdlet, respectively. With Get-RoutingGroupConnector, you can return a list of all available routing group connectors if you don't specify an identity or server. If you want to see only the routing group connectors configured on a particular server, use the Server parameter.

When you are creating or updating a routing group connector using New-Routing-GroupConnector or Set-RoutingGroupConnector, you specify source and target servers. The source and target servers must be Exchange 2007 Hub Transport servers or Exchange Server 2003 or Exchange 2000 Server bridgehead servers. By using the Bidirectional parameter, you can specify whether the connector is used for one-way or two-way mail flow. If you specify a two-way connector, a reciprocal connector is created in the target routing group.

Samples 15-13–15-16 provide the syntax and usage for the Get-RoutingGroup-Connector, New-RoutingGroupConnector, Set-RoutingGroupConnector, and Remove-RoutingGroupConnector cmdlets. With the Set-RoutingGroupConnector cmdlet, you can use the –MaxMessageSize parameter to set the maximum size for messages that are relayed between Exchange 2007 Hub Transport servers and Exchange 2003 or Exchange 2000 bridgehead servers.

Sample 15-13   Get-RoutingGroupConnector cmdlet syntax and usage

```
Syntax
Get-RoutingGroupConnector [-Identity
'RoutingGroup\ConnectorIdentity']
  [-DomainController 'DCName']
```

```
Usage
Get-RoutingGroupConnector

Get-RoutingGroupConnector -Identity 'Exchange Administrator
Group\Exchange 2003 Interop'
```

Sample 15-14   New-RoutingGroupConnector cmdlet syntax and usage

```
Syntax
New-RoutingGroupConnector -Name 'Name'
  -SourceTransportServers 'SourceServer1', 'SourceServer2',...
  -TargetTransportServers 'TransportServer1', 'TransportServer2',...
  [-BiDirectional <$true | $false>]
  [-Cost ConnectorCost]
  [-PublicFolderReferralsEnabled <$true | $false>]
```

```
Usage
New-RoutingGroupConnector -Name 'Exchange 2003 Interop'
  -SourceTransportServers 'Exchange2007Server12.cpandl.com'
  -TargetTransportServers 'Exchange2003Server08.cpandl.com'
  -Cost 100
  -BiDirectional $true
```

Sample 15-15   Set-RoutingGroupConnector cmdlet syntax and usage

Syntax
Set-RoutingGroupConnector -Identity **'Group\Connector Identity'**
[-Name **'Name'**]
[-SourceTransportServers 'SourceServer1', 'SourceServer2',...]
[-TargetTransportServers 'TransportServer1', 'TransportServer2',...]
[-BiDirectional <$true | $false>]
[-Cost **ConnectorCost**]
[-Instance **'SiteIdentity'**]
[-MaxMessageSize <'**Size**' | 'Unlimited'>]
[-PublicFolderReferralsEnabled <$true | $false>]

Usage
Set-RoutingGroupConnector -Identity 'Exchange Administrator
Group\Exchange 2003 Interop' -Name 'Exchange 2003 Interop'
 -SourceTransportServers 'Exchange2007Server12.cpandl.com'
 -TargetTransportServers 'Exchange2003Server08.cpandl.com'
 -Cost 100
 -BiDirectional $true

Sample 15-16   Remove-RoutingGroupConnector cmdlet syntax and usage

Syntax
Remove-RoutingGroupConnector [-Identity
'RoutingGroup\ConnectorIdentity']

Usage
Remove-RoutingGroupConnector -Identity 'Exchange Administrator
Group\Exchange 2003 Interop'

Completing Transport Server Setup

After you install Transport servers running Exchange Server 2007, you need to finalize the configuration by creating and configuring a postmaster mailbox and performing any other necessary tasks. For Exchange organizations with only Hub Transport servers, you should enable antispam features. For Exchange organizations with Edge Transport servers, you need to subscribe the Edge Transport servers to your Exchange organization. For either type of Exchange organization, you may also want to configure journal and transport rules on your Hub Transport servers.

Configuring the Postmaster Address and Mailbox

Every organization that sends and receives mail must have a postmaster address. This is the e-mail address listed on non-delivery reports and other delivery status notification reports created by Exchange Server. To view your Exchange organization's postmaster address, enter the following command at the Exchange Management Shell prompt:

```
get-TransportServer | Format-List Name,ExternalPostMasterAddress
```

Because each Transport server in your organization can have a different postmaster address, this command lists the Transport server name associated with each postmaster address, as shown in this sample output:

```
Name: Corpsvr127
ExternalPostmasterAddress : postmaster@cpand1.com

Name: Corpsvr192
ExternalPostmasterAddress : postmaster@cpand1.com
```

To change the postmaster address, you can use the ExternalPostMasterAddress parameter of the Set-TransportServer cmdlet, as shown in this example:

```
set-TransportServer -Identity 'CorpSvr127'
 -ExternalPostMasterAddress 'nondelivery@cpand1.com'
```

If you want the postmaster address to be able to receive mail, you must either create a mailbox and associate it with the postmaster address or assign the postmaster address as a secondary e-mail address for an existing mailbox. See Chapter 8, "Mailbox Administration," for more information.

Configuring Transport Limits

Exchange Server 2007 automatically places receive size, send size, and number of recipient limits on messages being routed through an Exchange organization. By default, the maximum message size that can be received by or sent by recipients in the organization is 10240 KB and messages can have no more than 5,000 recipients.

You can view or change the default limits by completing the following steps:

1. Start Exchange Management Console. On an Edge Transport server, select Edge Transport. On a Hub Transport server, expand the Server Configuration node, and then select the Hub Transport node.

2. In the main pane, select the Global Settings node and then double-click Transport Settings. This displays the Transport Settings Properties dialog box with the General tab selected by default.

3. To set a maximum receive size limit, select the Maximum Receive Size check box and then type the desired receive limit in the related text box. The valid input range is 0 to 2097151 KB. If you clear the check box or use a value of 0, no limit is imposed on the message size that can be received by recipients in the organization.

4. To set a maximum send size limit, select the Maximum Send Size check box and then type the desired send limit in the related text box. The valid input range is 0 to 2097151 KB. If you clear the check box or use a value of 0, no limit is imposed on the message size that can be sent by senders in the organization.

5. To set a maximum number of recipients limit, select the Maximum Number Of Recipients check box and then type the desired limit in the related text box. The valid input range is 0 to 2147483647. If you clear the check box or use a value of 0, no limit is imposed on the number of recipients in a message. Note that Exchange handles an unexpanded distribution group as one recipient.

6. Click OK to apply your settings.

In the Exchange Management Shell, you assign the desired transport limits using the Set-TransportConfig cmdlet, as shown in Sample 15-17. The MaxReceiveSize and MaxSendSize parameters set the maximum receive size and maximum send size, respectively. The MaxRecipientEnvelopeLimit sets the maximum number of recipients in a message. When you use the MaxReceiveSize and MaxSendSize parameters, you must specify the units for values using KB for kilobytes, MB for megabytes, or GB for gigabytes. Your changes are made at the organization level and apply to the entire Exchange Server 2007 organization.

Sample 15-17   Setting transport limits

```
Syntax
Set-TransportConfig [-MaxReceiveSize <'MaxSize' | 'Unlimited'>]
 [-MaxSendSize <'MaxSize' | 'Unlimited'>]
 [-MaxRecipientEnvelopeLimit <'MaxRecipients' | 'Unlimited'>]
```

```
Usage
Set-TransportConfig -MaxReceiveSize '15MB' -MaxSendSize '15MB'
 -MaxRecipientEnvelopeLimit '1000'
```

Configuring the Transport Dumpster

When a Hub Transport server uses cluster continuous replication (CCR) or local continuous replication (LCR), the server uses the transport dumpster to maintain a queue of messages that were recently delivered to recipients on a clustered mailbox server. During failover in instances where CCR is used, the clustered mailbox server to which Exchange mailbox services are being failed over requests every Hub Transport server in the Active Directory site to resubmit mail from their transport dumpster queues. With LCR, you can manually perform a similar procedure to recover messages from transport dumpster queues using the Restore-StorageGroupCopy cmdlet.

You can view or change the transport dumpster configuration by completing the following steps:

1. Start Exchange Management Console. On an Edge Transport server, select Edge Transport. On a Hub Transport server, expand the Server Configuration node, and then select the Hub Transport node.

2. In the main pane, select the Global Settings node and then double-click Transport Settings. This displays the Transport Settings Properties dialog box with the General tab selected by default.

3. The Maximum Size Per Storage Group text box specifies the maximum size of the transport dumpster for each storage group. Size this setting to accommodate all messages being sent in the recovery period—the period of time from failure to failover and full recovery (which could be calculated according to the formula RecoveryWindowSizeInMinutes * MessagesPerMinute * AverageMessageSize). The valid input range for this parameter is 0 to 2097151 MB.

4. The Maximum Retention Time text box specifies how long an e-mail message should remain in the transport dumpster. When LCR or CCR is used, transport servers should retain messages in the queue for a period of time that is long enough to allow messages to be recovered. The default retention period is 7 days. The valid input range is 0 to 24855 days. If you set the retention period to 0 days, you disable the transport dumpster completely.

5. Click OK to apply your settings.

In the Exchange Management Shell, you configure the transport dumpster using the Set-TransportConfig cmdlet, as shown in Sample 15-18. The MaxDumpsterSizePerStorageGroup and MaxDumpsterTime parameters set the maximum size and maximum retention time for the transport dumpster, respectively. When you use the MaxDumpsterSizePerStorageGroup parameter, you must specify the units for values using KB for kilobytes, MB for megabytes, GB for gigabytes, or TB for terabytes. When you use the MaxDumpsterTime parameter, you set the time span in the following format: DD.HH:MM:SS. The example sets the maximum dumpster time to 3 days, 12 hours.

Sample 15-18   Setting transport limits

```
Syntax
Set-TransportConfig [-MaxDumpsterSizePerStorageGroup 'MaxSize']
 [-MaxDumpsterTime <'TimeSpan'>]
```

```
Usage
Set-TransportConfig -MaxDumpsterSizePerStorageGroup '2GB'
 -MaxDumpsterTime '3.12:00:00'
```

Enabling Antispam Features

By default, Edge Transport servers have antispam features enabled and Hub Transport servers do not. In an Exchange organization with Edge Transport servers, this is the desired configuration: you want your Edge Transport servers to run antispam filters on messages before they are routed into the Exchange organization. After Edge Transport servers have filtered messages, you don't need to filter them again—which is why Hub Transport servers have this feature disabled.

If your organization doesn't use Edge Transport servers and has only Hub Transport servers, you may want to enable antispam features on Hub Transport servers that have network adapters that connect to the Internet. In this way, you can filter incoming messages for spam. You can enable or disable antispam features on Hub Transport servers using the Set-TransportServer cmdlet. To enable these features, set the AntispamAgentsEnabled parameter to $true. To disable these features, set the AntispamAgentsEnabled parameter to $false.

The following example shows how you can enable antispam features on a Hub Transport server named CorpSvr127:

```
Set-TransportServer –Identity 'CorpSvr127' –AntispamAgentsEnabled $true
```

You then need to restart the Microsoft Exchange Transport service on the server or simply restart the server itself. If you exit and restart the Exchange Management Console, you'll then see the Antispam tab in the details pane. (Expand the Server Configuration node, and then select the Hub Transport node.)

You can now configure the transport server's antispam features as discussed in the section of this chapter entitled "Configuring Antispam and Message Filtering Options." When you turn on antispam features, a transport server can automatically get updates for spam signatures, IP reputation, and antispam definitions through automatic updates, provided that you've done the following:

- Conformed to Microsoft's licensing requirements
- Enabled Automatic Updates for use on the server
- Specifically enabled and configured antispam updates

To obtain antispam updates through automatic updates, Microsoft requires an Exchange Enterprise Client Access License (CAL) for each mailbox user or the purchase of Microsoft Forefront Security For Exchange Server 2007. You can configure automatic updates using the Windows Update utility in Control Panel. Click Start, click Control Panel\Security, and then click Windows Update to start this utility. You can also configure Automatic Updates through Group Policy. Once you've ensured that automatic updates are enabled, you can check a transport server's antispam update configuration by completing the following steps:

1. Start Exchange Management Console. On an Edge Transport server, select Edge Transport. On a Hub Transport server, expand the Server Configuration node, and then select the Hub Transport node.

2. Right-click the transport server for which you are configuring antispam updates and then select Enable Anti-Spam Updates. This starts the Enable Anti-Spam Updates Wizard.

3. Under Update Mode, select Automatic to ensure the server automatically retrieves and applies available updates.

4. Generally, you'll want a server to retrieve updates for both spam signatures and IP reputation. However, if you don't use IP allow or block lists or other features that use IP reputation details, you may not want to retrieve this information.

5. Under Update Service, ensure that the Use Microsoft Update check box is selected. This enables the server to download and install antispam definition updates using Microsoft Update.

6. Click Enable and then click Finish.

Subscribing Edge Transport Servers

When your Exchange organization uses Edge Transport servers, you must subscribe the Edge Transport server to your Exchange organization prior to performing other configuration tasks on the Edge Transport server. Creating a subscription allows the EdgeSync service running on designated Hub Transport servers to establish one-way replication of recipient and configuration information from your internal Active Directory database to the ADAM database on an Edge Transport server. After you create an Edge subscription, synchronization is automatic. Should problems occur, however, you can force synchronization or remove the Edge subscription.

Creating an Edge Subscription

A subscribed Edge Transport server receives the following from the EdgeSync service:

- Send connector configurations
- Accepted domain configurations
- Remote domain configurations

- Safe Senders lists
- Recipients

Any manually configured accepted domains, message classifications, remote domains, and Send connectors are deleted as part of the subscription process and the related Exchange management interfaces are locked out as well. To manage these features after a subscription is created, you must do so within the Exchange organization and have the EdgeSync service update the Edge Transport server.

Also as part of the subscription process, you must select an Active Directory hub site for the subscription. The Hub Transport server or servers in the hub site are the servers responsible for replicating Active Directory information to the Edge Transport server.

You can create a subscription for an Edge Transport server by completing the following steps:

1. Log on to the Edge Transport server for which you are creating a subscription using an administrator account.

2. At the Exchange Management Shell prompt, type the following command:

   ```
   New-EdgeSubscription -file "C:\EdgeSubscriptionExport.xml"
   ```

3. When prompted, confirm that it is okay to delete any manually configured accepted domains, message classifications, remote domains, and Send connectors by pressing A (which answers Yes to all deletion prompts).

4. Copy the EdgeSubscriptionExport.xml file to a Hub Transport server in your Exchange organization.

5. Log on to a Hub Transport server in your Exchange organization using an account with Exchange administration privileges.

6. On the Hub Transport server, start Exchange Management Console. Expand the Organization Configuration node, and then select the Hub Transport node.

7. In the details pane, the Edge Subscriptions tab lists existing subscriptions by Edge Transport server name and associated Active Directory site.

8. Right-click an open area of the details pane, and then select New Edge Subscription. This starts the New Edge Subscription Wizard, as shown in Figure 15-3.

9. On the New Edge Subscription page, use the Active Directory Site drop-down list to choose the Active Directory site for replication.

10. Click Browse. In the Select The Subscription File dialog box, locate and then select the Edge Subscription file to import. Click Open.

11. On the New Edge Subscription page, click New to begin the subscription process.

12. On the Completion page, click Finish. Initial synchronization will begin, as discussed in "Synchronizing Edge Subscriptions."

Figure 15-3   Create a new Edge Subscription.

After you've completed steps 1–5, you can use the New-EdgeSubscription cmdlet to start a subscription. Sample 15-19 provides the syntax and usage. By default, the CreateInboundSendConnector parameter is set to $true, which ensures that a Send connector from the Edge Transport server to Hub Transport servers is created. By default, the CreateInternetSendConnector parameter is set to true, which ensures that a Send connector to the Internet is created.

Sample 15-19   New-EdgeSubscription cmdlet syntax and usage

```
Syntax
New-EdgeSubscription -FileName 'FilePath'
 -Site 'SiteName'
 [-CreateInboundSendConnector <$true | $false>]
 [-CreateInternetSendConnector <$true | $false>]
```

```
Usage
New-EdgeSubscription -FileName 'Z:\EdgeSubscriptionExport.xml'
 -Site 'Default-First-Site-Name'
```

Getting Edge Subscription Details

In the Exchange Management Console, you can view Edge subscriptions by expanding the Organization Configuration node, selecting the Hub Transport node, and then clicking the Edge Subscriptions tab. Each Edge subscription is listed by Edge Transport server name and associated Active Directory site.

As Sample 15-20 shows, you can use the Get-EdgeSubscription cmdlet to get information about Edge subscriptions as well. If you do not provide an identity with this cmdlet, configuration information for all Edge Subscriptions is returned.

Sample 15-20   Get-EdgeSubscription cmdlet syntax and usage

```
Syntax
Get-EdgeSubscription -Identity 'EdgeTransportServerName'
```

```
Usage
Get-EdgeSubscription -Identity 'EdgeSvr04'
```

Synchronizing Edge Subscriptions

During the configuration of an Edge subscription, you specified an Active Directory site to associate with the subscription. Hub Transport servers in this site run the Edge-Sync service and are responsible for synchronizing configuration data between Active Directory Domain Service and ADAM on the Edge Transport server. By default, the EdgeSync service synchronizes configuration data hourly and recipient data every four hours.

If you've just created a new subscription and synchronization has occurred, you should verify that replication is taking place as expected by completing the following steps:

1. On the Edge Transport server, start Exchange Management Shell.

2. Verify that a Send connector was created to send Internet mail by typing the command **get-sendconnector**.

3. Verify that there is at least one entry for accepted domains by typing **get-accepteddomain**.

If you suspect a problem with synchronization and you want to start immediate synchronization of configuration data for all Edge subscriptions, complete the following steps:

1. Start Exchange Management Shell.

2. At an Exchange Management Shell prompt, type the following command

   ```
   start-edgesynchronization -Server ServerName
   ```

   where *ServerName* is the name of the Hub Transport server on which you want to run the command, such as:

   ```
   start-edgesynchronization -Server mailserver25
   ```

If you are running the command on the Hub Transport server, you can omit the –Server parameter.

Verifying Edge Subscriptions

The easiest way to verify the subscription status of Edge Transport servers is to run the Test-EdgeSynchronization cmdlet. This cmdlet provides a report of the synchronization status and you also can use it to verify that a specific recipient has been synchronized to the ADAM directory service on an Edge Transport server.

Sample 15-21 provides the syntax and usage for the Test-EdgeSynchronization cmdlet. By default, the cmdlet verifies configuration objects and recipient objects. To have the cmdlet only verify configuration data, set ExcludeRecipientTest to $true. Use the –VerifyRecipient parameter to specify the e-mail address of a recipient to verify.

Sample 15-21   Test-EdgeSubscription cmdlet syntax and usage

```
Syntax
Test-EdgeSynchronization [-ExcludeRecipientTest <$true | $false>]
  [-MaxReportSize <'MaxNumberofObjectsToCheck' | 'Unlimited'>]
  [-MonitoringContext <$true | $false>]

Test-EdgeSynchronization -VerifyRecipient 'RecipientEmailAddress'
```

```
Usage
Test-EdgeSynchronization -ExcludeRecipientTest $true

Test-EdgeSynchronization -MaxReportSize 500

Test-EdgeSynchronization -VerifyRecipient 'williams@cpandl.com'
```

Removing Edge Subscriptions

If you replace or decommission an Edge Transport server, you no longer need the related Edge subscription and can remove it. Removing an Edge subscription:

- Stops synchronization of information from the Active Directory Domain Service to ADAM.

- Removes all the accounts that are stored in ADAM.

- Removes the Edge Transport server from the source server list of any Send connector.

You can remove an Edge Subscription by completing the following steps:

1. Log on to a Hub Transport server using an account with Exchange administrator privileges.

2. In Exchange Management Console, expand the Organization Configuration node, and then select the Hub Transport node.

3. In the details pane, on the Edge Subscriptions tab, right-click the subscription that you no longer need, and then select Remove.

4. When prompted to confirm, click Yes.

In the Exchange Management Shell, you can remove an Edge Subscription by passing the identity of the subscription to remove to the Remove-EdgeSubscription cmdlet. Sample 15-22 provides the syntax and usage.

Sample 15-22   Remove-EdgeSubscription cmdlet syntax and usage

```
Syntax
Remove-EdgeSubscription -Identity 'EdgeTransportServerName'
```

```
Usage
Remove-EdgeSubscription -Identity 'EdgeSvr04'
```

Configuring Journal Rules

As discussed in Chapter 13, "Implementing Managed Folders and Managed Records," journaling allows you to forward copies of messaging items and related reports automatically to an alternate location. You can use journaling to verify compliance with policies implemented in your organization and to help ensure that your organization can meet its legal and regulatory requirements. One way to implement journaling is to do so through managed folder settings. You can also enable journaling for the entire organization using journal rules.

Creating Journal Rules

You can target journal rules for:

- **Internal messaging items**   Tracks messaging items sent and received by recipients inside your Exchange 2007 organization.

- **External messaging items**   Tracks messaging items sent to recipients or from senders outside your Exchange 2007 organization.

- **Global messaging items**   Tracks all messaging items, including those already processed by journal rules that only track internal or external messaging items.

When you enable journal rules for one or more of these scopes, the rules are executed on your organization's Hub Transport servers. Journal rules can be targeted to all recipients or to specific recipients. For example, you can create a rule to journal all messages sent to the AllEmployees distribution group.

You can create a journal rule by completing the following steps:

1. In Exchange Management Console, expand the Organization Configuration node, and select the Hub Transport node.

2. On the Journaling tab, right-click an open area of the details pane, and then select New Journal Rule. This starts the New Journal Rule Wizard.

3. In the Rule Name text box, type a descriptive name for the rule.

4. You now need to provide the journal e-mail address. Click Browse. In the Select Recipient dialog box, select the recipient to which Exchange Server should forward journal reports.

5. Use the Scope options to set the scope as Global, Internal, or External.

6. If you want the rule to apply to a specific recipient rather than to all recipients, select the Journal E-Mail For Recipient check box, and then click Browse. In the Select Recipient dialog box, select the recipient for which journal reports should be created and then click OK.

7. By default, journal rules are enabled. If you want to create the rule but not enable it, clear the Enable Rule check box.

8. Click New to create the rule. On the Completion page, click Finish.

Managing Journal Rules

To manage journal rules, you can right-click and then select one of the following options:

- **Disable Rule**   Disables the journal rule so that it is no longer applied.

- **Remove**   Removes the journal rule.

- **Properties**   Allows you to edit the properties of the journal rule.

In the Exchange Management Shell, you can manage journal rules using the following cmdlets: New-JournalRule, Set-JournalRule, Get-JournalRule, and Remove-Journal-Rule.

Configuring Transport Rules

Transport rules allow you to screen messaging items and apply actions to those that meet specific conditions. When you enable transport rules, all Hub Transport servers in your Exchange organization screen messages according to the rules you've defined.

Understanding Transport Rules

Transport rules have conditions, actions, and exceptions that you can apply. Conditions you can screen for include:

- **From People**   Allows you to screen messages from a specific recipient.

- **From A Member Of A Distribution List**   Allows you to screen messages from a member of a distribution list.

- **Sent To People**   Allows you to screen messages sent to a specific recipient.

- **Sent To A Member Of A Distribution List**   Allows you to screen messages sent to a member of a distribution list.

- **Sent To Users Inside Or Outside The Corporation**   Allows you to screen messages sent by users inside the organization or received from users outside the organization.

- **When Any Of The Recipients In The To Field Is People**   Allows you to screen messages sent to specific recipients.

- **When Any Of The Recipients In The Cc Field Is People**   Allows you to screen messages copied to specific recipients.

- **When Any Of The Recipients In The From Field Is People**   Allows you to screen messages sent by specific recipients.

- **When The Subject Field Contains Specific Words**   Allows you to screen messages that have specific words in their subject line.

- **When The Subject Field Or The Message Body Contains Specific Words**   Allows you to screen messages that have specific words in their subject line or message body.

- **With A Spam Confidence Level (SCL) Rating That Is Greater Than Or Equal To Limit**   Allows you to screen messages that have a spam confidence level (SCL) rating that is greater than or equal to a limit that you set.

- **When The Size Of Any Attachment Is Greater Than Or Equal To Limit**   Allows you to screen messages with attachments that are greater than or equal to the size limit that you set.

When a message meets all of the conditions you specify in a transport rule, the message is handled according to the actions you've defined. Actions you can apply to messages that meet your transport rule conditions include:

- **Log An Event With Message**   Logs an event in the application logs with the message you specify.

- **Prepend The Subject With String**   Inserts a string you specify into the message subject.

- **Apply Message Classification**   Applies a message classification, such as Privileged, Confidential, Company Internal, or Attachment Removed.

- **Append Disclaimer Text**   Appends disclaimer text to the message.

- **Add A Recipient To The To Field Addresses**   Adds the recipients you specify to the To field of the message.

- **Copy The Message To Addresses**   Adds the recipients you specify to the Cc field of the message.

- **Blind Carbon Copy (Bcc) The Message To Addresses**   Adds the recipients you specify to the Bcc field of the message.

- **Redirect The Message To Addresses**   Redirects the message to the recipients you specify.

- **Send Bounce Message**   Drops the message and sends a bounce message to the sender.

- **Silently Drop The Message**   Drops the message and provides no notification of this action.

Transport rules can also have exceptions. Exception criteria are similar to condition criteria. For example, you can exclude messages from certain people or from certain members of distribution lists. You can also exclude messages sent to certain people or to particular members of a distribution list.

Creating Transport Rules

You can create a transport rule by completing the following steps:

1. In Exchange Management Console, expand the Organization Configuration node, and select the Hub Transport node.

2. On the Transport Rules tab, right-click an open area of the details pane, and then select New Transport Rule. This starts the New Transport Rule Wizard.

3. In the Rule Name text box, type a descriptive name for the rule and optionally enter a descriptive comment.

4. By default, transport rules are enabled. If you want to create the rule but not enable it, clear the Enable Rule check box.

5. Click Next. You now need to specify the conditions for the rule. When you select a condition's check box, you must then edit the rule description by clicking the link or links provided and specifying any required value. For example, to configure the From People condition, you select the From People check box and then click the People link under Edit The Rule Description (Click An Underlying Value). In the Select Senders dialog box, you then click Add to display the Select Recipient dialog box. You use the Select Recipient dialog box to select the recipient to which the condition should apply, and then click OK.

6. Click Next. You now need to specify the actions to take when a message meets the conditions you specified. When you select the check box for an action, you

must then edit the rule description by clicking the link or links provided and specifying any required value.

7. Click Next. You now need to specify any exceptions. When you select the check box for an exception, you must then edit the rule description by clicking the link or links provided and specifying any required value.

8. Click Next, and then click New to create the rule.

9. On the Completion page, click Finish.

Managing Transport Rules

You can manage transport rules in several different ways. You can edit their properties or disable them. When you've created multiple rules, you can also change their priority to determine the precedence order for application in case there are conflicts between rules. When multiple rules apply to a message, the rule with the highest priority is the one that your Hub Transport server applies.

To manage transport rules, you can right-click and then select one of the following options:

- **Change Priority**   Allows you to set the priority of the rule. The valid range for priorities depends on the number of rules you've configured.

- **Disable Rule**   Disables the transport rule so that it is no longer applied.

- **Remove**   Removes the transport rule.

- **Properties**   Allows you to edit the properties of the transport rule.

In the Exchange Management Shell, you can manage transport rules using the following cmdlets: New-TransportRule, Set-TransportRule, Get-TransportRule, and Remove-TransportRule.

Managing Message Pickup and Replay

To support message routing and delivery, Hub Transport and Edge Transport servers maintain several special directories:

- **Pickup**   A folder to which users and applications can manually create and submit new messages for delivery.

- **Replay**   A folder for messages bound for or received from non-SMTP mail connectors.

The sections that follow discuss how the Pickup and Replay directories are used and configured.

Understanding Message Pickup and Replay

When a Hub Transport or Edge Transport server receives incoming mail from a server using a non-SMTP connector, it stores the message in the Replay directory and then resubmits it for delivery using SMTP. When a Hub Transport or Edge Transport server has messages to deliver to a non-SMTP connector, it stores the message in the Replay directory and then resubmits it for delivery to the foreign connector. In this way, messages received from non-SMTP connectors are processed and routed, and messages to non-SMTP connectors are delivered.

Your Transport servers automatically process any correctly formatted .eml message file copied into the Pickup directory. Exchange considers a message file that is copied into the Pickup directory to be correctly formatted if it:

- Is a text file that complies with the basic SMTP message format and can also use Multipurpose Internet Mail Extensions (MIME) header fields and content.

- Has an .eml file name extension, zero or one e-mail address in the Sender field, and one or more e-mail addresses in the From field.

- Has at least one e-mail address in the To, Cc, or Bcc fields and a blank line between the header fields and the message body.

Transport servers check the Pickup directory for new message files every five seconds. Although you can't modify this polling interval, you can adjust the rate of message file processing by using the PickupDirectoryMaxMessagesPerMinute parameter on the Set-TransportServer cmdlet. The default value is 100 messages per minute. When a transport server picks up a message, it checks the message against the maximum message size, the maximum header size, the maximum number of recipients, and other messaging limits. By default, the maximum message size is 10 megabytes (MB), the maximum header size is 64 kilobytes (KB), and the maximum number of recipients is 100. You change these limits using the Set-TransportServer cmdlet. If a message file doesn't exceed any assigned limits, the Transport server renames the message file using a .tmp extension and then converts the .tmp file to an e-mail message. After the message is successfully queued for delivery, the Transport server issues a "close" command and deletes the .tmp file from the Pickup directory.

Your Transport servers automatically process any correctly formatted .eml message file copied into the Replay directory. Exchange considers a message file that is copied into the Replay directory to be correctly formatted if it:

- Is a text file that complies with the basic SMTP message format and can also use MIME header fields and content.

- Has an .eml file name extension and its X-Header fields occur before all regular header fields.

- Has a blank line between the header fields and the message body.

Transport servers check the Replay directory for new message files every five seconds. Although you can't modify this polling interval, you can adjust the rate of message file processing. To do this, use the PickupDirectoryMaxMessagesPerMinute parameter of the Set-TransportServer cmdlet. This parameter controls the rate of processing for both the Pickup directory and the Replay directory. The Transport server renames the message file using a .tmp extension and then converts the .tmp file to an e-mail message. After the message is successfully queued for delivery, the server issues a "close" command and deletes the .tmp file from the Replay directory.

Exchange considers any improperly formatted e-mail messages received in the Pickup or Replay directory to be undeliverable and renames them from the standard message name (*MessageName*.eml) to a bad message name (*MessageName*.bad). As this is considered a type of message-processing failure, a related error is generated as well in the event logs. In addition, if you restart the Microsoft Exchange Transport service when there are .tmp files in the Pickup, Replay, or both directories, all .tmp files are renamed as .eml files and are reprocessed. This can lead to duplicate message transmissions.

Configuring and Moving the Pickup and Replay Directories

Because of the way message pickup and replay works, Transport servers do not perform any security checks on messages submitted through these directories. This means that if you've configured antispam, antivirus, sender filtering, or recipient filtering actions on a Send connector, those checks are not performed on the Pickup or Replay directories. To ensure that the Pickup and Replay directories are not compromised by malicious users, specific security permissions are applied, which must be tightly controlled.

For the Pickup and Replay directories, you must configure the following permissions:

- Full Control for Administrator
- Full Control for Local System
- Read, Write, and Delete Subfolders and Files for Network Service

As may be necessary for balancing the load across a server's disk drives or ensuring ample free space for messages, you can move the Pickup and Replay directories to new locations. You move the location of the Pickup directory by using the PickupDirectoryPath parameter on the Set-TransportServer cmdlet. You move the location of the Replay directory by using the ReplayDirectoryPath parameter on the Set-TransportServer cmdlet. With either parameter, successfully changing the directory location depends on the rights that are granted to the Network Service account on the new directory location and whether the new directory already exists. Keep the following in mind:

- If the new directory does not already exist and the Network Service account has the rights to create folders and apply permissions at the new location, the new directory is created and the correct permissions are applied to it.

- If the new directory already exists, the existing folder permissions are not checked or changed. Exchange assumes you've already set the appropriate permissions.

Sample 15-23 provides the syntax and usage for moving the Pickup and Replay directories. If you want to move both the Pickup and the Replay directories, you should do this in two separate commands.

Sample 15-23   Changing the Pickup directory

```
Syntax
Set-TransportServer -Identity 'ServerIdentity'
  [-PickupDirectoryPath 'LocalFolderPath']
  [-ReplayDirectoryPath 'LocalFolderPath']
```

```
Usage
Set-TransportServer -Identity 'CorpSvr127'
  -PickupDirectoryPath 'g:\Pickup'
```

Changing the Message Processing Speed

By default, Transport servers simultaneously and separately process the Pickup and Replay directories. Transport servers scan the Pickup and Replay directories for new message files once every 5 seconds (or 12 times per minute) and process messages copied to either directory at a rate of 100 messages per minute, per directory. As the polling interval is not configurable, this means the maximum number of messages that can be processed in either the Pickup or Replay directory during each polling interval, by default, is approximately 8 (100 messages per minute divided by 12 messages processed per minute).

Although the polling interval is not configurable, the maximum number of messages that can be processed during each polling interval is configurable. You assign the desired processing rate using the PickupDirectoryMaxMessagesPerMinute parameter, as this processing speed is used with both the Pickup and the Replay directories. You may want to adjust the message processing rate in these situations:

- If the server is unable to keep up with message processing, you may want to decrease the number of messages processed per minute to reduce processor and memory utilization.

- If the server is handling message transport for a large organization and you are seeing delays in message transport because of an abundance of messages in the Pickup, Replay, or both directories, you may want to increase the number of messages processed per minute, providing that the server can handle the additional workload.

You assign the desired processing rate using the PickupDirectoryMaxMessagesPer-Minute parameter of the Set-TransportServer cmdlet, as shown in Sample 15-24, and this processing speed is used with both the Pickup and the Replay directories. Your Transport server then attempts to process messages in each directory independently at the rate specified. You can use a per-minute message processing value between 1 and 20000.

Sample 15-24   Changing the message processing speed

```
Syntax
Set-TransportServer -Identity 'ServerIdentity'
  [-PickupDirectoryMaxMessagesPerMinute 'Speed']
```

```
Usage
Set-TransportServer -Identity 'CorpSvr127'
  -PickupDirectoryMaxMessagesPerMinute '500'
```

Configuring Messaging Limits for the Pickup Directory

You can set messaging limits for the Pickup directory for message header sizes, maximum message sizes, and maximum recipients per message. The default message header size is 64 KB. To change this setting, you can set the PickupDirectoryMaxHeader-Size parameter of the Set-TransportServer cmdlet to the desired size. The valid input range for this parameter is 32,768 to 2,147,483,647 bytes. When you specify a value, you must qualify the units for that value by ending with one of the following suffixes:

- B for bytes
- KB for kilobytes
- MB for megabytes
- GB for gigabytes

The following example sets the maximum header size to 256 KB:

```
Set-TransportServer -PickupDirectoryMaxHeaderSize: '256KB'
```

The default maximum message size is 10 MB. To change this setting, you can set the PickupDirectoryMaxMessageSize parameter of the Set-TransportServer cmdlet to the desired size. The valid input range for this parameter is 65,536 to 2,147,483,647 bytes. When you specify a value, you must qualify the units for that value. The following example sets the maximum message size to 10 MB:

```
Set-TransportServer -PickupDirectoryMaxMessageSize: '10MB'
```

The default maximum recipients per message is 100. To change this setting, you can set the PickupDirectoryMaxRecipientsPerMessage parameter of the Set-TransportServer cmdlet to the desired size. The valid input range for this parameter is 1 to 10,000. The following example sets the maximum recipients to 500:

```
Set-TransportServer –PickupDirectoryMaxRecipientsPerMessage: '500'
```

Creating and Managing Accepted Domains

An accepted domain is any SMTP namespace for which an Exchange organization sends or receives e-mail. Accepted domains include those domains for which the Exchange organization is authoritative, as well as those domains for which the Exchange organization relays mail.

Understanding Accepted Domains, Authoritative Domains, and Relay Domains

An organization may have more than one SMTP domain. The set of e-mail domains your organization uses are its authoritative domains. An accepted domain is considered authoritative when the Exchange organization hosts mailboxes for recipients in this SMTP domain. Transport servers should always accept e-mail that is addressed to any of the organization's authoritative domains. By default, when you install the first Hub Transport server, one accepted domain is configured as authoritative for the Exchange organization, and this default accepted domain is based on the FQDN of your forest root domain.

In many cases, an organization's internal domain name may differ from its external domain name. You must create an accepted domain to match your external domain name. You must also create an e-mail address policy that assigns your external domain name to user e-mail addresses. For example, your internal domain name may be cpandl.local, while your external domain name is cpandl.com. When you configure DNS, the DNS MX records for your organization will reference cpandl.com, and you will want to assign this SMTP namespace to users by creating an e-mail address policy.

When e-mail is received from the Internet by a Transport server and the recipient of the message is not a part of your organization's authoritative domains, the sending server is trying to relay messages through your Transport servers. To prevent abuse of your servers, Transport servers reject all e-mail that is not addressed to a recipient in your organization's authoritative domains. However, at times you may need to relay e-mail from another domain, such as e-mail from a partner or subsidiary. In this case, you can configure accepted domains as relay domains. When your Transport servers receive the e-mail for a configured relay domain, they will relay the messages to an e-mail server in that domain.

You can configure a relay domain as an internal relay domain or as an external relay domain. You configure an internal relay domain when there are contacts from the relay domain in the global address list. If your organization contains more than one forest and has configured global address list synchronization, the SMTP domain for one forest may be configured as an internal relay domain in a second forest. Messages from the Internet that are addressed to recipients in internal relay domains are received and processed by your Edge Transport servers. They are then relayed to your Hub Transport servers, which, in turn, route the messages to the Hub Transport servers in the recipient forest. Configuring an SMTP domain as an internal relay domain ensures that all e-mail addressed to the relay domain is accepted by your Exchange organization.

You configure an external relay domain when you want to relay messages to an e-mail server that is both outside your Exchange organization and outside the boundaries of your organization's network perimeter. For this configuration to work, your DNS servers must have an MX record for the external relay domain that references a public IP address for the relaying Exchange 2007 organization. When your Edge Transport servers receive the messages for recipients in the external relay domain, they route the messages to the mail server for the external relay domain. You must also configure a Send connector from the Edge Transport server to the external relay domain. The external relay domain may also be using your organization's Edge Transport server as a smart host for outgoing mail.

Viewing Accepted Domains

You can view the accepted domains configured for your organization by completing the following steps:

1. In Exchange Management Console, expand the Organization Configuration node, and then select the Hub Transport node.

2. On the Accepted Domains tab, accepted domains are listed by name, SMTP domain name, and domain type. The domain type is listed as Authoritative, External Relay, or Internal Relay.

You can use the Get-AcceptedDomain cmdlet to list accepted domains or to get information on a particular accepted domain as well. If you do not provide an identity with this cmdlet, configuration information for all accepted domains is displayed. Sample 15-25 provides the syntax and usage, as well as sample output, for the Get-Accepted-Domain cmdlet.

Sample 15-25   Get-AcceptedDomain cmdlet syntax and usage

```
Syntax
Get-AcceptedDomain [-Identity 'DomainIdentity']
```

```
Usage
Get-AcceptedDomain -Identity 'cpandl.com'
```

```
Output
Name                    DomainType              Default
----                    ----------              -------
cpandl.com              Authoritative           True
```

Creating Accepted Domains

You can create accepted domains for your organization by completing the following steps:

1. In Exchange Management Console, expand the Organization Configuration node, and select the Hub Transport node.

2. On the Accepted Domains tab, right-click an open area of the details pane, and then select New Accepted Domain. This starts the New Accepted Domain Wizard, as show in Figure 15-4.

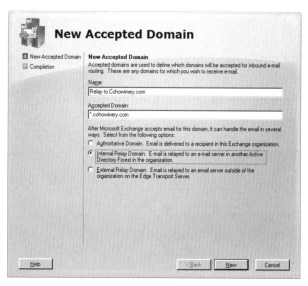

Figure 15-4   Create a new accepted domain.

3. On the New Accepted Domain page, use the Name text box to identify the accepted domain. You can use a descriptive name that identifies the purpose of the accepted domain or simply enter the actual SMTP domain name.

4. In the Accepted Domain text box, type the SMTP domain name for which the Exchange organization will accept e-mail messages. If you want to accept e-mail for the specified domain only, enter the full domain name, such as **cpandl.com**.

If you want to accept e-mail for the specified domain and child domains, type *(a wildcard character), then a period, and then the domain name, such as *.cpandl.com.

> **Note** Only domain names you specify can be used as part of an e-mail address policy. Because of this, if you want to use a subdomain as part of an e-mail address policy, you must either explicitly configure the subdomain as an accepted domain or use a wildcard character to include the parent domain and all related subdomains.

5. Select one of the following options to set the accepted domain type:

   ❑ Authoritative Domain. E-Mail Is Delivered To A Recipient In This Exchange Organization

   ❑ Internal Relay Domain. E-Mail Is Relayed To An E-Mail Server In Another Active Directory Forest In The Organization

   ❑ External Relay Domain. E-Mail Is Relayed To An E-Mail Server Outside The Organization By The Edge Transport Server

6. Click New to create the accepted domain.

7. On the Completion page, click Finish.

In the Exchange Management Shell, you can use the New-AcceptedDomain cmdlet to create accepted domains. Sample 15-26 provides the syntax and usage.

Sample 15-26 New-AcceptedDomain cmdlet syntax and usage

```
Syntax
New-AcceptedDomain -Name 'Name'
 -DomainName 'DomainName'
 -DomainType <'Authoritative'|'InternalRelay'|'ExternalRelay'>
```

```
Usage
new-AcceptedDomain -Name 'Relay to Cohowinery.com'
 -DomainName '*.cohowinery.com'
 -DomainType 'InternalRelay'
```

Changing the Accepted Domain Type and Identifier

You can change an accepted domain's type and identifier by completing the following steps:

1. In Exchange Management Console, expand the Organization Configuration node, and select the Hub Transport node.

2. On the Accepted Domains tab, right-click the accepted domain you want to change, and then select Properties.

3. In the Properties dialog box, enter a new identifier, use the options provided to change the accepted domain type as necessary, and then click OK.

In the Exchange Management Shell, you can use the Set-AcceptedDomain cmdlet to modify accepted domains. Sample 15-27 provides the syntax and usage. Use the AddressBookEnabled parameter to enable recipient filtering for this accepted domain. You should set this parameter to $true only if all the recipients in this accepted domain are replicated to the ADAM database on the Edge Transport servers. For authoritative domains and internal relay domains, the default value is $true. For external relay domains, the default value is $false.

Sample 15-27   Set-AcceptedDomain cmdlet syntax and usage

```
Syntax
Set-AcceptedDomain -Identity 'AcceptedDomainIdentity'
  [-Name 'Name']
  [-DomainType <'Authoritative'|'InternalRelay'|'ExternalRelay'>]
  [-AddressBookEnabled <$true | $false>]
  [-MakeDefault <$true | $false>]
```

```
Usage
Set-AcceptedDomain -Identity 'Relay to Cohowinery.com'
  -DomainType 'ExternalRelay'
```

Removing Accepted Domains

You can remove an accepted domain that is no longer needed by completing the following steps:

1. In Exchange Management Console, expand the Organization Configuration node, and select the Hub Transport node.

2. On the Accepted Domains tab, right-click the accepted domain you want to remove, and then select Remove.

3. When prompted to confirm, click Yes.

In the Exchange Management Shell, you can use the Remove-AcceptedDomain cmdlet to remove accepted domains. Sample 15-28 provides the syntax and usage.

Sample 15-28   Remove-AcceptedDomain cmdlet syntax and usage

```
Syntax
Remove-AcceptedDomain -Identity 'AcceptedDomainIdentity'
```

```
Usage
Remove-AcceptedDomain -Identity 'Relay to Cohowinery.com'
```

Creating and Managing E-mail Address Policies

E-mail address policies allow you to generate or rewrite e-mail addresses automatically for each recipient in your organization based on specific criteria you set. Exchange Server uses e-mail address policies in two key ways:

- Whenever you create a new recipient, Exchange Server sets the recipient's default e-mail address based on the applicable e-mail address policy.

- Whenever you apply an e-mail address policy, Exchange Server automatically rewrites the e-mail addresses for recipients to which the policy applies.

Every Exchange organization has a default e-mail address policy, which is required to create e-mail addresses for recipients. You can create additional e-mail address policies as well—for example, if your organization's internal domain name is different from its external domain name. You must create an accepted domain to match your external domain name and an e-mail address policy that assigns your external domain name to user e-mail addresses.

Viewing E-mail Address Policies

You can view the e-mail address policies configured for your organization by completing the following steps:

1. In Exchange Management Console, expand the Organization Configuration node, and then select the Hub Transport node.

2. On the E-mail Address Policies tab, e-mail address policies are listed by name, priority, last modified time, and applied status. The applied status is listed as True for a policy that has been applied to recipients and False for a policy that has not been applied to recipients.

You can use the Get-EmailAddressPolicy cmdlet to list e-mail address policies or to get information on a particular e-mail address policy. If you do not provide an identity with this cmdlet, configuration information for all e-mail address policies is displayed. Sample 15-29 provides the syntax and usage, as well as sample output, for the Get-EmailAddressPolicy cmdlet.

Sample 15-29   Get-EmailAddressPolicy cmdlet syntax and usage

```
Syntax
Get-EmailAddressPolicy [-Identity 'PolicyIdentity']
```

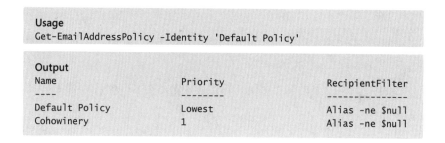

```
Usage
Get-EmailAddressPolicy -Identity 'Default Policy'
```

```
Output
Name                          Priority                    RecipientFilter
----                          --------                    ---------------
Default Policy                Lowest                      Alias -ne $null
Cohowinery                    1                           Alias -ne $null
```

Creating E-mail Address Policies

You can create e-mail address policies for your organization by completing the following steps:

1. In Exchange Management Console, expand the Organization Configuration node, and select the Hub Transport node.

2. On the E-mail Address Policies tab, right-click an open area of the details pane, and then select New E-mail Address Policy. This starts the New E-mail Address Policy Wizard, as shown in Figure 15-5.

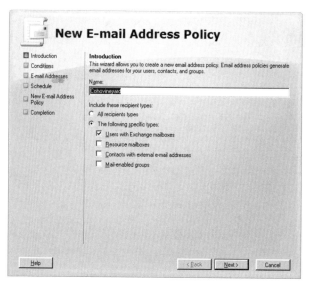

Figure 15-5   Create a new e-mail address policy.

3. On the Introduction page, use the Name text box to identify the e-mail address policy. You can use a descriptive name that identifies the purpose of the e-mail address policy or simply enter the actual SMTP domain name to which it applies.

4. Use the Include These Recipient Types options to specify the types of recipients to include in the policy. Select either All Recipient Types or select The Following Specific Types and then select the check boxes for the types of recipients to which you want to apply the policy.

5. Click Next. On the Conditions page, you can now set the filter conditions. The following types of conditions are available:

❑ **Recipient Is In A State Or Province**   Filters recipients based on the value of the State/Province field on the Address And Phone tab in the related Properties dialog box. Click the related In The Specified State Or Province link. In the Specify State Or Province dialog box, type a state or province to use as a filter condition, and then press Enter or click Add. Repeat as necessary, and then click OK.

❑ **Recipient Is In A Department**   Filters recipients based on the value of the Department field on the Organization tab in the related Properties dialog box. Click the related In The Specified Department(s) link. In the Specify Department dialog box, type a department to use as a filter condition, and then press Enter or click Add. Repeat as necessary, and then click OK.

❑ **Recipient Is In A Company**   Filters recipients based on the value of the Company field on the Organization tab in the related Properties dialog box. Click the related In The Specified Company link. In the Specify Company dialog box, type a company name to use as a filter condition, and then press Enter or click Add. Repeat as necessary, and then click OK.

6. On the E-mail Address page, click the small arrow to the right of Add, and then select SMTP Address. The SMTP E-mail Address dialog box appears, as shown in Figure 15-6.

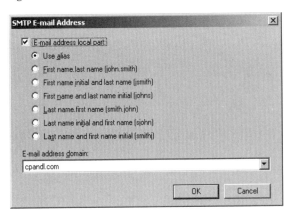

Figure 15-6   Select options to generate e-mail addresses.

7. Use the E-mail Address Local Part options to specify how to generate or rewrite e-mail addresses automatically for each recipient to which the policy applies. You can use the Exchange alias or parts of the user name in various orders.

8. Use the E-mail Address Domain drop-down list to select the e-mail address domain, and then click OK.

9. Click Next. If you want to create and apply the policy immediately, select Immediately. To schedule the policy application, select At The Following Time, and then set the date and time to apply the policy.

10. Click Next, and then click New to create and apply the policy or schedule the policy to be applied. After the policy is applied, e-mail addresses for recipients to which the policy applies will be rewritten.

11. On the Completion page, click Finish.

In the Exchange Management Shell, you create and apply e-mail address policies using separate tasks. You can create e-mail address policies using the New-EmailAddress-Policy cmdlet. You apply e-mail address policies using the Update- EmailAddressPolicy cmdlet. Samples 15-30 and 15-31 provide the syntax and usage for these cmdlets.

Note   Any time you receive an error regarding missing aliases, you should run the Update-EmailAddressPolicy cmdlet with the FixMissingAlias parameter set to $true. This tells Exchange to generate an alias for recipients who do not have an alias.

Sample 15-30   New-EmailAddressPolicy cmdlet syntax and usage

```
Syntax
New-EmailAddressPolicy -Name 'PolicyName'
 [-IncludedRecipients 'RecipientTypes']
 [-ConditionalCompany 'CompanyNameFilter1', 'CompanyNameFilter2',... ]
 [-ConditionalDepartment 'DeptNameFilter1',' DeptNameFilter2', ... ]
 [-ConditionalStateOrProvince 'StateNameFilter1', 'StateNameFilter2', ... ]
 [-Priority 'Priority']
 [-EnabledEmailAddressTemplates 'AddressTemplate']
 [-DisbledEmailAddressTemplates 'AddressTemplate']
```

```
Usage
New-EmailAddressPolicy -Name 'Primary E-Mail Address Policy'
-IncludedRecipients 'MailboxUsers, MailContacts, MailGroups'
 -ConditionalCompany 'City Power & Light'
 -ConditionalDepartment 'Sales','Marketing'
 -ConditionalStateOrProvince 'Washington','Idaho','Oregon'
 -Priority 'Lowest'
 -EnabledEmailAddressTemplates 'SMTP:%g.%s@cpandl.com'
```

Sample 15-31   Update-EmailAddressPolicy cmdlet syntax and usage

```
Syntax
Update-EmailAddressPolicy -Identity 'PolicyIdentity'
 [-FixMissingAlias <$true | $false>]
```

```
Usage
Update-EmailAddressPolicy -Identity 'Primary E-Mail Address Policy'

Update-EmailAddressPolicy -Identity 'Primary E-Mail Address Policy'
 -FixMissingAlias $true
```

Editing and Applying E-mail Address Policies

You can manage e-mail address policies in several different ways. You can edit their properties or apply them to rewrite e-mail addresses automatically for each recipient to which the policy applies. You can also change their priority to determine the precedence order for application in case there are conflicts between policies. When multiple policies may apply to a recipient, the policy with the highest priority is the one that applies.

You can change the way e-mail address policies work by completing the following steps:

1. In Exchange Management Console, expand the Organization Configuration node, and select the Hub Transport node.

2. On the E-mail Address Policies tab, right-click the e-mail address policy you want to change, and then select Edit. This starts the Edit E-mail Address Policy Wizard.

3. Follow steps 3–11 in "Creating E-mail Address Policies."

You can change the priority of an e-mail address policy by completing the following steps:

1. In Exchange Management Console, right-click the policy, and then select Change Priority.

2. In the Change E-mail Address Policy Priority dialog box, type the desired priority, and then click OK.

   Note   The valid range for priorities depends on the number of policies you've configured.

You can apply an e-mail address policy immediately or at a scheduled time by completing the following steps:

1. In Exchange Management Console, right-click the policy, and then select Apply. This starts the Apply E-mail Address Policy Wizard.

2. If you want to create and apply the policy immediately, select Immediately. To schedule the policy application, select At The Following Time, and then set the date and time to apply the policy.

3. Click Next, and then click Apply.

4. On the Completion page, click Finish.

In the Exchange Management Shell, you can use the Set-EmailAddressPolicy cmdlet to modify e-mail address policies, as shown in Sample 15-32. The Update-EmailAddress-Policy cmdlet, used to apply policies, was discussed previously.

Sample 15-32   Set-EmailAddressPolicy cmdlet syntax and usage

```
Syntax
Set-EmailAddressPolicy -Identity 'PolicyIdentity']
  [-Name 'PolicyName']
  [-IncludedRecipients 'RecipientTypes']
  [-ConditionalCompany 'CompanyNameFilter1', 'CompanyNameFilter2',... ]
  [-ConditionalDepartment 'DeptNameFilter1',' DeptNameFilter2', ... ]
  [-ConditionalStateOrProvince 'StateNameFilter1', 'StateNameFilter2', ... ]
  [-Priority 'Priority']
  [-EnabledEmailAddressTemplates 'AddressTemplate']
  [-DisbledEmailAddressTemplates 'AddressTemplate']
```

```
Usage
Set-EmailAddressPolicy  -Identity 'Primary E-Mail Address Policy'
  -Name 'Cpandl.com E-Mail Address Policy'
  -IncludedRecipients 'MailboxUsers,
  -ConditionalCompany 'City Power & Light'
  -ConditionalDepartment 'Sales'
  -ConditionalStateOrProvince 'Washington'
  -Priority '2'
  -EnabledEmailAddressTemplates 'SMTP:%g.%s@cpandl.com'
```

Removing E-mail Address Policies

You can remove an e-mail address policy that is no longer needed by completing the following steps:

1. In Exchange Management Console, expand the Organization Configuration node, and select the Hub Transport node.

2. On the E-mail Address Policies tab, right-click the e-mail address policy you want to remove, and then select Remove.

3. When prompted to confirm, click Yes.

In the Exchange Management Shell, you can use the Remove-EmailAddressPolicy cmdlet to remove e-mail address policies. Sample 15-33 provides the syntax and usage.

Sample 15-33 Remove-EmailAddressPolicy cmdlet syntax and usage

```
Syntax
Remove-EmailAddressPolicy -Identity 'EmailAddressPolicyIdentity'
```

```
Usage
Remove-EmailAddressPolicy -Identity 'Cpandl.com
E-Mail Address Policy'
```

Creating and Managing Remote Domains

Remote domain settings help you manage mail flow for most types of automated messages, including out-of-office messages, automatic replies, automatic forwarding, delivery reports, and nondelivery reports. Remote domain settings also control some automated message formatting options, such as whether to display a sender's name on a message or only the sender's e-mail address. Your Exchange organization has a default remote domain policy that sets the global defaults. You can create additional policies to create managed connections for specific remote domains as well.

Viewing Remote Domains

You can view the remote domains configured for your organization by completing the following steps:

1. In Exchange Management Console, expand the Organization Configuration node, and then select the Hub Transport node.

2. On the Remote Domain tab, remote domains are listed by name and the domain to which they apply. The Default remote domain applies to all remote domains, unless you override it with specific settings.

You can use the Get-RemoteDomain cmdlet to list remote domains or to get information on a particular remote domain. If you do not provide an identity with this cmdlet, configuration information for all remote domains is displayed. Sample 15-34 provides the syntax and usage, as well as sample output, for the Get-RemoteDomain cmdlet.

Sample 15-34 Get-RemoteDomain cmdlet syntax and usage

```
Syntax
Get-RemoteDomain [-Identity 'DomainIdentity']
```

```
Usage
Get-RemoteDomain -Identity 'cpandl.com'
```

```
Output
Name                           ContentType                  Status
----                           -----------                  ------
Default                        MimeHtmlText
Cohowinery                     MimeHtmlText
```

Creating Remote Domains

You can create remote domains for your organization by completing the following
steps:

1. In Exchange Management Console, expand the Organization Configuration
   node, and select the Hub Transport node.

2. On the Remote Domain tab, right-click an open area of the details pane, and then
   select New Remote Domain. This starts the New Remote Domain Wizard, as
   shown in Figure 15-7.

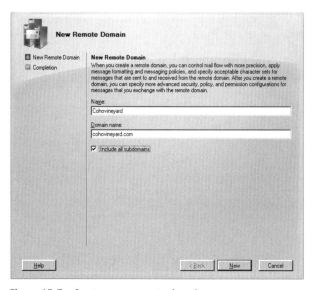

Figure 15-7 Create a new remote domain.

3. On the New Remote Domain page, use the Name text box to identify the remote
   domain. You can use a descriptive name that identifies the purpose of the remote
   domain or simply enter the actual SMTP domain name.

4. In the Domain Name text box, type the SMTP domain name for which you want to manage connections. If you want to manage connections for the specified domain and its child domains, select the Include All Subdomains check box.

5. Click New to create the remote domain.

6. On the Completion page, click Finish.

In the Exchange Management Shell, you can use the New-RemoteDomain cmdlet to create remote domains. Sample 15-35 provides the syntax and usage. The way you set the DomainName parameter determines whether the remote domain includes subdomains. You insert a period before the domain name to include child domains.

Sample 15-35   New-RemoteDomain cmdlet syntax and usage

```
Syntax
New-RemoteDomain -Name 'Name'
 -DomainName 'DomainName'
```

```
Usage for parent domain only
new-RemoteDomain -Name 'Cohowinery Managed Connection'
 -DomainName 'cohowinery.com'
```

```
Usage for parent domain and child domains
new-RemoteDomain -Name 'Cohowinery Managed Connection'
 -DomainName '.cohowinery.com'
```

Configuring Messaging Options for Remote Domains

Remote domains are used to control how automated messages are used and some types of messaging format options. To change the default configuration for a remote domain, follow these steps:

1. In Exchange Management Console, expand the Organization Configuration node, and select the Hub Transport node.

2. On the Remote Domain tab, right-click the remote domain you want to change, and then select Properties.

3. On the General tab, specify whether and how out-of-office messages are sent to the remote domain. The options are:

    ❑ **Allow None**   Blocks all out-of-office messages.

    ❑ **Allow External Out-Of-Office Messages Only**   Allows out-of-office messages to be received by the Exchange organization, but does not allow the organization's out-of-office messages to be sent.

❑ **Allow External Out-Of-Office Messages And Out-Of-Office Messages Set By Outlook 2003 Or Earlier Clients And Set On Exchange Server 2003 Or Earlier** Allows out-of-office messages to be received by the Exchange organization and receipt of out-of-office messages generated by Microsoft Outlook 2003, Exchange 2003, or earlier.

❑ **Allow Internal Out-Of-Office Messages And Out-Of-Office Messages Set By Outlook 2003 Or Earlier Clients And Set On Exchange Server 2003 Or Earlier** Allows out-of-office messages to be sent from the Exchange organization and sending of out-of-office messages generated by Outlook 2003, Exchange 2003, or earlier.

4. On the Format Of Original Message Sent As Attachment To Journal Report tab, specify how Exchange should format messages attached to journal reports. Allow messaging options by selecting the related check boxes, or disallow messaging options by clearing the related check boxes. The options available are:

❑ **Allow Automatic Replies** Allows the sender to be notified that the message was received.

❑ **Allow Automatic Forward** Allows Exchange Server to forward or deliver a duplicate message to a new recipient.

❑ **Allow Delivery Reports** Allows Exchange Server to return delivery confirmation reports to the sender.

❑ **Allow Non-Delivery Reports** Allows Exchange Server to return nondelivery confirmation reports to the sender.

❑ **Display Sender's Name On Messages** Allows both the sender's name and e-mail address to appear on outbound e-mail messages.

5. By default, text word-wrapping is disabled, which means that Exchange enforces no maximum line length. If you'd like message text to wrap at a specific line length, you can enable text word-wrapping at a specific column position, such as 72 characters. Select the Use Message Text Line Wrap At Column check box, and then enter the column position for text line wrap.

6. If you want to send Transport Neutral Encapsulation Format (TNEF) message data to the remote domain rather than Exchange Rich-Text format, select Never Use under Exchange Rich-Text Format.

7. To set a specific MIME and non-MIME character set, enter the character set code in the text boxes provided. Click OK to save your settings.

In the Exchange Management Shell, you can use the Set-RemoteDomain cmdlet to configure remote domains. Sample 15-36 provides the syntax and usage.

Sample 15-36   Set-RemoteDomain cmdlet syntax and usage

```
Syntax
Set-RemoteDomain -Identity 'RemoteDomainIdentity'
   [-AllowedOOFType <'External'|'InternalLegacy'|'ExternalLegacy'|'None'>]
   [-AutoForwardEnabled <$true | $false>]
   [-AutoReplyEnabled <$true | $false>]
   [-CharacterSet 'CharacterSet']
   [-ContentType <'MimeHtmlText'|'MimeText'|'MimeHtml'>]
   [-DeliveryReportEnabled <$true | $false>]
   [-DisplaySenderName <$true | $false>]
   [-LineWrapSize 'Size']
   [-MeetingForwardNotificationEnabled <$true | $false>]
   [-Name 'Name']
   [-NDREnabled <$true | $false>]
   [-NonMimeCharacterSet 'CharacterSet']
   [-TNEFEnabled <$true | $false>]
```

```
Usage
Set-RemoteDomain -Identity 'Cohowinery'
   -DeliveryReportEnabled $false
```

Removing Remote Domains

You can remove a remote domain that is no longer needed by completing the following steps:

1. In Exchange Management Console, expand the Organization Configuration node, and select the Hub Transport node.

2. On the Remote Domain tab, right-click the remote domain you want to remove, and then select Remove.

3. When prompted to confirm, click Yes.

In the Exchange Management Shell, you can use the Remove-RemoteDomain cmdlet to remove remote domains. Sample 15-37 provides the syntax and usage.

Sample 15-37   Remove-RemoteDomain cmdlet syntax and usage

```
Syntax
Remove-RemoteDomain -Identity 'RemoteDomainIdentity'
```

```
Usage
Remove-RemoteDomain -Identity 'Cohowinery'
```

Configuring Antispam and Message Filtering Options

Every minute users spend dealing with unsolicited commercial e-mail (spam) or other unwanted e-mail is a minute they cannot do their work and deal with other issues. To deter spammers and other senders from whom users don't want to receive messages, you can use message filtering to block these people from sending messages to your organization. Not only can you filter messages that claim to be from a particular sender or that are sent to a particular receiver, you can also establish connection filtering rules based on real-time block lists. The sections that follow discuss these and other antispam options.

As you configure message filtering, keep in mind that Exchange Server 2007 is designed to combat the most commonly used spammer techniques, but cannot block all of them. Like the techniques of those who create viruses, the techniques of those who send spam frequently change, and you won't be able to prevent all unwanted e-mail from going through. You should, however, be able to substantially reduce the flow of spam into your organization.

Filtering Spam and Other Unwanted E-mail by Sender

Sometimes, when you are filtering spam or other unwanted e-mail, you'll know specific e-mail addresses or e-mail domains from which you don't want to accept messages. In this case, you can block messages from these senders or e-mail domains by configuring sender filtering. Another sender from which you probably don't want to accept messages is a blank sender. If the sender is blank, it means the From field of the e-mail message wasn't filled in and the message is probably from a spammer.

Sender filtering is enabled by default. To configure filtering according to the sender of the message, follow these steps:

1. Start Exchange Management Console. On an Edge Transport server, select Edge Transport, and then click the Anti-Spam tab in the details pane. On a Hub Transport server for which you've enabled spam filtering, expand the Organization Configuration node, select Hub Transport, and then click the Anti-Spam tab in the details pane.

2. Right-click Sender Filtering, and then select Properties. The Sender Filtering Properties dialog box appears.

3. On the Blocked Senders tab (shown in Figure 15-8), the Senders list box shows the current sender filters, if any.

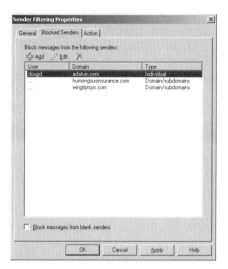

Figure 15-8   Use sender filtering to set restrictions on addresses and domains that can send mail to your organization.

4. You can add a sender filter by clicking Add. In the Add Blocked Senders dialog box, select Individual E-mail Address if the filter is for a specific e-mail address, or select Domain if you want to filter all e-mail sent from a particular domain. Type the e-mail address or domain name, as appropriate, and then click OK.

5. You can remove a filter by selecting it and then clicking Remove.

6. To edit a filter, double-click the filter entry, enter a new value, and then click OK.

7. On the Blocked Senders tab, you can also filter messages that don't have an e-mail address in the From field. To do this, select the Block Messages From Blank Senders check box.

8. On the Action tab, specify how messages from blocked senders are to be handled. If you want to ensure that Exchange doesn't waste processing power and other resources dealing with messages from filtered senders, select the Reject Message check box. If you want to mark messages as being from a blocked sender and continue processing them, select Stamp Message With Blocked Sender And Continue Processing. Click OK.

Filtering Spam and Other Unwanted E-mail by Recipient

In any organization, you'll have users whose e-mail addresses change, perhaps because they request it, leave the company, or change office locations. Although you might be able to forward e-mail to these users for a time, you probably won't want to forward e-mail indefinitely. At some point, you, or someone else in the organization, will decide it's time to delete the user's account, mailbox, or both. If the user is subscribed to mailing lists or other services that deliver automated e-mail, the automated messages continue to come in, unless you manually unsubscribe the user or reply to each e-mail that you don't want to receive the messages. That's a measure that wastes time, but Exchange administrators often find themselves doing this. It's much easier to add the old or invalid e-mail address to a recipient filter list and specify that Exchange shouldn't accept messages for users who aren't in the Exchange directory. Once you do this, Exchange won't attempt to deliver messages for filtered or invalid recipients, and you won't see related nondelivery reports (NDRs), either.

Recipient filtering is enabled by default. To configure filtering according to the message recipient, follow these steps:

1. Start Exchange Management Console. On an Edge Transport server, select Edge Transport, and then click the Anti-Spam tab in the details pane. On a Hub Transport server for which you've enabled spam filtering, expand the Organization Configuration node, select Hub Transport, and then click the Anti-Spam tab in the details pane.

2. Right-click Recipient Filtering, and then select Properties. The Recipient Filtering Properties dialog box appears.

3. On the Blocked Recipients tab (shown in Figure 15-9), the Recipients list box shows the current recipient filters, if any.

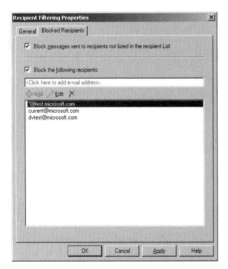

Figure 15-9   Use recipient filtering to set restrictions for specific or invalid recipients.

4. You can filter messages that are sent to recipients who don't have e-mail addresses and aren't listed as recipients in your Exchange organization. To do this, select the Block Messages Sent To Recipients Not Listed In the Recipient List check box.

5. Before you can add other recipient filters, you must select the Block The Following Recipients check box. You can then add a recipient filter by typing the address you'd like to filter and then clicking Add. Addresses can refer to a specific e-mail address, such as walter@microsoft.com, or a group of e-mail addresses designated with the wildcard character (*), such as *@microsoft.com to filter all e-mail addresses from microsoft.com, or *@*.microsoft.com, to filter all e-mail addresses from child domains of microsoft.com.

6. You can remove a filter by selecting it and then clicking Remove.

7. To edit a filter, double-click the filter entry, enter a new value, and then press Enter. Click OK.

Filtering Connections with Real-Time Block Lists

If you find that sender and recipient filtering isn't enough to stem the flow of spam into your organization, you might want to consider subscribing to a real-time block list service. Here's how this works:

■ You subscribe to a real-time block list service. Typically, you'll have to pay a monthly service fee. In return, the service lets you query their servers for known sources of unsolicited e-mail and known relay servers.

■ The service provides you with domains you can use for validation and a list of status codes to watch for. You configure Exchange to use the specified domains and enter connection filtering rules to match the return codes. Then you configure any exceptions for recipient e-mail addresses or sender IP addresses.

■ Each time an incoming connection is made, Exchange performs a lookup of the source IP address in the block list domain. A "host not found" error is returned to indicate the IP address is not on the block list and that there is no match. If there is a match, the block list service returns a status code that indicates the suspected activity. For example, a status code of 127.0.0.3 might mean that the IP address is from a known source of unsolicited e-mail.

■ If there is a match between the status code returned and the filtering rules you've configured, Exchange returns an error message to the user or server attempting to make the connection. The default error message says that the IP address has been blocked by a connection filter rule, but you can specify a custom error message to return instead.

The sections that follow discuss applying real-time block lists, setting provider priority, defining custom error messages to return, and configuring block list exceptions. These are all tasks you'll perform when you work with real-time block lists.

Applying Real-Time Block Lists

Before you get started, you'll need to know the domain of the block list service provider, and you should also consider how you want to handle the status codes the provider returns. Exchange allows you to specify that any return status code is a match, that only a specific code matched to a bit mask is a match, or that any of several status codes that you designate can match.

Table 15-1 shows a list of typical status codes that might be returned by a provider service. Rather than filter all return codes, in most cases, you'll want to be as specific as possible about the types of status codes that match. This ensures that you don't accidentally filter valid e-mail. For example, based on the list of status codes of the provider, you might decide that you want to filter known sources of unsolicited e-mail and known relay servers, but not filter known sources of dial-up user accounts, which might or might not be sources of unsolicited e-mail.

Table 15-1   Typical Status Codes Returned by Block List Provider Services

Return Status Code	Code Description	Code Bit Mask
127.0.0.2	Dial-up user account	0.0.0.2
127.0.0.3	Known source of unsolicited e-mail	0.0.0.3
127.0.0.4	Known relay server	0.0.0.4
127.0.0.5	Dial-up user account using a known source of unsolicited e-mail	0.0.0.5
127.0.0.6	Dial-up user account using a known relay server	0.0.0.6
127.0.0.7	Known source of unsolicited e-mail and a known relay server	0.0.0.7
127.0.0.9	Dial-up user, known source of unsolicited e-mail, and known relay server	0.0.0.9

You can filter connections using real-time block lists by completing the following steps:

1. Start Exchange Management Console. On an Edge Transport server, select Edge Transport, and then click the Anti-Spam tab in the details pane. On a Hub Transport server for which you've enabled spam filtering, expand the Organization Configuration node, select Hub Transport, and then click the Anti-Spam tab in the details pane.

2. Right-click IP Block List Providers, and then select Properties. The IP Block List Providers Properties dialog box appears.

3. Click the Providers tab. The Block List Providers list box shows the current Block List providers, if any.

4. Click Add to add a Block List provider. The Add IP Block List Provider dialog box appears, shown in Figure 15-10.

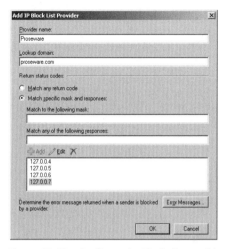

Figure 15-10   Configure the Block List provider.

5. Type the name of the provider in the Provider Name text box.

6. In the Lookup Domain text box, type the domain name of the block list provider service, such as **proseware.com**.

7. Under Return Status Codes, select Match Any Return Code to match any return code (other than an error) received from the provider service or select one or more of the following options:

   ❑ **Match Specific Mask And Responses**   Select this option to match a specific mask and return codes from the provider service.

   ❑ **Match To The Following Mask**   Select this option to match a specific return code from the provider service. For example, if the return code for a known relay server is 127.0.0.4 and you want to match this specific code, you would type the mask **0.0.0.4**.

   ❑ **Match Any Of The Following Responses**   Select this option to match specific values in the return status codes. Type a return status code to match, and then click Add. Repeat as necessary for each return code that you want to add.

8. Click OK to start using real-time block lists from the block list provider.

Setting Priority and Enabling Block List Providers

You can configure multiple block list providers. Each provider is listed in priority order, and if Exchange makes a match using a particular provider, the other providers are not checked for possible matches. In addition to priority, providers can also be enabled or disabled. If you disable a provider, it is ignored when looking for possible status code matches.

You can set block list provider priority and enable or disable providers by completing the following steps:

1. Start Exchange Management Console. On an Edge Transport server, select Edge Transport, and then click the Anti-Spam tab in the details pane. On a Hub Transport server for which you've enabled spam filtering, expand the Organization Configuration node, select Hub Transport, and then click the Anti-Spam tab in the details pane.

2. Right-click IP Block List Providers, and then select Properties. The IP Block List Providers Properties dialog box appears.

3. Click the Providers tab. The Block List Providers list box shows the current block list providers in priority order.

4. To change the priority of a provider, select it, and then click the Move Up or Move Down button to change its order in the list.

5. To disable a provider, select it, and then click Disable.

6. To enable a provider, select it, and then click Enable. Click OK to close the Properties dialog box.

Specifying Custom Error Messages to Return

When a match is made between the status code returned and the filtering rules you've configured for block list providers, Exchange returns an error message to the user or server attempting to make the connection. The default error message says that the IP address has been blocked by a connection filter rule. If you want to override the default error message, you can specify a custom error message to return on a per-rule basis. The error message can contain the following substitution values:

- %0 to insert the connecting IP address
- %1 to insert the name of the connection filter rule
- %2 to insert the domain name of the block list provider service

Some examples of custom error messages include the following:

- The IP address (%1) was blocked and not allowed to connect.
- %1 was rejected by %2 as a potential source of unsolicited e-mail.

Using the substitution values, you can create a custom error message for each block list provider by following these steps:

1. Start Exchange Management Console. On an Edge Transport server, select Edge Transport, and then click the Anti-Spam tab in the details pane. On a Hub Transport server for which you've enabled spam filtering, expand the Organization Configuration node, select Hub Transport, and then click the Anti-Spam tab in the details pane.

2. Right-click IP Block List Providers, and then select Properties. The IP Block List Providers Properties dialog box appears.

3. On the Providers tab, the Block List Providers list box shows the current Block List providers in priority order. Select the block list provider for which you want to create a custom error message, and then click Edit.

4. In the Edit IP Block List Provider dialog box, click Error Messages.

5. In the IP Block List Provider Error Message dialog box, select Custom Error Message, and then type the error message to return. Click OK twice.

Defining Block List Exceptions and Global Allow/Block Lists

Sometimes, you'll find that an IP address, a network, or an e-mail address shows up incorrectly on a block list. The easiest way to correct this problem is to create a block list exception that indicates that the specific IP address, network, or e-mail address shouldn't be filtered.

Creating or Removing Connection Filter Exceptions for E-mail Addresses

You can define connection filter exceptions for e-mail addresses by completing the following steps:

1. Start Exchange Management Console. On an Edge Transport server, select Edge Transport, and then click the Anti-Spam tab in the details pane. On a Hub Transport server for which you've enabled spam filtering, expand the Organization Configuration node, select Hub Transport, and then click the Anti-Spam tab in the details pane.

2. Right-click IP Block List Providers, and then select Properties. The IP Block List Providers Properties dialog box appears.

3. On the Exceptions tab, any current exceptions are listed by e-mail address. Type the e-mail address to add as an exception, such as **abuse@adatum.com**, and then click Add.

4. To delete an exception, select an existing e-mail address, and then click Remove.

5. Click OK to save your settings.

Creating or Removing Global Allowed Lists for IP Addresses and Networks

Exchange will accept e-mail from any IP address or network on the global allowed list. To define allowed entries for IP addresses and networks, complete the following steps:

1. Start Exchange Management Console. On an Edge Transport server, select Edge Transport, and then click the Anti-Spam tab in the details pane. On a Hub Transport server, expand the Organization Configuration node, select Hub Transport, and then click the Anti-Spam tab in the details pane.

2. Right-click IP Allow List, and then select Properties. The IP Allow List Properties dialog box appears.

3. On the Allowed Addresses tab, you'll see a list of current IP addresses and networks that are configured on the allowed list.

4. Click Add to add an IP address or network to the allowed list:

   ❑ To allow a single IP address, type the IP address in the text box provided, such as **192.168.10.45**, and then click OK.

   ❑ To allow all IP addresses on a network, type the network address, such as **192.168.0.0/24**, and then click OK.

5. To remove an existing entry from the allowed list, click the entry and then click Remove.

6. Click OK to save your settings.

Creating or Removing Global Block Lists for IP Addresses and Networks

Exchange will reject e-mail from any IP address or network on the block list. To define block list entries for IP addresses and networks, complete the following steps:

1. Start Exchange Management Console. On an Edge Transport server, select Edge Transport, and then click the Anti-Spam tab in the details pane. On a Hub Transport server, expand the Organization Configuration node, select Hub Transport, and then click the Anti-Spam tab in the details pane.

2. Right-click IP Block List, and then select Properties. The IP Block List Properties dialog box appears.

3. On the Blocked Addresses tab, you'll see a list of current IP addresses and networks that are configured on the block list. Click Add to add an IP address or network to the block list:

   ❑ To block a single IP address, type the IP address in the text box provided, such as **192.168.10.45**, and then click OK.

   ❑ To block all IP addresses on a network, type the network address, such as **192.168.0.0/24**, and then click OK.

4. To remove an entry from the block list, select the entry, and then click Remove.

5. Click OK to save your settings.

Preventing Internal Servers from Being Filtered

Typically, you don't want Exchange to apply Sender ID or connection filters to servers on your organization's network or to internal SMTP servers deployed in a perimeter zone. One way to ensure this is to configure message delivery options for your organization's transport servers so that they don't apply filters to IP addresses from internal servers and your perimeter network.

You can configure which IP addresses to ignore by completing the following steps:

1. Start Exchange Management Console. On an Edge Transport server, select Edge Transport. On a Hub Transport server, expand the Server Configuration node, and then select the Hub Transport node.

2. In the main pane, select the Global Settings node and then double-click Transport Settings. This displays the Transport Settings Properties dialog box with the General tab selected by default.

3. On the Message Delivery tab, you'll see a list of any existing IP addresses that are being ignored.

4. You can enter IP addresses and IP address ranges in the Internet Protocol Version 4 (IPv4) format, Internet Protocol Version 6 (IPv6) format, or both formats. Click the option button to the right of the Add button and then do one of the following:

   ❑ Select IP Address to enter the IP address of a server or a network that should not be filtered. In the dialog box provided, type a server IP address or network address and then click OK.

   ❑ Select IP Address And Mask to enter the IP address and subnet mask of a server that should not be filtered. In the dialog box provided, type the server's IP address and subnet mask, and then click OK.

   ❑ Select IP Address Range to enter a range of IP addresses on your organization's network that should not be filtered. In the dialog box provided, type a start IP address and an end IP address for the range of addresses, and then click OK.

5. Repeat step 4 as necessary. To modify a previous entry, select the entry, and then click Edit. To remove an existing entry, select the entry, and then click the Remove button.

6. Click OK to save your settings.

Chapter 16

Managing Client Access Servers

Microsoft Outlook Web Access, Exchange ActiveSync, and Outlook Anywhere are essential technologies for enabling users to access Microsoft Exchange anywhere at any time. As you know from previous chapters, Outlook Web Access lets users access Exchange over the Internet or over a wireless network using a standard Web browser; Exchange ActiveSync lets users access Exchange through a wireless carrier using mobile devices, such as smart phones and Pocket PCs; and Outlook Anywhere lets users access Exchange mailboxes from the Internet using remote procedure call (RPC) over Hypertext Transfer Protocol (HTTP). When users access Exchange mail and public folders over the Internet or a wireless network, HTTP virtual servers hosted by Client Access servers are working behind the scenes to grant access and transfer files. As you'll learn in this chapter, managing mobile access and HTTP virtual servers is a bit different from other tasks you'll perform as an Exchange administrator—and not only because you'll use the Internet Information Services (IIS) Manager snap-in to perform many of the management tasks.

Managing Web and Mobile Access

When you install the Client Access Server role on an Exchange server, Outlook Web Access and Exchange ActiveSync are automatically configured for use. This makes them fairly easy to manage, but there are some essential concepts you need to know to manage these implementations more effectively. This section explains these concepts.

> **Note** Before you can install the Client Access Server role on an Exchange server, you must install and configure Internet Information Services (IIS). Microsoft has released several different versions of IIS. IIS 7.0 is the version discussed in this chapter.

Using Outlook Web Access and Exchange ActiveSync with HTTP Virtual Servers

Outlook Web Access, Exchange ActiveSync, and a default HTTP virtual server are installed automatically when you install a Client Access server. In most cases, you only need to open the appropriate ports on your organization's firewall to allow users to access Exchange data. Then you simply tell users the Uniform Resource Locator (URL) path that they need to type in their browser's Address field. Users can then access Outlook Web Access or Exchange ActiveSync when they're off-site. The URLs for Outlook Web Access and Exchange ActiveSync are different. Typically, the Outlook Web Access

URL is *https://yourserver.yourdomain.com/owa* and the Exchange ActiveSync URL is *https://yourserver.yourdomain.com/Microsoft-Server-ActiveSync.*

You can configure Outlook Web Access and Exchange ActiveSync for single-server and multiserver environments. In a single-server environment, you use one Client Access server for all your Web and mobile access needs. In a multiple server environment, you can instruct users to access different URLs to access different Client Access servers, or you could use a technique such as Round Robin Domain Name System (DNS) to load-balance between multiple servers automatically while giving all users the same access URLs.

You can use Outlook Web Access and Exchange ActiveSync with firewalls. You configure your network to use a perimeter network with firewalls in front of the designated Client Access servers and then open ports 80 and 443 to the Internet Protocol (IP) addresses of your Client Access servers. If SSL is enabled, and you want all Outlook Web Access clients to use SSL exclusively, you don't need to open port 80.

Working with HTTP Virtual Servers

When you install a Client Access server, Exchange Setup installs and configures a default HTTP virtual server for use. The default HTTP virtual server allows authenticated users to access their messaging data from the Web. In Exchange Management Shell, you can use the Get-OWAVirtualDirectory cmdlet to view information about virtual directories, the New-OWAVirtualDirectory cmdlet to create an OWA directory if one does not exist, the Remove-OWAVirtualDirectory to remove an OWA directory, and the Test-OWAConnectivity cmdlet to test OWA connectivity.

HTTP virtual servers provide the services users need to access Exchange from the Web. If you examine the directory structure for the default HTTP virtual server, you'll find several important directories, including:

- **Autodiscover**   Autodiscover is used to enable the Autodiscover service for mobile devices. By default, this directory is configured for integrated authentication only.

- **Exchange Web Services**   Exchange Web Services (EWS) is used to enable developers to interact with Exchange mailboxes and messaging items using HTTP.

- **Exadmin**   Exadmin is used for Web-based administration of the HTTP virtual server. By default, this directory is configured for integrated authentication only.

- **Exchange**   Exchange is the directory to which users connect to access their mailboxes. By default, this directory is configured for both basic and integrated Windows authentication, with the default domain set to the pre-Windows 2000 domain name, such as ADATUM.

- **ExchWeb**   ExchWeb is used with Outlook Web Access and provides calendaring, address book, and other important control functions. By default, this directory is configured for anonymous access, but the bin directory (which provides the controls) is restricted and uses both basic and integrated Windows authentication.

- **Microsoft-Server-ActiveSync**   Microsoft-Server-ActiveSync is the directory to which Exchange ActiveSync users connect to access their Exchange data. By default, this directory is configured for basic authentication.

- **OAB**   OAB is the directory that provides the Offline Address Book (OAB) to clients. By default, this directory is configured for anonymous access.

- **OWA**   OWA is the directory to which users connect in their Web browsers to start an Outlook Web Access session. By default, this directory is configured for both basic and integrated Windows authentication.

- **Public**   Public is the directory to which users connect to access the default Public Folders tree. By default, this directory is configured for both basic and integrated Windows authentication, with the default domain set to the pre-Windows 2000 domain name, such as ADATUM.

- **UnifiedMessaging**   UnifiedMessaging is used to enable access to unified messaging services from the Web. By default, this directory is configured for integrated Windows authentication.

This section examines key tasks that you use to manage HTTP virtual servers and their related directories.

Enabling and Disabling Outlook Web Access Features

In Exchange 2007, Microsoft uses the term *segmentation* to refer to your ability to enable and disable the various features within Outlook Web Access. Segmentation settings applied to the OWA virtual directory on Client Access servers control the features available to users. If a server has multiple OWA virtual directories or you have multiple Client Access servers, you must configure each directory and server separately. Table 16-1 provides a summary of the segmentation features that are enabled by default for use with Outlook Web Access.

Table 16-1   An Overview of Segmentation Features

Feature	When this feature is enabled, users can...
All Address Lists	View all the available address lists. When this feature is disabled, users can only view the default global address lists.
Calendar	Access their calendars in Outlook Web Access.
Change Password	Change their passwords in Outlook Web Access.
Contacts	Access their contacts in Outlook Web Access.

Table 16-1   An Overview of Segmentation Features

Feature	When this feature is enabled, users can...
E-mail Signature	Customize their signatures and include a signature in outgoing messages.
Exchange ActiveSync Integration	Remove mobile devices, initiate mobile wipe, view their device passwords, and review their mobile access logs.
Journal	Access their journals in Outlook Web Access.
Junk E-mail Filtering	Filter junk e-mail using Outlook Web Access.
Notes	Access their notes in Outlook Web Access.
Premium Client	Use Premium features if they have a Premium access license.
Public Folders	Browse and read items in public folders using Outlook Web Access.
Recover Deleted Items	View items that have been deleted from Deleted Items and choose whether to recover them.
Reminders And Notifications	Receive new e-mail notifications, task reminders, calendar reminders, and automatic folder updates.
Rules	Customize rules in Outlook Web Access.
S/MIME	Download the S/MIME control and use it to read and compose signed and encrypted messages.
Search Folders	Access their Search folders in Outlook Web Access.
Spelling Checker	Access the spelling checker in Outlook Web Access.
Tasks	Access their tasks in Outlook Web Access.
Theme Selection	Change the color scheme in Outlook Web Access.
Unified Messaging Integration	Access their voice mail and faxes in Outlook Web Access. They can also configure voice mail options.

You can enable or disable segmentation features by completing the following steps:

1. In Exchange Management Console, expand the Server Configuration node, and then select the Client Access node.

2. In the upper portion of the details pane, you'll see a list of your organization's Client Access servers. Select the server you want to configure, as shown in Figure 16-1.

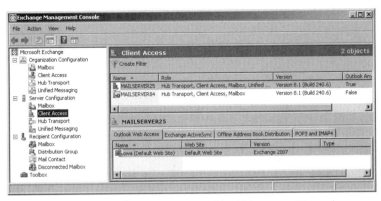

Figure 16-1   Select the Client Access server with which you want to work.

3. In the lower portion of the details pane, you'll see a list of option tabs for the selected server. On the Outlook Web Access tab, right-click the virtual directory for which you want to implement segmentation, and then select Properties. Typically, you'll want to configure the OWA virtual directory on the Default Web Site, as this directory is used by default for Outlook Web Access.

4. On the Segmentation tab, select a feature you want to enable or disable. Click Enable to enable the feature. Click Disable to disable the feature. Click OK.

In Exchange Management Shell, you can enable or disable segmentation features using the Set-OwaVirtualDirectory cmdlet. To enable or disable these features for individual users, use the Set-CASMailbox cmdlet.

Configuring Ports, IP Addresses, and Host Names Used by HTTP Virtual Servers

Each HTTP virtual server has one or more bindings. A binding is a unique combination of ports, IP addresses, and host names that identifies an HTTP virtual server. For unsecure connections, the default port is Transmission Control Protocol (TCP) port 80. For secure connections, the default port is TCP port 443. The default IP address setting is to use any available IP address. The default host name is the Client Access server's DNS name.

When the server is multihomed, or when you use it to provide Outlook Web Access or Exchange ActiveSync services for multiple domains, the default configuration isn't ideal. On a multihomed server, you'll usually want messaging protocols to respond only on a specific IP address. To do this, you need to change the default settings. On a server that provides Outlook Web Access and Exchange ActiveSync services for multiple domains, you'll usually want to specify an additional host name for each domain.

When you are working with IIS 7.0, you can change the identity of an HTTP virtual server by completing the following steps:

1. If you want the HTTP virtual server to use a new IP address, you must configure the IP address before trying to specify it on the HTTP virtual server. For details, see "Configuring Static IP Addresses" in Chapter 17 of *Windows Server 2008 Administrator's Pocket Consultant* (Microsoft Press, 2008).

2. Start IIS Manager. Click Start, point to Programs or All Programs as appropriate, point to Administrative Tools, and select Internet Information Services (IIS) Manager.

   Note By default, IIS Manager connects to the services running on the local computer. If you want to connect to a different server, select the Start Page node in the left pane and then click the Connect To A Server link. This starts the Connect To Server Wizard. Follow the prompts to connect to the remote server. Keep in mind that with IIS 7.0, the Web Management Service (WMSVC) must be configured and running on the remote server. For more information, see "Enabling and Configuring Remote Administration" in Chapter 3 of *Internet Information Services (IIS) 7.0 Administrator's Pocket Consultant* (Microsoft Press, 2007).

3. In IIS Manager, each HTTP virtual server is represented as a Web site. The Default Web Site represents the default HTTP virtual server. Double-click the entry for the server with which you want to work, and then double-click Web Sites.

4. In the left pane, select the Web site that you want to manage, and then select Bindings on the Actions pane.

5. As Figure 16-2 shows, you can now use the Site Bindings dialog box to configure multiple identities for the virtual server.

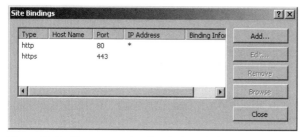

Figure 16-2 You can use the Site Bindings dialog box to configure multiple identities for the virtual server.

6. Use the Site Bindings dialog box to manage the site's bindings by using the following settings:

   ❏ **Add**   Adds a new identity. To add a new identity, click Add. In the Add Site Binding dialog box, select the binding type, IP address, and TCP port to use. Optionally, type a host header name or select an SSL certificate as appropriate for the binding type. Click OK when you have finished.

   ❏ **Edit**   Allows you to edit the currently selected identity. To edit an identity, click the identity, and then click Edit. In the Edit Site Binding dialog box, select an IP address and TCP port to use. Optionally, type a host header name or select an SSL certificate as appropriate for the binding type. Click OK when you have finished.

   ❏ **Remove**   Allows you to remove the currently selected identity. To remove an identity, click the identity, and then click Remove. When prompted to confirm, click Yes.

   ❏ **Browse**   Allows you to test an identity. To test an identity, click the identity, and then click Browse. IIS Manager will then open a browser window and connect to the selected binding.

7. Click OK twice.

Enabling SSL on HTTP Virtual Servers

SSL is a protocol for encrypting data that is transferred between a client and a server. Without SSL, servers pass data in cleartext to clients, which could be a security risk in an enterprise environment. With SSL, servers pass data encoded using 40-bit or 128-bit encryption.

Although HTTP virtual servers are configured to use SSL on port 443 automatically, the server won't use SSL unless you've created and installed a valid X.509 certificate. When you install the Client Access Server role on your Exchange server, a default X.509 certificate is created for Exchange Server 2007. You can view the default X.509 certificate by completing the following steps:

1. Log on locally to the Client Access server. Start IIS Manager. Click Start, point to Programs or All Programs as appropriate, point to Administrative Tools, and then select Internet Information Services (IIS) Manager.

2. In IIS Manager, select the server node and then double-click the Server Certificates feature.

3. On the Server Certificates page, you'll see a list of certificates the Web server can use. The default X.509 certificate for Exchange Server has the name Microsoft Exchange and is issued to the Exchange server configured with the Client Access

Server role. Click the certificate entry, and then click View in the Actions pane to view detailed information regarding the certificate. By default, this certificate is valid for one year from the date you install the Client Access Server role.

4. For a long-term solution, you'll need to create a permanent certificate for the Client Access server. This certificate can be a domain certificate, a self-signed certificate, or a third-party certificate. In the Actions pane, you'll see related options. Click Create Certificate Request, Create Domain Certificate, or Create Self-Signed Certificate as appropriate for the type of certificate you want to create. This starts the Request Certificate Wizard. Use the wizard to create a new certificate. For additional virtual servers on the same Exchange server, you'll want to assign an existing certificate.

5. For a general certificate request or a domain certificate, send the certificate request to a third-party certification authority (CA) or your organization's CA as appropriate. When you receive the certificate back from the CA, open the Server Certificates page again and click Complete Certificate Request in the Actions pane. Now you'll be able to process the pending request and install the certificate.

Once you've installed the certificate, you should test the certificate with an external client by accessing OWA from a remote computer. Clients won't automatically trust self-signed certificates or certificates issues by your CA. Because of this, you may see an error stating that there is a problem with the Web site's security certificate. In this case, follow these steps to have the client trust the certificate:

1. Click the Continue To This Website link. When you continue to the site, a Certificate Error option appears to the right of the address field.

2. Click the Certificate Error option to display a related error dialog box, and then click View Certificates to display the Certificate dialog box.

3. On the General tab of the Certificate dialog box, you'll see an error stating the CA Root Certificate isn't trusted. To enable trust, click Install Certificate. This starts the Certificate Import Wizard.

4. Accept the default settings by clicking Next twice and then clicking Finish. Click OK twice. The browser will now trust the certificate, and you shouldn't see the certificate error again for this client.

Restricting Incoming Connections and Setting Time-Out Values

You control incoming connections to an HTTP virtual server in several ways: you can set a maximum limit on the bandwidth used, you can set a limit on the number of simultaneous connections, and you can set a connection time-out value.

Normally, virtual servers have no maximum bandwidth limits and accept an unlimited number of connections, and this is an optimal setting in most environments. However, when you're trying to prevent a virtual server from becoming overloaded, you might want to limit the bandwidth available to the site and the number of simultaneous connections. When either limit is reached, no other clients are permitted to access the server. The clients must wait until the connection load on the server decreases.

The connection time-out value determines when idle user sessions are disconnected. With the default HTTP virtual server, sessions time out after they've been idle for 120 seconds (2 minutes). It's a sound security practice to disconnect idle sessions and force users to log back on to the server. If you don't disconnect idle sessions within a reasonable amount of time, unauthorized persons could gain access to your messaging system through a browser window left unattended on a remote terminal.

You can modify connection limits and time-outs by completing the following steps:

1. Start IIS Manager. Click Start, point to Programs or All Programs as appropriate, point to Administrative Tools, and then select Internet Information Services (IIS) Manager.

2. In IIS Manager, each HTTP virtual server is represented by a Web site. The Default Web Site represents the default HTTP virtual server. Double-click the entry for the server with which you want to work, and then double-click Web Sites.

3. In the left pane, select the Web site that you want to manage, and then click Limits in the Actions pane. This displays the Edit Web Site Limits dialog box, as shown in Figure 16-3.

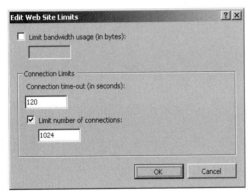

Figure 16-3 Use the Edit Web Site Limits dialog box to limit connections and set time-out values for each virtual server.

4. To remove maximum bandwidth limits, clear the Limit Bandwidth Usage check box. To set a maximum bandwidth limit, select the Limit Bandwidth Usage check box and then set the desired limit in bytes.

5. The Connection Time-Out field controls how long idle user sessions remain connected to the server. The default value is 120 seconds. Type a new value to change the current time-out value.

6. To remove connection limits, clear the Limit Number Of Connections check box. To set a connection limit, select the Limit Number Of Connections check box, and then type a limit.

7. Click OK.

Redirecting Users to Alternate URLs

Sometimes, you may find that you want to redirect users to alternate URLs. For example, you may want users to type **http://mail.cpandl.com** and get redirected to *https://mail.cpandl.com/owa*.

You can redirect users from one URL to another by completing the following steps:

1. Start IIS Manager. Click Start, point to Programs or All Programs as appropriate, point to Administrative Tools, and then select Internet Information Services (IIS) Manager.

2. In IIS Manager, navigate to the level you want to manage. You manage redirection for an entire site at the site level. You manage redirection for a directory at the directory level.

3. In the main pane, double-click the HTTP Redirect feature. This displays the HTTP Redirect page.

> **Note**   With IIS 7.0, HTTP redirection is an optional role service. Therefore, if the HTTP Redirect feature is not available, you'll need to install the related role service by using Server Manager's Add Role Services Wizard

4. On the HTTP Redirect page, select Redirect Requests To This Destination.

5. In the Redirect Requests To This Destination text box, type the Uniform Resource Locator (URL) to which the user should be redirected. To redirect the user to a different server, type the full path, starting with **http://** or **https://**, such as **https://mailer2.cpandl.com/owa**. To redirect the user to a virtual directory on the same server, type a slash mark (/) followed by the directory name, such as **/owa**. Click Apply to save your settings.

Controlling Access to the HTTP Server

HTTP virtual servers support several authentication methods, including:

- **Anonymous authentication**   With anonymous authentication, IIS automatically logs users on with an anonymous or guest account. This allows users to access resources without being prompted for user name and password information.

- **ASP.NET Impersonation** With ASP.NET Impersonation, a managed code application can run either as the user authenticated by IIS or as a designated account that you specify when configuring this mode.

- **Basic authentication** With basic authentication, users are prompted for logon information. When entered, this information is transmitted unencrypted (as cleartext) across the network. If you've configured secure communications on the server, as described in the section of this chapter entitled "Enabling SSL on HTTP Virtual Servers," you can require that clients use SSL. When you use SSL with basic authentication, the logon information is encrypted before transmission.

- **Integrated Windows authentication** With integrated Windows authentication, IIS uses standard Windows security to validate the user's identity. Instead of prompting for a user name and password, clients relay the logon credentials that users supply when they log on to Windows. These credentials are fully encrypted without the need for SSL, and they include the user name and password needed to log on to the network. Only Microsoft Internet Explorer browsers support this feature.

- **Digest authentication** With digest authentication, user credentials are transmitted securely between clients and servers. Digest authentication is a feature of HTTP 1.1 and uses a technique that can't be easily intercepted and decrypted. This feature is available only when IIS is configured on a server running Windows Server 2003 and is part of a Windows 2000 Server or later Active Directory domain. The client is required to use a domain account, and the request is made by Internet Explorer 5.0 or later.

- **ASP.NET Forms–based authentication** With ASP.NET Forms–based authentication, you manage client registration and authentication at the application level instead of relying on the authentication mechanisms in IIS. As the mode name implies, users register and provide their credentials using a logon form. By default, this information is passed as cleartext. To avoid this, you should use SSL encryption for the logon page and other internal application pages.

When you install IIS 7.0 on a Client Access server, you are required to enable basic authentication, digest authentication, and Windows authentication. These authentication methods, along with anonymous authentication, are used to control access to the server's virtual directories. A virtual directory is simply a folder path that is accessible by a URL. For example, you could create a virtual directory called Data that is physically located on C:\CorpData\Data and accessible using the URL *https:// myserver.mydomain.com/Data*.

Table 16-2 summarizes the default authentication settings for each directory. You should rarely change the default settings. However, if your organization has special needs, you can change the authentication settings at the virtual directory level.

Table 16-2   Default Authentication Settings for Virtual Directories

Virtual Directory	Anonymous Authentication	Basic Authentication	Digest Authentication	Windows Authentication
Autodiscover	No	Yes	No	Yes
EWS	No	No	No	Yes
Exadmin	No	Yes	No	Yes
Exchange	No	Yes	No	Yes
Exchweb	No	Yes	No	Yes
Microsoft-Server-ActiveSync	No	Yes	No	No
OAB	No	No	No	Yes
OWA	No	Yes	No	No
Public	No	Yes	No	Yes
Unified Messaging	No	No	No	Yes

As the table shows, the default public folder tree is accessible through basic and integrated Windows authentication. If you want to grant public access to this folder tree or restrict the tree so that only integrated Windows authentication is allowed, you can do so by editing the individual security settings on the related virtual directory.

The authentication settings on virtual directories are different from authentication settings on the virtual server itself. By default, the virtual server allows anonymous access. This means that anyone can access the server's home page without authenticating themselves. If you disable anonymous access at the server level and enable some other type of authentication, users need to authenticate themselves twice: once for the server and once for the virtual directory they want to access.

You can change the authentication settings for an entire site or for a particular virtual directory by completing the following steps:

1. Start IIS Manager. Click Start, point to Programs or All Programs as appropriate, point to Administrative Tools, and then select Internet Information Services (IIS) Manager.

2. In IIS Manager, navigate to the level you want to manage and then double-click the Authentication feature. On the Authentication page, shown in Figure 16-4, you should see the available authentication modes. If a mode you want to use is not available, you'll need to install and enable the related role service using Server Manager's Add Role Services Wizard.

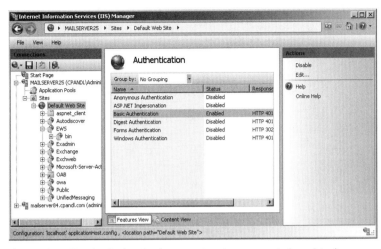

Figure 16-4   Use the Authentication page to set access control on virtual directories. Virtual directories can have different authentication settings than the virtual server.

3. To enable or disable anonymous access, select Anonymous Authentication, and then click Enable or Disable as appropriate.

   Note   With anonymous access, IIS uses an anonymous user account for access to the server. The anonymous user account is named IUSR_*ServerName*, such as IUSR_Mailer1. If you use this account, you don't need to set a password. Instead, let IIS manage the password. If you want to use a different account, click Edit, and then click Set to specify the user name and password for a different account to use for anonymous access.

4. To configure other authentication methods, select the authentication method, and then click Enable or Disable as appropriate. Keep the following in mind:

   ❑ Disabling basic authentication might prevent some clients from accessing resources remotely. Clients can log on only when you enable an authentication method that they support.

   ❑ A default domain isn't set automatically. If you enable basic authentication, you can choose to set a default domain that should be used when no domain information is supplied during the logon process. Setting the default domain is useful when you want to ensure that clients authenticate properly.

   ❑ With basic and digest authentication, you can optionally specify the realm that can be accessed. Essentially, a *realm* is the DNS domain name or Web address that will use the credentials that have been authenticated against the default domain. If default domain and realm are set to the same value, the internal Windows domain name may be exposed to external users during the user name and password challenge/response.

❏ If you enable ASP.NET Impersonation, you can specify the identity to impersonate. By default, IIS uses pass-through authentication, and the identity of the authenticated user is impersonated. You can also specify a specific user if necessary.

❏ If you enable forms authentication, you can set the logon URL and cookies settings used for authentication.

❏ If you enable passport authentication, all other authentication settings are ignored. As a result, the server will use this technique to authenticate only for the specified resource.

Starting, Stopping, and Pausing HTTP Virtual Servers and Web Sites

HTTP virtual servers run under a server process that you can start, stop, and pause, much like other server processes. For example, if you're changing the configuration of a virtual server or performing other maintenance tasks, you might need to stop the virtual server, make the changes, and then restart it. When a virtual server is stopped, it doesn't accept connections from users and can't be used to deliver or retrieve mail.

An alternative to stopping a virtual server is to pause it. Pausing a virtual server prevents new client connections, but it doesn't disconnect current connections. When you pause an HTTP virtual server, active clients can continue to retrieve documents, messages, and public folder data in their Web browser. No new connections are accepted, however.

The master process for all HTTP virtual servers is the World Wide Web Publishing Service. Stopping this service stops all virtual servers using the process, and all connections are disconnected immediately. Starting this service restarts all virtual servers that were running when you stopped the World Wide Web Publishing Service.

You can start, stop, or pause an HTTP virtual server by completing the following steps:

1. Start IIS Manager. Click Start, point to Programs or All Programs as appropriate, point to Administrative Tools, and then select Internet Information Services (IIS) Manager.

2. In IIS Manager, each HTTP virtual server is represented by a Web site. The Default Web Site represents the default HTTP virtual server. Double-click the entry for the server you want to work with, and then double-click Web Sites.

3. Select the virtual server you want to manage. Using the options in the Actions pane, you can now do the following:

    ❏ Select Start to start the virtual server.

❑   Select Stop to stop the virtual server.

❑   Select Restart to stop and then start the virtual server.

If you suspect there's a problem with the World Wide Web Publishing Service or other related IIS services, you can use the following technique to restart all IIS services:

1. Start IIS Manager. Click Start, point to Programs or All Programs as appropriate, point to Administrative Tools, and then select Internet Information Services (IIS) Manager.

2. Select the entry for the server you want to work with, and then select Restart in the Actions Pane.

Configuring URLs and Authentication for OAB

Outlook 2007 clients can retrieve the Offline Address Book (OAB) from a Web distribution point. The default distribution point is the OAB virtual directory on the Default Web Site. Each distribution point has three associated properties:

■ **PollInterval**   The time interval during which the distribution service should poll the generation server for new updates (in minutes).

■ **ExternalUrl**   The URL from which Outlook clients outside the corporate network can access the OAB.

■ **InternalUrl**   The URL form which Outlook clients inside the corporate network can access the OAB.

You can configure Web distribution points by completing the following steps:

1. In Exchange Management Console, expand the Server Configuration node, and then select the Client Access node.

2. In the upper portion of the details pane, you'll see a list of your organization's Client Access servers. Select the server with which you want to work.

3. In the lower portion of the details pane, on the Offline Address Book Distribution tab, you'll see an entry for each OAB Web distribution point configured on the server.

4. Right-click the distribution point you want to configure and then select Properties.

5. On the General tab, set the desired polling interval using the Polling Interval text box. The default interval is 480 minutes.

6. On the URLs tab, enter the desired internal and external URLs in the text boxes provided and then click OK.

Configuring URLs and Authentication for OWA

When you install a Client Access server, the server is configured with a Default Web Site and the virtual directories discussed previously. Through the OWA virtual directory, you can set the base URL for these directories so that different URLs are used for internal access and external access. You can also configure different authentication mechanisms for each directory.

You can configure OWA virtual directory URLs and authentication by completing the following steps:

1. In Exchange Management Console, expand the Server Configuration node, and then select the Client Access node.

2. In the upper portion of the details pane, you'll see a list of your organization's Client Access servers. Select the server with which you want to work.

3. In the lower portion of the details pane, on the Outlook Web Access tab, you'll see an entry for the OWA virtual directory used by Exchange Server.

4. Right-click the OWA virtual directory and then select Properties.

5. On the General tab, enter the internal and external URLs in the text boxes provided.

6. On the Authentication tab, forms-based authentication is configured by default with the logon format set to Domain\User Name. Only change this configuration if you have specific requirements that necessitate a change.

7. Click OK to save your settings.

You can configure authentication for other non-OWA virtual directories by completing the following steps:

1. In Exchange Management Console, expand the Server Configuration node, and then select the Mailbox node.

2. In the upper portion of the details pane, you'll see a list of your organization's Mailbox servers. Select the server with which you want to work.

3. In the lower portion of the details pane, on the WebDAV tab, you'll see an entry for the non-OWA virtual directories used by Exchange Server.

4. Right-click the virtual directory you want to work with, and then select Properties.

5. On the Authentication tab, integrated Windows authentication and basic authentication are enabled by default. Only change this configuration if you have specific requirements that necessitate a change.

6. Click OK to save your settings.

Configuring URLs and Authentication for Exchange ActiveSync

When you install a Client Access server, the server is configured with a Default Web Site that has a virtual directory for Exchange ActiveSync. The URL for this directory can be set so that different URLs are used for internal access and external access and so that different authentication mechanisms can be used.

You can configure the Exchange ActiveSync URLs and authentication by completing the following steps:

1. In Exchange Management Console, expand the Server Configuration node, and then select the Client Access node.

2. In the upper portion of the details pane, you'll see a list of your organization's Client Access servers. Select the server with which you want to work.

3. In the lower portion of the details pane, on the Exchange ActiveSync tab, you'll see an entry for each virtual directory used by Exchange Server for ActiveSync.

4. Right-click the virtual directory you want to configure and then select Properties.

5. On the General tab, enter the internal and external URLs in the text boxes provided.

6. On the Authentication tab, by default, basic authentication is enabled and client certificates are ignored. If your organization uses client certificates, you can clear the Basic Authentication check box and then select either Accept Client Certificates or Require Client Certificates as appropriate.

7. Click OK to save your settings.

Configuring POP3 and IMAP4

Exchange Server 2007 supports Internet Message Access Protocol 4 (IMAP4) and Post Office Protocol 3 (POP3). IMAP4 is a protocol for reading mail and accessing public and private folders on remote servers. Clients can log on to an Exchange server and use IMAP4 to download message headers and then read messages individually while online. POP3 is a protocol for retrieving mail on remote servers. Clients can log on to an Exchange server and then use POP3 to download their mail for offline use.

By default, POP3 (version 3) and IMAP4 (rev 1) are disabled in Exchange Server 2007 and no longer have associated HTTP virtual servers. This is primarily because Outlook Web Access, Exchange ActiveSync, and Outlook Anywhere offer so much more that they are the preferred way for users to access Exchange Server. If you still have users who want to use POP3 and IMAP4 to access Exchange Server, you can configure this, but you should try to move these users to Outlook Web Access, Exchange ActiveSync, or Outlook Anywhere.

Enabling the Exchange POP3 and IMAP4 Services

Clients that retrieve mail using POP3 or IMAP4 send mail using Simple Mail Transport Protocol (SMTP). SMTP is the default mail transport in Exchange Server 2007. To enable POP3 and IMAP4, you must first start the POP3 and IMAP4 services on the Client Access servers that will provide these services. You must then configure these services to start automatically in the future. You should also review the related settings for each service and make changes as necessary to optimize the way these services are used in your Exchange organization.

You can enable and configure POP3 for automatic startup by completing these steps:

1. Start the Services utility by clicking Start, selecting Administrative Tools, and then selecting Services.

2. Right-click Microsoft Exchange POP3, and then select Properties.

3. On the General tab, under Startup Type, select Automatic, and then click Apply.

4. Under Service Status, click Start, and then click OK.

You can enable and configure IMAP4 for automatic startup by completing these steps:

1. Start the Services utility by clicking Start, clicking Administrative Tools, and then selecting Services.

2. Right-click Microsoft Exchange IMAP4, and then click Properties.

3. On the General tab, under Startup Type, select Automatic, and then click Apply.

4. Under Service Status, click Start, and then click OK.

POP3 and IMAP4 have related IP address and TCP port configuration settings. The default IP address setting is to use any available IP address. On a multihomed server, however, you'll usually want messaging protocols to respond on a specific IP address. To do this, you need to change the default setting.

The default port setting depends on the messaging protocol being used and whether SSL is enabled or disabled. For users to be able to retrieve mail using POP3 and IMAP4, you must open the related messaging ports on your organization's firewalls. Table 16-3 shows the default port settings for key protocols used by Exchange Server 2007.

Table 16-3   Standard and Secure Port Settings for Messaging Protocols

Protocol	Default Port	Default Secure Port
SMTP	25	
HTTP	80	443
IMAP4	143	993
POP3	110	995

In Exchange Management Shell, you can manage POP3 and IMAP4 using the following cmdlets:

- **Get-POPSettings**   Lists POP3 configuration settings.

- **Set-POPSettings**   Configures POP3 settings.

- **Test-POPConnectivity**   Tests the POP3 configuration.

- **Get-IMAPSettings**   Lists IMAP4 configuration settings.

- **Set-IMAPSettings**   Configures IMAP4 settings.

- **Test-IMAPConnectivity**   Tests the IMAP4 configuration.

Configuring POP3 and IMAP4 Bindings

The bindings for POP3 and IMAP4 use a unique combination of an IP address and a TCP port. To change the IP address or port number for POP3 or IMAP4, complete the following steps:

1. In Exchange Management Console, expand the Server Configuration node, and then select the Client Access node.

2. In the upper portion of the details pane, you'll see a list of your organization's Client Access servers. Select the server with which you want to work.

3. In the lower portion of the details pane, on the POP3 and IMAP4 tabs, you'll see separate entries for POP3 and IMAP4.

4. Right-click POP3 or IMAP4 as appropriate for the protocol you want to work with, and then select Properties.

    ❑   On the General tab, you'll see the last modification date for the protocol settings as well as the status of the related Exchange service.

    ❑   On the Binding tab, you'll see the currently assigned IP addresses and ports used for TLS or unencrypted connections and SSL connections. The default configuration is as follows: POP3 and IMAP4 are configured to use all available IPv4 and IPv6 addresses, POP3 uses port 110 for TLS or unencrypted connections and port 995 for SSL connections, and IMAP4 uses port 143 for TLS or unencrypted connections and port 993 for SSL connections.

5. Select the Binding tab. To configure IP addresses and ports for TLS or unencrypted connections, use the following options on the TLS Or Unencrypted Connections panel:

    ❑   **Add**   Adds a TCP port on a per-IP address basis or all unassigned IP address basis. Click Add, and then specify the IP address and port you want to use.

❏ **Edit**   Allows you to edit the IP address and port settings for the currently selected entry in the Address list box.

❏ **Remove**   Allows you to remove the IP address and port settings for the currently selected entry in the Address list box.

> **Note**   The IP address/TCP port combination must be unique. You can assign the same port as long as the protocol is configured to use a different IP address.

6. To configure IP addresses and ports for secure connections, use the following options on the Secure Sockets Layer (SSL) Connections panel:

❏ **Add**   Adds a TCP port on a per-IP address basis or an all unassigned IP address basis. Click Add, and then specify the IP address and port you want to use.

❏ **Edit**   Allows you to edit the IP address and port settings for the currently selected entry in the Address list box.

❏ **Remove**   Allows you to remove the IP address and port settings for the currently selected entry in the Address list box.

7. Click OK to save your settings. When you add new ports, you must open the related messaging ports on your organization's firewalls.

8. Use the Services utility to restart the Exchange POP3 or IMAP4 service. Restarting the service applies the new settings.

Configuring POP3 and IMAP4 Authentication

By default, POP3 and IMAP4 clients pass connection information and message data through an insecure connection. If corporate security is a high priority, however, your information security team might require mail clients to connect over secure communication channels. You have several options for configuring secure communications, including plain-text authentication logon using integrated Windows authentication and a fully secure logon using TLS.

You configure communications using plaintext authentication logon with or without integrated Windows authentication by completing the following steps:

1. In Exchange Management Console, expand the Server Configuration node, and then select the Client Access node.

2. In the upper portion of the details pane, you'll see a list of your organization's Client Access servers. Select the server with which you want to work.

3. In the lower portion of the details pane, on the POP3 and IMAP4 tab, you'll see separate entries for POP3 and IMAP4.

4. Right-click POP3 or IMAP4 as appropriate for the protocol you want to work with and then select Properties.

5. On the Authentication tab, do one of the following and then click OK:

   ❑ Select Plain Text Logon (Basic Authentication) to use unsecure plain text for communications.

   ❑ Select Plain Text Authentication Logon (Integrated Windows Authentication) to use plain text for communications with integrated Windows authentication.

6. Use the Services utility to restart the Exchange POP3 or IMAP4 service. Restarting the service applies the new settings.

You configure secure TLS communications by completing the following steps:

1. Ensure that an X.509 certificate is installed on your organization's Client Access servers as discussed in "Enabling SSL on HTTP Virtual Servers" earlier in this chapter.

2. Configure the server to require secure TLS communications as follows:

   a. In Exchange Management Console, expand the Server Configuration node, and then select the Client Access node.

   b. In the upper portion of the details pane, you'll see a list of your organization's Client Access servers. Select the server with which you want to work.

   c. In the lower portion of the details pane, on the POP3 and IMAP4 tab, you'll see separate entries for POP3 and IMAP4.

   d. Right-click POP3 or IMAP4 as appropriate for the protocol you want to work with, and then select Properties.

   e. On the Authentication tab, select the Secure Logon option and ensure that the certificate name in the X.509 Certificate Name text box is the correct one to use for TLS connections. If not, enter the name of the appropriate certificate. Click OK.

3. Use the Services utility to restart the Exchange POP3 or IMAP4 service. Restarting the service applies the new settings.

4. Configure the mail client to use TLS by completing the following steps:

   a. In Office Outlook 2007, select Account Settings on the Tools menu.

   b. In the Account Settings dialog box, click Change.

   c. In the Change E-Mail Account dialog box, click More Settings.

   d. On the Advanced tab in the Internet E-Mail Settings dialog box, select TLS or Auto as the type of encrypted connection.

   e. Click OK. Click Nextm and then click Finish. Click Close.

Configuring Connection Settings for POP3 and IMAP4

You can control incoming connections to POP3 and IMAP4 in two ways. You can set a limit on the number of simultaneous connections, and you can set a connection time-out value.

POP3 and IMAP4 normally accept a maximum of 2000 connections each and a maximum of 16 connections from a single user, and in most environments these are acceptable settings. However, when you're trying to prevent a server from becoming overloaded, you might want to restrict the number of simultaneous connections even further. Once the limit is reached, no other clients are permitted to access the server. The clients must wait until the connection load on the server decreases.

The connection time-out value determines when idle connections are disconnected. Normally, unauthenticated connections time out after they've been idle for 60 seconds and authenticated connections time out after they've been idle for 1800 seconds (30 minutes). In most situations, these time-out values are sufficient. Still, at times you'll want to increase the time-out values, and this primarily relates to clients who get disconnected when downloading large files. If you discover that clients are being disconnected during large downloads, the time-out values are one area to examine. You'll also want to look at the maximum command size. By default, the maximum command size is restricted to 45 bytes.

You can modify connection limits and time-outs by completing the following steps:

1. In Exchange Management Console, expand the Server Configuration node, and then select the Client Access node.

2. In the upper portion of the details pane, you'll see a list of your organization's Client Access servers. Select the server with which you want to work.

3. In the lower portion of the details pane, on the POP3 and IMAP4 tab, you'll see separate entries for POP3 and IMAP4.

4. Right-click POP3 or IMAP4 as appropriate for the protocol you want to work with and then select Properties. In the Properties dialog box, click the Connection tab.

5. To set time-out values for authenticated and unauthenticated connections, enter the desired values in the Authenticated Time-Out and Unauthenticated Time-Out text boxes respectively. The valid range for authenticated connections is from 30 to 86,400 seconds. The valid range for unauthenticated connections is from 10 to 3,600 seconds.

6. To set connection limits, enter the desired limits in the text boxes on the Connection Limits panel. The valid input range for maximum connections is from 1 to 25,000. The valid input range for maximum connections from a single IP address is from 1 to 1,000. The valid input range for maximum connections

from a single user is from 1 to 1,000. The valid input range for maximum command size is form 40 to 1,024 bytes.

7. Click OK to save your settings. Use the Services utility to restart the Exchange POP3 or IMAP4 service. Restarting the service applies the new settings.

Configuring Message Retrieval Settings for POP3 and IMAP4

Message retrieval settings for POP3 and IMAP4 control the following options:

- **Message formatting**   Message format options allow you to set rules that POP3 and IMAP4 use to format messages before clients read them. By default, when POP3 or IMAP4 clients retrieve messages, the message body is converted to the best format for the client and message attachments are identified with a Multipurpose Internet Mail Extensions (MIME) content type based on the attachment's file extension. You can change this behavior by applying new message MIME formatting rules. Message MIME formatting rules determine the formatting for elements in the body of a message. Message bodies can be formatted as plain text, HTML, HTML and alternative text, enriched text, or enriched text and alternative text.

- **Message sort order**   Message sort order options allow you to control the time sorting of messages during new message retrieval. By default, POP3 and IMAP4 sort messages in descending order according to the time/date stamp. This ensures that the most recent messages are listed first. You can also sort messages by ascending order, which would place newer messages lower in the message list.

- **Calendar Retrieval**   Calendar retrieval settings control the technique used for retrieval of calendar items. By default, POP3 and IMAP4 use the iCalendar standard for retrieval of calendar items. Alternatively, you can specify an internal or external URL with which users can access their calendar information, or you can specify a custom URL for the organization's OWA server.

You can modify message retrieval settings by completing the following steps:

1. In Exchange Management Console, expand the Server Configuration node, and then select the Client Access node.

2. In the upper portion of the details pane, you'll see a list of your organization's Client Access servers. Select the server with which you want to work.

3. In the lower portion of the details pane, on the POP3 and IMAP4 tab, you'll see separate entries for POP3 and IMAP4.

4. Right-click POP3 or IMAP4 as appropriate for the protocol you want to work with and then select Properties. In the Properties dialog box, click the Retrieval Settings tab.

5. Use the Message MIME Format list to choose the desired body format for messages. As discussed previously, the options are Text, HTML, HTML And Alternative Text, Enriched Text, Enriched Text And Alternative Text, or Best Body Format.

6. Use the Message Sort Order list to specify the default sort order for message retrieval. Select Descending for descending sort order during message retrieval or Ascending for ascending sort order.

7. Use the Calendar Retrieval options to specify the technique to use for retrieving calendar items. As discussed previously, the options are iCalendar, Intranet URL, Internet URL, or Custom. If you select Custom, specify the URL of the organization's OWA server in the additional text box provided.

8. Click OK to save your settings. Use the Services utility to restart the Exchange POP3 or IMAP4 service. Restarting the service applies the new settings.

Deploying Outlook Anywhere

Outlook Anywhere provides secure Internet-based access to Exchange Server. When you enable and configure this feature, users can use RPC over HTTP to connect to their Exchange mailboxes, eliminating the need for virtual private network (VPN) connections. Because Outlook Anywhere uses the same URLs and namespaces that you use for Exchange ActiveSync and Outlook Web Access, no additional configuration is required beyond the initial setup. Because RPC over HTTP is secure, unauthenticated requests from Outlook clients are blocked from accessing Exchange Server.

You can deploy Outlook Anywhere by performing the following procedures:

1. Install a valid SSL certificate on the Exchange Server.

2. Install RPC Over HTTP Proxy Windows networking.

3. Enable Outlook Anywhere.

These procedures are discussed in the sections that follow.

Installing an SSL Certificate on the Exchange Server

For Outlook Anywhere to work, a default SSL certificate is created for Exchange Server during installation of a Client Access server. If you don't want to use the default SSL certificate, you can use another one, such as one issued by your organization's certificate authority (CA) or a third-party certificate service. The first time users access Exchange Server using Outlook Web Access, they'll need to specify that the trust the server certificate. See "Enabling SSL on HTTP Virtual Servers" earlier in this chapter.

Because Outlook requests use HTTP over SSL, you must allow port 443 through your firewall. If you already use Outlook Web Access with SSL or Exchange ActiveSync with SSL, port 443 should already be open and you do not have to open any additional ports.

Installing the RPC Over HTTP Proxy

For Outlook Anywhere to work, you should install the RPC Over HTTP Proxy Windows networking component on the Exchange Server during installation of a Client Access server. If for some reason this component was not installed, uninstalled, or becomes corrupted, you must reinstall it. The technique you use with Windows Server 2003 is different from the one for Windows Server 2008.

With Windows Server 2003, you install this component by completing the following steps:

1. In Control Panel, select Add Or Remove Programs.

2. In Add Or Remove Programs, click Add/Remove Windows Components.

3. In the Windows Components Wizard, select Networking Services, and then click Details. Be careful not to clear the Networking Services check box.

4. In the Networking Services dialog box, select the RPC Over HTTP Proxy check box, and then click OK.

5. Click Next to let the wizard start configuring components.

6. When prompted, insert the Windows Server 2003 CD into the appropriate CD-ROM drive, and then click OK.

7. Click Finish.

With Windows Server 2008, you install this component by completing the following steps:

1. Start Server Manager. Click Start, point to Programs or All Programs as appropriate, point to Administrative Tools, and then select Server Manager. Or click the Server Manager button on the Quick Launch toolbar.

2. In Server Manager, select the Features node in the left pane and then click Add Features. This starts the Add Features Wizard.

3. On the Select Features page, select RPC Over HTTP Proxy. If you see a prompt about additional required services, click Add Required Role Services to ensure that these additional services are installed.

4. Click Next three times and then click Install. When the Add Features Wizard finishes the installation, click Close.

Determining Whether Outlook Anywhere Is Enabled

In Exchange Management Console, you can determine whether Outlook Anywhere is enabled by expanding the Server Configuration node and then selecting the Client Access node. In the upper portion of the details pane, Client Access servers are listed by name, role, Exchange version, and Outlook Anywhere Enabled status.

You can use the Get-OutlookAnywhere cmdlet to list similar information about Outlook Anywhere for all Client Access servers in your organization. If you use the −Server parameter, you can limit the results to a specific server. If you use the −Identity parameter, you can examine a particular virtual directory on a server. Sample 16-1 provides the syntax, usage, and sample output.

Sample 16-1   Get-OutlookAnywhere cmdlet syntax and usage

```
Syntax
Get-OutlookAnywhere [-Server 'ServerName']

Get-OutlookAnywhere [-Identity 'VirtualDirectoryIdentity']


Usage
Get-OutlookAnywhere

Get-OutlookAnywhere -Server 'CorpSvr127'

Get-OutlookAnywhere -Identity 'CorpSvr127\Rpc (Default Web Site)'
```

```
Output
ServerName               : MAILSERVER25
SSLOffloading            : False
ExternalHostname         : mailserver25.cpandl.com
ClientAuthenticationMethod : Basic
IISAuthenticationMethods : {Basic}
MetabasePath             : IIS://MAILSERVER25.cpandl.com/W3SVC/1/
                           ROOT/Rpc
Path                     : C:\Windows\System32\RpcProxy
Server                   : MAILSERVER25
AdminDisplayName         :
ExchangeVersion          : 0.1 (8.0.535.0)
Name                     : Rpc (Default Web Site)
DistinguishedName        : CN=Rpc (Default Web
Site),CN=HTTP,CN=Protocols,CN=MAILSERVER25,CN=Servers,CN=Exchange
AdministrativeGroup (FYDIBOHF23SPDLT),CN=Administrative
Groups,CN=First Organization,CN=Microsoft
Exchange,CN=Services,CN=Configuration,DC=cpandl,DC=com
Identity                 : MAILSERVER25\Rpc (Default Web Site)
Guid                     : e7333d25-8ad7-47ce-8120-f65ccc2279c8
ObjectCategory           : cpandl.com/Configuration/Schema/ms-Exch-
Rpc-Http-Virtual-Directory
ObjectClass              : {top, msExchVirtualDirectory,
msExchRpcHttpVirtualDirectory}
WhenChanged              : 1/22/2008 5:02:32 PM
WhenCreated              : 1/22/2008 5:02:32 PM
OriginatingServer        : MAILSERVER25.cpandl.com
IsValid                  : True
```

Enabling and Modifying Outlook Anywhere

You can deploy Outlook Anywhere by enabling the feature on at least one Client Access server in each site of your Exchange organization. To enable Outlook Anywhere, complete the following steps:

1. In Exchange Management Console, expand the Server Configuration node, and then select the Client Access node.

2. In the upper portion of the details pane, you'll see a list of your organization's Client Access servers. Right-click the server on which you want to enable Outlook Anywhere, and select Enable Outlook Anywhere.

3. In the Enable Outlook Anywhere Wizard, type the external host name for the Client Access server, such as **mailer1.cpandl.com**.

4. Select an available external authentication method. You can select Basic Authentication or NTLM Authentication. NT LAN Manager (NTLM) authentication is more secure than basic authentication.

5. Only select the Allow Secure Channel (SSL) Offloading check box if you have configured an advanced firewall server, such as Microsoft Internet Acceleration and Security (ISA) Server to work with Exchange 2007 and handle your SSL processing.

6. Click Enable to apply your settings and enable Outlook Anywhere, and then click Finish.

In the Exchange Management Shell, you can enable Outlook Anywhere using the Enable-OutlookAnywhere cmdlet. Sample 16-2 provides the syntax and usage.

Sample 16-2   Enable-OutlookAnywhere cmdlet syntax and usage

```
Syntax
Enable-OutlookAnywhere -Server 'ServerName'
 -ExternalHostName 'ExternalHostName'
 -ExternalAuthenticationMethod <'Basic' | 'NTLM'>
 -SSLOffloading <$true|$false>
```

```
Usage
Enable-OutlookAnywhere -Server 'CAServer21'
 -ExternalHostName 'mailer1.cpandl.com'
 -ExternalAuthenticationMethod 'Basic'
 -SSLOffloading $false
```

If you want to modify the Outlook Anywhere configuration, you can use the Set-OutlookAnywhere cmdlet to do this. Sample 16-3 provides the syntax and usage.

Sample 16-3   Set-OutlookAnywhere cmdlet syntax and usage

```
Syntax
Set-OutlookAnywhere -Identity 'VirtualDirectoryIdentity'
[-ExternalHostName 'ExternalHostName']
[-ExternalAuthenticationMethod <'Basic' | 'NTLM'>]
[-SSLOffloading <$true|$false>]
```

```
Usage
Set-OutlookAnywhere -Identity 'CorpSvr127\Rpc (Default Web Site)'
-ExternalHostName 'mailer1.cpandl.com'
-ExternalAuthenticationMethod 'NTLM'
-SSLOffloading $true
```

Disabling Outlook Anywhere

If you no longer want a particular Client Access server to allow Outlook clients to use Outlook Anywhere, you can disable this feature by completing the following steps:

1. In Exchange Management Console, expand the Server Configuration node, and then select the Client Access node.

2. In the upper portion of the details pane, you'll see a list of your organization's Client Access servers. Right-click the server on which you want to enable Outlook Anywhere, and select Disable Outlook Anywhere.

3. When prompted to confirm, click Yes.

In the Exchange Management Shell, you can disable Outlook Anywhere using the Disable-OutlookAnywhere cmdlet. Sample 16-4 provides the syntax and usage.

Sample 16-4   Disable-OutlookAnywhere cmdlet syntax and usage

```
Syntax
Disable-OutlookAnywhere -Server 'ServerName'
```

```
Usage
Disable-OutlookAnywhere -Server 'CAServer21'
```

Managing Exchange Server Features for Mobile Devices

Mobile access to Exchange Server is supported on any device running Windows Mobile software, including Pocket PC 2002, Pocket PC 2003, and Windows Mobile 5.0. Devices running Windows Mobile 5.0 with Messaging & Security Feature Pack

(MSFP) and later versions of Windows Mobile software include extensions for cellular phones that permit the use of additional features, including:

- Autodiscovery
- Direct Push
- Exchange ActiveSync Mailbox Policy
- Remote Device Wipe
- Password Recovery
- Direct File Access
- Remote File Access
- WebReady Document Viewing

In Exchange Server, these features are all enabled by default. The sections that follow discuss how these features work and how related options are configured.

Understanding and Using Autodiscovery

Autodiscovery simplifies the provisioning process for mobile devices by returning the required Exchange settings after a user enters his or her e-mail address and password. This eliminates the need to configure mobile carriers in Exchange Server, as well as the need to download and install the carriers list on mobile devices.

Autodiscovery is enabled by default, and the Default Web Site associated with a particular Web site has an associated Autodiscover virtual directory through which devices can be provisioned.

You can manage Autodiscovery using Exchange Management Shell. To get detailed information about the Autodiscovery configuration, type the following command:

```
Get-AutodiscoverVirtualDirectory -Server MyServer
```

where *MyServer* is the name of the Client Access server you want to examine. Included in the detailed information is the identity of the Autodiscovery virtual directory, which you can use with related cmdlets.

By default, Autodiscover is configured to use basic and integrated Windows authentication. Using the Set-AutoDiscoverVirtualDirectory cmdlet, you can enable or disable these authentication methods as well as digest authentication. You can also set the internal and external URLs for Autodiscovery. Neither URL is set by default.

To disable Autodiscovery, type the following command:

```
Remove-AutodiscoverVirtualDirectory -Server MyServer
```

where *MyServer* is the name of the Client Access server on which this feature should be disabled.

If you later want to enable Autodiscovery, you can type the following command:

```
New-AutodiscoverVirtualDirectory -Server MyServer
```

where *MyServer* is the name of the Client Access server on which this feature should be enabled for the Default Web Site.

Samples 16-5 to 16-8 provide the full syntax and usage for the Get-AutodiscoverVirtual-Directory, New-AutodiscoverVirtualDirectory, Set-AutodiscoverVirtualDirectory and Remove-AutodiscoverVirtualDirectory cmdlets, respectively.

Sample 16-5   Get-AutodiscoverVirtualDirectory cmdlet syntax and usage

```
Syntax
Get-AutodiscoverVirtualDirectory -Identity 'DirectoryIdentity'

Get-AutodiscoverVirtualDirectory -Server 'ServerName'
```

```
Usage
Get-AutodiscoverVirtualDirectory
-Identity 'CorpMailSvr25\Autodiscover(Default Web Site)'
```

Sample 16-6   New-AutodiscoverVirtualDirectory cmdlet syntax and usage

```
Syntax
New-AutodiscoverVirtualDirectory [-ApplicationRoot 'RootPath']
  [-AppPoolId 'AppPoolIdentity']
  [-ExternalURL 'ExternalURL']
  [-InternalURL 'InternalURL']
  [-WebSiteName 'WebSiteName']
  [-BasicAuthentication <$true | $false>]
  [-DigestAuthentication <$true | $false>]
  [-WindowsAuthentication <$true | $false>]
```

```
Usage
New-AutodiscoverVirtualDirectory  -WebSiteName 'Default Web Site'
  -BasicAuthentication $true -DigestAuthentication $false
  -WindowsAuthentication $true
```

Sample 16-7   Set-AutodiscoverVirtualDirectory cmdlet syntax and usage

```
Syntax
Set-AutodiscoverVirtualDirectory -Identity 'DirectoryIdentity'
 [-ExternalURL 'ExternalURL']
 [-InternalURL 'InternalURL']
 [-BasicAuthentication <$true | $false>]
 [-DigestAuthentication <$true | $false>]
 [-WindowsAuthentication <$true | $false>]
```

```
Usage
Set-AutodiscoverVirtualDirectory
-Identity 'CorpMailSvr25\Autodiscover(Default Web Site)'
-BasicAuthentication $false -DigestAuthentication $false
–WindowsAuthentication $true
```

Sample 16-8   Remove-AutodiscoverVirtualDirectory cmdlet syntax and usage

```
Syntax
Remove-AutodiscoverVirtualDirectory -Identity 'DirectoryIdentity'
```

```
Usage
Remove-AutodiscoverVirtualDirectory
-Identity 'CorpMailSvr25\Autodiscover(Default Web Site)'
```

Understanding and Using Direct Push

Direct Push automates the synchronization process, enabling a mobile device to make requests to keep itself up-to-date. When the HTTP virtual server used with ActiveSync has SSL enabled, Direct Push allows a mobile device to issue long-lived Hypertext Transfer Protocol Secure (HTTPS) monitoring requests to Exchange Server. Exchange Server monitors activity in the related user's mailbox. If new mail arrives or other changes are made to the mailbox—such as modifications to calendar or contact items—Exchange sends a response to the mobile device, stating that changes have occurred and that the device should initiate synchronization with Exchange Server. The device then issues a synchronization request. When synchronization is complete, the device issues another long-lived HTTPS monitoring request.

Port 443 is the default TCP port used with SSL. For Direct Push to work, port 443 must be opened between the Internet and the organization's Internet-facing Client Access server or servers. You do not need to open port 443 to all of your Client Access servers—only those to which users can establish connections. The Client Access server receiving the request automatically proxies the request so that it can be handled appropriately.

If necessary, this may also mean proxying requests between the mobile device and the Client Access server in the user's home site. A user's home site is the Active Directory site where the mailbox server hosting his or her mailbox is located.

> **Tip** Microsoft recommends increasing the maximum time-out value for connections to 30 minutes. In addition, if there is a firewall between the Client Access server in the user's home site and the Mailbox server in the user's home site, TCP port 135 must be opened on the intervening firewall. TCP port 135 is used by the RPC locator service.

Understanding and Using Exchange ActiveSync Mailbox Policy

Exchange ActiveSync Mailbox Policy makes it possible to enhance the security of mobile devices used to access your Exchange servers. For example, you can use policy to require a password of a specific length and to configure devices to automatically prompt for a password after a period of inactivity.

Each mailbox policy you create has a name and a specific set of rules with which it is associated. Because you can apply policies separately to mailboxes when you create or modify them, you can create different policies for different groups of users. For example, you can have one policy for users and another policy for managers. You can also create separate policies for departments within the organization. For example, you can have separate policies for Marketing, Customer Support, and Technology.

Viewing Existing Exchange Active Sync Mailbox Policies

When the Client Access server role is installed on an Exchange server, the setup process creates a default Exchange ActiveSync policy. This default policy allows ActiveSync to be used without restrictions or password requirements. All users with mailboxes have this policy applied by default. You can modify the settings of this policy to change the settings for all users or create new policies for specific groups of users.

In Exchange Management Console, you can view the currently configured Exchange ActiveSync Mailbox policies by expanding the Organization Configuration node, and then selecting Client Access. In the details pane, you'll see a list of current policies.

In the Exchange Management Shell, you can list policies using the Get-ActiveSyncMailboxPolicy cmdlet. Sample 16-9 provides the syntax, usage, and sample output. If you do not provide an identity with this cmdlet, all available Exchange ActiveSync Mailbox policies are listed.

Sample 16-9   Get-ActiveSyncMailboxPolicy cmdlet syntax and usage

Syntax
Get-ActiveSyncMailboxPolicy [-Identity **'PolicyIdentity'**]

Usage
Get-ActiveSyncMailboxPolicy

Get-ActiveSyncMailboxPolicy
-Identity 'Primary ActiveSync Mailbox Policy'

Output

```
AllowNonProvisionableDevices                        : False
AlphanumericDevicePasswordRequired                  : False
AttachmentsEnabled                                  : True
DeviceEncryptionEnabled                             : False
RequireStorageCardEncryption                        : False
DevicePasswordEnabled                               : True
PasswordRecoveryEnabled                             : False
DevicePolicyRefreshInterval                         : unlimited
AllowSimpleDevicePassword                           : True
MaxAttachmentSize                                   : 9192KB
. . .
AllowBrowser                                        : True
AllowConsumerEmail                                  : True
AllowRemoteDesktop                                  : False
AllowInternetSharing                                : False
AllowBluetooth                                      : HandsfreeOnly
MaxCalendarAgeFilter                                : All
MaxEmailAgeFilter                                   : All
RequireSignedSMIMEAlgorithm                         : SHA1
RequireEncryptionSMIMEAlgorithm                     : TripleDES
AllowSMIMEEncryptionAlgorithmNegotiation : AllowAnyAlgorithmNegotiation
MinDevicePasswordComplexCharacters                  : 3
MaxEmailBodyTruncationSize                          : 2048
MaxEmailHTMLBodyTruncationSize                      : unlimited
UnapprovedInROMApplicationList                      : {}
ApprovedApplicationList                             : {}
AllowExternalDeviceManagement                       : False
MailboxPolicyFlags                                  : 0
AdminDisplayName                                    :
ExchangeVersion                                     : 0.1 (8.0.535.0)
Name                                                : Primary ActiveSync Mailbox
Policy
DistinguishedName                  : CN=Primary ActiveSync Mail
box Policy,CN=Mobile Mailbox Policies,CN=FirstOrganization,
CN=Microsoft Exchange,CN=Services,CN=Configuration,DC=cpandl,DC=com
```

```
Identity                                    : Primary ActiveSync Mailbox
Policy
Guid                                        : 87a141cf-6ce2-4043-90bf-
8f97568095df
ObjectCategory                              : cpand1.com/Configuration/
Schema/ms-Exch-Mobile-Mailbox-Policy
ObjectClass                                 : {top, msExchRecipientTemplate,
msExchMobileMailboxPolicy}
WhenChanged                                 : 2/12/2008 6:10:36 PM
WhenCreated                                 : 2/12/2008 6:07:30 PM
OriginatingServer                           : MAILSERVER25.cpand1.com
IsValid                                     : True
```

Creating Exchange ActiveSync Mailbox Policies

The Exchange ActiveSync Mailbox policies you create apply to your entire organization. You apply policies separately after you create them, as discussed in the "Assigning Exchange ActiveSync Mailbox Policies" section of this chapter.

In Exchange Management Console, you can create a new policy by completing the following steps:

1. Start Exchange Management Console. Expand the Organization Configuration node, and then select Client Access.

2. In the details pane, you'll see the Exchange ActiveSync Mailbox Policy node. Right-click an open area of the details pane, and select New Exchange ActiveSync Mailbox Policy.

3. As shown in Figure 16-5, type a descriptive name for the policy, and then use the following options to configure the policy:

   ❑ **Allow Non-Provisionable Devices**   Non-provisionable devices are older devices that do not support the Autodiscover service. If you select this option, these older devices can connect to Exchange 2007 by using Exchange ActiveSync.

   ❑ **Allow Attachments To Be Downloaded To Device**   Enables attachments to be downloaded to mobile devices. If you do not select this option, any message attachments are not downloaded with user messages.

   ❑ **Require Alphanumeric Passwords**   Requires that a password contain numeric and alphanumeric characters. If you do not select this option, users can use simple passwords, which may not be secure.

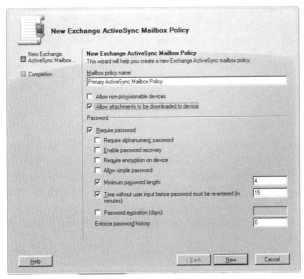

Figure 16-5   Create the Exchange ActiveSync Mailbox policy.

- ❑ **Enable Password Recovery**   Enables the device password to be recovered from the server. If you do not select this option and the user forgets his or her password, you will not be able to reset the device password and the user will be unable to access his or her mailbox using the device.

- ❑ **Require Encryption On Device**   Requires mobile devices to use encryption. Since encrypted data cannot be accessed without the appropriate password, this helps to protect the data on the device. If you select this option, Exchange will only allow devices to download data if they use encryption.

- ❑ **Allow Simple Password**   Allows the user to use a non-complex password instead of a password that meets the minimum complexity requirements.

- ❑ **Minimum Password Length**   Allows you to set a minimum password length. You must select the related check box to the desired minimum password length, such as eight characters. The longer the password, the more secure it is. A good minimum password length is between 8 and 12 characters.

❑ **Time Without User Input Before Password Must Be Re-Entered** Allows you to specify the length of time (in minutes) that a device can go without user input before it locks. You must select the related check box to the desired time interval, such as 15.

❑ **Password Expiration** Allows you to specify the maximum length of time users can keep a password before they have to change it. You can use this option to require users to change their passwords periodically. A good password expiration value is between 30 and 90 days.

❑ **Enforce Password History** Allows you to specify how frequently old passwords can be reused. the maximum length of time users can keep a password before they have to change it. You can use this option to discourage users from changing back and forth between a common set of passwords. To disable this option, set the size of the password history to zero. To enable this option, set the desired size of the password history. A good value is between 3 and 6.

4. Click New to create the policy, and then click Finish. Optimize the configuration, as discussed in "Optimizing Exchange Active Sync Mailbox Policies."

In the Exchange Management Shell, you can create new Exchange ActiveSync Mailbox policies using the New-ActiveSyncMailboxPolicy cmdlet. Sample 16-10 provides the syntax and usage.

Sample 16-10 New-ActiveSyncMailboxPolicy cmdlet syntax and usage

```
Syntax
New-ActiveSyncMailboxPolicy -Name 'Name'
[-AllowBluetooth <Disable | HandsfreeOnly | Allow>]
[-AllowBrowser <$true | $false>]
[-AllowCamera <$true | $false>]
[-AllowConsumerEmail <$true | $false>]
[-AllowDesktopSync <$true | $false>]
[-AllowExternalDeviceManagement <$true | $false>]
[-AllowHTMLEmail <$true | $false>]
[-AllowInternetSharing <$true | $false>]
[-AllowIrDA <$true | $false>]
[-AllowNonProvisionableDevices <$true | $false>]
[-AllowPOPIMAPEmail <$true | $false>]
[-AllowRemoteDesktop <$true | $false>]
[-AllowSimpleDevicePassword <$true | $false>]
[-AllowSMIMEEncryptionAlgorithmNegotiation <BlockNegotiation |
OnlyStrongAlgorithmNegotiation | AllowAnyAlgorithmNegotiation>]
[-AllowSMIMESoftCerts <$true | $false>]
[-AllowStorageCard <$true | $false>]
[-AllowTextMessaging <$true | $false>]
[-AllowUnsignedApplications <$true | $false>]
```

```
[-AllowUnsignedInstallationPackages <$true | $false>]
[-AllowWiFi <$true | $false>]
[-AlphanumericDevicePasswordRequired < $true | $false>]
[-ApprovedApplicationList 'AppList']
[-AttachmentsEnabled <$true | $false>]
[-DeviceEncryptionEnabled <$true | $false>]
[-DevicePasswordEnabled <$true | $false>]
[-DevicePasswordExpiration <'dd.hh.mm:ss' | 'Unlimited'>]
[-DevicePasswordHistory NumPasswords]
[-DomainController <Fqdn>]
[-IsDefaultPolicy <$true | $false>]
[-MaxAttachmentSize <'SizeKB' | 'Unlimited'>]
[-MaxCalendarAgeFilter <All | TwoWeeks | OneMonth | ThreeMonths
| SixMonths>]
[-MaxDevicePasswordFailedAttempts <Unlimited>]
[-MaxEmailAgeFilter <All | OneDay | ThreeDays | OneWeek | TwoWeeks
| OneMonth>]
[-MaxEmailBodyTruncationSize <Unlimited>]
[-MaxEmailHTMLBodyTruncationSize <'MaxSizeKB' | 'Unlimited'>]
[-MaxInactivityTimeDeviceLock <'hh.mm:ss' | 'Unlimited'>]
[-MinDevicePasswordComplexCharacters 'MinNumberOfComplexCharacters']
[-MinDevicePasswordLength 'MinPasswordLength']
[-PasswordRecoveryEnabled <$true | $false>]
[-RequireDeviceEncryption <$true | $false>]
[-RequireEncryptedSMIMEMessages <$true | $false>]
[-RequireEncryptionSMIMEAlgorithm <TripleDES | DES | RC2128bit
| RC264bit | RC240bit>]
[-RequireManualSyncWhenRoaming <$true | $false>]
[-RequireSignedSMIMEAlgorithm <SHA1 | MD5>]
[-RequireSignedSMIMEMessages <$true | $false>]
[-RequireStora geCardEncryption <$true | $false>]
[-TemplateInstance <PSObject>]
[-UnapprovedInROMApplicationList 'AppList']
[-UNCAccessEnabled <$true | $false>]
[-WSSAccessEnabled <$true | $false>]
```

Usage
```
New-ActiveSyncMailboxPolicy -Name 'Primary ActiveSync Mailbox Policy'
 -AllowNonProvisionableDevices $true
 -DevicePasswordEnabled $true
 -AlphanumericDevicePasswordRequired $true
 -MaxInactivityTimeDeviceLock '00.15:00'
 -MinDevicePasswordLength '8'
 -PasswordRecoveryEnabled $true
 -DeviceEncryptionEnabled $true
 -AttachmentsEnabled $true
```

Optimizing Exchange ActiveSync Mailbox Policies

When you create an Exchange ActiveSync Mailbox policy, some additional settings are configured automatically. By default, access to both Windows file shares and Microsoft Windows SharePoint Services is allowed. If you specified that passwords were required, by default, the number of failed attempts allowed is eight. If the policy allows devices to download attachments, there is no default limit on the attachment size. You can modify these and other policy settings by completing the following steps:

1. In Exchange Management Console, right-click the policy, and select Properties.

2. On the General tab, shown in Figure 16-6, use the options to configure whether non-provisionable devices are allowed.

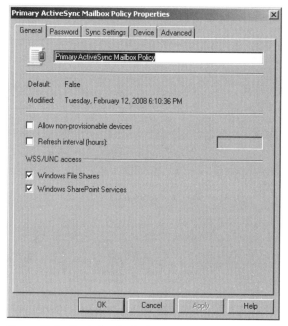

Figure 16-6 Optimize the Exchange ActiveSync Mailbox policy.

3. If you don't want users to be able to access file shares, SharePoint Services, or both from their mobile devices, clear the Windows File Shares and Windows SharePoint Services check boxes.

4. On the Password tab, you must select the Require Password check box to set controls for device passwords. The options available are the same as when you are creating a policy, with one addition: Number Of Failed Attempts Allowed. To limit the number of failed password attempts that can be made before a user's account is locked, select this check box, and then set the allowed limit.

5. On the Sync Settings tab, you can configure general device sync options. For past calendar and e-mail items, you can specify whether all items should be synced or only items from a specific period of time, such as the last two weeks. If you want to limit message size, select the Limit Message Size check box, and then enter the size limit in kilobytes (KB), such as 512. If you allow attachments and you want to limit the size of attachments that users can download, select the Maximum Attachment Size (KB) check box, and then enter the size limit in kilobytes (KB), such as 900.

6. On the Device tab, you can configure device-specific settings. To allow the use of a device-specific setting, select the related Allow check box. To prevent the uses of a device-specific setting, clear the related Allow check box. You can:

   ❑ Allow or disallow the device to access remove storage, such as memory cards.

   ❑ Allow or disallow the device to connect to a camera.

   ❑ Allow or disallow the device to connect to a wireless network.

   ❑ Allow or disallow the device to connect to other devices using infrared.

   ❑ Allow or disallow another device to share the device's Internet connection.

   ❑ Allow or disallow the device to connect to synchronize with a desktop computer.

7. Using the Allow Bluetooth list, you can specify whether and how the device can use Bluetooth. To allow the device to use Bluetooth, select Allow. To allow the device to use Bluetooth only in hands-free mode, select Handsfree Only. To prevent the device from using Bluetooth, select Disable.

8. On the Advanced tab, you can configure allowed or blocked applications. To enable features of the mobile device, you can:

   ❑ Select Allow Browser to allow the device to use Pocket Internet Explorer.

   ❑ Select Allow Consumer Mail to all the device to access e-mail accounts other than Microsoft Exchange.

   ❑ Select Allow Unsigned Applications to allow the device to execute unsigned applications.

   ❑ Select Allow Unsigned Installation Applications to allow the device to install unsigned applications.

9. Click OK to apply your settings.

In the Exchange Management Shell, you can modify Exchange ActiveSync Mailbox policies using the Set-ActiveSyncMailboxPolicy cmdlet. Sample 16-11 provides the syntax and usage.

Sample 16-11   Set-ActiveSyncMailboxPolicy cmdlet syntax and usage

```
Syntax
Set-ActiveSyncMailboxPolicy -Identity 'Name'
```

```
Usage
Set-ActiveSyncMailboxPolicy -Identity 'Primary ActiveSync
Mailbox Policy'
 -AllowNonProvisionableDevices $false
 -DevicePasswordEnabled $true
 -AlphanumericDevicePasswordRequired $true
 -MaxInactivityTimeDeviceLock '00:08:00'
 -MinDevicePasswordLength '6'
 -MaxDevicePasswordFailedAttempts '5'
```

Assigning Exchange ActiveSync Mailbox Policies

Mailbox servers automatically apply the default Exchange ActiveSync Mailbox policy through implicit inheritance when you create a new mailbox. Any mailbox that has implicitly inherited policy automatically applies the current default policy and its settings. When you modify the default policy or configure a new default policy, you change the Exchange ActiveSync settings for all mailbox users that implicitly inherit the default policy.

To set a new default policy and have it automatically applied through inheritance, follow these steps:

1. Start Exchange Management Console. Expand the Organization Configuration node, and then select Client Access.

2. In the details pane, you'll see a list of current policies. The current default policy has the value True in the Default column. To make another policy the default and apply this policy to all users in the Exchange organization, right-click the policy and then select Set As Default.

To prevent a mailbox from implicitly inheriting the default policy and its settings, you can explicitly assign a policy to the mailbox by completing the following steps:

1. In Exchange Management Console, expand the Recipient Configuration node, and then select the Mailbox node.

2. Right-click the mailbox with which you want to work, and then select Properties.

3. On the Mailbox Features tab, select Exchange ActiveSync, and then click Properties.

4. Click Browse. In the Select ActiveSync Mailbox Policy dialog box, select the policy you want to assign, and then click OK. Click OK twice to apply your settings.

Note   When you explicitly assign an Exchange ActiveSync policy, the mailbox applies only the settings from that policy and is not affected by the default policy. However, if you delete the Exchange ActiveSync policy being applied to the mailbox, the default policy will once again be inherited implicitly and applied.

In Exchange Management Shell, you can assign an Exchange ActiveSync Mailbox policy to a mailbox using the ActiveSyncMailboxPolicy parameter of the Set-CASMailbox cmdlet. Sample 16-12 provides the syntax and usage.

Sample 16-12   Assigning Exchange ActiveSync Mailbox policy to a mailbox

```
Syntax
Set-CASMailbox -Identity 'MailboxIdentity'
 -ActiveSyncMailboxPolicy 'PolicyIdentity'
```

```
Usage
Set-CASMailbox -Identity 'markh@cpandl.com'
 -ActiveSyncMailboxPolicy 'Primary ActiveSync Mailbox Policy'
```

Removing Exchange ActiveSync Mailbox Policies

When you no longer need an Exchange ActiveSync Mailbox policy, you can remove it, provided that it isn't the current default policy. In Exchange Management Console, right-click the policy, and select Remove. When prompted to confirm, click Yes to delete the policy. If users are assigned to the policy, they will stop using the policy and implicitly inherit the current default policy.

In Exchange Management Shell, you can remove an Exchange ActiveSync Mailbox policy using the Remove-ActiveSyncMailboxPolicy cmdlet. Sample 16-13 provides the syntax and usage.

Sample 16-13   Remove-ActiveSyncMailboxPolicy cmdlet syntax and usage

```
Syntax
Remove-ActiveSyncMailboxPolicy -Identity 'Name'
```

```
Usage
Remove-ActiveSyncMailboxPolicy -Identity 'Primary ActiveSync
Mailbox Policy'
```

Understanding and Using Remote Device Wipe

Although passwords help to protect mobile devices, they don't prevent access to the device. Malicious individuals may still gain access to data. In the event that a device is lost or stolen, you can use Remote Device Wipe to instruct a mobile device to delete all its data.

Remotely Wiping a Device

An administrator or the owner of the device can prevent the compromising of sensitive data by initiating a remote device wipe. After you initiate a remote device wipe and the device receives the request, the device confirms the remote wipe request by sending a confirmation message and then removes all its data the next time it connects to Exchange Server. Not only does this return the device to its factory default condition, but it also removes any data stored on any storage card inserted into the device. Wiping the data prevents it from being compromised.

The easiest way to wipe a device remotely is to have the device owner initiate the wipe using Outlook Web Access. When the device acknowledges the request, the user will get a confirmation e-mail. Alternately, an administrator can log on to Outlook Web Access as the device owner and initiate the remote wipe. To do this, follow these steps:

1. Start Internet Explorer. In the Address field, type the Outlook Web Access URL, such as **https://mail.cpandl.com/owa**, and then press Enter to access this page.

2. When prompted, provide the logon credentials of the user whose device you want to wipe. Do not provide your administrator credentials.

3. On the Outlook Web Access toolbar, click Options.

4. The left pane of the Options view provides a list of options. Scroll down, and then click Mobile Devices.

5. The user's mobile devices are listed in the details pane. Select the device you want to wipe, and then click Wipe All Data From Device.

6. Confirm the action when prompted.

7. Click Remove Device From List.

> **Note**   You can use Outlook Web Access for remote device wiping only if the user has used the device previously to access Exchange Server and if you have enabled the Segmentation feature of Exchange Active Directory Integration (which is the default configuration).

> **Caution**   Because wiping a device will cause complete data loss, you should do this only when you've contacted the user directly (preferably in person) and confirmed that the mobile device has been lost and that he or she understands the consequences of wiping the device. If your organization has a formal policy regarding the wiping of lost devices that may contain sensitive company data, be sure you follow this policy and get any necessary approvals.

In Exchange Management Shell, you can list the mobile devices registered as partners for a user's mailbox using the Get-MobileDeviceStatistics cmdlet. The device identity you want is the DeviceId string. If the user has multiple mobile devices, be sure to consult also the DeviceModel and DeviceOperatorNetwork values.

After you know the mobile device identity, you can issue a remote device wipe command using the Clear-ActiveSyncDevice cmdlet. You'll then need to confirm that you want to wipe the device when prompted by pressing the Y key. Samples 16-14 and 16-15 provide the syntax and usage for Get-MobileDeviceStatistics and Clear-ActiveSyncDevice cmdlets, respectively. With Get-MobileDeviceStatistics, you can specify either the unique identity of the remove device or the user mailbox you want to work with. The GetMailboxLog parameter retrieves mailbox logs and usage information. Use the OutputPath parameter to direct the statistics to a specific folder path or the NotificationEmailAddresses parameter to e-mail the statistics to specified e-mail addresses.

Note   If you determine that you've made a mistake in issuing a remote wipe, you should immediately issue a cancellation request using the Clear-ActiveSyncDevice cmdlet. Here, set the Cancel parameter to $true. The remove device will only process the cancellation request if the remote wipe has not yet been initiated.

Sample 16-14   Get-MobileDeviceStatistics cmdlet syntax and usage

```
Syntax
Get-MobileDeviceStatistics -Identity 'DeviceIdentity'

Get-MobileDeviceStatistics -Mailbox 'MailboxIdentity'
[-GetMailboxLog <$true | $false>]
[-NotificationEmailAddresses 'EmailAddress1', 'EmailAddress2', . . .]
[-OutputPath 'Path']
[-ShowRecoveryPassword <$true | $false>]
```

```
Usage
Get-MobileDeviceStatistics -Mailbox 'David Pelton'
```

Sample 16-15   Clear-ActiveSyncDevice cmdlet syntax and usage

```
Syntax
Clear-ActiveSyncDevice -Identity 'MobileDeviceIdentity'
[-Cancel <$true | $false>]
[-NotificationEmailAddresses 'EmailAddress1', 'EmailAddress2', . . .]
```

```
Usage
Clear-ActiveSyncDevice -Identity 'Mobile_DavidP'

Clear-ActiveSyncDevice -Identity 'Mobile_DavidP' -Cancel $true
```

Reviewing the Remote Wipe Status

When you initiate a remote wipe, the mobile device removes all its data the next time it connects to Exchange Server. You can review the remote wipe status using an alternate syntax for the Get-MobileDeviceStatistics cmdlet. Instead of passing the cmdlet the Mailbox parameter, use the Identity parameter to specify the DeviceId string of the device you wiped. The statistics returned will include these output parameters:

- **DeviceWipeRequestTime**   The time you request a remote wipe

- **DeviceWipeSentTime**   The time the server sent the remote wipe command to the device

- **DeviceWipeAckTime**   The time when the device acknowledged receipt of the remote wipe command

If there is a DeviceWipeSentTime timestamp, the device has connected to Exchange Server and Exchange Server sent the device the remote wipe command. If there is a DeviceWipeAckTime timestamp, the device acknowledged receipt of the remote wipe and has started to wipe its data.

Understanding and Using Password Recovery

Users can create passwords for their mobile devices. If a user forgets his or her password, you can obtain a recovery password that unlocks the device and lets the user create a new password. The user can also recover his or her device password by using Outlook Web Access.

To use Outlook Web Access to recover a user's device password, complete the following steps:

1. Start Internet Explorer. In the Address field, type the Outlook Web Access URL, such as **https://mail.cpandl.com/owa**, and then press Enter to access this page.

2. When prompted, provide the user's logon credentials. Do not provide your administrator credentials.

3. On the Outlook Web Access toolbar, click Options.

4. The left pane of the Options view provides a list of options. Scroll down, and then click Mobile Devices.

5. The user's mobile devices are listed in the details pane. Select the device for which you are recovering the password.

6. Click Display Device Password.

You also can display the device recovery password by completing the following steps:

1. In Exchange Management Console, expand the Recipient Configuration node, and then select the Mailbox node.

2. Right-click the user's mailbox, and then select Manage Mobile Device. The device recovery password is displayed in the Manage Mobile Device dialog box.

In Exchange Management Shell, you can display the device recovery password using the ShowRecoveryPassword parameter of the Get-ActiveSyncDeviceStatistics cmdlet. Sample 16-16 provides the syntax and usage.

Sample 16-16   Recovering a device password

```
Syntax
Get-ActiveSyncDeviceStatistics -Mailbox 'MailboxIdentity'
 -ShowRecoveryPassword $true
```

```
Usage
Get-ActiveSyncDeviceStatistics -Mailbox 'HelenB@cpand1.com'
 -ShowRecoveryPassword $true
```

Understanding and Configuring Direct File Access

By default, Exchange Server 2007 allows users to access files directly through Outlook Web Access. This means that users will be able to access files attached to e-mail messages. You can configure how users interact with files using one of three options in the Exchange Management Console:

- **Allow**   Allows users to access files of the specified types and sends the users' browser information that allows the files to be displayed or opened in the proper applications.

- **Block**   Prevents users from accessing files of the specified types.

- **Force Save**   Forces users to save files of the specified types prior to opening them.

Table 16-4 lists the default file extensions and default Multipurpose Internet Mail Extensions (MIME) values that Exchange Server allows, blocks, or sets to force save by default. These settings are applied to the OWA virtual directory on Client Access servers. If a server has multiple OWA virtual directories or you have multiple Client Access servers, you must configure each directory and server separately.

Note   If there are conflicts between the allow, block, and force save lists, the allow list takes precedence. This means that the allow list settings override the block list and the force save list. As updates are applied to Exchange Server, the default lists may change. Be sure to check the currently applied defaults.

Table 16-4   Default File Extensions and Default MIME Values for Direct File Access

Option	Default File Name Extensions	Default MIME Values
Allow	.avi, .bmp, .doc, .docm, .docx, .gif, .jpg, .mp3, .one, .pdf, .png, .ppsm, .ppsx, .ppt, .pub, .rpmsg, .rtf, .tif, .tiff, .txt, .vsd, .wav, .wma, .wmv, .xls, .xlsb, .xlsm, .xlsx, .zip	image/jpeg, image/png, image/gif, image/bmp
Block	.ade, .adp, .asx, .app, .asp, .aspx, .asx, .asx, .bas, .bat, .cer, .chm, .cmd, .com, .cpl, .crt, .csh, .der, .exe, .fxp, .gadget, .hlp, .hta, .htc, .inf, .ins, .isp, .its, .js, .jse, .ksh, .lnk, .mad, .maf, .mag, .mam, .maq, .mar, .mas, .mat, .mau, .mav, .maw, .mda, .mdb, .mde, .mdt, .mdw, .mdz, .mht, .mhtml, .msc,.msh, .msh1, .mshxml, .msh1xml, .msi, .msp,.mst, .ops, .pcd, .pif, .plg, .prf,.prg, .ps1, .ps2, .psc1, .psc2, .ps1xml, .ps2xml, .pst, .reg, .scf, .scr, .sct, .shb, .shs, .spl, .swf, .tmp, .url, .vb, .vbe, .vbs, .vsmacros, .vss, .vst, .vsw, .ws, .wsc, .wsf, .wsh, .xml	application/hta, application/javascript, application/msaccess, application/prg, application/x-javascript, application/xml, text/javascript, text/scriptlet, text/xml, x-internet-signup
Force Save	.vsmacros, .mshxml, .aspx, .xml, .wsh, .wsf, .wsc, .vsw, .vst, .vss, .vbs, .vbe, .url, .tmp, .swf, .spl, . shs, .shb, .sct, .scr, .scf, .reg, .pst, .prg, .prf, .plg, .pif, .pcd, .ops, .mst, .msp, .msi, .msh, .msc, .mdz, .mdw, .mdt, .mde, .mdb, .mda, .maw, .mav, .mau, .mat, .mas, .mar, .maq, .mam, .mag, .maf, .mad, .lnk, .ksh, .jse, .its, .isp, .ins, .inf, .hta, .hlp, .fxp, .exe, .dir, .dcr, .csh, .crt, .cpl, .com, .cmd, .chm, .cer, .bat, .bas, .asx, .asp, .app, .adp, .ade, .ws, .vb, .js	Application/x-shockwave-flash, Application/octet-stream, Application/futuresplash, Application/x-director

Exchange Server considers all file extensions and MIME types not listed on the allow, block, or force save list to be unknown files and file types. The default setting for unknown file types is force save.

Based on the user's selection, the configuration of his or her network settings, or both, Exchange divides all client connections into one of two classes:

- **Public Computer**   A public computer is a computer being used on a public network.

- **Private Computer**   A private computer is a computer on a private network.

You can enable or disable direct access to files separately for public computers and private computers. However, the allow, block, and force save settings for both types of computers are shared and applied to both public and private computers in the same way.

You can configure direct file access by completing the following steps:

1. In Exchange Management Console, expand the Server Configuration node, and then select the Client Access node.

2. In the upper portion of the details pane, you'll see a list of your organization's Client Access servers. Select the server you want to configure.

3. In the lower portion of the details pane, you'll see a list of option tabs for the selected server. On the Outlook Web Access tab, right-click the virtual directory for which you are configuring direct file access, and then select Properties. Typically, you'll want to configure the OWA virtual directory on the Default Web Site, as this directory is used by default for Outlook Web Access.

4. To enable or disable direct file access for public computers, on the Public Computer File Access tab, select or clear the Enable Direct File Access check box, as appropriate (see Figure 16-7).

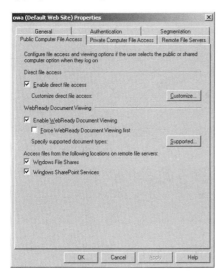

Figure 16-7   Enable or disable direct file access for public computers.

5. To enable or disable direct file access for private computers, on the Private Computer File Access tab, select or clear the Enable Direct File Access check box, as appropriate.

6. On either the Public Computer File Access tab or Private Computer File Access tab, click the Customize button on the Direct File Access panel. The Direct File Access Settings dialog box appears, as shown in Figure 16-8.

Figure 16-8 Configure the direct file access settings.

7. In the Direct File Access Settings dialog box, you can configure allowed files by clicking Allow. The Allow List dialog box appears. Use the following techniques to configure allowed files, and then click OK:

   ❑ To allow a new file extension, type it in the text box provided. Be sure to include the period, such as **.xhtml**, and then press Enter or click Add.

   ❑ To allow a new MIME type, enter it in the text box provided. Be sure to include the full MIME type designator, such as **text/xhtml**, and then press Enter or click Add.

   ❑ To stop allowing a file extension or MIME type, select it, and then click the Remove button.

8. In the Direct File Access Settings dialog box, you can configure blocked files by clicking Block. The Block List dialog box appears. Use the following techniques to configure blocked files, and then click OK:

   ❑ To block a new file extension, type it in the text box provided. Be sure to include the period, such as **.src**, and then press Enter or click Add.

   ❑ To block a new MIME type, enter it in the text box provided. Be sure to include the full MIME type designator, such as **application/src**, and then press Enter or click Add.

❑ To stop blocking a file extension or MIME type, select it, and then click the Remove button.

9. In the Direct File Access Settings dialog box, you can configure allowed files by clicking Force Save. The Force Save List dialog box appears. Use the following techniques to configure force-saved files, and then click OK:

   ❑ To force save a new file extension, type it in the text box provided. Be sure to include the period, such as **.aap**, and then press Enter or click Add.

   ❑ To force save a new MIME type, enter it in the text box provided. Be sure to include the full MIME type designator, such as **application/stream**, and then press Enter or click Add.

   ❑ To stop force saving a file extension or MIME type, select it, and then click the Remove button.

10. In the Direct File Access Settings dialog box, you can configure allowed files using the selection list on the Unknown Files panel. Set the desired action to Allow, Block, or Force Save. Click OK to save your settings, and then click OK to close the Properties dialog box for the virtual directory you selected.

In Exchange Management Shell, you can use the Set-OwaVirtualDirectory cmdlet to manage the direct file-access configuration. Set the Identity parameter to the identity of the virtual directory on the server with which you want to work, such as:

```
Set-OwaVirtualDirectory -Identity 'Corpsvr127\owa (Default Web Site)'
 -DirectFileAccessOnPublicComputersEnabled $false
 -DirectFileAccessOnPrivateComputersEnabled $true
```

If you are unsure of the virtual directory identity value, use the Get-OwaVirtualDirectory cmdlet to retrieve a list of available virtual directories on a named server, as shown in the following example:

```
Get-OwaVirtualDirectory -Server 'Corpsvr127'
```

Understanding and Configuring Remote File Access

By default, Exchange Server 2007 allows users to access files remotely through Outlook Web Access as long as they have a Premium Client Access License. This means users will be able to access Windows SharePoint Services and Universal Naming Convention (UNC) file shares on SharePoint sites. SharePoint sites consist of Web Parts and Windows ASP.NET–based components that allow users to share documents, tasks, contacts, events, and other information. When you configure UNC file shares on SharePoint sites, you enable users to share folders and files.

You can enable or disable direct remote access to Windows file shares and Windows SharePoint Services separately for public computers and private computers. To configure remote file access, complete the following steps:

1. In Exchange Management Console, expand the Server Configuration node, and then select the Client Access node.

2. In the upper portion of the details pane, you'll see a list of your organization's Client Access servers. Select the server you want to configure.

3. In the lower portion of the details pane, you'll see a list of option tabs for the selected server. On the Outlook Web Access tab, right-click the virtual directory for which you are configuring remote file access, and then select Properties. Typically, you'll want to configure the OWA virtual directory on the Default Web Site, as this directory is used by default for Outlook Web Access.

4. To configure remote file access for public computers, on the Public Computer File Access tab, use the following techniques to configure remote file access from public computers:

   ❑ Enable UNC file shares for remote access by selecting the Windows File Shares check box.

   ❑ Disable UNC file shares for remote access by clearing the Windows File Shares check box.

   ❑ Enable Web Parts and SharePoint for remote access by selecting the Windows SharePoint Services check box.

   ❑ Disable Web Parts and SharePoint for remote access by clearing the Windows SharePoint Services check box.

5. To configure remote file access for private computers, on the Private Computer File Access tab, select or clear the Windows File Shares and Windows SharePoint Services check boxes, as appropriate.

6. On the Remote File Servers tab (shown in Figure 16-9), you can specify the host names of servers from which clients are denied or allowed access using block and allow lists, respectively. If there is a conflict between the block list and the allow list, the block list takes precedence.

7. To configure the block list, click Block. Use the following techniques to configure the block list, and then click OK:

   ❑ To add a server to the block list, type the fully qualified domain name of the server, such as **mailsvr83.cpandl.com**, and then press Enter or click Add.

   ❑ To remove a server from the block list, select the host entry, and then click the Remove button.

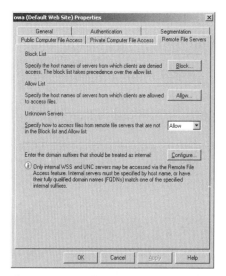

Figure 16-9   Configure remote file server options.

8. To configure the allow list, click Allow. Use the following techniques to configure the allow list, and then click OK:

   ❑ To add a server to the allow list, type the fully qualified domain name of the server, such as **mailsvr83.cpandl.com**, and then press Enter or click Add.

   ❑ To remove a server from the allow list, select the host entry, and then click the Remove button.

9. Servers that are not listed on either the allow list or the block list are considered to be unknown servers. By default, access to unknown servers is allowed. On the Remote File Servers tab, use the Unknown Servers selection list to allow or block unknown servers.

10. Users only have access to shares hosted on internal servers. For a server to be considered an internal server, you must tell Exchange about the domain suffixes that should be handled as internal. On the Remote File Servers tab, click the Configure button. Use the following techniques to configure your internal domain suffixes, and then click OK:

   ❑ To add a domain suffix, type the fully qualified domain name of the suffix, such as **cpandl.com**, and then press Enter or click Add.

   ❑ To remove a domain suffix, select the suffix entry, and then click the Remove button.

In the Exchange Management Shell, you can use the Set-OwaVirtualDirectory cmdlet to manage the direct file access configuration. Set the Identity parameter to the identity of the virtual directory on the server you want to work with, such as:

```
Set-OwaVirtualDirectory -Identity 'Corpsvr127\owa (Default Web Site)'
 -UNCAccessOnPublicComputersEnabled $false
 -UNCAccessOnPrivateComputersEnabled $true
 -WSSAccessOnPublicComputersEnabled $false
 -WSSAccessOnPrivateComputersEnabled $true
```

If you are unsure of the virtual directory identity value, use the Get-OwaVirtualDirectory cmdlet to retrieve a list of available virtual directories on a named server, as shown in the following example:

```
Get-OwaVirtualDirectory -Server 'Corpsvr127'
```

Understanding and Using WebReady Document Viewing

WebReady Document Viewing allows users to view common file types in Outlook Web Access without having the applications associated with those file types installed on their computer. This allows users to view the following files:

- Adobe PDF documents with the .pdf extension.
- Microsoft Office Excel spreadsheets with the.xls and .xlsx extensions.
- Microsoft Office Word documents with the .doc, .docx, .dot, and .rtf extensions.
- Microsoft Office PowerPoint presentations with the .pps, .ppt, and .pptx extensions.

For attachments, the following related MIME types are supported, as well as related open XML formats for presentations, spreadsheets, and word processing documents:

- application/msword
- application/pdf
- application/vnd.ms-excel
- application/vnd.ms-powerpoint
- application/x-msexcel
- application/x-mspowerpoint

Note WebReady Document Viewing works by converting documents in supported formats to HTML so that they can be viewed as a Web page in Outlook Web Access. Thus, when an e-mail message has an attachment in a supported format, WebReady Document Viewing allows the document to be viewed without having to first download the document to the user's computer or open a helper application.

When there are conflicting settings between the direct file, remote file, and WebReady Document Viewing settings, you can force clients to use WebReady Document Viewing first, if you want. This means that the documents will be opened within Internet Explorer rather than in a related application, such as Microsoft Office Word.

You can enable or disable WebReady Document Viewing separately for public computers and private computers. However, supported document settings for both types of computers are shared and applied to both public and private computers in the same way.

To configure WebReady Document Viewing, complete the following steps:

1. In Exchange Management Console, expand the Server Configuration node, and then select the Client Access node.

2. In the upper portion of the details pane, you'll see a list of your organization's Client Access servers. Select the server you want to configure.

3. In the lower portion of the details pane, you'll see a list of option tabs for the selected server. On the Outlook Web Access tab, right-click the virtual directory for which you are configuring WebReady Document Viewing, and then select Properties. Typically, you'll want to configure the OWA virtual directory on the Default Web Site, as this directory is used by default for Outlook Web Access.

4. Use the following techniques to configure WebReady Document Viewing from public computers:

   ❑ Enable WebReady Document Viewing by selecting the Enable WebReady Document Viewing check box.

   ❑ Disable WebReady Document Viewing by clearing the Enable WebReady Document Viewing check box.

   ❑ Force the use of WebReady Document Viewing first by selecting the Force WebReady Document Viewing First check box.

   ❑ Allow documents with supported WebReady Document Viewing formats to be opened in related applications by clearing the Force WebReady Document Viewing First check box.

5. To configure WebReady Document Viewing for private computers, on the Private Computer File Access tab, select or clear the Enable WebReady Document Viewing and Force WebReady Document Viewing First check boxes, as appropriate.

6. On either the Public Computer File Access tab or Private Computer File Access tab, click the Supported button on the WebReady Document Viewing panel. The WebReady Document Viewing Settings dialog box appears, as shown in Figure 16-10.

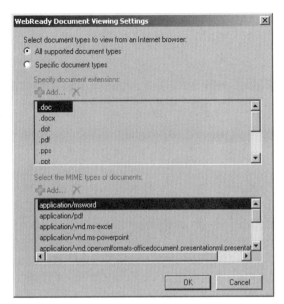

Figure 16-10 Configure WebReady Document Viewing.

7. To allow all supported document types to be used with WebReady Document Viewing, select All Supported Document Types, and then click OK.

8. To customize the supported document types, click Specific Document Types. Use the following techniques to configure supported document types:

   ❑ To stop allowing a document extension or MIME type, select it, and then click the Remove button.

   ❑ To restore a previously removed document extension, under Specify Document Extensions, click the Add button, select the document extension to add, and then click OK.

   ❑ To restore a previously removed MIME type, under Specify The MIME Types Of Documents, click the Add button, select the MIME type to add, and then click OK.

9. Click OK to close the Properties dialog box for the virtual directory.

In the Exchange Management Shell, you can use the Set-OwaVirtualDirectory cmdlet to manage the WebReady Document Viewing configuration. Set the Identity parameter to the identity of the virtual directory on the server with which you want to work, such as:

```
Set-OwaVirtualDirectory -Identity 'Corpsvr127\owa (Default Web Site)'
 -WebReadyDocumentViewingAccessOnPublicComputersEnabled $false
 -WebReadyDocumentViewingOnPrivateComputersEnabled $true
```

If you are unsure of the virtual directory identity value, use the Get-OwaVirtualDirectory cmdlet to retrieve a list of available virtual directories on a named server, as shown in the following example:

```
Get-OwaVirtualDirectory -Server 'Corpsvr127'
```

Part IV

Exchange Server 2007
Optimization and Maintenance

In this part:

Chapter 17
Microsoft Exchange Server 2007 Maintenance, Monitoring, and Queuing

With the exception of backup and recovery, no administration tasks are more important than maintenance, monitoring, and queue tracking. You must maintain Microsoft Exchange Server 2007 to ensure proper flow and recoverability of message data. You need to monitor Exchange Server to ensure that services and processes are functioning normally, and you need to track Exchange Server queues to ensure that messages are being processed.

Understanding Troubleshooting Basics

In the Exchange Management Console, you'll find several tools in the Toolbox to help you troubleshoot messaging problems. These tools include:

- **Database Recovery Management/Database Troubleshooter**   Can help you identify problems with Exchange databases by checking the disks a server is using for messaging to ensure that they are accessible, have free space, and are mounted. You can then troubleshoot database mount problems, analyze log drive space, review database-related event logs, repair a database, or create a recovery storage group.

- **Mailflow Troubleshooter**   Can help you troubleshoot message delivery delays, unexpected nondelivery reports, and problems with Edge Transport server synchronization. Can also help you find lost messages.

- **Performance Troubleshooter**   Can help you troubleshoot performance issues related to delays while using Microsoft Office Outlook, frequent Remote Procedure Call (RPC) dialog box display in Outlook, and higher-than-expected RPC operations.

Using the troubleshooting tools is straightforward, and you can follow these steps to get started:

1. In Exchange Management Console, access the Toolbox node.
2. Double-click the troubleshooter with which you want to work.

Note The first time you start the troubleshooter, you'll need to specify your update and error reporting options. You can configure the troubleshooter to either check for updates automatically on startup or to not check for updates. If you want to report errors to Microsoft, join the customer experience improvement program. Otherwise, specify that you don't want to join the program.

3. After the troubleshooter checks for updates or you manually check for updates by clicking Check For Updates Now, click Go To Welcome Screen.

4. Enter the required troubleshooting parameters, and then click Next.

5. Follow the prompts and select the appropriate options to perform troubleshooting tasks.

As part of your standard operating procedure, you should track changes in the configuration of your Exchange servers. The Exchange Management Shell provides the following cmdlets for obtaining detailed information on the current configuration of your Exchange servers:

- **Get-ExchangeServer** Displays the general configuration details for Exchange servers

- **Get-TransportServer** Displays configuration details for servers with the Hub Transport or Edge Transport Server role

- **Get-MailboxServer** Displays configuration details for servers with the Mailbox Server role

- **Get-ClientAccessServer** Displays configuration details for servers with the Client Access Server role

- **Get-UMServer** Displays configuration details for servers with the Unified Messaging Server role

To get related details for a specific server, you pass a cmdlet the identity of the server, as shown in the following example:

```
Get-TransportServer mailserver25 | fl
```

To get related details for all servers, omit the Identity parameter, as shown in the following example:

```
Get-TransportServer | fl
```

When you finalize the configuration of your Exchange servers, you should use these cmdlets to store the configuration details for each server role. To store the configuration details in a file, redirect the output to a file, as shown in the following example:

```
Get-TransportServer mailserver25 | fl >
c:\SavedConfigs\transport2008-0418.txt
```

If you then store the revised configuration on a per-role basis any time you make significant changes, you can use this information during troubleshooting to help resolve problems that may be related to configuration changes. To compare two configuration files, you can use the file compare command, fc, at an elevated, administrator command prompt. When you use the following syntax with the fc command, the output is the difference between two files:

```
fc FilePath1 FilePath2
```

where *FilePath1* is the full file path to the first file and *FilePath2* is the full file path to the second file, such as:

```
fc c:\SavedConfigs\transport08-0418.txt c:\SavedConfigs\
transport08-0521.txt
```

Because the files contain configuration details for specific dates, the changes shown in the output represent the configuration changes that you've made to the server.

Performing Tracking and Logging Activities in the Organization

This section examines message tracking, protocol logging, and diagnostic logging. You use these features to monitor Exchange Server and to troubleshoot messaging problems.

Using Message Tracking

You use message tracking on Transport servers to monitor the flow of messages into the organization and within it. With message tracking enabled, Exchange Server maintains daily log files, with a running history of all messages transferred within the organization. You use the logs to determine the status of a message, such as whether a message has been sent, received, or is waiting in the queue to be delivered. Because Exchange Server handles postings to public folders in much the same way as e-mail messages, you can also use message tracking to monitor public folder usage.

> **Tip**   Tracking logs can really save the day when you're trying to troubleshoot delivery and routing problems. The logs are also useful in fending off problem users who blame e-mail for their woes. Users can't claim they didn't receive e-mails if you can find the messages in the logs.

Configuring Messaging Tracking

By default, all Hub Transport and Edge Transport servers perform message tracking. You can enable or disable message tracking on a per-server basis by setting the Message-TrackingLogEnabled parameter of the Set-TransportServer cmdlet to $true or $false, as appropriate. The following example disables message tracking on MailServer16:

```
Set-TransportServer -Identity 'MailServer16'
 -MessageTrackingLogEnabled $false
```

Tip   You can configure basic message tracking options in the Exchange Management Console. Expand the Server Organization node and then select the Hub Transport node. In the main pane, double-click the server you want to configure to display the related Properties dialog box. On the Log Settings tab, select or clear the Enable Message Tracking Logging check box. If you enable message tracking, you can specify the log file path by clicking Browse, selecting a folder for logging, and then clicking OK.

Each Transport server in your organization can have different message tracking settings that control:

- Where logs are stored

- How logging is performed

- The maximum log size and maximum log directory size

- How long logs are retained

By default, message tracking logs are stored in the C:\Program Files\Microsoft\ Exchange Server\TransportRoles\Logs\MessageTracking directory. To improve performance, you may want to move the tracking logs to a separate disk. Before you do this, however, you should create the directory you want to use and set the following required permissions:

- Full Control For Administrator

- Full Control For Local System

- Read, Write, And Delete Subfolders And Files For Network Service

After you've created the directory and set the required permissions, you can change the location of the tracking logs to any local directory by setting the MessageTrackingLog-Path parameter of the Set-TransportServer cmdlet to the desired local directory. The following example sets the message tracking directory as G:\Tracking on MailServer16:

```
Set-TransportServer -Identity 'MailServer16'
 -MessageTrackingLogPath 'G:\Tracking'
```

Note   When you change the location of the message tracking directory, Exchange Server does not copy any existing tracking logs from the old directory to the new one. You must manually copy the old logs to the new location if you want all the logs to be in the same location.

By default, all Hub Transport and Edge Transport servers perform extended message tracking, which allows you to perform searches based on message subject lines, header information, sender, and recipient. If you don't want to collect information on potentially sensitive subject lines, you can disable subject line tracking by setting the

MessageTrackingLogSubjectLoggingEnabled parameter of the Set-TransportServer cmdlet to $false, as shown in the following example:

```
Set-TransportServer -Identity 'MailServer16'
 -MessageTrackingLogSubjectLoggingEnabled $false
```

Exchange Server continues to write to message tracking logs until a log grows to a specified maximum size, at which point Exchange Server creates a new log and then uses this log to track current messages. By default, the maximum log file size is 10 megabytes (MB). You can change this behavior by setting the MessageTrackingLog-MaxFileSize parameter to the desired maximum file size. You must qualify the desired file size using B for bytes, KB for kilobytes, MB for megabytes, or GB for gigabytes. The following example sets the message log file size to 50 MB:

```
Set-TransportServer -Identity 'MailServer16'
 -MessageTrackingLogMaxFileSize '50MB'
```

Exchange Server uses circular logging to delete the oldest message tracking logs automatically when tracking logs reach a maximum age or when the maximum log directory size is reached. By default, the maximum age is 30 days and the maximum log directory size is 250 MB. You can use the MessageTrackingLogMaxAge parameter to set the maximum allowed age in the following format:

DD.HH:MM:SS

where DD is the number of days, HH is the number of hours, MM is the number of minutes, and SS is the number of seconds. The following example sets the maximum age for logs to 90 days:

```
Set-TransportServer -Identity 'MailServer16'
 -MessageTrackingLogMaxAge '90.00:00:00'
```

You can set the maximum log directory size using the MessageTrackingLogMaxDirectory-Size parameter. As with the maximum log file size, the qualifiers are B, KB, MB, and GB. The following example sets the maximum log directory size to 2 GB:

```
Set-TransportServer -Identity 'MailServer16'
 -MessageTrackingLogMaxDirectorySize '2GB'
```

Searching Through the Tracking Logs

You use the Message Tracking tool to search through the message tracking logs. The tracking logs are useful in troubleshooting problems with routing and delivery. You can search the logs in several ways:

- By message ID
- By sender
- By server that processed the messages
- By event ID

- By date

- By subject

To begin a search, you must specify one or more of the previously listed identifiers as the search criteria. You must also identify a server in the organization that has processed the message in some way. This server can be the sender's server, the recipient's server, or a server that relayed the message.

To search through the message tracking logs, complete the following steps:

1. In Exchange Management Console, select the Toolbox node, and then double-click Message Tracking. After the Troubleshooting Assistant checks for updates to the Message Tracking tool, click Go To Welcome Screen, and you'll see the Message Tracking Parameters page, shown in Figure 17-1.

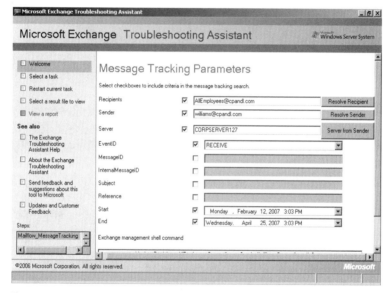

Figure 17-1   Use the Message Tracking tool to search for user messages, system messages, and postings to public folders.

2. Set the search criteria using the following options:

   ❑ **Recipients**   Sets the name of a recipient listed on the To, Cc, or Bcc fields of the message. Click Resolve Recipient to obtain the full e-mail address of the recipient.

   ❑ **Sender**   Sets the name of the sender listed in the From field of the message. Click Resolve Sender to obtain the full e-mail address of the recipient.

❏ **Server**   Sets the name of the Transport server that processed the message within the organization. Click Server From Sender to obtain the full server name.

❏ **Event ID**   Specifies the ID of the event for which you want to search, such as a RECEIVE, SEND, or FAIL event.

❏ **Message ID**   Specifies the ID of the message for which you want to search.

❏ **Subject**   Specifies the subject of the message for which you want to search.

❏ **Reference**   Specifies a reference within the message for which you want to search.

3. You can search for messages from a starting date and time to an ending date and time. Click the Start Selection list to display a calendar. Locate and then click the desired start date on the calendar. Then click the End Selection list to display a calendar. Locate and then click the desired end date on the calendar.

> **Note**   To search for messages, you're required to identify only the name of a server that processed the message within the organization and the search interval. All other search parameters are optional. Keep in mind that only messages that match *all* of the search criteria you've specified are displayed. If you want to perform a broader search, specify a limited number of parameters. If you want to focus the search precisely, specify multiple parameters.

4. Scroll down and then click Next to begin the search. Messages matching the search criteria are displayed.

5. Select a message, and then click Next to view its message tracking history.

Reviewing Message Tracking Logs Manually

Exchange Server creates message tracking logs daily and stores them in the C:\Program Files\Microsoft\Exchange Server\TransportRoles\Logs\MessageTracking directory. Each log file is named by the date on which it was created, using the format MSGTRKYYYYMMDD-N.log, such as MSGTRK20080925-1.log for the first log created on September 25, 2008.

The message tracking log stores each message event on a single line. The information on a particular line is organized by comma-separated fields. Logs begin with a header that shows the following information:

■ A statement that identifies the file as a message tracking log file

■ The version of the Exchange Server that created the file

■ The date on which the log file was created

■ A comma-delimited list of fields contained in the body of the log file

Table 17-1 summarizes message event fields and their meaning. Not all of the fields are tracked for all message events.

Table 17-1   Message Tracking Log Fields

Log Field	Description
Date-Time	The connection date and time
Client-ip	The IP address of the client making the request
Client-hostname	The hostname of the client making the request
Server-hostname	The server on which the log entry was generated
Server-ip	The IP address of the server on which the log entry was generated
Source-context	The context of the event source
Connector-id	The identity of the connector used
Source	The messaging component for which the event is being logged, such as StoreDriver
Event-id	The type of event being logged, such as Submit
Internal-message-id	The internal identifier used by Exchange to track the message
Message-id	The message identifier
Recipient-address	The e-mail addresses of the message recipients
Recipient-status	The status of the recipient e-mail address
Total-bytes	The total size of the message in bytes
Recipient-count	The total number of recipients
Related-recipient-address	The e-mail addresses of any related recipients
Reference	The references, if any
Message-subject	The subject of the message
Sender-address	The distinguished name of the sender's e-mail address
Return-path	The return path on the message
Security-info	Any related security information on the message

You can view the message tracking log files with any standard text editor, such as Microsoft Notepad. You can also import the message tracking log files into a spreadsheet or a database. Follow these steps to import a message tracking log file into Microsoft Office Excel 2007:

1. Start Microsoft Office Excel 2007. Click the Microsoft Office Button and then click Open. Use the Open dialog box to select the message tracking log file you want to open. Click Open.

2. The Text Import Wizard starts automatically. The wizard should detect all the appropriate settings, so click Finish immediately.

3. The log file should now be imported. You can view, search, and print the message tracking log as you would any other spreadsheet.

Using Protocol Logging

Protocol logging allows you to track Simple Mail Transfer Protocol (SMTP) communications that occur between Exchange servers as part of message routing and delivery. You use protocol logging to troubleshoot problems with the Send and Receive connectors that are configured on Hub Transport and Edge Transport servers. However, you shouldn't use protocol logging to monitor Exchange activity. This is primarily because protocol logging is process- and resource-intensive, which means that an Exchange server has to perform a lot of work to log protocol activity.

Configuring Protocol Logging

By default, Hub Transport and Edge Transport servers do not perform protocol logging. As long as you know the identity of the connector with which you want to work, you can configure protocol logging for a specified connector. To retrieve a list of available Send and Receive connectors for a server, use the Get-SendConnector and Get-ReceiveConnector cmdlets, respectively. If you run either cmdlet without specifying additional parameters, a list of all available Send or Receive connectors is returned.

You enable or disable protocol logging on a per-connector basis. For Send connectors, you use the Set-SendConnector cmdlet to enable protocol logging. For Receive connectors, you use the Set-ReceiveConnector cmdlet to enable protocol logging. Both cmdlets have a ProtocolLoggingLevel parameter that you can set to Basic to enable protocol logging or to None to disable protocol logging, as shown in this example:

```
set-ReceiveConnector -Identity 'Corpsvr127\Custom Receive Connector'
 -ProtocolLoggingLevel 'Basic'
```

Although you enable protocol logging on a per-connector basis, you configure the other protocol logging parameters on a per-server basis for either all Send connectors or all Receive connectors. As with message tracking logs, Exchange Server uses circular logging to delete the oldest protocol logs automatically when tracking logs reach a maximum age or when the maximum log directory size is reached. If you decide to move the protocol log directories, you should create the directories you want to use and then set the following required permissions:

- Full Control For Administrator

- Full Control For Local System

- Read, Write, And Delete Subfolders And Files For Network Service

Because the parameters are similar to those for message tracking, I'll summarize the available parameters. Table 17-2 shows the Send connector parameters for configuring protocol logging. Table 17-3 shows the Receive connector parameters for configuring protocol logging.

> **Tip** You can configure send and receive protocol log paths in the Exchange Management Console. Expand the Server Organization node, and then select the Hub Transport node. In the main pane, double-click the server you want to configure to display the related Properties dialog box. On the Log Settings tab, the Protocol log panel shows the current send and receive protocol log paths. You can specify the log file path by clicking the appropriate Browse button, selecting a folder for logging, and then clicking OK.

Table 17-2   Send Connector Parameters for Protocol Logging

Parameter	Description	Default
SendProtocolLogPath	Sets the local file path for protocol logging of Send connectors	C:\Program Files\Microsoft\ Exchange Server\ TransportRoles\Logs\ ProtocolLog\SmtpSend
SendProtocolLogMax-FileSize	Sets the maximum size for Send connector protocol logs	10 MB
SendProtocolLogMax-DirectorySize	Sets the maximum size for the Send connector protocol directory	250 MB
SendProtocolLogMax-Age	Sets the maximum age for Send connector protocol logs	30.00:00:00

Table 17-3   Receive Connector Parameters for Protocol Logging

Parameter	Description	Default
ReceiveProtocolLog-Path	Sets the local file path for protocol logging of Receive connectors	C:\Program Files\Microsoft\Exchange Server\TransportRoles\Logs\ ProtocolLog\SmtpReceive
ReceiveProtocolLog-MaxFileSize	Sets the maximum size for Receive connector protocol logs	10 MB

Table 17-3   Receive Connector Parameters for Protocol Logging

Parameter	Description	Default
ReceiveProtocolLog-MaxDirectorySize	Sets the maximum size for the Receive connector protocol directory	250 MB
ReceiveProtocolLog-MaxAge	Sets the maximum age for Receive connector protocol logs	30.00:00:00

Working with Protocol Logging Properties and Fields

Exchange Server creates protocol logs daily and stores them in either the C:\Program Files\Microsoft\Exchange Server\TransportRoles\Logs\ProtocolLog\SmtpSend or C:\Program Files\Microsoft\Exchange Server\TransportRoles\Logs\Protocol-Log\SmtpReceive directory as appropriate for the type of connector being logged. Each log file is named by the date on which it was created, using the format SENDYYYYMMDD-N.log or RECVYYYYMMDD-N.log, such as SEND20080925-1.log for the first Send connector log created on September 25, 2008.

The protocol log stores each SMTP protocol event on a single line. The information on a particular line is organized by comma-separated fields. Logs begin with a header that shows the following information:

- A statement that identifies the file as either a Send connector protocol log or a Receive connector protocol log

- The date on which the log file was created

- The version of the Exchange Server that created the file

- A comma-delimited list of fields contained in the body of the log file

Table 17-4 summarizes SMTP protocol event fields and their meanings. Not all of the fields are tracked for all protocol events. You can view the protocol log files with any standard text editor, such as Notepad. You can also import the protocol log files into a spreadsheet or a database, as discussed previously.

Table 17-4   Protocol Log Fields

Log Field	Description
Date-time	The date and time of the protocol event.
Connector-id	The distinguished name of the connector associated with the event.
Session-id	The globally unique identifier of the SMTP session. Each event for a particular session has the same identifier.
Sequence-number	The number of the event within an SMTP session. The first event has a sequence number of 0.

Table 17-4   Protocol Log Fields

Log Field	Description
Local-endpoint	The local endpoint of the SMTP session, identified by the Internet Protocol (IP) address and Transmission Control Protocol (TCP) port.
Remote-endpoint	The remote endpoint of the SMTP session, identified by the IP address and TCP port.
Event	The type of protocol event: + for Connect, - for Disconnect, > for Send, < for Receive, and * for Information.
Data	The data associated with the SMTP event.
Context	The context for the SMTP event.

Enabling Protocol Logging for HTTP

Client Access servers have HTTP virtual servers and use IIS to provide the related services. In IIS 7.0, protocol logging for HTTP is a feature that you must enable by installing the HTTP Logging module. Once you install and enable the module, you can enable protocol logging on each virtual server separately or for the server as a whole to track access to Outlook Web Access, Exchange ActiveSync, Outlook Anywhere, and the HTTP virtual servers in general.

To enable protocol logging for HTTP, complete the following steps:

1. Start Internet Information Services (IIS) Manager. Click Start, point to Programs or All Programs as appropriate, point to Administrative Tools, and select Internet Information Services (IIS) Manager.

   Note   By default, IIS Manager connects to the services running on the local computer. If you want to connect to a different server, select the Start Page node in the left pane and then click the Connect To A Server link. This starts the Connect To Server Wizard. Follow the prompts to connect to the remote server. Keep in mind that with IIS 7.0, the Web Management Service (WMSVC) must be configured and running on the remote server. For more information, see "Enabling and Configuring Remote Administration" in Chapter 3 of *Internet Information Services (IIS) 7.0 Administrator's Pocket Consultant* (Microsoft Press, 2007).

2. In IIS Manager, each HTTP virtual server is represented as a Web site. The Default Web Site represents the default HTTP virtual server. Double-click the entry for the server with which you want to work, and then double-click Web Sites.

3. In the left pane, select the Web site that you want to manage, and then double-click Logging in the main pane to open the Logging feature as shown in Figure 17-2.

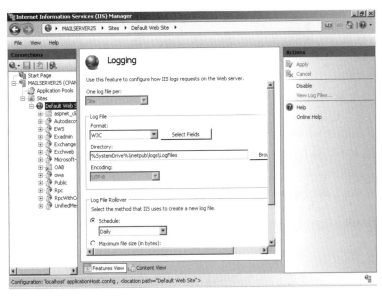

Figure 17-2 Customize logging by selecting the desired options.

4. If all logging options are dimmed and the server is configured for per-site logging, you can click Enable in the Actions pane to enable logging for this site. Otherwise, if logging is configured per server, you'll need to configure logging at the server level rather than at the site level; the procedure is similar.

5. Use the Format selection list to choose one of the following log formats:

    ❑ **W3C Extended Log File Format**   Writes the log in ASCII text following the World Wide Web Consortium (W3C) extended log file format. Fields are space-delimited, and each entry is written on a new line. This style is the default.

    ❑ **Microsoft IIS Log File Format**   Writes the log in ASCII text following the IIS log file format. Fields are tab-delimited, and each entry is written on a new line.

    ❑ **NCSA Common Log File Format**   Writes the log in ASCII text following the National Center for Supercomputing Applications (NCSA) common log file format. Fields are space-delimited, and each entry is written on a new line.

    Tip   W3C Extended Log File Format is the preferred logging format. Unless you're certain that another format meets your needs, you should use this format.

6. Use the Log File Directory text box to set the main folder for log files. By default, log files are written to a subdirectory of %SystemDrive%\inetpub\logs\ LogFiles.

7. On the Log File Rollover Panel, select Schedule and then use the related selection list to choose a log time period. In most cases, you'll want to create daily or weekly logs, so select either Daily or Weekly.

8. If you selected W3C Extended Log File Format, click Select Fields, choose the fields that should be recorded in the logs. Click Apply.

Working with HTTP Protocol Logs

On Client Access servers, HTTP protocol log files can help you detect and trace problems with HTTP, Outlook Web Access, Exchange ActiveSync, and Outlook Anywhere. By default, Exchange Server writes protocol log files to a subdirectory of %SystemDrive%\inetpub\logs\LogFiles. You can use the logs to determine the following:

- Whether a client was able to connect to a specified virtual server and, if not, what problem occurred

- Whether a client was able to send or receive protocol commands and, if not, what error occurred

- Whether a client was able to send or receive data

- How long it took to establish a connection

- How long it took to send or receive protocol commands

- How long it took to send or receive data

- Whether server errors are occurring and, if so, what types of errors are occurring

- Whether server errors are related to Windows or to the protocol itself

- Whether a user is connecting to the server using the proper logon information

Most protocol log files are written as ASCII text. This means you can view them in Notepad or another text editor. You can import these protocol log files into Office Excel 2007 in much the same way as you import tracking logs.

Log files, written as space-delimited or tab-delimited text, begin with a header that shows the following information:

- A statement that identifies the protocol or service used to create the file

- The protocol, service, or software version

- A date and timestamp

- A space-delimited or tab-delimited list of fields contained in the body of the log file

Using Connectivity Logging

Connectivity logging allows you to track the connection activity of outgoing message delivery queues. You use connectivity logging on Transport servers to troubleshoot problems with messages reaching their designated destination mailbox server, Send connector, or domain.

Configuring Connectivity Logging

By default, Hub Transport and Edge Transport servers do not perform connectivity logging. You can enable or disable connectivity logging on a per-server basis by setting the ConnectivityLogEnabled parameter of the Set-TransportServer cmdlet to $true or $false, as appropriate. The following example enables connectivity logging on MailServer16:

```
Set-TransportServer -Identity 'MailServer16'
 -ConnectivityLogEnabled $false
```

> **Tip**   You can configure basic connectivity logging options in the Exchange Management Console. Expand the Server Organization node and then select the Hub Transport node. In the main pane, double-click the server you want to configure to display the related Properties dialog box. On the Log Settings tab, select or clear the Enable Connectivity Logging check box. If you enable connectivity logging, you can specify the log file path by clicking Browse, selecting a folder for logging, and then clicking OK.

Each Transport server in your organization can have different connectivity logging settings:

- Use the ConnectivityLogPath parameter to move the log directory to a new location. The default location is C:\Program Files\Microsoft\ExchangeServer\ TransportRoles\Logs\Connectivity directory.

- Use the ConnectivityLogMaxFileSize parameter to set the maximum log file size. The default maximum log file size is 10 MB.

- Use the ConnectivityLogMaxDirectorySize parameter to set the maximum log directory size. The default maximum log directory size is 250 MB.

- Use the ConnectivityLogMaxAge parameter to set the maximum log file age. The default maximum age is 30.00:00:00.

As with other logs, Exchange Server uses circular logging to delete the oldest connectivity logs automatically when tracking logs reach a maximum age or when the maximum log directory size is reached. If you decide to move the protocol log directories, you should create the directories you want to use and set the following required permissions:

- Full Control For Administrator
- Full Control For Local System
- Read, Write, And Delete Subfolders And Files For Network Service

Working with Connectivity Log Properties and Fields

Exchange Server creates connectivity logs daily and stores them in the C:\Program Files\Microsoft\Exchange Server\TransportRoles\Logs\Connectivity directory. Each log file is named by the date on which it was created, using the format CONNECTLOGYYYYMMDD-N.log, such as CONNECTLOG20080925-1.log for the first connectivity log created on September 25, 2008.

The connectivity log stores outgoing queue connection events on a single line. The information on a particular line is organized by comma-separated fields. Logs begin with a header that shows the following information:

- A statement that identifies the file as a connectivity log
- The date on which the log file was created
- The version of Exchange Server that created the file
- A comma-delimited list of fields contained in the body of the log file

Table 17-5 summarizes connectivity logging fields and their meanings. Not all of the fields are tracked for all outgoing queue connection events. You can view the connectivity log files with any standard text editor, such as Notepad. You can also import the connectivity log files into a spreadsheet or a database, as discussed previously.

Table 17-5   Connectivity Log Fields

Log Field	Description
Date-time	The date and time of the outgoing queue connection event.
Session	The globally unique identifier of the SMTP session. Each event for a particular session has the same identifier. For Messaging Application Programming Interface (MAPI) sessions, this field is blank.
Destination	The name of the destination Mailbox server, smart host, or domain.
Direction	The direction of the event: + for Connect, - for Disconnect, > for Send, and < for Receive.
Description	The data associated with the event, including the number and size of messages transmitted, Domain Name Server (DNS) mail exchanger (MX) information, connection success messages, and connection failure messages.

Monitoring Events, Services, Servers, and Resource Usage

As an Exchange administrator, you should routinely monitor event logs, services, servers, and resource usage. These elements are the keys to ensuring that the Exchange organization is running smoothly. Because you can't be on-site 24 hours a day, you can set alerts to notify you when problems occur.

Viewing Events

System and application events generated by Exchange Server are recorded in the Windows event logs. The primary log that you'll want to check is the application log. In this log, you'll find the key events recorded by Exchange Server services. Keep in mind that related events might be recorded in other logs, including the directory service, DNS server, security, and system logs. For example, if the server is having problems with a network card and this card is causing message delivery failures, you'll have to use the system log to pinpoint the problem.

You access the application log by completing the following steps:

1. Click Start, point to All Programs, point to Administrative Tools, and then select Computer Management.

2. If you want to view the logs on another computer, in the console tree, right-click the Computer Management entry, and choose Connect To Another Computer from the shortcut menu. You can now choose the server for which you want to manage logs.

3. Double-click the System Tools node, double-click Event Viewer, and then double-click the Windows Logs node. You should now see a list of logs.

4. Select the Application log, as shown in Figure 17-3.

Entries in the main panel of Event Viewer provide an overview of when, where, and how an event occurred. To obtain detailed information on an event, double-click its entry. The event level precedes the date and time of the event. Event levels include the following:

- **Information**   An informational event, generally related to a successful action.

- **Warning**   Details for warnings are often useful in preventing future system problems.

- **Error**   An error such as the failure of a service to start.

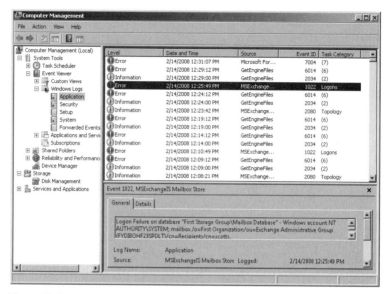

Figure 17-3 Event Viewer displays events for the selected log.

In addition to level, date, and time, the summary and detailed event entries provide the following information:

- **Source** The application, service, or component that logged the event.

- **Event ID** An identifier for the specific event.

- **Task Category** The category of the event, which is sometimes used to further describe the related action.

- **User** The user account that was logged on when the event occurred.

- **Computer** The name of the computer where the event occurred.

- **Description** In the detailed entries, this provides a text description of the event.

- **Data** In the detailed entries, this provides any data or error code output created by the event.

Use the event entries to detect and diagnose Exchange performance problems. Exchange-related event sources include the following:

- **Microsoft Forefront Security** Helps you track activities related to Microsoft Forefront Security and licensed antispam/antivirus engines. Watch for errors related to signature file updates for the antispam and antivirus engines. If you've improperly configured Microsoft Forefront Security, or if Microsoft Forefront Security is unable to access the Internet to retrieve updates, you'll see update errors. You'll see additional errors from the GetEngineFiles source because there are no updates to process. Additional related sources for Microsoft Forefront Security include: FSCController, FSCMonitor, FSCRealtimeScanner, FSCStatisticsService, FSCTransportScanner, FSEIMC, and FSEMailPickup.

- **MSExchangeIS, MSExchangeIS Mailbox Store, MSExchangeIS Public Store** Help you track activities related to the Microsoft Exchange Information Store service, mailbox stores and public folder stores. If a user is having problems logging on to Exchange, you may see multiple logon errors. You may also see lots of logon errors if someone is trying to hack into an Exchange mailbox.

- **ESE, ESE Backup, ESENT** Help you track activities related to the Extensible Storage Engine (ESE) used by Exchange Server 2007. Watch for logging and recovery errors, which may indicate a problem with the database engine; also watch for errors when the ESE backs up the information store. If you want to track the status of online defragmentation, look for Event ID 703.

- **EXCDO EXOLEDB** Helps you track activities related to the Exchange Calendaring agent and Exchange OLEDB respectively. Watch for initialization errors or other errors that may be indicative of problems with this features.

- **Exchange Migration** Helps you track import, export, and move operations related to Exchange mailboxes. When you are performing these tasks in the background or using scripts, watch for failure errors that may indicate that you need to repeat the procedure.

- **MSExchangeADAccess** Helps you track activities related to the Exchange Active Directory Provider, which is used for retrieving information for Active Directory and performing the DNS lookups that Exchange uses to locate domain controllers and global catalog servers. Watch for topology discovery failures and DNS lookup failures, which can indicate problems with the DNS configuration as well as with the Active Directory site configuration.

- **MSExchange Anti-Spam Update** Helps you track activities related to Windows Update. When you've configured Microsoft Exchange to use Windows Update to retrieve antispam updates, watch for errors regarding update failure. You may need to change the Windows Update configuration or the way updates are retrieved.

- **MSExchange Assistants, MSExchange System Attendant Mailbox** Help you track activities related to the Microsoft Exchange Mailbox Assistants service and the Microsoft Exchange System Attendant Mailbox feature respectively. The Microsoft Exchange Mailbox Assistants service performs background processing of mailboxes and public folder data in the Information Store. Watch for processing errors, which can indicate database structure problems. You can use the Exchange Server Database Utilities engine (eseutil.exe) to perform offline checks and repairs of database. After you create a backup of a database, use Eseutil /G to check for problems and Eseutil /P to repair the database. Additional related sources include MSExchangeMailboxAssistants and MSExchangeSA.

- **MS Exchange Edge Sync**   Helps you track activities related to edge synchronization processes. The Microsoft Exchange EdgeSync service uses the Exchange Active Directory Provider to obtain information about the Active Directory topology. If the service cannot locate a suitable domain controller, the service will fail to initialize and edge synchronization will fail as well.

- **MSExchange Messaging Policies**   Helps you track activities related to messaging policies, including transport and journal rules. Watch for load failures, which can indicate a configuration problem that needs to be resolved.

- **MS Exchange IMAP4, MS Exchange POP3, MS Exchange OWA**   Help you track activities related to IMAP4, POP3, and OWA respectively. Keep in mind Outlook Anywhere requires the RPC Over HTTP Proxy component. If you enable Outlook Anywhere but don't install this component, you'll see errors for the MSExchange RPC Over HTTP Autoconfig source stating the this component is not installed or is not configured correctly. Additional related sources include MS Exchange IMAP4 Service and MS Exchange POP3 Service.

- **MSExchange Transport Service, MSExchange Unified Messaging**   Help you track activities related to the Microsoft Exchange Transport service and the Microsoft Exchange Unified Messaging service respectively. Watch for errors that can indicate configuration issues. For example, if you haven't created a dial plan, you'll see errors for the Microsoft Exchange Unified Messaging service. Additional related sources include MSExchangeTransport, MSExchangeServiceHost, and MSExchangeMailSubmission.

- **MSExchangeFDS, MSExchangeRepl**   Help you track activities related to the Microsoft Exchange File Distribution service. This service is responsible for synchronizing Offline Address Books and generating related files for distribution. Watch for errors regarding synchronization and directory generation. The Microsoft Exchange File Distribution service generates OAB data in a subfolder of the OAB Distribution share. By default, this share is located under %SystemDrive%\Program Files\Microsoft\Exchange Server\ExchangeOAB. The Exchange Servers group must have read access to the share, the directory, and subdirectories of the directory. If for some reason the automatically generated directory is not created, you should create the required directory. The related error message provides the expected directory name.

Managing Essential Services

Most of Exchange Server's key components run as system services. If an essential service stops, its related functionality will not be available and Exchange Server won't work as expected. When you are troubleshooting Exchange Server problems, you'll want to check to ensure that essential services are running as expected early in your troubleshooting process. To manage system services, you'll use the Services node in the Computer Management console. You can start Computer Management and access the Services entry by completing the following steps:

1. Choose Start, choose Programs or All Programs as appropriate, point to Administrative Tools, and then select Computer Management. Or select Computer Management in the Administrative Tools folder.

2. If you want to manage the services on another computer, right-click the Computer Management entry in the console tree, and select Connect To Another Computer on the shortcut menu. You can now choose the system whose services you want to manage.

3. Expand the Services And Applications node, and then select Services.

As Figure 17-4 shows, you'll now see the available services. Services are listed by:

- **Name**   The name of the service.

- **Description**   A short description of the service and its purpose.

- **Status**   The status of the service. If the entry is blank, the service is stopped.

- **Startup Type**   The startup setting for the service.

- **Log On As**   The account the service logs on as. The default in most cases is the local system account.

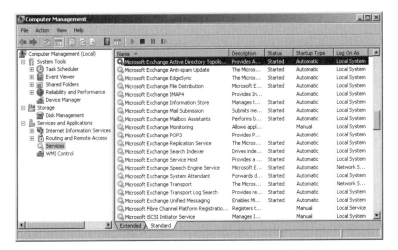

Figure 17-4   View the status of essential services during troubleshooting.

Tip   Any service that has a startup type of Automatic should have a status of Started. If a service has a startup type of Automatic and the status is blank, the service is not running and you should start it.

If a service is stopped and it should be started, you'll need to restart it. If you suspect a problem with a service, you may want to stop and then restart it. To start, stop, or restart a service, complete the following steps:

1. Access the Services node in the Computer Management console.

2. Right-click the service you want to manage, and then select Start, Stop, or Restart, as appropriate.

Monitoring Exchange Messaging Components

When you are troubleshooting or optimizing a server for performance, you can use performance monitoring to track the activities of Exchange messaging components. Performance Monitor graphically displays statistics for the set of performance parameters you've selected for display. These performance parameters are referred to as *counters*. Performance Monitor displays information for only the counters you're tracking. Thousands of counters are available, and these counters are organized into groupings called *performance objects*.

When you install Exchange Server 2007 on a computer, Performance Monitor is updated with a set of objects and counters for tracking Exchange performance. You'll find dozens of related performance objects for everything from the Microsoft Exchange Availability Service to the Microsoft Exchange Journaling Agent to Microsoft Exchange Outlook Web Access.

You can select which counters you want to monitor by completing the following steps:

1. In Exchange Management Console, select the Toolbox node, and then double-click Performance Monitor. This opens the Exchange Server Performance Monitor.

2. Select the System Monitor entry in the left pane, as shown in Figure 17-5.

3. The Performance Monitor tool has several views and view types. Ensure that you are viewing current activity by clicking View Current Activity on the toolbar or pressing Ctrl+T. You can switch between the view types, (Line, Histogram Bar, and Report) by clicking the Change Graph Type button or pressing Ctrl+G.

4. To add counters, click Add on the toolbar or press Ctrl+I. This displays the Add Counters dialog box shown in Figure 17-6.

5. In the Select Counters From Computer combo box, enter the Universal Naming Convention (UNC) name of the IIS server you want to work with, such as **MailServer18** or choose <Local computer> to work with the local computer.

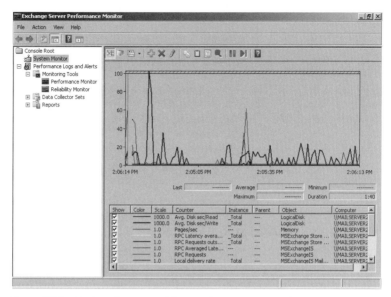

Figure 17-5   Track performance objects and counters to monitor server performance.

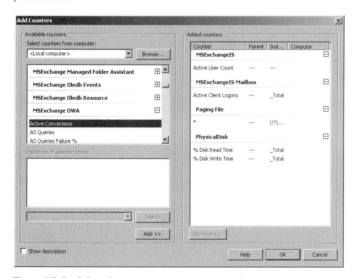

Figure 17-6   Select the counters you want to monitor.

> **Note** You'll need to be at least a member of the Performance Monitor Users group in the domain or the local computer to perform remote monitoring. When you use performance logging, you'll need to be at least a member of the Performance Log Users group in the domain or the local computer to work with performance logs on remote computers.

6. In the Available Counters panel, Performance Objects are listed alphabetically. If you select an object entry by clicking it, all related counters are selected. If you expand an object entry, you can see all the related counters and you can then select individual counters by clicking them. For example, you could expand the entry for the Active Server Pages object and then select Requests Failed Total, Requests Not Found, Requests Queued, and Requests Total counters.

7. When you select an object or any of its counters, you see the related instances. Choose All Instances to select all counter instances for monitoring. Or select one or more counter instances to monitor. For example, you could select instances of Anonymous Users/Sec for individual Web sites or for all Web sites.

8. When you've selected an object or a group of counters for an object as well as the object instances, click Add to add the counters to the graph. Repeat steps 5 through 7 to add other performance parameters.

9. Click Close when you're finished adding counters. You can delete counters later by clicking their entry in the lower portion of the Performance window and then clicking Delete.

Using Performance Alerting

In Windows Server 2008, Data Collector Sets are used to collect performance data. When you configure Data Collector Sets to alert you when specific criteria are met, you are using performance alerting. Windows performance alerting provides a fully automated method for monitoring server performance and reporting when certain performance thresholds are reached. You can use performance alerting to track the following:

- Memory usage
- CPU utilization
- Disk usage
- Messaging components

Using notifications, you can then provide automatic notification when a server exceeds a threshold value.

Tracking Memory Usage

Physical and virtual memory is critical to normal system operation. When a server runs low on memory, system performance can suffer and message processing can grind to a halt. To counter this problem, you should configure performance alerting to watch memory usage. You can then increase the amount of virtual memory available on the server or add additional random access memory (RAM) as needed.

You configure a memory alert by completing the following steps:

1. In Exchange Management Console, click the Toolbox node, and then double-click Performance Monitor. This opens the Exchange Server Performance Monitor.

2. Expand the Performance Logs And Alerts and the Data Collector Sets nodes, and then select User Defined. You should see a list of current alerts (if any) in the right pane.

3. Right-click the User-Defined node in the left pane, point to New, and then choose Data Collector Set.

4. In the Create New Data Collector Set Wizard, type a name for the Data Collector Set, such as **Memory Usage Alert**. Select the Create Manually option and then click Next.

5. On the What Type Of Data Do You Want To Include page, the Create Data Logs option is selected by default. Select the Performance Counter Alert check box and then click Next.

6. On the Which Performance Counters Would You Like To Log page, click Add. This displays the Add Counter dialog box. Because you are configuring memory alerts, expand the Memory object in the Performance Object list. Select Available Mbytes by clicking it, and then click Add.

7. Expand the Paging File object in the Performance Object list. Click %Usage. In the Instances Of Selected Object panel, select _Total, and then click Add. Click OK.

8. On the Which Performance Counters Would You Like To Log page, you'll see the counters you've added. In the Performance Counters panel, select Available Mbytes, as shown in Figure 17-7, and then set the Alert When list to Below, and then enter a Limit value that is approximately 5 percent of the total physical memory (RAM) on the server for which you are configuring alerting. For example, if the server has 2 GB of RAM, you would set the value to 100 MB to alert you when the server is running low on available memory.

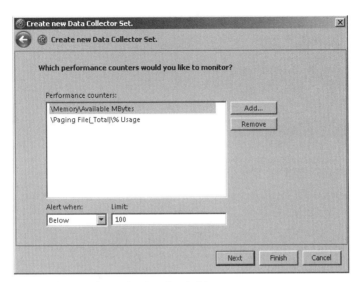

Figure 17-7   Configure the alert threshold.

9. In the Performance Counters panel, select %Usage. Set the Alert When list to Above, and then type **98** as the Limit value. This ensures that you are alerted when more than 98 percent of the paging file is being used.

10. Click Next and then click Finish. This saves the Data Collector Set and closes the wizard.

11. In the left pane, select the related Data Collector Set and then double-click the data collector for the alert in the main pane. This displays the data collector Properties dialog box.

12. On the Alerts tab, use the Sample Interval options to set a sample interval (see Figure 17-8). The sample interval specifies when new data is collected. Don't sample too frequently, however, because you'll use system resources and might cause the server to seem unresponsive. By default, the Performance Monitor will check the values of the configured counters every 15 seconds. A better value may be once every 10 to 30 minutes.

13. On the Alert Action tab, select the Log An Entry In The Application Event Log check box. Selecting this option ensures that an event is logged when the alert occurs.

14. Click OK to close the Properties dialog box. By default, alerting is configured to start manually. To start alerting, select the User Defined node in the left pane, click the alert in the main pane to select it, and then click the Start button on the toolbar.

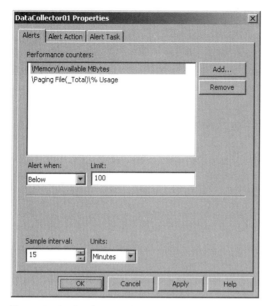

Figure 17-8   Set the sample interval.

To manage an alert, select the User Defined node in the left pane, right-click the alert in the main pane, and then select one of the following options:

- **Delete**   Deletes the alert.
- **Properties**   Displays the alert's Properties dialog box.
- **Start**   Activates alerting.
- **Stop**   Halts alerting.

Tracking CPU Utilization

You can use a CPU utilization alert to track the usage of a server's CPUs. When CPU utilization is too high, Exchange Server can't effectively process messages or manage other critical functions. As a result, performance can suffer greatly. CPU utilization at 100 percent for an extended period of time can be an indicator of serious problems on a server. Typically, you'll need to reboot a server when the CPU utilization is stuck at maximum utilization (100 percent).

You'll also want to closely track process threads that are waiting to execute. A relatively high number of waiting threads can be an indicator that a server's processors need to be upgraded.

You configure a CPU utilization alert by completing the following steps:

1. In Exchange Management Console, click the Toolbox node, and then double-click Performance Monitor. This opens the Exchange Server Performance Monitor.

2. Expand the Performance Logs And Alerts and the Data Collector Sets nodes, and then select User Defined. You should see a list of current alerts (if any) in the right pane.

3. Right-click the User-Defined node in the left pane, point to New, and then choose Data Collector Set.

4. In the Create New Data Collector Set Wizard, type a name for the Data Collector Set, such as **CPU Utilization Alert**. Select the Create Manually option and then click Next.

5. On the What Type Of Data Do You Want To Include page, the Create Data Logs option is selected by default. Select the Performance Counter Alert check box and then click Next.

6. On the Which Performance Counters Would You Like To Log page, click Add. This displays the Add Counter dialog box. Because you are configuring CPU alerts, expand the Processor object in the Performance Object list. Click % Processor Time. In the Instances Of Selected Object panel, select _Total, and then click Add.

7. Expand the System object in the Performance Object list. Click Processor Queue Length, and then click Add. Click OK.

8. On the Which Performance Counters Would You Like To Log page, you'll see the counters you've added. Select % Processor Time and then set the Alert When list to Above, and then type **98** as the Limit value. This ensures that you are alerted when processor utilization is more than 98 percent.

9. In the Performance Counters panel, select Processor Queue Length and then set the Alert When list to Above, and then type **10** as the Limit value. This ensures that you are alerted when more than 10 processes are waiting to execute, which can be an indicator that a server's processors need to be upgraded.

10. Click Next and then click Finish. This saves the Data Collector Set and closes the wizard.

11. Finish configuring the alert by following steps 10 through 14 under "Tracking Memory Usage."

Tracking Disk Usage

Exchange Server uses disk space for data storage, logging, tracking, and virtual memory. When hard disks run out of space, the Exchange server malfunctions and data gets lost. To prevent serious problems, you should monitor free disk space closely on all drives used by Exchange Server.

You'll also want to track closely the number of system requests that are waiting for disk access. A relatively high value for a particular disk can affect server performance and is also a good indicator that a disk is being overutilized. To resolve this problem, you'll want to try to shift part of the disk's workload to other disks.

You configure disk usage alerting by completing the following steps:

1. In Exchange Management Console, click the Toolbox node, and then double-click Performance Monitor. This opens the Exchange Server Performance Monitor.

2. Expand the Performance Logs And Alerts and the Data Collector Sets nodes, and then select User Defined. You should see a list of current alerts (if any) in the right pane.

3. Right-click the User-Defined node in the left pane, point to New, and then choose Data Collector Set.

4. In the Create New Data Collector Set Wizard, type a name for the Data Collector Set, such as **Disk Usage Alert**. Select the Create Manually option and then click Next.

5. On the What Type Of Data Do You Want To Include page, the Create Data Logs option selected by default. Select the Performance Counter Alert check box and then click Next.

6. On the Which Performance Counters Would You Like To Log page, click Add. This displays the Add Counter dialog box. Because you are configuring disk alerts, expand the LogicalDisk object in the Performance Object list. Click % Free Space. In the Instances Of Selected Object panel, select all individual logical disk instances except _Total, and then click Add.

7. Expand the PhysicalDisk object in the Performance Object list. Click Current Disk Queue Length. In the Instances Of Selected Object panel, select all individual physical disk instances except _Total, and then click Add. Click OK.

8. On the Which Performance Counters Would You Like To Log page, you'll see the counters you've added. Select the first logical disk instance and then set the Alert When list to Below, and then type **5** as the Limit value. This ensures that you are alerted when available free space is less than 5 percent. Repeat this procedure for each logical disk.

9. In the Performance Counters panel, select the first physical disk instance and then set the Alert When list to Above, and then type **2** as the Limit value. This ensures that you are alerted when more than two system requests are waiting for disk access. Repeat this procedure for each physical disk.

10. Click Next and then click Finish. This saves the Data Collector Set and closes the wizard.

11. Finish configuring the alert by following steps 10 through 14 under "Tracking Memory Usage."

Working with Queues

As an Exchange administrator, it's your responsibility to monitor Exchange queues regularly. Hub Transport and Edge Transport servers use queues to hold messages while they are processing them for routing and delivery. If messages remain in a queue for an extended period, there could be a problem. For example, if an Exchange server is unable to connect to the network, you'll find that messages aren't being cleared out of queues.

Understanding Exchange Queues

As discussed in the "Working with the Exchange Server Message Queues" section of Chapter 5, "Microsoft Exchange Server 2007 Administration Essentials," queues are temporary holding locations for messages that are waiting to be processed, and Exchange Server 2007 uses an Extensible Storage Engine (ESE) database for queue storage. Exchange Server 2007 uses the following types of queues:

- **Submission queue**   The submission queue is a persistent queue that is used by the Categorizer to store temporarily all messages that have to be resolved, routed, and processed by Transport agents. All messages that are received by a Transport server enter processing in the submission queue. Messages are submitted through SMTP-receive, the Pickup directory, or the store driver. Each Transport server has only one submission queue. Messages that are in the submission queue cannot be in other queues at the same time.

  Edge Transport servers use the Categorizer to route messages to the appropriate destinations. Hub Transport servers use the Categorizer to expand distribution lists, to identify alternative recipients, and to apply forwarding addresses. After the Categorizer retrieves the necessary information about recipients, it uses that information to apply policies, route the message, and perform content conversion. After categorization, the Transport server moves the message to a delivery queue or to the unreachable queue.

- **Mailbox delivery queue**   Mailbox delivery queues hold messages that are being delivered to a mailbox server by using encrypted Exchange RPC. Only Hub Transport servers have mailbox delivery queues, and they use the queue to store temporarily messages that are being delivered to mailbox recipients whose mailbox data is stored on a mailbox server that is located in the same site as the Hub Transport server. Hub Transport servers will have one mailbox delivery queue for each destination mailbox server associated with messages currently being routed. After queuing the message, the Hub Transport server delivers the messages to the distinguished name of the mailbox store.

■ **Remote delivery queue**   Remote delivery queues hold messages that are being delivered to a remote server by using SMTP. Both Hub Transport servers and Edge Transport servers can have remote delivery queues, and they use the queue to store temporarily messages that are being routed to remote destinations. On an Edge Transport server, these destinations are external SMTP domains or SMTP connectors. On a Hub Transport server, these destinations are outside the Active Directory site in which the Hub Transport server is located. Transport servers will have one remote delivery queue for each remote destination associated with messages currently being routed. After queuing the message, the Transport server delivers it to the appropriate domain, smart host, IP address, or Active Directory site.

■ **Poison message queue**   The poison message queue is used to hold messages that are detected to be potentially harmful to Exchange Server 2007 after a server failure. Messages that contain errors that are potentially fatal to Exchange Server 2007 are delivered to the poison message queue. Each Transport server has one poison message queue. While this queue is persistent, it typically is empty and, as a result, is not displayed in queue viewing interfaces. By default, all messages in the poison message queue are suspended and can be manually deleted.

■ **Unreachable queue**   The unreachable queue contains messages that cannot be routed to their destinations. Each Transport server has one unreachable queue. Although this queue is persistent, it typically is empty and, as a result, is not displayed in queue viewing interfaces.

When a Transport server receives a message, a transport mail item is created and saved in the appropriate queue within the queue database. Exchange Server assigns each mail item a unique identifier when it stores the mail item in the database. If a mail item is being routed to more than one recipient, the mail item can have more than one destination and, in this case, there will be a routed mail item for each destination. A routed mail item is a reference to the transport mail item, and it is the routed mail item that Exchange queues for delivery.

Accessing the Queue Viewer

You access system and link queues by completing the following steps:

1. In Exchange Management Console, select the Toolbox node, and then double-click Queue Viewer. This opens the Queue Viewer.

2. By default, the Queue Viewer connects to the queuing database on the local server (if applicable). To connect to a different server, on the Action menu, select Connect To Server. In the Connect To Server dialog box, click Browse. Select the Exchange Server with which you want to work, and then click OK. Click Connect.

3. As shown in Figure 17-9, the Queue Viewer provides an overview of the status of each active queue.

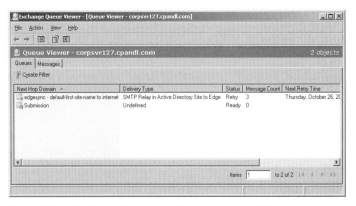

Figure 17-9   The Queue Viewer provides an overview of the status of each active queue.

❑   A folder icon indicates an active state.

❑   A folder icon with a green check mark indicates the queue has a reader status.

❑   A folder icon with a blue button and a small down arrow indicates a retry state.

❑   A folder icon with a red exclamation point indicates a warning state, such as Not Available or Error.

Managing Queues

You usually won't see messages in queues because they're processed and routed quickly. Messages come into a queue, Exchange Server performs a lookup or establishes a connection, and then Exchange Server either moves the message to a new queue or delivers it to its destination.

Understanding Queue Summaries and Queue States

Messages remain in a queue when there's a problem. To check for problem messages, use the Queue Viewer to examine the number of messages in the queues. If you see a queue with a consistent or growing number of messages, there might be a problem. Again, normally, messages should come into a queue and then be processed fairly quickly. Because of this, the number of messages in a queue should gradually decrease over time as the messages are processed, providing no new messages come into the queue.

Whenever you click the Queues tab in Queue Viewer, you get a summary of the currently available queues for the selected server. Although queue summaries provide important details for troubleshooting message flow problems, you do have to know what to look for. The connection status is the key information to look at first. This value tells you the state of the queue. States you'll see include these:

- **Ready**   A ready queue is needed to allow messages to be transported. When queues are ready, they can have a connection allocated to them.

- **Retry**   A connection attempt has failed and the server is waiting to retry.

- **Scheduled**   The server is waiting for a scheduled connection time.

- **Remote**   The server is waiting for a remote dequeue command (TURN/ETRN).

- **Suspended**   The queue is suspended, and none of its messages can be processed for routing. Messages can enter the queue, however, as long as the Exchange routing Categorizer is running. You must resume the queue to resume normal queue operations.

Administrators can choose to enable or disable connections to queues by suspending them. If a queue is suspended, it is unable to route and deliver messages.

You can change the queue state to Ready by clicking the Resume command. When you do this, Exchange Server should immediately enable the queue, which allows messages to be routed and delivered from it. If a queue is in the retry state, you can force an immediate retry using the Retry command.

Other summary information that you might find useful in troubleshooting includes:

- **Next Hop Domain**   Tells you the type of the queue, such as whether it is a submission queue or an unreachable queue. For mailbox delivery and remote delivery queues, this field tells you the next hop domain. Messages queued for delivery to an EdgeSync server list the associated site and destination, such as EdgeSync–Default-First-Site Name To Internet.

- **Message Count**   Tells you the total number of messages waiting in the queue. If you see a large number, you could have a connectivity or routing problem.

- **Next Retry Time**   When the connection state is Retry, this column tells you when another connection attempt will be made. You can click the Retry command to attempt a connection immediately.

- **Last Retry Time**   When the connection state is Retry, this column tells you when the last retry attempt was made.

- **Last Error**   Tells you the error code and details of the last error to occur in a particular queue. This can help you determine why a queue is having delivery problems.

Refreshing the Queue View

Use the queue summaries and queue state information to help you find queuing problems, as discussed in the earlier section of this chapter entitled, "Understanding Queue Summaries and Queue States." By default, the queue view is refreshed every 30 seconds and the maximum number of message items that can be listed on each page is 1,000.

To change the viewing options, follow these steps:

1. In Queue Viewer, on the View menu, click Options.

2. To turn off automatic refresh, clear the Auto-Refresh Screen check box. Otherwise, enable automatic refresh by selecting the Auto-Refresh Screen check box.

3. In the Refresh Interval text box, type a specific refresh rate in seconds.

4. Type the desired maximum number of messaging items to be displayed per page in the Number Of Items To Display text box. Click OK.

Working with Messages in Queues

To manage queues, you must enumerate messages. This process allows you to examine queue contents and perform management tasks on messages within a particular queue.

The easiest way to enumerate messages is to do so in sets of 1,000. To display the first 1,000 messages in a queue, follow these steps:

1. On the Queues tab in Queue Viewer, you should see a list of available queues. Double-click a queue to enumerate the first 1,000 messages, as shown in Figure 17-10.

2. After you enumerate messages in a queue, you can examine message details by double-clicking the entries for individual messages.

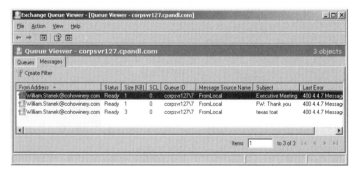

Figure 17-10 The Queue Viewer provides a summary for each message in a queue.

You can also create a filter to search for specific types of messages. To do this, follow these steps:

1. Double-click the queue with which you want to work. This enumerates the first 1,000 messages in the queue, as discussed previously.

2. If you haven't previously created a filter, click Create Filter.

3. Use the first selection list to specify the field you want to use for filtering messages. You can filter messages by: Date Received, Expiration Time, From Address, Internet Message ID, Last Error, Message Source Name, Queue ID, SCL, Size (KB), Source IP, Status, and Subject.

4. Use the second selection list to specify the filter criteria. The available filter criteria depend on the filter field and include: Equals, Does Not Equal, Contains, Does Not Contain, Greater Than, and Less Than.

5. Use the text box provided to specify the exact criteria to match. For example, if you are filtering messages using the Status field, you may want to see all messages where the Status field equals Retry. Your filter is automatically applied, and you can examine message details by double-clicking the entries for individual messages.

6. To stop filtering, click the Remove Filter button.

Forcing Connections to Queues

In many cases, you can change the queue state to Ready by forcing a connection. Simply right-click the queue, and then select Retry. When you do this, Exchange Server should immediately enable connections to the queue, and this should allow messages to be routed to and delivered from it.

Suspending and Resuming Queues

When you suspend a queue, all message transfer out of that queue stops. This means that messages can continue to enter the queue, but no messages will leave it. To restore normal operations, you must resume the queue.

You suspend and resume a queue by completing the following steps:

1. On the Queues tab in Queue Viewer, you should see a list of available queues. Right-click a queue, and then select Suspend.

2. When you're done troubleshooting, right-click the queue, and then select Resume.

Another way to suspend messages in a queue is to do so selectively. In this way, you can control the transport of a single message or several messages that might be causing problems on the server. For example, if a large message is delaying the delivery of other messages, you can suspend that message until other messages have left the queue. Afterward, you can resume the message to resume normal delivery.

To suspend and then resume individual messages, complete the following steps:

1. On the Queues tab in Queue Viewer, you should see a list of available queues. Double-click the queue with which you want to work.

2. Right-click the problem message, and then select Suspend. You can select multiple messages using Shift and Ctrl.

3. When you're ready to resume delivery of the message, right-click the problem message, and then select Resume.

Deleting Messages from Queues

You can remove messages from queues, if necessary. To do this, follow these steps:

1. On the Queues tab in Queue Viewer, you should see a list of available queues. Double-click the queue with which you want to work.

2. Right-click the problem message. You can select multiple messages using Shift and Ctrl, and then right-click. Select one of the following options from the shortcut menu:

   ❏ **Remove (With NDR)**   Deletes the selected messages from the queue and notifies the sender with a nondelivery report (NDR)

   ❏ **Remove (Without Sending NDR)**   Deletes the message(s) from the queue without sending an NDR to the sender

3. When prompted, click Yes to confirm the deletion.

Deleting messages from a queue removes them from the messaging system permanently. You can't recover the deleted messages.

Chapter 18

Backing Up and Restoring Microsoft Exchange Server 2007

Microsoft Exchange Server 2007 is critically important to your organization. If a mailbox server crashes, you are faced with the possibility of every user on that server losing days, weeks, or even months of work. If your primary Client Access server crashes and you don't have any alternates, users won't be able to remotely access messages, calendars, address lists, and more. If your primary Transport server crashes and you don't have any alternates, messages will not be properly routed and delivered. To ensure access to Exchange Server and protect your users' data, you need to extend your Exchange organization to meet the availability expectations and implement a backup and recovery plan. Backing up Exchange Server can protect against database corruption, hardware failures, accidental loss of user messages, and even natural disasters. As an administrator, your job is to make sure that backups are performed and that backup media are stored in a secure location.

Understanding the Essentials of Exchange Server Availability, Backup, and Recovery

Backing up and recovering Exchange data is a bit different from backing up other types of data, primarily because Exchange Server 2007 has different units of backup and recovery than Windows. You not only work with files and drives, you also work with the information store and the data structures it contains. As you know from previous chapters, the information store can contain one or more storage groups and, in turn, each storage group can contain one or more databases.

Ensuring Data Availability

With Exchange Server 2007, it is easier than ever to design a fault-tolerant architecture that ensures the availability of most messaging services. Simply by deploying multiple Hub Transports, Edge Transports, and Client Access servers and placing the additional servers within the appropriate Active Directory sites, you can ensure availability of key messaging services if a primary Hub Transport, Edge Transport, or Client Access server fails.

When it comes to mailbox servers, you can use several techniques to improve availability and avoid having to restore from backups, including:

- **Continuous replication** Exchange 2007 includes asynchronous log shipping technology that you can use to create and maintain a copy of a storage group. If you are using clustered mailbox servers, you can use cluster continuous replication or standby continuous replication to create a copy of a storage group on another server. If you are using nonclustered mailbox servers, you can use local continuous replication to create a copy of a storage group on another set of disks.

- **Deleted item retention**   Deleted item retention allows users themselves to restore a single item or entire folders in Microsoft Office Outlook.

- **Deleted mailbox retention**   Deleted mailbox retention allows administrators to restore deleted mailboxes without having to restore the mailboxes from backups.

- **Multiple mailbox databases**   By using multiple mailbox databases and distributing users across these databases, you can reduce significantly the impact of the loss of a single database and allow for faster restores when needed.

Backing Up Exchange Server: The Basics

To create a complete backup of an Exchange server, you must back up the following:

- Exchange configuration data, which includes the configuration settings for the Exchange organization. You take configuration settings from Active Directory and the Windows registry. Configuration data doesn't include any user data.

- Exchange user data, which includes Exchange mailbox databases, public folder databases, and transaction logs. If you want to be able to recover mailbox and public folder databases, you must back up this data. User data doesn't contain Exchange configuration settings.

- System State data for the operating system, which includes essential system files needed to recover the local system. All computers have System State data, which you must back up in addition to other files to restore a complete working system.

- Folders and drives that contain Windows and Exchange files. Normally, this means backing up the root drive C, which includes the special partition for Exchange Server.

Storage groups and databases are the units of backup and recovery for the information store. Storage groups are the smallest units of backup, and mailboxes are the smallest units of recovery. This means that you have the following backup and recovery options for the information store:

- Backup options
  - ❏ You can back up the entire information store.
  - ❏ You can back up sets of storage groups.
  - ❏ You can back up individual storage groups.

■ Recovery options

❑ You can recover the entire information store.

❑ You can recover sets of storage groups.

❑ You can recover individual storage groups.

❑ You can recover groups of databases.

❑ You can recover individual databases.

❑ You can recover individual mailboxes.

The ability to recover an individual database from backup is a great improvement over early releases of Exchange Server, but you should know about some fundamental issues before you try to do so. These issues pertain to transactions, transaction logs, and transaction logging modes.

Exchange Server uses transactions to control database changes. You can think of a transaction as a logical unit of work that contains one or more operations that affect the information store. If Exchange Server executes all of the operations in a transaction successfully, it marks the transaction as successful and permanently commits the changes. If one or more of the operations in a transaction fails to complete, Exchange Server marks the transaction as failed and removes any changes that the transaction created. The process of removing changes is referred to as *rolling back* the transaction.

Transaction logs are units of storage for transactions. Exchange Server writes each transaction to a log file and maintains the log files according to the logging mode. With standard logging, Exchange Server reserves 1 megabyte (MB) of disk space for the active transaction log. Exchange Server commits or rolls back transactions based on their success or failure. When the contents of the log reach 1 MB, Exchange Server creates a new log file. Because Exchange Server maintains the transaction logs until the next full backup, you can recover Exchange Server to the last transaction.

Note   The active transaction log is named E##.log, where ## is the unique identifier for the storage group. Additional transaction logs are named E##00000001.log, E##00000002.log, and so on.

The ability to recover mailboxes selectively from backup is an improvement over Exchange 2000 Server; as with recovering databases, you should know about some fundamental issues before you try to recover individual mailboxes. These issues pertain to recovery storage groups.

Recovery storage groups are special types of storage groups that Exchange Server reserves for recovery operations. Using a recovery storage group, you can restore mailboxes from any of the regular storage groups in an Exchange organization. You can recover individual or multiple mailboxes at the same time, provided that the databases for those mailboxes are in the same storage group. You cannot, however, use recovery storage groups to restore public folder databases. Because you link each recovery storage group to an existing storage group, you can mount only databases from the linked storage group in the recovery storage group.

Note   Don't confuse this recovery procedure with those used for disconnected mailbox recovery. You use disconnected mailbox recovery to recover deleted, disconnected, or otherwise unavailable mailboxes, as long as those mailboxes are available for recovery from an existing mailbox database. You use the recovery storage group to recover mailboxes from a previous backup of a mailbox database.

Creating a Disaster Recovery Plan Based on Exchange Roles

With Exchange Server 2007, you need to tailor your recovery plan to the roles installed on your Exchange servers. Because configuration data for Exchange Server 2007 is stored in Active Directory, you can fully restore some server roles by running the Exchange Setup program with the /mode:recoverserver command on a server. With other roles, running this command restores the Exchange configuration, but you will need to recover the critical Exchange data from backup.

Note   Recoverserver mode is only for recovering a server or moving a server to new hardware while maintaining the same server name. When you run Setup in this mode, Setup reads configuration data from Active Directory for a server with the same name as the server from which you are running Setup. This mode doesn't migrate custom settings stored locally or databases; it only migrates settings stored in Active Directory.

Use the following guidelines for your recovery planning:

- **Mailbox servers**   You cannot fully restore the Mailbox Server role by running the Exchange Setup program with the /mode:recoverserver command. You must restore mailbox servers from a backup that includes the necessary Exchange data and the System State data. Mailbox servers store Exchange database files, including both mailbox and public folder databases, and Exchange transaction log files specific to each storage group. You must back up these files with an Exchange-aware backup application. You can also rebuild replicated public folder data through the normal replication process if there are available replicas. Mailbox servers also store full-text indexing information specific to each mailbox database in a storage group. You do not need to back up full-text indexes, because you need to rebuild them, as discussed in the "Content Indexing" section of Chapter 11, "Managing Microsoft Exchange Server 2007 Data and Storage Groups." Other types of Exchange databases on mailbox servers include: free/busy information and the Offline Address Book (OAB). This information can be rebuilt by automated maintenance and then replicated.

- **Hub Transport servers**   You can restore the Hub Transport Server role and make it fully functional by running Exchange Setup with the /mode:recoverserver command. Hub Transport servers store all essential configuration data in Active Directory. These servers also store some limited configuration data in the registry. You back up the registry when you perform a System State data backup. In addition to configuration data, Hub Transport servers store queues in database files and any logs you've enabled, including message tracking, protocol, and connectivity logs. Queues store messages actively being processed, and logs are primarily used for historical reference and troubleshooting. Queues and logs are not essential to restoring Hub Transport server functionality. That said, you could mount message queues on a new server if you recover them from a failed server.

- **Edge Transport servers**   The Edge Transport Server role is designed to function on a stand-alone server. Edge Transport servers store configuration data, queues, replicated data from Active Directory, and any logs you've enabled, including message tracking, protocol, and connectivity logs. These servers also store some limited configuration data in the registry. You back up the registry when you perform a System State data backup. Replicated data from Active Directory is stored in Active Directory Application Mode (ADAM). Queues store messages actively being processed, and logs are primarily used for historical reference and troubleshooting. Replicated data, queues, and logs are not essential to restoring Edge Transport server functionality. Replicated data can be resynchronized as necessary, and both queues and logs are created automatically as necessary. If you've applied custom settings to an Edge Transport server, such as those for content filtering, you can create a backup of the configuration, as discussed in the "Cloning Edge Transport Server Configurations" section of this chapter.

- **Client Access servers**   You can restore the Client Access Server role to its initial default state by running Exchange Setup with the /mode:recoverserver command. However, any custom changes you've made to Hypertext Transfer Protocol (HTTP) virtual servers running on a Client Access server are not restored. Changes to HTTP virtual servers are stored in the Internet Information Server configuration data. Although you could restore the IIS configuration data from backup to recover the custom settings, this is not recommended, as you may experience errors on the Client Access server if the IIS configuration data and the recovered Active Directory settings aren't exactly in sync. These servers store some limited configuration data in the registry. You back up the registry by performing a System State data backup. To restore a Client Access server, you can build a new server with a new name by running Exchange Setup, or you can restore the old server with the same name by running Exchange Setup with the /mode:recoverserver command. When Setup finishes, you then need to apply the same customizations that you had on the server before, re-creating additional Web sites and virtual directories as necessary. To apply the setting changes, you should restart IIS.

■ **Unified Messaging servers**   The Unified Messaging Server role stores all of its essential configuration data in Active Directory, and you can restore a server restored to its initial default state by running the Exchange Setup program with the /mode:recoverserver command. Unified Messaging servers store some limited configuration data in the registry. You can back up the registry by performing a System State data backup. In addition to configuration data, Unified Messaging (UM) servers store queues in database files and any logs you've enabled. Queues store messages actively being processed, and logs are primarily used for historical reference and troubleshooting. Queues and logs are not essential to restoring UM server functionality. You can mount message queues on a new server if you can recover them from a failed server. In addition, you can restore any custom audio files used for prompts automatically through replication if you have other UM servers in the organization.

Finalizing Your Exchange Server Disaster Recovery Plan

As you've seen, creating a backup and recovery plan for Exchange Server 2007 requires forethought on your part. As part of your planning, you also need take a close look at the overall architecture of your Exchange organization and make any changes required to ensure that the architecture meets the availability and recoverability expectations of your bosses. You need to review:

■ The number of Exchange servers to use in your organization. Do you need multiple servers to ensure high availability? Do you need multiple servers to improve performance? Do you need multiple servers because the organization spans several geographic areas?

■ The number of storage groups for each Exchange server, as well as how the groups are organized. Do you need to create storage groups for each department or division in the organization? Do you need to create storage groups for different business functions? Do you need to create separate storage groups for public folders and other types of data?

■ The number and type of databases for each storage group. Do you need to create separate databases for different departments, divisions, and business functions? Do you need to create separate databases for different types of public folder data?

After you've reviewed the architecture of the Exchange organization and implemented any necessary changes, you can create a backup and recovery plan to support that organization. You'll need to figure out what data you need to back up, how often you should back up the data, and more. To help you create a plan, consider the following:

■ **How important is the mailbox or public folder database you're backing up?** The importance of the data can go a long way in helping you determine when and how you should back up the database. For critical data, such as a department's mailbox database, you'll want to have redundant backup sets that extend back for several backup periods. For less important data, such as public folders for nonessential documents, you won't need such an elaborate backup plan, but you'll need to back up the data regularly and ensure that you can recover the data easily.

- **How quickly do you need to recover the data?** Time is an important factor in creating a backup plan. You might need to get critical data, such as the primary mailbox database, back online swiftly. To do this, you might need to alter your backup plan. For example, you might need to create multiple mailbox databases and place them in different storage groups on different servers. You can then recover individual databases, individual storage groups, or individual servers as the situation warrants.

- **Do you have the equipment to perform backups?** If you don't have backup hardware, you can't perform backups. To perform timely backups, you might need several backup devices and several sets of backup media. Backup hardware includes tape drives, tape library systems, storage arrays, and removable disk drives.

- **Who will be responsible for the backup and recovery plan?** Ideally, someone should be the primary contact for the Exchange backup and recovery plan. This person might also be responsible for performing the actual backup and recovery of Exchange Server.

- **What is the best time to schedule backups?** Scheduling backups when system use is as low as possible speeds up the backup process. However, because you can't always schedule backups for off-peak hours, you'll need to carefully plan when you back up data.

- **Do you need to store backups off-site?** Storing copies of backup tapes off-site is essential to recovering Exchange Server in the case of a natural disaster. In your off-site storage location, you should also include copies of all the software you might need to recover Exchange Server.

Choosing Backup Options

As you'll find when you work with data backup and recovery, there are many techniques for backing up data. The techniques you use depend on the type of data you're backing up, how convenient you want the recovery process to be, and other factors.

You can perform backups online (with Exchange services running) or offline (with Exchange services stopped). With online backups, you can archive the following:

- Exchange configuration data

- Exchange user data

- System State data

- Files and folders that contain Windows and Exchange files

With offline backups, you can't archive Exchange configuration or user data. This means that you can only archive the following:

- System State data

- Files and folders that contain Windows and Exchange files

Real World   With Exchange Server 2007 running on Microsoft Windows Server 2003 or later, you have the option of using the Volume Shadow Copy Service (VSS) to perform online backups. VSS creates point-in-time snapshots of data at the beginning of the backup process. The snapshot data is then used to create the backup rather than working with the server's hard disk. This allows normal operations to continue while the backup occurs and ensures that the backup is consistent, even if the data changes while the backup is in progress. Shadow copies of Exchange data can be made only if the backup software you are using supports the Exchange VSS extensions.

The basic types of backups you'll want to perform with Exchange Server are as follows:

- **Normal/full backups**   Back up all Exchange data that has been selected, including the related databases and the current transaction logs. A normal backup tells Exchange Server you've performed a complete backup, which allows Exchange Server to clear out the transaction logs.

- **Copy backups**   Back up all Exchange data that has been selected, including the related databases and the current transaction logs. Unlike a normal backup, a copy backup doesn't tell Exchange Server you've performed a complete backup and, as a result, the backup does not clear the log files. This allows you to perform other types of Exchange backups later.

- **Differential backups**   Designed to create backup copies of all data that has changed since the last normal backup. Backs up only transaction log files and not the actual databases. Does not clear the log files. To recover Exchange Server, you must apply the most recent normal backup and the most recent differential backup.

- **Incremental backups**   Designed to create backups of data that has changed since the most recent normal or incremental backup. Backs up only transaction log files and not the actual databases. Clears the log files after the incremental backup completes. To recover Exchange Server, you must apply the most recent full backup and then apply each incremental backup after the full backup. You must apply transaction logs in order.

In your backup plan, you'll probably want to perform full backups on a weekly basis and supplement them with nightly differential or incremental backups. You might also want to create an extended backup set for monthly and quarterly backups that you rotate to off-site storage.

Performing Backup and Recovery on Windows Server 2003

Windows Server 2003 provides a backup utility called Backup for creating backups on local and remote systems. Backup has special extensions that allow you to create online backups of Exchange Server 2007. You use Backup to do the following:

- Archive Exchange configuration and user data

- Access media pools reserved for Backup

- Access remote Exchange servers through My Network Places

- Create snapshots of the System State for backup and restore

- Schedule backups through the Task Scheduler

- Recover Exchange configuration and user data

You create backups using the Backup utility's Backup tab or the Backup Wizard. Both techniques make use of default options set for the Backup utility. You can view or change the default options by clicking Tools and then selecting Options. The account you use for backup and restore should be a member of both the Backup Operators and Server Operators groups.

Getting Started with the Backup Utility for Windows Server 2003

You can access the Backup utility in several ways:

- On the Start menu, select Run. In the Run dialog box, type **ntbackup,** and then click OK.

- On the Start menu, select Programs or All Programs as appropriate, select Accessories, select System Tools, and then select Backup.

The first time you use the Backup utility, it starts in basic wizard mode. As an administrator, you'll want to use advanced mode, because it gives you more options. Clear the Always Start In Wizard Mode check box, and then click Advanced Mode. You should now see the main Backup utility interface. As shown in Figure 18-1, the standard interface has the following four tabs, which provide easy access to key features:

- **Welcome**   Introduces Backup and provides buttons for starting the Backup Wizard, the Restore Wizard, and the Automated System Recovery Wizard.

- **Backup**   Provides the main interface for selecting data to back up. You can back up data on local and mapped network drives.

- **Restore And Manage Media** Provides the main interface for restoring archived data. You can restore data to the original location or to an alternate location anywhere on the network.

- **Schedule Jobs** Provides a month-by-month job schedule for backups. You can view executed jobs as well as jobs scheduled for future dates.

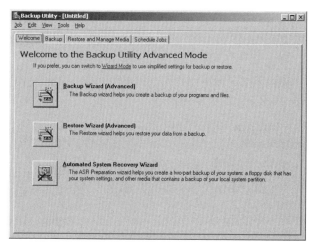

Figure 18-1   The Windows Backup utility provides a user-friendly interface for backup and restore.

Backing Up Exchange Server with the Backup Wizard

The procedures you use to work with the Backup Wizard are similar to those you use to back up data manually. You can perform backups with Exchange Server online or offline. For online backups, verify that the Exchange System Attendant and Microsoft Information Store services are running before starting a backup. For offline backups, verify that all Exchange services are stopped before performing a backup.

You start and work with the wizard by completing the following steps:

1. Start the Backup utility in advanced mode. On the Welcome tab, click Backup Wizard. If wizard mode is enabled, click Advanced Mode, and then click Backup Wizard.

2. Click Next. Select Back Up Selected Files, Drives, Or Network Data, and then click Next again.

3. As shown in Figure 18-2, choose the user data you want to back up. You make selections by selecting or clearing the check boxes associated with a particular drive or folder. When you select a top-level folder, all the subfolders are selected.

When you clear a check box for a top-level folder, check boxes for the related subfolders are cleared as well. Key backup options for Exchange Server are as follows:

❑ To create a full backup that includes all Exchange servers in the organization, you need to select the Microsoft Information Store node of each individual server. Expand Microsoft Exchange Server, expand the node for the first server that you want to back up, and then select the Microsoft Information Store check box. Afterward, expand the node for the next server that you want to back up, and then select the Microsoft Information Store check box, and so on.

❑ To back up specific Exchange servers, expand Microsoft Exchange Server, expand the node for the server that you want to back up, and then select the Microsoft Information Store check box.

❑ To back up all user databases on a specific Exchange server, expand Microsoft Exchange Server, expand the node for the server that you want to back up, and then select the Microsoft Information Store check box.

❑ To back up individual databases on an Exchange server, expand Microsoft Exchange Server, expand a server, expand Information Store, expand the storage group you want to work with, and then select the check box for the database you want to back up.

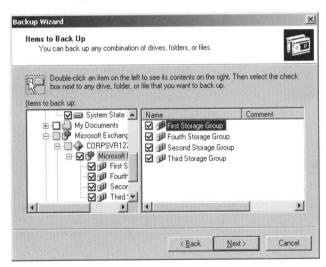

Figure 18-2   Choose the Exchange data to back up.

4. If you want to back up configuration data, choose additional items. Key options are as follows:

   ❑ To back up Exchange Server 2007 and Windows settings, select all hard disk drives where Windows and Exchange Server are installed. Normally, this means backing up the root of the C drive and the drives used by Exchange Server.

   ❑ To back up the Windows registry and Active Directory settings, expand My Computer, and then select the System State check box. System State data includes essential system files needed to recover the local system. All computers have System State data, which you must back up in addition to other files to restore a complete working system.

5. Click Next, and then select the Backup Media Type. Choose File if you want to back up to a file. Choose a storage device if you want to back up files and folders to a tape or removable disk.

6. Select the backup file or media you want to use. If you're backing up to a file, select a location from those available, or click Browse to specify a file location and name. If you're backing up to a tape or removable disk, choose the tape or disk you want to use. Afterward, type a name for the backup you are creating, such as **Exchange Backup January 2008**.

   Note   When you write backups to a file, the backup file normally has the .bkf file extension. You can use another file extension if you want. Note also that you use Removable Storage to manage tapes and removable disks.

7. Click Next. Click Advanced if you want to override default options or schedule the backup to be run as a job. Then follow steps 8 through 11. Otherwise, skip to step 12.

8. Select the type of backup to perform. The available types are: Normal, Copy, Differential, Incremental, and Daily. Click Next.

9. You can now set the following options for verification and compression, and then click Next:

   ❑ **Verify Data After Backup**   Instructs Backup to verify data after the backup procedure is completed. If you select this option, every file on the backup tape is compared to the original file. Verifying data can protect against write errors or failures, but requires more time than a backup without verification.

   ❑ **If Possible, Compress The Backup Data To Save Space**   Allows Backup to compress data as it's written to the storage device. This option is available only if the device supports hardware compression, and only if the drives are compatible to read the compressed information, which might mean that only a drive from the same manufacturer can recover the data.

10. Set options for copying data to the designated file, tape, or removable disk. To add the backup after existing data, select Append This Backup To The Existing Backups. To overwrite existing data, select Replace The Existing Backups. If you're overwriting data, you can specify that only the owner and an administrator can access the archive file by selecting the Allow Only The Owner And Administrator Access To The Backup Data check box. Click Next.

11. Determine when the backup will run. Select Now to run the backup now, and then click Next. Select Later to schedule the backup for a specific date. If you want to schedule the backup for a later date, type a job name, click Set Schedule, set a run schedule, and then click OK. When you click Next, if you've scheduled the backup, you'll have to enter an account name and password to add it to the schedule. This account must have Backup Operator privileges or be a member of a group that has Backup Operator privileges.

12. Click Finish to start the backup. You can cancel the backup by clicking Cancel in the Backup Progress dialog box. When the backup completes, click Close to complete the process, or click Report to view the backup log.

Note Backup selection scripts and backup logs are stored in %Userprofile%\Local Settings\Application Data\Microsoft\WindowsNT\NTBackup\Data. Backup selection scripts are saved with the .bks extension. Backup logs are saved with the .log extension. You can view these files with any standard text editor, such as Microsoft Notepad.

Backing Up Exchange Server Manually

You don't have to use a wizard to back up Exchange Server 2007. You can perform backups with Exchange Server online or offline, provided that you keep in mind the following:

- You can perform online backups only when key Exchange services are running. Verify that the Exchange System Attendant and Microsoft Information Store services are running before starting a backup.

- You can perform offline backups only when all Exchange services are stopped. Verify that all Exchange services are stopped before starting a backup.

You can configure backups manually by completing the following steps:

1. Start Backup. If wizard mode is enabled, click Advanced Mode, and then click the Backup tab, shown in Figure 18-3. Otherwise, just click the Backup tab.

2. Clear any existing selections on the Backup tab by selecting New from the Job menu and clicking Yes when prompted.

3. Select the items you want to back up by selecting or clearing the check boxes associated with a particular drive or folder. When you select a top-level folder, all

the subfolders are selected. When you clear a check box for a top-level folder, check boxes for the related subfolders are cleared as well. Key backup options for Exchange Server are as follows:

❑ To create a full backup that includes all Exchange servers in the organization, you need to select the Microsoft Information Store node of each individual server. Expand Microsoft Exchange Server, expand the node for the first server that you want to back up, and then select the Microsoft Information Store check box. Afterward, expand the node for the next server that you want to back up, select the Microsoft Information Store check box, and so on.

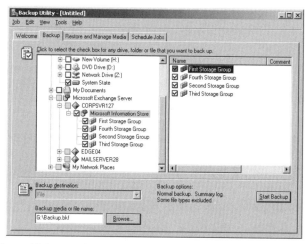

Figure 18-3 Use the Backup tab to configure backups by hand, and then click Start Backup.

❑ To back up specific Exchange servers, expand Microsoft Exchange Server, expand the node for the server that you want to back up, and then select the Microsoft Information Store check box.

❑ To back up all user databases on a specific Exchange server, expand Microsoft Exchange Server, expand the node for the server that you want to back up, and then select the Microsoft Information Store check box.

❑ To back up individual databases on an Exchange server, expand Microsoft Exchange Server, expand a server, expand Information Store, expand the storage group with which you want to work, and then select the check box for the database you want to back up.

4. If you want to back up configuration data, choose additional items. The key options are as follows:

   ❑ To back up Exchange Server 2007 and Windows settings, select all hard disk drives where Windows and Exchange Server are installed. Normally, this means backing up the root of the C drive and the drives used by Exchange Server.

   ❑ To back up the Windows registry and Active Directory settings, expand My Computer, and then select the System State check box. System State data includes essential system files needed to recover the local system. All computers have System State data, which you must back up in addition to other files to restore a complete working system.

5. Use the Backup Destination drop-down list to choose the media type for the backup. Choose File if you want to back up to a file. Choose a storage device if you want to back up files and folders to a tape or removable disk.

   Note   When you write backups to a file, the backup file normally has the .bkf file extension. You can use another file extension if you want. Note also that you use Removable Storage to manage tapes and removable disks.

6. In Backup Media Or File Name, select the backup file or media you want to use. If you're backing up to a file, type a path and filename for the backup file, or click Browse to find a file. If you're backing up to a tape or removable disk, choose the tape or disk you want to use.

7. Click Start Backup. The Backup Job Information dialog box appears, shown in Figure 18-4. You use the options in this dialog box as follows:

   ❑ **Backup Description**   Sets the backup label, which applies to the current backup only.

   ❑ **Append This Backup To The Media**   Adds the backup after existing data.

   ❑ **Replace The Data On The Media With This Backup**   Overwrites existing data.

   ❑ **If The Media Is Overwritten, Use This Label To Identify The Media**   Sets the media label, which is changed only when you're writing to a blank tape or overwriting existing data.

8. Click Advanced if you want to override the default options. The advanced options are as follows:

   ❑ **Back Up Data That Is In Remote Storage**   Archives placeholder files for Remote Storage with the backup. This ensures that you can recover an entire file system with necessary Remote Storage references intact.

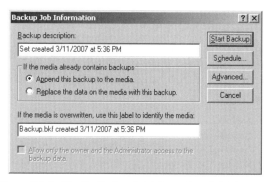

Figure 18-4   Use the Backup Job Information dialog box to configure backup options and information as necessary, and then click Start Backup.

❏ **Verify Data After Backup**   Instructs Backup to verify data after the backup procedure is completed. If you select this check box, Backup compares every file on the backup tape to the original file. Verifying data can protect against write errors or failures.

❏ **If Possible, Compress The Backup Data To Save Space**   Allows Backup to compress data as it's written to the storage device. This option is available only if the device supports hardware compression, and only if the drives are compatible to read the compressed information, which might mean that only a drive from the same manufacturer can recover the data.

❏ **Automatically Back Up System Protected Files With The System State**   Backs up all the system files in the %SystemRoot% folder in addition to the boot files that are included with the System State data.

❏ **Backup Type**   The type of backup to perform. The available types are: Normal, Copy, Differential, Incremental, and Daily.

9. Click Schedule if you want to schedule the backup for a later date. When prompted to save the backup settings, click Yes. Type a name for the backup selection script, and then click Save. In the Set Account Information dialog box, type the account name and password to run the scheduled backup job. In the Scheduled Job Options dialog box, type a job name, click Properties, and then set a run schedule. Skip the remaining steps.

> **Note**   Backup selection scripts and backup logs are stored in %Userprofile%\ Local Settings\Application Data\Microsoft\WindowsNT\NTBackup\Data. Backup selection scripts are saved with the .bks extension. Backup logs are saved with the .log extension. You can view these files with any standard text editor, such as Notepad.

10. Click Finish to start the backup operation. You can cancel the backup by clicking Cancel in the Set Information and Backup Progress dialog boxes.

11. When the backup is completed, click Close to complete the process, or click Report to view the backup log.

Recovering Exchange Server on Windows Server 2003

With the Windows Backup utility, you can restore Exchange Server 2007 using the Restore Wizard or the Restore tab within the Backup program. You can perform recovery on individual databases and storage groups or on all databases on a particular server. The recovery procedure you use depends on the types of backups you have available.

If you use normal backups and differential backups, you can recover an Exchange database or storage group to the point of failure by completing the following steps:

1. Restore the most recent normal (full) backup, as described in the sections of this chapter entitled "Recovering Exchange Server with the Restore Wizard" or "Recovering Exchange Server Manually." Don't set the Last Backup Set option, and don't mount the database after restore.

2. Restore the most recent differential backup as described in the sections of this chapter entitled "Recovering Exchange Server with the Restore Wizard" and "Recovering Exchange Server Manually." Be sure to set the Last Backup Set option and mount the database after restore. This starts the log file replay after the restore completes.

3. Check the related mailbox and public folder databases to make sure that the data recovery was successful.

If you use normal backups and incremental backups, you can recover an Exchange database or storage group to the point of failure by completing the following steps:

1. Restore the most recent normal (full) backup, as described in the sections of this chapter entitled "Recovering Exchange Server with the Restore Wizard" and "Recovering Exchange Server Manually." Don't set the Last Backup Set option, and don't mount the database after restore.

2. Apply each incremental backup in order. Restore the first incremental backup created after the normal backup, then the second, and so on, as described in the sections of this chapter entitled "Recovering Exchange Server with the Restore Wizard" and "Recovering Exchange Server Manually."

3. When restoring the last incremental backup, be sure to set the Last Backup Set option and mount the database after restore. This starts the log file replay after the restore completes.

4. Check the related mailbox and public folder databases to make sure that the data recovery was successful.

Recovering Exchange Server with the Restore Wizard

To recover Exchange Server 2007 with the Restore Wizard, follow these steps:

1. Restore system and configuration data before restoring the user data by following these instructions:

   ❑ When restoring configuration data, stop all services being used by Exchange Server, as well as all IIS services—IIS Admin and World Wide Web Publishing Service. Exit Exchange Management Console. Restart the Microsoft Exchange Information Store service.

   ❑ When restoring user data, dismount the affected databases before starting the recovery operation. During recovery, Exchange services are stopped temporarily.

   ❑ When recovering an entire server, make sure that you restore drives, System State data, Exchange configuration data, and Exchange user data.

2. Start the Backup utility in advanced mode. On the Welcome tab, click Restore Wizard. If wizard mode is enabled, click Advanced Mode, click Restore Wizard, and then click Next.

3. As shown in Figure 18-5, you can now choose the data you want to restore. The left view displays files organized by volume. The right view displays media sets. If the media set you want to work with isn't shown, or if there is no media information, click Browse, and then type the path to the catalog for the backup.

   ❑ To recover Exchange data, select the information store storage groups you want to restore. You must select each storage group individually. If you want to restore an individual mailbox database or the log files for a storage group, expand the Storage Group node, and then select the mailbox database and Log File nodes, as appropriate.

   ❑ To recover regular file data, select the check box next to any drive, folder, or file that you want to restore. You can't restore regular file data and Exchange data in the same operation. You need to restore each in turn and probably want to start with the regular file data.

   ❑ To restore System State data, select the System State check box and check boxes for other data you want to restore. If you're restoring to the original location, the current system state is replaced by the System State data you're restoring. If you restore to an alternate location, only the registry, system volume, and system boot files are restored. You can restore System State data only on a local system.

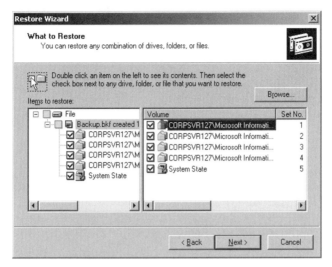

Figure 18-5   In the Restore Wizard, select the Exchange data you want to restore.

> **Tip**   By default, Active Directory and other replicated data, such as Sysvol, aren't restored on domain controllers. This information is instead replicated to the domain controller after you restart it, which prevents accidentally overwriting essential domain information.

4. Click Next. In the Restore To text box, type the name of the computer on which you want to restore files, such as **Mailer1**, or click Browse to search for the computer.

5. In the Temporary Location For Log And Patch Files text box, type the folder path for a temporary restore location, such as **C:\Temp**.

6. If this is the last backup set you need to recover, select the Last Restore Set and Mount Database After Restore check boxes.

7. Click Next. If they're available, you can choose to restore security and system files using the following check boxes:

   ❑ **Restore Security Settings**   Restores security settings for Exchange data, files, and folders on New Technology File System (NTFS) volumes.

   ❑ **Restore Junction Points, Not The Folders And File Data They Reference**
   Restores network drive mappings, but doesn't restore the actual data to the mapped network drive. Essentially, you're restoring the folder that references the network drive.

   ❑ **Preserve Existing Volume Mount Points**   Ensures that existing mount points are preserved during the restore operation.

❑ **When Restoring Replicated Data Sets, Mark The Restored Data As The Primary Data For All Replicas**   Useful if you're restoring replicated data and want the restored data to be published to subscribers. If you don't choose this option, the data might not be replicated, because it will appear older than existing data on the subscribers.

8. Click Next, and then click Finish. If prompted, type the path and name of the backup set to use. You can cancel the backup by clicking Cancel in the Operation Status and Restore Progress dialog boxes.

9. When the restore is completed, click Close to complete the process or click Report to view a backup log containing information about the restore operation.

Always check the related mailbox and public folder databases to make sure that the data recovery was successful.

Recovering Exchange Server Manually

You don't have to use the Restore Wizard to recover Exchange Server 2007. You can recover Exchange data manually by completing the following steps:

1. Restore system and configuration data before restoring the user data by following these instructions:

   ❑ When restoring configuration data, stop all services being used by Exchange Server, as well as all IIS services (IIS Admin and World Wide Web Publishing Service). Exit Exchange Management Console. Restart the Microsoft Exchange Information Store service.

   ❑ When restoring user data, dismount the affected databases before starting the recovery operation. During recovery, Exchange services are stopped temporarily.

   ❑ When recovering an entire server, make sure that you restore drives, System State data, Exchange configuration data, and Exchange user data.

2. Start Backup. If wizard mode is enabled, click Advanced Mode, and then click the Restore And Manage Media tab. Otherwise, just click the Restore And Manage Media tab.

3. Choose the data you want to restore, as shown in Figure 18-6. The left view displays files organized by volume. The right view displays media sets. If the media set you want to work with isn't shown, or if there is no media information, right-click File in the left pane, and then select Catalog File. You can then type the path to the catalog for the backup:

   ❑ To recover Exchange data, select the check boxes for the information store storage groups you want to restore. You must select each storage group individually. If you want to restore an individual mailbox database or the log files for a storage group, expand the storage group node, and then select the mailbox database and log file node check boxes, as appropriate.

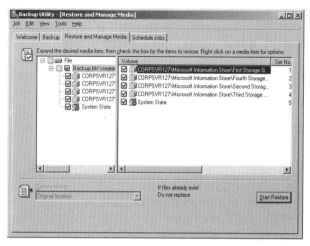

Figure 18-6   Use the Restore And Manage Media tab to specify the Exchange data to restore.

❏   To recover regular file data, select the check box next to any drive, folder, or file that you want to restore. You can't restore regular file data and Exchange data in the same operation. You need to restore each in turn and probably want to start with the regular file data.

❏   To restore System State data, select the System State check box and check boxes for other data you want to restore. If you're restoring to the original location, the current system state is replaced by the System State data you're restoring. If you restore to an alternate location, only the registry, Sysvol, and system boot files are restored. You can restore System State data only on a local system.

Tip   By default, Active Directory and other replicated data, such as Sysvol, aren't restored on domain controllers. Instead, this information is replicated to the domain controller after you restart it, which prevents accidentally over-writing essential domain information.

4. Use the Restore Files To drop-down list to choose the restore location. The options are as follows:

❏   **Original Location**   Restores data to the folder or files it was in when it was backed up.

❑ **Alternate Location**   Restores data to a folder that you designate, thereby preserving the directory structure. After you select this option, enter the folder path to use or click Browse to select the folder path.

❑ **Single Folder**   Restores all files to a single folder without preserving the directory structure. After you select this option, enter the folder path to use or click Browse to select the folder path.

5. Specify how you want to restore files. Click Tools, and then select Options. The Options dialog box appears with the Restore folder selected. The available options are as follows:

❑ **Do Not Replace The Files On My Computer (Recommended)**   Select this option if you don't want to copy over existing files.

❑ **Replace The File On Disk Only If The File On Disk Is Older**   Select this option to replace older files on disk with newer files from the backup.

❑ **Always Replace The File On My Computer**   Select this option to replace all files on disk with files from the backup.

6. Click Start Restore. The Restoring Database Store dialog box appears.

7. In the Restore To text box, type the name of the computer on which you want to restore files, such as **Mailer1**, or click Browse to search for the computer.

8. In Temporary Location For Log And Patch Files, type the folder path for a temporary restore location, such as **C:\Temp**.

9. If this is the last backup set you need to recover, select the Last Restore Set and Mount Database After Restore check boxes.

10. Click OK to start the restore operation. If prompted, enter the path and name of the backup set to use. You can cancel the backup by clicking Cancel in the Operation Status and Restore Progress dialog boxes.

11. When the restore is completed, click Close to complete the process or click Report to view a backup log containing information about the restore operation.

Always check the related mailbox and public folder databases to make sure that the data recovery was successful.

Performing Backup and Recovery on Windows Server 2008

Windows Server 2008 provides a different toolset for performing backup and recovery procedures. These tools include Windows Server Backup, Wbadmin, Startup Repair, and Complete PC Restore.

Getting Started with Windows Server Backup

Windows Server 2008 provides Windows Server Backup for creating backups and for recovery using backups. You can install Windows Server Backup by following these steps:

1. In Server Manager, select the Features node in the left pane, and then click Add Features. This starts the Add Features Wizard.

2. On the Select Features page, expand the Windows Server Backup Features node, and then select the Windows Server Backup and Windows Command-line options. Click Next.

3. Click Install. When the wizard finishes installing the selected features, click Close. From now on, Windows Server Backup will be available as an option on the Administrative Tools menu and as an option under the Storage node in Server Manager.

When you start Windows Server Backup the first time, you'll see a warning that no backup has been configured for the computer. You clear this warning by creating a backup using the Backup Once feature or by scheduling backups to run automatically by using the Backup Schedule feature. Only members of the Administrators and the Backup Operators groups have full authority to back up and restore any type of file, regardless of who owns the file and the permissions set on it.

Windows Server Backup provides extensions for working with system state and application data. All computers have System State data, which must be backed up in addition to other files to restore a complete working system. Windows Server Backup creates block-level backups of application data using VSS.

Real World   The original implementation of Windows Server Backup allows you to perform full, copy, and incremental backups. While you can schedule a full or incremental backup to be performed one or more times each day, you cannot use this feature to create separate run schedules for performing both full and incremental backups. Further, you cannot select the day or days of the week to run backups. This occurs because each server has a single master schedule that is set to run one or more times daily. An update to Windows Server Backup is expected to allow you to create multiple master schedules for any day of the week or month. When you implement this update, you'll be able to configure separate schedules for full and incremental backups on the same server. You'll also be able to select the days of the week or month for backups. If your servers have a single master schedule, you can work around this limitation by configuring Windows Server Backup to perform daily incremental backups and then creating a scheduled task via the Task Scheduler that uses the command-line Wbadmin utility to create a full backup on the desired day of the week or month.

When you start Windows Server Backup, the utility connects to the local computer by default. This allows you to easily manage backups on the local computer. If you want to manage backups on a remote computer, you'll need to connect to the computer by following these steps:

1. Start Windows Server Backup. In the Action pane or on the Action menu, click Connect To Another Computer.

2. Select Another Computer, and then type the server's name or IP address. Alternatively, if network discovery is enabled, click Browse, choose the remote computer in the dialog box provided, and then click OK.

3. Click Finish to establish a connection to the remote computer.

When you use Windows Server Backup, the first backup of a server is always a full backup. The full backup process clears the archive bits on files so that Windows Server Backup can track which files are updated subsequently. Whether Windows Server Backup subsequently performs full or incremental backups depends on the default performance settings that you configure. In Windows Server Backup, click the Configure Performance Settings option to configure the desired default setting for backups. Once you've configured the default performance settings, you can start a backup by selecting Backup Once on the Action menu or in the Action pane. You can configure a backup schedule by clicking Backup Schedule on the Action menu or in the Action pane.

Backing Up Exchange Server on Windows Server 2008

As part of your planning for each server you plan to back up, you should consider which volumes you want to back up and whether backups will include system state recovery data, application data, or both. Although you can manually back up to shared volumes and DVD media, you will need a separate, dedicated hard disk for running scheduled backups. After you configure a disk for scheduled backups, Windows Server Backup automatically manages the disk usage and automatically reuses the space of older backups when creating new backups. Once you schedule backups, you'll need to check periodically to ensure that backups are being performed as expected and that the backup schedule meets current needs.

When you create or schedule backups, you will need to specify the volumes that you want to include, and this will affect the ways you can recover your servers and your data. As part of the backup process, you also will need to specify a storage location for backups. Keep the following in mind when you are choosing storage locations:

■ When you use an internal hard disk for storing backups, you are limited in how you can recover your system. You can recover the data from a volume, but you cannot rebuild the entire disk structure.

■ When you use an external hard disk for storing backups, the disk will be dedicated for storing your backups and will not be visible in Windows Explorer.

Choosing this option will format the selected disk or disks, removing any existing data.

■ When you use a remote shared folder for storing backups, your backup will be overwritten each time you create a new backup. Do not choose this option if you want to store multiple backups for each server.

■ When you use removable media or DVDs for storing backups, you can recover only entire volumes, not applications or individual files. The media you use must be at least 1 GB in size.

You can schedule automated backups for a server by following these steps:

1. In Windows Server Backup, you are connected to the local server by default. As necessary, connect to the remote server with which you want to work.

2. Click Backup Schedule on the Action menu or in the Action pane. This starts the Backup Schedule Wizard. Click Next.

3. On the Select Backup Type page, note the backup size listed under the Full Server option. This is the storage space required to back up the server data, applications, and system state. Volumes that contain operating system files or applications are included in the backup by default and cannot be excluded. To back up all volumes on the server, select the Full Server option and then click Next. To back up selected volumes on the server, click Custom and then click Next.

4. If you selected Custom, the Select Backup Items page is displayed. Select the check boxes for the volumes that you want to back up and clear the check boxes for the volumes that you want to exclude.

5. On the Specify Backup Time page, you can specify how often and when you want to run backups. To perform backups daily at a specific time, choose Once A Day and then select the time to start running the daily backup. To perform backups multiple times each day, choose More Than Once A Day. Next, click a start time under Available Time, and then click Add to move the time to the Scheduled Time list. Repeat this step for each start time that you want to add. Click Next when you are ready to continue.

6. On the Select Destination Disk page, select the external disk that you want to use for scheduled backups. If the disk that you want to use is not listed, click Show All Available Disks. Then select the check box next to the disk that you want to use to store the backups.

> **Note**   Each external disk can store up to 512 backups, depending on the amount of data contained in each backup. You can select multiple disks. If you do so, Windows Server Backup will rotate among them.

7. When you click Next, you'll see a warning prompt informing you that the selected disk will be formatted and any existing data will be deleted. Click Yes.

8. On the Label Destination Disk page, the disk that you selected is listed. A label that includes the disk type, server name, the current date, the current time, and a disk size is assigned to the disk. If you need to recover data from the backup stored on the disk, you will need this information to identify the disk. Therefore, be sure to record this information. With external disks, you may want to attach a printed label containing this information.

9. On the Confirmation page, review the details, and then click Finish. The wizard will then format the disk. The formatting process may take several minutes or considerably longer depending on the size of the disk.

10. On the Summary page, click Close. Your backups are now scheduled for the selected server.

You can manually back up servers using Windows Server Backup by following these steps:

1. Start Windows Server Backup. You are connected to the local server by default. As necessary, connect to the remote server with which you want to work.

2. Click Backup Once on the Action menu or in the Action pane. This starts the Backup Once Wizard. Click Next.

3. If you want to back up the server using the same options that you use for the Backup Schedule Wizard, select The Same Options, click Next, and then click Backup to perform the backup. Skip the remaining steps.

4. If you want to back up the server using different options, select Different Options, click Next, and then follow the remaining steps in this procedure.

5. On the Select Backup Type page, note the backup size listed under the Full Server option. This is the storage space required to back up the server data, applications, and system state. To back up all volumes on the server, select the Full Server option and then click Next. To back up selected volumes on the server, click Custom and then click Next.

6. If you selected Custom, the Select Backup Items page is displayed. Select the check boxes for the volumes that you want to back up and clear the check boxes for the volumes that you want to exclude. If you want to back up the system state and all critical operating system volumes, select the Enable System Recovery check box. Click Next.

7. On the Specify Destination Type page, do one of the following:

   ❑ If you want to back up to local drives, select Local Drives and then click Next. On the Backup Destination page, select the internal or external disc or DVD drive to use as the backup target. Backups are compressed when stored on a DVD. As a result, the size of the backup on a DVD might be smaller than the volume on the server. If the backup target is a removable media drive, the backup is verified automatically after the wizard writes the backup data. Clear the Verify After Writing check box if you do not want to verify the backup. Click Next.

❑   If you want to back up to a remote shared folder, select Remote Shared Folder and then click Next. On the Specify Remote Folder page, type the UNC path to the remote folder, such as **\\BackupServer18\backups**. If you want the backup to be accessible to everyone who has access to the shared folder, select Inherit under Access Control. If you want to restrict access to the shared folder to the current user, administrators, and backup operators, select Do Not Inherit under Access Control. Click Next. When prompted to provide access credentials, type the user name and password for an account authorized to access and write to the shared folder.

8. On the Specify VSS Backup Type page, specify whether you want to perform a copy backup or a VSS full backup. Choose Copy Backup if you are using a separate backup utility to backup application data. Otherwise choose VSS Full Backup to fully back up the selected volumes, including all application data.

9. Click Next and then click Backup. The Backup Progress dialog box shows you the progress of the backup process. If you click Close, the backup will continue to run in the background.

Performing a Full Server Recovery

Windows Server 2008 includes startup repair features that can recover a server in case of corrupted or missing system files. The startup repair process can also recover from some types of boot failures involving the boot manager. If these processes fail and the boot manager is the reason you cannot start the server, you can use the Windows Server 2008 installation disc or a recovery partition to restore the boot manager and enable startup.

If Startup Repair fails and you are not able to start the server, you can attempt to recover the server from a backup by following these steps:

1. Insert the Windows disc into the DVD drive and turn on the computer. If needed, press the required key to boot from the disc. The Install Windows Wizard should appear.

2. Specify the language settings to use, and then click Next.

3. Click Repair Your Computer. Setup searches the hard disk drives for an existing Windows installation and then displays the results in the System Recovery Options Wizard. If you are recovering the operating system onto separate hardware, the list should be empty and there should be no operating system on the computer. Click Next.

4. On the System Recovery Options page, click Windows Complete PC Restore. This starts the Windows Complete PC Restore Wizard.

5. Click Use The Latest Available Backup (Recommended) and then click Next. Or click Restore A Different Backup and then click Next.

6. If you chose to restore a different backup, on the Select The Location Of The Backup page, do one of the following:

   ❏ Click the computer that contains the backup that you want to use, and then click Next. On the Select The Backup To Restore page, click the backup that you want to use, and then click Next.

   ❏ Click Advanced to browse for a backup on the network, and then click Next. Browse the network to select the backup to restore and then click Next.

7. On the Choose How To Restore The Backup page, perform the following optional tasks, and then click Next:

   ❏ Select the Format And Repartition Disks check box to delete existing partitions and reformat the destination disks to be the same as the backup.

   ❏ Click the Exclude Disks button and then select the check boxes associated with any disks that you want to exclude from being formatted and partitioned. The disk that contains the backup that you are using is automatically excluded.

   ❏ Click Install Drivers to install device drivers for the hardware to which you are recovering.

   ❏ Click Advanced to specify whether the computer is restarted and the disks are checked for errors immediately after the recovery operation is completed.

8. On the Confirmation page, review the details for the restoration, and then click Finish. The Windows Complete PC Restore Wizard will then restore the operating system or the full server as appropriate for the options you've selected.

Recovering Exchange Server

In cases where you only need to recover Exchange data, you don't need to initiate a full server recovery. Instead, you can recover an Exchange database or storage group to the point of failure by restoring the most recent normal (full) backup and then applying each incremental backup in order.

With this in mind, you can recover Exchange data by following these steps:

1. Start Windows Server Backup. In the Action pane or on the Action menu, click Recover. This starts the Recovery Wizard.

2. On the Getting Started page, specify whether you will recover data from the local computer or another computer, and then click Next. For example, if you are logged on to CorpPC185 and want to recover data from MailServer284, select Another Server, regardless of whether the data for the server is stored on a local drive or remote share.

3. If you are recovering data from another computer, specify whether the backup that you want to restore is on a local drive or a remote shared folder, click Next, and then specify location-specific settings. When you are recovering from a local drive, on the Select Backup Location page, select the location of the backup from the drop-down list. When you are recovering from a remote shared folder, on the Specify Remote Folder page, type the path to the folder that contains the backup. In the remote folder, the backup should be stored at \WindowsImageBackup\ComputerName.

4. If you are recovering from the local computer and there are multiple backups, on the Select Backup Location page, select the location of the backup on the drop-down list.

5. On the Select Backup Date page, select the date and time of the backup you want to restore using the calendar and the time list. Backups are available for dates shown in bold. Click Next.

6. On the Select Recovery Type page, click Files And Folders, and then click Next. On the Select Items To Recover page, under Available items, click the plus sign (+) to expand the list until the Exchange folder you want is visible. Click a folder to display the contents of the folder in the adjacent pane, click each item that you want to restore, and then click Next.

> **Note**   The original implementation of Windows Server Backup requires you to use the Files And Folders option to recover Exchange data. While you can use this option to recover data, you cannot use this option to dynamically handle Exchange's databases and perform roll-forward recovery. An Exchange Server extension for Windows Server Backup is expected to be available that will allow you to perform roll-forward recovery. When this option is available, you'll select Applications as what you want to recover. You'll then work your way from the last full backup through the incremental backups. When you are recovering the most recent incremental backup, you'll then select Do Not Perform A Roll-Forward Recovery to ensure that the databases are recovered in a ready mode.

7. On the Specify Recovery Options page, under Recovery Destination, specify whether you want to restore data to its original location (non-system files only) or an alternate location. For an alternate location, type the path to the desired restore location or click Browse to select it.

8. Under When Backup Finds Existing Files And Folders, choose a recovery technique to apply when files and folders already exist in the recovery location. You can create copies so that you have both versions of the file or folder, overwrite existing files with recovered files, or skip duplicate files and folders to preserve existing files.

9. On the Confirmation page, review the details, and then click Recover to restore the specified items.

Restoring Mailboxes Selectively from Backup

You use recovery storage groups to restore mailboxes selectively from any of the regular storage groups in an Exchange organization. The process of using a recovery storage group to restore mailbox data works like this:

1. On the server for which you are recovering mailboxes, create a recovery storage group, and link it to the storage group containing the databases where the mailboxes you want to restore were originally located. A server can only have one recovery storage group at a time.

2. Use a backup utility, such as Windows Backup, to restore the mailbox databases for the linked storage group, and then mount the databases in the recovery storage group you previously created. Mailboxes in the recovery storage group are disconnected and are not accessible to users.

3. Use the Troubleshooting Assistant to select the mailboxes to restore, and restore them to the original mailbox database. The wizard copies data from the mailboxes in the recovery databases and merges it with data in the corresponding mailboxes in the specified database.

4. When you are finished using the recovery storage group, dismount the recovery databases and remount the recovery storage group. By dismounting the recovery databases, you allow normal recovery operations of Exchange Server to resume. By removing the recovery storage group, you remove the recovery databases and the recovery storage group itself.

Although restoring mailboxes from backups is a lengthy process, it is the best way to selectively recover mailboxes. Keep in mind that you don't have to use recovery storage groups to recover all the mailboxes in a given mailbox database. In this case, you simply restore the entire mailbox database.

Step 1: Creating and Using Recovery Storage Groups

Regardless of whether you are using Exchange Server 2007 Standard Edition or Exchange Server 2007 Enterprise Edition, each Exchange server in your organization can have a recovery storage group. If you need to recover mailboxes stored on multiple

Exchange servers, you don't have to create a recovery storage group on each server. Instead, you can create one recovery storage group and use this for your recovery operations.

Before you create a recovery storage group, plan carefully for the additional storage requirements. During the recovery process, several types of files are created:

- **Transaction**   Transaction files, stored in the recovery transaction log folder, are given the file prefix R00 by default. You'll find a temporary log file that is used as temporary workspace for processing transactions (R00tmp.log) and a transaction log file that is the primary transaction log file for the recovery group. The total space required for transaction files is at least as much as that of the databases for which you plan to restore mailboxes.

- **System**   System files, stored in the recovery system folder, are given the file prefix R00 by default. You'll find a transaction checkpoint file that contains recovered file fragments (R00.chk).

- **Database**   Database files, stored in the recovery database folder, include the database (.edb) files for all mailbox database databases. The total space required for system files is the same as that of the original mailbox database databases.

To create a recovery storage group, follow these steps:

1. In Exchange Management Console, select the Toolbox node. Double-click Database Recovery Management.

2. After the Troubleshooting Assistant checks for updates, click Go To Welcome Screen.

3. Enter an identifying label for the activity, such as **Database Recovery**.

4. In the Server Name text box, enter the name of the server on which you want to create the recovery group and the domain controller you want to query during recovery, and then click Next.

5. The Troubleshooting Assistant will check connectivity to Active Directory and Exchange Server. Afterward, the troubleshooter will analyze the Exchange database configuration by checking the disks a server is using for messaging to ensure that they are accessible, have free space, and are mounted.

6. Click Create A Recovery Storage Group.

7. Select the Storage Group to link with the Recovery Storage group and then click Next. You can mount only databases from the linked storage group in the recovery storage group.

8. You'll see the default location for the transaction logs, system files, and database files. If you want to change the location of these files, use the Browse buttons to the right of the related text boxes to set new file locations.

9. Click Create Recovery Storage Group. When the creation process finishes, note the results. Each database should be listed as added successfully, and the recovery storage group should be listed as created successfully. If there are problems, they'll typically be due to running out of free space, and you'll need to resolve this by clearing up the required space.

10. Click Go Back To Task Center. Do not close the Troubleshooting Assistant.

Step 2: Restoring and Mounting the Recovery Databases

When you create the recovery storage group, all databases in the linked storage group are made available automatically for recovery. You then need to restore the databases using Windows Backup, making sure to apply the last full (normal) backup and any subsequent differential or incremental backups as necessary. When the restore operation is complete, you can mount the database to the recovery storage group.

With Windows Server 2003, you restore the data by completing the following steps:

1. Start Windows Backup. If wizard mode is enabled, click Advanced Mode, and then click the Restore And Manage Media tab. Otherwise, just click the Restore And Manage Media tab.

2. Expand the backup media containing the last full backup of the Exchange server information store, and then select the check box for the storage group that contains the databases with which you want to work. If you want to restore an individual mailbox database, expand the storage group node, and then select the check box for the mailbox database and any associated log files.

3. Click Start Restore. The Restoring Database Store dialog box appears.

4. In the Restore To text box, type the name of the computer on which you want to restore files, such as **Mailer1**, or click Browse to search for the computer.

5. In the Temporary Location For Log And Patch Files text box, type the folder path for a temporary restore location, such as **C:\Temp**.

6. If this is the last backup set you need to recover, select the Last Restore Set and Mount Database After Restore check boxes.

7. Click OK to start the restore operation. When the restore is completed, click Close to complete the process. Keep in mind the databases aren't recovered to the Exchange information store—they are written to the recovery storage group.

8. If you need to apply differential or incremental backups, repeat this procedure, making sure to select the correct backup media. With differential backups, you need to restore only the last differential backup. With incremental backups, you must restore each incremental backup sequentially, starting with the first one made after the last full (normal) backup.

With Windows Server 2003, you restore the data by completing the following steps:

1. Start Windows Server Backup. In the Action pane or on the Action menu, click Recover. This starts the Recovery Wizard.

2. On the Select Backup Location page, select the location of the backup from the drop-down list.

3. On the Select Backup Date page, select the date and time of the last full backup. Backups are available for dates shown in bold. Click Next.

4. On the Select Recovery Type page, click Files And Folders, and then click Next. On the Select Items To Recover page, expand the backup media containing the last full backup of the Exchange server information store, and then select the check box for the storage group that contains the databases with which you want to work. If you want to restore an individual mailbox database, expand the storage group node, and then select the check box for the mailbox database and any associated log files. Click Next.

5. On the Specify Recovery Options page, under Recovery Destination, specify that you are restoring data to an alternate location. Type the path to the desired restore location, such as **C:\Temp**, or click Browse to select it.

6. Under When Backup Finds Existing Files And Folders, choose a recovery technique to apply when files and folders already exist in the recovery location. You can create copies so that you have both versions of the file or folder, overwrite existing files with recovered files, or skip duplicate files and folders to preserve existing files.

7. On the Confirmation page, review the details, and then click Recover to restore the specified items.

8. If you need to apply incremental backups, repeat this procedure, being sure to select the correct backup media. With incremental backups, you must restore each incremental backup sequentially, starting with the first one made after the last full (normal) backup.

After you restore the data, you need to mount the database by following these steps:

1. In the Troubleshooting Assistant, click Mount Or Dismount Databases In The Recovery Storage Group.

2. Select the check boxes for the databases to mount, and then click Mount Selected Database.

3. Review the Mount Or Dismount Databases Report to ensure that the mount operations were successful.

4. Scroll down, and then click Go Back To Task Center. Do not close the Troubleshooting Assistant.

Step 3: Selecting and Restoring Mailboxes

Now that you've recovered the databases and mounted them in the recovery storage group, you can use the Troubleshooting Assistant to select mailboxes and restore them. The Troubleshooting Assistant copies data from the mailboxes in the recovery databases and allows you to merge it with the existing data in the mailboxes of the original database.

You can use the Troubleshooting Assistant to select and extract mailbox data by completing the following steps:

1. In the Troubleshooting Assistant, click Merge Or Copy Mailbox Contents.

2. The mounted databases in the recovery storage groups are listed by name. Select the database with which you want to work, and then click Gather Merge Information.

3. The details for the database mounted in the recovery storage group and the original database in the linked storage group are listed by name, item count, and total size.

4. At this point, you can choose to swap the entire database configurations or continue with mailbox selection. If you select the Swap Database Configurations check box and then click Next, the database mounted from backup for recovery is moved to the linked storage group and becomes the active database in the original database location. Only select this check box if you want to completely replace the original database.

5. To continue merging individual mailbox data, click Next, and then click Perform Pre-Merge Tasks.

6. On the Select Mailboxes For Copy Or Merge page, a list of matched mailboxes is provided. All matched mailboxes are selected by default. However, only select the check boxes for the recovered mailboxes you want to merge with the original mailboxes.

    Note   To save a list of the matched mailboxes to a file, click Save. In the Save As dialog box, select a save location, type a file name for the saved data, and then click Save.

7. To set advanced options, click Show Advanced Options. You can now match all source mailboxes to a single destination mailbox; set filter options for start date, end date, and message subject; and set a maximum bad item limit.

8. Click Perform Merge Action to merge or copy mailbox contents from the database in the recovery storage group to the original database.

9. Note any errors listed on the Error tab. To print a report of the errors, click Print Report. To export the errors to a file, click Export Report. In the Export Report

dialog box, select a save location, type a file name for the saved data, and then click Save.

10. On the Information tab, review the list of mailboxes that were restored. To print a report of the mailboxes restored, click Print Report. To export the list to a file, click Export Report. In the Export Report dialog box, select a save location, type a file name for the saved data, and then click Save.

11. Click Go Back To Task Center. Do not close the Troubleshooting Assistant.

Step 4: Dismounting Recovery Databases and Removing the Recovery Storage Group

When you are finished using the recovery storage group, you should dismount the recovery databases by completing the following steps:

1. In the Troubleshooting Assistant, click Mount Or Dismount Databases In The Recovery Storage Group.

2. The currently mounted databases are listed. Because you are done working with the recovery storage group, select the check boxes for all mounted databases, and then click Dismount Selected Database.

3. Review the Mount Or Dismount Databases Report to ensure that the dismount operations were successful.

4. Scroll down, and then click Go Back To Task Center.

5. Click Remove The Recovery Storage Group.

6. When you click Perform Remove RSG Action, the Troubleshooting Assistant removes the recovery databases and the recovery storage group.

7. Review the results to ensure that the remove operations were successful. Click Go Back To Task Center.

Performing Additional Backup and Recovery Tasks

You may want to perform several additional backup and recovery tasks. These include:

- Recovering a server using Setup/mode:recoverserver
- Cloning Edge Transport server configurations
- Troubleshooting database mount problems
- Mounting databases on alternate servers

These tasks are discussed in the sections that follow.

Using the Recover Server Mode

You use Setup with the /mode:recoverserver to recover a server that was once fully functional or to move a server to new hardware and maintain the same name. You should not use this as a repair tool, to recover from a failed install, to recover from a failed uninstall, or to reconfigure a server. In addition, this recovery process does not restore customized settings that were stored on the server or in Exchange databases.

When you use the /mode:recoverserver command with Exchange Setup, the new server needs to have the same name as the server that it will be replacing and have a matching drive configuration for drives that had Exchange data on them. With this in mind, you can recover Exchange on a new server by completing the following steps:

1. Reset the domain computer account for the lost server. In Active Directory Users And Computers, right-click the computer name, and then click Reset Account.

2. Install the new server, making sure you give it the same name as the old server and a matching drive configuration for drives that had Exchange data on them.

3. Join the server to the domain, and restart the server if necessary.

4. Insert the Exchange Server 2007 disc in the CD/DVD-ROM drive. At a command prompt change to the Exchange source directory on the CD/DVD. (The Exchange source folder is the folder that identifies the processor type, such as \amd64.)

5. At the command prompt, type **Setup /mode:recoverserver**. This tells Setup to read the configuration information from Active Directory for a server with the same name as the server from which you are running Setup. Setup then installs the Exchange roles and files on the new server using the settings that were stored in Active Directory.

Cloning Edge Transport Server Configurations

Most Edge Transport server settings are set by default, either because they are updated from the Web, such as with antispam data, or because they are replicated from Active Directory through the EdgeSync process. If you haven't modified the settings or created custom settings, no Edge Transport server data needs to be backed up, and you could fully recover Edge Transport services simply by setting up a new Edge Transport server. If you've modified or customized the settings, you can clone the configuration to capture any settings you've changed.

On an Edge Transport server, you'll find two scripts in the C:\Program Files\Microsoft\ Exchange Server\Scripts directory. If you run the first script, ExportEdgeConfig.ps1, Exchange will export all user-configured settings and store the data in an .xml file. If you copy the .xml file or a backup of the .xml file to a new Edge Transport server and run the second script, ImportEdgeConfig.ps1, Exchange will import all user-configured settings in the .xml file.

Troubleshooting Database Mount Problems

Sometimes, you may find that a database won't mount. This may be because a required log file is missing or because the database is corrupted. You can diagnose many database mount problems using the Troubleshooting Assistant.

You can use the Troubleshooting Assistant to troubleshoot a database mount problem by completing the following steps:

1. In Exchange Management Console, select the Toolbox node. Double-click Database Recovery Management.

2. After the Troubleshooting Assistant checks for updates, click Go To Welcome Screen.

3. Enter an identifying label for the activity, such as **Database Recovery**.

4. In the Server Name text box, enter the name of the server on which you want to create the recovery group and the domain controller you want to query during recovery. Then click Next.

5. The Troubleshooting Assistant will check connectivity to Active Directory and Exchange Server. Afterward, the troubleshooter will analyze the Exchange database configuration by checking the disks a server is using for messaging to ensure that they are accessible, have free space, and are mounted.

6. Click Repair Database.

7. On the Select Repair Options page, select the storage group in which the problem database is located, and then click Next.

8. Any dismounted databases in the previously selected storage group are listed and can be selected for troubleshooting.

9. When you've selected the database or databases for troubleshooting, click Analyze Selected Database. The database status is provided, along with a possible solution for resolving the problem.

Mounting Mailbox Databases on Alternate Servers

Thanks to the database portability feature in Exchange Server 2007, you can mount a mailbox database on a server other than the server on which you created the database. Database portability is not supported for public folder databases. Public folder databases are replicated automatically. If you create a public folder database on a server, all public folder data will be replicated to other public folder servers as part of the normal replication process.

You can move a mailbox database to a new server by completing the following steps:

1. Your first step in moving a database to a new server is to commit any uncommitted transaction log files to the database by running the following command at a command prompt:

   ```
   eseutil /r ENN
   ```

   where ENN specifies the log file prefix of the transaction logs you intend to replay into the database. Generally, the name of the log file for the first storage group is E00.log, the name of the log file for the second storage group is E01.log, and so on.

   Note If there are no transaction logs to commit, you can skip step 1.

2. Your next step is to create a new Mailbox database on the new server, as discussed in the "Creating Mailbox Databases" section of Chapter 12, "Mailbox and Public Folder Database Administration." Do not mount the database. The new database must have the same name as the name configured on the previous Exchange server. You can use the Get-StorageGroup cmdlet to obtain the required database name. Set the Identity parameter to the identity of the original storage group, such as:

   ```
   get-StorageGroup -Identity 'CORPSVR127\Third Storage Group'
   ```

3. After you create the database, you must enable the database to be overwritten by a restore operation. You can do this by setting the AllowFileRestore parameter of the Set-MailboxDatabase cmdlet to $true, as shown in the following example:

   ```
   Set-MailboxDatabase –Identity 'CORPSVR84\First Storage Group\
   Accounting DB'
    –AllowFileRestore $true
   ```

4. Move the database files (.edb files, log files, and content indexing catalog) to the appropriate location on the new server. You must put the files in the exact locations the new server expects these files to be in. You set these locations when you created the database.

5. Mount the database using the Mount-Database cmdlet, as shown in the following example:

   ```
   Mount-Database –Identity 'CORPSVR84\First Storage Group\
   Accounting DB'
   ```

6. After you mount the database, you must modify the user account settings with Move-Mailbox -ConfigurationOnly so that the accounts point to the mailbox on the new mailbox server. To use Move-Mailbox -ConfigurationOnly to move all

of the users from the old database to the new database, run the following command:

```
Get-MailboxStatistics -Database 'NewDatabaseIdenity'
 | Move-Mailbox -ConfigurationOnly
-TargetDatabase 'NewDatabaseIdentity'
```

where *NewDatabaseIdentity* is the name of the new database in both instances, such as:

```
Get-MailboxStatistics
-Database 'CORPSVR84\First Storage Group\Accounting DB'
 | Move-Mailbox -ConfigurationOnly
-TargetDatabase 'CORPSVR84\First Storage Group\Accounting DB'
```

Note   Only mailboxes that have been opened or that have mail are moved with this command. If there are new mailboxes that have no mail or that have not been opened, these mailboxes will not be created.

Mailbox users will be redirected to the new mailbox location automatically once Active Directory replication has completed.

Index

About the Author

William R. Stanek (*http://www.williamstanek.com*) has more than 20 years of hands-on experience with advanced programming and development. He is a leading technology expert, an award-winning author, and a pretty-darn-good instructional trainer. Over the years, his practical advice has helped millions of programmers, developers, and network engineers all over the world. He has written more than 70 books. Current or forthcoming books include *Windows Command-Line Administrator's Pocket Consultant* Second Edition, *Windows Server 2008 Administrator's Pocket Consultant*, *Microsoft SQL Server 2008 Administrator's Pocket Consultant*, and *Windows Server 2008 Inside Out*.

William has been involved in the commercial Internet community since 1991. His core business and technology experience comes from more than 11 years of military service. He has substantial experience in developing server technology, encryption, and Internet solutions. He has written many technical white papers and training courses on a wide variety of topics. He frequently serves as a subject matter expert and consultant.

William has an MS with distinction in information systems and a BS in computer science, magna cum laude. He is proud to have served in the Persian Gulf War as a combat crewmember on an electronic warfare aircraft. He flew on numerous combat missions into Iraq and was awarded nine medals for his wartime service, including one of the United States of America's highest flying honors, the Air Force Distinguished Flying Cross. Currently, he resides in the Pacific Northwest with his wife and children.

What do you think of this book?

We want to hear from you!

Do you have a few minutes to participate in a brief online survey?

Microsoft is interested in hearing your feedback so we can continually improve our books and learning resources for you.

To participate in our survey, please visit:

www.microsoft.com/learning/booksurvey/

...and enter this book's ISBN-10 number or ISBN-13 number (located above barcode on back cover*). As a thank-you to survey participants in the United States and Canada, each month we'll randomly select five respondents to win one of five $100 gift certificates from a leading online merchant. At the conclusion of the survey, you can enter the drawing by providing your e-mail address, which will be used for prize notification only.

Thanks in advance for your input. Your opinion counts!

Microsoft®
Press

*Where to find the ISBN on back cover

ISBN-13: 000-0-0000-0000-0
ISBN-10: 0-0000-0000-0

0 0 0 0 0

0 000000 000000

Example only. Each book has unique ISBN.

www.microsoft.com/learning/booksurvey/